# RESPONDING TO LITERATURE

### Orange Level

## Senior Consultants

**ARTHUR N. APPLEBEE**
*State University of New York at Albany*

**JUDITH A. LANGER**
*State University of New York at Albany*

## Authors

**MARGARET GRAUFF FORST**

**JULIE WEST JOHNSON**

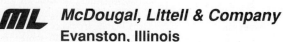

**McDougal, Littell & Company**
**Evanston, Illinois**
New York • Dallas • Sacramento • Columbia, SC

ISBN 0-8123-7077-5 (softcover)
ISBN 0-8123-7071-6 (hardbound)

Copyright © 1992 by McDougal, Littell & Company
Box 1667, Evanston, Illinois 60204

# Acknowledgments

**F. E. Albi** "Moco Limping" by David Nava Monreal. Courtesy of Dr. F. E. Albi, Editor.

**Margaret Walker Alexander** "Lineage" from *For My People* by Margaret Walker. Copyright 1942 by Yale University Press. Reprinted by permission of the author.

**Isaac Asimov** "The Feeling of Power" from *The Best Science Fiction of Isaac Asimov* by Isaac Asimov. Copyright © 1986 by Nightfall, Inc. Reprinted by permission of the author.

**Toni Cade Bambara** "My Delicate Heart Condition" by Toni Cade Bambara. Copyright © 1965 by Toni Cade Bambara. Reprinted by permission of the author.

**Robert Bly** "Ode to the Watermelon" by Pablo Neruda, from *Neruda and Vallejo: Selected Poems*. Chosen and translated by Robert Bly. Copyright © 1971 by Beacon Press, Boston. Copyright © 1971 by Robert Bly; reprinted with his permission.

**Brandt & Brandt Literary Agents, Inc.** "The Most Dangerous Game" by Richard Connell. Copyright 1924 by Richard Connell. Copyright renewed 1952 by Richard Connell. "The Possibility of Evil" by Shirley Jackson. Copyright © 1965 by Stanley Edgar Hyman. Reprinted by permission of Brandt & Brandt Literary Agents, Inc.

**Gwendolyn Brooks** "The Bean Eaters" from Blacks by Gwendolyn Brooks. Copyright © 1987 by The David Company, Chicago. Reprinted by permission of the author.

**Curtis Brown, Ltd.** "Rhinoceros" from *Heroes, Advise Us* by Adrien Stoutenburg. Copyright © 1964 by Adrien Stoutenburg. "Ape" by Babette Deutsch, from *Collected Poems of Babette Deutsch*. Copyright © 1967 by Babette Deutsch. Reprinted by permission of Curtis Brown, Ltd.

**City Lights Books** "Nodding against the wall, the flowers sneeze" from *Scattered Poems* by Jack Kerouac. Copyright © 1970, 1971 by the estate of Jack Kerouac. Reprinted by permission of City Lights Books.

**Joan Daves** "I Have a Dream" by Martin Luther King, Jr. Copyright © 1963 by Martin Luther King, Jr. Reprinted by permission of Joan Daves.

**Descant, The Texas Christian University Literary Journal** "Everybody Knows Tobie" by Daniel Garza. Copyright © 1963 by *Descant*.

**Delacorte Press** "The Lie" from *Welcome to the Monkey House* by Kurt Vonnegut, Jr. Copyright © 1962 by Kurt Vonnegut, Jr. Used by permission of Delacorte Press/Seymour Lawrence, a division of Bantam, Doubleday, Dell Publishing Group, Inc.

**Doubleday** "My Papa's Waltz" from *The Collected Poems of Theodore Roethke* by Theodore Roethke. Copyright © 1942 by Hearst Magazines, Inc. "The Seeing See Little" from *Three Days to See* by Helen Keller. Copyright 1933 by Helen Keller. "The Birds" from *Kiss Me Again, Stranger* by Daphne du Maurier. Copyright 1952 by Daphne du Maurier. Used by permission of Doubleday, a division of Bantam, Doubleday, Dell Publishing Group, Inc., and Curtis Brown, Ltd., London.

**E. P. Dutton** "All Cats Are Gray" by Andre Norton, from *The Many Worlds of Science Fiction* edited by Ben Bova. Copyright © 1971 by Ben Bova. Reprinted by permission of the publisher, Dutton Children's Books, a division of Penguin USA, Inc.

*(continued on page 660)*

## SENIOR CONSULTANTS

The senior consultants guided all conceptual development for the *Responding to Literature* series. They participated actively in shaping tables of contents and prototype materials for all major components and features, and they reviewed completed units to ensure consistency with current research and the philosophy of the series.

**Arthur N. Applebee,** Professor of Education, State University of New York at Albany; Director, Center for the Learning and Teaching of Literature

**Judith A. Langer,** Professor of Education, State University of New York at Albany; Co-Director, Center for the Learning and Teaching of Literature

## AUTHORS

The authors of this text wrote lessons for the literary selections.

**Margaret Grauff Forst,** Lake Forest High School, Lake Forest, Illinois

**Julie West Johnson,** New Trier Township High School, Winnetka, Illinois

## ACADEMIC CONSULTANTS

The academic consultants worked with the senior consultants to establish the theoretical framework for the series and the pedagogical design of the lessons. The consultants reviewed prototype lessons for the student book and Teacher's Guide, read selected units to ensure philosophical consistency, and suggested writing assignments.

**Susan Hynds,** Director of English Education, Syracuse University, Syracuse, New York

**James Marshall,** Associate Professor of English and Education, University of Iowa, Iowa City

**Robert E. Probst,** Professor of English Education, Georgia State University, Atlanta

**William Sweigart,** Assistant Professor of English, Indiana University Southeast, New Albany; formerly, Research Associate, Center for the Study of Writing, University of California at Berkeley

## LITERARY CONSULTANTS

The literary consultants commented on the table of contents for this text, suggested reorganizations, additions, and deletions, and supplied bibliographies for use in the Teacher's Guide.

**Carlos J. Cumpián,** Editor and Researcher, Hispanic Literature, Chicago, Illinois

**Peter Jaffe-Notier,** Instructor of World Literature, Lyons Township High School, La Grange, Illinois

**Michael W. Smith,** Department of Curriculum and Instruction, University of Wisconsin, Madison

## CONSULTANT-REVIEWERS

The consultant-reviewers responded to the table of contents, evaluated the lesson design, and reviewed selections for the purpose of assessing effectiveness and appropriateness for students and teachers.

**Elizabeth Anderson,** English Department Chairman, Olathe South High School, Olathe, Kansas

**Nancy J. Boersma,** Coordinator of English, White Plains Public Schools, White Plains, New York

**Jennifer C. Boyd,** Instructor of English, Nampa High School, Nampa, Idaho

**Helen Brown,** Educational Consultant, Baton Rouge, Louisiana

**Marilyn K. Buehler,** Arizona State Teacher of the Year 1989, English Instructor, North High School, Phoenix, Arizona

**Patrick Cates,** Chairman, English Department, Lubbock High School, Lubbock, Texas

**Charles R. Chew,** Director, Division of Communications Arts and Social Science Instruction, New York State Department of Education, Albany, New York

**Barry D. Gelsinger,** English Department Chair, Westminster High School, Westminster, Maryland

**Catherine C. Hatala,** Curriculum Coordinator, Humanities, School District of Philadelphia, Pennsylvania

**F. William Horchler,** Chairman, English Department, East Bladen High School, Elizabethtown, North Carolina

**Vicki Montgomery,** Language Arts Coordinator, Renton School District, Renton, Washington

**Jack Pelletier,** Chair, Mira Loma High School English Department, Sacramento, California

**Carolyn Phipps,** Executive Director, Tennessee Council of Teachers of English; Oakhaven High School, Memphis, Tennessee

**Sue Wilson,** Department Chairman, Wade Hampton High School, Greenville, South Carolina

## STUDENT ADVISORS

The student advisors reviewed literary selections to assess their appeal for ninth-grade students.

**Annamaria Babbo, John Borysek, Noel C. Bush, De Anna Moore, Jeff Winterfield, Ramu Yalamanchi**

---

Design: **Design 5**

Tests and Vocabulary Worksheets: **Sense and Nonsense**

Teacher's Guide Lessons: **Brown Publishing Network**

Multimodal Activities: **Verneva E. McPike,** Classroom Teacher, Livonia Public Schools, Livonia, Michigan

# Contents

**ONE READER'S RESPONSE**                                                    x

    James Thurber            The Secret Life of Walter Mitty

**RESPONDING IN WRITING**                                                    xv

---

## Unit *1*  THE SHORT STORY                                                  1

**ON THE EDGE OF YOUR SEAT: SUSPENSE**                                        2

    Richard Connell         The Most Dangerous Game     4
    Liam O'Flaherty         The Sniper     20
    Hernando Téllez         Lather and Nothing Else     27
                    *Translated from the Spanish*
    Frank Stockton         The Lady, or the Tiger?     33

**INTERACTIONS: FOCUS ON CHARACTERS**                                        38

    Langston Hughes         Thank You, M'am     40
    O. Henry         The Ransom of Red Chief     45
    Shirley Jackson         The Possibility of Evil     55

**RITES OF PASSAGE: STRUGGLES OF PERSONAL GROWTH**                           62

    Sylvia Plath         Initiation     64
    Doris Lessing         Through the Tunnel     74
    Toni Cade Bambara         My Delicate Heart Condition     83

**DIFFERENT VIEWPOINTS: UNDERSTANDING THE NARRATOR**                         88

    James Hurst         The Scarlet Ibis     90
    Eugenia Collier         Marigolds     101
    Marjorie Kinnan Rawlings     A Mother in Mannville     110
    Daniel Garza         Everybody Knows Tobie     118

### THE INDIVIDUAL IN COMMUNITY: DEFINING PERSONAL VALUES — 124

| | | |
|---|---|---|
| **Guy de Maupassant** | The Necklace<br>*Translated from the French* | 126 |
| **Kurt Vonnegut, Jr.** | The Lie | 134 |
| **Amy Tan** | Two Kinds | 145 |
| **Jean McCord** | The Cave | 156 |

### OUT OF THIS WORLD: SCIENCE FICTION AND THE MACABRE — 166

| | | |
|---|---|---|
| **Isaac Asimov** | The Feeling of Power | 168 |
| **Andre Norton** | All Cats Are Gray | 178 |
| **Edgar Allan Poe** | The Masque of the Red Death | 185 |
| **Daphne du Maurier** | The Birds | 193 |

REVIEWING CONCEPTS — 217

## Unit 2  NONFICTION — 218

### SHADES OF THE PAST: CHILDHOOD MEMORIES — 220

| | | |
|---|---|---|
| **Maya Angelou** | Mrs. Flowers<br>from *I Know Why the Caged Bird Sings* | 222 |
| **Truman Capote** | A Christmas Memory | 230 |
| **James Thurber** | The Night the Bed Fell | 242 |
| **Agnes de Mille** | from *Dance to the Piper*<br>(Performing Arts) | 248 |

### VOICES OF EXPERIENCE: PEOPLE AND PLACES — 252

| | | |
|---|---|---|
| **Beryl Markham** | West with the Night | 254 |
| **Loren Eiseley** | Obituary of a Bone Hunter<br>(Archaeology) | 265 |
| **Eddy Harris** | from *Mississippi Solo* | 274 |

### MEDITATIONS: THOUGHTS AND OPINIONS — 280

| | | |
|---|---|---|
| **Mark Twain** | How to Tell a Story | 282 |
| **Helen Keller** | The Seeing See Little | 287 |

| Richard Selzer | The Knife (Medicine) | 294 |
| Patrick McManus | A Dog for All Seasons | 301 |

## PERSUASION: THE ART OF ARGUMENT — 304

| Martin Luther King, Jr. | I Have a Dream (Political Issue) | 306 |
| Farley Mowat | from A Whale for the Killing (Environment) | 313 |
| Ellen Goodman | Primal Screen (Social Issue) | 321 |

## REVIEWING CONCEPTS — 323

## Unit 3 POETRY — 324

### OBSERVATIONS: IDEAS IN POETRY — 326

| Yoshino Hiroshi | Sunset Colors | 328 |
| Gwendolyn Brooks | The Bean Eaters | 328 |
| Margaret Walker | Lineage | 333 |
| Alice Walker | Women | 333 |
| Babette Deutsch | Ape | 338 |
| David Nava Monreal | Moco Limping | 338 |

### SHAPE AND SOUND: MUSIC AND MOVEMENT IN POETRY — 340

| William Blake | A Poison Tree | 342 |
| Elinor Wylie | Velvet Shoes | 342 |
| Anonymous | Barbara Allen's Cruelty | 349 |
| David Wagoner | The Shooting of John Dillinger Outside the Biograph Theater, July 22, 1934 | 349 |
| Matsuo Bashō | Haiku | 359 |
| Yosa Buson | | |
| Wallace Stevens | | |
| Jack Kerouac | | |

**TRANSFORMATIONS: THE MAGIC OF LANGUAGE** **360**

| | | |
|---|---|---|
| **Gloria Oden** | The Way It Is | 362 |
| **Langston Hughes** | Mother to Son | 362 |
| **Adrien Stoutenburg** | Rhinoceros | 368 |
| **Denise Levertov** | The Sharks | 368 |
| **Deborah Austin** | Dandelions | 373 |
| **Demetrio Herrera** | Training | 373 |

**SENSATIONS: POETRY AS EXPERIENCE** **376**

| | | |
|---|---|---|
| **Carl Sandburg** | Jazz Fantasia | 378 |
| **Theodore Roethke** | My Papa's Waltz | 378 |
| **e. e. cummings** | Spring is like a perhaps hand | 383 |
| **Emily Dickinson** | A Bird Came Down the Walk | 383 |
| **Pablo Neruda** | Ode to the Watermelon | 389 |
| | *Translated from the Spanish* | |
| **Featured Poet: Robert Frost** | Fire and Ice | 392 |
| | Nothing Gold Can Stay | 392 |
| | Birches | 392 |

**REVIEWING CONCEPTS** **399**

*Unit* **4** **THE HOMERIC EPIC** **400**

**INTRODUCTION** **402**

| | | |
|---|---|---|
| **Homer** | from *The Odyssey* | 406 |
| | *Translated from the Greek by Robert Fitzgerald* | |
| | The Cyclops | 406 |
| | The Homecoming | 421 |
| **Edna St. Vincent Millay** | An Ancient Gesture | 439 |
| **Dorothy Parker** | Penelope | 439 |

## Unit 5   MODERN DRAMA   442

| | | |
|---|---|---|
| **William Gibson** | *The Miracle Worker* | 446 |
| **Anton Chekhov** | *A Marriage Proposal* | 511 |
| | *Translated from the Russian* | |

REVIEWING CONCEPTS   521

## Unit 6   SHAKESPEAREAN DRAMA   522

INTRODUCTION   524

| | | |
|---|---|---|
| **William Shakespeare** | *The Tragedy of Romeo and Juliet* | 530 |

BIOGRAPHIES OF AUTHORS   636

INDEX OF ESSENTIAL VOCABULARY   648

INDEX OF LITERARY TERMS   652

INDEX OF WRITING MODES AND FORMATS   654

INDEX OF AUTHORS AND TITLES   657

PRONUNCIATION KEY: INSIDE BACK COVER

# Dear Student,

As a reader and as a thinker, you are unique. Your process of reading literature reflects your individuality. As you read, you make predictions about what intrigues you. You question words, sentences, and passages that are confusing to you. You understand what you read in your own special way, a way that comes as much from your own experiences, ideas, and feelings as from the writer's words.

As you read a work, you think and rethink meaning, arriving at a concept, or vision, that is uniquely your own. *Responding to Literature* gives you the tools to develop this vision of what a work means.

*Responding to Literature* helps you begin your reading process by

- giving you enough background to understand what's going on from the first line or paragraph
- previewing the words you need to know
- focusing on issues from your own experience that are important to the work you are about to read

*Responding to Literature* supports your reading process by

- defining essential words as you come to them
- helping you through difficult pieces

*Responding to Literature* extends your reading process by

- guiding you to rethink the work as a whole
- suggesting interesting issues to discuss and write about
- challenging you to make new connections with your own experiences and with the world around you

*Responding to Literature* is a series for the way you really read, the way you really think, the way you really write. As you use this first book in the series, you will learn new ways of exploring literature, and you will discover personal meanings in works that are part of your literary heritage.

*The Authors and Editors*

Alongside the following story is a transcription of the spoken comments made by ninth-grader Cole Thompson while reading "The Secret Life of Walter Mitty" for the first time. Her comments will give you a glimpse into the mind of a reader actively engaged in the process of reading. To get the most benefit from Cole's response, first read the story. Question, predict, and make meaning as you read. Then read Cole's response and notice the ways in which her reading process resembles your own, even though her comments are probably quite different.

# The Secret Life of Walter Mitty

Writer:
JAMES THURBER

Student Reader:
COLE THOMPSON

E'RE GOING THROUGH!" The Commander's voice was like thin ice breaking. He wore his full-dress uniform, with the heavily braided white cap pulled down rakishly over one cold gray eye. "We can't make it, sir. It's spoiling for a hurricane, if you ask me." "I'm not asking you, Lieutenant Berg," said the Commander. "Throw on the power lights! Rev her up to 8,500! We're going through!" The pounding of the cylinders increased: ta-pocketa-pocketa-pocketa-*pocketa-pocketa*. The Commander stared at the ice forming on the pilot window. He walked over and twisted a row of complicated dials. "Switch on No. 8 auxiliary!" he shouted. "Switch on No. 8 auxiliary!" repeated Lieutenant Berg. "Full strength in No. 3 turret!" shouted the Commander. The crew, bending to their various tasks in the huge hurtling eight-engined Navy hydroplane, looked at each other and grinned. "The Old Man'll get us through," they said to one another. "The Old Man ain't afraid of Hell!" . . .

"Not so fast! You're driving too fast!" said Mrs. Mitty. "What are you driving so fast for?"

"Hmm?" said Walter Mitty. He looked at his wife, in the seat

*"I like the effect of the 'pocketa-pocketa'"*
(making meaning)

*"You feel the suspense right here. Something bad's going to happen."*
(predicting)

*"This reminds me of my mom when we're driving."*
(making meaning)

beside him, with shocked astonishment. She seemed grossly unfamiliar, like a strange woman who had yelled at him in a crowd. "You were up to fifty-five," she said. "You know I don't like to go more than forty. You were up to fifty-five." Walter Mitty drove on toward Waterbury in silence, the roaring of the SN202 through the worst storm in twenty years of Navy flying fading in the remote, intimate airways of his mind. "You're tensed up again," said Mrs. Mitty. "It's one of your days. I wish you'd let Dr. Renshaw look you over."

Walter Mitty stopped the car in front of the building where his wife went to have her hair done. "Remember to get those overshoes while I'm having my hair done," she said. "I don't need overshoes," said Mitty. She put her mirror back into her bag. "We've been all through that," she said, getting out of the car. "You're not a young man any longer." He raced the engine a little. "Why don't you wear your gloves? Have you lost your gloves?" Walter Mitty reached in a pocket and brought out the gloves. He put them on, but after she had turned and gone into the building and he had driven on to a red light, he took them off again. "Pick it up, brother!" snapped a cop as the light changed, and Mitty hastily pulled on his gloves and lurched ahead. He drove around the streets aimlessly for a time, and then he drove past the hospital on his way to the parking lot.

. . . "It's the millionaire banker, Wellington McMillan," said the pretty nurse. "Yes?" said Walter Mitty, removing his gloves slowly. "Who has the case?" "Dr. Renshaw and Dr. Benbow, but there are two specialists here, Dr. Remington from New York and Mr. Pritchard-Mitford from London. He flew over." A door opened down a long, cool corridor and Dr. Renshaw came out. He looked distraught and haggard. "Hello, Mitty," he said. "We're having the devil's own time with McMillan, the millionaire banker and close personal friend of Roosevelt. Obstreosis of the ductal tract. Tertiary. Wish you'd take a look at him." "Glad to," said Mitty.

In the operating room there were whispered introductions: "Dr. Remington, Dr. Mitty. Mr. Pritchard-Mitford, Dr. Mitty." "I've read your book on streptothricosis," said Pritchard-Mitford, shaking hands. "A brilliant performance, sir." "Thank you," said Walter Mitty. "Didn't know you were in the States, Mitty," grumbled Remington. "Coals to Newcastle bringing Mitford and me up here for a tertiary." "You are very kind," said Mitty. A huge, complicated machine, connected to the operating table, with many tubes and wires, began at this moment to go pocketa-pocketa-pocketa. "The new anaesthetizer is giving way!" shouted an intern. "There is no one in the East who knows how to fix it!" "Quiet, man!" said Mitty, in a low, cool voice. He sprang to the machine, which was

*"The mother's all uptight . . . I mean the wife."*

(making meaning)

*"The names are getting confusing."*

(questioning)

*"I don't know this word* [streptothricosis].*"*

(questioning)

now going pocketa-pocketa-queep-pocketa-queep. He began fingering delicately a row of glistening dials. "Give me a fountain pen!" he snapped. Someone handed him a fountain pen. He pulled a faulty piston out of the machine and inserted the pen in its place. "That will hold for ten minutes," he said. "Get on with the operation." A nurse hurried over and whispered to Renshaw, and Mitty saw the man turn pale. "Coreopsis has set in," said Renshaw nervously. "If you would take over, Mitty?" Mitty looked at him and at the craven figure of Benbow, who drank, and at the grave, uncertain faces of the two great specialists. "If you wish," he said. They slipped a white gown on him; he adjusted a mask and drew on thin gloves; nurses handed him shining. . . .

"Back it up, Mac! Look out for that Buick!" Walter Mitty jammed on the brakes. "Wrong lane, Mac," said the parking-lot attendant, looking at Mitty closely. "Gee. Yeh," muttered Mitty. He began cautiously to back out of the lane marked "Exit Only." "Leave her sit there," said the attendant. "I'll put her away." Mitty got out of the car. "Hey, better leave the key." "Oh," said Mitty, handing the man the ignition key. The attendant vaulted into the car, backed it up with insolent skill, and put it where it belonged.

They're so damn cocky, thought Walter Mitty, walking along Main Street; they think they know everything. Once he had tried to take his chains off, outside New Milford, and he had got them wound around the axles. A man had had to come out in a wrecking car and unwind them, a young, grinning garageman. Since then Mrs. Mitty always made him drive to a garage to have the chains taken off. The next time, he thought, I'll wear my right arm in a sling; they won't grin at me then. I'll have my right arm in a sling, and they'll see I couldn't possibly take the chains off myself. He kicked at the slush on the sidewalk. "Overshoes," he said to himself, and he began looking for a shoe store.

When he came out into the street again, with the overshoes in a box under his arm, Walter Mitty began to wonder what the other thing was his wife had told him to get. She had told him twice, before they set out from their house for Waterbury. In a way he hated these weekly trips to town—he was always getting something wrong. Kleenex, he thought, Squibb's, razor blades? No. Toothpaste, toothbrush, bicarbonate, carborundum, initiative and referendum? He gave it up. But she would remember it. "Where's the what's-its-name?" she would ask. "Don't tell me you forgot the what's-its-name?" A newsboy went by shouting something about the Waterbury trial.

. . . "Perhaps this will refresh your memory." The District Attorney suddenly thrust a heavy automatic at the quiet figure on the witness stand. "Have you ever seen this before?" Walter Mitty

*"I like the way they're describing the way the machine's breaking."*

(making meaning)

*"It reminds me of a movie I saw last night—Beverly Hills Cop II. There was a car scene like this."*

(making meaning)

*"I don't know what garageman means."*

(questioning)

*"This reminds me of Sesame Street, where the boy sets out to get three things and on the way he forgets."*

(making meaning)

*"It's all these lives. There are lots of changes from life to life. I think that's neat."*

(making meaning)

took the gun and examined it expertly. "This is my Webley-Vickers 50.80," he said calmly. An excited buzz ran around the courtroom. The judge rapped for order. "You are a crack shot with any sort of firearms, I believe?" said the District Attorney, insinuatingly. "Objection!" shouted Mitty's attorney. "We have shown that the defendant could not have fired the shot. We have shown that he wore his right arm in a sling on the night of the fourteenth of July." Walter Mitty raised his hand briefly and the bickering attorneys were stilled. "With any known make of gun," he said evenly, "I could have killed Gregory Fitzhurst at three hundred feet *with my left hand*." Pandemonium broke loose in the courtroom. A woman's scream rose above the bedlam, and suddenly a lovely, dark-haired girl was in Walter Mitty's arms. The District Attorney struck at her savagely. Without rising from his chair, Mitty let the man have it on the point of the chin. "You miserable cur!" . . .

"Puppy biscuit," said Walter Mitty. He stopped walking, and the buildings of Waterbury rose up out of the misty courtroom and surrounded him again. A woman who was passing laughed. "He said 'Puppy biscuit,'" she said to her companion. "That man said 'Puppy biscuit' to himself." Walter Mitty hurried on. He went into an A.&P., not the first one he came to but a smaller one farther up the street. "I want some biscuit for small, young dogs," he said to the clerk. "Any special brand, sir?" The greatest pistol shot in the world thought a moment. "It says 'Puppies Bark for It' on the box," said Walter Mitty.

His wife would be through at the hairdresser's in fifteen minutes, Mitty saw in looking at his watch, unless they had trouble drying it; sometimes they had trouble drying it. She didn't like to get to the hotel first; she would want him to be there waiting for her as usual. He found a big leather chair in the lobby, facing a window, and he put the overshoes and the puppy biscuit on the floor beside it. He picked up an old copy of *Liberty* and sank down into the chair. "Can Germany Conquer the World Through the Air?" Walter Mitty looked at the pictures of bombing planes and of ruined streets.

. . . "The cannonading has got the wind up in young Raleigh, sir," said the sergeant. Captain Mitty looked up at him through tousled hair. "Get him to bed," he said wearily. "With the others. I'll fly alone." "But you can't, sir," said the sergeant anxiously. "It takes two men to handle that bomber, and the Archies are pounding the hell out of the air. Von Richtman's circus is between here and Saulier." "Somebody's got to get that ammunition dump," said Mitty. "I'm going over. Spot of brandy?" He poured a drink for the sergeant and one for himself. War thundered and whined around the dugout and battered at the door. There was a rending of wood,

*"This is kind of confusing in here. I'm not real familiar with some of the terms."*

(questioning)

*"This part of the story reminds me of* To Kill a Mockingbird: *the way the man proved the black man couldn't have hurt the woman."*

(making meaning)

*"I don't know what the word* cur *means."*

(questioning)

*"This is kind of funny. They're making a big deal out of biscuits."*

*"I wonder if puppy biscuits is one of the things he's trying to remember to get."*

(predicting)

*"There's suspense here. I can just see all these men rushing around."*

(making meaning)

and splinters flew through the room. "A bit of a near thing," said Captain Mitty carelessly. "The box barrage is closing in," said the sergeant. "We only live once, Sergeant," said Mitty, with his faint, fleeting smile. "Or do we?" He poured another brandy and tossed it off. "I never see a man could hold his brandy like you, sir," said the sergeant. "Begging your pardon, sir." Captain Mitty stood up and strapped on his huge Webley-Vickers automatic. "It's forty kilometers through hell, sir," said the sergeant. Mitty finished one last brandy. "After all," he said softly, "what isn't?" The pounding of the cannon increased; there was the rat-tat-tatting of machine guns, and from somewhere come the menacing pocketa-pocketa-pocketa of the new flamethrowers. Walter Mitty walked to the door of the dugout humming "Auprès de Ma Blonde." He turned and waved to the sergeant. "Cheerio!" he said. . . .

*"I think this ['We only live once'] is really true."*
(making meaning)

*"Mitty is drinking a lot."*
(making meaning)

Something struck his shoulder. "I've been looking all over this hotel for you," said Mrs. Mitty. "Why do you have to hide in this old chair? How did you expect me to find you?" "Things close in," said Walter Mitty vaguely. "What?" Mrs. Mitty said. "Did you get the what's-its-name? The puppy biscuit? What's in that box?" "Overshoes," said Mitty. "Couldn't you have put them on in the store?" "I was thinking," said Walter Mitty. "Does it ever occur to you that I am sometimes thinking?" She looked at him. "I'm going to take your temperature when I get you home," she said.

*"I think this word [cheerio] means goodbye. But I thought of the cereal."*
(making meaning)

*"It bothers me the way she's always uptight about everything."*
(making meaning)

They went out through the revolving doors that made a faintly derisive whistling sound when you pushed them. It was two blocks to the parking lot. At the drugstore on the corner she said, "Wait here for me. I forgot something. I won't be a minute." She was more than a minute. Walter Mitty lighted a cigarette. It began to rain, rain with sleet in it. He stood up against the wall of the drugstore, smoking. . . . He put his shoulders back and his heels together. "To hell with the handkerchief," said Walter Mitty scornfully. He took one last drag on his cigarette and snapped it away. Then, with that faint, fleeting smile playing about his lips, he faced the firing squad; erect and motionless, proud and disdainful, Walter Mitty the Undefeated, inscrutable to the last.

*"It sounds like something my mom would say when she's going to the store."*
(making meaning)

*"I think this is a good description. The way he acts."*
(making meaning)

After reading and commenting on "The Secret Life of Walter Mitty," Cole was asked to express her overall impressions of the story. She responded as follows:

*"I think that the writer had a good idea. It was kind of confusing to know when the scene was switched. There are parts that I didn't think needed to be there, for example, the attorney part. I like when Mitty is trying to figure out what he's supposed to be getting, and I think it's neat to fantasize about being in different worlds. He's pretending that he's in different times, different situations."*

# Responding in Writing

Everyone who reads and writes belongs to a special community, a community of readers and writers. You too are part of this community. When you read, you discover meaning that reflects who you are as well as what the writer is trying to communicate. When you write, you discover ideas about yourself, about the world, and about what you read.

Important aspects of studying the literature in this book are writing *about* the literature and writing *from* the literature. Much of the writing you will do will be shared with the other members of your classroom community. Some pieces will be shared with members of the broader community. Others will be personal writing for you alone.

On the following pages you will find practical information that you can apply in many different writing situations. You can use this information as a reference as you develop skill in reading literature and writing about it.

## The Reader's Journal

Like all readers, you observe, question, predict, and compare as you read. You experience feelings such as excitement and amusement. One place to record these responses to literature is in a reader's journal or reading log. Your journal then can serve as a rich source of writing ideas. Your journal can also serve as the place to record notes as you prepare for a writing assignment.

Here are some tips for keeping a journal:

**GUIDE:**

*Keeping a Journal*

- Carry your journal with you or keep it in an accessible place.
- Date and label your journal entries.
- Record words, passages, and lines that trigger ideas, along with your responses to these ideas.
- Set aside part of your journal for the journal writing that is suggested throughout this book.
- Set aside another part of your journal for observations, quotations, and imaginative writing that is not tied to a literary selection.

**ACTIVITY 1:** *Using a Journal*

Scan "The Secret Life of Walter Mitty." Take notes that will help you write about the Mittys' day from Mrs. Mitty's point of view. Mark your journal entry with the label "Second reading" or with another appropriate phrase. Save these notes to use as you work through this writing handbook.

## The Writing Process

Writing is a process unique to each writer and to each writing situation. However, certain activities need to take place during most writing experiences. Following are some of these activities:

- **Exploring ideas:** reflecting on what you know, what you need to know, and where you might find what you need
- **Gathering material:** remembering, imagining, reading, observing, interviewing, discussing
- **Discovering connections:** exploring how ideas fit together, allowing new ideas to surface, elaborating and pushing ideas to their limits
- **Eliminating barriers to communication:** rethinking content, reshaping structure, refining mechanics and usage

In many books about writing, each of these activities is described in connection with a specific stage of the writing process: prewriting, drafting and discovery, revision (and editing), or publishing and presenting. In reality, though, any of the activities can take place at any point in the process, depending on how the writing experience is progressing.

## The Writer as Decision-Maker

During the writing process, writers make a series of decisions that give direction or redirection to their writing. These decisions concern the key issues of purpose, audience, subject, point of view, and form. Following is a list of questions to guide you in thinking about these issues as you plan your writing, as you get your ideas down on paper, and as you revise your work.

**GUIDE:**

*Making Key Decisions*

**Purpose**

Is a purpose stated in the assignment?

What are my personal goals?

What do I really want to do in this piece: express ideas or feelings? inform? entertain? analyze? persuade?

How do I want my audience to respond?

**Audience**

Who will read my writing?

What do my readers know?

What might they need to know?

What might they find interesting?

**Subject**

What exactly am I writing about: my own thoughts and feelings? a piece of literature? information from sources outside the book?

What information must I pull together or research?

Will I need to fill in details from my imagination?

How detailed will I need to be for my audience?

**Point of View**

In whose voice am I writing: my own? that of a character in a story? that of an imagined person?

What does the narrator, or "voice," know? think? feel?

**Form**

Is a form named in the assignment?

What is the most effective organization to accomplish my purpose?

What should the final product look like?

☞ **ACTIVITY 2:** *Making Decisions*

*The following assignment is an example of the kinds of writing assignments in this book. This assignment is based on the story "The Secret Life of Walter Mitty."*

**Assignment:** *Put yourself in Mrs. Mitty's shoes. Describe your day with Walter in a letter to your mother.*

*Assume that you've been given this assignment. Begin planning your writing, either by exploring further the ideas about Mrs. Mitty that you wrote for Activity 1 or by drafting some preliminary paragraphs. Think about purpose, audience, subject, point of view, and form only as much as seems comfortable for you at this time. Save any writing that you do.*

## The Writer as Problem-Solver

Everyone's writing process is personal. Many writers, however, experience the same kinds of difficulties. The questions they ask tend to sound like these:

1. Where do I start? Where do I get ideas? What do I do with them?

2. Who can help me? When should I ask for help?

3. How do I know what's wrong with my writing? How do I fix it?

On this page and the following pages are some strategies to help you deal with these common problems.

## Strategies: *Clustering and Brainstorming*

The notes in your reader's journal can be a good starting point for many writing assignments. When you need to explore further the ideas in your journal, to generate new ideas, or to discover connections among ideas, you might want to try the technique of clustering. A cluster is a diagram showing a central idea and related ideas. To begin a cluster, write a central idea in the middle of a page and draw a circle around it. Outside the circle, write related ideas. Circle each one and draw a line connecting it to the central idea.

This cluster shows the central idea "Walter Mitty" surrounded by words and phrases that describe his qualities.

**GRAPHIC:**

*Cluster Diagram*

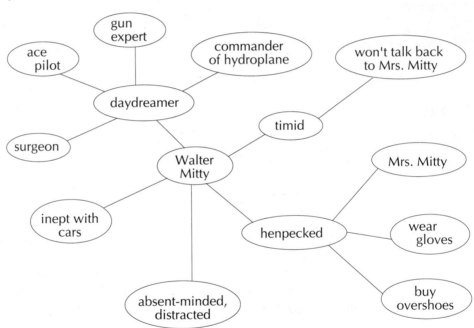

This particular cluster diagram would be useful for writing a character sketch of Mitty. Clustering is also a useful technique for writing poems, recording feelings about literature, and creating metaphors.

### ACTIVITY 3: *Creating a Cluster Diagram*

*Create a cluster of ideas about Mrs. Mitty. Use the ideas in your journal as a starting point and fill in details, real and imagined. When you finish, think about the "voice" in which Mrs. Mitty might speak.*

**Brainstorming** is similar to clustering. In brainstorming, though, you write down every idea that comes to mind, whether it is related or not. Brainstorming can be done alone, but it is even more productive when done in a group.

## STRATEGIES: *Charts and Diagrams*

Charts and diagrams can help you to discover connections as well as to pinpoint where you need to gather more material. The following two types of charts are especially useful for assignments in which you must understand and explain a sequence of events. The charts can be completed as you read—or reread— a work of literature.

**GRAPHIC:**

*Story-Sequence Map*

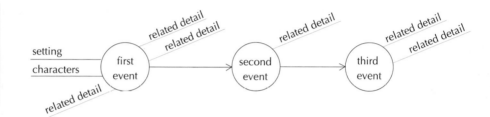

**GRAPHIC:**

*Time Line*

event 1   event 2   event 3   event 4   event 5   event 6   event 7   event 8

(dates, days, times of day)

The next two types of graphics are useful tools for organizing ideas when an assignment asks you to compare and contrast two or more subjects. You might begin such an assignment by listing the qualities of each subject on a comparison/contrast chart and then identifying similarities and differences on that same chart. Another approach would be to use a Venn diagram to record the similarities and differences you want to write about.

**GRAPHIC:**

*Comparison/ Contrast Chart*

| First Subject | Second Subject | Similarities | Differences |
|---|---|---|---|
| | | | |
| | | | |
| | | | |
| | | | |
| | | | |

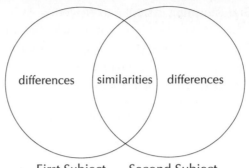

differences | similarities | differences

First Subject    Second Subject

∞ **ACTIVITY 4:** *Using Graphics for Writing*

*1. Trace the events of Mrs. Mitty's day, using a story-sequence map or a time line. Use the notes in your journal and the writing you did for Activity 2. Add imaginary details as needed.*

*2. Use a comparison/contrast chart or Venn diagram to show how Mr. and Mrs. Mitty are alike and different from each other. Use information from the two cluster diagrams: the sample one about Walter Mitty and the one you created for Activity 3. Add details if necessary.*

## STRATEGIES: *Peers as Partners*

Because you are part of a community of readers and writers, you can work with a partner at any point in the writing process. You can co-develop a writing plan, bounce ideas off a friend, ask a classmate to read a draft or a cleaned-up copy, or in some cases team-write a piece. Involving peers in your problem-solving process can help you in exploring and clarifying ideas, in seeing a subject from a different perspective, and in identifying and eliminating problems in communication.

When you want some feedback on a piece of writing, you can read it to a class-mate and then ask that person two simple questions: What do you like? What don't you like?

A way to get more detailed feedback, especially for longer pieces, is to give a class-mate the piece of writing along with the following thought-provoking questions. You can use the answers to these questions as a guide for talking about your writing with your partner.

• What did you like the best? the least?

• What message do you think I am trying to get across? Summarize it for me.

• What do you want to know more about? What parts went on too long?

• Did the beginning work for you? Did the ending?

• Did you have any trouble following my ideas?

## STRATEGIES: *Self-Evaluation*

Sometimes a first draft of a piece of writing presents few barriers to communication and therefore needs little revision. Other times you may have to write several drafts, perhaps going back to do more research or to rethink the ideas. When trying to figure out what's wrong with a piece of writing that just isn't working, you can start with a quick check like the following:

- The main point I am trying to make is _____.
- I want my reader to respond to my writing by thinking or feeling that _____ .
- In looking back over the piece, I like _____. I don't like _____.

At this point you'll want to review the personal goals you set when identifying the purpose of your writing and to decide how close you've come to meeting your goals. You'll also want to read your writing aloud, listening for ideas that are unclear or unnecessary, ideas that don't connect logically, abrupt transitions from one idea to the next, a dull or choppy style, and words that don't sound quite right or aren't right for your audience. You might use the following checklists to guide your analysis.

### Checklist for Rethinking Content

- Have I discovered what's most important in my writing and expressed the focus or main idea clearly in my draft?
- Have I included all the ideas my readers need in order to understand my message? Have I left anything out?
- Are my ideas presented so they can be easily understood?

### Checklist for Reworking Structure

- Do the details relate directly to my focus or main idea?
- Is the material organized effectively so that the relationship between ideas is clear?
- Do the sentences and paragraphs flow smoothly?

## STRATEGIES: *The Final Edit*

It would be wonderful to know perfectly all the rules of grammar, spelling, capitalization, punctuation, and usage, all the synonyms for every word, all the meanings for every word you read or hear. The next best thing is to know where to get the information you need to refine your writing. Here are some ideas:

- To check spelling: dictionary, spelling dictionary, computer spellchecker
- To check punctuation, capitalization, grammar, and usage: composition and grammar textbook such as *The Writer's Craft*
- To check word meanings and synonyms: dictionary, thesaurus

One point to check carefully when writing about literature is the accuracy of your quotations and of your spellings of any names and titles. The literature itself is your source for this information.

### ACTIVITY 5: *Wrapping Up the Lesson*

*Complete the assignment that asks you to write a letter in the voice of Mrs. Mitty. Use the materials that you developed for Activities 1 through 4. As an alternative, compare and contrast Mr. and Mrs. Mitty in a report to the Mittys written by a marriage counselor. Use the information on the chart you developed for Activity 4.*

## The Writer as Learner

After you have completed a piece of writing, you'll want to reflect on your writing process. Questions like these can help you to focus on various aspects of the writing and learning experience:

- Am I pleased with my final product?
- Did I become involved in my topic?
- Did I learn something from writing about it?
- Which aspects of the writing process were easiest for me? Which were the most difficult?
- What aspect of writing is becoming easier?
- What was the biggest problem I encountered? How did I solve the problem? How might I avoid the problem next time?
- When I compare this piece of writing with others in my working folder or portfolio, can I see changes in my writing style? in my writing skill?
- Have I seen anything in the writing done by my peers or by professional writers that I would like to try myself?

Another way to learn from a writing experience is through an objective evaluation of your final product. The evaluation may be conducted by a teacher or a peer reader. The goal is the same: to contribute to your growth as a writer and to heighten your sense of writing as communication.

# STRATEGIES: *The Evaluation Task*

Each kind of writing has certain characteristics unique to that writing. An evaluator, however, can assess the strengths and weaknesses of most writing using general guidelines in three key areas: (1) content, (2) form, and (3) grammar, usage, and mechanics.

The following is a description of a well-developed piece of writing. You might use the description when you are acting as a peer evaluator and when judging whether your own work is ready for a final evaluation or in need of further revision.

**GUIDE:**

*Evaluating Content*

**The content of a well-developed piece of writing . . .**

Is clearly focused throughout the piece

Maintains a consistent tone and point of view

Uses precise verbs, nouns, and modifiers and incorporates descriptive and figurative language as appropriate

Elaborates on the ideas with supporting details, examples, and summaries as appropriate

Demonstrates a clear sense of purpose

Demonstrates a clear sense of audience through choice of language and details

**GUIDE:**

*Evaluating Form*

**The form of a well-developed piece of writing . . .**

Maintains clear relationships among ideas through effective transitions

Demonstrates an awareness of correct and effective paragraphing

Includes sentences with a variety of structures

**GUIDE:**

*Evaluating Grammar, Usage, and Mechanics*

**The final draft of a well-developed piece of writing . . .**

Demonstrates understanding and application of editing and proofreading skills

Contains few, if any, minor errors in grammar and usage

Contains few, if any, minor errors in spelling, capitalization, and punctuation

## ACTIVITY 6: *Evaluating Process and Product*

*Evaluate the assignment that you completed for Activity 5. First reflect on your writing process, using Guide: Learning from the Writing Process. Next apply the three evaluating guides to your own writing. Assess strengths to build on and weaknesses to remedy. Then ask a classmate to do the same, and compare the results.*

# The Writer as Communicator

When the time comes to share your writing, you have many choices. A few of these choices are listed below.

**OPTIONS:**

*Publishing and Presenting*

- Trade papers with the classmate who helped you refine your ideas.
- Trade papers with a classmate unfamiliar with your work.
- Read your writing to a small group of classmates or to the class.
- Ask a classmate to read your writing aloud.
- Read your writing to younger children or to adults in your family or community.
- Discuss the ideas explored in your writing and the conclusions you arrived at.
- Choose appropriate ideas to share in a discussion and save others for future use.
- Present a dramatic reading with sound effects.
- Tape-record a reading of the piece.
- Stage your work as simple Readers Theater or as a more elaborate performance.
- Publish a booklet of your own writing or of writing by many contributors.
- Display your writing in the classroom or school.
- Submit your writing to the school newspaper or literary magazine.
- Mail your writing to a magazine or newspaper with a wider circulation.
- Add your writing to your notebook or portfolio for later sharing.

Whatever option you choose, share your work in the spirit of learning and growing in your role as communicator.

## ☞ ACTIVITY 7: *Publishing and Presenting*

*Brainstorm with two or three classmates about ways to share your writing about "The Secret Life of Walter Mitty." Choose one way, plan how to share, and then follow through on your plan.*

*"Literature is news
that stays news."*

EZRA POUND

*Page from a Notebook,* 1921, ROGER DE LA FRESNAYE.

# The Short Story

*"A story always involves, in a dramatic way, the mystery of personality."*

FLANNERY O'CONNOR

# On the Edge of Your Seat: Suspense

PERHAPS YOU'VE FELT IT: the inner tension that builds when the action in a story gets exciting or the hero or heroine is in trouble. At those moments you may wonder, "What is going to happen next?" and eagerly turn the pages to learn the character's fate. Stories that create an excited curiosity in the reader usually involve an element of danger or an unexpected twist that takes the reader by surprise. Adventure stories are full of uncertainty about who will survive, how the hero or heroine will triumph, when evil will be defeated, where help will come from. The unpredictability of events adds to the reader's enjoyment of the story.

The stories in this section keep the reader guessing right up to the last line. In "The Secret Life of Walter Mitty," the excitement lies only in Walter Mitty's fantasies; his real life is dull, predictable, and safe. In the stories you are about to read, the stakes are much higher—and your experience is likely to be more intense. As you read, you may find yourself sitting on the edge of your seat.

*Diver*, 1919,
FRANS MASEREEL.
From *Passionate Journey* by Frans Masereel. © Europa Verlag, Zurich, Switzerland.

# Literary Vocabulary

## INTRODUCED IN THIS SECTION

**Plot.** Plot refers to the actions and events in a literary work. The basic plot of "The Secret Life of Walter Mitty" is not only simple but a bit boring: Mitty takes his wife to the hairdresser and runs a few errands. However, the plots of Mitty's daydreams are much more complex, as well as being full of danger and romance.

**Suspense.** Suspense is the excitement or tension that readers feel as they become involved in a story and eager to know the outcome.

**Conflict.** The plot of a story always involves some sort of conflict, or struggle between opposing forces. In Walter Mitty's first daydream, the conflict is between Commander Mitty and the storm that threatens his hydroplane and crew. The conflict in the basic plot of the story is between the timid Mitty and his overbearing wife. All these conflicts are **external** in that they involve a character pitted against an outside force—nature, a physical obstacle, or another character. An **internal conflict** is one that occurs within a character.

**Climax.** Often called a turning point, the climax is the moment when the reader's interest and emotional intensity reach the highest point. The climax usually occurs toward the end of a story, after the reader has understood the conflict and gotten emotionally involved with the characters. The climax sometimes, but not always, points to the resolution of the conflict. In Walter Mitty's first daydream, for instance, the climax occurs when Mitty acts decisively and the crew is reassured that "the Old Man'll get us through." The climax of the basic plot of the story is harder to spot. The conflict between Mitty and his wife reaches a peak when Mitty finally talks back to her: "Does it ever occur to you that I am sometimes thinking?" When Mrs. Mitty regains her control, however, Mitty is defeated, except in his dreams.

# The Most Dangerous Game

RICHARD CONNELL

A biography of Connell appears on page 638.

## Approaching the Story

The thrill of the hunt! For those under its influence, hunting has a powerful pull. "The Most Dangerous Game" is a story about big game hunters, people with the desire—as well as the money and the time—to travel the world seeking bigger and more challenging animals to hunt. For such people, big game hunting may be either a sport or a career. In either case, danger and the excitement of the chase are part of the appeal.

## Building Vocabulary

These essential words are footnoted within the story.

**palpable** (pal´ pə bəl): "Can't see it," remarked Rainsford, trying to peer through the dank tropical night that was **palpable** as it pressed its thick, warm blackness in upon the yacht. (page 5)

**tangible** (tan´ jə bəl): Sometimes I think evil is a **tangible** thing—with wavelengths, just as sound and light have. (page 5)

**quarry** (kwôr´ ē): I suppose the first three shots I heard was when the hunter flushed his **quarry**. (page 7)

**affable** (af´ ə bəl): He was finding the general a most thoughtful and **affable** host. (page 9)

**condone** (kən dōn´): "Surely your experiences in the war—" "Did not make me **condone** coldblooded murder," finished Rainsford stiffly. (page 11)

**scruples** (skr<u>oo</u>´ pəlz): "Your **scruples** are quite ill-founded." (page 11)

**futile** (fy<u>oo</u>t´ ʹl): He saw that straight flight was **futile**; inevitably it would bring him face to face with the sea. (page 14)

**imperative** (im per´ ə tiv): His need for rest was **imperative**. (page 14)

## Connecting Writing and Reading

Why do some people like to hunt? In your journal, list reasons that people might have for hunting. As you read, think about the motives of the hunters in this story.

O FF THERE TO the right —somewhere—is a large island," said Whitney. "It's rather a mystery—"

"What island is it?" Rainsford asked.

"The old charts call it 'Ship-Trap Island,'" Whitney replied. "A suggestive name, isn't it? Sailors have a curious dread of the place. I don't know why. Some superstition—"

"Can't see it," remarked Rainsford, trying to peer through the dank tropical night that was palpable[1] as it pressed its thick, warm blackness in upon the yacht.

"You've good eyes," said Whitney, with a laugh, "and I've seen you pick off a moose moving in the brown fall bush at four hundred yards; but even you can't see four miles or so through a moonless Caribbean night."

"Nor four yards," admitted Rainsford. "Ugh! It's like moist black velvet."

"It will be light in Rio," promised Whitney. "We should make it in a few days. I hope the jaguar guns have come from Purdey's. We should have some good hunting up the Amazon. Great sport, hunting."

"The best sport in the world," agreed Rainsford.

"For the hunter," amended Whitney. "Not for the jaguar."

"Don't talk rot, Whitney," said Rainsford. "You're a big-game hunter, not a philosopher. Who cares how a jaguar feels?"

"Perhaps the jaguar does," observed Whitney.

"Bah! They've no understanding."

"Even so, I rather think they understand one thing—fear. The fear of pain and the fear of death."

"Nonsense," laughed Rainsford. "This hot weather is making you soft, Whitney. Be a realist. The world is made up of two classes—the hunters and the huntees. Luckily, you and I are hunters. Do you think we've passed that island yet?"

"I can't tell in the dark. I hope so."

"Why?" asked Rainsford.

"The place has a reputation—a bad one."

"Cannibals?" suggested Rainsford.

"Hardly. Even cannibals wouldn't live in such a Godforsaken place. But it's gotten into sailor lore, somehow. Didn't you notice that the crew's nerves seemed a bit jumpy today?"

"They were a bit strange, now you mention it. Even Captain Nielsen—"

"Yes, even that tough-minded old Swede, who'd go up to the devil himself and ask him for a light. Those fishy blue eyes held a look I never saw there before. All I could get out of him was: 'This place has an evil name among seafaring men, sir.' Then he said to me, very gravely, 'Don't you feel anything?'—as if the air about us was actually poisonous. Now, you mustn't laugh when I tell you this—I did feel something like a sudden chill.

"There was no breeze. The sea was as flat as a plate-glass window. We were drawing near the island then. What I felt was a—a mental chill; a sort of sudden dread."

"Pure imagination," said Rainsford. "One superstitious sailor can taint the whole ship's company with his fear."

"Maybe. But sometimes I think sailors have an extra sense that tells them when they are in danger. Sometimes I think evil is a tangible[2] thing—with wavelengths, just as sound and light have. An evil place can, so to speak, broadcast vibrations of evil. Anyhow, I'm glad we're getting out of this zone. Well, I think I'll turn in now, Rainsford."

"I'm not sleepy," said Rainsford. "I'm going to smoke another pipe up on the afterdeck."

"Good night, then, Rainsford. See you at breakfast."

"Right. Good night, Whitney."

---

1. **palpable** (pal′ pə bəl): that can be touched or felt.
2. **tangible** (tan′ jə bəl): that can be touched or felt; having actual form and substance.

There was no sound in the night as Rainsford sat there but the muffled throb of the engine that drove the yacht swiftly through the darkness and the swish and ripple of the wash of the propeller.

Rainsford, reclining in a steamer chair, indolently puffed on his favorite briar. The sensuous drowsiness of the night was on him. "It's so dark," he thought, "that I could sleep without closing my eyes; the night would be my eyelids—"

An abrupt sound startled him. Off to the right he heard it, and his ears, expert in such matters, could not be mistaken. Again he heard the sound, and again. Somewhere, off in the blackness, someone had fired a gun three times.

Rainsford sprang up and moved quickly to the rail, mystified. He strained his eyes in the direction from which the reports had come, but it was like trying to see through a blanket. He leaped upon the rail and balanced himself there, to get greater elevation; his pipe, striking a rope, was knocked from his mouth. He lunged for it; a short, hoarse cry came from his lips as he realized he had reached too far and had lost his balance. The cry was pinched off short as the blood-warm waters of the Caribbean Sea closed over his head.

He struggled up to the surface and tried to cry out, but the wash from the speeding yacht slapped him in the face and the salt water in his open mouth made him gag and strangle. Desperately he struck out with strong strokes after the receding lights of the yacht, but he stopped before he had swum fifty feet. A certain coolheadedness had come to him; it was not the first time he had been in a tight place. There was a chance that his cries could be heard by someone aboard the yacht, but that chance was slender and grew more slender as the yacht raced on. He wrestled himself out of his clothes, and shouted with all his power. The lights of the yacht became faint and ever-vanishing fireflies; then they were blotted out entirely by the night.

Rainsford remembered the shots. They had come from the right, and doggedly he swam in that direction, swimming with slow, deliberate strokes, conserving his strength. For a seemingly endless time he fought the sea. He began to count his strokes; he could do possibly a hundred more and then—

Rainsford heard a sound. It came out of the darkness, a high screaming sound, the sound of an animal in an extremity of anguish and terror.

He did not recognize the animal that made the sound. He did not try to. With fresh vitality, he swam toward the sound. He heard it again; then it was cut short by another noise, crisp, staccato.

"Pistol shot," muttered Rainsford, swimming on.

Ten minutes of determined effort brought another sound to his ears—the most welcome he had ever heard—the muttering and growling of the sea breaking on a rocky shore. He was almost on the rocks before he saw them; on a night less calm he would have been shattered against them. With his remaining strength he dragged himself from the swirling waters. Jagged crags appeared to jut up into the opaqueness; he forced himself upward, hand over hand. Gasping, his hands raw, he reached a flat place at the top. Dense jungle came down to the very edge of the cliffs. What perils that tangle of trees and underbrush might hold for him did not concern Rainsford just then. All he knew was that he was safe from his enemy, the sea, and that utter weariness was on him. He flung himself down at the jungle edge and tumbled headlong into the deepest sleep of his life.

When he opened his eyes, he knew from the position of the sun that it was late in the afternoon. Sleep had given him new vigor; a sharp hunger was picking at him. He looked about him, almost cheerfully.

"Where there are pistol shots, there are men. Where there are men, there is food," he thought. But what kind of men, he wondered, in so forbidding a place? An unbroken front of snarled and ragged jungle fringed the shore.

He saw no sign of a trail through the closely knit web of weeds and trees; it was easier to go along the shore, and Rainsford floundered along by the water. Not far from where he landed, he stopped.

Some wounded thing, by the evidence a large animal, had thrashed about in the underbrush. The jungle weeds were crushed down and the moss was lacerated; one patch of weeds was stained crimson. A small, glittering object not far away caught Rainsford's eye, and he picked it up. It was an empty cartridge.

"A twenty-two," he remarked. "That's odd. It must have been a fairly large animal, too. The hunter had his nerve to tackle it with a light gun. It's clear that the brute put up a fight. I suppose the first three shots I heard was when the hunter flushed his quarry[3] and wounded it. The last shot was when he trailed it here and finished it.

He examined the ground closely and found what he had hoped to find—the print of hunting boots. They pointed along the cliff in the direction he had been going. Eagerly he hurried along, now slipping on a rotten log or a loose stone, but making headway; night was beginning to settle down on the island.

Bleak darkness was blacking out the sea and jungle when Rainsford sighted the lights. He came upon them as he turned a crook in the coastline, and his first thought was that he had come upon a village, for there were many lights. But as he forged along, he saw to his great astonishment that all the lights were in one enormous building—a lofty structure with pointed towers plunging upward into the gloom. His eyes made out the shadowy outlines of a palatial chateau; it was set on a high bluff, and on three sides of it cliffs dived down to where the sea licked greedy lips in the shadows.

"Mirage," thought Rainsford. But it was no mirage, he found, when he opened the tall, spiked, iron gate. The stone steps were real enough; the massive door with a leering gargoyle for a knocker was real enough; yet about it all hung an air of unreality.

He lifted the knocker, and it creaked up stiffly, as if it had never before been used. He let it fall, and it startled him with its booming loudness. He thought he heard steps within; the door remained closed. Again Rainsford lifted the heavy knocker, and let it fall. The door opened then, opened as suddenly as if it were on a spring, and Rainsford stood blinking in the river of glaring gold light that poured out. The first thing Rainsford's eyes discerned was the largest man Rainsford had ever seen—a gigantic creature, solidly made and black-bearded to the waist. In his hand the man held a long-barreled revolver, and he was pointing it straight at Rainsford's heart.

Out of the snarl of beard two small eyes regarded Rainsford.

"Don't be alarmed," said Rainsford, with a smile which he hoped was disarming. "I'm no robber. I fell off a yacht. My name is Sanger Rainsford of New York City."

The menacing look in his eyes did not change. The revolver pointed as rigidly as if the giant was a statue. He gave no sign that he understood Rainsford's words or that he had even heard them. He was dressed in uniform, a black uniform trimmed with gray astrakhan.

"I'm Sanger Rainsford of New York," Rainsford began again. "I fell off a yacht. I am hungry."

The man's only answer was to raise with his thumb the hammer of his revolver. Then Rainsford saw the man's free hand go to his forehead in a military salute, and he saw him click his heels together and stand at attention.

---

3. **quarry** (kwôr′ ē): anything that is being hunted.

Another man was coming down the broad marble steps, an erect, slender man in evening clothes. He advanced to Rainsford and held out his hand.

In a cultivated voice marked by a slight accent that gave it added precision and deliberateness, he said: "It is a very great pleasure and honor to welcome Mr. Sanger Rainsford, the celebrated hunter, to my home."

Automatically Rainsford shook the man's hand.

"I've read your book about hunting snow leopards in Tibet, you see," explained the man. "I am General Zaroff."

Rainsford's first impression was that the man was singularly handsome; his second was that there was an original, almost bizarre quality about the general's face. He was a tall man past middle age, for his hair was a vivid white; but his thick eyebrows and pointed military mustache were as black as the night from which Rainsford had come. His eyes, too, were black and very bright. He had high cheek bones, a sharp-cut nose, a spare, dark face, the face of a man used to giving orders, the face of an aristocrat. Turning to the giant in uniform, the general made a sign. The giant put away his pistol, saluted, withdrew.

"Ivan is an incredibly strong fellow," remarked the general, "but he has the misfortune to be deaf and dumb. A simple fellow, but, I'm afraid, like all his race, a bit of a savage."

"Is he Russian?"

"He is a Cossack,"[4] said the general, and his smile showed red lips and pointed teeth. "So am I."

"Come," he said, "we shouldn't be chatting here. We can talk later. Now you want clothes, food, rest. You shall have them. This is a most restful spot."

Ivan had reappeared, and the general spoke to him with lips that moved but gave forth no sound.

"Follow Ivan, if you please, Mr. Rainsford," said the general. "I was about to have my dinner when you came. I'll wait for you. You'll find that my clothes will fit you, I think."

It was to a huge, beam-ceilinged bedroom with a canopied bed big enough for six men that Rainsford followed the silent giant. Ivan laid out an evening suit, and Rainsford, as he put it on, noticed that it came from a London tailor who ordinarily cut and sewed for none below the rank of duke.

The dining room to which Ivan conducted him was in many ways remarkable. There was a medieval magnificence about it. It suggested a baronial hall of feudal times[5] with its oaken panels, its high ceiling, its vast refectory table where twoscore men could sit down to eat. About the hall were the mounted heads of many animals—lions, tigers, elephants, moose, bears; larger or more perfect specimens Rainsford had never seen. At the great table the general was sitting, alone.

"You'll have a cocktail, Mr. Rainsford," he suggested. The cocktail was surpassingly good; and, Rainsford noted, the table appointments were the finest—the linen, the crystal, the silver, the china.

They were eating borsch, the rich, red soup with sour cream so dear to Russian palates. Half apologetically General Zaroff said, "We do our best to preserve the amenities of civilization here. Please forgive any lapses. We are well off the beaten track, you know. Do you think the champagne has suffered from its long ocean trip?"

"Not in the least," declared Rainsford. He was finding the general a most thoughtful and

---

4. **Cossack** (käs′ ak′): a member of a favored military caste of frontiersman and border guards of southern Russia during the time of the Czars, famous as horsemen and cavalrymen.

5. **baronial** (bə rō′ nē əl) **hall of feudal times:** the residence, usually a spacious house or castle, of a European nobleman in the Middle Ages.

affable [6] host, a true cosmopolite. But there was one small trait of the general's that made Rainsford uncomfortable. Whenever he looked up from his plate he found the general studying him, appraising him narrowly.

"Perhaps," said General Zaroff, "you were surprised that I recognized your name. You see, I read all books on hunting published in English, French, and Russian. I have but one passion in my life, Mr. Rainsford, and it is the hunt."

"You have some wonderful heads here," said Rainsford as he ate a particularly well cooked filet mignon. "That Cape buffalo is the largest I ever saw."

"Oh, that fellow. Yes, he was a monster."

"Did he charge you?"

"Hurled me against a tree," said the general. "Fractured my skull. But I got the brute."

"I've always thought," said Rainsford, "that the Cape buffalo is the most dangerous of all big game."

For a moment the general did not reply; he was smiling his curious, red-lipped smile. Then he said slowly, "No. You are wrong, sir. The Cape buffalo is not the most dangerous big game." He sipped his wine. "Here in my preserve on this island," he said in the same slow tone, "I hunt more dangerous game."

Rainsford expressed his surprise. "Is there big game on this island?"

The general nodded. "The biggest."

"Really?"

"Oh, it isn't here naturally, of course. I have to stock the island."

"What have you imported, General?" Rainsford asked. "Tigers?"

The general smiled. "No," he said. "Hunting tigers ceased to interest me some years ago. I exhausted their possibilities, you see. No thrill left in tigers, no real danger. I live for danger, Mr. Rainsford."

The general took from his pocket a gold cigarette case and offered his guest a long black cigarette with a silver tip; it was perfumed and gave off a smell like incense.

"We will have some capital hunting, you and I," said the general. "I shall be most glad to have your society."

"But what game—" began Rainsford.

"I'll tell you," said the general. "You will be amused, I know. I think I may say, in all modesty, that I have done a rare thing. I have invented a new sensation. May I pour you another glass of port, Mr. Rainsford?"

"Thank you, General."

The general filled both glasses, and said, "God makes some men poets. Some He makes kings, some beggars. Me He made a hunter. My hand was made for the trigger, my father said. He was a very rich man with a quarter of a million acres in the Crimea, and he was an ardent sportsman. When I was only five years old he gave me a little gun, specially made in Moscow for me, to shoot sparrows with. When I shot some of his prize turkeys with it, he did not punish me; he complimented me on my marksmanship. I killed my first bear in the Caucasus [7] when I was ten. My whole life has been one prolonged hunt. I went into the army—it was expected of noblemen's sons—and for a time commanded a division of Cossack cavalry, but my real interest was always the hunt. I have hunted every kind of game in every land. It would be impossible for me to tell you how many animals I have killed."

The general puffed at his cigarette.

"After the debacle in Russia, [8] I left the country, for it was imprudent for an officer of

---

6. **affable** (af′ ə bəl): easy to approach and talk to; friendly.

7. **Crimea** (krī mē′ ə) . . . **Caucasus** (kô′ kə səs): regions in southern U.S.S.R.

8. **debacle** (di bä′ kəl) **in Russia:** a reference to the Russian Revolution of 1917, in which the Communists overthrew the Czar.

the Czar to stay there. Many noble Russians lost everything. I, luckily, had invested heavily in American securities, so I shall never have to open a tearoom in Monte Carlo or drive a taxi in Paris. Naturally, I continued to hunt—grizzlies in your Rockies, crocodiles in the Ganges, rhinoceroses in East Africa. It was in Africa that the Cape buffalo hit me and laid me up for six months. As soon as I recovered, I started for the Amazon to hunt jaguars, for I had heard they were unusually cunning. They weren't." The Cossack sighed. "They were no match at all for a hunter with his wits about him and a high-powered rifle. I was bitterly disappointed. I was lying in my tent with a splitting headache one night when a terrible thought pushed its way into my mind. Hunting was beginning to bore me! And hunting, remember, had been my life. I have heard that in America, businessmen often go to pieces when they give up the business that has been their life."

"Yes, that's so," said Rainsford.

The general smiled. "I had no wish to go to pieces," he said. "I must do something. Now, mine is an analytical mind, Mr. Rainsford. Doubtless that is why I enjoy the problems of the chase."

"No doubt, General Zaroff."

"So," continued the general, "I asked myself why the hunt no longer fascinated me. You are much younger than I am, Mr. Rainsford, and have not hunted as much, but you perhaps can guess the answer."

"What was it?"

"Simply this: hunting had ceased to be what you call 'a sporting proposition.' It had become too easy. I always got my quarry. Always. There is no greater bore than perfection."

The general lit a fresh cigarette.

"No animal had a chance with me any more. That is no boast; it is a mathematical certainty. The animal had nothing but his legs and his instinct. Instinct is no match for reason. When I thought of this it was a tragic

moment for me, I can tell you."

Rainsford leaned across the table, absorbed in what his host was saying.

"It came to me as an inspiration what I must do," the general went on.

"And that was?"

The general smiled the quiet smile of one who has faced an obstacle and surmounted it with success. "I had to invent a new animal to hunt," he said.

"A new animal? You're joking."

"Not at all," said the general. "I never joke about hunting. I needed a new animal. I found one. So I bought this island, built this house, and here I do my hunting. The island is perfect for my purposes—there are jungles with a maze of trails in them, hills, swamps—"

"But the animal, General Zaroff?"

"Oh," said the general, "it supplies me with the most exciting hunting in the world. No other hunting compares with it for an instant. Every day I hunt, and I never grow bored now, for I have a quarry with which I can match my wits."

Rainsford's bewilderment showed in his face.

"I wanted the ideal animal to hunt," explained the general. "So, I said: 'What are the attributes of an ideal quarry?' And the answer was, of course: 'It must have courage, cunning, and, above all, it must be able to reason.'"

"But no animal can reason," objected Rainsford.

"My dear fellow," said the general, "there is one that can."

"But you can't mean—" gasped Rainsford.

"And why not?"

"I can't believe you are serious, General Zaroff. This is a grisly joke."

"Why should I not be serious? I am speaking of hunting."

"Hunting? General Zaroff, what you speak of is murder."

The general laughed with entire good

nature. He regarded Rainsford quizzically. "I refuse to believe that so modern and civilized a young man as you seem to be harbors romantic ideas about the value of human life. Surely your experiences in the war—"

"Did not make me condone[9] coldblooded murder," finished Rainsford stiffly.

Laughter shook the general. "How extraordinarily droll you are!" he said. "One does not expect nowadays to find a young man of the educated class, even in America, with such a naive, and, if I may say so, mid-Victorian point of view. It's like finding a snuffbox in a limousine. Ah, well, doubtless you had Puritan ancestors. So many Americans appear to have had. I'll wager you'll forget your notions when you go hunting with me. You've a genuine new thrill in store for you, Mr. Rainsford."

"Thank you. I'm a hunter, not a murderer."

"Dear me," said the general, quite unruffled. "Again that unpleasant word. But I think I can show you that your scruples[10] are quite ill-founded."

"Yes?"

"Life is for the strong, to be lived by the strong, and, if need be, taken by the strong. The weak of the world were put here to give the strong pleasure. I am strong. Why should I not use my gift? If I wish to hunt, why should I not? I hunt the scum of the earth—sailors from tramp ships—lascars, blacks, Chinese, whites, mongrels—a thoroughbred horse or hound is worth more than a score of them."

"But they are men," said Rainsford hotly.

"Precisely," said the general. "That is why I use them. It gives me pleasure. They can reason, after a fashion. So they are dangerous."

"But where do you get them?"

The general's left eyelid fluttered down in a wink. "This island is called Ship-Trap," he answered. "Sometimes an angry god of the high seas sends them to me. Sometimes, when Providence is not so kind, I help Providence a bit. Come to the window with me."

Rainsford went to the window and looked out toward the sea.

"Watch! Out there!" exclaimed the general, pointing into the night. Rainsford's eyes saw only blackness, and then, as the general pressed a button, far out to sea Rainsford saw the flash of lights.

The general chuckled. "They indicate a channel," he said, "where there's none; giant rocks with razor edges crouch like a sea monster with wide-open jaws. They can crush a ship as easily as I crush this nut." He dropped a walnut on the hardwood floor and brought his heel grinding down on it. "Oh, yes," he said, casually, as if in answer to a question, "I have electricity. We try to be civilized here."

"Civilized? And you shoot down men?"

A trace of anger was in the general's black eyes, but it was there for but a second, and he said, in his most pleasant manner, "Dear me, what a righteous young man you are! I assure you I do not do the thing you suggest. That would be barbarous. I treat these visitors with every consideration. They get plenty of good food and exercise. They get into splendid physical condition. You shall see for yourself tomorrow."

"What do you mean?"

"We'll visit my training school," smiled the general. "It's in the cellar. I have about a dozen pupils down there now. They're from the Spanish bark *San Lucar* that had the bad luck to go on the rocks out there. A very inferior lot, I regret to say. Poor specimens and more accustomed to the deck than to the jungle."

He raised his hand, and Ivan, who served as waiter, brought thick Turkish coffee. Rainsford, with an effort, held his tongue in check.

"It's a game, you see," pursued the general blandly. "I suggest to one of them that we go

---

9. **condone** (kən dōn'): forgive or overlook.
10. **scruples** (skrōō' pəlz): doubts or hesitations about doing something because it may be morally wrong.

hunting. I give him a supply of food and an excellent hunting knife. I give him three hours' start. I am to follow, armed only with a pistol of the smallest caliber and range. If my quarry eludes me for three whole days, he wins the game. If I find him"—the general smiled—"he loses."

"Suppose he refuses to be hunted?"

"Oh," said the general, "I give him his option, of course. He need not play that game if he doesn't wish to. If he does not wish to hunt, I turn him over to Ivan. Ivan once had the honor of serving as official knouter[11] to the Great White Czar, and he has his own ideas of sport. Invariably, Mr. Rainsford, invariably they choose the hunt."

"And if they win?"

The smile on the general's face widened. "To date I have not lost," he said.

Then he added, hastily: "I don't wish you to think me a braggart, Mr. Rainsford. Many of them afford only the most elementary sort of problem. Occasionally I strike a tartar. One almost did win. I eventually had to use the dogs."

"The dogs?"

"This way, please. I'll show you."

The general steered Rainsford to a window. The lights from the windows sent a flickering illumination that made grotesque patterns on the courtyard below, and Rainsford could see moving about there a dozen or so huge black shapes. As they turned toward him, their eyes glittered greenly.

"A rather good lot, I think," observed the general. "They are let out at seven every night. If anyone should try to get into my house—or out of it—something extremely regrettable would occur to him." He hummed a snatch of song from the Folies Bergère.[12]

"And now," said the general, "I want to show you my new collection of heads. Will you come with me to the library?"

"I hope," said Rainsford, "that you will excuse me tonight, General Zaroff. I'm really not feeling at all well."

"Ah, indeed?" the general inquired solicitously. "Well, I suppose that's only natural, after your long swim. You need a good, restful night's sleep. Tomorrow you'll feel like a new man, I'll wager. Then we'll hunt, eh? I've one rather promising prospect—"

Rainsford was hurrying from the room.

"Sorry you can't go with me tonight," called the general. "I expect rather fair sport—a big, strong fellow. He looks resourceful—Well, good night, Mr. Rainsford; I hope you have a good night's rest."

The bed was good, and the pajamas of the softest silk, and he was tired in every fiber of his being, but nevertheless Rainsford could not quiet his brain with the opiate of sleep. He lay, eyes wide open. Once he thought he heard stealthy steps in the corridor outside his room. He sought to throw open the door; it would not open. He went to the window and looked out. His room was high up in one of the towers. The lights of the chateau were out now, and it was dark and silent; but there was a fragment of sallow moon, and by its wan light he could see, dimly, the courtyard. There, weaving in and out in the pattern of shadow, were black, noiseless forms. The hounds heard him at the window and looked up, expectantly, with their green eyes. Rainsford went back to the bed and lay down. By many methods he tried to put himself to sleep. He had achieved a doze when, just as morning began to come, he heard, far off in the jungle, the faint report of a pistol.

General Zaroff did not appear until luncheon. He was dressed faultlessly in the tweeds

---

11. **knouter** (nout′ ər): a person who whipped criminals in Russia.

12. **Folies Bergère** (fō lē′ ber zher′) *French:* an elaborately costumed French theatrical revue featuring musical skits and dancing.

of a country squire. He was solicitous about the state of Rainsford's health.

"As for me," sighed the general, "I do not feel so well. I am worried, Mr. Rainsford. Last night I detected traces of my old complaint."

To Rainsford's questioning glance the general said: "Ennui. Boredom."

Then, taking a second helping of crêpes suzette, the general explained: "The hunting was not good last night. The fellow lost his head. He made a straight trail that offered no problems at all. That's the trouble with these sailors; they have dull brains to begin with, and they do not know how to get about in the woods. They do excessively stupid and obvious things. It's most annoying. Will you have another glass of Chablis, Mr. Rainsford?"

"General," said Rainsford firmly, "I wish to leave this island at once."

The general raised his thickets of eyebrows; he seemed hurt. "But, my dear fellow," the general protested, "you've only just come. You've had no hunting—"

"I wish to go today," said Rainsford. He saw the dead black eyes of the general on him, studying him. General Zaroff's face suddenly brightened.

He filled Rainsford's glass with venerable Chablis from a dusty bottle.

"Tonight," said the general, "we will hunt—you and I."

Rainsford shook his head. "No, General," he said. "I will not hunt."

The general shrugged his shoulders and delicately ate a hothouse grape. "As you wish, my friend," he said. "The choice rests entirely with you. But may I not venture to suggest that you will find my idea of sport more diverting than Ivan's?"

He nodded toward the corner where the giant stood, scowling, his thick arms crossed on his hogshead of chest.

"You don't mean—" cried Rainsford.

"My dear fellow," said the general, "have I not told you I always mean what I say about hunting? This is really an inspiration. I drink to a foeman worthy of my steel—at last."

The general raised his glass, but Rainsford sat staring at him.

"You'll find this game worth playing," the general said enthusiastically. "Your brain against mine. Your woodcraft against mine. Your strength and stamina against mine. Outdoor chess! And the stake is not without value, eh?"

"And if I win—" began Rainsford huskily.

"I'll cheerfully acknowledge myself defeated if I do not find you by midnight of the third day," said General Zaroff. "My sloop will place you on the mainland near a town."

The general read what Rainsford was thinking.

"Oh, you can trust me," said the Cossack. "I will give you my word as a gentleman and a sportsman. Of course you, in turn, must agree to say nothing of your visit here."

"I'll agree to nothing of the kind," said Rainsford.

"Oh," said the general, "in that case—But why discuss that now? Three days hence we can discuss it over a bottle of Veuve Cliquot, unless—"

The general sipped his wine.

Then a businesslike air animated him. "Ivan," he said to Rainsford, "will supply you with hunting clothes, food, a knife. I suggest you wear moccasins; they leave a poorer trail. I suggest, too, that you avoid a big swamp in the southeast corner of the island. We call it Death Swamp. There's quicksand there. One foolish fellow tried it. The deplorable part of it was that Lazarus followed him. You can imagine my feelings, Mr. Rainsford. I loved Lazarus; he was the finest hound in my pack. Well, I must beg you to excuse me now, I always take a siesta after lunch. You'll hardly have time for a nap, I fear. You'll want to start, no doubt. I shall not follow till dusk. Hunting at night is so much more exciting than by day, don't you think? Au revoir,[13] Mr. Rainsford, au revoir."

General Zaroff, with a deep, courtly bow, strolled from the room.

From another door came Ivan. Under one arm he carried khaki hunting clothes, a haversack of food, a leather sheath containing a long-bladed hunting knife; his right hand rested on a cocked revolver thrust in the crimson sash about his waist. . . .

Rainsford had fought his way through the bush for two hours. "I must keep my nerve. I must keep my nerve," he said through tight teeth.

He had not been entirely clearheaded when the château gates snapped shut behind him. His whole idea at first was to put distance between himself and General Zaroff, and, to this end, he had plunged along, spurred on by the sharp rowels of something very like panic. Now he had got a grip on himself, and stopped, and was taking stock of himself and the situation.

He saw that straight flight was futile;[14] inevitably it would bring him face to face with the sea. He was in a picture with a frame of water, and his operations, clearly, must take place within that frame.

"I'll give him a trail to follow," muttered Rainsford, and he struck off from the rude paths he had been following into the trackless wilderness. He executed a series of intricate loops; he doubled on his trail again and again, recalling all the lore of the fox hunt, and all the dodges of the fox. Night found him legweary, with hands and face lashed by the branches, on a thickly wooded ridge. He knew it would be insane to blunder on through the dark, even if he had the strength. His need for rest was imperative,[15] and he thought, "I have played the fox, now I must play the cat of the fable." A big tree with a thick trunk and outspread branches was nearby, and, taking care

to leave not the slightest mark, he climbed up into the crotch, and stretching out on one of the broad limbs, after a fashion, rested. Rest brought him new confidence and almost a feeling of security. Even so zealous a hunter as General Zaroff could not trace him there, he told himself; only the devil himself could follow that complicated trail through the jungle after dark. But, perhaps, the general was a devil—

An apprehensive night crawled slowly by like a wounded snake, and sleep did not visit Rainsford, although the silence of a dead world was on the jungle. Toward morning, when a dingy gray was varnishing the sky, the cry of some startled bird focused Rainsford's attention in that direction. Something was coming through the bush, coming slowly, carefully, coming by the same winding way Rainsford had come. He flattened himself down on the limb, and through a screen of leaves almost as thick as tapestry, he watched. The thing that was approaching was a man.

It was General Zaroff. He made his way along with his eyes fixed in utmost concentration on the ground before him. He paused, almost beneath the tree, dropped to his knees, and studied the ground. Rainsford's impulse was to hurl himself down like a panther, but he saw that the general's right hand held something metallic—a small automatic pistol.

The hunter shook his head several times, as if he were puzzled. Then he straightened up and took from his case one of his black cigarettes; its pungent, incenselike smoke floated up to Rainsford's nostrils.

Rainsford held his breath. The general's eyes had left the ground and were traveling

---

13. **au revoir** (ō′ rə vwär′) *French*: until we meet again; goodbye.
14. **futile** (fyo͞ot′ 'l): useless, hopeless, ineffective.
15. **imperative** (im per′ ə tiv): absolutely necessary; urgent.

inch by inch up the tree. Rainsford froze there, every muscle tensed for a spring. But the sharp eyes of the hunter stopped before they reached the limb where Rainsford lay; a smile spread over his brown face. Very deliberately he blew a smoke ring into the air; then he turned his back on the tree and walked carelessly away, back along the trail he had come. The swish of the underbrush against his hunting boots grew fainter and fainter.

The pent-up air burst hotly from Rainsford lungs. His first thought made him feel sick and numb. The general could follow a trail through the woods at night; he could follow an extremely difficult trail. He must have uncanny powers. Only by the merest chance had the Cossack failed to see his quarry.

Rainsford's second thought was even more terrible. It sent a shudder of cold horror through his whole being. Why had the general smiled? Why had he turned back?

Rainsford did not want to believe what his reason told him was true, but the truth was as evident as the sun that had by now pushed through the morning mists. The general was playing with him! The general was saving him for another day's sport! The Cossack was the cat; he was the mouse. Then it was that Rainsford knew the full meaning of terror.

"I will not lose my nerve. I will not."

He slid down from the tree, and struck off again into the woods. His face was set, and he forced the machinery of his mind to function. Three hundred yards from his hiding place he stopped where a huge, dead tree leaned precariously on a smaller, living one. Throwing off his sack of food, Rainsford took his knife from its sheath and began to work with all his energy.

The job was finished at last, he threw himself down behind a fallen log a hundred feet away. He did not have to wait long. The cat was coming again to play with the mouse.

Following the trail with the sureness of a bloodhound came General Zaroff. Nothing

escaped those searching black eyes, no crushed blade of grass, no bent twig, no mark, no matter how faint, in the moss. So intent was the Cossack on his stalking that he was upon the thing Rainsford had made before he saw it. His foot touched the protruding bough that was the trigger. Even as he touched it, the general sensed his danger and leaped back with the agility of an ape. But he was not quite quick enough; the dead tree, delicately adjusted to rest on the cut living one, crashed down and struck the general a glancing blow on the shoulder as it fell; but for his alertness, he must have been smashed beneath it. He staggered, but he did not fall; nor did he drop his revolver. He stood there, rubbing his injured shoulder, and Rainsford, with fear again gripping his heart, heard the general's mocking laugh ring through the jungle.

"Rainsford," called the general, "if you are within sound of my voice, as I suppose you are, let me congratulate you. Not many men know how to make a Malay man-catcher. Luckily, for me, I too have hunted in Malacca. You are proving interesting, Mr. Rainsford. I am going now to have my wound dressed; it's only a slight one. But I shall be back. I shall be back."

When the general, nursing his bruised shoulder, had gone, Rainsford took up his flight again. It was flight now, a desperate, hopeless flight, that carried him on for some hours. Dusk came, then darkness, and still he pressed on. The ground grew softer under his moccasins; the vegetation grew ranker, denser; insects bit him savagely. Then, as he stepped forward, his foot sank into the ooze. He tried to wrench it back, but the muck sucked viciously at his foot as if it were a giant leech. With a violent effort, he tore his foot loose. He knew where he was now. Death Swamp and its quicksand.

His hands were tight closed as if his nerve were something tangible that someone in the darkness was trying to tear from his grip. The softness of the earth had given him an idea. He stepped back from the quicksand a dozen feet or so and, like some huge prehistoric beaver, he began to dig.

Rainsford had dug himself in in France when a second's delay meant death. That had been a placid pastime compared to his digging now. The pit grew deeper; when it was above his shoulders, he climbed out, and from some hard saplings cut stakes and sharpened them to a fine point. These stakes he planted in the bottom of the pit with the points sticking up. With flying fingers he wove a rough carpet of weeds and branches and with it he covered the mouth of the pit. Then, wet with sweat and aching with tiredness, he crouched behind the stump of a lightning-charred tree.

He knew his pursuer was coming; he heard the padding sound of feet on the soft earth, and the night breeze brought him the perfume of the general's cigarette. It seemed to Rainsford that the general was coming with unusual swiftness; he was not feeling his way along, foot by foot. Rainsford, crouching there, could not see the general, nor could he see the pit. He lived a year in a minute. Then he felt an impulse to cry aloud with joy, for he heard the sharp crackle of the breaking branches as the cover of the pit gave way; he heard the sharp scream of pain as the pointed stakes found their mark. He leaped up from concealment. Then he cowered back. Three feet from the pit a man was standing, with an electric torch in his hand.

"You've done well, Rainsford," the voice of the general called. "Your Burmese tiger pit has claimed one of my best dogs. Again you score. I think, Mr. Rainsford, I'll see what you can do against my whole pack. I'm going home for a rest now. Thank you for a most amusing evening."

At daybreak, Rainsford, lying near the swamp, was awakened by a sound that made him know that he had new things to learn about fear. It was a distant sound, faint and wavering, but he knew it. It was the baying of a pack of hounds.

Rainsford knew he could do one of two things. He could stay where he was and wait. That was suicide. He could flee. That was postponing the inevitable. For a moment he stood there, thinking. An idea that held a wild chance came to him, and tightening his belt, he headed away from the swamp.

The bay of the hounds grew nearer, then still nearer, nearer, ever nearer. On the ridge Rainsford climbed a tree. Down a watercourse, not a quarter of a mile away, he could see the bush moving. Straining his eyes, he saw the lean figure of General Zaroff. Just ahead of him Rainsford made out another figure whose wide shoulders surged through the tall jungle weeds. It was the giant Ivan, and he seemed pulled forward by some unseen force. Rainsford knew that Ivan must be holding the pack in leash.

They would be on him any minute now. His mind worked frantically. He thought of a native trick he had learned in Uganda. He slid down the tree. He caught hold of a springy young sapling, and to it he fastened his hunting knife, with the blade pointing down the trail. With a bit of wild grapevine he tied back the sapling. Then he ran for his life. The hounds raised their voices as they hit the fresh scent. Rainsford knew now how an animal at bay feels.

He had to stop to get his breath. The baying of the hounds stopped abruptly, and Rainsford's heart stopped too. They must have reached the knife.

He shinnied excitedly up a tree and looked back. His pursuers had stopped. But the hope that was in Rainsford's brain when he climbed died, for he saw in the shallow valley that General Zaroff was still on his feet. But Ivan was not. The knife, driven by the recoil of the springing tree, had not wholly failed.

Rainsford had hardly tumbled to the ground when the pack took up the cry again.

"Nerve, nerve, nerve!" he panted, as he dashed along. A blue gap showed between the trees dead ahead. Ever nearer drew the hounds. Rainsford forced himself on toward that gap. He reached it. It was the shore of the sea. Across the cove he could see the gloomy gray stone of the chateau. Twenty feet below him the sea rumbled and hissed. Rainsford hesitated. He heard the hounds. Then he leaped far out into the sea. . . .

When the general and his pack reached the place by the sea, the Cossack stopped. For some minutes he stood regarding the blue-green expanse of water. He shrugged his shoulders. Then he sat down, took a drink of brandy from a silver flask, lit a perfumed cigarette, and hummed a bit from *Madame Butterfly*.[16]

General Zaroff had an exceedingly good dinner in his great paneled dining hall that evening. With it he had a bottle of Pol Roger and half a bottle of Chambertin. Two slight annoyances kept him from perfect enjoyment. One was the thought that it would be difficult to replace Ivan; the other was that his quarry escaped him. Of course, the American hadn't played the game—so thought the general as he tasted his after-dinner liqueur. In his library he read, to soothe himself, from the works of Marcus Aurelius.[17] At ten he went up to his bedroom. He was deliciously tired, he said to himself, as he locked himself in. There was a little moonlight, so, before turning on his light, he went to the window and looked down at the courtyard. He could see the great hounds, and he called: "Better luck another time," to them. Then he switched on the light.

A man, who had been hiding in the curtain of the bed, was standing there.

"Rainsford!" screamed the general. "How did you get here?"

"Swam," said Rainsford. "I found it quicker than walking through the jungle."

The general sucked in his breath and smiled. "I congratulate you," he said. "You have won the game."

Rainsford did not smile. "I am still a beast at bay," he said, in a low, hoarse voice. "Get ready, General Zaroff."

The general made one of his deepest bows. "I see," he said. "Splendid! One of us is to furnish a repast for the hounds. The other will sleep in this very excellent bed. On guard, Rainsford. . . ."

He had never slept in a better bed, Rainsford decided.

---

16. *Madame Butterfly:* an opera composed by Giacomo Puccini.

17. **Marcus Aurelius** (ô rē′ lē əs): a Roman emperor and philosopher.

# *Thinking About the Story*

## A PERSONAL RESPONSE

*sharing
impressions*

**1.** What did you think about General Zaroff as you read this story? Take a minute to describe your thoughts in your journal.

*constructing
interpretations*

**2.** Why does General Zaroff hunt humans?

**Think about**
- Zaroff's descriptions of different kinds of quarry
- his range of experiences as a hunter
- his feelings about other humans

**3.** How does Rainsford change during the story?

**Think about**
- what Rainsford says about hunting
- physical changes he undergoes during the story
- his experience as a quarry

**4.** Why do you think Rainsford wins the game?

**5.** How would you explain the meaning of the title of the story?

## A CREATIVE RESPONSE

**6.** Ivan is General Zaroff's unusual servant. Imagine what Ivan's thoughts might be as he accompanies the general on the hunt for Rainsford.

## A CRITICAL RESPONSE

**7.** Analyze some of the conflicts in this story.

**Think about**
- the different aspects of General Zaroff's personality
- the decisions Rainsford makes
- what is involved in the hunt itself

**8.** Most countries today have laws limiting the kinds and number of animals that can be hunted. As a result, some people have chosen to go on photo safaris rather than hunting safaris. Look at the reasons for hunting that you identified in your journal. Which of those reasons might hold true for photo safaris?

# Analyzing the Writer's Craft

## PLOT AND SUSPENSE

Think about events in the story that aroused your curiosity about or anticipation of what might happen next. When did you feel the most uncertainty about what was to come?

**Building a Literary Vocabulary.** Plot refers to the actions and events in a story. The feeling of excitement or tension that readers experience as they become involved in a story is called suspense. A suspenseful story makes the reader eager to know the outcome of the plot.

**Application: Measuring Suspense.** Create a line graph to show the strength of your feeling of suspense in response to each major event of the story. On the horizontal line, list the major events of the plot, such as *Rainsford hears about the island* and *Rainsford falls overboard*. On the vertical line, make a suspense scale by listing the numbers from 1 (feeling of least suspense) to 10 (most suspense). Then place a dot on the graph above each event and across from the number that indicates your level of suspense. When you have finished, draw a line that connects the dots. Get together with a few of your classmates to compare your line graphs.

# Connecting Reading and Writing

**1.** Early in the story Rainsford says to Whitney, "The world is made up of two classes—the hunters and the huntees." Decide whether you agree or disagree with Rainsford's statement and express your opinion in a **letter** to a newspaper editor.

Option: Write a brief **exposition** of your opinion for a person who likes to hunt.

**2.** Some readers think that the character of General Zaroff is a logical extension of Rainsford's character—that Rainsford would have become like Zaroff if he had not encountered the general. Take a position on this issue and explain your conclusion in a **persuasive speech** to a group of animal rights activists.

Option: Pretend you are Zaroff's and Rainsford's high school guidance counselors and write a **report** in which you compare the two as boys.

**3.** What do you suppose Rainsford has learned from his unusual experience with General Zaroff? Summarize his thoughts after he returns to New York in an **interview** with a reporter.

Option: Write a **diary entry** in which Rainsford records what he learned.

**4.** Describe the legend of Zaroff's island in an **article** for a sensational tabloid.

Option: Compose a **rap song** about General Zaroff.

# The Sniper
## LIAM O'FLAHERTY

A biography of O'Flaherty appears on page 644.

## Approaching the Story

In struggling to gain independence from England to become a unified country, Ireland has endured internal warfare for most of the twentieth century. "The Sniper" is set in Dublin during a civil war in 1922-1923. At that time, one group of citizens, known as the Irish Free State Army, agreed to England's proposal that Ireland become a free republic, but within the British Empire. Another group, the Irish Republican Army, or the Republicans, wanted complete independence from England. The use of tanks and heavy artillery in the clash between these two groups often resulted in the death of innocent civilians.

## Building Vocabulary

These essential words are footnoted within the story.

**beleaguered** (bē lē´ gərd): Around the **beleaguered** Four Courts the heavy guns roared. (page 21)

**ascetic** (ə set´ ik), **fanatic** (fə nat´ ik): His face was the face of a student, thin and **ascetic**, but his eyes had the cold gleam of the **fanatic**. (page 21)

**ruse** (ro͞oz): His **ruse** had succeeded. (page 23)

**remorse** (ri môrs´): He became bitten by **remorse**. (page 23)

## Connecting Writing and Reading

In your journal, name all the reasons you can think of that a person might be your enemy. Then choose the three reasons that you think are the most valid and explain why. As you read this story, notice the feelings of the sniper toward those he considers his enemies.

THE LONG JUNE twilight faded into night. Dublin[1] lay enveloped in darkness but for the dim light of the moon that shone through fleecy clouds, casting a pale light as of approaching dawn over the streets and the dark waters of the Liffey. Around the beleaguered[2] Four Courts the heavy guns roared. Here and there through the city, machine guns and rifles broke the silence of the night, spasmodically, like dogs barking on lone farms. Republicans and Free Staters were waging civil war.

On a roof-top near O'Connell Bridge, a Republican sniper lay watching. Beside him lay his rifle and over his shoulders were slung a pair of field glasses. His face was the face of a student, thin and ascetic,[3] but his eyes had the cold gleam of the fanatic.[4] They were deep and thoughtful, the eyes of a man who is used to looking at death.

He was eating a sandwich hungrily. He had eaten nothing since morning. He had been too excited to eat. He finished the sandwich, and, taking a flask from his pocket, he took a short draught. Then he returned the flask to his pocket. He paused for a moment, considering whether he should risk a smoke. It was dangerous. The flash might be seen in the darkness and there were enemies watching. He decided to take the risk.

Placing a cigarette between his lips, he struck a match. There was a flash and a bullet whizzed over his head. He dropped immediately. He had seen the flash. It came from the opposite side of the street.

He rolled over the roof to a chimney stack in the rear, and slowly drew himself up behind it, until his eyes were level with the top of the parapet. There was nothing to be seen—just the dim outline of the opposite housetop against the blue sky. His enemy was under cover.

Just then an armored car came across the bridge and advanced slowly up the street. It stopped on the opposite side of the street, fifty yards ahead. The sniper could hear the dull panting of the motor. His heart beat faster. It was an enemy car. He wanted to fire, but he knew it was useless. His bullets would never pierce the steel that covered the gray monster.

Then round the corner of a side street came an old woman, her head covered by a tattered shawl. She began to talk to the man in the turret of the car. She was pointing to the roof where the sniper lay. An informer.

The turret opened. A man's head and shoulders appeared, looking toward the sniper. The sniper raised his rifle and fired. The head fell heavily on the turret wall. The woman darted toward the side street. The sniper fired again. The woman whirled round and fell with a shriek into the gutter.

Suddenly from the opposite roof a shot rang out and the sniper dropped his rifle with a curse. The rifle clattered to the roof. The sniper thought the noise would wake the dead. He stooped to pick the rifle up. He couldn't lift it. His forearm was dead.

"Blast!" he muttered, "I'm hit."

Dropping flat onto the roof, he crawled back to the parapet. With his left hand he felt the injured right forearm. There was no pain—just a deadened sensation, as if the arm had been cut off.

Quickly he drew his knife from his pocket, opened it on the breastwork of the parapet, and ripped open the sleeve. There was a small

1. **Dublin** (dub′ lən): a seaport city on the east coast of Ireland at the mouth of the Liffey River.
2. **beleaguered** (bē lē′ gərd): attacked from all sides to prevent escape; encircled.
3. **ascetic** (ə set′ ik): severe and self-denying.
4. **fanatic** (fə nat′ ik): a person who is unreasonably enthusiastic about a cause or belief.

*Barricade II* (detail), 1984,
KAREL HRUSKA.
Collection of the artist.

hole where the bullet had entered. On the other side there was no hole. The bullet had lodged in the bone. It must have fractured it. He bent the arm below the wound. The arm bent back easily. He ground his teeth to overcome the pain.

Then, taking out a field dressing, he ripped open the packet with his knife. He broke the neck of the iodine bottle and let the bitter fluid drip into the wound. A paroxysm of pain swept through him. He placed the cotton wadding over the wound and wrapped the dressing over it. He tied the ends with his teeth.

Then he lay against the parapet, and, closing his eyes, he made an effort of will to overcome the pain.

In the street beneath all was still. The armored car had retired speedily over the bridge, with the machine gunner's head hanging lifelessly over the turret. The woman's corpse lay still in the gutter.

The sniper lay still for a long time nursing his wounded arm and planning escape. Morning must not find him wounded on the roof. The enemy on the opposite roof covered his escape. He must kill that enemy and he could not use his rifle. He had only a revolver to do it. Then he thought of a plan.

Taking off his cap, he placed it over the muzzle of his rifle. Then he pushed the rifle slowly over the parapet, until the cap was visible from the opposite side of the street. Almost immediately there was a report, and a bullet pierced the center of the cap. The sniper slanted the rifle forward. The cap slipped down into the street. Then, catching the rifle in the middle, the sniper dropped his left hand over the roof and let it hang, lifelessly. After a few moments he let the rifle drop to the street. Then he sank to the roof, dragging his hand with him.

Crawling quickly to the left, he peered up at the corner of the roof. His ruse[5] had succeeded. The other sniper, seeing the cap and rifle fall, thought he had killed his man. He was now

standing before a row of chimney pots, looking across, with his head clearly silhouetted against the western sky.

The Republican sniper smiled and lifted his revolver above the edge of the parapet. The distance was about fifty yards—a hard shot in the dim light, and his right arm was paining him like a thousand devils. He took a steady aim. His hand trembled with eagerness. Pressing his lips together, he took a deep breath through his nostrils and fired. He was almost deafened with the report, and his arm shook with the recoil.

Then when the smoke cleared, he peered across and uttered a cry of joy. His enemy had been hit. He was reeling over the parapet in his death agony. He struggled to keep his feet, but he was slowly falling forward, as if in a dream. The rifle fell from his grasp, hit the parapet, fell over, bounded off the pole of a barber's shop beneath, and then clattered on the pavement.

Then the dying man on the roof crumpled up and fell forward. The body turned over and over in space and hit the ground with a dull thud. Then it lay still.

The sniper looked at his enemy falling, and he shuddered. The lust of battle died in him. He became bitten by remorse.[6] The sweat stood out in beads on his forehead. Weakened by his wound and the long summer day of fasting and watching on the roof, he revolted from the sight of the shattered mass of his dead enemy. His teeth chattered, he began to gibber to himself, cursing the war, cursing himself, cursing everybody.

He looked at the smoking revolver in his hand, and with an oath he hurled it to the roof at his feet. The revolver went off with the concussion and the bullet whizzed past the sniper's

---

5. **ruse** (rōōz): a trick or plan for fooling someone.

6. **remorse** (ri môrs′): a deep and continuing sense of guilt.

head. He was frightened back to his senses by the shock. His nerves steadied. The cloud of fear scattered from his mind, and he laughed.

Taking the flask from his pocket, he emptied it at a draught. He felt reckless under the influence of the spirit. He decided to leave the roof now and look for his company commander, to report. Everywhere around was quiet. There was not much danger in going through the streets. He picked up his revolver and put it in his pocket. Then he crawled down through the skylight to the house underneath.

When the sniper reached the laneway on the street level, he felt a sudden curiosity as to the identity of the enemy sniper whom he had killed. He decided that he was a good shot, whoever he was. He wondered did he know him. Perhaps he had been in his own company before the split in the army. He decided to risk going over to have a look at him. He peered around the corner into O'Connell Street. In the upper part of the street there was heavy firing, but around here all was quiet.

The sniper darted across the street. A machine gun tore up the ground around him with a hail of bullets, but he escaped. He threw himself downward beside the corpse. The machine gun stopped.

Then the sniper turned over the dead body and looked into his brother's face.

# Thinking About the Story

## A PERSONAL RESPONSE

*sharing impressions*

**1.** How did you react to the discovery revealed in the last sentence? Use your journal to explore your thoughts and feelings in writing.

*constructing interpretations*

**2.** Why do you think the sniper decides to look at the gunman he killed?

**3.** How does the sniper define who his enemy is throughout the story?

**Think about**
- the causes of the conflict
- his reasons for each of the killings

**4.** What are some of the sniper's feelings about his actions?

**Think about**
- why his eyes are described as having "the cold gleam of the fanatic"
- how he responds to the first two killings
- how he feels immediately after he sees his enemy fall from the parapet

## A CREATIVE RESPONSE

**5.** If the sniper had not looked at his enemy's face and recognized him, what difference would that have made in this story?

## A CRITICAL RESPONSE

**6.** Go back through the story and point out passages that you think are the most suspenseful.

**7.** Many readers find this story a convincing statement against war. Explain why you agree or disagree with this interpretation.

# *A*nalyzing the Writer's Craft

## CLIMAX

What is the moment in "The Sniper" when your interest and involvement with the story reach a high point?

**Building a Literary Vocabulary.** In dramatic or narrative literature, the moment of peak interest and intensity is called the climax, or turning point.

Often the climax is the moment in the story when the outcome becomes clear. In "The Most Dangerous Game," for example, the climax occurs in the final sentence when the reader realizes that Rainsford has beaten General Zaroff at his own game.

**Application: Understanding Climax.** With a few classmates, agree on what event marks the climax of "The Sniper." Then create a chart or diagram that shows the events leading up to that climax. Share your group's chart with the class.

## Connecting Reading and Writing

**1.** It has been said that in war no side really wins. Decide whether you agree or disagree with this statement. Then, using examples from this story and from another source (such as a movie or newspaper), express your opinion in a **letter** to the Secretary of Defense.

Option: Write a **song** about war.

**2.** Imagine the next meeting between the main character of "The Sniper" and his parents. Present their conversation in a **scene** from a story.

Option: Create a **dramatic dialogue.**

**3.** Imagine that you are the sniper and that you have been asked to deliver the eulogy at your brother's funeral. No one there knows that you are responsible for your brother's death. Write the **eulogy** that the sniper might deliver.

Option: Write a **poem** about his brother that the sniper might compose.

**4.** Speculate about possible interpretations of the word *brother* in "The Sniper" in a **speech** to deliver to your class.

Option: Interview several of your classmates and write a **summary** of their interpretations.

# Lather and Nothing Else

HERNANDO TÉLLEZ
Translated from the Spanish

A biography of Téllez appears on page 646.

## *Approaching the Story*

"Lather and Nothing Else" takes place in a Latin American country where an underground revolutionary movement is pitted against the existing government. Usually, revolutionaries use guerrilla warfare, or surprise attacks. When rebel forces work secretly for change in this way, it is difficult for any one person to know who the enemy is.

In this story, the action takes place in an old-fashioned barber shop where the barber uses a straight razor sharpened on a strop, or thick band of leather.

## *Building Vocabulary*

These essential words are footnoted within the story.

**foray** (fôr´ ā): I estimated he had a four-days' growth of beard, the four days he had been gone on the last **foray** after our men. (page 28)

**nape** (nāp): I finished tying the knot against his **nape**. (page 28)

**rejuvenated** (ri jōō´ və nāt´ ed): Torres was **rejuvenated**. (page 29)

**indelible** (in del´ ə bəl), **stanched** (stôncht): The blood would go flowing, along the floor, warm, **indelible,** not to be **stanched,** until it reached the street. (page 30)

**avenger** (ə venj´ ər): And others would say, "The **avenger** of our people. A name to remember." (page 30)

## *Connecting Writing and Reading*

In your journal, copy the following situations that require a decision:
- choosing the three people who should be cut from a school team
- deciding the winner in a talent competition
- deciding how to punish someone who has vandalized the school

For each situation, indicate whether you would want to make the decision yourself or whether you would want someone else to make it for you, and why. As you read "Lather and Nothing Else," think carefully about the complex decision the barber, who is telling the story, must make.

# Lather and Nothing Else

H E CAME IN without a word. I was stropping my best razor. And when I recognized him, I started to shake. But he did not notice. To cover my nervousness, I went on honing the razor. I tried the edge with the tip of my thumb and took another look at it against the light.

Meanwhile, he was taking off his cartridge-studded belt with the pistol holster suspended from it. He put it on a hook in the wardrobe and hung his cap above it. Then he turned full around toward me and, loosening his tie, remarked, "It's hot as the devil. I want a shave." With that he took his seat.

I estimated he had a four-days' growth of beard, the four days he had been gone on the last foray[1] after our men. His face looked burnt, tanned by the sun.

I started to work carefully on the shaving soap. I scraped some slices from the cake, dropped them into the mug, then added a little lukewarm water, and stirred with the brush. The lather soon began to rise.

"The fellows in the troop must have just about as much beard as I." I went on stirring up lather.

"But we did very well, you know. We caught the leaders. Some of them we brought back dead; others are still alive. But they'll all be dead soon."

"How many did you take?" I asked.

"Fourteen. We had to go pretty far in to find them. But now they're paying for it. And not one will escape; not a single one."

He leaned back in the chair when he saw the brush in my hand, full of lather. I had not yet put the sheet on him. I was certainly flustered. Taking a sheet from the drawer, I tied it around my customer's neck.

He went on talking. He evidently took it for granted that I was on the side of the existing regime.

"The people must have gotten a scare with what happened the other day," he said.

"Yes," I replied, as I finished tying the knot against his nape,[2] which smelt of sweat.

"Good show, wasn't it?"

"Very good," I answered, turning my attention now to the brush. The man closed his eyes wearily and awaited the cool caress of the lather.

I had never had him so close before. The day he ordered the people to file through the schoolyard to look upon the four rebels hanging there, my path had crossed his briefly. But the sight of those mutilated bodies kept me from paying attention to the face of the man who had been directing it all and whom I now had in my hands.

It was not a disagreeable face, certainly. And the beard, which aged him a bit, was not unbecoming. His name was Torres. Captain Torres.

I started to lay on the first coat of lather. He kept his eyes closed.

"I would love to catch a nap," he said, "but there's a lot to be done this evening."

I lifted the brush and asked, with pretended indifference: "A firing party?"

"Something of the sort," he replied, "but slower."

"All of them?"

"No, just a few."

---

1. **foray** (fôr′ ā): a sudden attack or raid.
2. **nape** (nāp): back part of the neck.

I went on lathering his face. My hands began to tremble again. The man could not be aware of this, which was lucky for me. But I wished he had not come in. Probably many of our men had seen him enter the shop. And with the enemy in my house I felt a certain responsibility.

I would have to shave his beard just like any other, carefully, neatly, just as though he were a good customer, taking heed that not a single pore should emit a drop of blood. Seeing to it that the blade did not slip in the small whorls. Taking care that the skin was left clean, soft, shining, so that when I passed the back of my hand over it not a single hair should be felt. Yes. I was secretly a revolutionary, but at the same time I was a conscientious barber, proud of the way I did my job. And that four-day beard presented a challenge.

I took up the razor, opened the handle wide, releasing the blade, and started to work, downward from one sideburn. The blade responded to perfection. The hair was tough and hard; not very long, but thick. Little by little the skin began to show through. The razor gave out its usual sound as it gathered up layers of soap mixed with bits of hair. I paused to wipe it clean, and taking up the strop once more went about improving its edge, for I am a painstaking barber.

The man, who had kept his eyes closed, now opened them, put a hand out from under the sheet, felt of the part of his face that was emerging from the lather, and said to me, "Come at six o'clock this evening to the school."

"Will it be like the other day?" I asked, stiff with horror.

"It may be even better," he replied.

"What are you planning to do?"

"I'm not sure yet. But we'll have a good time."

Once more he leaned back and shut his eyes. I came closer, the razor on high.

"Are you going to punish all of them?" I timidly ventured.

"Yes, all of them."

The lather was drying on his face. I must hurry. Through the mirror, I took a look at the street. It appeared about as usual; there was the grocery shop with two or three customers. Then I glanced at the clock, two-thirty.

The razor kept descending. Now from the other sideburn downward. It was a blue beard, a thick one. He should let it grow like some poets, or some priests. It would suit him well. Many people would not recognize him. And that would be a good thing for him, I thought, as I went gently over all the throat line. At this point you really had to handle your blade skillfully, because the hair, while scantier, tended to fall into small whorls. It was a curly beard. The pores might open, minutely, in this area and let out a tiny drop of blood. A good barber like myself stakes his reputation on not permitting that to happen to any of his customers.

And this was indeed a special customer. How many of ours had he sent to their death? How many had he mutilated? It was best not to think about it. Torres did not know I was his enemy. Neither he nor the others knew it. It was a secret shared by very few, just because that made it possible for me to inform the revolutionaries about Torres's activities in the town and what he planned to do every time he went on one of his raids to hunt down rebels. So it was going to be very difficult to explain how it was that I had him in my hands and then let him go in peace, alive, cleanshaven.

His beard had now almost entirely disappeared. He looked younger, several years younger than when he had come in. I suppose that always happens to men who enter and leave barbershops. Under the strokes of my razor, Torres was <u>rejuvenated</u>;[3] yes, because I

---

3. **rejuvenated** (ri jōō′ və nāt′ ed): brought back to youthful strength or appearance.

am a good barber, the best in this town, and I say this in all modesty.

A little more lather here under the chin, on the Adam's apple, right near the great vein. How hot it is! Torres must be sweating just as I am. But he is not afraid. He is a tranquil man, who is not even giving thought to what he will do to his prisoners this evening. I, on the other hand, polishing his skin with this razor but avoiding the drawing of blood, careful with every stroke—I cannot keep my thoughts in order.

Confound the hour he entered my shop! I am a revolutionary but not a murderer. And it would be so easy to kill him. He deserves it. Or does he? No! No one deserves the sacrifice others make in becoming assassins. What is to be gained by it? Nothing. Others and still others keep coming, and the first kill the second, and then these kill the next, and so on until everything becomes a sea of blood. I could cut his throat, so, swish, swish! He would not even have time to moan, and with his eyes shut he would not even see the shine of the razor or the gleam in my eye.

But I'm shaking like a regular murderer. From his throat a stream of blood would flow on the sheet, over the chair, down on my hands, onto the floor. I would have to close the door. But the blood would go flowing, along the floor, warm, <u>indelible,</u>[4] not to be <u>stanched,</u>[5] until it reached the street like a small scarlet river.

I'm sure that with a good strong blow, a deep cut, he would feel no pain. He would not suffer at all. And what would I do then with the body? Where would I hide it? I would have to flee, leave all this behind, take shelter far away, very far away. But they would follow until they caught up with me. "The murderer of Captain Torres. He slit his throat while he was shaving him. What a cowardly thing to

do." And others would say, "The <u>avenger</u>[6] of our people. A name to remember"—my name here. "He was the town barber. No one knew he was fighting for our cause."

And so, which will it be? Murderer or hero? My fate hangs on the edge of this razor blade. I can turn my wrist slightly, put a bit more pressure on the blade, let it sink in. The skin will yield like silk, like rubber, like the strop. There is nothing more tender than a man's skin, and the blood is always there, ready to burst forth. A razor like this cannot fail. It is the best one I have.

But I don't want to be a murderer. No, sir. You came in to be shaved. And I do my work honorably. I don't want to stain my hands with blood. Just with lather, and nothing else. You are an executioner; I am only a barber. Each one to his job. That's it. Each one to his job.

The chin was now clean, polished, soft. The man got up and looked at himself in the glass. He ran his hand over the skin and felt its freshness, its newness.

"Thanks," he said. He walked to the wardrobe for his belt, his pistol, and his cap. I must have been very pale, and I felt my shirt soaked with sweat. Torres finished adjusting his belt buckle, straightened his gun in its holster, and, smoothing his hair mechanically, put on his cap. From his trousers pocket he took some coins to pay for the shave. And he started toward the door. On the threshold he stopped for a moment, and turning toward me he said,

"They told me you would kill me. I came to find out if it was true. But it's not easy to kill. I know what I'm talking about."

---

4. **indelible** (in del′ ə bəl): unable to be erased or blotted out.

5. **stanched** (stôncht): stopped.

6. **avenger** (ə venj′ ər): one who gets revenge for; one who punishes someone who has done wrong.

## A PERSONAL RESPONSE

*sharing impressions*

**1.** Which character do you have the strongest feeling about, Torres or the barber? Describe your reaction in your journal.

*constructing interpretations*

**2.** In your view, does the barber make the right decision? Explain why or why not.

**3.** Why does the barber decide not to kill Torres?
### *Think about*
- how the barber performs his work
- his involvement in the revolutionary movement
- his thoughts about murder

**4.** What kind of person do you think Torres is?
### *Think about*
- the barber's description of him
- what he tells the barber during the shave
- why he puts himself into the barber's hands
- his final words before leaving

## A CREATIVE RESPONSE

**5.** What if the barber had killed Captain Torres? Imagine what the barber's thoughts and actions would be after doing so.

## A CRITICAL RESPONSE

**6.** What do you think is the climax of this story? Be ready to defend your choice.
### *Think about*
- the definition of climax as a turning point and the moment when interest and intensity reach a peak
- the point in the story when the outcome became clear to you

**7.** Although this story takes place in a Latin American country and "The Sniper" takes place in Ireland, the two stories are both about civil war. What other points do you think the two stories have in common?

# *Analyzing the Writer's Craft*

## CONFLICT

What kinds of problems does the barber face?

**Building a Literary Vocabulary.** The struggle between opposing forces that is the basis for the plot of a story is called conflict. External conflicts can occur between characters, between a character and society, or between a character and nature. Rainsford in "The Most Dangerous Game" faces external conflicts with General Zaroff as well as with the jungle environment. Internal conflicts occur between opposing tendencies within a character. In "The Sniper," the sniper's remorse after he kills the other gunman indicates his internal conflict over killing.

**Application: Evaluating Conflicts.** Get together in a group and go back through the story to look for passages that indicate conflicts that the barber faces. Make a list of the conflicts and circle the ones that are internal. Then evaluate which of the conflicts is the most important one in the story.

# *Connecting Reading and Writing*

**1.** How would this episode be different if Captain Torres had told the story? Let him give his interpretation of the episode in a **report** to his commander.

Option: Write a **scene** from the story as told by Torres.

**2.** Write about a difficult decision that you had to make and compare your decision to the barber's. Present your comparison in a **diary entry.**

Option: Write your comparison in the form of a news reporter's **interview** with you.

**3.** Analyze the different aspects of the story that make it suspenseful, such as the references to blood. Present your analysis in a **poster** for a film version of the story.

Option: Explain your analysis in an **exposition** written for someone who has not read the story.

**4.** If the barber of this story, the sniper, and General Zaroff got together, what do you think they would say to one another? Imagine their meeting in a **comic strip.**

Option: Write a **dramatic skit** showing the meeting.

# The Lady, or the Tiger?

### FRANK R. STOCKTON

A biography of Stockton appears on page 646.

## *Approaching the Story*

To enter into the fictional world of this story, take your imagination back through the centuries, back to the time of the Roman Empire, when a person's life might depend on the whims and fancies of a single person, a tyrannical king. The king in this story adheres to the practice of holding public—and often bloody—spectacles in the central arena. Now, the practice of pitting a person against another person or an animal for the amusement of spectators was common throughout ancient times. However, this king considers himself enlightened. He uses the arena as a means of administering justice.

*I*N THE VERY olden time, there lived a semibarbaric king, whose ideas, though somewhat polished and sharpened by the progressiveness of distant Latin neighbors,[1] were still large, florid, and untrammeled, as became the half of him which was barbaric.[2] He was a man of exuberant fancy, and, withal, of an authority so irresistible that, at his will, he turned his varied fancies into facts. He was greatly given to self–communing; and, when he and himself agreed upon anything, the thing was done. When every member of his domestic and political systems moved smoothly in its appointed course, his nature was bland[3] and genial; but whenever there was a little hitch and some of his orbs got out of their orbits, he was blander and more genial still, for nothing pleased him so much as to make the crooked straight and crush down uneven places.

Among the borrowed notions by which his barbarism had become semifixed was that of the public arena, in which, by exhibitions of manly and beastly valor, the minds of his subjects were refined and cultured.

But even here the exuberant and barbaric fancy asserted itself. The arena of the king was built, not to give the people an opportunity of hearing the rhapsodies of dying gladiators, nor to enable them to view the inevitable conclusion of a conflict between religious opinions and hungry jaws, but for purposes far better adapted to widen and develop the mental energies of the people. This vast amphitheater, with its encircling galleries, its mysterious vaults, and its unseen passages, was an agent of

---

1. **Latin neighbors:** people who lived in countries that were part of the Roman Empire.
2. **barbaric** (bär ber′ ik): uncivilized; cruel and brutal.
3. **bland** (bland): mild; suave.

poetic justice, in which crime was punished or virtue rewarded by the decrees of an impartial and incorruptible chance.

When a subject was accused of a crime of sufficient importance to interest the king, public notice was given that on an appointed day the fate of the accused person would be decided in the king's arena, a structure which well deserved its name. Although its form and plan were borrowed from afar, its purpose emanated solely from the brain of this man, who, every barleycorn a king,[4] knew no tradition to which he owed more allegiance than pleased his fancy and who ingrafted on every adopted form of human thought and action the rich growth of his barbaric idealism.

When all the people had assembled in the galleries and the king, surrounded by his court, sat high up on his throne of royal state on one side of the arena, he gave a signal, a door beneath him opened, and the accused subject stepped out into the amphitheater. Directly opposite him, on the other side of the enclosed space, were two doors, exactly alike and side by side. It was the duty and the privilege of the person on trial to walk directly to these doors and open one of them. He could open either door he pleased; he was subject to no guidance or influence but that of the aforementioned impartial and incorruptible chance. If he opened the one, there came out of it a hungry tiger, the fiercest and most cruel that could be procured, which immediately sprang upon him and tore him to pieces, as a punishment for his guilt. The moment that the case of the criminal was thus decided, doleful iron bells were clanged, great wails went up from the hired mourners posted on the outer rim of the arena, and the vast audience, with bowed heads and downcast hearts, wended slowly their homeward way, mourning greatly that one so young and fair, or so old and respected, should have merited so dire a fate.

But if the accused person opened the other door, there came forth from it a lady, the most suitable to his years and station that his majesty could select among his fair subjects; and to this lady he was immediately married, as a reward for his innocence. It mattered not that he might already possess a wife and family or that his affections might be engaged upon an object of his own selection. The king allowed no such subordinate arrangements to interfere with his great scheme of retribution[5] and reward. The exercises, as in the other instance, took place immediately and in the arena. Another door opened beneath the king, and a priest, followed by a band of choristers and dancing maidens blowing joyous airs on golden horns and treading an epithalamic measure,[6] advanced to where the pair stood, side by side, and the wedding was promptly and cheerily solemnized. Then the gay brass bells rang forth their merry peals, the people shouted glad hurrahs, and the innocent man, preceded by children strewing flowers on his path, led his bride to his home.

This was the king's semibarbaric method of administering justice. Its perfect fairness is obvious. The criminal could not know out of which door would come the lady. He opened either he pleased, without having the slightest idea whether, in the next instant, he was to be devoured or married. On some occasions the tiger came out of one door and on some out of the other. The decisions of this tribunal[7] were not only fair, they were positively determinate. The accused person was instantly punished if

---

4. **every barleycorn a king:** the barleycorn is an obsolete unit of measurement (about one-third of an inch, or the length of a grain of barley); this phrase is equivalent to "every inch a king."
5. **retribution** (re′ trə byo͞o′ shən): a punishment that one deserves for a wrong he or she has done.
6. **treading an epithalamic** (ep′ i thə lā′ mik) **measure:** dancing a wedding dance.
7. **tribunal** (trī byo͞o′ nəl): a court of justice.

he found himself guilty, and, if innocent, he was rewarded on the spot, whether he liked it or not. There was no escape from the judgments of the king's arena.

The institution was a very popular one. When the people gathered together on one of the great trial days, they never knew whether they were to witness a bloody slaughter or a hilarious wedding. This element of uncertainty lent an interest to the occasion which it could not otherwise have attained. Thus, the masses were entertained and pleased, and the thinking part of the community could bring no charge of unfairness against this plan; for did not the accused person have the whole matter in his own hands?

This semibarbaric king had a daughter as blooming as his most florid fancies and with a soul as fervent and imperious as his own. As is usual in such cases, she was the apple of his eye and was loved by him above all humanity. Among his courtiers[8] was a young man of that fineness of blood and lowness of station common to the conventional heroes of romance who love royal maidens. This royal maiden was well satisfied with her lover, for he was handsome and brave to a degree unsurpassed in all this kingdom, and she loved him with an ardor[9] that had enough of barbarism in it to make it exceedingly warm and strong. This love affair moved on happily for many months, until one day the king happened to discover its existence. He did not hesitate nor waver in regard to his duty in the premises. The youth was immediately cast into prison, and a day was appointed for his trial in the king's arena. This, of course, was an especially important occasion, and his majesty, as well as all the people, was greatly interested in the workings and development of this trial. Never before had such a case occurred; never before had a subject dared to love the daughter of a king. In afteryears such things became commonplace enough, but then they were, in no slight degree, novel and startling.

The tiger cages of the kingdom were searched for the most savage and relentless beasts, from which the fiercest monster might be selected for the arena, and the ranks of maiden youth and beauty throughout the land were carefully surveyed by competent judges, in order that the young man might have a fitting bride in case fate did not determine for him a different destiny. Of course, everybody knew that the deed with which the accused was charged had been done. He had loved the princess, and neither he, she, nor anyone else thought of denying the fact, but the king would not think of allowing any fact of this kind to interfere with the workings of the tribunal, in which he took such great delight and satisfaction. No matter how the affair turned out, the youth would be disposed of, and the king would take an aesthetic pleasure in watching the course of events, which would determine whether or not the young man had done wrong in allowing himself to love the princess.

The appointed day arrived. From far and near the people gathered and thronged the great galleries of the arena, and crowds, unable to gain admittance, massed themselves against its outside walls. The king and his court were in their places opposite the twin doors—those fateful portals so terrible in their similarity.

All was ready. The signal was given. A door beneath the royal party opened, and the lover of the princess walked into the arena. Tall, beautiful, fair, his appearance was greeted with a low hum of admiration and anxiety. Half the audience had not known so grand a youth had lived among them. No wonder the princess loved him! What a terrible thing for him to be there!

---

8. **courtiers** (kôrt′ ē ərz): attendants or servants at a royal court.

9. **ardor** (är′ dər): an intense feeling; passion.

As the youth advanced into the arena, he turned, as the custom was, to bow to the king, but he did not think at all of that royal personage; his eyes were fixed upon the princess who sat to the right of her father. Had it not been for the moiety[10] of barbarism in her nature, it is probable that lady would not have been there, but her intense and fervid soul would not allow her to be absent on an occasion in which she was so terribly interested.

From the moment that the decree had gone forth, that her lover should decide his fate in the king's arena, she had thought of nothing, night or day, but this great event and the various subjects connected with it. Possessed of more power, influence, and force of character than anyone who had ever before been interested in such a case, she had done what no other person had done—she had possessed herself of the secret of the doors. She knew in which of the two rooms that lay behind those doors stood the cage of the tiger, with its open front, and in which waited the lady. Through these thick doors, heavily curtained with skins on the inside, it was impossible that any noise or suggestion should come from within to the person who should approach to raise the latch of one of them; but gold and the power of a woman's will had brought the secret to the princess.

And not only did she know in which room stood the lady ready to emerge, all blushing and radiant, should her door be opened, but she knew who the lady was. It was one of the fairest and loveliest of the damsels of the court who had been selected as the reward of the accused youth should he be proved innocent of the crime of aspiring to one so far above him, and the princess hated her. Often had she seen, or imagined that she had seen, this fair creature throwing glances of admiration upon the person of her lover, and sometimes she thought these glances were perceived and even returned. Now and then she had seen them talking together; it was but for a moment or two, but much can be said in a brief space. It may have been on most unimportant topics, but how could she know that? The girl was lovely, but she had dared to raise her eyes to the loved one of the princess; and, with all the intensity of the savage blood transmitted to her through long lines of wholly barbaric ancestors, she hated the woman who blushed and trembled behind that silent door.

When her lover turned and looked at her, and his eye met hers as she sat there paler and whiter than anyone in the vast ocean of anxious faces about her, he saw, by that power of quick perception which is given to those whose souls are one, that she knew behind which door crouched the tiger and behind which stood the lady. He had expected her to know it. He understood her nature, and his soul was assured that she would never rest until she had made plain to herself this thing, hidden to all other lookers-on, even to the king. The only hope for the youth in which there was any element of certainty was based upon the success of the princess in discovering this mystery, and the moment he looked upon her, he saw she had succeeded, as in his soul he knew she would succeed.

Then it was that his quick and anxious glance asked the question: "Which?" It was as plain to her as if he shouted it from where he stood. There was not an instant to be lost. The question was asked in a flash; it must be answered in another.

Her right arm lay on the cushioned parapet before her. She raised her hand and made a slight, quick movement toward the right. No one but her lover saw her. Every eye but his was fixed on the man in the arena.

He turned, and with a firm and rapid step he walked across the empty space. Every heart

---

10. **moiety** (moi′ ə tē): a half; either of two equal, or more or less equal, parts.

stopped beating, every breath was held, every eye was fixed immovably upon that man. Without the slightest hesitation, he went to the door on the right and opened it.

Now, the point of the story is this: Did the tiger come out of that door, or did the lady?

The more we reflect upon this question, the harder it is to answer. It involves a study of the human heart which leads us through devious mazes of passion, out of which it is difficult to find our way. Think of it, fair reader, not as if the decision of the question depended upon yourself, but upon that hotblooded, semibarbaric princess, her soul at a white heat beneath the combined fires of despair and jealousy. She had lost him, but who should have him?

How often, in her waking hours and in her dreams, had she started in wild horror and covered her face with her hands as she thought of her lover opening the door on the other side of which waited the cruel fangs of the tiger!

But how much oftener had she seen him at the other door! How in her grievous reveries had she gnashed her teeth and torn her hair, when she saw his start of rapturous delight as he opened the door of the lady! How her soul had burned in agony when she had seen him rush to meet that woman, with her flushing cheek and sparkling eye of triumph; when she had seen him lead her forth, his whole frame kindled with the joy of recovered life; when she had heard the glad shouts from the multitude, and the wild ringing of the happy bells; when she had seen the priest, with his joyous followers, advance to the couple and make them man and wife before her very eyes; and when she had seen them walk away together upon their path of flowers, followed by the tremendous shouts of the hilarious multitude, in which her one despairing shriek was lost and drowned!

Would it not be better for him to die at once and go to wait for her in the blessed regions of semibarbaric futurity?

And yet, that awful tiger, those shrieks, that blood!

Her decision had been indicated in an instant, but it had been made after days and nights of anguished deliberation. She had known she would be asked, she had decided what she would answer, and, without the slightest hesitation, she had moved her hand to the right.

The question of her decision is one not to be lightly considered, and it is not for me to presume to set myself up as the one person able to answer it. And so I leave it with all of you: Which came out of the opened door—the lady, or the tiger?

# Interactions:
# Focus on Characters

*T*HINK OF THE opening of a fairy tale: Once upon a time there lived a beautiful princess. Compare that opening with the opening of a newspaper story: On June 9, John Smith lost control of his car and hit another vehicle driving north on Lake Shore Drive. The fairy tale is idealized and set in an unspecified place and time. The news story is objective and filled with facts. Despite their obvious differences, however, the two stories have something important in common. They are both about people.

Short stories usually focus on people, too—people who are interesting enough to read about. Often, a character in a story is unusual or faced with a dramatic choice or trapped in a difficult situation. In "The Sniper," for example, the sniper's thoughts and his struggle to stay alive engage a reader emotionally. The story would be far less gripping if it were only a report about three shootings.

Like "The Most Dangerous Game" and "The Sniper," which show enemies trying to outwit each other, most stories focus on more than one person. The interaction between the different characters is at the heart of the story.

In this section, you will read about several different characters. Some of them may seem strange to you, but some may be similar to people you know. Some of them may even remind you of yourself.

*Students*, 1969,
ISABEL BISHOP.
Collection of Greenwich Country Day School, Connecticut.

# *Literary Vocabulary*

## INTRODUCED IN THIS SECTION

**Character.** Characters are the people (and occasionally animals or fantasy creatures) who participate in the action of a literary work. Characters are either **main** or **minor,** depending upon the extent of their development and on their importance in a story. Rainsford and Zaroff are both main characters in "The Most Dangerous Game"; Zaroff's servant Ivan is a minor character.

**Characterization.** Characterization refers to the techniques that a writer uses to develop characters. There are four basic methods of characterization.

**1. Through physical description:** In "The Most Dangerous Game," General Zaroff is described as tall, past middle age, with white hair but with eyes, eyebrows, and mustache "as black as the night." The unusual darkness in Zaroff's physical appearance is an early indication of the evil in his nature.

**2. Through a character's speech, thoughts, feelings, or actions:** At the beginning of the story, Rainsford callously remarks, "Who cares how a jaguar feels?" Later, when Rainsford becomes one of the hunted, the reader finds out how he has changed: "Rainsford knew now how an animal at bay feels."

**3. Through the speech, feelings, thoughts, or actions of other characters:** When he first meets General Zaroff, Rainsford notices "an original, almost bizarre quality about the general's face."

**4. Through direct comments about a character's nature:** "The Lady, or the Tiger?" includes several interpretive comments. For example, the king is characterized as "a man of exuberant fancy" whose "nature was bland and genial."

**Irony.** Irony is a contrast between what is expected and what actually exists or happens. **Verbal irony** occurs when a character says one thing and means another, such as saying "Lovely evening, isn't it?" on a cold, rainy night. When verbal irony is especially bitter or harsh, it is called sarcasm. **Situational irony** is the contrast between what a character expects and what actually happens. Rainsford's situation is ironic in that the ruthless hunter becomes the frightened quarry. **Dramatic irony** refers to the contrast between what a character knows and what the reader knows.

## REVIEWED IN THIS SECTION

**Climax**

# Thank You, M'am

### LANGSTON HUGHES

A biography of Hughes appears on page 641.

## *Approaching the Story*

Langston Hughes is most famous for his poetry, but he also wrote short stories, novels, plays, and song lyrics. Like much of his work, "Thank You, M'am" is about African Americans living in a poor neighborhood of a large American city. The time period is the late 1950's, after Elvis Presley had recorded the rock-and-roll hit "Blue Suede Shoes."

## *Connecting Writing and Reading*

What do you think is the most appropriate response to juvenile crime? Should teenage offenders be punished severely or given a second chance? Imagine that you are a judge deciding on a sentence for a teenage, first-time offender. In your journal, list the sentence you would impose for each of the following offenses:

**1.** spray painting graffiti on a neighbor's garage

**2.** snatching a purse

**3.** shoplifting a pair of earrings

**4.** breaking into a vending machine to steal change

**5.** driving while drunk

**6.** sneaking into a theater without paying

While you read "Thank You, M'am," evaluate one woman's response to a young offender.

S HE WAS A large woman with a large purse that had everything in it but hammer and nails. It had a long strap, and she carried it slung across her shoulder. It was about eleven o'clock at night, and she was walking alone, when a boy ran up behind her and tried to snatch her purse. The strap broke with the single tug the boy gave it from behind. But the boy's weight and the weight of the purse combined caused him to lose his balance so, instead of taking off full blast as he had hoped, the boy fell on his back on the sidewalk, and his legs flew up. The large woman simply turned around and kicked him right square in his blue jeaned sitter. Then she reached down, picked the boy up by his shirt front, and shook him until his teeth rattled.

After that the woman said, "Pick up my pocketbook, boy, and give it here."

She still held him. But she bent down enough to permit him to stoop and pick up her purse. Then she said, "Now ain't you ashamed of yourself?"

Firmly gripped by his shirt front, the boy said, "Yes'm."

The woman said, "What did you want to do it for?"

The boy said, "I didn't aim to."

She said, "You a lie!"

By that time two or three people passed, stopped, turned to look, and some stood watching.

"If I turn you loose, will you run?" asked the woman.

"Yes'm," said the boy.

"Then I won't turn you loose," said the woman. She did not release him.

"I'm very sorry, lady, I'm sorry," whispered the boy.

"Um-hum! And your face is dirty. I got a great mind to wash your face for you. Ain't you got nobody home to tell you to wash your face?"

"No'm," said the boy.

"Then it will get washed this evening," said the large woman starting up the street, dragging the frightened boy behind her.

He looked as if he were fourteen or fifteen, frail and willow-wild, in tennis shoes and blue jeans.

The woman said, "You ought to be my son. I would teach you right from wrong. Least I can do right now is to wash your face. Are you hungry?"

"No'm," said the being-dragged boy. "I just want you to turn me loose."

"Was I bothering you when I turned that corner?" asked the woman.

"No'm."

"But you put yourself in contact with me," said the woman. "If you think that that contact is not going to last awhile, you got another thought coming. When I get through with you, sir, you are going to remember Mrs. Luella Bates Washington Jones."

Sweat popped out on the boy's face and he began to struggle. Mrs. Jones stopped, jerked him around in front of her, put a half nelson[1] about his neck, and continued to drag him up the street. When she got to her door, she dragged the boy inside, down a hall, and into a large kitchenette-furnished room at the rear of the house. She switched on the light and left the door open. The boy could hear other roomers laughing and talking in the large house. Some of their doors were open, too, so he knew he and the woman were not alone. The woman still had him by the neck in the middle of her room.

She said, "What is your name?"

"Roger," answered the boy.

"Then, Roger, you go to that sink and wash

---

1. **half nelson** (haf nel′ sən): wrestling hold in which one arm is placed under the opponent's arm from behind with the hand pressed against the back of the neck.

your face," said the woman, whereupon she turned him loose—at last. Roger looked at the door—looked at the woman—looked at the door—*and went to the sink.*

"Let the water run until it gets warm," she said. "Here's a clean towel."

"You gonna take me to jail?" asked the boy, bending over the sink.

"Not with that face, I would not take you nowhere," said the woman. "Here I am trying to get home to cook me a bite to eat and you snatch my pocketbook! Maybe you ain't been to your supper either, late as it be. Have you?"

"There's nobody home at my house," said the boy.

"Then we'll eat," said the woman. "I believe you're hungry—or been hungry—to try to snatch my pocketbook."

"I wanted a pair of blue suede shoes," said the boy.

"Well, you didn't have to snatch *my* pocketbook to get some suede shoes," said Mrs. Luella Bates Washington Jones. "You could of asked me."

"M'am?"

The water dripping from his face, the boy looked at her. There was a long pause. A very long pause. After he had dried his face and not knowing what else to do dried it again, the boy turned around, wondering what next. The door was open. He could make a dash for it down the hall. He could run, run, run, run, *run!*

The woman was sitting on the daybed. After awhile she said, "I were young once and I wanted things I could not get."

There was another long pause. The boy's mouth opened. Then he frowned, but not knowing he frowned.

The woman said, "Um-hum! You thought I was going to say *but,* didn't you? You thought I was going to say, *but I didn't snatch people's pocketbooks.* Well, I wasn't going to say that." Pause. Silence. "I have done things, too, which I would not tell you, son—neither tell God, if he didn't already know. So you set down while I fix us something to eat. You might run that comb through your hair so you will look presentable."

In another corner of the room behind a screen was a gas plate and an icebox. Mrs. Jones got up and went behind the screen. The woman did not watch the boy to see if he was going to run now, nor did she watch her purse which she left behind her on the daybed. But the boy took care to sit on the far side of the room where he thought she could easily see him out of the corner of her eye, if she wanted to. He did not trust the woman *not* to trust him. And he did *not* want to be mistrusted now.

"Do you need somebody to go to the store," asked the boy, "maybe to get some milk or something?"

"Don't believe I do," said the woman, "unless you just want sweet milk yourself. I was going to make cocoa out of this canned milk I got here."

"That will be fine," said the boy.

She heated some lima beans and ham she had in the icebox, made the cocoa, and set the table. The woman did not ask the boy anything about where he lived, or his folks, or anything else that would embarrass him. Instead, as they ate, she told him about her job in a hotel beauty shop that stayed open late, what the work was like, and how all kinds of women came in and out, blondes, redheads, and Spanish. Then she cut him a half of her ten-cent cake.

"Eat some more, son," she said.

When they were finished eating she got up and said, "Now, here, take this ten dollars and buy yourself some blue suede shoes. And next time, do not make the mistake of latching onto *my* pocketbook *nor nobody else's*—because shoes come by devilish like that will burn your feet. I got to get my rest now. But I wish you would behave yourself, son, from here on in."

She led him down the hall to the front door and opened it. "Goodnight! Behave yourself, boy!" she said, looking out into the street.

The boy wanted to say something else other than, "Thank you, m'am," to Mrs. Luella Bates Washington Jones, but he couldn't do so as he turned at the barren stoop and looked back at the large woman in the door. He barely managed to say "Thank you" before she shut the door. And he never saw her again.

# Thinking About the Story

## A PERSONAL RESPONSE

*sharing impressions*

**1.** What are your overall impressions of the characters in this story? Record your impressions in your journal.

*constructing interpretations*

**2.** Do you think that Mrs. Jones does the right thing? Explain.

**3.** How does Mrs. Jones's response to the attempted purse snatching compare to the punishment you thought would be appropriate for purse snatching?

**4.** What do you think motivates Mrs. Jones to help Roger?
  ***Think about***
  • what she says about the way he looks
  • what she says about her life

## A CREATIVE RESPONSE

**5.** How do you think the encounter with Mrs. Jones will affect Roger's life?

**6.** What might have happened if Mrs. Jones had called the police?

## A CRITICAL RESPONSE

**7.** Explain what point in the story you think marks the climax.
  ***Think about***
  • climax as a turning point, when the outcome of the story becomes clear
  • at what point you know for sure that Roger is not going to steal Mrs. Jones's purse

**8.** Discuss whether Mrs. Jones's response to Roger could be adapted by law enforcement institutions when dealing with teenage, first-time offenders.

# *Analyzing the Writer's Craft*

## CHARACTER AND CHARACTERIZATION

In "Thank You, M'am" only two people appear, Roger and Mrs. Jones. What are these two people like? How do you learn about them?

**Building a Literary Vocabulary.** Characters are the people (and occasionally animals or fantasy creatures) who participate in the action of a story. In "Thank You, M'am," both Roger and Mrs. Jones are main characters because they are both essential to the story: the events of the plot are based on what they as characters do, say, think, and feel.

Characterization refers to the techniques that a writer uses to develop characters. Describing physical appearance is one way to communicate something about a character. A character's inner nature may be revealed through his or her speech, thoughts, feelings, and actions—as well as through direct comments about the character's nature. Character may also be revealed through the speech, thoughts, feelings, and actions of the other characters.

**Application: Analyzing Character and Characterization.** With a group of your classmates, create report cards for Roger and Mrs. Jones. Grade them on five or six traits, such as honesty and judgment. The report cards should cover two grading periods, one at the beginning of the story and one at the end. In the comments column, list which of the following technique(s) of characterization were used to develop the trait you've identified.

- physical description
- character's own speech, thoughts, feelings, or actions
- another character's speech, thoughts, feelings, or actions
- direct comments about the character

# *Connecting Reading and Writing*

**1.** Write to an older person who helped you at some time in the past. In a **letter,** tell that person how you feel about him or her.

Option: Express your feelings about that person in a **poem.**

**2.** Imagine a meeting between Mrs. Jones and Roger ten years after this story takes place. Consider your answer to question 5 as a foundation and present their meeting in a brief **story.**

Option: Create a dramatic **dialogue** between the two characters.

**3.** Survey at least twenty of your classmates and write a **summary** of their suggestions for curbing juvenile crime.

Option: Write an **editorial** analyzing the pros and cons of using only one method to deal with juvenile crime.

# The Ransom of Red Chief

## O. HENRY

A biography of O. Henry appears on page 640.

### *Approaching the Story*

O. Henry was the pen name of William Sydney Porter, a popular writer who lived during the late nineteenth and early twentieth centuries. Many of O. Henry's stories present simple people in uncontrollable circumstances. Often, the stories are humorous and have surprise endings. "The Ransom of Red Chief" is one of O. Henry's best-known works.

### *Building Vocabulary*

These essential words are footnoted within the story.

**undeleterious** (un del´ ə tir´ ē əs): It contained inhabitants of as **undeleterious** and self-satisfied a class of peasantry as ever clustered around a Maypole. (page 46)

**dastardly** (das´ tərd lē): I expected to see [the villagers] . . . beating the countryside for the **dastardly** kidnappers. (page 48)

**peremptory** (pər emp´ tə rē): I thought it best to send a **peremptory** letter to old man Dorset that day, demanding the ransom and dictating how it should be paid. (page 49)

**surreptitiously** (sʉr´ əp tish´ əs lē): I . . . posted my letter **surreptitiously**, and came away. (page 50)

**renegade** (ren´ ə gād ): "I suppose you'll think I'm a **renegade**, but I couldn't help it." (page 51)

**depredation** (dep´ rə dā´ shən): "I tried to be faithful to our articles of **depredation**." (page 51)

**impudent** (im´ pyo͞o dənt): "Great pirates of Penzance," says I; "of all the **impudent**—" (page 52)

**spendthrift** (spend´ thrift´): I think Mr. Dorset is a **spendthrift**. (page 52)

### *Connecting Writing and Reading*

In your journal, predict what the story will be about. As you read, evaluate your prediction against what actually occurs.

# The Ransom of Red Chief

I T LOOKED LIKE a good thing, but wait till I tell you. We were down South, in Alabama—Bill Driscoll and myself—when this kidnapping idea struck us. It was, as Bill afterward expressed it, "during a moment of temporary mental apparition";[1] but we didn't find that out till later.

There was a town down there, as flat as a flannel cake, and called Summit, of course. It contained inhabitants of as <u>undeleterious</u>[2] and self-satisfied a class of peasantry as ever clustered around a Maypole.

Bill and me had a joint capital of about six hundred dollars, and we needed just two thousand dollars more to pull off a fraudulent town lot scheme in Western Illinois with. We talked it over on the front steps of the hotel. Philoprogenitiveness,[3] says we, is strong in semirural communities; therefore, and for other reasons, a kidnapping project ought to do better there than in the radius of newspapers that send reporters out in plain clothes to stir up talk about such things. We knew that Summit couldn't get after us with anything stronger than constables and, maybe, some lackadaisical bloodhounds and a diatribe or two in the *Weekly Farmers' Budget*. So, it looked good.

We selected for our victim the only child of a prominent citizen named Ebenezer Dorset.

The father was respectable and tight, a mortgage fancier and a stern, upright collection-plate passer and forecloser. The kid was a boy of ten, with bas-relief[4] freckles and hair the color of the cover of the magazine you buy at the newsstand when you want to catch a train. Bill and me figured that Ebenezer would melt down for a ransom of two thousand dollars to a cent. But wait till I tell you.

About two miles from Summit was a little mountain, covered with a dense cedar brake. On the rear elevation of this mountain was a cave. There we stored provisions.

One evening after sundown, we drove in a buggy past old Dorset's house. The kid was in the street, throwing rocks at a kitten on the opposite fence.

"Hey, little boy!" says Bill, "would you like to have a bag of candy and a nice ride?"

The boy catches Bill neatly in the eye with a piece of brick.

"That will cost the old man an extra five hundred dollars," says Bill, climbing over the wheel.

That boy put up a fight like a welterweight cinnamon bear; but, at last, we got him down in the bottom of the buggy and drove away. We took him up to the cave, and I hitched the horse in the cedar brake. After dark I drove the buggy to the little village, three miles away, where we had hired it, and walked back to the mountain.

---

1. **apparition** (ap′ ə rish′ ən): anything that appears unexpectedly or in an extraordinary way; Bill means "aberration," or unsoundness of mind. Throughout the story, Bill and Sam misuse big words in an attempt to sound educated and "high class."
2. **undeleterious** (un del′ ə tir′ ē əs): harmless to health or well-being; not injurious.

3. **philoprogenitiveness** (fil′ ō prō jen′ ə tiv′ nis): love of offspring.
4. **bas-relief** (bä′ ri lēf′) *French:* sculpture in which figures are carved in a flat surface so that they project only a little from the background.

Bill was pasting court plaster[5] over the scratches and bruises on his features. There was a fire burning behind the big rock at the entrance of the cave, and the boy was watching a pot of boiling coffee, with two buzzard tailfeathers stuck in his red hair. He points a stick at me when I come up, and says, "Ha! cursed paleface, do you dare to enter the camp of Red Chief, the terror of the plains?"

"He's all right now," says Bill, rolling up his trousers and examining some bruises on his shins. "We're playing Indian. We're making Buffalo Bill's show look like magic-lantern views of Palestine in the town hall.[6] I'm Old Hank, the Trapper, Red Chief's captive, and I'm to be scalped at daybreak. By Geronimo! that kid can kick hard."

Yes, sir, that boy seemed to be having the time of his life. The fun of camping out in a cave had made him forget that he was a captive himself. He immediately christened me Snake-eye, the Spy, and announced that, when his braves returned from the warpath, I was to be broiled at the stake at the rising of the sun.

Then we had supper; and he filled his mouth full of bacon and bread and gravy, and began to talk. He made a during-dinner speech something like this,

"I like this fine. I never camped out before, but I had a pet 'possum once, and I was nine last birthday. I hate to go to school. Rats ate up sixteen of Jimmy Talbot's aunt's speckled hen's eggs. Are there any real Indians in these woods? I want some more gravy. Does the trees moving make the wind blow? We had five puppies. What makes your nose so red, Hank? My father has lots of money. Are the stars hot? I whipped Ed Walker twice, Saturday. I don't like girls. You dassent catch toads unless with a string. Do oxen make any noise? Why are oranges round? Have you got beds to sleep on in this cave? Amos Murray has got six toes. A parrot can talk, but a monkey or a fish can't.

How many does it take to make twelve?"

Every few minutes he would remember that he was a pesky redskin, and pick up his stick rifle and tiptoe to the mouth of the cave to rubber[7] for the scouts of the hated paleface. Now and then he would let out a war whoop that made Old Hank the Trapper shiver. That boy had Bill terrorized from the start.

"Red Chief," says I to the kid, "would you like to go home?"

"Aw, what for?" says he. "I don't have any fun at home. I hate to go to school. I like to camp out. You won't take me back home again, Snake-eye, will you?"

"Not right away," says I. "We'll stay here in the cave awhile."

"All right!" says he. "That'll be fine. I never had such fun in all my life."

We went to bed about eleven o'clock. We spread down some wide blankets and quilts and put Red Chief between us. We weren't afraid he'd run away. He kept us awake for three hours, jumping up and reaching for his rifle and screeching, "Hist! pard," in mine and Bill's ears, as the fancied crackle of a twig or the rustle of a leaf revealed to his young imagination the stealthy approach of the outlaw band. At last, I fell into a troubled sleep and dreamed that I had been kidnapped and chained to a tree by a ferocious pirate with red hair.

Just at daybreak, I was awakened by a series of awful screams from Bill. They weren't yells, or howls, or shouts, or whoops, or yawps, such

---

5. **court plaster** (kôrt plas′ tər): cloth covered with an adhesive material, formerly used to protect minor skin wounds.
6. **Buffalo Bill's show . . . town hall:** Driscoll thinks that Red Chief's game makes a Wild West frontier show look as tame and boring as a slide-show travelogue.
7. **rubber:** short for *rubberneck*—to stretch the neck and look around curiously.

as you'd expect from a manly set of vocal organs—they were simply indecent, terrifying, humiliating screams, such as women emit when they see ghosts or caterpillars. It's an awful thing to hear a strong, desperate, fat man scream incontinently in a cave at daybreak.

I jumped up to see what the matter was. Red Chief was sitting on Bill's chest, with one hand twined in Bill's hair. In the other he had the sharp case knife we used for slicing bacon; and he was industriously and realistically trying to take Bill's scalp, according to the sentence that had been pronounced upon him the evening before.

I got the knife away from the kid and made him lie down again. But, from that moment, Bill's spirit was broken. He laid down on his side of the bed, but he never closed an eye again in sleep as long as that boy was with us. I dozed off for a while, but along toward sunup I remembered that Red Chief had said I was to be burned at the stake at the rising of the sun. I wasn't nervous or afraid, but I sat up and lit my pipe and leaned against a rock.

"What are you getting up so soon for, Sam?" asked Bill.

"Me?" says I. "Oh, I got a kind of a pain in my shoulder. I thought sitting up would rest it."

"You're a liar!" says Bill. "You're afraid. You was to be burned at sunrise, and you was afraid he'd do it. And he would, too, if he could find a match. Ain't it awful, Sam? Do you think anybody will pay out money to get a little imp like that back home?"

"Sure," said I. "A rowdy kid like that is just the kind that parents dote on. Now, you and the Chief get up and cook breakfast, while I go up on the top of this mountain and reconnoitre."

I went up on the peak of the little mountain and ran my eye over the contiguous vicinity. Over toward Summit I expected to see the sturdy yeomanry of the village armed with scythes and pitchforks beating the countryside for the <u>dastardly</u>[8] kidnappers. But what I saw was a peaceful landscape dotted with one man ploughing with a dun mule. Nobody was dragging the creek; no couriers dashed hither and yon, bringing tidings of no news to the distracted parents. There was a sylvan attitude of somnolent sleepiness pervading that section of the external outward surface of Alabama that lay exposed to my view. "Perhaps," says I to myself, "it has not yet been discovered that the wolves have borne away the tender lambkin from the fold. Heaven help the wolves!" says I, and I went down the mountain to breakfast.

When I got to the cave, I found Bill backed up against the side of it, breathing hard, and the boy threatening to smash him with a rock half as big as a coconut.

"He put a red-hot boiled potato down my back," explained Bill, "and then mashed it with his foot, and I boxed his ears. Have you got a gun about you, Sam?"

I took the rock away from the boy and kind of patched up the argument. "I'll fix you," says the kid to Bill. "No man ever yet struck the Red Chief but what he got paid for it. You better beware!"

After breakfast, the kid takes a piece of leather with strings wrapped around it out of his pocket and goes outside the cave unwinding it.

"What's he up to now?" says Bill, anxiously. "You don't think he'll run away, do you, Sam?"

"No fear of it," says I. "He don't seem to be much of a homebody. But we've got to fix up some plan about the ransom. There don't seem to be much excitement around Summit on account of his disappearance, but maybe they haven't realized yet that he's gone. His folks may think he's spending the night with Aunt Jane or one of the neighbors. Anyhow, he'll be

8. **dastardly** (das′ tərd lē): mean, sneaky, and cowardly.

missed today. Tonight we must get a message to his father demanding the two thousand dollars for his return."

Just then we heard a kind of war whoop, such as David might have emitted when he knocked out the champion Goliath.[9] It was a sling that Red Chief had pulled out of his pocket, and he was whirling it around his head.

I dodged, and heard a heavy thud and a kind of a sigh from Bill, like a horse gives out when you take his saddle off. A rock the size of an egg had caught Bill just behind his left ear. He loosened himself all over and fell in the fire across the frying pan of hot water for washing the dishes. I dragged him out and poured cold water on his head for half an hour.

By and by, Bill sits up and feels behind his ear and says: "Sam, do you know who my favorite Biblical character is?"

"Take it easy," says I. "You'll come to your senses presently."

"King Herod,"[10] says he. "You won't go away and leave me here alone, will you, Sam?"

I went out and caught that boy and shook him until his freckles rattled.

"If you don't behave," says I, "I'll take you straight home. Now, are you going to be good, or not?"

"I was only funning," says he, sullenly. "I didn't mean to hurt Old Hank. But what did he hit me for? I'll behave, Snake-eye, if you won't send me home, and if you'll let me play the Black Scout today."

"I don't know the game," says I. "That's for you and Mr. Bill to decide. He's your playmate for the day. I'm going away for a while, on business. Now come in and make friends with him and say you are sorry for hurting him, or home you go, at once."

I made him and Bill shake hands, and then I took Bill aside and told him I was going to Poplar Cove, a little village three miles from the cave, to find out what I could about how the kidnapping had been regarded in Summit. Also, I thought it best to send a peremptory[11] letter to old man Dorset that day, demanding the ransom and dictating how it should be paid.

"You know, Sam," says Bill, "I've stood by you without batting an eye in earthquakes, fire, and flood—in poker games, dynamite outrages, police raids, train robberies, and cyclones. I never lost my nerve yet till we kidnapped that two-legged skyrocket of a kid. He's got me going. You won't leave me long with him, will you, Sam?"

"I'll be back some time this afternoon," says I. "You must keep the boy amused and quiet till I return. And now we'll write the letter to old Dorset."

Bill and I got paper and pencil and worked on the letter while Red Chief, with a blanket wrapped around him, strutted up and down, guarding the mouth of the cave. Bill begged me tearfully to make the ransom fifteen hundred dollars instead of two thousand. "I ain't attempting," says he, "to decry the celebrated moral aspect of parental affection, but we're dealing with humans; and it ain't human for anybody to give up two thousand dollars for that forty-pound chunk of freckled wildcat. I'm willing to take a chance at fifteen hundred dollars. You can charge the difference up to me."

So, to relieve Bill, I acceded, and we collaborated a letter that ran this way:

---

9. **David . . . Goliath** (gə lī′ əth): a reference to the Bible story in which the young David kills the Philistine giant Goliath with a stone from a sling.
10. **King Herod** (her′ əd): the ruler of Galilee who, according to the New Testament, ordered the killing of all male children under two years of age in an effort to slay the infant Jesus.
11. **peremptory** (pər emp′ tə rē): expecting to be obeyed without question.

Ebenezer Dorset, Esq.:

We have your boy concealed in a place far from Summit. It is useless for you or the most skillful detectives to attempt to find him. Absolutely, the only terms on which you can have him restored to you are these: We demand fifteen hundred dollars in large bills for his return, the money to be left at midnight tonight at the same spot and in the same box as your reply—as hereinafter described. If you agree to these terms, send your answer in writing by a solitary messenger tonight at half-past eight o'clock. After crossing Owl Creek on the road to Poplar Cove, there are three large trees about a hundred yards apart, close to the fence of the wheat field on the right-hand side. At the bottom of the fence post, opposite the third tree, will be found a small pasteboard box.

The messenger will place the answer in this box and return immediately to Summit.

If you attempt any treachery or fail to comply with our demand as stated, you will never see your boy again.

If you pay the money as demanded, he will be returned to you safe and well within three hours. These terms are final, and if you do not accede to them no further communication will be attempted.

Two Desperate Men

I addressed this letter to Dorset, and put it in my pocket. As I was about to start, the kid comes up to me and says,

"Aw, Snake-eye, you said I could play the Black Scout while you was gone."

"Play it, of course," says I. "Mr. Bill will play with you. What kind of game is it?"

"I'm the Black Scout," says Red Chief, "and I have to ride to the stockade to warn the settlers that the Indians are coming. I'm tired of playing Indian myself. I want to be the Black Scout."

"All right," says I. "It sounds harmless to me. I guess Mr. Bill will help you foil the pesky savages."

"What am I to do?" asks Bill, looking at the kid suspiciously.

"You are the hoss," says Black Scout. "Get down on your hands and knees. How can I ride to the stockade without a hoss?"

"You'd better keep him interested," said I, "till we get the scheme going. Loosen up."

Bill gets down on his all fours, and a look comes in his eyes like a rabbit's when you catch it in a trap.

"How far is it to the stockade, kid?" he asks, in a husky manner of voice.

"Ninety miles," says the Black Scout. "And you have to hurry yourself to get there on time. Whoa, now!"

The Black Scout jumps on Bill's back and digs his heels in his side.

"For Heaven's sake," says Bill, "hurry back, Sam, as soon as you can. I wish we hadn't made the ransom more than a thousand. Say, you quit kicking me, or I'll get up and warm you good."

I walked over to Poplar Cove and sat around the post office and store, talking with the chaw bacons[12] that came in to trade. One whiskerando[13] says that he hears Summit is all upset on account of Elder Ebenezer Dorset's boy having been lost or stolen. That was all I wanted to know. I bought some smoking tobacco, referred casually to the price of black-eyed peas, posted my letter surreptitiously,[14] and came away. The postmaster said the mail carrier would come by in an hour to take the mail on to Summit.

When I got back to the cave, Bill and the boy were not to be found. I explored the vicin-

---

12. **chaw bacon** (chô bā' kən): a rustic bumpkin, hick, or yokel.
13. **whiskerando** (hwis' kər an' dō): an old-timer.
14. **surreptitiously** (sʉr' əp tish' əs lē): in a sly, secret way.

ity of the cave and risked a yodel or two, but there was no response.

So I lighted my pipe and sat down on a mossy bank to await developments.

In about half an hour I heard the bushes rustle, and Bill wobbled out into the little glade in front of the cave. Behind him was the kid, stepping softly like a scout, with a broad grin on his face. Bill stopped, took off his hat, and wiped his face with a red hand-kerchief. The kid stopped about eight feet behind him.

"Sam," says Bill, "I suppose you'll think I'm a renegade,[15] but I couldn't help it. I'm a grown person with masculine proclivities and habits of self-defense, but there is a time when all sys-tems of egotism and predominance fail. The boy is gone. I have sent him home. All is off. There was martyrs in old times," goes on Bill, "that suffered death rather than give up the particular graft they enjoyed. None of 'em ever was subjugated to such supernatural tortures as I have been. I tried to be faithful to our articles of depredation;[16] but there came a limit."

"What's the trouble, Bill?" I asks him.

"I was rode," says Bill, "the ninety miles to the stockade, not barring an inch. Then, when the settlers was rescued, I was given oats. Sand ain't a palatable substitute. And then, for an hour I had to try to explain to him why there was nothin' in holes, how a road can run both ways, and what makes the grass green. I tell you, Sam, a human can only stand so much. I takes him by the neck of his clothes and drags him down the mountain. On the way he kicks my legs black and blue from the knees down, and I've got to have two or three bites on my thumb and hand cauterized.

"But he's gone"—continues Bill—"gone home. I showed him the road to Summit and kicked him about eight feet nearer there at one kick. I'm sorry we lose the ransom, but it was either that or Bill Driscoll to the mad-house."

Bill is puffing and blowing, but there is a look of ineffable peace and growing content on his rose-pink features.

"Bill," says I, "there isn't any heart disease in your family, is there?"

"No," says Bill, "nothing chronic[17] except malaria and accidents. Why?"

"Then you might turn around," says I, "and have a look behind you."

Bill turns and sees the boy, and loses his complexion and sits down plump on the ground and begins to pluck aimlessly at grass and little sticks. For an hour I was afraid of his mind. And then I told him that my scheme was to put the whole job through immediately and that we would get the ran-som and be off with it by midnight if old Dorset fell in with our proposition. So Bill braced up enough to give the kid a weak sort of a smile and a promise to play the Russian in a Japanese war with him as soon as he felt a little better.

I had a scheme for collecting the ransom without danger of being caught by counterplots that ought to commend itself to professional kidnappers. The tree under which the answer was to be left—and the money later on—was close to the road fence with big, bare fields on all sides. If a gang of constables should be watching for anyone to come for the note, they could see him a long way off crossing the fields or in the road. But no, sirree! At half-past eight I was up in that tree as well hidden as a tree toad, waiting for the messenger to arrive.

Exactly on time, a half-grown boy rides up the road on a bicycle, locates the pasteboard

---

15. **renegade** (ren′ ə gād′): a person who abandons his or her principles to join the other side; a traitor.
16. **depredation** (dep′ rə dā′ shən): the act of robbing or laying waste; the state of being robbed or laid waste.
17. **chronic** (krän′ ik): long lasting; colloquially, it is used to mean "serious."

box at the foot of the fence post, slips a folded piece of paper into it, and pedals away again back toward Summit.

I waited an hour and then concluded the thing was square. I slid down the tree, got the note, slipped along the fence till I struck the woods, and was back at the cave in another half an hour. I opened the note, got near the lantern, and read it to Bill. It was written with a pen in a crabbed hand, and the sum and substance of it was this:

Two Desperate Men
Gentlemen:

I received your letter today by post, in regard to the ransom you ask for the return of my son. I think you are a little high in your demands, and I hereby make you a counterproposition, which I am inclined to believe you will accept. You bring Johnny home and pay me two hundred and fifty dollars in cash, and I agree to take him off your hands. You had better come at night, for the neighbors believe he is lost, and I couldn't be responsible for what they would do to anybody they saw bringing him back.

Very respectfully,
Ebenezer Dorset

"Great pirates of Penzance," says I; "of all the <u>impudent</u>—"[18]

But I glanced at Bill, and hesitated. He had the most appealing look in his eyes I ever saw on the face of a dumb or a talking mute.

"Sam," says he, "what's two hundred and fifty dollars, after all? We've got the money. One more night of this kid will send me to a bed in Bedlam.[19] Besides being a thorough gentleman, I think Mr. Dorset is a <u>spendthrift</u>[20] for making us such a liberal offer. You ain't going to let the chance go, are you?"

"Tell you the truth, Bill," says I, "this little he ewe lamb has somewhat got on my nerves

too. We'll take him home, pay the ransom, and make our getaway."

We took him home that night. We got him to go by telling him that his father had bought a silver-mounted rifle and a pair of moccasins for him, and we were going to hunt bears the next day.

It was just twelve o'clock when we knocked at Ebenezer's front door. Just at that moment when I should have been abstracting the fifteen hundred dollars from the box under the tree, according to the original proposition, Bill was counting out two hundred and fifty dollars into Dorset's hand.

When the kid found out we were going to leave him at home, he started up a howl like a calliope and fastened himself as tight as a leech to Bill's leg. His father peeled him away gradually, like a porous plaster.

"How long can you hold him?" asks Bill.

"I'm not as strong as I used to be," says old Dorset, "but I think I can promise you ten minutes."

"Enough," says Bill. "In ten minutes I shall cross the Central, Southern, and Middle Western states and be legging it trippingly for the Canadian border."

And, as dark as it was, and as fat as Bill was, and as good a runner as I am, he was a good mile and a half out of Summit before I could catch up with him.

---

18. **impudent** (im′ pyo͞o dənt): shamelessly bold or disrespectful.

19. **Bedlam** (bed′ ləm): popular name for Bethlehem Royal Hospital, founded in London in 1247, the first asylum for the insane to be built in England. The word *bedlam* came to mean any mental hospital or general uproar.

20. **spendthrift** (spend′ thrift): one who spends money carelessly.

# Thinking About the Story

## A PERSONAL RESPONSE

*sharing
impressions*

**1.** Did you like this story? Jot down your response in your journal.

**2.** Explain how accurate or inaccurate your prereading prediction was.

*constructing
interpretations*

**3.** What unexpected elements, or twists, did O. Henry incorporate into this story?

**Think about**
- events and characters usually associated with a kidnapping
- how the events and characters in this story differ from those expected in a kidnapping

**4.** Discuss the character of Red Chief, identifying ways in which he behaves impudently. Is his impudence that of a typical ten-year-old or is it exaggerated?

## A CREATIVE RESPONSE

**5.** What might the story be like if it were told by Red Chief instead of by Sam?

## A CRITICAL RESPONSE

**6.** How does the choice of words used by Bill and Sam create humor in the story? Point out specific passages to support your ideas.

**Think about**
- how you would describe the words used—as lofty? slangy?
- whether these words fit the characters or the situation
- ways in which words are misused

# Analyzing the Writer's Craft

## IRONY

You may have noticed that this story contains elements that do not conform to expectations. A speaker may say one thing and imply just the opposite. The outcome of a situation may be quite different from the one you anticipated. A character's words may take on a meaning that he is unaware of because he lacks information known to you, the reader.

**Building a Literary Vocabulary.** The contrasts just described are forms of irony. The three types of irony are reviewed on the next page.

- Verbal irony refers to the contrast between what is said and what is meant. For instance, Sam calls Red Chief a "lamb" but actually means that the boy is devilish, not sweet and gentle.
- Situational irony refers to the contrast between what a character or the reader expects and what actually occurs. The twist at the end of the story when the kidnappers end up paying the ransom is an illustration of situational irony.
- Dramatic irony refers to the contrast between what a character knows and what the reader or audience knows. For example, Bill's speech expressing his relief at Red Chief's departure is ironic because the reader knows that Red Chief is standing behind Bill as he speaks.

**Application: Identifying Irony.** Working with a partner, list two or three other examples of irony in this story. Analyze why each example is ironic and identify the type of irony it represents. Then working as a class, combine your findings in a chart. This chart should have three columns, one for each type of irony. Which type of irony predominates in this story?

## Connecting Reading and Writing

**1.** Retell an incident in the story from Red Chief's point of view, using your response to question 5 as a starting point. Present Red Chief's thoughts in a **diary entry.**

Option: Write an **interview** that you might have with Red Chief.

**2.** Assess the positives and negatives of this story and express an opinion about whether it is worth reading. Give your opinion in a **review column.**

Option: Express your opinion in a **letter** to a publisher.

**3.** Read another story by O. Henry. Compare and contrast the characters, plots, and language of the stories in a **chart,** which a classmate can use to decide whether he or she would like to read the other story.

Option: Write an **expository essay** comparing the two stories to submit to a literary journal.

**4.** Write a humorous piece, fact-based or entirely fictional, about an experience with an imaginative, energetic child like Red Chief. Relate this experience as a short **anecdote** to amuse your classmates.

Option: Write a **list** of do's and don't's for a teenager hired to babysit a child like Red Chief.

# The Possibility of Evil

## SHIRLEY JACKSON

A biography of Jackson appears on page 641.

*A*pproaching the Story

"The Possibility of Evil" takes place in a small town, the sort of community where everyone knows everyone else. At the center of the story is Miss Adela Strangeworth, an elderly woman who has lived all her life in the small town that her grandfather helped establish.

MISS ADELA Strangeworth came daintily along Main Street on her way to the grocery. The sun was shining, the air was fresh and clear after the night's heavy rain, and everything in Miss Strangeworth's little town looked washed and bright. Miss Strangeworth took deep breaths and thought that there was nothing in the world like a fragrant summer day.

She knew everyone in town, of course; she was fond of telling strangers—tourists who sometimes passed through the town and stopped to admire Miss Strangeworth's roses—that she had never spent more than a day outside this town in all her long life. She was seventy-one, Miss Strangeworth told the tourists, with a pretty little dimple showing by her lip, and she sometimes found herself thinking that the town belonged to her. "My grandfather built the first house on Pleasant Street," she would say, opening her blue eyes wide with the wonder of it. "This house, right here. My family has lived here for better than a hundred years. My grandmother planted these roses,

and my mother tended them, just as I do. I've watched my town grow; I can remember when Mr. Lewis, Senior, opened the grocery store, and the year the river flooded out the shanties on the low road, and the excitement when some young folks wanted to move the park over to the space in front of where the new post office is today. They wanted to put up a statue of Ethan Allen"[1]—Miss Strangeworth would frown a little and sound stern—"but it should have been a statue of my grandfather. There wouldn't have been a town here at all if it hadn't been for my grandfather and the lumber mill."

Miss Strangeworth never gave away any of her roses, although the tourists often asked her. The roses belonged on Pleasant Street, and it bothered Miss Strangeworth to think of people wanting to carry them away, to take them into strange towns and down strange streets. When the new minister came, and the ladies were

---

1. **Ethan Allen** (ē' thən al' ən): American Revolutionary soldier who led the Green Mountain Boys in the capture of Fort Ticonderoga.

gathering flowers to decorate the church, Miss Strangeworth sent over a great basket of gladioli; when she picked the roses at all, she set them in bowls and vases around the inside of the house her grandfather had built.

Walking down Main Street on a summer morning, Miss Strangeworth had to stop every minute or so to say good morning to someone or to ask after someone's health. When she came into the grocery, half a dozen people turned away from the shelves and the counters to wave at her or call out good morning.

"And good morning to you, too, Mr. Lewis," Miss Strangeworth said at last. The Lewis family had been in the town almost as long as the Strangeworths; but the day young Lewis left high school and went to work in the grocery, Miss Strangeworth had stopped calling him Tommy and started calling him Mr. Lewis, and he had stopped calling her Addie and started calling her Miss Strangeworth. They had been in high school together, and had gone to picnics together, and to high-school dances and basketball games; but now Mr. Lewis was behind the counter in the grocery, and Miss Strangeworth was living alone in the Strangeworth house on Pleasant Street.

"Good morning," Mr. Lewis said, and added politely, "Lovely day."

"It is a very nice day," Miss Strangeworth said, as though she had only just decided that it would do after all. "I would like a chop, please, Mr. Lewis, a small, lean veal chop. Are those strawberries from Arthur Parker's garden? They're early this year."

"He brought them in this morning," Mr. Lewis said.

"I shall have a box," Miss Strangeworth said. Mr. Lewis looked worried, she thought, and for a minute she hesitated, but then she decided that he surely could not be worried over the strawberries. He looked very tired indeed. He was usually so chipper, Miss Strangeworth thought, and almost commented; but it was far too personal a subject to be introduced to Mr. Lewis, the grocer, so she only said, "And a can of cat food and, I think, a tomato."

Silently, Mr. Lewis assembled her order on the counter, and waited. Miss Strangeworth looked at him curiously and then said, "It's Tuesday, Mr. Lewis. You forgot to remind me."

"Did I? Sorry."

"Imagine your forgetting that I always buy my tea on Tuesday," Miss Strangeworth said gently. "A quarter pound of tea, please, Mr. Lewis."

"Is that all, Miss Strangeworth?"

"Yes thank you, Mr. Lewis. Such a lovely day, isn't it?"

"Lovely," Mr. Lewis said.

Miss Strangeworth moved slightly to make room for Mrs. Harper at the counter. "Morning, Adela," Mrs. Harper said, and Miss Strangeworth said, "Good morning, Martha."

"Lovely day," Mrs. Harper said, and Miss Strangeworth said, "Yes, lovely," and Mr. Lewis, under Mrs. Harper's glance, nodded.

"Ran out of sugar for my cake frosting," Mrs. Harper explained. Her hand shook slightly as she opened her pocketbook. Miss Strangeworth wondered, glancing at her quickly, if she had been taking proper care of herself. Martha Harper was not as young as she used to be, Miss Strangeworth thought. She probably could use a good strong tonic.

"Martha," she said, "you don't look well."

"I'm perfectly all right," Mrs. Harper said shortly. She handed her money to Mr. Lewis, took her change and her sugar, and went out without speaking again. Looking after her, Miss Strangeworth shook her head slightly. Martha definitely did *not* look well.

Carrying her little bag of groceries, Miss Strangeworth came out of the store into the bright sunlight and stopped to smile down on the Crane baby. Don and Helen Crane were really the two most <u>infatuated</u>[2] young parents she had ever known, she thought indulgently,[3] looking at the delicately embroidered baby cap and the lace-edged carriage cover.

"That little girl is going to grow up expecting luxury all her life," she said to Helen Crane.

Helen laughed. "That's the way we want her to feel," she said. "Like a princess."

"A princess can see a lot of trouble sometimes," Miss Strangeworth said dryly. "How old is Her Highness now?"

"Six months next Tuesday," Helen Crane said, looking down with rapt wonder at her child. "I've been worrying, though, about her. Don't you think she ought to move around more? Try to sit up, for instance?"

"For plain and fancy worrying," Miss Strangeworth said, amused, "give me a new mother every time."

"She just seems—slow," Helen Crane said.

"Nonsense. All babies are different. Some of them develop much more quickly than others."

"That's what my mother says." Helen Crane laughed, looking a little bit ashamed.

"I suppose you've got young Don all upset about the fact that his daughter is already six months old and hasn't yet begun to learn to dance?"

"I haven't mentioned it to him. I suppose she's just so precious that I worry about her all the time."

"Well, apologize to her right now," Miss Strangeworth said. "*She* is probably worrying about why you keep jumping around all the time." Smiling to herself and shaking her old head, she went on down the sunny street, stopping once to ask little Billy Moore why he wasn't out riding in his daddy's shiny new car; and talking for a few minutes outside the library with Miss Chandler, the librarian, about the new novels to be ordered and paid for by the annual library appropriation. Miss Chandler seemed absent-minded and very much as though she were thinking about something else. Miss Strangeworth noticed that Miss Chandler had not taken much trouble with her hair that morning, and sighed. Miss Strangeworth hated sloppiness.

Many people seemed disturbed recently, Miss Strangeworth thought. Only yesterday the Stewarts' fifteen-year-old Linda had run crying down her own front walk and all the way to school, not caring who saw her. People around town thought she might have had a fight with the Harris boy, but they showed up together at the soda shop after school as usual, both of them looking grim and bleak. Trouble at home, people concluded, and sighed over the problems of trying to raise kids right these days.

From halfway down the block, Miss Strangeworth could catch the heavy scent of her roses, and she moved a little more quickly. The perfume of roses meant home, and home meant the Strangeworth House on Pleasant Street. Miss Strangeworth stopped at her own front gate, as she always did, and looked with deep pleasure at her house, with the red and pink and white roses massed along the narrow lawn, and the rambler going up along the porch; and the neat, the unbelievably trim lines of the house itself, with its slimness and its washed white look. Every window sparkled, every curtain hung stiff and straight, and even the stones of the front walk were swept and clear. People around town wondered how old Miss Strangeworth managed to keep the house looking the way it did, and there was a legend about a tourist once mistaking it for the local

---

2. **infatuated** (in fach′ ōō āt′ ed): completely carried away by love or attraction.

3. **indulgently** (in dul′ jənt lē): kindly or without strictness.

museum and going all through the place without finding out about his mistake. But the town was proud of Miss Strangeworth and her roses and her house. They had all grown together.

Miss Strangeworth went up her front steps, unlocked her front door with her key, and went into the kitchen to put away her groceries. She debated about having a cup of tea and then decided that it was too close to midday dinnertime; she would not have the appetite for her little chop if she had tea now. Instead she went into the light, lovely sitting room, which still glowed from the hands of her mother and her grandmother, who had covered the chairs with bright chintz[4] and hung the curtains. All the furniture was spare and shining, and the round hooked rugs on the floor had been the work of Miss Strangeworth's grandmother and her mother. Miss Strangeworth had put a bowl of her red roses on the low table before the window, and the room was full of their scent.

Miss Strangeworth went to the narrow desk in the corner and unlocked it with her key. She never knew when she might feel like writing letters, so she kept her notepaper inside and the desk locked. Miss Strangeworth's usual stationery was heavy and cream-colored, with STRANGEWORTH HOUSE engraved across the top; but, when she felt like writing her other letters, Miss Strangeworth used a pad of various-colored paper bought from the local newspaper shop. It was almost a town joke, that colored paper, layered in pink and green and blue and yellow; everyone in town bought it and used it for odd, informal notes and shopping lists. It was usual to remark, upon receiving a note written on a blue page, that so-and-so would be needing a new pad soon—here she was, down to the blue already. Everyone used the matching en-velopes for tucking away recipes, or keeping odd little things in, or even to hold cookies in the school lunchboxes. Mr. Lewis sometimes gave them to the children for carrying home penny candy.

Although Miss Strangeworth's desk held a trimmed quill pen that had belonged to her grandfather, and a gold-frosted fountain pen that had belonged to her father, Miss Strangeworth always used a dull stub of pencil when she wrote her letters; and she printed them in a childish block print. After thinking for a minute, although she had been phrasing the letter in the back of her mind all the way home, she wrote on a pink sheet: DIDNT YOU EVER SEE AN IDIOT CHILD BEFORE? SOME PEOPLE JUST SHOULDN'T HAVE CHILDREN SHOULD THEY?

She was pleased with the letter. She was fond of doing things exactly right. When she made a mistake, as she sometimes did, or when the letters were not spaced nicely on the page, she had to take the discarded page to the kitchen stove and burn it at once. Miss Strangeworth never delayed when things had to be done.

After thinking for a minute, she decided that she would like to write another letter, perhaps to go to Mrs. Harper, to follow up the ones she had already mailed. She selected a green sheet this time and wrote quickly: HAVE YOU FOUND OUT YET WHAT THEY WERE ALL LAUGHING ABOUT AFTER YOU LEFT THE BRIDGE CLUB ON THURSDAY? OR IS THE WIFE REALLY ALWAYS THE LAST ONE TO KNOW?

Miss Strangeworth never concerned herself with facts; her letters all dealt with the more <u>negotiable</u>[5] stuff of suspicion. Mr. Lewis would never have imagined for a minute that his

---

4. **chintz** (chints): brightly colored, flowered cotton with a shiny surface.
5. **negotiable** (ni gō′ shē ə bəl): open to debate, compromise, or bargaining; flexible.

grandson might be lifting petty cash[6] from the store register if he had not had one of Miss Strangeworth's letters. Miss Chandler, the librarian, and Linda Stewart's parents would have gone unsuspectingly ahead with their lives, never aware of possible evil lurking nearby, if Miss Strangeworth had not sent letters opening their eyes. Miss Strangeworth would have been genuinely shocked if there *had* been anything between Linda Stewart and the Harris boy; but, as long as evil existed unchecked in the world, it was Miss Strangeworth's duty to keep her town alert to it. It was far more sensible for Miss Chandler to wonder what Mr. Shelley's first wife had really died of than to take a chance on not knowing. There were so many wicked people in the world and only one Strangeworth left in the town. Besides, Miss Strangeworth liked writing her letters.

She addressed an envelope to Don Crane after a moment's thought, wondering curiously if he would show the letter to his wife, and using a pink envelope to match the pink paper. Then she addressed a second envelope, green, to Mrs. Harper. Then an idea came to her and she selected a blue sheet and wrote: YOU NEVER KNOW ABOUT DOCTORS. REMEMBER THEY'RE ONLY HUMAN AND NEED MONEY LIKE THE REST OF US. SUPPOSE THE KNIFE SLIPPED ACCIDENTALLY. WOULD DR. BURNS GET HIS FEE AND A LITTLE EXTRA FROM THAT NEPHEW OF YOURS?

She addressed the blue envelope to old Mrs. Foster, who was having an operation next month. She had thought of writing one more letter, to the head of the school board, asking how a chemistry teacher like Billy Moore's father could afford a new convertible, but, all at once, she was tired of writing letters. The three she had done would do for one day. She could write more tomorrow; it was not as though they all had to be done at once.

She had been writing her letters—some-

times two or three every day for a week, sometimes no more than one in a month—for the past year. She never got any answers, of course, because she never signed her name. If she had been asked, she would have said that her name, Adela Strangeworth, a name honored in the town for so many years, did not belong on such trash. The town where she lived had to be kept clean and sweet, but people everywhere were lustful and evil and degraded,[7] and needed to be watched; the world was so large, and there was only one Strangeworth left in it. Miss Strangeworth sighed, locked her desk, and put the letters into her big black leather pocketbook, to be mailed when she took her evening walk.

She broiled her little chop nicely, and had a sliced tomato and a good cup of tea ready when she sat down to her midday dinner at the table in her dining room, which could be opened to seat twenty-two, with a second table, if necessary, in the hall. Sitting in the warm sunlight that came through the tall windows of the dining room, seeing her roses massed outside, handling the heavy, old silverware and the fine, translucent china, Miss Strangeworth was pleased; she would not have cared to be doing anything else. People must live graciously, after all, she thought, and sipped her tea. Afterward, when her plate and cup and saucer were washed and dried and put back onto the shelves where they belonged, and her silverware was back in the mahogany silver chest, Miss Strangeworth went up the graceful staircase and into her bedroom, which was the front room overlooking the roses, and had been her mother's and her grandmother's. Their Crown Derby dresser set and furs had

---

6. **petty cash:** money (bills and coins) kept on hand for minor expenses.

7. **degraded** (dē grād′ əd): in a state of corruption and loss of dignity and humanity; disgraceful; dishonorable; disrespectful.

been kept there, their fans and silver-backed brushes and their own bowls of roses; Miss Strangeworth kept a bowl of white roses on the bed table.

She drew the shades, took the rose satin spread from the bed, slipped out of her dress and her shoes, and lay down tiredly. She knew that no doorbell or phone would ring; no one in town would dare to disturb Miss Strangeworth during her afternoon nap. She slept, deep in the rich smell of roses.

After her nap she worked in her garden for a little while, sparing herself because of the heat; then she came in to her supper. She ate asparagus from her own garden, with sweet-butter sauce and a soft-boiled egg; and, while she had her supper, she listened to a late-evening news broadcast and then to a program of classical music on her small radio. After her dishes were done and her kitchen set in order, she took up her hat—Miss Strangeworth's hats were proverbial[8] in the town; people believed that she had inherited them from her mother and her grandmother—and, locking the front door of her house behind her, set off on her evening walk, pocketbook under her arm. She nodded to Linda Stewart's father, who was washing his car in the pleasantly cool evening. She thought that he looked troubled.

There was only one place in town where she could mail her letters, and that was the new post office, shiny with red brick and silver letters. Although Miss Strangeworth had never given the matter any particular thought, she had always made a point of mailing her letters very secretly; it would, of course, not have been wise to let anyone see her mail them. Consequently, she timed her walk so she could reach the post office just as darkness was starting to dim the outlines of the trees and the shapes of people's faces, although no one could ever mistake Miss Strangeworth, with her dainty walk and her rustling skirts.

There was always a group of young people around the post office, the very youngest roller-skating upon its driveway, which went all the way around the building and was the only smooth road in town; and the slightly older ones already knowing how to gather in small groups and chatter and laugh and make great, excited plans for going across the street to the soda shop in a minute or two. Miss Strangeworth had never had any self-consciousness before the children. She did not feel that any of them were staring at her unduly or longing to laugh at her; it would have been most reprehensible for their parents to permit their children to mock Miss Strangeworth of Pleasant Street. Most of the children stood back respectfully as Miss Strangeworth passed, silenced briefly in her presence, and some of the older children greeted her, saying soberly, "Hello, Miss Strangeworth."

Miss Strangeworth smiled at them and quickly went on. It had been a long time since she had known the name of every child in town. The mail slot was in the door of the post office. The children stood away as Miss Strangeworth approached it, seemingly surprised that anyone should want to use the post office after it had been officially closed up for the night and turned over to the children. Miss Strangeworth stood by the door, opening her black pocketbook to take out the letters, and heard a voice which she knew at once to be Linda Stewart's. Poor little Linda was crying again, and Miss Strangeworth listened carefully. This was, after all, her town, and these were her people; if one of them was in trouble she ought to know about it.

"I can't tell you, Dave," Linda was saying—so she *was* talking to the Harris boy, as Miss Strangeworth had supposed—"I just *can't*. It's just *nasty*."

"But why won't your father let me come

---

8. **proverbial** (prō vʉr′ bē əl): well known because commonly referred to.

around any more? What on earth did I do?"

"I can't tell you. I just wouldn't tell you for *anything*. You've got to have a dirty, dirty mind for things like that."

"But something's happened. You've been crying and crying, and your father is all upset. Why can't *I* know about it, too? Aren't I like one of the family?"

"Not any more, Dave, not any more. You're not to come near our house again; my father said so. He said he'd horsewhip you. That's all I can tell you: You're not to come near our house any more."

"But I didn't *do* anything."

"Just the same, my father said . . ."

Miss Strangeworth sighed and turned away. There was so much evil in people. Even in a charming little town like this one, there was still so much evil in people.

She slipped her letters into the slot, and two of them fell inside. The third caught on the edge and fell outside, onto the ground at Miss Strangeworth's feet. She did not notice it because she was wondering whether a letter to the Harris boy's father might not be of some service in wiping out this potential badness. Wearily Miss Strangeworth turned to go home to her quiet bed in her lovely house, and never heard the Harris boy calling to her to say that she had dropped something.

"Old lady Strangeworth's getting deaf," he said, looking after her and holding in his hand the letter he had picked up.

"Well, who cares?" Linda said. "Who cares any more, anyway?"

"It's for Don Crane," the Harris boy said, "this letter. She dropped a letter addressed to Don Crane. Might as well take it on over. We pass his house anyway." He laughed. "Maybe it's got a check or something in it, and he'd be just as glad to get it tonight instead of tomorrow."

"Catch old lady Strangeworth sending any-body a check," Linda said. "Throw it in the post office. Why do anyone a favor?" She sniffled. "Doesn't seem to me anybody around here cares about us," she said. "Why should we care about them?"

"I'll take it over anyway," the Harris boy said. "Maybe it's good news for them. Maybe they need something happy tonight, too. Like us."

Sadly, holding hands, they wandered off down the dark street, the Harris boy carrying Miss Strangeworth's pink envelope in his hand.

Miss Strangeworth awakened the next morning with a feeling of intense happiness and, for a minute wondered why, and then remembered that this morning three people would open her letters. Harsh, perhaps, at first, but wickedness was never easily banished, and a clean heart was a scoured heart. She washed her soft old face and brushed her teeth, still sound in spite of her seventy-one years, and dressed herself carefully in her sweet, soft clothes and buttoned shoes. Then, coming downstairs and reflecting that perhaps a little waffle would be agreeable for breakfast in the sunny dining room, she found the mail on the hall floor and bent to pick it up. A bill, the morning paper, a letter in a green envelope that looked oddly familiar. Miss Strangeworth stood perfectly still for a minute, looking down at the green envelope with the penciled printing, and thought: It looks like one of my letters. Was one of my letters sent back? No, because no one would know where to send it. How did this get here?

Miss Strangeworth was a Strangeworth of Pleasant Street. Her hand did not shake as she opened the envelope and unfolded the sheet of green paper inside. She began to cry silently for the wickedness of the world when she read the words:

LOOK OUT AT WHAT USED TO BE YOUR ROSES.

# Rites of Passage: Struggles of Personal Growth

**E**ACH STORY YOU will read in this section portrays someone about your age in the process of growing up. Growing and changing are seldom easy but almost always interesting. Thinking back, you probably can identify some childhood landmark accomplishments, such as learning to ride a bicycle or finishing grade school. You may also remember a more internal sign of growth: perhaps when you first had a crush on someone or when you struggled to get over the loss of a beloved pet. All of these growth experiences helped to shape your perceptions of yourself and others.

When a personal experience leads to growth or change—usually to a new level of maturity—you have undergone what is known as a rite of passage. Most young people undergo public or ceremonial rites of passage into adulthood: learning to drive a car or receiving a high school diploma, for example. However, rites of passage are more often personal and internal, unique to each individual.

The characters in the following stories go through private rites of passage that lead to important moments of awareness and growth. As a reader, you may identify with these characters as they face difficult situations, make decisions, and try to understand what it means to grow up.

*Woman from Martinique,*
1946-47, HENRI MATISSE.
Bibliothèque Nationale, Paris.

# Literary Vocabulary

**Psychological Realism.** The literary technique in which a writer explores the thoughts of a character confronted by a difficult moral choice is called psychological realism. Psychological means "having to do with the workings of the mind." Realism is a literary technique that aims for a truthful representation of life. "Lather and Nothing Else" is an example of psychological realism because the reader knows the barber's thoughts while he shaves his enemy.

**Symbol.** A symbol is a person, place, activity, or object that stands for something beyond itself. Cultural symbols are those whose meanings can be understood by people in the same culture. For example, most people recognize roses as a symbol of love. Literary symbols take on meaning within the context of a literary work. In "The Possibility of Evil," Miss Strangeworth's roses symbolize her position of prominence in the town: "tourists . . . stopped to admire Miss Strangeworth's roses." The roses also stand for tradition and family background, as she proudly points out: "'My grandmother planted these roses, and my mother tended them, just as I do.'" The destruction of Miss Strangeworth's roses at the end of the story is a symbolic destruction of her power.

**Setting.** Setting is the time and place of the action of a story. Some stories, such as "The Secret Life of Walter Mitty," have only a minimal description of the setting. In "The Most Dangerous Game," the setting is described in such detail as to seem to become an active participant in the hunt. In stories such as "The Sniper," the historical period as well as the particular place of the action greatly influence the story.

**Description.** Description helps a reader understand exactly what something is like. The opening paragraph of "The Sniper" describes important sights and sounds of a Dublin street to convey the experience of being in that city during a war.

# Initiation

## SYLVIA PLATH

A biography of Plath appears on page 644.

## Approaching the Story

"Initiation" concerns one girl's experience with a high school sorority, a highly selective social club for girls much like a fraternity for boys. As the story opens, Millicent is participating in the sorority's hazing ceremony, a series of humiliating tasks that girls hoping to become members must complete.

## Building Vocabulary

These essential words are footnoted within the story.

**initiation** (i nish´ ē ā´ shen): She could not think of anyone who had ever been invited into the high school sorority and failed to get through **initiation** time. (page 65)

**elect** (ē lekt´): What girl would not want to be one of the **elect**? (page 65)

**malicious** (mə lish´ əs): There was something about her tone that annoyed Millicent. It was almost **malicious**. (page 67)

**comradeship** (käm´ rəd ship´): Why, this was wonderful, the way she felt a sudden **comradeship** with a stranger. (page 69)

**prestige** (pres tēzh´): "But it sure gives a girl **prestige** value." (page 71)

## Connecting Writing and Reading

Most teenagers feel pressured to behave in certain ways. The pressure may come from adults or from friends and classmates. In your journal, name some pressures that you feel and briefly note your response to these pressures. As you read this story, notice the way Millicent responds to pressure to join a sorority.

*T*HE BASEMENT ROOM was dark and warm, like the inside of a sealed jar, Millicent thought, her eyes getting used to the strange dimness. The silence was soft with cobwebs, and from the small, rectangular window set high in the stone wall there sifted a faint bluish light that must be coming from the full October moon. She could see now that what she was sitting on was a woodpile next to the furnace.

Millicent brushed back a strand of hair. It was stiff and sticky from the egg that they had broken on her head as she knelt blindfolded at the sorority altar a short while before. There had been a silence, a slight crunching sound, and then she had felt the cold, slimy egg-white flattening and spreading on her head and sliding down her neck. She had heard someone smothering a laugh. It was all part of the ceremony.

Then the girls had led her here, blindfolded still, through the corridors of Betsy Johnson's house and shut her in the cellar. It would be an hour before they came to get her, but then Rat Court would be all over and she would say what she had to say and go home.

For tonight was the grand finale, the trial by fire. There really was no doubt now that she would get in. She could not think of anyone who had ever been invited into the high school sorority and failed to get through initiation[1] time. But even so, her case would be quite different. She would see to that. She could not exactly say what had decided her revolt, but it definitely had something to do with Tracy and something to do with the heather birds.

What girl at Lansing High would not want to be in her place now? Millicent thought, amused. What girl would not want to be one of the elect,[2] no matter if it did mean five days of initiation before and after school, ending in the climax of Rat Court on Friday night when

they made the new girls members? Even Tracy had been wistful when she heard that Millicent had been one of the five girls to receive an invitation.

"It won't be any different with us, Tracy," Millicent had told her. "We'll still go around together like we always have, and next year you'll surely get in."

"I know, but even so," Tracy had said quietly, "you'll change, whether you think you will or not. Nothing ever stays the same."

And nothing does, Millicent had thought. How horrible it would be if one never changed . . . if she were condemned to be the plain, shy Millicent of a few years back for the rest of her life. Fortunately there was always the changing, the growing, the going on.

It would come to Tracy, too. She would tell Tracy the silly things the girls had said, and Tracy would change also, entering eventually into the magic circle. She would grow to know the special ritual as Millicent had started to last week.

"First of all," Betsy Johnson, the vivacious blonde secretary of the sorority, had told the five new candidates over sandwiches in the school cafeteria last Monday, "first of all, each of you has a big sister. She's the one who bosses you around, and you just do what she tells you."

"Remember the part about talking back and smiling," Louise Fullerton had put in, laughing. She was another celebrity in high school, pretty and dark and vice-president of the student council. "You can't say anything unless your big sister asks you something or tells you to talk to someone. And you can't smile, no matter how you're dying to." The girls had laughed a little nervously, and then the bell

---

1. **initiation** (i nish′ ē ā′ shən): a ceremony by which one is admitted as a member into a group or organization.

2. **elect** (ē lekt′): the one, or few, chosen.

had rung for the beginning of afternoon classes.

It would be rather fun for a change, Millicent mused, getting her books out of her locker in the hall, rather exciting to be part of a closely knit group, the exclusive set at Lansing High. Of course, it wasn't a school organization. In fact, the principal, Mr. Cranton, wanted to do away with initiation week altogether, because he thought it was undemocratic and disturbed the routine of school work. But there wasn't really anything he could do about it. Sure, the girls had to come to school for five days without any lipstick on and without curling their hair, and of course everybody noticed them, but what could the teachers do?

Millicent sat down at her desk in the big study hall. Tomorrow she would come to school, proudly, laughingly, without lipstick, with her brown hair straight and shoulder length, and then everybody would know, even the boys would know, that she was one of the elect. Teachers would smile helplessly, thinking perhaps: So now they've picked Millicent Arnold. I never would have guessed it.

A year or two ago, not many people would have guessed it. Millicent had waited a long time for acceptance, longer than most. It was as if she had been sitting for years in a pavilion outside a dance floor, looking in through the windows at the golden interior, with the lights clear and the air like honey, wistfully watching the couples waltzing to the never-ending music, laughing in pairs and groups together, no one alone.

But now at last, amid a week of fanfare and merriment, she would answer her invitation to enter the ballroom through the main entrance marked "Initiation." She would gather up her velvet skirts, her silken train, or whatever the disinherited princesses wore in the story books, and come into her rightful kingdom. . . . The bell rang to end study hall.

"Millicent, wait up!" It was Louise Fullerton behind her, Louise who had always before been very nice, very polite, friendlier than the rest, even long ago, before the invitation had come.

"Listen," Louise walked down the hall with her to Latin, their next class, "are you busy right after school today? Because I'd like to talk to you about tomorrow."

"Sure. I've got lots of time."

"Well, meet me in the hall after homeroom then, and we'll go down to the drugstore or something."

Walking beside Louise on the way to the drugstore, Millicent felt a surge of pride. For all anyone could see, she and Louise were the best of friends.

"You know, I was so glad when they voted you in," Louise said.

Millicent smiled. "I was really thrilled to get the invitation," she said frankly, "but kind of sorry that Tracy didn't get in, too."

Tracy, she thought. If there is such a thing as a best friend, Tracy has been just that this last year.

"Yes, Tracy," Louise was saying, "she's a nice girl, and they put her up on the slate, but . . . well, she had three blackballs against her."

"Blackballs? What are they?"

"Well, we're not supposed to tell anybody outside the club, but seeing as you'll be in at the end of the week I don't suppose it hurts." They were at the drugstore now.

"You see," Louise began explaining in a low voice after they were seated in the privacy of the booth, "once a year the sorority puts up all the likely girls that are suggested for membership. . . ."

Millicent sipped her cold, sweet drink slowly, saving the ice cream to spoon up last. She listened carefully to Louise who was going on," . . . and then there's a big meeting, and all the girls' names are read off and each girl is discussed."

"Oh?" Millicent asked mechanically, her voice sounding strange.

"Oh, I know what you're thinking," Louise laughed. "But it's really not as bad as all that. They keep it down to a minimum of catting.[3] They just talk over each girl and why or why not they think she'd be good for the club. And then they vote. Three blackballs eliminate a girl."

"Do you mind if I ask you what happened to Tracy?" Millicent said.

Louise laughed a little uneasily. "Well, you know how girls are. They notice little things. I mean, some of them thought Tracy was just a bit *too* different. Maybe you could suggest a few things to her."

"Like what?"

"Oh, like maybe not wearing knee socks to school, or carrying that old bookbag. I know it doesn't sound like much, but well, it's things like that which set someone apart. I mean, you know that no girl at Lansing would be seen dead wearing knee socks, no matter how cold it gets, and it's kiddish and kind of green[4] to carry a bookbag."

"I guess so," Millicent said.

"About tomorrow," Louise went on. "You've drawn Beverly Mitchell for a big sister. I wanted to warn you that she's the toughest, but if you get through all right it'll be all the more credit for you."

"Thanks, Lou," Millicent said gratefully, thinking, this is beginning to sound serious. Worse than a loyalty test, this grilling over the coals. What's it supposed to prove anyway? That I can take orders without flinching? Or does it just make them feel good to see us run around at their beck and call?

"All you have to do really," Louise said, spooning up the last of her sundae, "is be very meek and obedient when you're with Bev and do just what she tells you. Don't laugh or talk back or try to be funny, or she'll just make it harder for you, and believe me, she's a great

one for doing that. Be at her house at seven-thirty."

And she was. She rang the bell and sat down on the steps to wait for Bev. After a few minutes the front door opened and Bev was standing there, her face serious.

"Get up, gopher,"[5] Bev ordered.

There was something about her tone that annoyed Millicent. It was almost <u>malicious</u>.[6] And there was an unpleasant anonymity about the label "gopher," even if that was what they always called the girls being initiated. It was degrading, like being given a number. It was a denial of individuality.

Rebellion flooded through her.

"I said get up. Are you deaf?"

Millicent got up, standing there.

"Into the house, gopher. There's a bed to be made and a room to be cleaned at the top of the stairs."

Millicent went up the stairs mutely. She found Bev's room and started making the bed. Smiling to herself, she was thinking: How absurdly funny, me taking orders from this girl like a servant.

Bev was suddenly there in the doorway. "Wipe that smile off your face," she commanded.

There seemed something about this relationship that was not all fun. In Bev's eyes, Millicent was sure of it, there was a hard, bright spark of exultation.

On the way to school, Millicent had to walk behind Bev at a distance of ten paces, carrying her books. They came up to the drugstore where

---

3. **catting** (kat′ iŋ): making mean and spiteful remarks.

4. **green:** unsophisticated, inexperienced, naive.

5. **gopher** (gō′ fər), also spelled **gofer:** a person expected to run errands and cater to others; a "go for."

6. **malicious** (mə lish′ əs): having, showing, or caused by the desire to harm another or do mischief.

there already was a crowd of boys and girls from Lansing High waiting for the show.

The other girls being initiated were there, so Millicent felt relieved. It would not be so bad now, being part of the group.

"What'll we have them do?" Betsy Johnson asked Bev. That morning Betsy had made her "gopher" carry an old colored parasol through the square and sing "I'm Always Chasing Rainbows."

"I know," Herb Dalton, the good-looking basketball captain, said.

A remarkable change came over Bev. She was all at once very soft and coquettish.

"You can't tell them what to do," Bev said sweetly. "Men have nothing to say about this little deal."

"All right, all right," Herb laughed, stepping back and pretending to fend off a blow.

"It's getting late," Louise had come up. "Almost eight-thirty. We'd better get them marching on to school."

The "gophers" had to do a Charleston[7] step all the way to school, and each one had her own song to sing, trying to drown out the other four. During school, of course, you couldn't fool around, but even then, there was a rule that you mustn't talk to boys outside of class or at lunchtime . . . or any time at all after school. So the sorority girls would get the most popular boys to go up to the "gophers" and ask them out, or try to start them talking, and sometimes a "gopher" was taken by surprise and began to say something before she could catch herself. And then the boy reported her and she got a black mark.

Herb Dalton approached Millicent as she was getting an ice cream at the lunch counter that noon. She saw him coming before he spoke to her, and looked down quickly, thinking: He is too princely, too dark and smiling. And I am much too vulnerable. Why must he be the one I have to be careful of?

I won't say anything, she thought, I'll just smile very sweetly.

She smiled up at Herb very sweetly and mutely. His return grin was rather miraculous. It was surely more than was called for in the line of duty.

"I know you can't talk to me," he said, very low. "But you're doing fine, the girls say. I even like your hair straight and all."

Bev was coming toward them, then, her red mouth set in a bright, calculating smile. She ignored Millicent and sailed up to Herb.

"Why waste your time with gophers?" she caroled gaily. "Their tongues are tied, but completely."

Herb managed a parting shot. "But that one keeps *such* an attractive silence."

Millicent smiled as she ate her sundae at the counter with Tracy. Generally, the girls who were outsiders now, as Millicent had been, scoffed at the initiation antics as childish and absurd to hide their secret envy. But Tracy was understanding, as ever.

"Tonight's the worst, I guess, Tracy," Millicent told her. "I hear that the girls are taking us on a bus over to Lewiston and going to have us performing in the square."

"Just keep a poker face outside," Tracy advised. "But keep laughing like mad inside."

Millicent and Bev took a bus ahead of the rest of the girls; they had to stand up on the way to Lewiston Square. Bev seemed very cross about something. Finally she said, "You were talking with Herb Dalton at lunch today."

"No," said Millicent honestly.

"Well, I *saw* you smile at him. That's practically as bad as talking. Remember not to do it again."

Millicent kept silent.

---

7. **Charleston** (chärls′ tən): a lively dance popular during the 1920's.

"It's fifteen minutes before the bus gets into town," Bev was saying then. "I want you to go up and down the bus asking people what they eat for breakfast. Remember, you can't tell them you're being initiated."

Millicent looked down the aisle of the crowded bus and felt suddenly quite sick. She thought: How will I ever do it, going up to all those stony-faced people who are staring coldly out of the window. . . .

"You heard me, gopher."

"Excuse me, madam," Millicent said politely to the lady in the first seat of the bus, "but I'm taking a survey. Could you please tell me what you eat for breakfast?"

"Why . . . er . . . just orange juice, toast, and coffee," she said.

"Thank you very much." Millicent went on to the next person, a young business man. He ate eggs sunny side up, toast and coffee.

By the time Millicent got to the back of the bus, most of the people were smiling at her. They obviously know, she thought, that I'm being initiated into something.

Finally, there was only one man left in the corner of the back seat. He was small and jolly, with a ruddy, wrinkled face that spread into a beaming smile as Millicent approached. In his brown suit with the forest-green tie he looked something like a gnome or a cheerful leprechaun.

"Excuse me, sir," Millicent smiled, "but I'm taking a survey. What do you eat for breakfast?"

"Heather birds' eyebrows on toast," the little man rattled off.

"*What?*" Millicent exclaimed.

"Heather birds' eyebrows," the little man explained. "Heather birds live on the mythological moors and fly about all day long, singing wild and sweet in the sun. They're bright purple and have *very* tasty eyebrows."

Millicent broke out into spontaneous laugh-

ter. Why, this was wonderful, the way she felt a sudden comradeship[8] with a stranger.

"Are you mythological, too?"

"Not exactly," he replied, "but I certainly hope to be someday. Being mythological does wonders for one's ego."

The bus was swinging into the station now; Millicent hated to leave the little man. She wanted to ask him more about the birds.

And from that time on, initiations didn't bother Millicent at all. She went gaily about Lewiston Square from store to store asking for broken crackers and mangoes, and she just laughed inside when people stared and then brightened, answering her crazy questions as if she were quite serious and really a person of consequence.[9] So many people were shut up tight inside themselves like boxes, yet they would open up, unfolding quite wonderfully, if only you were interested in them. And really, you didn't have to belong to a club to feel related to other human beings.

One afternoon Millicent had started talking with Liane Morris, another of the girls being initiated, about what it would be like when they were finally in the sorority.

"Oh, I know pretty much what it'll be like," Liane had said. "My sister belonged before she graduated from high school two years ago."

"Well, just what *do* they do as a club?" Millicent wanted to know.

"Why, they have a meeting once a week . . . each girl takes turns entertaining at her house. . . ."

"You mean it's just a sort of exclusive social group. . . ."

"I guess so . . . though that's a funny way of

---

8. **comradeship** (käm′ rəd ship′): a relationship arising from the sharing of mutual interests and activities.
9. **consequence:** importance or influence.

*The Adolescent,* 1956, RAPHAEL SOYER.
By permission of the Soyer family.

putting it. But it sure gives a girl prestige[10] value. My sister started going steady with the captain of the football team after she got in. Not bad, I say."

No, it wasn't bad, Millicent had thought, lying in bed on the morning of Rat Court and listening to the sparrows chirping in the gutters. She thought of Herb. Would he ever have been so friendly if she were without the sorority label? Would he ask her out (if he ever did) just for herself, no strings attached?

Then there was another thing that bothered her. Leaving Tracy on the outskirts. Because that is the way it would be; Millicent had seen it happen before.

Outside, the sparrows were still chirping, and as she lay in bed Millicent visualized them, pale gray-brown birds in a flock, one like the other, all exactly alike.

And then, for some reason, Millicent thought of the heather birds. Swooping carefree over the moors, they would go singing and crying out across the great spaces of air, dipping and darting, strong and proud in their freedom and their sometime loneliness. It was then that she made her decision.

Seated now on the woodpile in Betsy Johnson's cellar, Millicent knew that she had come triumphant through the trial of fire, the searing period of the ego which could end in two kinds of victory for her. The easiest of which would be her coronation as a princess, labeling her conclusively as one of the select flock.

The other victory would be much harder, but she knew that it was what she wanted. It was not that she was being noble or anything.

It was just that she had learned there were other ways of getting into the great hall, blazing with lights, of people and of life.

It would be hard to explain to the girls tonight, of course, but she could tell Louise later just how it was. How she had proved something to herself by going through everything, even Rat Court, and then deciding not to join the sorority after all. And how she could still be friends with everybody. Sisters with everybody. Tracy, too.

The door behind her opened and a ray of light sliced across the soft gloom of the basement room.

"Hey Millicent, come on out now. This is it." There were some of the girls outside.

"I'm coming," she said, getting up and moving out of the soft darkness into the glare of light, thinking: This is it, all right. The worst part, the hardest part, the part of initiation that I figured out myself.

But just then, from somewhere far off, Millicent was sure of it, there came a melodic fluting, quite wild and sweet, and she knew that it must be the song of the heather birds as they went wheeling and gliding against wide blue horizons through vast spaces of air, their wings flashing quick and purple in the bright sun.

Within Millicent another melody soared, strong and exuberant, a triumphant answer to the music of the darting heather birds that sang so clear and lilting over the far lands. And she knew that her own private initiation had just begun.

---

10. **prestige** (pres tēzh′): status or reputation.

# Thinking About the Story

## A PERSONAL RESPONSE

*sharing impressions*

**1.** What are your thoughts about Millicent's decision? Briefly note your thoughts in your journal.

*constructing interpretations*

**2.** How would you explain the meaning of the last sentence in the story?

**3.** Why does Millicent make the decision she does?
### Think about
- her relationships with Tracy and Bev
- the things she has to do during initiation week
- what she finds out about being in a sorority
- the effect of her conversation with the older man on the bus

**4.** Compare Millicent's situation with the pressures you wrote about in your prereading journal entry.

**5.** How does Millicent change during the story?

## A CREATIVE RESPONSE

**6.** If Herb Dalton had told Millicent that he would take her out as soon as she was in the sorority, how might her final decision have been affected?

## A CRITICAL RESPONSE

**7.** Go back through the story and find the point at which you think Millicent begins to change her mind about initiations. Be prepared to explain your answer.

**8.** What do you think heather birds symbolize for Millicent?
### Think about
- how she felt when the man on the bus first spoke of them
- how they are described toward the end of the story
- how they differ from the sparrows she hears outside her window

**9.** Analyze the way the description in the first two paragraphs prepares the reader for the rest of the story.
### Think about
- the feelings you have as you read the paragraphs
- the sights, sounds, and physical sensations that the language conveys
- the comparisons made

# *Analyzing the Writer's Craft*

## PSYCHOLOGICAL REALISM

Do you think Millicent's decision is a difficult one for her to make? Think about how you learn about her decision.

**Building a Literary Vocabulary.** The literary technique in which a writer explores the thoughts of a character confronted by a difficult moral choice is called psychological realism. Sylvia Plath used this technique in portraying Millicent's experience during initiation week. The reader knows what Millicent is thinking and feeling throughout the week and so can follow the way she gradually reaches her decision.

**Application: Understanding Psychological Realism.** With a partner go through the first half of the story and look for passages that help explain Millicent's reasons for wanting to join a sorority in the first place. List those reasons on a sheet of paper. Then look for passages in the second half that show Millicent beginning to change her mind, and jot down her reasons for not joining a sorority. These two lists give you examples of some of Millicent's needs and desires. Now imagine what she might say in any one of the following situations:

- her appearance before Rat Court
- the next time she meets Herb Dalton
- the next time she meets Bev Mitchell

With your partner act out any one of these scenes in front of the class.

# *Connecting Reading and Writing*

**1.** Consider how Millicent might feel about her decision after ten years have passed. In an **interview** with Millicent, indicate her thoughts on the subject and the shape her life has taken.

Option: Have Millicent write a **letter** to Tracy recalling her decision.

**2.** Millicent learns that there are "other ways of getting into the great hall, blazing with lights, of people and of life." Explain what she has learned in a **poem.**

Option: Present her views in a brief **essay** that she might write on a college application.

**3.** Should sororities and fraternities be allowed in high schools, as they were in the 1950's? Take a position and argue it in a **speech.**

Option: Write a **newspaper editorial** arguing your position.

# Through the Tunnel

### DORIS LESSING

A biography of Lessing appears on page 642.

## *Approaching the Story*

Jerry, the main character of "Through the Tunnel," is an English boy of eleven on a seaside vacation with his widowed mother. This story takes place in a foreign country, but Jerry's experience is something all young people can understand.

## *Building Vocabulary*

These essential words are footnoted within the story.

**contrition** (kən trish´ ən): **Contrition** sent him running after her. (page 75)

**supplication** (sup´ lə kā´ shən): He had swum in and was on the rocks beside them, smiling with a desperate, nervous **supplication**. (page 76)

**defiant** (dē fī´ ənt), **beseeching** (bē sēch´ iŋ): "I want some swimming goggles," he panted, **defiant** and **beseeching**. (page 77)

**incredulous** (in krej´ oo ləs): He was **incredulous** and then proud to find he could hold his breath without strain for two minutes. (page 78)

## *Connecting Writing and Reading*

Think about times in your life when you took risks to achieve something. What did you risk losing? In your journal, list risks that you have taken and evaluate whether each risk was worth taking. As you read this story, compare Jerry's risks with yours.

GOING TO THE shore on the first morning of the vacation, the young English boy stopped at a turning of the path and looked down at a wild and rocky bay, and then over the crowded beach he knew so well from other years. His mother walked on in front of him, carrying a bright striped bag in one hand. Her other arm, swinging loose, was very white in the sun. The boy watched that white, naked arm, and turned his eyes, which had a frown behind them, toward the bay and back again to his mother. When she felt he was not with her, she swung around. "Oh, there you are, Jerry!" she said. She looked impatient, then smiled. "Why, darling, would you rather not come with me? Would you rather—" She frowned, conscientiously worrying over what amusements he might secretly be longing for, which she had been too busy or too careless to imagine. He was very familiar with that anxious, apologetic smile. Contrition[1] sent him running after her. And yet, as he ran, he looked back over his shoulder at the wild bay; and all morning, as he played on the safe beach, he was thinking of it.

Next morning, when it was time for the routine of swimming and sunbathing, his mother said, "Are you tired of the usual beach, Jerry? Would you like to go somewhere else?"

"Oh, no!" he said quickly, smiling at her out of that unfailing impulse of contrition—a sort of chivalry. Yet, walking down the path with her, he blurted out, "I'd like to go and have a look at those rocks down there."

She gave the idea her attention. It was a wild-looking place, and there was no one there; but she said, "Of course, Jerry. When you've had enough, come to the big beach. Or just go straight back to the villa, if you like." She walked away, that bare arm, now slightly reddened from yesterday's sun, swinging. And he almost ran after her again, feeling it unbearable that she should go by herself, but he did not.

She was thinking, Of course he's old enough to be safe without me. Have I been keeping him too close? He mustn't feel he ought to be with me. I must be careful.

He was an only child, eleven years old. She was a widow. She was determined to be neither possessive nor lacking in devotion. She went worrying off to her beach.

As for Jerry, once he saw that his mother had gained her beach, he began the steep descent to the bay. From where he was, high up among red-brown rocks, it was a scoop of moving bluish green fringed with white. As he went lower, he saw that it spread among small promontories and inlets of rough, sharp rock, and the crisping, lapping surface showed stains of purple and darker blue. Finally, as he ran sliding and scraping down the last few yards, he saw an edge of white surf and the shallow, luminous movement of water over white sand and, beyond that, a solid, heavy blue.

He ran straight into the water and began swimming. He was a good swimmer. He went out fast over the gleaming sand, over a middle region where rocks lay like discolored monsters under the surface, and then he was in the real sea—a warm sea where irregular cold currents from the deep water shocked his limbs.

When he was so far out that he could look back not only on the little bay but past the promontory that was between it and the big beach, he floated on the buoyant surface and looked for his mother. There she was, a speck of yellow under an umbrella that looked like a slice of orange peel. He swam back to shore, relieved at being sure she was there, but all at once very lonely.

On the edge of a small cape that marked the side of the bay away from the promontory was a loose scatter of rocks. Above them, some boys were stripping off their clothes. They

---

1. **contrition** (kən trish′ ən): a feeling of sorrow for doing wrong.

came running, naked, down to the rocks. The English boy swam toward them, but kept his distance at a stone's throw. They were of that coast; all of them were burned smooth dark brown and speaking a language he did not understand. To be with them, of them, was a craving that filled his whole body. He swam a little closer; they turned and watched him with narrowed, alert dark eyes. Then one smiled and waved. It was enough. In a minute, he had swum in and was on the rocks beside them, smiling with a desperate, nervous supplication.[2] They shouted cheerful greetings at him; and then, as he preserved his nervous, uncomprehending smile, they understood that he was a foreigner strayed from his own beach, and they proceeded to forget him. But he was happy. He was with them.

They began diving again and again from a high point into a well of blue sea between rough, pointed rocks. After they had dived and come up, they swam around, hauled themselves up, and waited their turn to dive again. They were big boys—men, to Jerry. He dived, and they watched him; and when he swam around to take his place, they made way for him. He felt he was accepted and he dived again, carefully, proud of himself.

Soon the biggest of the boys poised himself, shot down into the water, and did not come up. The others stood about, watching. Jerry, after waiting for the sleek brown head to appear, let out a yell of warning; they looked at him idly and turned their eyes back toward the water. After a long time, the boy came up on the other side of a big dark rock, letting the air out of his lungs in a sputtering gasp and a shout of triumph. Immediately the rest of them dived in. One moment, the morning seemed full of chattering boys; the next, the air and the surface of the water were empty. But through the heavy blue, dark shapes could be seen moving and groping.

Jerry dived, shot past the school of under-water swimmers, saw a black wall of rock looming at him, touched it, and bobbed up at once to the surface, where the wall was a low barrier he could see across. There was no one visible; under him, in the water, the dim shapes of the swimmers had disappeared. Then one, and then another of the boys came up on the far side of the barrier of rock, and he understood that they had swum through some gap or hole in it. He plunged down again. He could see nothing through the stinging salt water but the blank rock. When he came up the boys were all on the diving rock, preparing to attempt the feat again. And now, in a panic of failure, he yelled up, in English, "Look at me! Look!" and he began splashing and kicking in the water like a foolish dog.

They looked down gravely, frowning. He knew the frown. At moments of failure, when he clowned to claim his mother's attention, it was with just this grave, embarrassed inspection that she rewarded him. Through his hot shame, feeling the pleading grin on his face like a scar that he could never remove, he looked up at the group of big brown boys on the rock and shouted, *"Bonjour! Merci! Au revoir! Monsieur, monsieur!"*[3] while he hooked his fingers round his ears and waggled them.

Water surged into his mouth; he choked, sank, came up. The rock, lately weighted with boys, seemed to rear up out of the water as their weight was removed. They were flying down past him, now, into the water; the air was full of falling bodies. Then the rock was empty in the hot sunlight. He counted one, two, three. . . .

At fifty, he was terrified. They must all be drowning beneath him, in the watery caves of

---

2. **supplication** (sup' lə kā' shən): a humble request, prayer, or petition.

3. ***Bonjour! Merci! Au revoir! Monsieur, monsieur!*** (bon zho͞or' mer sē' ō' rə vwär' mə syʉr') *French:* Good day! Thank you! Goodbye! Sir, sir!

the rock! At a hundred, he stared around him at the empty hillside, wondering if he should yell for help. He counted faster, faster, to hurry them up, to bring them to the surface quickly, to drown them quickly—anything rather than the terror of counting on and on into the blue emptiness of the morning. And then, at a hundred and sixty, the water beyond the rock was full of boys blowing like brown whales. They swam back to the shore without a look at him.

He climbed back to the diving rock and sat down, feeling the hot roughness of it under his thighs. The boys were gathering up their bits of clothing and running off along the shore to another promontory. They were leaving to get away from him. He cried openly, fists in his eyes. There was no one to see him, and he cried himself out.

It seemed to him that a long time had passed, and he swam out to where he could see his mother. Yes, she was still there, a yellow spot under an orange umbrella. He swam back to the big rock, climbed up, and dived into the blue pool among the fanged and angry boulders. Down he went, until he touched the wall of rock again. But the salt was so painful in his eyes that he could not see.

He came to the surface, swam to shore, and went back to the villa to wait for his mother. Soon she walked slowly up the path, swinging her striped bag, the flushed, naked arm dangling beside her. "I want some swimming goggles," he panted, defiant[4] and beseeching.[5]

She gave him a patient, inquisitive look as she said casually, "Well, of course, darling."

But now, now, now! He must have them this minute, and no other time. He nagged and pestered until she went with him to a shop. As soon as she had bought the goggles, he grabbed them from her hand, as if she were going to claim them for herself, and was off, running down the steep path to the bay.

Jerry swam out to the big barrier rock, adjusted the goggles, and dived. The impact of the water broke the rubber-enclosed vacuum, and the goggles came loose. He understood that he must swim down to the base of the rock from the surface of the water. He fixed the goggles tight and firm, filled his lungs, and floated, face down, on the water. Now, he could see. It was as if he had eyes of a different kind—fish eyes that showed everything clear and delicate and wavering in the bright water.

Under him, six or seven feet down, was a floor of perfectly clean, shining white sand, rippled firm and hard by the tides. Two grayish shapes steered there, like long, rounded pieces of wood or slate. They were fish. He saw them nose toward each other, poise motionless, make a dart forward, swerve off, and come around again. It was like a water dance. A few inches above them the water sparkled as if sequins were dropping through it. Fish again—myriads of minute fish, the length of his fingernail, were drifting through the water, and in a moment he could feel the innumerable tiny touches of them against his limbs. It was like swimming in flaked silver. The great rock the big boys had swum through rose sheer out of the white sand—black, tufted lightly with greenish weed. He could see no gap in it. He swam down to its base.

Again and again he rose, took a big chestful of air, and went down. Again and again he groped over the surface of the rock, feeling it, almost hugging it in the desperate need to find the entrance. And then, once, while he was clinging to the black wall, his knees came up and he shot his feet out forward and they met no obstacle. He had found the hole.

He gained the surface, clambered about the stones that littered the barrier rock until he found a big one, and, with this in his arms, let himself down over the side of the rock. He

---

4. **defiant** (dē fī′ ənt): with bold opposition and willingness to challenge or fight.
5. **beseeching** (bē sēch′ iŋ): earnestly asking, begging.

dropped, with the weight, straight to the sandy floor. Clinging tight to the anchor of stone, he lay on his side and looked in under the dark shelf at the place where his feet had gone. He could see the hole. It was an irregular, dark gap; but he could not see deep into it. He let go of his anchor, clung with his hands to the edge of the hole, and tried to push himself in.

He got his head in, found his shoulders jammed, moved them in sidewise, and was inside as far as his waist. He could see nothing ahead. Something soft and clammy touched his mouth; he saw a dark frond moving against the grayish rock, and panic filled him. He thought of octopuses, of clinging weed. He pushed himself out backward and caught a glimpse, as he retreated, of a harmless tentacle of seaweed drifting in the mouth of the tunnel. But it was enough. He reached the sunlight, swam to shore, and lay on the diving rock. He looked down into the blue well of water. He knew he must find his way through that cave, or hole, or tunnel, and out the other side.

First, he thought, he must learn to control his breathing. He let himself down into the water with another big stone in his arms, so that he could lie effortlessly on the bottom of the sea. He counted. One, two, three. He counted steadily. He could hear the movement of blood in his chest. Fifty-one, fifty-two. . . . His chest was hurting. He let go of the rock and went up into the air. He saw that the sun was low. He rushed to the villa and found his mother at her supper. She said only "Did you enjoy yourself?" and he said "Yes."

All night the boy dreamed of the water-filled cave in the rock, and as soon as breakfast was over he went to the bay.

That night, his nose bled badly. For hours he had been under water, learning to hold his breath, and now he felt weak and dizzy. His mother said, "I shouldn't overdo things, darling, if I were you."

That day and the next, Jerry exercised his lungs as if everything, the whole of his life, all

that he would become, depended upon it. Again his nose bled at night, and his mother insisted on his coming with her the next day. It was a torment to him to waste a day of his careful self-training, but he stayed with her on that other beach, which now seemed a place for small children, a place where his mother might lie safe in the sun. It was not his beach.

He did not ask for permission, on the following day, to go to his beach. He went, before his mother could consider the complicated rights and wrongs of the matter. A day's rest, he discovered, had improved his count by ten. The big boys had made the passage while he counted a hundred and sixty. He had been counting fast, in his fright. Probably now, if he tried, he could get through the long tunnel, but he was not going to try yet. A curious, most unchildlike persistence, a controlled impatience, made him wait. In the meantime, he lay underwater on the white sand, littered now by stones he had brought down from the upper air, and studied the entrance to the tunnel. He knew every jut and corner of it, as far as it was possible to see. It was as if he already felt its sharpness about his shoulders.

He sat by the clock in the villa, when his mother was not near, and checked his time. He was incredulous[6] and then proud to find he could hold his breath without strain for two minutes. The words "two minutes," authorized by the clock, brought close the adventure that was so necessary to him.

In another four days, his mother said casually one morning, they must go home. On the day before they left, he would do it. He would do it if it killed him, he said defiantly to himself. But two days before they were to leave—a day of triumph when he increased his count by fifteen—his nose bled so badly that he turned dizzy and had to lie limply over the big rock like a bit of seaweed, watching the thick red blood flow on to the rock and trickle slowly

---

6. **incredulous** (in krej′ o͞o ləs): doubtful, disbelieving.

down to the sea. He was frightened. Supposing he turned dizzy in the tunnel? Supposing he died there, trapped? Supposing—his head went around, in the hot sun, and he almost gave up. He thought he would return to the house and lie down, and next summer, perhaps, when he had another year's growth in him—*then* he would go through the hole.

But even after he had made the decision, or thought he had, he found himself sitting up on the rock and looking down into the water; and he knew that now, this moment, when his nose had only just stopped bleeding, when his head was still sore and throbbing—this was the moment when he would try. If he did not do it now, he never would. He was trembling with fear that he would not go; and he was trembling with horror at that long, long tunnel under the rock, under the sea. Even in the open sunlight, the barrier rock seemed very wide and very heavy; tons of rock pressed down on where he would go. If he died there, he would lie until one day—perhaps not before next year—those big boys would swim into it and find it blocked.

He put on his goggles, fitted them tight, tested the vacuum. His hands were shaking. Then he chose the biggest stone he could carry and slipped over the edge of the rock until half of him was in the cool, enclosing water and half in the hot sun. He looked up once at the empty sky, filled his lungs once, twice, and then sank fast to the bottom with the stone. He let it go and began to count. He took the edges of the hole in his hands and drew himself into it, wriggling his shoulders in sidewise as he remembered he must, kicking himself along with his feet.

Soon he was clear inside. He was in a small rockbound hole filled with yellowish-gray water. The water was pushing him up against the roof. The roof was sharp and pained his back. He pulled himself along with his hands—fast, fast—and used his legs as levers.

His head knocked against something; a sharp pain dizzied him. Fifty, fifty-one, fifty-two. . . . He was without light, and the water seemed to press upon him with the weight of rock. Seventy-one, seventy-two. . . . There was no strain on his lungs. He felt like an inflated balloon, his lungs were so light and easy, but his head was pulsing.

He was being continually pressed against the sharp roof, which felt slimy as well as sharp. Again he thought of octopuses, and wondered if the tunnel might be filled with weed that could tangle him. He gave himself a panicky, convulsive kick forward, ducked his head, and swam. His feet and hands moved freely, as if in open water. The hole must have widened out. He thought he must be swimming fast, and he was frightened of banging his head if the tunnel narrowed.

A hundred, a hundred and one. . . . The water paled. Victory filled him. His lungs were beginning to hurt. A few more strokes and he would be out. He was counting wildly; he said a hundred and fifteen, and then, a long time later, a hundred and fifteen again. The water was a clear jewel-green all around him. Then he saw, above his head, a crack running up through the rock. Sunlight was falling through it, showing the clean, dark rock of the tunnel, a single mussel shell, and darkness ahead.

He was at the end of what he could do. He looked up at the crack as if it were filled with air and not water, as if he could put his mouth to it to draw in air. A hundred and fifteen, he heard himself say inside his head—but he had said that long ago. He must go on into the blackness ahead, or he would drown. His head was swelling, his lungs cracking. A hundred and fifteen, a hundred and fifteen pounded through his head, and he feebly clutched at rocks in the dark, pulling himself forward, leaving the brief space of sunlit water behind. He felt he was dying. He was no longer quite conscious. He struggled on in the darkness between lapses into unconsciousness. An immense, swelling pain filled his head, and then the darkness cracked with an explosion of green light. His hands, groping forward, met nothing; and his feet, kicking back, propelled him out into the open sea.

He drifted to the surface, his face turned up to the air. He was gasping like a fish. He felt he would sink now and drown; he could not swim the few feet back to the rock. Then he was clutching it and pulling himself up onto it. He lay face down, gasping. He could see nothing but a red-veined, clotted dark. His eyes must have burst, he thought; they were full of blood. He tore off his goggles and a gout of blood went into the sea. His nose was bleeding, and the blood had filled the goggles.

He scooped up handfuls of water from the cool, salty sea, to splash on his face, and did not know whether it was blood or salt water he tasted. After a time, his heart quieted, his eyes cleared, and he sat up. He could see the local boys diving and playing half a mile away. He did not want them. He wanted nothing but to get back home and lie down.

In a short while, Jerry swam to shore and climbed slowly up the path to the villa. He flung himself on his bed and slept, waking at the sound of feet on the path outside. His mother was coming back. He rushed to the bathroom, thinking she must not see his face with bloodstains, or tearstains, on it. He came out of the bathroom and met her as she walked into the villa, smiling, her eyes lighting up.

"Have a nice morning?" she asked, laying her hand on his warm brown shoulder.

"Oh, yes, thank you," he said.

"You look a bit pale." And then, sharp and anxious, "How did you bang your head?"

"Oh, just banged it," he told her.

She looked at him closely. He was strained; his eyes were glazed-looking. She was worried. And then she said to herself, Oh, don't fuss! Nothing can happen. He can swim like a fish.

They sat down to lunch together.

"Mummy," he said, "I can stay under water for two minutes—three minutes, at least." It came bursting out of him.

"Can you, darling?" she said. "Well, I shouldn't overdo it. I don't think you ought to swim any more today."

She was ready for a battle of wills, but he gave in at once. It was no longer of the least importance to go to the bay.

# Thinking About the Story

## A PERSONAL RESPONSE

*sharing impressions*

**1.** In your journal record your reaction to Jerry's swim through the tunnel.

*constructing interpretations*

**2.** How does Jerry seem to feel about himself and his swim at the end of the story?

**3.** Why do you think it is so important to Jerry to swim through the tunnel?

### Think about
- his age and family situation
- his interactions with the older boys
- the risks involved

**4.** How would you describe Jerry's relationship with his mother?

### Think about
- the concerns his mother has
- why Jerry is described as both "defiant and beseeching"
- why Jerry doesn't tell his mother about the risk he has taken

## A CREATIVE RESPONSE

**5.** If Jerry had failed to make it through the tunnel (yet had survived the attempt), how might the story have ended?

## A CRITICAL RESPONSE

**6.** What elements of psychological realism do you see in the portrayal of Jerry's struggle?

### Think about
- psychological realism as a technique in which the writer reveals the thoughts of a character confronted by a difficult moral choice
- what you know of Jerry's fears and desires at various points in the story
- what, if any, moral choice Jerry makes

**7.** Describe some rites of passage common today among adolescents and explain what risks are involved.

# Analyzing the Writer's Craft

Jerry notices the contrast between the beach where he and his mother usually swim and the bay where the boys swim. What might these two locations represent to Jerry?

**Building a Literary Vocabulary.** Setting is the time and place of the action of a story. A symbol is a person, place, object, or activity that stands for something beyond itself. In "Through the Tunnel" key parts of the setting have symbolic meaning. For example, the beach where Jerry and his mother usually go is described as "a place for small children, a place where his mother might lie safe in the sun." This sheltered beach, with its sense of security, seems to represent Jerry's ties to childhood

and dependency—both of which he longs to shed. In contrast, the bay where the older boys swim is bounded by "small promontories and inlets of rough, sharp rock." Jerry is drawn to the wild, rocky bay because for him it represents the danger and mystery of the older, masculine world he wants to be part of.

**Application: Interpreting Symbol.** Working with two or three classmates, reread the descriptions of the tunnel and of Jerry's feelings about it. On a sheet of paper, list possible symbolic interpretations of the tunnel, supported by evidence from the story. Then present your group's interpretations to the class as an oral presentation.

# Connecting Reading and Writing

**1.** The line between courage and foolishness is often a thin one. Decide whether Jerry's action is brave or foolish and argue your position in a **letter** to Jerry.

Option: Interview twelve classmates and write a **report** summarizing their opinions about the wisdom of Jerry's action.

**2.** Think of several prominent symbols of maturity and status for teenagers today. Explore the meanings of these symbols in a short **pamphlet** for incoming freshmen.

Option: Write about these symbols in **notes** for a speech for freshmen orientation.

**3.** Does Jerry's mother allow him too little, just enough, or too much freedom? Explain your response in a **note** to Jerry's mother.

Option: Write a **diary entry** for Jerry in which he gives his opinion about this issue.

**4.** How do you think Jerry would react if, twenty years from the time of this story, his own son seemed to be drawn to risky behavior? Describe Jerry's response in a **letter** to an advice columnist.

Option: Write a **script** for a conversation between Jerry and his son.

# My Delicate Heart Condition

TONI CADE BAMBARA

A biography of Bambara appears on page 636.

## *Approaching the Story*

"My Delicate Heart Condition" features Harriet Watkins, a girl who tells the story in her own words. Harriet has an especially colorful, often humorous way of talking. She begins her story abruptly, and because she sometimes refers to people, locations, and events without explaining who or what they are, the reader has to infer a great deal.

MY COUSIN JOANNE has not been allowed to hang out with me for some time because she went and told Aunt Hazel that I scare her to death whenever she sleeps over at our house or I spend the weekend at hers. The truth is I sometimes like to tell stories about bloodthirsty vampires or ugly monsters that lurk in clothes closets or giant beetles that eat their way through the shower curtain, like I used to do at camp to entertain the kids in my bunk. But Joanne always cries and that makes the stories even weirder, like background music her crying. And too—I'm not going to lie about it—I get spookier on purpose until all the little crybabies are stuffing themselves under their pillows and throwing their sneakers at me and making such a racket that Mary the counselor has to come in and shine her flashlight around the bunkhouse. I play like I'm asleep. The rest of them are too busy blub-bering and finding their way out from under blankets to tell Mary that it's me. Besides, once they get a load of her standing against the moonlight in that long white robe of hers looking like a ghost, they just start up again and pretty soon the whole camp is awake. Anyway, that's what I do for fun. So Joanne hasn't been around. And this year I'll have to go to the circus by myself and to camp without her. My mother said on the phone to Aunt Hazel—"Good, keep Jo over there and maybe Harriet'll behave herself if she's got no one to show off to." For all the years my mother's known me, she still doesn't understand that my behaving has got nothing to do with who I hang out with. A private thing between me and me or maybe between me and the Fly family since they were the ones that first got me to sit through monster movies and with-stand all the terror I could take.

For four summers now, me and the Fly fam-ily have had this thing going. A battle of nerves, you might say. Each year they raise the rope closer and closer to the very top of the tent—I hear they're going to perform outdoors this year and be even higher—and they stretch the rope further across the rings where the clowns and the pony riders perform. Each year they get bolder and more daring with their rope dancing and swinging by the legs and flinging themselves into empty space making everyone throw up their hands and gasp for air until Mr. Fly at the very last possible second swings out on his bar to catch them up by the tips of their heels. Everyone just dies and clutches at their hearts. Everybody but me. I sit there calmly. I've trained myself. Joanne used to die and duck her head under the benches and stay there till it was all over.

Last summer they really got bold. On the final performance just before the fair closed, and some revival type tent show comes in and all the kids go off to camp, the Fly family performed without a net. I figured they'd be up to something so I made sure my stomach was like steel. I did ten push-ups before breakfast, twenty sit-ups before lunch, skipped dinner altogether. My brother Teddy kidded me all day—"Harriet's trying out for the Olympics." I passed up the icie man on the corner and the pizza and sausage stand by the schoolyard and the cotton candy and jelly apple lady and the pickle and penny candy boy, in fact I passed up all the stands that lead from the street down the little roadway to the fair grounds that used to be a swamp when we first moved from Baltimore to Jamaica, Long Island. It wasn't easy, I'm not going to lie, but I was taking no chances. Between the balloon man and the wheel of fortune was the usual clump of ladies from church who came night after night to try to win the giant punch bowl set on the top shelf above the wheel, but had to settle night after night for a jar of gumdrops or salt and pepper shakers or some other little thing from the bottom shelf. And from the wheel of for-

tune to the tent was at least a million stands selling B. B. bats and jawbreakers and gingerbread and sweet potato pie and frozen custard and—like I said it wasn't easy. A million ways to tempt you, to unsettle your stomach, and make you lose the battle with the Fly family.

I sat there almost enjoying the silly clowns who came tumbling out of a steamer trunk no bigger than the one we have in the basement where my mother keeps my old report cards and photographs and letters and things. And I almost enjoyed the fire-eater and the knife thrower, but I was so close up I could see how there wasn't any real thrill. I almost enjoyed the fat-leg girls who rode the ponies two at a time and standing up, but their costumes weren't very pretty—just an ordinary polo shirt like you get if you run in the PAL meets[1] and short skirts you can wear on either side like the big girls wear at the roller rink. And I almost enjoyed the jugglers except that my Uncle Bubba can juggle the dinner plates better any day of the week so long as Aunt Hazel isn't there to stop him. I was impatient and started yawning. Finally all the clowns hitched up their baggy pants and tumbled over each other out of the ring and into the dark, the jugglers caught all the things that were up in the air and yawning just like me went off to the side. The pony girls brought their horses to a sudden stop that raised a lot of dust, then jumped down into the dirt and bowed. Then the ringmaster stepped into the circle of light and tipped his hat which was a little raggedy from where I was sitting and said—"And now, Ladieeez and Gentlemen, what you've alll been waiting forrr, the Main aTTRACtion, the FLY FAMILEEE." And everyone jumped up to shout like crazy as they came running out on their toes to stand in the light and then climb the ropes. I took a deep breath and fold-

1. **PAL meets:** sports events organized for neighborhood children by the Police Athletic League.

ed my arms over my chest and a kid next to me went into hiding, acting like she was going to tie her shoelaces.

There used to be four of them—the father, a big guy with a bald head and a bushy mustache and shoulders and arms like King Kong; a tall lanky mother whom you'd never guess could even climb into a high chair or catch anything heavier than a Ping-Pong ball to look at her; the oldest son who looked like his father except he had hair on his head but none on his face and a big face it was, so that no matter how high up he got you could always tell whether he was smiling or frowning or counting; the younger boy about thirteen, maybe, had a vacant stare like he was a million miles away feeding his turtles or something, anything but walking along a tightrope or flying through the air with his family. I had always liked to watch him because he was as cool as I was. But last summer the little girl got into the act. My grandmother says she's probably a midget 'cause no self-respecting mother would allow her child to be up there acting like a bird. "Just a baby," she'd say. "Can't be more than six years old. Should be home in bed. Must be a midget." My grandfather would give me a look when she started in and we'd smile at her together.

They almost got to me that last performance, dodging around with new routines and two at a time so that you didn't know which one Mr. Fly was going to save at the last minute. But he'd fly out and catch the little boy and swing over to the opposite stand where the big boy was flying out to catch them both by the wrists and the poor woman would be left kind of dangling there, suspended, then she'd do this double flip which would kill off everyone in the tent except me, of course, and swing out on the very bar she was on in the first place. And then they'd mess around two or three flying at once just to confuse you until the big drum roll started and out steps the lit-

tle girl in a party dress and a huge blindfold wrapped around her little head and a pink umbrella like they sell down in Chinatown. And I almost—I won't lie about it—I almost let my heart thump me off the bench. I almost thought I too had to tie my shoelaces. But I sat there. Stubborn. And the kid starts bouncing up and down on the rope like she was about to take off and tear through the canvas roof. Then out swings her little brother, and before you know it, Fly Jr. like a great eagle with his arms flapping grabs up the kid, eyeband in his teeth, and swoops her off to the bar that's already got Mrs., Mr., and Big Bro on it, and surely there's no room for him. And everyone standing on their feet clutching at their faces. Everyone but me. Cause I know from the getgo[2] that Mr. and Mrs. are going to leave the bar to give Jr. room and fly over to the other side. Which is exactly what they do. The lady in front of me, Mrs. Perez, who does all the sewing in our neighborhood, gets up and starts shaking her hands like ladies do to get the fingernail polish dry and she says to me with her eyes jammed shut "I must go finish the wedding gowns. Tell me later who died." And she scoots through the aisle, falling all over everybody with her eyes still shut and never looks up. And Mrs. Caine taps me on the back and leans over and says, "Some people just can't take it." And I smile at her and at her twins who're sitting there with their mouths open. I fold my arms over my chest and just dare the Fly family to do their very worst.

The minute I got to camp, I ran up to the main house where all the counselors gather to say hello to the parents and talk with the directors. I had to tell Mary the latest doings with the Fly family. But she put a finger to her mouth like she sometimes does to shush me. "Let's not have any scary stuff this summer,

2. **getgo** (get′ gō): start; beginning.

Harriet," she said, looking over my shoulder at a new kid. This new kid, Willie, was from my old neighborhood in Baltimore so we got friendly right off. Then he told me that he had a romantic heart so I quite naturally took him under my wing and decided not to give him a heart attack with any ghost tales. Mary said he meant "<u>rheumatic</u>"[3] heart, but I don't see any difference. So I told Mary to move him out of George's tent and give him a nicer counselor who'd respect his romantic heart. George used to be my play boyfriend when I first came to camp as a little kid and didn't know any better. But he's not a nice person. He makes up funny nicknames for people which aren't funny at all. Like calling Eddie Michaels the Watermelon Kid or David Farmer Charcoal Plenty which I really do not appreciate and especially from a counselor. And once he asked Joanne, who was the table monitor, to go fetch a pail of milk from the kitchen. And the minute she got up, he started hatching a plot, trying to get the kids to hide her peanut butter sandwich and put spiders in her soup. I had to remind everyone at the table that Joanne was my first cousin by blood, and I would be forced to waste the first bum that laid a hand on her plate. And ole George says, "Oh don't be a dumbhead, Harriet. Jo's so stupid she won't even notice." And I told him right then and there that I was not his play girlfriend anymore and would rather marry the wolfman than grow up and be his wife. And just in case he didn't get the message, that night around the campfire when we were all playing Little Sally Walker sittin' in a saucer and it was my turn to shake it to the east and to shake it to the west and to shake it to the very one that I loved the best—I shook straight for Mr. Nelson the lifeguard, who was not only the ugliest person in camp but the arch enemy of ole George.

And that very first day of camp last summer when Willie came running up to me to get in line for lunch, here comes George talking some simple stuff about "What a beautiful head you have, Willie. A long, smooth, streamlined head. A sure sign of superior gifts. Definitely genius proportions." And poor Willie went for it, grinning and touching his head, which if you want to know the truth is a bullet head and that's all there is to it. And he's turning to me every which way, like he's modeling his head in a fashion show. And the minute his back is turned, ole George makes a face about Willie's head and all the kids in the line bust out laughing. So I had to beat up a few right then and there and finish off the rest later in the shower for being so stupid, laughing at a kid with a romantic heart.

One night in the last week of August when the big campfire party is held, it was very dark and the moon was all smoky, and I just couldn't help myself and started in with a story about the great caterpillar who was going to prowl through the tents and nibble off everybody's toes. And Willie started this whimpering in the back of his throat so I had to switch the story real quick to something cheerful. But before I could do that, ole George picked up my story and added a wicked witch who puts spells on city kids who come to camp, and a hunchback dwarf that chopped up tents and bunk beds, and a one-eyed phantom giant who gobbled up the hearts of underprivileged kids. And every time he got to the part where the phantom ripped out a heart, poor Willie would get louder and louder until finally he started rolling around in the grass and screaming and all the kids went crazy and scattered behind the rocks almost kicking the fire completely out as they dashed off into the darkness yelling bloody murder. And the counselors could hardly round us all up—me, too, I'm not going to lie about it. Their little circles of flashlight bobbing in and out of the bushes along the

---

3. **rheumatic** (r$\overline{oo}$ mat′ ik): painfully inflamed.

patches of pine, bumping into each other as they scrambled for us kids. And poor Willie rolling around something awful, so they took him to the infirmary.

I was sneaking some gingersnaps in to him later that night when I hear Mary and another senior counselor fussing at ole George in the hallway.

"You've been picking on that kid ever since he got here, George. But tonight was the limit——"

"I wasn't picking on him, I was just trying to tell a story——"

"All that talk about hearts, gobblin' up hearts, and underpriv——"

"Yeh, you were directing it all at the little kid. You should be——"

"I wasn't talking about him. They're all underprivileged kids, after all. I mean all the kids are underprivileged."

I huddled back into the shadows and almost banged into Willie's iron bed. I was hoping he'd open his eyes and wink at me and tell me he was just fooling. That it wasn't so bad to have an underprivileged heart. But he just slept. "I'm an underprivileged kid too," I thought to myself. I knew that it was a special camp, but I'd never realized. No wonder Aunt Hazel screamed so about my scary stories and my mother flicked off the TV when the monsters came on and Mary was always shushing me. We all had bad hearts. I crawled into the supply cabinet to wait for Willie to wake up so I could ask him about it all. I ate all the gingersnaps but I didn't feel any better. You have a romantic heart, I whispered to myself settling down among the bandages. You will have to be very careful.

It didn't make any difference to Aunt Hazel that I had changed, that I no longer told scary stories or dragged my schoolmates to the latest creature movie, or raced my friends to the edge of the roof, or held my breath, or ran under the train rail when the train was already in sight. As far as she was concerned, I was still the same ole spooky kid I'd always been. So Joanne was kept at home. My mother noticed the difference, but she said over the phone to my grandmother, "She's acting very ladylike these days, growing up." I didn't tell her about my secret, that I knew about my heart. And I was kind of glad Joanne wasn't around 'cause I would have blabbed it all to her and scared her to death. When school starts again, I decided, I'll ask my teacher how to outgrow my underprivileged heart. I'll train myself, just like I did with the Fly family.

"Well, I guess you'll want some change to go to the fair again, hunh?" my mother said coming into my room and dumping things in her pocketbook.

"No," I said. "I'm too grown up for circuses."

She put the money on the dresser anyway. I was lying, of course. I was thinking what a terrible strain it would be for Mrs. Perez and everybody else if while sitting there, with the Fly family zooming around in the open air a million miles above the ground, little Harriet Watkins should drop dead with a fatal heart attack behind them.

"I lost," I said out loud.

"Lost what?"

"The battle with the Fly family."

She just stood there a long time looking at me, trying to figure me out, the way mothers are always doing but should know better. Then she kissed me goodbye and left for work.

# Different Viewpoints: Understanding the Narrator

*I*N MANY STORIES, a main character narrates the events in his or her own words. For example, in "My Delicate Heart Condition," Harriet humorously tells about herself and recounts a summer experience that had a strong impact on her. Similarly, the events of "The Ransom of Red Chief" are told by the story's main character, Sam, who relates the details of the disastrous kidnapping. When a character in the story acts as the narrator, the reader has the advantage of learning directly the character's thoughts and feelings—of seeing the action through that character's eyes. Sometimes, however, the reader might be curious about what other characters are feeling, thinking, or seeing. Even though the narrator may provide a version of that information, the wary reader may wonder, "How accurate is this explanation of the situation?" or "Can I trust what the narrator says?" The answers to these questions may be a key factor in interpreting the story.

The stories in this section are told by narrators who are the main characters. The differences among the viewpoints result from the differences in the narrators' ages and proximity to the incidents they relate. Two stories are told by adults looking back on childhood, one story is narrated by an adult focusing on a recent experience, and the last story is told by a young boy describing something that just happened to him. Try to understand and judge the narrator in these stories just as you would any other character.

# $L$*iterary Vocabulary*

**Narrator.** The narrator is the person or voice who tells the story. The narrator can be a character in the story, such as Harriet in "My Delicate Heart Condition," or a voice from outside the action, as in "Initiation" and "Through the Tunnel."

**Point of View.** Point of view refers to the narrative method, or the kind of narrator, used in a literary work. Point of view is usually either first person or third person. In the **first-person point of view,** the narrator is a character in the story who tells everything in his or her own words. **Third-person point of view** means that a story is told by a narrative voice outside the action, not by one of the characters. If a story is told from an omniscient, or all-knowing, third-person point of view, the narrator sees into the minds of more than one character. For example, in "Through the Tunnel" the narrator reveals both the mother's and the boy's thoughts and feelings. If a story is told from a third-person limited point of view, the narrator tells only what one character thinks, feels, and observes. In "Initiation" the reader's understanding of the story is limited to Millicent's understanding and perceptions; the narrator does not reach into the mind of any other character.

**Foreshadowing.** Foreshadowing is a writer's use of hints or clues to indicate events that will occur later in the story. The use of this technique creates suspense while at the same time preparing the reader for what is to come.

**Flashback.** A flashback is a conversation, an episode, or an event that happened before the beginning of a story. Sometimes, a flashback interrupts the chronological flow of a story to give the reader information helpful in understanding a character's present situation. In "Lather and Nothing Else," the barber's memory of seeing Captain Torres in the schoolyard is a flashback. It interrupts his act of shaving to show how harsh Torres is in punishing the rebels. Some stories are told almost entirely in flashback, as a narrator tries to interpret a past experience.

REVIEWED IN THIS SECTION

**Symbol    Conflict**

# The Scarlet Ibis

## JAMES HURST

A biography of Hurst appears on page 641.

## Approaching the Story

In "The Scarlet Ibis" an adult narrator recalls growing up with his younger brother and reflects upon his own feelings and motivations during that time. The story takes place on the family's cotton farm in the deep South, a hot, humid area lush with vegetation. The date is 1918, when the United States is beginning to get involved in World War I.

## Building Vocabulary

These essential words are footnoted within the story.

**invalid** (in´ və lid): It was bad enough having an **invalid** brother, but having one who possibly was not all there was unbearable. (page 91)

**imminent** (im´ ə nənt): With success so **imminent**, we decided not to tell anyone until he could actually walk. (page 94)

**infallibility** (in fal´ ə bil´ ə tē): I began to believe in my own **infallibility**. (page 95)

**exotic** (eg zät´ ik): We stood around it, awed by its **exotic** beauty. (page 96)

**vermilion** (vər mil´ yən): He lay . . . with his head thrown far back, making his **vermilion** neck appear unusually long and slim. (page 98)

**heresy** (her´ i sē): I lay there crying, sheltering my fallen scarlet ibis from the **heresy** of rain. (page 98)

## Connecting Writing and Reading

In your journal, copy the following list of actions that seem cruel. Identify those actions that, under certain circumstances, may not really be cruel because they could help someone.

- Hitting someone
- Refusing to help someone
- Forcing someone to do something
- Calling someone names
- Ridiculing someone
- Frightening someone

During your reading of this story, think about whether the narrator's treatment of his brother is cruel.

*I*T WAS IN the clove of seasons, summer was dead but autumn had not yet been born, that the ibis lit in the bleeding tree.[1] The flower garden was stained with rotting brown magnolia petals and ironweeds grew rank amid the purple phlox. The five o'clocks by the chimney still marked time, but the oriole nest in the elm was untenanted and rocked back and forth like an empty cradle. The last graveyard flowers were blooming, and their smell drifted across the cotton field and through every room of our house, speaking softly the names of our dead.

It's strange that all this is still so clear to me, now that summer has long since fled and time has had its way. A grindstone stands where the bleeding tree stood, just outside the kitchen door, and now if an oriole sings in the elm, its song seems to die up in the leaves, a silvery dust. The flower garden is prim, the house a gleaming white, and the pale fence across the yard stands straight and spruce. But sometimes (like right now), as I sit in the cool, green-draped parlor, the grindstone begins to turn, and time with all its changes is ground away—and I remember Doodle.

Doodle was just about the craziest brother a boy ever had. Of course, he wasn't crazy crazy like old Miss Leedie, who was in love with President Wilson and wrote him a letter every day, but was a nice crazy, like someone you meet in your dreams. He was born when I was six and was, from the outset, a disappointment. He seemed all head, with a tiny body which was red and shriveled like an old man's. Everybody thought he was going to die—everybody except Aunt Nicey, who had delivered him. She said he would live because he was born in a caul,[2] and cauls were made from Jesus' nightgown. Daddy had Mr. Heath, the carpenter, build a little mahogany coffin for him. But he didn't die, and when he was three months old, Mama and Daddy decided they might as well name him. They named him William Armstrong, which is like tying a big tail on a small kite. Such a name sounds good only on a tombstone.

I thought myself pretty smart at many things, like holding my breath, running, jumping, or climbing the vines in Old Woman Swamp, and I wanted more than anything else someone to race to Horsehead Landing, someone to box with, and someone to perch with in the top fork of the great pine behind the barn, where across the fields and swamps you could see the sea. I wanted a brother. But Mama, crying, told me that even if William Armstrong lived, he would never do these things with me. He might not, she sobbed, even be "all there." He might, as long as he lived, lie on the rubber sheet in the center of the bed in the front bedroom where the white marquisette curtains billowed out in the afternoon sea breeze, rustling like palmetto fronds.

It was bad enough having an invalid[3] brother, but having one who possibly was not all there was unbearable, so I began to make plans to kill him by smothering him with a pillow. However, one afternoon as I watched him, my head poked between the iron posts of the foot of the bed, he looked straight at me and grinned. I skipped through the rooms, down the echoing halls, shouting, "Mama, he smiled. He's all there! He's all there!" and he was.

When he was two, if you laid him on his stomach, he began to move himself, straining terribly. The doctor said that with his weak heart this strain would probably kill him, but it

---

1. **bleeding tree:** reference to a certain tree prevalent in the South; the name derives from the fact that the tree emits a milky substance whenever a branch is broken from it.
2. **caul** (kôl): a membrane sometimes surrounding the head of a child at birth.
3. **invalid** (in' və lid): ill, disabled, or weak and sickly.

didn't. Trembling, he'd push himself up, turning first red, then a soft purple, and finally collapse back onto the bed like an old worn-out doll. I can still see Mama watching him, her hand pressed tight across her mouth, her eyes wide and unblinking. But he learned to crawl (it was his third winter), and we brought him out of the front bedroom, putting him on the rug before the fireplace. For the first time he became one of us.

As long as he lay all the time in bed, we called him William Armstrong, even though it was formal and sounded as if we were referring to one of our ancestors, but with his creeping around on the deerskin rug and beginning to talk, something had to be done about his name. It was I who renamed him. When he crawled, he crawled backwards, as if he were in reverse and couldn't change gears. If you called him, he'd turn around as if he were going in the other direction, then he'd back right up to you to be picked up. Crawling backward made him look like a doodlebug, so I began to call him Doodle, and in time even Mama and Daddy thought it was a better name than William Armstrong. Only Aunt Nicey disagreed. She said caul babies should be treated with special respect since they might turn out to be saints. Renaming my brother was perhaps the kindest thing I ever did for him, because nobody expects much from someone called Doodle.

Although Doodle learned to crawl, he showed no signs of walking, but he wasn't idle. He talked so much that we all quit listening to what he said. It was about this time that Daddy built him a go-cart and I had to pull him around. At first I just paraded him up and down the piazza, but then he started crying to be taken out into the yard, and it ended up by my having to lug him wherever I went. If I so much as picked up my cap, he'd start crying to go with me and Mama would call from wherever she was, "Take Doodle with you."

He was a burden in many ways. The doctor had said that he mustn't get too excited, too hot, too cold, or too tired and that he must always be treated gently. A long list of don'ts went with him, all of which I ignored once we got out of the house. To discourage his coming with me, I'd run with him across the ends of the cotton rows and careen him around corners on two wheels. Sometimes I accidentally turned him over, but he never told Mama. His skin was very sensitive, and he had to wear a big straw hat whenever he went out. When the going got rough and he had to cling to the sides of the go-cart, the hat slipped all the way down over his ears. He was a sight. Finally, I could see I was licked. Doodle was my brother and he was going to cling to me forever, no matter what I did, so I dragged him across the burning cotton field to share with him the only beauty I knew, Old Woman Swamp. I pulled the go-cart through the saw-tooth fern, down into the green dimness where the palmetto fronds whispered by the stream. I lifted him out and set him down in the soft rubber grass beside a tall pine. His eyes were round with wonder as he gazed about him, and his little hands began to stroke the rubber grass. Then he began to cry.

"For heaven's sake, what's the matter?" I asked, annoyed.

"It's so pretty," he said. "So pretty, pretty, pretty."

After that day Doodle and I often went down into Old Woman Swamp. I would gather wildflowers, wild violets, honeysuckle, yellow jasmine, snakeflowers, and water lilies, and with wire grass we'd weave them into necklaces and crowns. We'd bedeck ourselves with our handiwork and loll about thus beautified, beyond the touch of the everyday world. Then when the slanted rays of the sun burned orange in the tops of the pines, we'd drop our jewels into the stream and watch them float away toward the sea.

There is within me (and with sadness I have watched it in others) a knot of cruelty borne by the stream of love, much as our blood sometimes bears the seed of our destruction, and at times I was mean to Doodle. One day I took him up to the barn loft and showed him his casket, telling him how we all had believed he would die. It was covered with a film of Paris green sprinkled to kill the rats, and screech owls had built a nest inside it.

Doodle studied the mahogany box for a long time, then said, "It's not mine."

"It is," I said. "And before I'll help you down from the loft, you're going to have to touch it."

"I won't touch it," he said sullenly.

"Then I'll leave you here by yourself," I threatened, and made as if I were going down.

Doodle was frightened of being left. "Don't go leave me, Brother," he cried, and he leaned toward the coffin. His hand, trembling, reached out, and when he touched the casket he screamed. A screech owl flapped out of the box into our faces, scaring us and covering us with Paris green. Doodle was paralyzed, so I put him on my shoulder and carried him down the ladder, and even when we were outside in the bright sunshine, he clung to me, crying, "Don't leave me. Don't leave me."

When Doodle was five years old, I was embarrassed at having a brother of that age who couldn't walk, so I set out to teach him. We were down in Old Woman Swamp and it was spring and the sick-sweet smell of bay flowers hung everywhere like a mournful song. "I'm going to teach you to walk, Doodle," I said.

He was sitting comfortably on the soft grass, leaning back against the pine. "Why?" he asked.

I hadn't expected such an answer. "So I won't have to haul you around all the time."

"I can't walk, Brother," he said.

"Who says so?" I demanded.

"Mama, the doctor—everybody."

"Oh, you can walk," I said, and I took him by the arms and stood him up. He collapsed onto the grass like a half-empty flour sack. It was as if he had no bones in his little legs.

"Don't hurt me, Brother," he warned.

"Shut up. I'm not going to hurt you. I'm going to teach you to walk." I heaved him up again, and again he collapsed.

This time he did not lift his face up out of the rubber grass. "I just can't do it. Let's make honeysuckle wreaths."

"Oh yes you can, Doodle," I said. "All you got to do is try. Now come on," and I hauled him up once more.

It seemed so hopeless from the beginning that it's a miracle I didn't give up. But all of us must have something or someone to be proud of, and Doodle had become mine. I did not know then that pride is a wonderful, terrible thing, a seed that bears two vines, life and death. Every day that summer we went to the pine beside the stream of Old Woman Swamp, and I put him on his feet at least a hundred times each afternoon. Occasionally I too became discouraged because it didn't seem as if he was trying, and I would say, "Doodle, don't you *want* to learn to walk?"

He'd nod his head, and I'd say, "Well, if you don't keep trying, you'll never learn." Then I'd paint for him a picture of us as old men, white-haired, him with a long white beard and me still pulling him around in the go-cart. This never failed to make him try again.

Finally one day, after many weeks of practicing, he stood alone for a few seconds. When he fell, I grabbed him in my arms and hugged him, our laughter pealing through the swamp like a ringing bell. Now we knew it could be done. Hope no longer hid in the dark palmetto thicket but perched like a cardinal in the lacy toothbrush tree, brilliantly visible. "Yes,

yes," I cried, and he cried it too, and the grass beneath us was soft and the smell of the swamp was sweet.

With success so <u>imminent</u>,[4] we decided not to tell anyone until he could actually walk. Each day, barring rain, we sneaked into Old Woman Swamp, and by cotton-picking time Doodle was ready to show what he could do. He still wasn't able to walk far, but we could wait no longer. Keeping a nice secret is very hard to do, like holding your breath. We chose to reveal all on October eighth, Doodle's sixth birthday, and for weeks ahead we mooned around the house, promising everybody a most spectacular surprise. Aunt Nicey said that, after so much talk, if we produced anything less tremendous than the Resurrection, she was going to be disappointed.

At breakfast on our chosen day, when Mama, Daddy, and Aunt Nicey were in the dining room, I brought Doodle to the door in the go-cart just as usual and had them turn their backs, making them cross their hearts and hope to die if they peeked. I helped Doodle up, and when he was standing alone I let them look. There wasn't a sound as Doodle walked slowly across the room and sat down at his place at the table. Then Mama began to cry and ran over to him, hugging him and kissing him. Daddy hugged him too, so I went to Aunt Nicey, who was thanks praying in the doorway, and began to waltz her around. We danced together quite well until she came down on my big toe with her brogans, hurting me so badly I thought I was crippled for life.

Doodle told them it was I who had taught him to walk, so everyone wanted to hug me, and I began to cry.

"What are you crying for?" asked Daddy, but I couldn't answer. They did not know that I did it for myself; that pride, whose slave I was, spoke to me louder than all their voices, and that Doodle walked only because I was ashamed of having a crippled brother.

Within a few months Doodle had learned to walk well and his go-cart was put up in the barn loft (it's still there) beside his little mahogany coffin. Now, when we roamed off together, resting often, we never turned back until our destination had been reached, and to help pass the time, we took up lying. From the beginning Doodle was a terrible liar and he got me in the habit. Had anyone stopped to listen to us, we would have been sent off to Dix Hill.

My lies were scary, involved, and usually pointless, but Doodle's were twice as crazy. People in his stories all had wings and flew wherever they wanted to go. His favorite lie was about a boy named Peter who had a pet peacock with a ten-foot tail. Peter wore a golden robe that glittered so brightly that when he walked through the sunflowers they turned away from the sun to face him. When Peter was ready to go to sleep, the peacock spread his magnificent tail, enfolding the boy gently like a closing go-to-sleep flower, burying him in the glorious iridescent, rustling vortex. Yes, I must admit it. Doodle could beat me lying.

Doodle and I spent lots of time thinking about our future. We decided that when we were grown we'd live in Old Woman Swamp and pick dog-tongue for a living. Beside the stream, he planned, we'd build us a house of whispering leaves and the swamp birds would be our chickens. All day long (when we weren't gathering dog-tongue) we'd swing through the cypresses on the rope vines, and if it rained we'd huddle beneath an umbrella tree and play stickfrog. Mama and Daddy could come and live with us if they wanted to. He even came up with the idea that he could marry Mama and I could marry Daddy. Of course, I was old enough to know this wouldn't work out, but the picture he painted was so beautiful and serene that all I could do was whisper Yes, yes.

---

4. **imminent** (im′ ə nənt): about to take place.

Once I had succeeded in teaching Doodle to walk, I began to believe in my own infallibility,[5] and I prepared a terrific development program for him, unknown to Mama and Daddy, of course. I would teach him to run, to swim, to climb trees, and to fight. He, too, now believed in my infallibility, so we set the deadline for these accomplishments less than a year away, when, it had been decided, Doodle could start to school.

That winter we didn't make much progress, for I was in school and Doodle suffered from one bad cold after another. But when spring came, rich and warm, we raised our sights again. Success lay at the end of summer like a pot of gold, and our campaign got off to a good start. On hot days, Doodle and I went down to Horsehead Landing, and I gave him swimming lessons or showed him how to row a boat. Sometimes we descended into the cool greenness of Old Woman Swamp and climbed the rope vines or boxed scientifically beneath the pine where he had learned to walk. Promise hung about us like the leaves, and wherever we looked, ferns unfurled and birds broke into song.

That summer, the summer of 1918, was blighted. In May and June there was no rain and the crops withered, curled up, then died under the thirsty sun. One morning in July a hurricane came out of the east, tipping over the oaks in the yard and splitting the limbs of the elm trees. That afternoon it roared back out of the west, blew the fallen oaks around, snapping their roots and tearing them out of the earth like a hawk at the entrails of a chicken. Cotton bolls were wrenched from the stalks and lay like green walnuts in the valleys between the rows, while the cornfield leaned over uniformly so that the tassels touched the ground. Doodle and I followed Daddy out into the cotton field, where he stood, shoulders sagging, surveying the ruin. When his chin sank down onto his chest, we were frightened, and

Doodle slipped his hand into mine. Suddenly Daddy straightened his shoulders, raised a giant knuckly fist, and with a voice that seemed to rumble out of the earth itself began cursing the weather and the Republican Party. Doodle and I, prodding each other and giggling, went back to the house, knowing that everything would be all right.

And during that summer, strange names were heard through the house: Chateau-Thierry, Amiens, Soissons, and in her blessing at the supper table, Mama once said, "And bless the Pearsons, whose boy Joe was lost at Belleau Wood."[6] So we came to that clove of seasons. School was only a few weeks away, and Doodle was far behind schedule. He could barely clear the ground when climbing up the rope vines, and his swimming was certainly not passable. We decided to double our efforts, to make that last drive and reach our pot of gold. I made him swim until he turned blue and row until he couldn't lift an oar. Wherever we went, I purposely walked fast, and although he kept up, his face turned red and his eyes became glazed. Once, he could go no further, so he collapsed on the ground and began to cry.

"Aw, come on, Doodle," I urged. "You can do it. Do you want to be different from everybody else when you start school?"

"Does it make any difference?"

"It certainly does," I said. "Now, come on," and I helped him up.

As we slipped through dog days, Doodle began to look feverish, and Mama felt his forehead, asking him if he felt ill. At night he didn't sleep well, and sometimes he had nightmares, crying out until I touched him and said, "Wake up, Doodle. Wake up."

---

5. **infallibility** (in fal′ ə bil′ ə tē): the state or condition of being incapable of error.
6. **Château-Thierry, Amiens, Soissons, . . . Belleau Wood** (shȧ tō′ tyer ē′, ȧ myan′, swȧ sōn′, be lō′): World War I battle sites.

It was Saturday noon, just a few days before school was to start. I should have already admitted defeat, but my pride wouldn't let me. The excitement of our program had now been gone for weeks, but still we kept on with a tired doggedness. It was too late to turn back, for we had both wandered too far into a net of expectations and left no crumbs behind.

Daddy, Mama, Doodle, and I were seated at the dining-room table having lunch. It was a hot day, with all the windows and doors open in case a breeze should come. In the kitchen Aunt Nicey was humming softly. After a long silence, Daddy spoke. "It's so calm, I wouldn't be surprised if we had a storm this afternoon."

"I haven't heard a rain frog," said Mama, who believed in signs, as she served the bread around the table.

"I did," declared Doodle. "Down in the swamp."

"He didn't," I said contrarily.

"You did, eh?" said Daddy, ignoring my denial.

"I certainly did," Doodle reiterated, scowling at me over the top of his iced-tea glass, and we were quiet again.

Suddenly, from out in the yard, came a strange croaking noise. Doodle stopped eating, with a piece of bread poised ready for his mouth, his eyes popped round like two blue buttons. "What's that?" he whispered.

I jumped up, knocking over my chair, and had reached the door when Mama called, "Pick up the chair, sit down again, and say excuse me."

By the time I had done this Doodle had excused himself and had slipped out into the yard. He was looking up into the bleeding tree. "It's a great big red bird!" he called.

The bird croaked loudly again, and Mama and Daddy came out into the yard. We shaded our eyes with our hands against the hazy glare of the sun and peered up through the still leaves. On the topmost branch a bird the size of a chicken, with scarlet feathers and long legs, was perched precariously. Its wings hung down loosely, and as we watched, a feather dropped away and floated slowly down through the green leaves.

"It's not even frightened of us," Mama said.

"It looks tired," Daddy added. "Or maybe sick."

Doodle's hands were clasped at his throat, and I had never seen him stand still so long. "What is it?" he asked.

Daddy shook his head. "I don't know, maybe it's—"

At that moment the bird began to flutter, but the wings were uncoordinated, and amid much flapping and a spray of flying feathers, it tumbled down, bumping through the limbs of the bleeding tree and landing at our feet with a thud. Its long, graceful neck jerked twice into an S, then straightened out, and the bird was still. A white veil came over the eyes and the long white beak unhinged. Its legs were crossed and its clawlike feet were delicately curved at rest. Even death did not mar its grace, for it lay on the earth like a broken vase of red flowers, and we stood around it, awed by its exotic[7] beauty.

"It's dead," Mama said.

"What is it?" Doodle repeated.

"Go bring me the bird book," said Daddy.

I ran into the house and brought back the bird book. As we watched, Daddy thumbed through its pages. "It's a scarlet ibis," he said, pointing to a picture. "It lives in the tropics—South America to Florida. A storm must have brought it here."

Sadly, we all looked back at the bird. A scarlet ibis! How many miles it had traveled to die like this, in *our* yard, beneath the bleeding tree.

"Let's finish lunch," Mama said, nudging us back toward the dining room.

---

7. **exotic** (eg zät′ ik): foreign; strangely beautiful.

"I'm not hungry," said Doodle, and he knelt down beside the ibis.

"We've got peach cobbler for dessert," Mama tempted from the doorway.

Doodle remained kneeling. "I'm going to bury him."

"Don't you dare touch him," Mama warned. "There's no telling what disease he might have had."

"All right," said Doodle. "I won't."

Daddy, Mama, and I went back to the dining-room table, but we watched Doodle through the open door. He took out a piece of string from his pocket and, without touching the ibis, looped one end around its neck. Slowly, while singing softly "Shall We Gather at the River," he carried the bird around to the front yard and dug a hole in the flower garden, next to the petunia bed. Now we were watching him through the front window, but he didn't know it. His awkwardness at digging the hole with a shovel whose handle was twice as long as he was made us laugh, and we covered our mouths with our hands so he wouldn't hear.

When Doodle came into the dining room, he found us seriously eating our cobbler. He was pale, and lingered just inside the screen door. "Did you get the scarlet ibis buried?" asked Daddy.

Doodle didn't speak but nodded his head.

"Go wash your hands, and then you can have some peach cobbler," said Mama.

"I'm not hungry," he said.

"Dead birds is bad luck," said Aunt Nicey, poking her head from the kitchen door. "Specially *red* dead birds!"

As soon as I had finished eating, Doodle and I hurried off to Horsehead Landing. Time was short, and Doodle still had a long way to go if he was going to keep up with the other boys when he started school. The sun, gilded with the yellow cast of autumn, still burned fiercely, but the dark green woods through which we passed were shady and cool. When we reached the landing, Doodle said he was too tired to swim, so we got into a skiff and floated down the creek with the tide. Far off in the marsh a rail was scolding, and over on the beach locusts were singing in the myrtle trees. Doodle did not speak and kept his head turned away, letting one hand trail limply in the water.

After we had drifted a long way, I put the oars in place and made Doodle row back against the tide. Black clouds began to gather in the southwest, and he kept watching them, trying to pull the oars a little faster. When we reached Horsehead Landing, lightning was playing across half the sky and thunder roared out, hiding even the sound of the sea. The sun disappeared and darkness descended, almost like night. Flocks of marsh crows flew by, heading inland to their roosting trees; and two egrets, squawking, arose from the oyster-rock shallows and careened away.

Doodle was both tired and frightened, and when he stepped from the skiff he collapsed onto the mud, sending an armada of fiddler crabs rustling off into the marsh grass. I helped him up, and as he wiped the mud off his trousers, he smiled at me ashamedly. He had failed and we both knew it, so we started back home, racing the storm. We never spoke (What are the words that can solder cracked pride?), but I knew he was watching me, watching for a sign of mercy. The lightning was near now, and from fear he walked so close behind me he kept stepping on my heels. The faster I walked, the faster he walked, so I began to run. The rain was coming, roaring through the pines, and then, like a bursting Roman candle, a gum tree ahead of us was shattered by a bolt of lightning. When the deafening peal of thunder had died, and in the moment before the rain arrived, I heard Doodle, who had fallen behind, cry out, "Brother, Brother, don't leave me! Don't leave me!"

The knowledge that Doodle's and my plans had come to naught was bitter, and that streak of cruelty within me awakened. I ran as fast as I could, leaving him far behind with a wall of rain dividing us. The drops stung my face like nettles, and the wind flared the wet glistening leaves of the bordering trees. Soon I could hear his voice no more.

I hadn't run too far before I became tired, and the flood of childish spite evanesced as well. I stopped and waited for Doodle. The sound of rain was everywhere, but the wind had died and it fell straight down in parallel paths like ropes hanging from the sky. As I waited, I peered through the downpour, but no one came. Finally I went back and found him huddled beneath a red nightshade bush beside the road. He was sitting on the ground, his face buried in his arms, which were resting on his drawn-up knees. "Let's go, Doodle," I said.

He didn't answer, so I placed my hand on his forehead and lifted his head. Limply, he fell backwards onto the earth. He had been bleeding from the mouth, and his neck and the front of his shirt were stained a brilliant red.

"Doodle! Doodle!" I cried, shaking him, but there was no answer but the ropy rain. He lay very awkwardly, with his head thrown far back, making his vermilion[8] neck appear unusually long and slim. His little legs, bent sharply at the knees, had never before seemed so fragile, so thin.

I began to weep, and the tear-blurred vision in red before me looked very familiar. "Doodle!" I screamed above the pounding storm and threw my body to the earth above his. For a long long time, it seemed forever, I lay there crying, sheltering my fallen scarlet ibis from the heresy[9] of rain.

---

8. **vermilion** (vər mil′ yən): bright red.
9. **heresy** (her′ i sē): something that contradicts what is generally thought of as right.

# *Thinking About the Story*

## A PERSONAL RESPONSE

*sharing impressions*

**1.** In your journal jot down several words and phrases that describe your feelings about the narrator.

*constructing interpretations*

**2.** Explain who, if anyone, you think is to blame for Doodle's death.

**3.** How would you judge the narrator's treatment of Doodle?
### Think about
- which actions seem cruel
- the reasons he gives for his actions
- the effect of his actions on Doodle

**4.** What is your opinion of Doodle's character?
### Think about
- his strengths and weaknesses
- why he does what his brother says to do
- how you would feel about him if he were your brother

**5.** Why do you think the narrator tells this story?

## A CREATIVE RESPONSE

**6.** Imagine that Doodle was only unconscious at the end of the story and that he later recovered. How might the narrator's treatment of Doodle be different?

## A CRITICAL RESPONSE

**7.** What symbols do you think add meaning to the story?
### Think about
- objects that have possible religious significance
- the connection between Doodle and the scarlet ibis

**8.** Find at least five phrases, sentences, or events in the story that foreshadow Doodle's death at the end.
### Think about
- the definition of foreshadowing as hints or clues in a story that indicate events that will occur later
- key words in the descriptive language in the story
- specific comments about death from the narrator

**9.** Compare the narrator's attitude about his brother's disabilities with the attitude commonly held toward the disabled today.

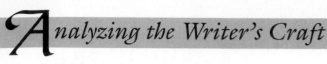

# Analyzing the Writer's Craft

## NARRATOR

Think about your own opinion of the narrator's guilt in this story. Do you think that any other character in the story, including Doodle himself, would judge the narrator's treatment of Doodle the same way you do? Why or why not?

**Building a Literary Vocabulary.** The narrator is the person or voice who tells the story. "The Scarlet Ibis" is told by a first-person narrator: all the events and characters are filtered through the mind of the narrator, who is himself a main character in the story. Because the narrator has such strong feelings about the events he relates, it is difficult to determine the exact meaning of those events. For example, is the narrator really guilty of his brother's death or does he just feel guilty?

**Application: Judging the Narrator.** Work together with your entire class to conduct a trial of the narrator, using passages from the story as evidence both for and against him. Someone should play the narrator and be prepared to answer all questions related to Doodle. The prosecution team, composed of three or four students, will need to go through the story to find evidence that will incriminate the narrator in his brother's death. The members of the defense team will have to find convincing evidence of the narrator's innocence and prepare themselves to refute the prosecution's charges. There should also be witnesses—the father, the mother, and Aunt Nicey—at the trial to testify for or against the narrator, and a judge to ensure the justice of the proceedings. The remainder of the class could serve as the jury.

# Connecting Reading and Writing

**1.** Retell the final episodes of Doodle's life from another character's point of view as **testimony** at the narrator's trial.

Option: Write another character's thoughts and feelings about Doodle in a **letter** to a relative.

**2.** Think about the degree of responsibility the narrator bears for Doodle's death. Present your conclusions as a lawyer's **closing argument** to the jury at the narrator's trial.

Option: Write an **analysis** of the narrator's trial for the editorial page of the local newspaper.

**3.** Write a **eulogy** about Doodle that you might deliver at his memorial service.

Option: Write about Doodle in a **poem.**

**4.** Doodle is symbolically linked with the scarlet ibis in this story. Think of a bird or other animal that could represent an aspect of your personality and develop the symbolic connection in a **character sketch** of yourself.

Option: Write about this symbolic connection in a **journal entry** that you will review periodically and possibly revise as you mature.

# Marigolds
## EUGENIA COLLIER

A biography of Collier appears on page 638.

## Approaching the Story

The narrator of "Marigolds" is an adult who recalls a memory from her childhood, a memory that is as much about the feelings she had as a girl of fourteen as it is about her actions. The event she remembers takes place during the Great Depression, a time of economic hardship for the entire country but especially for those who lived in the shantytowns of the rural South.

## Building Vocabulary

These essential words are footnoted within the story.

**futile** (fy$\overline{oo}$t´ ´l), **impoverished** (im päv´ ər ishd): **Futile** waiting was the sorrowful background music of our **impoverished** little community. (page 102)

**poignantly** (poin´ yənt lē): As I think of those days I feel most **poignantly** the tag end of summer. (page 103)

**stoicism** (stō´ i siz´ əm): Her face had Indian-like features and the stern **stoicism** that one associates with Indian faces. (page 104)

**perverse** (pər vʉrs´): For some **perverse** reason, we children hated those marigolds. (page 104)

**degradation** (deg´ rə dā´ shən): The smoldering emotions of that summer swelled in me and burst—the great need for my mother . . ., the hopelessness of our poverty and **degradation**. (page 107)

**contrition** (kən trish´ ən): Despite my wild **contrition** she never planted marigolds again. (page 107)

## Connecting Writing and Reading

Think about the kinds of things people do when they are unhappy. In your journal, briefly explain what unhappy people might do to themselves, to other people, and to things around them. Then as you read, notice how characters act when they suffer unhappiness or loss.

# Marigolds

WHEN I THINK of the hometown of my youth, all that I seem to remember is dust—the brown, crumbly dust of late summer—arid, sterile dust that gets into the eyes and makes them water, gets into the throat and between the toes of bare brown feet. I don't know why I should remember only the dust. Surely there must have been lush green lawns and paved streets under leafy shade trees somewhere in town; but memory is an abstract painting—it does not present things as they are, but rather as they *feel*. And so, when I think of that time and that place, I remember only the dry September of the dirt roads and grassless yards of the shantytown where I lived. And one other thing I remember, another incongruency of memory—a brilliant splash of sunny yellow against the dust—Miss Lottie's marigolds.

Whenever the memory of those marigolds flashes across my mind, a strange nostalgia comes with it and remains long after the picture has faded. I feel again the chaotic emotions of adolescence, illusive as smoke, yet as real as the potted geranium before me now. Joy and rage and wild animal gladness and shame become tangled together in the multicolored skein of fourteen-going-on-fifteen as I recall that devastating moment when I was suddenly more woman than child, years ago in Miss Lottie's yard. I think of those marigolds at the strangest times. I remember them vividly now as I desperately pass away the time waiting for you, who will not come.

I suppose that futile[1] waiting was the sorrowful background music of our impoverished[2] little community when I was young. The Depression that gripped the nation was no new thing to us, for the black workers of rural Maryland had always been depressed. I don't know what it was that we were waiting for; certainly not for the prosperity that was "just around the corner," for those were white folks' words, which we never believed. Nor did we wait for hard work and thrift to pay off in shining success as the American Dream[3] promised, for we knew better than that, too. Perhaps we waited for a miracle, amorphous in concept but necessary if one were to have the grit to rise before dawn each day and labor in the white man's vineyard until after dark, or to wander about in the September dust offering one's sweat in return for some meager share of bread. But God was *chary* with miracles in those days, and so we waited—and waited.

We children, of course, were only vaguely aware of the extent of our poverty. Having no radios, few newspapers, and no magazines, we were somewhat unaware of the world outside our community. Nowadays we would be called "culturally deprived," and people would write books and hold conferences about us. In those days everybody we knew was just as hungry and ill-clad as we were. Poverty was the cage in which we all were trapped, and our hatred of it was still the vague, undirected restlessness of the zoo-bred flamingo who knows that nature created him to fly free.

---

1. **futile** (fyo͞ot′ 'l): useless; hopeless; ineffective.

2. **impoverished** (im päv′ ər ishd): made poor; robbed of strength or power.

3. **American Dream:** the American ideal of attaining success through equality of opportunity afforded all citizens.

As I think of those days I feel most poignantly[4] the tag end of summer, the bright, dry times when we began to have a sense of shortening days and the imminence of the cold.

By the time I was fourteen my brother Joey and I were the only children left at our house, the older ones having left home for early marriage or the lure of the city, and the two babies having been sent to relatives who might care for them better than we. Joey was three years younger than I, and a boy, and therefore vastly inferior. Each morning our mother and father trudged wearily down the dirt road and around the bend, she to her domestic job, he to his daily unsuccessful quest for work. After a few chores around the tumbledown shanty, Joey and I were free to run wild in the sun with other children similarly situated.

For the most part, those days are ill-defined in my memory, running together and combining like a fresh watercolor painting left out in the rain. I remember squatting in the road, drawing a picture in the dust, a picture that Joey gleefully erased with one sweep of his dirty foot. I remember fishing for minnows in a muddy creek and watching sadly as they eluded my cupped hands, while Joey laughed uproariously. And I remember, that year, a strange restlessness of body and spirit, a feeling that something old and familiar was ending, and something unknown and therefore terrifying was beginning.

One day returns to me with special clarity for some reason, perhaps because it was the beginning of the experience that in some inexplicable way marked the end of innocence. I was loafing under the great oak tree in our yard, deep in some reverie that I have now forgotten except that it involved some secret thoughts of one of the Harris boys across the yard. Joey and a bunch of kids were bored now with the old tire suspended from an oak limb, which had kept them entertained for a while.

"Hey, Lizabeth," Joey yelled. He never talked when he could yell. "Hey, Lizabeth, let's us go somewhere."

I came reluctantly from my private world.

"Where at, Joey?"

The truth was that we were becoming tired of the formlessness of our summer days. The idleness whose prospect had seemed so beautiful during the busy days of spring now had degenerated to an almost desperate effort to fill up the empty midday hours.

"Let's go see can we find us some locusts on the hill," someone suggested.

Joey was scornful. "Ain't no more locusts there. Y'all got 'em all while they was still green."

The argument that followed was brief and not really worth the effort. Hunting locust trees wasn't fun any more by now.

"Tell you what," said Joey finally, his eyes sparkling. "Let's us go over to Miss Lottie's."

The idea caught on at once, for annoying Miss Lottie was always fun. I was still child enough to scamper along with the group over rickety fences and through bushes that tore our already raggedy clothes, back to where Miss Lottie lived. I think now that we must have made a tragicomic spectacle, five or six kids of different ages, each of us clad in only one garment—the girls in faded dresses that were too long or too short, the boys in patchy pants, their sweaty brown chests gleaming in the hot sun. A little cloud of dust followed our thin legs and bare feet as we tramped over the barren land.

When Miss Lottie's house came into view we stopped, ostensibly to plan our strategy but actually to reinforce our courage.

Miss Lottie's house was the most ramshackle of all our ramshackle homes. The sun and rain had long since faded its rickety frame siding

---

4. **poignantly** (poin′ yənt lē): in a manner that sharply, keenly, or painfully affects the feelings.

from white to a sullen gray. The boards themselves seemed to remain upright not from being nailed together but rather from leaning together like a house that a child might have constructed from cards.

A brisk wind might have blown it down, and the fact that it was still standing implied a kind of enchantment that was stronger than the elements. There it stood, and as far as I know is standing yet—a gray, rotting thing with no porch, no shutters, no steps, set on a cramped lot with no grass, not even weeds—a monument to decay.

In front of the house in a squeaky rocking chair sat Miss Lottie's son, John Burke, completing the impression of decay. John Burke was what was known as "queer-headed." Black and ageless, he sat, rocking day in and day out in a mindless stupor, lulled by the monotonous squeak-squawk of the chair. A battered hat atop his shaggy head shaded him from the sun. Usually John Burke was totally unaware of everything outside his quiet dream world. But if you disturbed him, if you intruded upon his fantasies, he would become enraged, strike out at you, and curse at you in some strange enchanted language which only he could understand. We children made a game of thinking of ways to disturb John Burke and then to elude his violent retribution.

But our real fun and our real fear lay in Miss Lottie herself. Miss Lottie seemed to be at least a hundred years old. Her big frame still held traces of the tall, powerful woman she must have been in youth, although it was now bent and drawn. Her smooth skin was a dark reddish-brown, and her face had Indian-like features and the stern stoicism[5] that one associates with Indian faces.

Miss Lottie didn't like intruders either, especially children. She never left her yard, and nobody ever visited her. We never knew how she managed those necessities that depend on human interaction—how she ate, for example,

or even whether she ate. When we were tiny children, we thought Miss Lottie was a witch, and we made up tales, that we half believed ourselves, about her exploits. We were far too sophisticated now, of course, to believe the witch-nonsense. But old fears have a way of clinging like cobwebs, and so when we sighted the tumbledown shack, we had to stop to reinforce our nerves.

"Look, there she," I whispered, forgetting that Miss Lottie could not possibly have heard me from that distance. "She fooling with them crazy flowers."

"Yeh, look at 'er."

Miss Lottie's marigolds were perhaps the strangest part of the picture. Certainly they did not fit in with the crumbling decay of the rest of her yard. Beyond the dusty brown yard, in front of the sorry gray house, rose suddenly and shockingly a dazzling strip of bright blossoms, clumped together in enormous mounds, warm and passionate and sun-golden. The old black witch-woman worked on them all summer, every summer, down on her creaky knees, weeding and cultivating and arranging, while the house crumbled and John Burke rocked. For some perverse[6] reason, we children hated those marigolds. They interfered with the perfect ugliness of the place; they were too beautiful; they said too much that we could not understand; they did not make sense. There was something in the vigor with which the old woman destroyed the weeds that intimidated us. It should have been a comical sight—the old woman with the man's hat on her cropped white head, leaning over the bright mounds, her big backside in the air—but it wasn't comical; it was something we could not name. We had to annoy her by whizzing a pebble into her

---

5. **stoicism** (stō′ i siz′ əm): stern control or holding in of emotion.

6. **perverse** (pər vurs′): stubbornly contrary; wrong, harmful, or against one's own interests.

flowers or by yelling a dirty word, then dancing away from her rage, reveling in our youth and mocking her age. Actually, I think it was the flowers we wanted to destroy, but nobody had the nerve to try it, not even Joey, who was usually fool enough to try anything.

"Y'all git some stones," commanded Joey now, and was met with instant giggling obedience as everyone except me began to gather pebbles from the dusty ground. "Come on, Lizabeth."

I just stood there peering through the bushes, torn between wanting to join the fun and feeling that it was all a bit silly.

"You scared, Lizabeth?"

I cursed and spat on the ground—my favorite gesture of phony bravado. "Y'all children get the stones. I'll show you how to use 'em."

I said before that we children were not consciously aware of how thick were the bars of our cage. I wonder now, though, whether we were not more aware of it than I thought. Perhaps we had some dim notion of what we were, and how little chance we had of being anything else. Otherwise, why would we have been so preoccupied with destruction? Anyway, the pebbles were collected quickly, and everybody looked at me to begin the fun.

"Come on, y'all."

We crept to the edge of the bushes that bordered the narrow road in front of Miss Lottie's place. She was working placidly kneeling over the flowers, her dark hand plunged into the golden mound. Suddenly "zing"—an expertly aimed stone cut the head off one of the blossoms.

"Who out there?" Miss Lottie's backside came down and her head came up as her sharp eyes searched the bushes. "You better git!"

We had crouched down out of sight in the bushes, where we stifled the giggles that insisted on coming. Miss Lottie gazed warily across the road for a moment, then cautiously returned to her weeding. "Zing"—Joey sent a pebble into the blooms, and another marigold was beheaded.

Miss Lottie was enraged now. She began struggling to her feet, leaning on a rickety cane and shouting, "Y'all git! Go on home!" Then the rest of the kids let loose with their pebbles, storming the flowers and laughing wildly and senselessly at Miss Lottie's impotent rage. She shook her stick at us and started shakily toward the road crying, "Git 'long! John Burke! John Burke, come help!"

Then I lost my head entirely, mad with the power of inciting such rage, and ran out of the bushes in the storm of pebbles, straight toward Miss Lottie chanting madly, "Old lady witch, fell in a ditch, picked up a penny and thought she was rich!" The children screamed with delight, dropped their pebbles and joined the crazy dance, swarming around Miss Lottie like bees and chanting, "Old lady witch!" while she screamed curses at us. The madness lasted only a moment, for John Burke, startled at last, lurched out of his chair, and we dashed for the bushes just as Miss Lottie's cane went whizzing at my head.

I did not join the merriment when the kids gathered again under the oak in our bare yard. Suddenly I was ashamed, and I did not like being ashamed. The child in me sulked and said it was all in fun, but the woman in me flinched at the thought of the malicious attack that I had led. The mood lasted all afternoon. When we ate the beans and rice that was supper that night, I did not notice my father's silence, for he was always silent these days, nor did I notice my mother's absence, for she always worked until well into evening. Joey and I had a particularly bitter argument after supper; his exuberance got on my nerves. Finally I stretched out upon the pallet in the room we shared and fell into a fitful doze.

When I awoke, somewhere in the middle of the night, my mother had returned, and I vaguely listened to the conversation that was audible through the thin walls that separated our rooms. At first I heard no words, only voices. My mother's voice was like a cool, dark room in summer—peaceful, soothing, quiet. I loved to listen to it; it made things seem all right somehow. But my father's voice cut through hers, shattering the peace.

"Twenty-two years, Maybelle, twenty-two years," he was saying, "and I got nothing for you, nothing, nothing."

"It's all right, honey, you'll get something. Everybody out of work now, you know that."

"It ain't right. Ain't no man ought to eat his woman's food year in and year out, and see his children running wild. Ain't nothing right about that."

"Honey, you took good care of us when you had it. Ain't nobody got nothing nowadays."

"I ain't talking about nobody else, I'm talking about *me*. God knows I try." My mother said something I could not hear, and my father cried out louder. "What must a man do, tell me that?"

"Look, we ain't starving. I git paid every week, and Mrs. Ellis is real nice about giving me things. She gonna let me have Mr. Ellis's old coat for you this winter—"

"Forget Mr. Ellis's coat! And forget his money! You think I want white folks' leavings? Oh, Maybelle"—and suddenly he sobbed, loudly and painfully, and cried helplessly and hopelessly in the dark night. I had never heard a man cry before. I did not know men ever cried. I covered my ears with my hands but could not cut off the sound of my father's harsh, painful, despairing sobs. My father was a strong man who would whisk a child upon his shoulders and go singing through the house. My father whittled toys for us and laughed so loud that the great oak seemed to laugh with him, and taught us how to fish and hunt rabbits. How could it be that my father was crying? But the sobs went on, unstifled, finally quieting until I could hear my mother's voice, deep and rich, humming softly as she used to hum to a frightened child.

The world had lost its boundary lines. My mother, who was small and soft, was now the strength of the family; my father, who was the rock on which the family had been built, was sobbing like the tiniest child. Everything was suddenly out of tune, like a broken accordion. Where did I fit into this crazy picture? I do not now remember my thoughts, only a feeling of great bewilderment and fear.

Long after the sobbing and the humming had stopped, I lay on the pallet, still as stone with my hands over my ears, wishing that I could cry and be comforted. The night was silent now except for the sound of the crickets and of Joey's soft breathing. But the room was too crowded with fear to allow me to sleep, and finally, feeling the terrible aloneness of 4 A.M., I decided to awaken Joey.

"Ouch! What's the matter with you? What you want?" he demanded disagreeably when I had pinched and slapped him awake.

"Come on, wake up."

"What for? Go 'way."

I was lost for a reasonable reply. I could not say, "I'm scared, and I don't want to be alone," so I merely said, "I'm going out. If you want to come, come on."

The promise of adventure awoke him. "Going out now? Where at, Lizabeth? What you going to do?"

I was pulling my dress over my head. Until now I had not thought of going out. "Just come on," I replied tersely.

I was just out the window and halfway down the road before Joey caught up with me.

"Wait, Lizabeth, where you going?"

I was running as if the Furies[7] were after me,

---

7. **Furies** (fyŏŏr′ ēz): in Greek and Roman mythology, female spirits with serpentine hair who punished wrongdoers.

as perhaps they were—running silently and furiously until I came to where I had half known I was headed—to Miss Lottie's yard.

The half-dawn light was more eerie than complete darkness, and in it the old house was like the ruin that my world had become—foul and crumbling, a grotesque creature. It looked haunted, but I was not afraid because I was haunted too.

"Lizabeth, you lost your mind?" panted Joey.

I had indeed lost my mind, for all the smoldering emotions of that summer swelled in me and burst—the great need for my mother who was never there, the hopelessness of our poverty and degradation,[8] the bewilderment of being neither child nor woman and yet both at once, the fear unleashed by my father's tears. And these feelings combined in one great impulse toward destruction.

"Lizabeth!"

I leaped furiously into the mounds of marigolds and pulled madly, trampling and pulling and destroying the perfect yellow blooms. The fresh smell of early morning and of dew-soaked marigolds spurred me on as I went tearing and mangling and sobbing while Joey tugged my dress or my waist crying, "Lizabeth stop, please stop!"

And then I was sitting in the ruined little garden among the uprooted and ruined flowers, crying and crying, and it was too late to undo what I had done. Joey was sitting beside me, silent and frightened, not knowing what to say. Then, "Lizabeth, look."

I opened my swollen eyes and saw in front of me a pair of large calloused feet; my gaze lifted to the swollen legs, the age-distorted body clad in a tight cotton night dress, and then the shadowed Indian face surrounded by stubby white hair. And there was no rage in the face now, now that the garden was destroyed and there was nothing any longer to be protected.

"M-miss Lottie!" I scrambled to my feet and just stood there and stared at her, and that was

the moment when childhood faded and womanhood began. The violent, crazy act was the last act of childhood. For as I gazed at the immobile face with sad, weary eyes, I gazed upon a kind of reality that is hidden to childhood. The witch was no longer a witch but only a broken old woman who had dared to create beauty in the midst of ugliness and sterility. She had been born in squalor and had lived in it all her life. Now at the end of that life she had nothing except a falling-down hut, a wrecked body, and John Burke, the mindless son of her passion. Whatever verve there was left in her, whatever was of love and beauty and joy that had not been squeezed out by life, had been there in the marigolds she had so tenderly cared for.

Of course I could not express the things that I knew about Miss Lottie as I stood there awkward and ashamed. The years have put words to the things I knew in that moment, and as I look back upon it, I know that that moment marked the end of innocence. . . . Innocence involves an unseeing acceptance of things at face value, an ignorance of the area below the surface. In that humiliating moment I looked beyond myself and into the depths of another person. This was the beginning of compassion, and one cannot have both compassion and innocence.

The years have taken me worlds away from that time and that place, from the dust and squalor of our lives and from the bright thing that I destroyed in a blind, childish striking out at God-knows-what. Miss Lottie died long ago, and many years have passed since I last saw her hut, completely barren at last, for despite my wild contrition[9] she never planted marigolds again. Yet, there are

---

8. **degradation** (deg' rə dā' shən): a state of corruption and loss of dignity and humanity.
9. **contrition** (kən trish' ən): feeling of sorrow or regret for wrong doing.

times when the image of those passionate yellow mounds returns with a painful poignancy. For one does not have to be ignorant and poor to find that one's life is barren as the dusty yards of one's town. And I too have planted marigolds.

# Thinking About the Story

## A PERSONAL RESPONSE

*sharing impressions*

**1.** What was the strongest emotion you felt as you read this story? Write about this emotion in your journal.

*constructing interpretations*

**2.** What does Lizabeth mean when she says that she too has planted marigolds?
### Think about
- her interpretation of Miss Lottie's reasons for planting marigolds
- her statement that "one does not have to be ignorant and poor to find that one's life is barren as the dusty yards of one's town"
- the "you" she addresses in the second paragraph of the story

**3.** Why does Lizabeth destroy the marigolds?
### Think about
- why the children like to annoy Miss Lottie
- how Lizabeth describes the unhappiness in her family
- how Lizabeth describes being "fourteen-going-on-fifteen"

**4.** How does the destruction of the marigolds signal the end of Lizabeth's childhood and the beginning of womanhood?

**5.** How do different characters in the story suffer unhappiness or loss?

## A CRITICAL RESPONSE

**6.** What does the use of flashback add to the story?
### Think about
- flashback as an event that happened before the beginning of the story
- how the story might have been different if it had been told by the child Lizabeth right after it happened
- how the incident continues to affect the adult narrator

**7.** Analyze the sources of the tensions that lead Lizabeth to destroy the marigolds. Support your analysis with examples from the story.

# *Analyzing the Writer's Craft*

Reread the description of John Burke sitting in front of his mother's house. What does his presence tell you about Miss Lottie's life?

**Building a Literary Vocabulary.** A symbol is a person, place, object, or activity that stands for something beyond itself. Usually, a son or daughter represents a parent's hopes and dreams for the future. Because of John Burke's infirmities, he is unable to function outside his own dream world, and in this story he can be seen as a symbol of Miss Lottie's frustrated hopes and desires. The narrator describes him as "completing the impression of decay" associated with Miss Lottie and her house.

**Application: Analyzing a Symbol.** Work in a small group to make a list of what the marigolds mean to Lizabeth, both as the adult narrator and as the child she remembers. Then make a list of what the marigolds mean to Miss Lottie. Compare the lists to analyze how a single symbol can have complex meaning in a story.

# *Connecting Reading and Writing*

**1.** Draw or find pictures that illustrate the story. Around the pictures create a **cluster diagram** of words associated with the pictures.

Option: Write a **proposal** to the publisher of this story explaining why your pictures would be the best illustrations.

**2.** Describe an incident in which you expressed your anger, either constructively or destructively. Create a **word search puzzle** of adjectives and verbs you associate with the incident, which might be used in a book of word games.

Option: Write a **script** for a skit that would portray the incident in flashback.

**3.** Support or challenge this quotation from the story: "One cannot have both compassion and innocence." Using specific examples from your reading and from real life, argue your opinion in a **sermon.**

Option: Argue your opinion in an **editorial**.

**4.** Analyze Lizabeth's character at fourteen, exploring both her positive and negative qualities. Present your analysis in a teacher's **note** to Lizabeth's parents.

Option: Create a **dialogue** between two of Lizabeth's close friends.

# A Mother in Mannville

MARJORIE KINNAN RAWLINGS

A biography of Rawlings appears on page 645.

## *A*pproaching the Story

The narrator of this story is a writer who, like many writers, feels a need for quiet and solitude to do her best work. She rents a cabin in the Carolina mountains that is owned by a nearby orphanage. The action takes place at a time when children without parents often had to live in institutions. The story revolves around the writer's encounter with Jerry, a child from the orphanage.

## *B*uilding Vocabulary

These essential words are footnoted within the story.

**integrity** (in teg´ rə tē): The word that comes to me is "**integrity**." (page 112)

**communion** (kə myoon´ yən): There is a strange **communion** between a boy and a dog. (page 113)

**impelled** (im peld´): He was suddenly **impelled** to speak of things he had not spoken of before. (page 113)

**anomalous** (ə näm´ ə ləs): He did not question the **anomalous** relation. (page 114)

## *C*onnecting Writing and Reading

Imagine a situation in which you are very busy. You meet someone who clearly wants to be your friend, but you do not want to be friends. In your journal describe three things you could do to resolve this conflict of needs. Then as you read "A Mother in Mannville," compare your resolutions to the one in this story.

THE ORPHANAGE IS high in the Carolina mountains. Sometimes in the winter the snowdrifts are so deep that the institution is cut off from the village below, from all the world. Fog hides the mountain peaks, the snow swirls down the valleys, and a wind blows so bitterly that the orphanage boys who take the milk twice daily to the baby cottage reach the door with fingers stiff in an agony of numbness.

"Or when we carry trays from the cookhouse for the ones that are sick," Jerry said, "we get our faces frostbit, because we can't put our hands over them. I have gloves," he added. "Some of the boys don't have any."

He liked the late spring, he said. The rhododendron was in bloom, a carpet of color, across the mountainsides, soft as the May winds that stirred the hemlocks. He called it laurel.

"It's pretty when the laurel blooms," he said. "Some of it's pink and some of it's white."

I was there in the autumn. I wanted quiet, isolation, to do some troublesome writing. I wanted mountain air to blow out the malaria from too long a time in the subtropics. I was homesick, too, for the flaming of maples in October, and for corn shocks and pumpkins and black-walnut trees and the lift of hills. I found them all, living in a cabin that belonged to the orphanage, half a mile beyond the orphanage farm. When I took the cabin, I asked for a boy or man to come and chop wood for the fireplace. The first few days were warm, I found what wood I needed about the cabin, no one came, and I forgot the order.

I looked up from my typewriter one late afternoon, a little startled. A boy stood at the door, and my pointer dog, my companion, was at his side and had not barked to warn me. The boy was probably twelve years old, but undersized. He wore overalls and a torn shirt, and was barefooted.

He said, "I can chop some wood today."

I said, "But I have a boy coming from the orphanage."

"I'm the boy."

"You? But you're small."

"Size don't matter, chopping wood," he said. "Some of the big boys don't chop good. I've been chopping wood at the orphanage a long time."

I visualized mangled and inadequate branches for my fires. I was well into my work and not inclined to conversation. I was a little blunt.

"Very well. There's the ax. Go ahead and see what you can do."

I went back to work, closing the door. At first the sound of the boy dragging brush annoyed me. Then he began to chop. The blows were rhythmic and steady, and shortly I had forgotten him, the sound no more of an interruption than a consistent rain. I suppose an hour and a half passed, for when I stopped and stretched, and heard the boy's steps on the cabin stoop, the sun was dropping behind the farthest mountain, and the valleys were purple with something deeper than the asters.

The boy said, "I have to go to supper now. I can come again tomorrow evening."

I said, "I'll pay you now for what you've done," thinking I should probably have to insist on an older boy. "Ten cents an hour?"

"Anything is all right."

We went together back of the cabin. An astonishing amount of solid wood had been cut. There were cherry logs and heavy roots of rhododendron, and blocks from the waste pine and oak left from the building of the cabin.

"But you've done as much as a man," I said. "This is a splendid pile."

I looked at him, actually, for the first time. His hair was the color of the corn shocks and his eyes, very direct, were like the mountain sky when rain is pending—gray, with a shadowing of that miraculous blue. As I spoke, a light came over him, as though the setting sun had touched him with the same suffused glory with which it touched the mountains. I gave him a quarter.

"You may come tomorrow," I said, "and thank you very much."

He looked at me, and at the coin, and seemed to want to speak, but could not, and turned away.

"I'll split kindling tomorrow," he said over his thin, ragged shoulder. "You'll need kindling and medium wood and logs and backlogs."

At daylight I was half wakened by the sound of chopping. Again it was so even in texture that I went back to sleep. When I left my bed in the cool morning, the boy had come and gone, and a stack of kindling was neat against the cabin wall. He came again after school in the afternoon and worked until time to return to the orphanage. His name was Jerry; he was twelve years old, and he had been at the orphanage since he was four. I could picture him at four, with the same grave gray-blue eyes and the same—independence? No, the word that comes to me is "integrity."[1]

The word means something very special to me, and the quality for which I use it is a rare one. My father had it—there is another of whom I am almost sure—but almost no man of my acquaintance possesses it with the clarity, the purity, the simplicity of a mountain stream. But the boy Jerry had it. It is bedded on courage, but it is more than brave. It is honest, but it is more than honesty. The ax handle broke one day. Jerry said the woodshop at the orphanage would repair it. I brought money to pay for the job, and he refused it.

"I'll pay for it," he said. "I broke it. I brought the ax down careless."

"But no one hits accurately every time," I told him. "The fault was in the wood of the handle. I'll see the man from whom I bought it."

It was only then that he would take the money. He was standing back of his own carelessness. He was a free-will agent, and he chose to do careful work; and if he failed, he took the responsibility without subterfuge.

And he did for me the unnecessary thing, the gracious thing, that we find done only by the great of heart. Things no training can teach, for they are done on the instant, with no predicated experience. He found a cubbyhole beside the fireplace that I had not noticed. There, of his own accord, he put kindling and "medium" wood, so that I might always have dry fire material ready in case of sudden wet weather. A stone was loose in the rough walk to the cabin. He dug a deeper hole and steadied it, although he came, himself, by a shortcut over the bank. I found that when I tried to return his thoughtfulness with such things as candy and apples, he was wordless. "Thank you" was perhaps an expression for which he had had no use, for his courtesy was instinctive. He only looked at the gift and at me, and a curtain lifted, so that I saw deep into the clear well of his eyes, and gratitude was there, and affection, soft over the firm granite of his character.

He made simple excuses to come and sit with me. I could no more have turned him away than if he had been physically hungry. I suggested once that the best time for us to visit was just before supper, when I left off my writing. After that, he waited always until my typewriter had been some time quiet. One day I worked until nearly dark. I went outside the cabin, having forgotten him. I saw him going up over the hill in the twilight toward the orphanage. When I sat down on my stoop, a place was warm from his body where he had been sitting.

He became intimate, of course, with my

---

1. **integrity** (in teg′ rə tē): honesty; the state of having standards and values that cannot be corrupted.

pointer, Pat. There is a strange communion[2] between a boy and a dog. Perhaps they possess the same singleness of spirit, the same kind of wisdom. It is difficult to explain, but it exists. When I went across the state for a weekend, I left the dog in Jerry's charge. I gave him the dog whistle and the key to the cabin, and left sufficient food. He was to come two or three times a day and let out the dog, and feed and exercise him. I should return Sunday night, and Jerry would take out the dog for the last time Sunday afternoon and then leave the key under an agreed hiding place.

My return was belated, and fog filled the mountain passes so treacherously that I dared not drive at night. The fog held the next morning, and it was Monday noon before I reached the cabin. The dog had been fed and cared for that morning. Jerry came early in the afternoon, anxious.

"The superintendent said nobody would drive in the fog," he said. "I came just before bedtime last night and you hadn't come. So I brought Pat some of my breakfast this morning. I wouldn't have let anything happen to him."

"I was sure of that. I didn't worry."

"When I heard about the fog, I thought you'd know."

He was needed for work at the orphanage, and he had to return at once. I gave him a dollar in payment, and he looked at it and went away. But that night he came in the darkness and knocked at the door.

"Come in, Jerry," I said, "if you're allowed to be away this late."

"I told maybe a story," he said. "I told them I thought you would want to see me."

"That's true," I assured him, and I saw his relief. "I want to hear about how you managed with the dog."

He sat by the fire with me, with no other light, and told me of their two days together.

The dog lay close to him, and found a comfort there that I did not have for him. And it seemed to me that being with my dog, and caring for him, had brought the boy and me, too, together, so that he felt that he belonged to me as well as to the animal.

"He stayed right with me," he told me, "except when he ran in the laurel. He likes the laurel. I took him up over the hill and we both ran fast. There was a place where the grass was high and I lay down in it and hid. I could hear Pat hunting for me. He found my trail and he barked. When he found me, he acted crazy, and he ran around and around me, in circles."

We watched the flames.

"That's an apple log," he said. "It burns the prettiest of any wood."

We were very close.

He was suddenly impelled[3] to speak of things he had not spoken of before, nor had I cared to ask him.

"You look a little bit like my mother," he said. "Especially in the dark, by the fire."

"But you were only four, Jerry, when you came here. You have remembered how she looked, all these years?"

"My mother lives in Mannville," he said.

For a moment, finding that he had a mother shocked me as greatly as anything in my life has ever done, and I did not know why it disturbed me. Then I understood my distress. I was filled with a passionate resentment that any woman should go away and leave her son. A fresh anger added itself. A son like this one—The orphanage was a wholesome place, the executives were kind, good people, the food was more than adequate, the boys were healthy, a ragged shirt was no hardship, nor the doing of clean labor. Granted, perhaps,

---

2. **communion** (kə myo͞on′ yən): a close relationship based on a deep understanding, often without words.
3. **impelled** (im peld′): forced; compelled; urged.

that the boy felt no lack, what blood fed the bowels of a woman who did not yearn over this child's lean body that had come in parturition out of her own? At four he would have looked the same as now. Nothing, I thought, nothing in life could change those eyes. His quality must be apparent to an idiot, a fool. I burned with questions I could not ask. In any case, I was afraid, there would be pain.

"Have you seen her, Jerry—lately?"

"I see her every summer. She sends for me."

I wanted to cry out, "Why are you not with her? How can she let you go away again?"

He said, "She comes up here from Mannville whenever she can. She doesn't have a job now."

His face shone in the firelight.

"She wanted to give me a puppy, but they can't let any one boy keep a puppy. You remember the suit I had on last Sunday?" He was plainly proud. "She sent me that for Christmas. The Christmas before that"—he drew a long breath, savoring the memory—"she sent me a pair of skates."

"Roller skates?"

My mind was busy, making pictures of her, trying to understand her. She had not, then, entirely deserted or forgotten him. But why, then—I thought, "I must not condemn her without knowing."

"Roller skates. I let the other boys use them. They're always borrowing them. But they're careful of them."

What circumstance other than poverty—

"I'm going to take the dollar you gave me for taking care of Pat," he said, "and buy her a pair of gloves."

I could only say, "That will be nice. Do you know her size?"

"I think it's $8\frac{1}{2}$," he said.

He looked at my hands.

"Do you wear $8\frac{1}{2}$?" he asked.

"No. I wear a smaller size, a 6."

"Oh! Then I guess her hands are bigger than yours."

I hated her. Poverty or no, there was other food than bread, and the soul could starve as quickly as the body. He was taking his dollar to buy gloves for her big stupid hands, and she lived away from him, in Mannville, and contented herself with sending him skates.

"She likes white gloves," he said. "Do you think I can get them for a dollar?"

"I think so," I said.

I decided that I should not leave the mountains without seeing her and knowing for myself why she had done this thing.

The human mind scatters its interests as though made of thistledown,[4] and every wind stirs and moves it. I finished my work. It did not please me, and I gave my thoughts to another field. I should need some Mexican material.

I made arrangements to close my Florida place. Mexico immediately, and doing the writing there, if conditions were favorable. Then, Alaska with my brother. After that, heaven knew what or where.

I did not take time to go to Mannville to see Jerry's mother, nor even to talk with the orphanage officials about her. I was a trifle abstracted about the boy, because of my work and plans. And after my first fury at her—we did not speak of her again—his having a mother, any sort at all, not far away, in Mannville, relieved me of the ache I had had about him. He did not question the anomalous[5] relation. He was not lonely. It was none of my concern.

He came every day and cut my wood and did small helpful favors and stayed to talk. The days had become cold, and often I let him

---

4. **thistledown** : the soft, fluffy down attached to the flower head of a thistle plant.

5. **anomalous** (ə näm′ ə ləs): not following the general rule.

come inside the cabin. He would lie on the floor in front of the fire, with one arm across the pointer, and they would both doze and wait quietly for me. Other days they ran with a common ecstasy through the laurel, and since the asters were now gone, he brought me back vermilion maple leaves, and chestnut boughs dripping with imperial yellow. I was ready to go.

I said to him, "You have been my good friend, Jerry. I shall often think of you and miss you. Pat will miss you too. I am leaving tomorrow."

He did not answer. When he went away, I remember that a new moon hung over the mountains, and I watched him go in silence up the hill. I expected him the next day, but he did not come. The details of packing my personal belongings, loading my car, arranging the bed over the seat, where the dog would ride, occupied me until late in the day. I closed the cabin and started the car, noticing that the sun was in the west and I should do well to be out of the mountains by nightfall. I stopped by the orphanage and left the cabin key and money for my light bill with Miss Clark.

"And will you call Jerry for me to say goodbye to him?"

"I don't know where he is," she said. "I'm afraid he's not well. He didn't eat his dinner this noon. One of the other boys saw him going over the hill into the laurel. He was supposed to fire the boiler this afternoon. It's not like him; he's unusually reliable."

I was almost relieved, for I knew I should never see him again, and it would be easier not to say goodbye to him.

I said, "I wanted to talk with you about his mother—why he's here—but I'm in more of a hurry than I expected to be. It's out of the question for me to see her now too. But here's some money I'd like to leave with you to buy things for him at Christmas and on his birthday. It will be better than for me to try to send him things. I could so easily duplicate—skates, for instance."

She blinked her honest spinster's eyes.

"There's not much use for skates here," she said.

Her stupidity annoyed me.

"What I mean," I said, "is that I don't want to duplicate things his mother sends him. I might have chosen skates if I didn't know she had already given them to him."

She stared at me.

"I don't understand," she said. "He has no mother. He has no skates."

# Thinking About the Story

## A PERSONAL RESPONSE

*sharing impressions*

**1.** How did you react when you discovered that Jerry has no mother? Write about your reaction in your journal.

*constructing interpretations*

**2.** What do you think motivates Jerry to lie about having a mother?
### Think about
- the kind of life he leads
- unfulfilled needs he might have
- his relationship with the narrator and her dog

**3.** How do Jerry and the narrator seem to feel about each other?
### Think about
- the things they do for each other
- the time they are willing to give each other
- their different reactions to the narrator's departure at the end of the story

**4.** What is your opinion about the way the narrator handles the conflict of needs that is described in the story?

**5.** Explain to what extent you think Jerry and the narrator display integrity.

## A CREATIVE RESPONSE

**6.** How might the story be different if the narrator were a man?

## A CRITICAL RESPONSE

**7.** What internal conflicts do you think Jerry and the narrator face? Support your answer with details from the story.
### Think about
- internal conflict as a struggle between opposing tendencies within a character
- actions of the characters that might reveal these opposing tendencies.

**8.** Both the narrator of "A Mother in Mannville" and Mrs. Jones from "Thank You, M'am" have an encounter with a young boy in difficult circumstances. Compare the two women's treatment of the boys, and explain how you think the boys are affected.

**9.** In 1936 Marjorie Kinnan Rawlings was working on her novel *The Yearling* at a mountain retreat in North Carolina. "A Mother in Mannville" was inspired by a boy from the nearby orphanage who became close to Rawlings during her stay. What effect does this information have on your interpretation of the story?

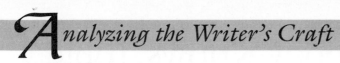

# Analyzing the Writer's Craft

## POINT OF VIEW

Think about how you learn about Jerry's character in this story.

**Building a Literary Vocabulary.** Point of view refers to the narrative method, or the kind of narrator, used in a story. Like "The Scarlet Ibis," "A Mother in Mannville" is written in the first-person point of view. The narrator is one of the two main characters of the story; everything that happens in the story is seen through her eyes. This means that the reader has only the narrator's interpretation of Jerry's actions, thoughts, and emotions.

**Application: Understanding Point of View.** Working with a classmate, list passages from the story where the narrator does the following:

- objectively describes Jerry's behavior
- speculates about the thoughts or feelings that may be responsible for those actions

Then come up with some alternative explanations for each of the behaviors that the narrator describes.

# Connecting Reading and Writing

**1.** Imagine that Jerry has just learned that the narrator has come to the orphanage to say goodbye to him. Have Jerry express his feelings about the narrator and his relationship with her in a **diary entry.**

Option: Have Jerry express his feelings in a **note** to the narrator.

**2.** Give the narrator a chance to explain her thoughts, feelings, and needs to Jerry after she learns the truth about his mother. Express her views in a **letter** to Jerry.

Option: Write a **script** for a dramatic scene between the narrator and Jerry.

**3.** Analyze Jerry's character in a **recommendation** for a job.

Option: Write an **outline** for a human-interest article on Jerry, to be published in the local newspaper.

**4.** Explain the meaning of integrity in **captions** for a photographic essay illustrating the quality.

Option: Write a brief **expository essay** on integrity addressed to your teacher.

# Everybody Knows Tobie

### DANIEL GARZA

*A*pproaching the Story

This story takes place in a small Texas town divided into two groups of people: gringos and Chicanos. *Gringo* is slang for an Anglo-American; *Chicano* refers to a Mexican American born in this country. Joey, the narrator of this story, is a Chicano who explains how he and his brother Tobie fit into their town.

HEN I WAS thirteen years old, my older brother, Tobie, had the town newspaper route. Everyone in the town knew him well because he had been delivering papers for a year and a half. Tobie used to tell me that he had the best route of all because his customers would pay promptly each month, and sometimes, he used to brag that the nice people of the town would tip him a quarter or maybe fifty cents at the end of the month because he would trudge up many stairs to deliver the paper personally.

The other newspaper boys were not as lucky as Tobie because sometimes their customers would not be at home when they went by to collect payment for that month's newspaper, or maybe at the end of the month the customers would just try to avoid the paper boys to keep from paying.

Yes, Tobie had it good. The biggest advantage, I thought, that Tobie had over all the newspaper boys was that he knew the gringos of the town so well that he could go into a gringo barbershop and get a haircut without having the barber tell him to go to the Mexican barber in our town, or maybe just embarrassing him in front of all the gringo customers in the shop as they often did when Chicano cotton pickers came into their places during the fall months.

The gringo barbers of my town were careful whom they allowed in their shops during the cotton harvest season in the fall. September and October and cotton brought Chicanos from the south to the north of Texas where I lived, and where the cotton was sometimes plentiful and sometimes scarce. *Chicanos* is what we say in our language, and it is slang among our people. It means the Mexicans of Texas. These Chicano cotton pickers came from the Rio Grande Valley in South Texas, and sometimes, even people from Mexico made the trip to the north of Texas. All these Chicanos came to my little town in which many gringos lived, and a few of us who spoke both English and Spanish.

When the Chicanos came to my town on Saturdays after working frightfully in the cotton fields all week, they would go to the town market for food, and the fathers would buy candy and ice cream for their flocks of little black-headed ones. The younger ones, the *jovenes*, would go to the local movie house. And then maybe those who had never been north of Texas before would go to the gringos' barbershops for haircuts, not knowing that they would be refused. The gringo barbers would be very careful not to let them come too close to their shops because the regular gringo customers would get mad, and sometimes they would curse the Chicanos.

"It's them darn pepper bellies again. Can't seem to get rid of 'em in the fall," the prejudiced gringos of my town would say. Some of the nicer people would only become uneasy at seeing so many Chicanos with long, black, greasy hair wanting haircuts.

The barbers of the town liked Tobie, and they invited him to their shops for haircuts. Tobie said that the barbers told him that they would cut his hair because he did not belong to that group of people who came from the south of Texas. Tobie understood. And he did not argue with the barbers because he knew how Chicanos from South Texas were, and how maybe gringo scissors would get all greasy from cutting their hair.

During that fall, Tobie encouraged me to go to the gringo's place for a haircut. "Joey, when are you going to get rid of that mop of hair?" he asked.

"I guess I'll get rid of it when Mr. Lopez learns how to cut flattops."

"Golly, Joey, Mr. Lopez is a good ole guy and all that, but if he doesn't know how to give flat-tops, then you should go to some other barber for flattops. Really, Kid-brother, that hair looks awful."

"Yeah, but I'm afraid."

"Afraid of what?" Tobie asked

"I'm afraid the barber will mistake me for one of those guys from South Texas and run me out of his shop."

"Oh, forget it," Tobie said. "Mr. Brewer . . . you know, the barber who cuts my hair . . . is a nice man, and he'll cut your hair. Just tell him you're my kid-brother."

I thought about this new adventure for several days, and then on Saturday, when there was no school, I decided on the haircut at Mr. Brewer's. I hurriedly rode my bike to town and parked it in the alley close to the barbershop. As I walked into the shop, I noticed that all of a sudden the gringos inside stopped their conversation and looked at me. The shop was silent for a moment. I thought then that maybe this was not too good and that I should leave. I remembered what Tobie had told me about being his brother, and about Mr. Brewer being a nice man. I was convinced that I belonged in the gringo barbershop.

I found an empty chair and sat down to wait my turn for a haircut. One gringo customer sitting next to me rose and explained to the barber that he had to go to the courthouse for something. Another customer left without saying anything. And then one, who was dressed in dirty coveralls and a faded khaki shirt, got up from Mr. Brewer's chair and said to him, "Say, Tom, looks like you got yourself a little tamale to clip."

Mr. Brewer smiled only.

My turn was next, and I was afraid. But I remembered again that this was all right because I was Tobie's brother, and everybody liked Tobie. I went to Mr. Brewer's chair. As I started to sit down, he looked at me and smiled a nice smile.

He said, "I'm sorry, Sonny, but I can't cut your hair. You go to Mr. Lopez's. He'll cut your hair."

Mr. Brewer took me to the door and pointed the way to Lopez's barbershop. He pointed with his finger and said, "See, over there behind that service station. That's his place. You go there. He'll clip your hair."

Tears were welling up in my eyes. I felt a

lump in my throat. I was too choked up to tell him that I was Tobie's brother, and that it was all right to cut my hair. I only looked at him as he finished giving directions. He smiled again and patted me on the back. As I left, Mr. Brewer said, "Say hello to Mr. Lopez for me, will you, Sonny?"

I did not turn back to look at Mr. Brewer. I kept my head bowed as I walked to Mr. Lopez's because tears filled my eyes, and these tears were tears of hurt to the pride and confidence that I had slowly gained in my gringo town.

I thought of many things as I walked slowly. Maybe this was a foolish thing that I had done. There were too many gringos in the town and too few of us who lived there all year long. This was a bad thing because the gringos had the right to say yes or no, and we could only follow what they said. It was useless to go against them. It was foolish. But I was different from the Chicanos who came from the south, much different. I did live in the town the ten months of the year when the other Chicanos were in the south or in Mexico. Then I remembered what the barber had told my brother about the South Texas people, and why the gringo customers had left while I was in Mr. Brewer's shop. I began to understand. But it was very hard for me to realize that even though I had lived among gringos all of my life I still had to go to my own people for such things as haircuts. Why wouldn't gringos cut my hair? I was clean. My hair was not long and greasy.

I walked into Mr. Lopez's shop. There were many Chicanos sitting in the chairs and even on the floor, waiting their turn for a haircut. Mr. Lopez paused from his work when he saw me enter and said, "Sorry, Joey, full up. Come back in a couple of hours."

I shrugged my shoulders and said OK. As I started to leave, I remembered what Mr. Brewer had told me to say to Mr. Lopez. "Mr. Lopez," I said, and all the Chicanos, the ones who were waiting, turned and looked at me with curious eyes. "Mr. Brewer told me to tell you hello."

Mr. Lopez shook his head approvingly, not digesting the content of my statement. The Chicanos looked at me again and began to whisper among themselves. I did not hear, but I understood.

I told Mr. Lopez that I would return later in the day, but I did not because there would be other Chicanos wanting haircuts on Saturday. I could come during the week when he had more time, and when all the Chicanos would be in the fields working.

I went away, feeling rejected both by the gringos and even my own people, the entire world I knew.

Back in the alley where my bike was parked, I sat on the curb for a long while thinking how maybe I did not fit into this town. Maybe my place was in the south of Texas where there were many of my kind of people, and where there were more Chicano barbershops and fewer gringo barbers. Yes, I thought, I needed a land where I could belong to one race. I was so concerned with myself that I did not notice a Chicano, a middle-aged man dressed in a new chambray shirt and faded denim pants, studying me.

He asked, "*Qué pasó, Chamaco?*"[1]

"*Nada,*"[2] I answered.

"Maybe the cotton has not been good for you this year."

"No, Señor. I live here in the town."

And then the Chicano said, "Chico, I mistook you for one of us."

Suddenly the Chicano became less interested in me and walked away unconcerned.

I could not have told him that I had tried for a haircut at the gringo's because he would

---

1. *Qué pasó, Chamaco?* (kä pä sö′ chä mä′ cō) *Spanish:* What happened, boy?
2. *Nada* (nä′ də) *Spanish:* nothing.

© 1990, Phillip Cantor, Chicago.

have laughed at me, and called me *pocho,* a Chicano who prefers gringo ways. These experienced Chicanos knew the ways of the gringos in the north of Texas.

After the Chicano had left me, I thought that maybe these things that were happening to me in the town would all pass in a short time. The entire cotton crop would soon be harvested, and the farmers around my town would have it baled and sold. Then the Chicanos would leave the north of Texas and journey back to their homes in the Valley in the south and to Mexico.

My town would be left alone for ten more months of the year, and in this time everything and everybody would be all right again. The gringo barbers would maybe think twice before sending me to Mr. Lopez's.

Early in November, the last of the cotton around my town had been harvested. The people of South Texas climbed aboard their big trucks with tall sideboards and canvas on the top to shield the sun, and they began their long journey to their homes in the border country.

The streets of the little town were now empty on Saturday. A few farmers came to town on Saturday and brought their families to do their shopping. Still, the streets were quiet and empty.

In my home there was new excitement for me. Tobie considered leaving his newspaper route for another job, one that would pay more money. And I thought that maybe he would let me take over his route. This was something very good. By taking his route, I would know all the gringos of the town, and maybe . . . maybe then the barbers would invite me to their shops as they had invited Tobie.

At supper that night I asked Tobie if he would take me on his delivery for a few days and then let me deliver the newspaper on my own.

Tobie said, "No, Joey. You're too young to handle money. Besides, the newspaper bag would be too heavy for you to carry on your shoulder all over town. No, I think I'll turn my route over to Red."

My father was quiet during this time, but soon he spoke, "Tobie, you give the route to Joey. He knows about money. And he needs to put a little muscle on his shoulders."

The issue was settled.

The next day Tobie took me to the newspaper office. Tobie's boss, a nice elderly man wearing glasses, studied me carefully, scratched his white head, and then asked Tobie, "Well, what do you think?"

"Oh," Tobie said, "I told him he was too young to handle this job, but he says he can do it."

"Yes, sir," I butted in enthusiastically.

Tobie's boss looked at me and chuckled, "Well, he's got enough spunk."

He thought some more.

Tobie spoke, "I think he'll make you a good delivery boy, sir."

A short silence followed while Tobie's boss put his thoughts down on a scratch pad on his desk.

Finally, the boss said, "We'll give him a try, Tobie." He looked at me. "But, Young'un, you'd better be careful with that money. It's your responsibility."

"Yes, sir," I gulped.

"OK, that's settled," the boss said.

Tobie smiled and said, "Sir, I'm taking him on my delivery for a few days so he can get the hang of it, and then I'll let him take over."

The boss agreed. I took his hand and shook it, and promised him that I would do my extra best. Then Tobie left, and I followed behind.

In a few days I was delivering the *Daily News* to all the gringos of the town and also to Mr. Brewer.

Each afternoon, during my delivery, I was careful not to go into Mr. Brewer's with the newspaper. I would carefully open the door and drop the paper in. I did this because I thought that maybe Mr. Brewer would remember me, and this might cause an embarrassing incident. But I did this a very few times because one afternoon Mr. Brewer was standing at the door. He saw me. I opened the door and quickly handed him the newspaper, but before I could shut the door he said, "Say, Sonny, aren't you the one I sent to Mr. Lopez's a while back?"

"Yes, sir," I said.

"Why'd you stay around here? Didn't your people go back home last week? You do belong to 'em, don't you?"

"No, sir," I said. "I live here in town."

"You mean to say you're not one of those . . . ?"

"No, sir."

"Well, I'll be durned." He paused and thought. "You know, Sonny, I have a young Meskin[3] boy who lives here in town come to this here shop for haircuts every other Saturday. His name is . . . durn, can't think of his name to save my soul . . . ."

"Tobie?"

"Yeah, yeah, that's his name. Fine boy. You know him?"

"Yes, sir. He's my older brother."

Then Mr. Brewer's eyes got bigger in astonishment. "Well, I'll be doubly durned." He paused and shook his head unbelievingly. "And I told you to go to Mr. Lopez's. Why didn't you speak up and tell me you was Tobie's brother. I woulda put you in that there chair and clipped you a pretty head of hair."

"Oh, I guess I forgot to tell you," I said.

"Well, from now on, Sonny, you come to this here shop, and I'll cut your hair."

"But what about your customers? Won't they get mad?"

"Naw. I'll tell 'em you're Tobie's brother, and everything will be all right. Everybody in town knows Tobie, and everybody likes him."

Then a customer walked into the barbershop. He looked at Mr. Brewer, and then at me, and then at my newspaper bag. And then the gringo customer smiled a nice smile at me.

"Well, excuse me, Sonny, got a customer waitin'. Remember now, come Saturday, and I'll clip your hair."

"OK, Mr. Brewer. Bye."

Mr. Brewer turned and said goodbye.

As I continued my delivery, I began to chuckle small bits of contentment to myself because Mr. Brewer had invited me to his shop for haircuts, and because the gringo customer had smiled at me, and because now all the gringos of the town would know me and maybe accept me.

Those incidents that had happened to me during the cotton harvest in my town—Mr. Brewer sending me to Mr. Lopez's for the haircut, and the Chicano cotton picker avoiding me after discovering that I was not one of his people, and the gringo customers leaving Mr. Brewer's barbershop because of me—all seemed so insignificant. And now I felt that delivering the *Daily News* to the businessmen had given me a place among them, and all because of the fact that everybody in my town knew Tobie.

---

3. **Meskin**: mispronunciation of *Mexican*.

# The Individual in Community: Defining Personal Values

CHILDREN LEARN BY imitating the people around them. They pick up spoken language as well as behavior and facial expressions. The most basic living skills, such as eating with a fork or with chopsticks, are learned from the family and the society in which a child lives.

As children grow older, they learn a set of values, again based on the values of the people around them. Developing personal values is often a difficult process. In "Everybody Knows Tobie," Joey is caught between the values of two groups of people, both of whom reject him. The Chicano cotton pickers do not consider him one of them, and the gringo citizens reject him for being a Chicano. Following his brother's lead, Joey learns that to be accepted by gringos he must differentiate himself from the Chicano cotton pickers. Thus, Joey ends up conforming to values that exclude people of his own heritage.

Sometimes a person forms positive values by successfully resisting the pressure to conform. In "Initiation," Millicent decides that she does not want to become just like the girls in the sorority. As Millicent goes through the process of rejecting the sorority's values, she discovers exactly what is important to her.

The stories in this section focus on characters making decisions about values. Each of the main characters is shown as part of a community that has a specific way of viewing life. The tension in the stories builds as the individuals try to discover how they fit into the communities in which they live. As you read these stories, see whether they reveal anything to you about your place in your own community.

# Literary Vocabulary

**Theme.** Theme is the central idea or message in a work of literature. Theme should not be confused with subject, or what the work is about. Rather, theme is a perception about life or humanity that a writer expresses about a subject. For example, the subject of "Everybody Knows Tobie" is racial prejudice. The theme is that racial prejudice reduces a person's sense of worth. The theme of this story, like most themes, is not stated directly. It is revealed through an interpretation of Jocy's experience. Joey knows that the gringos accept him not for who he is as a person but because he is Tobie's brother—sufficient proof for them that he is different from other Chicanos.

Most stories communicate several of the writer's perceptions, one of which usually predominates. A minor theme in "Everybody Knows Tobie" concerns the strong influence that an older brother has over a younger one.

One clue to the theme of a story is its title. By emphasizing the central symbol, the title of "The Scarlet Ibis" also points to the theme. Both the ibis and Doodle are unusual—the ibis for its outer beauty, Doodle for his inner beauty. Their deaths represent the frailty of beautiful living things that are out of place in ordinary life.

**Figurative Language.** Figurative language is language that communicates ideas beyond the literal meanings of the words. The words in a figurative expression are not literally true; rather, they create impressions in the reader's mind. One of the most common forms of figurative language is a simile. A **simile** is a comparison between two things that are actually unlike yet have something in common. A simile usually contains the word like or as. In "Through the Tunnel" Jerry is described as swimming out "over a middle region where rocks lay like discolored monsters under the surface." The rocks in this simile are compared to monsters to give the impression of danger and to illustrate Jerry's fear.

**Symbol    Irony    Conflict**

# The Necklace

### GUY DE MAUPASSANT
Translated from the French

A biography of de Maupassant appears on page 638.

## *A*pproaching the Story

"The Necklace" takes place in Paris, France, in the second half of the nineteenth century. For a young woman of the time, life had few opportunities. A rich young woman could look forward to a life of luxury, social activities, and entertainment. A middle-class woman was expected to find happiness in the care of her home and family. A poor woman could expect a life of drudgery. The only way that a young woman born into the middle class could join the upper class was to marry a rich man. However, to marry a rich man a young woman usually needed a dowry, or property given to a husband upon marriage. As you can imagine, wealth and status were desired by many but achieved by few.

## *B*uilding Vocabulary

These essential words are footnoted within the story.

**incessantly** (in ses´ ənt lē): She grieved **incessantly**. (page 127)

**disconsolate** (dis kän´ sə lit): The sight . . . roused in her **disconsolate** regrets and wild daydreams. (page 127)

**vexation** (veks ā´ shən), **anguish** (aŋ´ gwish): She would weep for days on end from **vexation**, regret, despair, and **anguish**. (page 127)

**pauper** (pô´ pər): "I'll look like a **pauper**." (page 128)

**adulation** (a´ jōō lā´ shən): She danced madly, . . . in a kind of happy cloud composed of all the **adulation**. (page 129)

**privations** (prī vā´ shənz): He [was] terrified . . . by the prospect of all the **privations** of the body and tortures of the spirit. (page 130)

**exorbitant** (eg zor´ bi tənt): Finally, all was paid back, everything including the **exorbitant** rates of the loan sharks. (page 131)

## *C*onnecting Writing and Reading

Think of some things that you value, things that are important to you. List these things in your journal. As you read "The Necklace," compare your values to those of the main character. Take brief notes in your journal to help you remember your thoughts.

**S**HE WAS ONE of those pretty and charming girls, born, as if by an accident of fate, into a family of clerks. With no dowry, no prospects, no way of any kind of being met, understood, loved, and married by a man both prosperous and famous, she was finally married to a minor clerk in the Ministry of Education.

She dressed plainly because she could not afford fine clothes, but was as unhappy as a woman who has come down in the world; for women have no family rank or social class. With them, beauty, grace, and charm take the place of birth and breeding. Their natural poise, their instinctive good taste, and their mental cleverness are the sole guiding principles that make daughters of the common people the equals of ladies in high society.

She grieved incessantly,[1] feeling that she had been born for all the little niceties and luxuries of living. She grieved over the shabbiness of her apartment, the dinginess of the walls, the worn-out appearance of the chairs, the ugliness of the draperies. All these things, which another woman of her class would not even have noticed, gnawed at her and made her furious. The sight of the little Breton[2] girl who did her humble housework roused in her disconsolate[3] regrets and wild daydreams. She would dream of silent chambers, draped with Oriental tapestries and lighted by tall bronze floor lamps, and of two handsome butlers in knee breeches, who, drowsy from the heavy warmth cast by the central stove, dozed in large overstuffed armchairs.

She would dream of great reception halls hung with old silks, of fine furniture filled with priceless curios,[4] and of small, stylish, scented sitting rooms just right for the four o'clock chat with intimate friends, with distinguished and sought-after men whose attention every woman envies and longs to attract.

When dining at the round table, covered for the third day with the same cloth, opposite her husband, who would raise the cover of the soup tureen, declaring delightedly, "Ah! a good stew! There's nothing I like better . . . ," she would dream of fashionable dinner parties, of gleaming silverware, of tapestries making the walls alive with characters out of history and strange birds in a fairyland forest; she would dream of delicious dishes served on wonderful china, of gallant compliments whispered and listened to with a sphinxlike[5] smile as one eats the rosy flesh of a trout or nibbles at the wings of a grouse.

She had no evening clothes, no jewels, nothing. But those were the things she wanted: she felt that was the kind of life for her. She so much longed to please, be envied, be fascinating and sought after.

She had a well-to-do friend, a classmate of convent-school days whom she would no longer go to see, simply because she would feel so distressed on returning home. And she would weep for days on end from vexation,[6] regret, despair, and anguish.[7]

Then one evening, her husband came home proudly holding out a large envelope.

"Look," he said, "I've got something for you."

She excitedly tore open the envelope and pulled out a printed card bearing these words:

"The Minister of Education and Mme.

---

1. **incessantly** (in ses′ ənt lē): without stopping.
2. **Breton** (bret′ 'n): from Brittany, a province in northwestern France.
3. **disconsolate** (dis kän′ sə lit): so unhappy that nothing will comfort.
4. **curios** (kyo͞or′ ē ōz′): rare or unusual articles.
5. **sphinxlike** (sfiŋks′ līk): mysterious; the Sphinx is a famous Egyptian statue with a mysterious smile.
6. **vexation** (veks ā′ shən): annoyance or distress.
7. **anguish** (aŋ′ gwish): great suffering; agony.

Georges Ramponneau[8] beg M. and Mme. Loisel[9] to do them the honor of attending an evening reception at the Ministerial Mansion on Friday, January 18."

Instead of being delighted, as her husband had hoped, she scornfully tossed the invitation on the table, murmuring, "What good is that to me?"

"But, my dear, I thought you'd be thrilled to death. You never get a chance to go out, and this is a real affair, a wonderful one! I had an awful time getting a card. Everybody wants one; it's much sought after, and not many clerks have a chance at one. You'll see all the most important people there."

She gave him an irritated glance and burst out impatiently, "What do you think I have to go in?"

He hadn't given that a thought. He stammered, "Why, the dress you wear when we go to the theater. That looks quite nice, I think."

He stopped talking, dazed and distracted to see his wife burst out weeping. Two large tears slowly rolled from the corners of her eyes to the corners of her mouth. He gasped, "Why, what's the matter? What's the trouble?"

By sheer willpower she overcame her outburst and answered in a calm voice while wiping the tears from her wet cheeks:

"Oh, nothing. Only I don't have an evening dress and therefore I can't go to that affair. Give the card to some friend at the office whose wife can dress better than I can."

He was stunned. He resumed. "Let's see, Mathilde.[10] How much would a suitable outfit cost—one you could wear for other affairs too—something very simple?"

She thought it over for several seconds, going over her allowance and thinking also of the amount she could ask for without bringing an immediate refusal and an exclamation of dismay from the thrifty clerk.

Finally, she answered hesitatingly, "I'm not sure exactly, but I think with four hundred francs[11] I could manage it."

He turned a bit pale, for he had set aside just that amount to buy a rifle so that, the following summer, he could join some friends who were getting up a group to shoot larks on the plain near Nanterre.[12]

However, he said, "All right. I'll give you four hundred francs. But try to get a nice dress."

As the day of the party approached, Mme. Loisel seemed sad, moody, and ill at ease. Her outfit was ready, however. Her husband said to her one evening, "What's the matter? You've been all out of sorts for three days."

And she answered, "It's embarrassing not to have a jewel or a gem—nothing to wear on my dress. I'll look like a pauper;[13] I'd almost rather not go to that party."

He answered, "Why not wear some flowers? They're very fashionable this season. For ten francs you can get two or three gorgeous roses."

She wasn't at all convinced. "No. . . . There's nothing more humiliating than to look poor among a lot of rich women."

But her husband exclaimed, "My, but you're silly! Go see your friend Mme. Forestier[14] and ask her to lend you some jewelry. You and she know each other well enough for you to do that."

She gave a cry of joy, "Why, that's so! I hadn't thought of it."

---

8. **Mme. Georges Ramponneau** (mȧ dȧm′ zhôrzh rəm′ pə nō).

9. **M. and Mme. Loisel** (mə syoor′, mȧ dȧm′ lwȧ zel′).

10. **Mathild**e (mȧ tēld′).

11. **four hundred francs** (fraŋks): The franc is the French monetary unit; four hundred francs would have been about eighty dollars at the time.

12. **Nanterre** (nän te r′): a town near Paris.

13. **pauper** (pô′ pər): one who is entirely without money; a poor person.

14. **Forestier** (fô rə styā′).

The next day she paid her friend a visit and told her of her predicament.

Mme. Forestier went toward a large closet with mirrored doors, took out a large jewel box, brought it over, opened it, and said to Mme. Loisel, "Pick something out, my dear."

At first her eyes noted some bracelets, then a pearl necklace, then a Venetian cross, gold and gems, of marvelous workmanship. She tried on these adornments in front of the mirror, but hesitated, unable to decide which to part with and put back. She kept on asking, "Haven't you something else?"

"Oh, yes, keep on looking. I don't know just what you'd like."

All at once she found, in a black satin box, a superb diamond necklace; and her pulse beat faster with longing. Her hands trembled as she took it up. Clasping it around her throat, outside her high-necked dress, she stood in ecstasy looking at her reflection.

Then she asked, hesitatingly, pleading, "Could I borrow that, just that and nothing else?"

"Why, of course."

She threw her arms around her friend, kissed her warmly, and fled with her treasure.

The day of the party arrived. Mme. Loisel was a sensation. She was the prettiest one there, fashionable, gracious, smiling, and wild with joy. All the men turned to look at her, asked who she was, begged to be introduced. All the Cabinet officials wanted to waltz with her. The minister took notice of her.

She danced madly, wildly, drunk with pleasure, giving no thought to anything in the triumph of her beauty, the pride of her success, in a kind of happy cloud composed of all the adulation,[15] of all the admiring glances, of all the awakened longings, of a sense of complete victory that is so sweet to a woman's heart.

She left around four o'clock in the morning. Her husband, since midnight, had been dozing in a small empty sitting room with three other gentlemen whose wives were having too good a time to leave.

He threw over her shoulders the wraps he had brought for going home, modest garments of everyday life whose shabbiness clashed with the stylishness of her evening clothes. She felt this and longed to escape, unseen by the other women who were draped in expensive furs.

Loisel held her back.

"Hold on! You'll catch cold outside. I'll call a cab."

But she wouldn't listen to him and went rapidly down the stairs. When they were on the street, they didn't find a carriage; and they set out to hunt for one, hailing drivers whom they saw going by at a distance.

They walked toward the Seine,[16] disconsolate and shivering. Finally on the docks they found one of those carriages that one sees in Paris only after nightfall, as if they were ashamed to show their drabness during daylight hours.

It dropped them at their door in the Rue des Martyrs,[17] and they climbed wearily up to their apartment. For her, it was all over. For him, there was the thought that he would have to be at the Ministry at ten o'clock.

Before the mirror, she let the wraps fall from her shoulders to see herself once again in all her glory. Suddenly she gave a cry. The necklace was gone.

Her husband, already half undressed, said, "What's the trouble?"

She turned toward him despairingly, "I . . . I . . . I don't have Mme. Forestier's necklace."

"What! You can't mean it! It's impossible!"

They hunted everywhere, through the folds of the dress, through the folds of the coat, in the pockets. They found nothing.

---

15. **adulation** (a′jōo lā′ shən): extreme admiration.
16. **Seine** (sen): the river that runs through Paris.
17. **Rue des Martyrs** (rōo dā mär′ tēr): "Street of the Martyrs"; a street in Paris.

He asked, "Are you sure you had it when leaving the dance?"

"Yes, I felt it when I was in the hall of the Ministry."

"But if you had lost it on the street, we'd have heard it drop. It must be in the cab."

"Yes, quite likely. Did you get its number?"

"No. Didn't you notice it either?"

"No."

They looked at each other aghast. Finally Loisel got dressed again.

"I'll retrace our steps on foot," he said, "to see if I can find it."

And he went out. She remained in her evening clothes, without the strength to go to bed, slumped in a chair in the unheated room, her mind a blank.

Her husband came in about seven o'clock. He had had no luck.

He went to the police station, to the newspapers to post a reward, to the cab companies, everywhere the slightest hope drove him.

That evening Loisel returned, pale, his face lined; still he had learned nothing.

"We'll have to write your friend," he said, "to tell her you have broken the catch and are having it repaired. That will give us a little time to turn around."

She wrote to his dictation.

At the end of a week, they had given up all hope.

And Loisel, looking five years older, declared, "We must take steps to replace that piece of jewelry."

The next day they took the case to the jeweler whose name they found inside. He consulted his records. "I didn't sell that necklace, madame," he said. "I only supplied the case."

Then they went from one jeweler to another hunting for a similar necklace, going over their recollections, both sick with despair and anxiety.

They found, in a shop in Palais Royal,[18] a string of diamonds that seemed exactly like the one they were seeking. It was priced at forty thousand francs. They could get it for thirty-six.

They asked the jeweler to hold it for them for three days. And they reached an agreement that he would take it back for thirty-four thousand if the one lost was found before the end of February.

Loisel had eighteen thousand francs he had inherited from his father. He would borrow the rest.

He went about raising the money, asking a thousand francs from one, four hundred from another, a hundred here, sixty there. He signed notes, made ruinous deals, did business with loan sharks, ran the whole gamut[19] of moneylenders. He compromised the rest of his life, risked his signature without knowing if he'd be able to honor it, and then, terrified by the outlook for the future, by the blackness of despair about to close around him, by the prospect of all the privations[20] of the body and tortures of the spirit, he went to claim the new necklace with the thirty-six thousand francs that he placed on the counter of the shopkeeper.

When Mme. Loisel took the necklace back, Mme. Forestier said to her frostily, "You should have brought it back sooner; I might have needed it."

She didn't open the case, an action her friend was afraid of. If she had noticed the substitution, what would she have thought? What would she have said? Would she have thought her a thief?

Mme. Loisel experienced the horrible life the needy live. She played her part, however,

---

18. **Palais Royal** (pà lā′ rɔ̄i yāl′): a section of Paris with expensive shops.

19. **ran the whole gamut** (gam′ et): covered the entire range or extent.

20. **privations** (prī vā′ shənz): absence of what is needed for a healthy existence.

with sudden heroism. That frightful debt had to be paid. She would pay it. She dismissed her maid; they rented a garret under the eaves.

She learned to do the heavy housework, to perform the hateful duties of cooking. She washed dishes, wearing down her shell-pink nails scouring the grease from pots and pans; she scrubbed dirty linen, shirts, and cleaning rags, which she hung on a line to dry; she took the garbage down to the street each morning and brought up water, stopping on each landing to get her breath. And, clad like a peasant woman, basket on arm, guarding sou[21] by sou her scanty allowance, she bargained with the fruit dealers, the grocer, the butcher, and was insulted by them.

Each month notes had to be paid and others renewed to give more time.

Her husband labored evenings to balance a tradesman's accounts, and at night, often, he copied documents at five sous a page.

And this went on for ten years.

Finally, all was paid back, everything including the exorbitant[22] rates of the loan sharks and accumulated compound interest.

Mme. Loisel appeared an old woman now. She became heavy, rough, harsh, like one of the poor. Her hair untended, her skirts askew, her hands red, her voice shrill, she even slopped water on her floors and scrubbed them herself. But, sometimes, while her husband was at work, she would sit near the window and think of that long-ago evening when, at the dance, she had been so beautiful and admired.

What would have happened if she had not lost that necklace? Who knows? Who can say? How strange and unpredictable life is! How little there is between happiness and misery!

Then one Sunday when she had gone for a walk on the Champs Élysées[23] to relax a bit from the week's labors, she suddenly noticed a woman strolling with a child. It was Mme. Forestier, still young looking, still beautiful, still charming.

Mme. Loisel felt a rush of emotion. Should she speak to her? Of course. And now that everything was paid off, she would tell her the whole story. Why not?

She went toward her. "Hello, Jeanne."

The other, not recognizing her, showed astonishment at being spoken to so familiarly by this common person. She stammered. "But . . . madame . . . I don't recognize . . . You must be mistaken."

"No, I'm Mathilde Loisel."

Her friend gave a cry, "Oh, my poor Mathilde, how you've changed!"

"Yes, I've had a hard time since last seeing you. And plenty of misfortunes—and all on account of you!"

"Of me . . . How do you mean?"

"Do you remember that diamond necklace you loaned me to wear to the dance at the Ministry?"

"Yes, but what about it?"

"Well, I lost it."

"You lost it! But you returned it."

"I brought you another just like it. And we've been paying for it for ten years now. You can imagine that wasn't easy for us who had nothing. Well, it's over now, and I am glad of it."

Mme. Forestier stopped short, "You mean to say you bought a diamond necklace to replace mine?"

"Yes. You never noticed, then? They were quite alike."

---

21. **sou** (so͞o): a French coin that was worth about a penny.
22. **exorbitant** (eg zor′ bi tənt): unreasonably high.
23. **Champs Élysées** (shan′ zā lē zā′): "Flysian Fields"; a famous and fashionable boulevard in Paris.

And she smiled with proud and simple joy. Mme. Forestier, quite overcome, clasped her by the hands. "Oh, my poor Mathilde. But mine was only paste.[24] Why, at most it was worth only five hundred francs!"

---

24. **paste** (pāst): a hard, brilliant glass used to make artificial gems.

# Thinking About the Story

## A PERSONAL RESPONSE

*sharing impressions*

**1.** How do you feel about Madame Loisel by the end of this story? In your journal jot down words and phrases that describe your feelings.

*constructing interpretations*

**2.** How does Madame Loisel change as a result of her experiences?
### Think about
- what Madam Loisel values in life
- the positive and negative qualities she exhibits
- whether any of her values or qualities change

**3.** Review the list of values that you created before reading. Compare yourself with Madame Loisel.

**4.** Find points in the story at which Madame Loisel and her husband make choices. Which do you think are the most important choices?
### Think about
- the key choices that the characters make
- the consequences of each choice
- whether the choices were foolish or sensible
- what might have happened if they had made different choices

## A CREATIVE RESPONSE

**5.** The narrator asks, "What would have happened if she [Madame Loisel] had not lost that necklace?" What do you think might have happened?

## A CRITICAL RESPONSE

**6.** What might the necklace symbolize for Madame Loisel?

***Think about***
- a symbol as a person, place, object, or activity that stands for something beyond itself
- the real value of the necklace
- why Madame Loisel wants the necklace in the first place

**7.** What things have changed and what things have not changed for women since the days of Madame Loisel? Use examples to support your opinions.

# *Analyzing the Writer's Craft*

## IRONY

Which events in this story were quite different from what you anticipated? Which events did not turn out the way that Madame Loisel expected?

**Building a Literary Vocabulary.** Irony of situation occurs when what happens in a story contrasts with what a reader or character expects. In this story, for example, both Madame Loisel and the reader suppose that because Madame Forestier is rich, the diamond necklace is real. In fact, the Loisels, who are poor, end up buying a real necklace.

**Application: Identifying Irony.** Working with a group of classmates, identify the five or six main events in this story. For each event decide whether the event is ironic or at least contains ironic elements. Share your conclusions with the class.

# *Connecting Reading and Writing*

**1.** This story ends when Madame Forestier reveals that the lost necklace was false. Tell what might have happened next in a **scene** from a story.

Option: Write the additional episode as the last stanza of a **narrative poem.**

**2.** Imagine that Madame Loisel seeks advice the day after the reception. Write her plea and the advisor's response in the form of a **dialogue** between Madame Loisel and a friend.

Option: Write **letters** to and from an advice columnist.

**3.** Apply the saying "Success is getting what you want, but happiness is wanting what you get" to the characters in "The Necklace." Present your ideas in **notes** for a speech.

Option: Explain your ideas in a brief **exposition** addressed to Madame Loisel.

**4.** Imagine that Madame Loisel is a teenager today. Adapt the story of "The Necklace" to a modern setting and write an **outline** for the story.

Option: Tell the story through **diary entries.**

# The Lie

## KURT VONNEGUT, JR.

A biography of Vonnegut appears on page 647.

## *Approaching the Story*

Being the child of well-to-do parents can mean many things. For Eli Remenzel in this story, it means that his family expects him to attend an exclusive preparatory school, a private residential high school that prepares students for college. Prep schools are often partially funded by wealthy graduates who still feel ties to the school. In some families, several successive generations have attended the same school, so that the prep school becomes part of family tradition.

## *Building Vocabulary*

These essential words are footnoted within the story.

**reserve** (ri zʉrv´): Sylvia enjoyed arguing with her husband about her lack of **reserve** and his excess of it. (page 136)

**inconceivable** (in´ kən sēv´ ə bəl): It was **inconceivable** to them that Eli could not go there. (page 138)

**wretchedly** (rech´ id lē): "I know," said Eli **wretchedly**. (page 139)

**expansively** (ek span´ siv lē): "Certainly, of course," said Doctor Remenzel **expansively**. (page 140)

**incredulity** (in´ krə do͞o´ lə tē): "A letter from me," said Doctor Warren, with growing **incredulity**. (page 140)

## *Connecting Writing and Reading*

In what areas of your life do you feel the most pressure to succeed? Make a pie graph in your journal showing how much pressure you feel in the following areas: academics, athletics, social relations, finances, other. For example, if you feel the most pressure to succeed as an athlete, you might label a large part of the pie graph "athletic pressure." As you read, note in your journal the pressures that you see affecting the characters in this story.

I T WAS EARLY springtime. Weak sunshine lay cold on old gray frost. Willow twigs against the sky showed the golden haze of fat catkins about to bloom. A black Rolls-Royce streaked up the Connecticut Turnpike from New York City. At the wheel was Ben Barkley, a black chauffeur.

"Keep it under the speed limit, Ben," said Doctor Remenzel. "I don't care how ridiculous any speed limit seems; stay under it. No reason to rush—we have plenty of time."

Ben eased off on the throttle. "Seems like in the springtime she wants to get up and go," he said.

"Do what you can to keep her down—OK?" said the doctor.

"Yes, sir!" said Ben. He spoke in a lower voice to the thirteen-year-old boy who was riding beside him, to Eli Remenzel, the doctor's son. "Ain't just people and animals feel good in the springtime," he said to Eli. "Motors feel good too."

"Um," said Eli.

"Everything feel good," said Ben. "Don't you feel good?"

"Sure, sure I feel good," said Eli emptily.

"Should feel good—going to that wonderful school," said Ben.

The wonderful school was the Whitehill School for Boys, a private preparatory school in North Marston, Massachusetts. That was where the Rolls-Royce was bound. The plan was that Eli would enroll for the fall semester, while his father, a member of the class of 1939, attended a meeting of the Board of Overseers of the school.

"Don't believe this boy's feeling so good, doctor," said Ben. He wasn't particularly serious about it. It was more a genial springtime blather.

"What's the matter, Eli?" said the doctor absently. He was studying blueprints, plans for a thirty-room addition to the Eli Remenzel Memorial Dormitory—a building named in honor of his great-great-grandfather. Doctor Remenzel had the plans draped over a walnut table that folded out of the back of the front seat. He was a massive, dignified man, a physician, a healer for healing's sake, since he had been born as rich as the Shah of Iran. "Worried about something?" he asked Eli without looking up from the plans.

"Nope," said Eli.

Eli's lovely mother, Sylvia, sat next to the doctor, reading the catalog of the Whitehill School. "If I were you," she said to Eli, "I'd be so excited I could hardly stand it. The best four years of your whole life are just about to begin."

"Sure," said Eli. He didn't show her his face. He gave her only the back of his head, a pinwheel of coarse brown hair above a stiff white collar, to talk to.

"I wonder how many Remenzels have gone to Whitehill," said Sylvia.

"That's like asking how many people are dead in a cemetery," said the doctor. He gave the answer to the old joke, and to Sylvia's question too. "All of 'em."

"If all the Remenzels who went to Whitehill were numbered, what number would Eli be?" said Sylvia. "That's what I'm getting at."

The question annoyed Doctor Remenzel a little. It didn't seem in very good taste. "It isn't the sort of thing you keep score on," he said.

"Guess," said his wife.

"Oh," he said, "you'd have to go back through all the records, all the way back to the end of the eighteenth century, even, to make any kind of a guess. And you'd have to decide whether to count the Schofields and the Haleys and the MacLellans as Remenzels."

"Please make a guess—" said Sylvia, "just people whose last names were Remenzel."

"Oh—" The doctor shrugged, rattled the plans. "Thirty maybe."

"So Eli is number thirty-one!" said Sylvia, delighted with the number. "You're number thirty-one, dear," she said to the back of Eli's head.

Doctor Remenzel rattled the plans again. "I don't want him going around saying something asinine, like he's number thirty-one," he said.

"Eli knows better than that," said Sylvia. She was a game, ambitious woman, with no money of her own at all. She had been married for sixteen years but was still openly curious and enthusiastic about the ways of families that had been rich for many generations.

"Just for my own curiosity—not so Eli can go around saying what number he is," said Sylvia, "I'm going to go wherever they keep the records and find out what number he is. That's what I'll do while you're at the meeting and Eli's doing whatever he has to do at the Admissions Office."

"All right," said Doctor Remenzel, "you go ahead and do that."

"I will," said Sylvia. "I think things like that are interesting, even if you don't." She waited for a rise[1] on that but didn't get one. Sylvia enjoyed arguing with her husband about her lack of reserve[2] and his excess of it, enjoyed saying, toward the end of arguments like that, "Well, I guess I'm just a simple-minded country girl at heart, and that's all I'll ever be; and I'm afraid you're going to have to get used to it."

But Doctor Remenzel didn't want to play that game. He found the dormitory plans more interesting.

"Will the new rooms have fireplaces?" said Sylvia. In the oldest part of the dormitory, several of the rooms had handsome fireplaces.

"That would practically double the cost of construction," said the doctor.

"I want Eli to have a room with a fireplace, if that's possible," said Sylvia.

"Those rooms are for seniors."

"I thought maybe through some fluke—" said Sylvia.

"What kind of fluke do you have in mind?" said the doctor. "You mean I should demand that Eli be given a room with a fireplace?"

"Not *demand*—" said Sylvia.

"Request firmly?" said the doctor.

"Maybe I'm just a simple-minded country girl at heart," said Sylvia, "but I look through this catalog, and I see all the buildings named after Remenzels, look through the back and see all the hundreds of thousands of dollars given by Remenzels for scholarships, and I just can't help thinking people named Remenzel are entitled to ask for a little something extra."

"Let me tell you in no uncertain terms," said Doctor Remenzel, "that you are not to ask for anything special for Eli—not anything."

"Of course I won't", said Sylvia. "Why do you always think I'm going to embarrass you?"

"I don't," he said.

"But I can still think what I think, can't I?" she said.

"If you have to," he said.

"I have to," she said cheerfully, utterly unrepentant. She leaned over the plans. "You think those people will like those rooms?"

"What people?" he said.

"The Africans," she said. She was talking about thirty Africans who, at the request of the State Department, were being admitted to Whitehill in the coming semester. It was because of them that the dormitory was being expanded.

"The rooms aren't for them," he said. "They aren't going to be segregated."

"Oh," said Sylvia. She thought about this awhile, and then she said, "Is there a chance Eli will have to have one of them for a roommate?"

---

1. **rise** (rīz): response to teasing or provoking; from the expression "a fish rising to the bait."
2. **reserve** (ri zɨrv'): strict control over the expression of thoughts and feelings.

"Freshmen draw lots for roommates," said the doctor. "That piece of information's in the catalog too."

"Eli?" said Sylvia.

"H'm?" said Eli.

"How would you feel about it if you had to room with one of those Africans?"

Eli shrugged listlessly.

"That's all right?" said Sylvia.

Eli shrugged again.

"I guess it's all right," said Sylvia.

"It had better be," said the doctor.

The Rolls-Royce pulled abreast of an old Chevrolet, a car in such bad repair that its back door was lashed shut with clothesline. Doctor Remenzel glanced casually at the driver, and then, with sudden excitement and pleasure, he told Ben Barkley to stay abreast of the car.

The doctor leaned across Sylvia, rolled down his window, yelled to the driver of the old Chevrolet, "Tom! Tom!"

The man was a Whitehill classmate of the doctor. He wore a Whitehill necktie, which he waved at Doctor Remenzel in gay recognition. And then he pointed to the fine young son who sat beside him, conveyed with proud smiles and nods that the boy was bound for Whitehill.

Doctor Remenzel pointed to the chaos of the back of Eli's head; beamed that his news was the same. In the wind blustering between the two cars they made a lunch date at the Holly House in North Marston, at the inn whose principal business was serving visitors to Whitehill.

"All right," said Doctor Remenzel to Ben Barkley, "drive on."

"You know," said Sylvia, "somebody really ought to write an article—" And she turned to look through the back window at the old car now shuddering far behind. "Somebody really ought to."

"What about?" said the doctor. He noticed that Eli had slumped way down in the front seat. "Eli!" he said sharply. "Sit up straight!" He turned his attention to Sylvia.

"Most people think prep schools are such snobbish things, just for people with money," said Sylvia, "but that isn't true." She leafed through the catalog and found the quotation she was after.

> "The Whitehill School operates on the assumption," she read, "that no boy should be deterred from applying for admission because his family is unable to pay the full cost of a Whitehill education. With this in mind, the Admissions Committee selects each year from approximately 3,000 candidates the 150 most promising and deserving boys, regardless of their parents' ability to pay the full $2,200 tuition. And those in need of financial aid are given it to the full extent of their need. In certain instances, the school will even pay for the clothing and transportation of a boy."

Sylvia shook her head. "I think that's perfectly amazing. It's something most people don't realize at all. A truck driver's son can come to Whitehill."

"If he's smart enough," he said.

"Thanks to the Remenzels," said Sylvia with pride.

"And a lot of other people too," said the doctor.

Sylvia read out loud again: "In 1799, Eli Remenzel laid the foundation for the present Scholarship Fund by donating to the school forty acres in Boston. The school still owns twelve of those acres, their current evaluation being $3,000,000."

"Eli!" said the doctor. "Sit up! What's the matter with you?"

Eli sat up again, but began to slump almost immediately, like a snowman in the sun. Eli had good reason for slumping, for actually hoping to die or disappear. He could not bring himself to say what the reason was. He slumped because he knew he had been denied admission to Whitehill. He had failed the entrance examinations. Eli's parents did not know this, because Eli had found the awful notice in the mail and had torn it up.

Doctor Remenzel and his wife had no doubts whatsoever about their son's getting into Whitehill. It was inconceivable[3] to them that Eli could not go there, so they had no curiosity as to how Eli had done on the examinations, were not puzzled when no report ever came.

"What all will Eli have to do to enroll?" said Sylvia, as the black Rolls-Royce crossed the Rhode Island border.

"I don't know," said the doctor. "I suppose they've got it all complicated now with forms to be filled out in quadruplicate, and punch-card machines and bureaucrats. This business of entrance examinations is all new, too. In my day a boy simply had an interview with the headmaster. The headmaster would look him over, ask him a few questions, and then say, 'There's a Whitehill boy.'"

"Did he ever say, 'There isn't a Whitehill boy'?" said Sylvia.

"Oh sure," said Doctor Remenzel, "if a boy was impossibly stupid or something. There have to be standards. There have always been standards. The African boys have to meet the standards, just like anybody else. They aren't getting in just because the State Department wants to make friends. We made that clear. Those boys had to meet the standards."

"And they did?" said Sylvia.

"I suppose," said Doctor Remenzel. "I heard they're all in, and they all took the same examination Eli did."

"Was it a hard examination, dear?" Sylvia asked Eli. It was the first time she'd thought to ask.

"Um," said Eli.

"What?" she said.

"Yes," said Eli.

"I'm glad they've got high standards," she said, and then she realized that this was a fairly silly statement. "Of course they've got high standards," she said. "That's why it's such a famous school. That's why people who go there do so well in later life."

Sylvia resumed her reading of the catalog again, opened out a folding map of "The Sward," as the campus of Whitehill was traditionally called. She read off the names of features that memorialized Remenzels—the Sanford Remenzel Bird Sanctuary, the George MacLellan Remenzel Skating Rink, the Eli Remenzel Memorial Dormitory, and then she read out loud a quatrain printed on one corner of the map:

*"When night falleth gently*
*Upon the green Sward,*
*It's Whitehill, dear Whitehill,*
*Our thoughts all turn toward."*

"You know," said Sylvia, "school songs are so corny when you just read them. But when I hear the Glee Club sing those words, they sound like the most beautiful words ever written, and I want to cry."

"Um," said Doctor Remenzel.

"Did a Remenzel write them?"

"I don't think so," said Doctor Remenzel. And then he said, "No—Wait. That's the *new* song. A Remenzel didn't write it. Tom Hilyer wrote it."

"The man in that old car we passed?"

"Sure," said Doctor Remenzel. "Tom wrote it. I remember when he wrote it."

"A scholarship boy wrote it?" said Sylvia. "I think that's awfully nice. He *was* a scholarship boy, wasn't he?"

"His father was an ordinary automobile mechanic in North Marston."

---

3. **inconceivable** (in' kən sēv' ə bəl): that cannot be imagined or believed; unthinkable.

"You hear what a democratic school you're going to, Eli?" said Sylvia.

Half an hour later Ben Barkley brought the limousine to a stop before the Holly House, a rambling country inn twenty years older than the Republic. The inn was on the edge of the Whitehill Sward, glimpsing the school's rooftops and spires over the innocent wilderness of the Sanford Remenzel Bird Sanctuary.

Ben Barkley was sent away with the car for an hour and a half. Doctor Remenzel shepherded Sylvia and Eli into a familiar, low-ceilinged world of pewter, clocks, lovely old woods, agreeable servants, elegant food and drink.

Eli, clumsy with horror of what was surely to come, banged a grandmother clock with his elbow as he passed, made the clock cry.

Sylvia excused herself. Doctor Remenzel and Eli went to the threshold of the dining room, where a hostess welcomed them both by name. They were given a table beneath an oil portrait of one of the three Whitehill boys who had gone on to become President of the United States.

The dining room was filling quickly with families. What every family had was at least one boy about Eli's age. Most of the boys wore Whitehill blazers—black, with pale-blue piping, with Whitehill seals on the breast pockets. A few, like Eli, were not yet entitled to wear blazers, were simply hoping to get in.

The doctor ordered a drink, then turned to his son and said, "Your mother has the idea that you're entitled to special privileges around here. I hope you don't have that idea too."

"No, sir," said Eli.

"It would be a source of greatest embarrassment to me," said Doctor Remenzel with considerable grandeur, "if I were ever to hear that you had used the name Remenzel as though you thought Remenzels were something special."

"I know," said Eli <u>wretchedly</u>.[4]

"That settles it," said the doctor. He had nothing more to say about it. He gave abbreviated salutes to several people he knew in the dining room, speculated as to what sort of party had reserved a long banquet table that was set up along one wall. He decided that it was for a visiting athletic team. Sylvia arrived, and Eli had to be told in a sharp whisper to stand when a woman came to a table.

Sylvia was full of news. The long table, she related, was for the thirty boys from Africa. "I'll bet that's more black people than have eaten here since this place was founded," she said softly. "How fast things change these days!"

"You're right about how fast things change," said Doctor Remenzel. "You're wrong about the black people who've eaten here. This used to be a busy part of the Underground Railroad."[5]

"Really?" said Sylvia. "How exciting." She looked all about herself in a birdlike way. "I think everything's exciting here. I only wish Eli had a blazer on."

Doctor Remenzel reddened. "He isn't entitled to one," he said.

"I know that," said Sylvia.

"I thought you were going to ask somebody for permission to put a blazer on Eli right away," said the doctor.

"I wouldn't do that," said Sylvia, a little offended now. "Why are you always afraid I'll embarrass you?"

"Never mind. Excuse me. Forget it," said Doctor Remenzel.

Sylvia brightened again, put her hand on Eli's arm, and look radiantly at a man in the dining-room doorway. "There's my favorite

---

4. **wretchedly** (rech′ id lē): very unhappily; miserably.

5. **Underground Railroad:** a system set up by opponents of slavery before the Civil War to help fugitive slaves escape to free states and Canada.

person in all the world, next to my son and husband," she said. She meant Dr. Donald Warren, headmaster of the Whitehill school. A thin gentleman in his early sixties, Doctor Warren was in the doorway with the manager of the inn, looking over the arrangements for the Africans.

It was then that Eli got up abruptly, fled the dining room, fled as much of the nightmare as he could possibly leave behind. He brushed past Doctor Warren rudely, though he knew him well, though Doctor Warren spoke his name. Doctor Warren looked after him sadly.

"I'll be darned," said Doctor Remenzel. "What brought that on?"

"Maybe he really *is* sick," said Sylvia.

The Remenzels had no time to react more elaborately, because Doctor Warren spotted them and crossed quickly to their table. He greeted them, some of his perplexity about Eli showing in his greeting. He asked if he might sit down.

"Certainly, of course," said Doctor Remenzel <u>expansively</u>.[6] "We'd be honored if you did. Heavens."

"Not to eat," said Doctor Warren. "I'll be eating at the long table with the new boys. I would like to talk, though." He saw that there were five places set at the table. "You're expecting someone?"

"We passed Tom Hilyer and his boy on the way," said Doctor Remenzel. "They'll be along in a minute."

"Good, good," said Doctor Warren absently. He fidgeted, looked again in the direction in which Eli had disappeared.

"Tom's boy will be going to Whitehill in the fall?" said Doctor Remenzel.

"H'm?" said Doctor Warren. "Oh—yes, yes. Yes, he will."

"Is he a scholarship boy, like his father?" said Sylvia.

"That's not a polite question," said Doctor Remenzel severely.

"I beg your pardon," said Sylvia.

"No, no—that's a perfectly proper question these days," said Doctor Warren. "We don't keep that sort of information very secret any more. We're proud of our scholarship boys, and they have every reason to be proud of themselves. Tom's boy got the highest score anyone's ever got on the entrance examinations. We feel privileged to have him."

"We never *did* find out Eli's score," said Doctor Remenzel. He said it with good-humored resignation, without expectation that Eli had done especially well.

"A good strong medium, I imagine," said Sylvia. She said this on the basis of Eli's grades in primary school, which had ranged from medium to terrible.

The headmaster looked surprised. "I didn't tell you his scores?" he said.

"We haven't seen you since he took the examinations," said Doctor Remenzel.

"The letter I wrote you—" said Doctor Warren.

"What letter?" said Doctor Remenzel. "Did we get a letter?"

"A letter from me," said Doctor Warren, with growing <u>incredulity</u>.[7] "The hardest letter I ever had to write."

Sylvia shook her head. "We never got any letter from you."

Doctor Warren sat back, looking very ill. "I mailed it myself," he said. "It was definitely mailed—two weeks ago."

Doctor Remenzel shrugged. "The U.S. mails don't lose much," he said, "but I guess that now and then something gets misplaced."

Doctor Warren cradled his head in his hands. "Oh, dear—oh, my, oh, Lord," he said. "I was surprised to see Eli here. I wondered

---

6. **expansively** (ek span′ siv lē): in an open, generous way.

7. **incredulity** (in′ krə dōō′ lə tē): complete inability to believe.

that he would want to come along with you."

"He didn't come along just to see the scenery," said Doctor Remenzel. "He came to enroll."

"I want to know what was in the letter," said Sylvia.

Doctor Warren raised his head, folded his hands. "What the letter said was this, and no other words could be more difficult for me to say: '*On the basis of his work in primary school and his scores on the entrance examinations, I must tell you that your son and my good friend Eli cannot possibly do the work required of boys at Whitehill.*'" Doctor Warren's voice steadied, and so did his gaze. "'*To admit Eli to Whitehill, to expect him to do Whitehill work,*'" he said, "'*would be both unrealistic and cruel.*'"

Thirty African boys, escorted by several faculty members, State Department men, and diplomats from their own countries, filed into the dining room.

And Tom Hilyer and his boy, having no idea that something had just gone awfully wrong for the Remenzels, came in, too, and said hello to the Remenzels and Doctor Warren gaily, as though life couldn't possibly be better.

"I'll talk to you more about this later, if you like," Doctor Warren said to the Remenzels, rising. "I have to go now, but later on—" He left quickly.

"My mind's a blank," said Sylvia. "My mind's a perfect blank."

Tom Hilyer and his boy sat down. Hilyer looked at the menu before him, clapped his hands and said, "What's good? I'm hungry." And then he said, "Say—where's your boy?"

"He stepped out for a moment," said Doctor Remenzel evenly.

"We've got to find him," said Sylvia to her husband.

"In time, in due time," said Doctor Remenzel.

"That letter," said Sylvia; "Eli knew about it. He found it and tore it up. Of course he did!" She started to cry, thinking of the hideous trap Eli had caught himself in.

"I'm not interested right now in what Eli's done," said Doctor Remenzel. "Right now I'm a lot more interested in what some other people are going to do."

"What do you mean?" said Sylvia.

Doctor Remenzel stood impressively, angry and determined. "I mean," he said, "I'm going to see how quickly people can change their minds around here."

"Please," said Sylvia, trying to hold him, trying to calm him, "we've got to find Eli. That's the first thing."

"The first thing," said Doctor Remenzel quite loudly, "is to get Eli admitted to Whitehill. After that we'll find him, and we'll bring him back."

"But darling—" said Sylvia.

"No 'but' about it," said Doctor Remenzel. "There's a majority of the Board of Overseers in this room at this very moment. Every one of them is a close friend of mine, or a close friend of my father. If they tell Doctor Warren Eli's in, that's it—Eli's in. If there's room for all these other people," he said, "there's darn well room for Eli too."

He strode quickly to a table nearby, sat down heavily, and began to talk to a fierce-looking and splendid old gentleman who was eating there. The old gentleman was chairman of the board.

Sylvia apologized to the baffled Hilyers and then went in search of Eli.

Asking this person and that person, Sylvia found him. He was outside—all alone on a bench in a bower of lilacs that had just begun to bud.

Eli heard his mother's coming on the gravel path, stayed where he was, resigned. "Did you find out," he said, "or do I still have to tell you?"

"About you?" she said gently. "About not getting in? Doctor Warren told us."

"I tore his letter up," said Eli.

"I can understand that," she said. "Your father and I have always made you feel that you had to go to Whitehill, that nothing else would do."

"I feel better," said Eli. He tried to smile, found he could do it easily. "I feel so much better now that it's over. I tried to tell you a couple of times—but I just couldn't. I didn't know how."

"That's my fault, not yours," she said.

"What's father doing?" said Eli.

Sylvia was so intent on comforting Eli that she'd put out of her mind what her husband was up to. Now she realized that Doctor Remenzel was making a ghastly mistake. She didn't want Eli admitted to Whitehill, could see what a cruel thing that would be.

She couldn't bring herself to tell the boy what his father was doing, so she said, "He'll be along in a minute, dear. He understands." And then she said, "You wait here, and I'll go get him and come right back."

But she didn't have to go to Doctor Remenzel. At that moment, the big man came out of the inn and caught sight of his wife and son. He came to her and to Eli. He looked dazed.

"Well?" she said.

"They—they all said no," said Doctor Remenzel, very subdued.

"That's for the best," said Sylvia. "I'm relieved. I really am."

"Who said no?" said Eli. "Who said no to what?"

"The members of the board," said Doctor Remenzel, not looking anyone in the eye. "I asked them to make an exception in your case—to reverse their decision and let you in."

Eli stood, his face filled with incredulity and shame that were instant. "You what?" he said, and there was no childishness in the way he said it. Next came anger. "You shouldn't have done that!" he said to his father.

Doctor Remenzel nodded. "So I've already been told."

"That isn't done!" said Eli. "How awful! You shouldn't have!"

"You're right," said Doctor Remenzel, accepting the scolding lamely.

"Now I *am* ashamed," said Eli, and he showed that he was.

Doctor Remenzel, in his wretchedness, could find no strong words to say. "I apologize to you both," he said at last. "It was a very bad thing to try."

"Now a Remenzel *has* asked for something," said Eli.

"I don't suppose Ben's back yet with the car?" said Doctor Remenzel. It was obvious that Ben wasn't. "We'll wait out here for him," he said. "I don't want to go back in there now."

"A Remenzel asked for something—as though a Remenzel were something special," said Eli.

"I don't suppose—" said Doctor Remenzel, and he left the sentence unfinished, dangling in the air.

"You don't suppose what?" said his wife, her face puzzled.

"I don't suppose," said Doctor Remenzel, "that we'll ever be coming here any more."

# Thinking About the Story

## A PERSONAL RESPONSE

*sharing
impressions*

**1.** What do you think about the family relationships in this story? Briefly note your thoughts in your journal.

*constructing
interpretations*

**2.** Who do you think feels the most pressure in this story, and why?

**3.** Compare the ways in which Doctor and Mrs. Remenzel react to the news that Eli has not been admitted to Whitehill.
### Think about
- their behavior when they hear the news
- the pressures that motivate their behavior
- the losses they each face

**4.** At the beginning of the story, Doctor Remenzel appears to dominate both his wife and his son. How does this family relationship change during the story?

**5.** What situations in the story do you think the title refers to?
### Think about
- who hides the truth in the story
- the different ways the truth is hidden
- why a character might choose to hide the truth

## A CREATIVE RESPONSE

**6.** How might the story be different if Eli had been accepted to Whitehill but still did not want to go?

## A CRITICAL RESPONSE

**7.** What events of the story would you describe as ironic?
### Think about
- dramatic irony as the contrast between what a character in a story knows about events and what the reader knows
- situational irony as the contrast between what the reader expects and what actually happens

**8.** How do the pressures that the Remenzel family face compare to the pressures faced by Monsieur and Madame Loisel in "The Necklace"?

## Analyzing the Writer's Craft

### THEME

What do you think of the relationships within the Remenzel family?

**Building a Literary Vocabulary.** Theme is the central idea or message in a work of literature. It is the writer's perception about life or humanity that is shared with the reader. Often a clue to theme occurs in the title of a story. Interestingly for "The Lie," the letters in *lie* also spell *Eli*. However, Kurt Vonnegut shows that behind Eli's lie about Whitehill is a family relationship that fosters dishonesty. At the beginning of the story, Doctor and Mrs. Remenzel are so ambitious for their son's future at Whitehill that they fail to notice his silence and withdrawal on the way to the school. This insensitivity to Eli's feelings in the car reflects their larger ignorance of his academic abilities, for it seems clear from his low score on the extrance examination that Eli is not "a Whitehill boy." Because Doctor and Mrs. Remenzel have lost touch with their son, Eli does not feel free to express himself honestly. Thus the theme, or what Vonnegut may be saying through Eli's lie, is that a child's dishonesty often results from the parents' failure to recognize the child's individual needs, desires, and abilities. At the end of the story, Mrs. Remenzel reinforces this theme by acknowledging her mistake.

**Application: Stating Themes.** Most stories include several themes, one of which usually predominates. Look at what Vonnegut says about hypocrisy by having Doctor Remenzel ask the board at Whitehill to make an exception for Eli. Then think about the point Vonnegut makes about social snobbery through Mrs. Remenzel. Get together with a group of three classmates and come up with a statement that expresses each of these themes. Then share your thematic statements with other members of your class.

## Connecting Reading and Writing

**1.** Analyze the character of Mrs. Remenzel in an **article** for the society page of the local newspaper.

Option: Analyze Mrs. Remenzel's character in a **character sketch**.

**2.** Choose one of the themes of "The Lie" and explain how that theme is expressed by the characters and events of the story. **Outline** your ideas for a friend who has not read the story and who has asked, "What is the story about?"

Option: Analyze the theme in an **expository essay** for a classmate who missed the discussion of this story.

**3.** In a **note** of warning to a good friend, describe a situation in which you told a lie, large or small, that was later discovered.

Option: Compose a **letter** that Eli might have written to Dr. Warren in response to the rejection notice.

# Two Kinds

### AMY TAN

A biography of Tan appears on page 646.

## *Approaching the Story*

During the 1930's and 1940's China was invaded by the Japanese and was racked by political upheavals that led to a bitter civil war. Some Chinese citizens escaped these dangers by emigrating to the United States. Here they settled in California, primarily in San Francisco, their point of entry. To many Chinese immigrants life in the United States was so different from life in war-torn China that anything seemed possible, especially for their children. The children were expected to pursue the American dream of material success, without sacrificing the traditional Chinese values of obedience and respect for one's elders. "Two Kinds" is told by a young woman who, like Amy Tan herself, is the daughter of Chinese immigrants.

## *Building Vocabulary*

These essential words are footnoted within the story.

**prodigy** (präd´ ə jē): "Of course, you can be **prodigy**, too." (page 146)

**preludes** (prel´ yo͞odz), **discordant** (dis kôrd´ 'nt): I learned to play only the most ear-splitting **preludes**, the most **discordant** hymns. (page 149)

**devastated** (dev´ əs tāt´ ed): But my mother's expression was what **devastated** me: a quiet, blank look that said she had lost everything. (page 151)

**fiasco** (fē äs´ kō): I assumed my talent-show **fiasco** meant I never had to play the piano again. (page 151)

## *Connecting Writing and Reading*

Imagine that your mother has decided that you should study to be a concert violinist. She tells you that you must practice for two hours after school every day, even though you would rather spend that time with your friends. How would you respond to your mother's expectations? Write a few phrases in your journal describing your probable response. Then during your reading of "Two Kinds," notice how the narrator responds to her mother's expectations.

# Two Kinds

MY MOTHER BELIEVED you could be anything you wanted to be in America. You could open a restaurant. You could work for the government and get good retirement. You could buy a house with almost no money down. You could become rich. You could become instantly famous.

"Of course, you can be <u>prodigy</u>,[1] too," my mother told me when I was nine. "You can be best anything. What does Auntie Lindo know? Her daughter, she is only best tricky."

America was where all my mother's hopes lay. She had come to San Francisco in 1949 after losing everything in China: her mother and father, her family home, her first husband, and two daughters, twin baby girls. But she never looked back with regret. There were so many ways for things to get better.

We didn't immediately pick the right kind of prodigy. At first my mother thought I could be a Chinese Shirley Temple.[2] We'd watch Shirley's old movies on TV as though they were training films. My mother would poke my arm and say, *"Ni kan"*—You watch. And I would see Shirley tapping her feet, or singing a sailor song, or pursing her lips into a very round O while saying, "Oh my goodness."

*"Ni kan,"* said my mother as Shirley's eyes flooded with tears. "You already know how. Don't need talent for crying!"

Soon after my mother got this idea about Shirley Temple, she took me to a beauty training school in the Mission district and put me in the hands of a student who could barely hold the scissors without shaking. Instead of getting big fat curls, I emerged with an uneven mass of crinkly black fuzz. My mother dragged me off to the bathroom and tried to wet down my hair.

"You look like Negro Chinese," she lamented, as if I had done this on purpose.

The instructor of the beauty training school had to lop off these soggy clumps to make my hair even again. "Peter Pan is very popular these days," the instructor assured my mother. I now had hair the length of a boy's, with straight-across bangs that hung at a slant two inches above my eyebrows. I liked the haircut and it made me actually look forward to my future fame.

In fact, in the beginning, I was just as excited as my mother, maybe even more so. I pictured this prodigy part of me as many different images, trying each one on for size. I was a dainty ballerina girl standing by the curtains, waiting to hear the right music that would send me floating on my tiptoes. I was like the Christ child lifted out of the straw manger, crying with holy indignity. I was Cinderella stepping from her pumpkin carriage with sparkly cartoon music filling the air.

In all of my imaginings, I was filled with a sense that I would soon become *perfect*. My mother and father would adore me. I would be beyond reproach. I would never feel the need to sulk for anything.

But sometimes the prodigy in me became impatient. "If you don't hurry up and get me out of here, I'm disappearing for good," it warned. "And then you'll always be nothing."

---

1. **prodigy** (präd′ ə jē): a child who is amazingly talented or intelligent.
2. **Shirley Temple:** a popular child movie star of the 1930's.

Every night after dinner, my mother and I would sit at the Formica kitchen table. She would present new tests, taking her examples from stories of amazing children she had read in *Ripley's Believe It or Not,* or *Good Housekeeping, Reader's Digest,* and a dozen other magazines she kept in a pile in our bathroom. My mother got these magazines from people whose houses she cleaned. And since she cleaned many houses each week, we had a great assortment. She would look through them all, searching for stories about remarkable children.

The first night she brought out a story about a three-year-old boy who knew the capitals of all the states and even most of the European countries. A teacher was quoted as saying the little boy could also pronounce the names of the foreign cities correctly.

"What's the capital of Finland?" my mother asked me, looking at the magazine story.

All I knew was the capital of California, because Sacramento was the name of the street we lived on in Chinatown. "Nairobi!" I guessed, saying the most foreign word I could think of. She checked to see if that was possibly one way to pronounce "Helsinki" before showing me the answer.

The tests got harder—multiplying numbers in my head, finding the queen of hearts in a deck of cards, trying to stand on my head without using my hands, predicting the daily temperatures in Los Angeles, New York, and London.

One night I had to look at a page from the Bible for three minutes and then report everything I could remember. "Now Jehoshaphat had riches and honor in abundance and . . . that's all I remember, Ma," I said.

And after seeing my mother's disappointed face once again, something inside of me began to die. I hated the tests, the raised hopes and failed expectations. Before going to bed that night, I looked in the mirror above the bathroom sink and when I saw only my face staring back—and that it would always be this ordinary face—I began to cry. Such a sad, ugly girl! I made high-pitched noises like a crazed animal, trying to scratch out the face in the mirror.

And then I saw what seemed to be the prodigy side of me—because I had never seen that face before. I looked at my reflection, blinking so I could see more clearly. The girl staring back at me was angry, powerful. This girl and I were the same. I had new thoughts, willful thoughts, or rather thoughts filled with lots of won'ts. I won't let her change me, I promised myself. I won't be what I'm not.

So now on nights when my mother presented her tests, I performed listlessly, my head propped on one arm. I pretended to be bored. And I was. I got so bored I started counting the bellows of the foghorns out on the bay while my mother drilled me in other areas. The sound was comforting and reminded me of the cow jumping over the moon. And the next day, I played a game with myself, seeing if my mother would give up on me before eight bellows. After a while I usually counted only one, maybe two bellows at most. At last she was beginning to give up hope.

Two or three months had gone by without any mention of my being a prodigy again. And then one day my mother was watching *The Ed Sullivan Show*[3] on TV. The TV was old and the sound kept shorting out. Every time my mother got halfway up from the sofa to adjust the set, the sound would go back on and Ed would be talking. As soon as she sat down, Ed would go silent again. She got up, the TV broke into loud piano music. She sat down. Silence. Up and down, back and forth, quiet and loud. It was like a stiff embraceless dance

---

3. ***The Ed Sullivan Show:*** a weekly variety-program television series of the 1950's and 1960's.

between her and the TV set. Finally she stood by the set with her hand on the sound dial.

She seemed entranced by the music, a little frenzied piano piece with this mesmerizing quality, sort of quick passages and then teasing lilting ones before it returned to the quick playful parts.

"*Ni kan,*" my mother said, calling me over with hurried hand gestures, "Look here."

I could see why my mother was fascinated by the music. It was being pounded out by a little Chinese girl, about nine years old, with a Peter Pan haircut. The girl had the sauciness of a Shirley Temple. She was proudly modest like a proper Chinese child. And she also did this fancy sweep of a curtsy, so that the fluffy skirt of her white dress cascaded slowly to the floor like the petals of a large carnation.

In spite of these warning signs, I wasn't worried. Our family had no piano and we couldn't afford to buy one, let alone reams of sheet music and piano lessons. So I could be generous in my comments when my mother badmouthed the little girl on TV.

"Play note right, but doesn't sound good! No singing sound," complained my mother.

"What are you picking on her for?" I said carelessly. "She's pretty good. Maybe she's not the best, but she's trying hard." I knew almost immediately I would be sorry I said that.

"Just like you," she said. "Not the best. Because you not trying." She gave a little huff as she let go of the sound dial and sat down on the sofa.

The little Chinese girl sat down also to play an encore of "Anitra's Dance" by Grieg. I remember the song, because later on I had to learn how to play it.

Three days after watching *The Ed Sullivan Show,* my mother told me what my schedule would be for piano lessons and piano practice. She had talked to Mr. Chong, who lived on the first floor of our apartment building. Mr. Chong was a retired piano teacher and my mother had traded housecleaning services for weekly lessons and a piano for me to practice on every day, two hours a day, from four until six.

When my mother told me this, I felt as though I had been sent to hell. I whined and then kicked my foot a little when I couldn't stand it anymore.

"Why don't you like me the way I am? I'm *not* a genius! I can't play the piano. And even if I could, I wouldn't go on TV if you paid me a million dollars!" I cried.

My mother slapped me. "Who ask you be genius?" she shouted. "Only ask you be your best. For you sake. You think I want you be genius? Hnnh! What for! Who ask you!"

"So ungrateful," I heard her mutter in Chinese. "If she had as much talent as she has temper, she would be famous now."

Mr. Chong, whom I secretly nicknamed Old Chong, was very strange, always tapping his fingers to the silent music of an invisible orchestra. He looked ancient in my eyes. He had lost most of the hair on top of his head and he wore thick glasses and had eyes that always looked tired and sleepy. But he must have been younger than I thought, since he lived with his mother and was not yet married.

I met Old Lady Chong once and that was enough. She had this peculiar smell like a baby that had done something in its pants. And her fingers felt like a dead person's, like an old peach I once found in the back of the refrigerator; the skin just slid off the meat when I picked it up.

I soon found out why Old Chong had retired from teaching piano. He was deaf. "Like Beethoven!" he shouted to me. "We're both listening only in our head!" And he would start to conduct his frantic silent sonatas.

Our lessons went like this. He would open the book and point to different things, explaining their purpose: "Key! Treble! Bass! No sharps or flats! So this is C major! Listen now and play after me!"

And then he would play the C scale a few times, a simple chord, and then, as if inspired by an old, unreachable itch, he gradually added more notes and running trills and a pounding bass until the music was really something quite grand.

I would play after him, the simple scale, the simple chord, and then I just played some nonsense that sounded like a cat running up and down on top of garbage cans. Old Chong smiled and applauded and then said, "Very good! But now you must learn to keep time!"

So that's how I discovered that Old Chong's eyes were too slow to keep up with the wrong notes I was playing. He went through the motions in half-time. To help me keep rhythm, he stood behind me, pushing down on my right shoulder for every beat. He balanced pennies on top of my wrists so I would keep them still as I slowly played scales and arpeggios. He had me curve my hand around an apple and keep that shape when playing chords. He marched stiffly to show me how to make each finger dance up and down, staccato like an obedient little soldier.

He taught me all these things, and that was how I also learned I could be lazy and get away with mistakes, lots of mistakes. If I hit the wrong notes because I hadn't practiced enough, I never corrected myself. I just kept playing in rhythm. And Old Chong kept conducting his own private reverie.

So maybe I never really gave myself a fair chance. I did pick up the basics pretty quickly, and I might have become a good pianist at that young age. But I was so determined not to try, not to be anybody different that I learned to play only the most ear-splitting <u>preludes</u>,[4] the most <u>discordant</u>[5] hymns.

Over the next year, I practiced like this, dutifully in my own way. And then one day I heard my mother and her friend Lindo Jong both talking in a loud bragging tone of voice so others could hear. It was after church, and I was leaning against the brick wall wearing a dress with stiff white petticoats. Auntie Lindo's daughter, Waverly, who was about my age, was standing farther down the wall about five feet away. We had grown up together and shared all the closeness of two sisters squabbling over crayons and dolls. In other words, for the most part, we hated each other. I thought she was snotty. Waverly Jong had gained a certain amount of fame as "Chinatown's Littlest Chinese Chess Champion."

"She bring home too many trophy," lamented Auntie Lindo that Sunday. "All day she play chess. All day I have no time do nothing but dust off her winnings." She threw a scolding look at Waverly, who pretended not to see her.

"You lucky you don't have this problem," said Auntie Lindo with a sigh to my mother.

And my mother squared her shoulders and bragged: "Our problem worser than yours. If we ask Jing-mei wash dish, she hear nothing but music. It's like you can't stop this natural talent."

And right then, I was determined to put a stop to her foolish pride.

A few weeks later, Old Chong and my mother conspired to have me play in a talent show which would be held in the church hall. By then, my parents had saved up enough to buy me a secondhand piano, a black Wurlitzer spinet with a scarred bench. It was the showpiece of our living room.

For the talent show, I was to play a piece called "Pleading Child" from Schumann's *Scenes from Childhood*. It was a simple, moody

---

4. **preludes** (prel′ yo͞odz): introductory musical works.

5. **discordant** (dis kôrd′ ′nt): not in harmony; clashing.

piece that sounded more difficult than it was. I was supposed to memorize the whole thing, playing the repeat parts twice to make the piece sound longer. But I dawdled over it, playing a few bars and then cheating, looking up to see what notes followed. I never really listened to what I was playing. I daydreamed about being somewhere else, about being someone else.

The part I liked to practice best was the fancy curtsy: right foot out, touch the rose on the carpet with a pointed foot, sweep to the side, left leg bends, look up and smile.

My parents invited all the couples from the Joy Luck Club[6] to witness my debut. Auntie Lindo and Uncle Tin were there. Waverly and her two older brothers had also come. The first two rows were filled with children both younger and older than I was. The littlest ones got to go first. They recited simple nursery rhymes, squawked out tunes on miniature violins, twirled Hula Hoops, pranced in pink ballet tutus, and when they bowed or curtsied, the audience would sigh in unison, "Awww," and then clap enthusiastically.

When my turn came, I was very confident. I remember my childish excitement. It was as if I knew, without a doubt, that the prodigy side of me really did exist. I had no fear whatsoever, no nervousness. I remember thinking to myself, This is it! This is it! I looked out over the audience, at my mother's blank face, my father's yawn, Auntie Lindo's stiff-lipped smile, Waverly's sulky expression. I had on a white dress layered with sheets of lace, and pink bow in my Peter Pan haircut. As I sat down I envisioned people jumping to their feet and Ed Sullivan rushing up to introduce me to everyone on TV.

And I started to play. It was so beautiful. I was so caught up in how lovely I looked that at first I didn't worry how I would sound. So it was a surprise to me when I hit the first wrong note and I realized something didn't sound quite right. And then I hit another and another followed that. A chill started at the top of my head and began to trickle down. Yet I couldn't stop playing, as though my hands were bewitched. I kept thinking my fingers would adjust themselves back, like a train switching to the right track. I played this strange jumble through two repeats, the sour notes staying with me all the way to the end.

When I stood up, I discovered my legs were shaking. Maybe I had just been nervous and the audience, like Old Chong, had seen me go through the right motions and had not heard anything wrong at all. I swept my right foot out, went down on my knee, looked up and smiled. The room was quiet, except for Old Chong, who was beaming and shouting, "Bravo! Bravo! Well done!" But then I saw my mother's face, her stricken face. The audience clapped weakly, and as I walked back to my chair, with my whole face quivering as I tried not to cry, I heard a little boy whisper loudly to his mother, "That was awful," and the mother whispered back, "Well, she certainly tried."

And now I realized how many people were in the audience, the whole world it seemed. I was aware of eyes burning into my back. I felt the shame of my mother and father as they sat stiffly throughout the rest of the show.

We could have escaped during intermission. Pride and some strange sense of honor must have anchored my parents to their chairs. And so we watched it all: the eighteen-year-old boy with a fake mustache who did a magic show and juggled flaming hoops while riding a unicycle. The girl with white makeup who sang from *Madama Butterfly* and got honorable mention. And the eleven-year-old boy who won first prize playing a tricky violin song that sounded like a busy bee.

After the show, the Hsus, the Jongs, and the

---

6. **Joy Luck Club:** the social group to which the family in this story belongs.

St. Clairs from the Joy Luck Club came up to my mother and father.

"Lots of talented kids," Auntie Lindo said vaguely, smiling broadly.

"That was somethin' else," said my father, and I wondered if he was referring to me in a humorous way, or whether he even remembered what I had done.

Waverly looked at me and shrugged her shoulders. "You aren't a genius like me," she said matter-of-factly. And if I hadn't felt so bad, I would have pulled her braids and punched her stomach.

But my mother's expression was what devastated[7] me: a quiet, blank look that said she had lost everything. I felt the same way, and it seemed as if everybody were now coming up, like gawkers at the scene of an accident, to see what parts were actually missing. When we got on the bus to go home, my father was humming the busy-bee tune and my mother was silent. I kept thinking she wanted to wait until we got home before shouting at me. But when my father unlocked the door to our apartment, my mother walked in and then went to the back, into the bedroom. No accusations. No blame. And in a way, I felt disappointed. I had been waiting for her to start shouting, so I could shout back and cry and blame her for all my misery.

I assumed my talent-show fiasco[8] meant I never had to play the piano again. But two days later, after school, my mother came out of the kitchen and saw me watching TV.

"Four clock," she reminded me as if it were any other day. I was stunned, as though she were asking me to go through the talent-show torture again. I wedged myself more tightly in front of the TV.

"Turn off TV," she called from the kitchen five minutes later.

I didn't budge. And then I decided. I didn't have to do what my mother said anymore. I wasn't her slave. This wasn't China. I had listened to her before and look what happened. She was the stupid one.

She came out from the kitchen and stood in the arched entryway of the living room. "Four clock," she said once again, louder.

"I'm not going to play anymore," I said nonchalantly. "Why should I? I'm not a genius."

She walked over and stood in front of the TV. I saw her chest was heaving up and down in an angry way.

"No!" I said, and I now felt stronger, as if my true self had finally emerged. So this was what had been inside me all along.

"No! I won't!" I screamed.

She yanked me by the arm, pulled me off the floor snapped off the TV. She was frighteningly strong, half pulling, half carrying me toward the piano as I kicked the throw rugs under my feet. She lifted me up and onto the hard bench. I was sobbing by now, looking at her bitterly. Her chest was heaving even more and her mouth was open, smiling crazily as if she were pleased I was crying.

"You want me to be someone that I'm not!" I sobbed. "I'll never be the kind of daughter you want me to be!"

"Only two kinds of daughters," she shouted in Chinese. "Those who are obedient and those who follow their own mind! Only one kind of daughter can live in this house. Obedient daughter!"

"Then I wish I wasn't your daughter. I wish you weren't my mother," I shouted. As I said these things I got scared. It felt like worms and toads and slimy things crawling out of my chest, but it also felt good, as if this awful side of me had surfaced, at last.

"Too late change this," said my mother shrilly.

And I could sense her anger rising to its breaking point. I wanted to see it spill over.

---

7. **devastated** (dev′ əs tāt′ ed): destroyed completely.
8. **fiasco** (fē äs′ kō): a complete or ridiculous failure.

And that's when I remembered the babies she had lost in China, the ones we never talked about. "Then I wish I'd never been born!" I shouted. "I wish I were dead! Like them."

It was as if I had said the magic words. Alakazam!—and her face went blank, her mouth closed, her arms went slack, and she backed out of the room, stunned, as if she were blowing away like a small brown leaf, thin, brittle, lifeless.

It was not the only disappointment my mother felt in me. In the years that followed, I failed her so many times, each time asserting my own will, my right to fall short of expectations. I didn't get straight As. I didn't become class president. I didn't get into Stanford. I dropped out of college.

For unlike my mother, I did not believe I could be anything I wanted to be. I could only be me.

And for all those years, we never talked about the disaster at the recital or my terrible accusations afterward at the piano bench. All that remained unchecked, like a betrayal that was now unspeakable. So I never found a way to ask her why she had hoped for something so large that failure was inevitable.

And even worse, I never asked her what frightened me the most: Why had she given up hope?

For after our struggle at the piano, she never mentioned my playing again. The lessons stopped. The lid to the piano was closed, shutting out the dust, my misery, and her dreams.

So she surprised me. A few years ago, she offered to give me the piano, for my thirtieth birthday. I had not played in all those years. I saw the offer as a sign of forgiveness, a tremendous burden removed.

"Are you sure?" I asked shyly. "I mean, won't you and Dad miss it?"

"No, this your piano," she said firmly. "Always your piano. You only one can play."

"Well, I probably can't play anymore," I said. "It's been years."

"You pick up fast," said my mother, as if she knew this was certain. "You have natural talent. You could been genius if you want to."

"No I couldn't."

"You just not trying," said my mother. And she was neither angry nor sad. She said it as if to announce a fact that could never be disproved. "Take it," she said.

But I didn't at first. It was enough that she had offered it to me. And after that, every time I saw it in my parents' living room, standing in front of the bay windows, it made me feel proud, as if it were a shiny trophy I had won back.

Last week I sent a tuner over to my parents' apartment and had the piano reconditioned, for purely sentimental reasons. My mother had died a few months before and I had been getting things in order for my father, a little bit at a time. I put the jewelry in special silk pouches. The sweaters she had knitted in yellow, pink, bright orange—all the colors I hated—I put those in moth-proof boxes. I found some old Chinese silk dresses, the kind with little slits up the sides. I rubbed the old silk against my skin, then wrapped them in tissue and decided to take them home with me.

After I had the piano tuned, I opened the lid and touched the keys. It sounded even richer than I remembered. Really, it was a very good piano. Inside the bench were the same exercise notes with handwritten scales, the same secondhand music books with their covers held together with yellow tape.

I opened up the Schumann book to the dark little piece I had played at the recital. It was on the left-hand side of the page, "Pleading Child." It looked more difficult than I remembered. I played a few bars, surprised at how easily the notes came back to me.

And for the first time, or so it seemed, I noticed the piece on the right-hand side. It was called "Perfectly Contented." I tried to play this one as well. It had a lighter melody but the same flowing rhythm and turned out to be quite easy. "Pleading Child" was shorter but slower; "Perfectly Contented" was longer, but faster. And after I played them both a few times, I realized they were two halves of the same song.

# Thinking About the Story

## A PERSONAL RESPONSE

*sharing impressions*

**1.** What words describe your feelings about the two main characters in the story? Write these words in your journal.

*constructing interpretations*

**2.** What might the narrator mean when she says that "Pleading Child" and "Perfectly Contented" are "two halves of the same song"?
### Think about
- why she plays the piano again after her mother dies
- how the songs might express her feelings about her relationship with her mother

**3.** Why do you think the narrator's feelings about being a prodigy change during the story?
### Think about
- her daydreams at the beginning of the story
- her response to her mother's expectations
- her own opinions about herself

**4.** Who do you think is right in the story, the mother or the daughter?
### Think about
- how realistic the mother's expectations are
- how the mother treats the daughter
- how the daughter treats the mother

## A CREATIVE RESPONSE

**5.** How might this story be different if the mother had not lost the two babies in China?

**6.** Explain to what extent the conflict between the narrator and her mother is resolved in the story. Support your interpretation with examples from the story.

**7.** Compare the ways in which Madame Loisel, Eli Remenzel, and the daughter in "Two Kinds" respond to the pressures and expectations of their communities or families.

**8.** Amy Tan wrote the following about the book from which "Two Kinds" is taken: "When I was writing, it was so much for my mother and myself. I wanted her to know what I thought about China and what I thought about growing up in this country. And I wanted those words to almost fall off the page so that she could just see the story, almost like a little curtain that would fall away." Analyze to what extent you think Tan succeeded at writing a story that can be easily visualized by all readers.

# Analyzing the Writer's Craft

## FIGURATIVE LANGUAGE: SIMILE

Comparisons often capture feelings and sensations better than direct descriptions do. For example, the narrator describes Old Lady Chong's fingers in two comparisons: "And her fingers felt like a dead person's, like an old peach I once found in the back of the refrigerator; the skin just slid off the meat when I picked it up." What effect do these comparisons have on you?

**Building a Literary Vocabulary.** Figurative language is language that communicates ideas beyond the literal meanings of the words. The comparisons of Old Lady Chong's fingers to those of a corpse and to a rotten peach are figurative expressions called similes. A simile compares two things in a phrase that contains *like* or *as*. The similes in the description of Old Lady Chong's fingers help the reader to imagine the feeling of loose skin over cold, shrunken flesh. The similes also show in a humorous way the perspective of a child who considers old age creepy.

**Application: Identifying Similes.** Working in a group, find at least five similes in the story. For each example, create a diagram similar to the one that follows.

**Example from story**

"And her fingers felt like a dead person's, like an old peach I once found in the back of the refrigerator; the skin just slid off the meat when I picked it up."

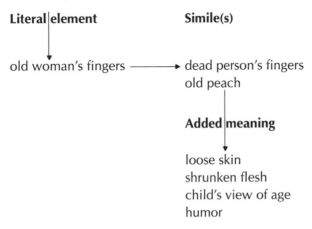

**Literal element**

old woman's fingers ⟶

**Simile(s)**

dead person's fingers
old peach

**Added meaning**

loose skin
shrunken flesh
child's view of age
humor

After you have diagramed five examples, choose the one simile that your group likes best and diagram it for your class on the board or on a large sheet of paper.

# Connecting Reading and Writing

**1.** Imagine that you are a school counselor and the narrator has come to you with her problem. How will you respond when she tells you about her conflict with her mother? Create a **dialogue** between yourself and the narrator.

Option: Write a **letter** of concern and advice to the mother, in the voice of a school counselor.

**2.** Review your prereading notes about how you would react to your parents' expectations for you to be a violinist. Write a **dramatic skit** that more fully portrays your response to your parents.

Option: Write about your response to your parents in a brief **story**.

**3.** In newspaper and magazine articles research the adjustments that children of immigrants must make. Use the information to create a set of **guidelines** for your school to follow in dealing with students from immigrant families.

Option: Write a **summary** of what you have learned.

# The Cave

JEAN McCORD

A biography of McCord appears on page 642.

## Approaching the Story

Like "Two Kinds," "The Cave" is told in the main character's own words. Charley recounts the central events in the story after having spent three days thinking about them. He speaks directly and conversationally, mentioning names and places as though he assumes the reader will be able to follow his train of thought. In the opening paragraphs, Charley refers to George, whose acquaintance with Charley is the basis for the story.

GEORGE IS GONE. He's either dead, or he's crawled off into one of the deep caves and laid himself down in darkness and silence to die. How long do you think it will take for an old man to die of a broken heart?

I know I'm to blame. I had my part in what happened, except right at the last when the guys went and did what they did. I wasn't in on that, but I might as well have been. It was the same in the end, anyway. When the work and the glory was gone, there was simply no reason for George to go on living.

Why do things happen like that in life? Things you do or cause to be done like me, and you don't even know what's going on, what it really means, at the time.

I was the only one who knew about him at first.

One Saturday morning in early spring, I'd left the house for a run. My bones are growing fast, and sometimes I get these aches in my knees. When I'm all scrunched up behind my desk in school, they ache all the more. The only thing that helps is to get away by myself and run along the banks of the Godalming River. My mother frequently says, "Charles, you eat like a horse these days." What she doesn't know is that I feel like a horse, too. I run along the trails on the riverbank for miles, the blood pounding in my throat, the clap of my hooves beating against the dirt, the wind tickling through my mane, before I finally collapse and throw myself down on the ground, and my hooves turn back into smelly canvas sneakers.

That morning I'd been galloping long and hard to get the kinks out of my knees. The riverbanks are high and steep where we live, overgrown with trees that lean outward and trails that wind along for miles. Once they were animal trails, I think; then the Chippewa Indians lived here and must have used them. Nobody knows all the trails; they run at different levels, dipping and rising with the contour of the banks. I'd gotten a little further than I'd ever been before, changing levels, first up high near the top of the cliffs, then running swiftly downhill by a crosstrail. I'd suddenly seen a new path angling up from the river road, had swung into it, and loped along uphill as far as I could until a stitch in my side made me stop.

There was a spring there, bubbling up into a little pool under the roots of a tree. I leaned over and drank like a horse drinks, lips barely touching water, sucking it up noisily. The water was as clear as sunlight, and cold, and tasted slightly brown from the leaves lying in it.

When I raised my head I was looking up the hill about twenty feet, and I saw something hidden behind some brush. I wish now I'd gone on and let it be, but my curiosity always drives me like I was some snoopy girl, fingering something in her best friend's dresser drawer. I went soundlessly up the hill in my sneakers, noticing there were no steps or trail to give this away, whatever it was. I got up to it and found it was the mouth of a cave, high on the hill with a perfect view up and down the river. It had been boarded over with two-by-fours and some rough, river-washed planks. A skinny door hung slightly open on leather hinges.

I started to stick my nose in the crack when, just then, a voice remarked behind my back, "Looking for something?" and I spun around so fast and so guilty I almost fell down the hill.

There was an old man sitting casually under a tree and keeping so still that I hadn't even seen him. But he had been watching me, probably since the moment I'd stopped to drink.

He looked so weird I recognized him right away for what he was, a bum, yet he wasn't like any other bum I'd ever seen. His hair was long and tangled, falling almost to his shoulders like a Bible prophet's, and his face was a mass of porcupine bristles, not having been shaved in weeks. His nose was a narrow, anxious-looking beak, but his brown eyes were as soft as the spring water, and his mouth was clamped on the broken stub of a pipe, unlit. I

took time to look him over instead of bolting as had been my first intention since there was that look in his eye that told me he was harmless. Besides, what was there to be afraid of? I hadn't done anything.

"Sit down, boy, if you like." He motioned me over.

I went and squatted, looking up and down at the view companionably.

After a while he spoke again. "Got a name?"

I almost said, "Yes, sir, Charles," but I stopped myself. "Charley," I grunted.

"Good name," he said. "Long lineage;[1] way back. You heard of Charlemagne?"[2]

"Yes." I looked at him curiously. I'd studied that in history class, but where had he heard about the guy?

"Same name. Means Charley the Greatest. A royal name. Dozens of crowned heads answered to it."

"Oh yeah?" I was interested in spite of myself. Now why hadn't the teacher mentioned that? It might have made that history class a little easier to take. But our history teacher always droned on, reading from our textbook like he was a hive of bees on a warm day. After a while, your ears got hypnotized and heard what he was saying, but the meaning was completely gone.

"Got a pretty royal name myself," the old bum was saying. "George. Same as six kings of England, two of Greece, a Pres. of the U.S. of A., and a saint who was quite a dragon hunter.[3] Not that it's ever brought me much."

---

1. **lineage** (lin′ ē ij): descent from an ancestor; family line.
2. **Charlemagne** (shär′ lə mān′): King of the Franks and emperor of the Roman Empire who lived from A.D. 742 to 814.
3. **a saint . . . dragon hunter:** the patron saint of England, a reference to St. George, a legendary dragon slayer.

He was looking ruefully at his pipe, which was quite empty. And then to make it look funny and make me laugh, which I did, he wriggled his big toe, which was sticking clean out of the tip of one shoe. I wished I had some tobacco to give him, but I didn't. Maybe another time.

"You live in there?" I jerked my thumb at the boards hiding the cave.

"Well, let's just say it's my Passport to Paradise."

Urrgh, I thought, this old boy's got a few bats flying round in his belfry. But he had my curiosity aroused again, just the same. I'll come back tomorrow and bring him some tobacco, I thought. I can take some from my Dad and he'll never miss it.

As it happened, I didn't return the next day because my folks made me go with them to visit Aunt Margaret.

A week later, Saturday again, I wrapped some tobacco in a handkerchief and headed back to see old George. Usually I would have gone to the clubhouse and spent the day with my gang. I belong to the Jesse James[4] gang. When you live in a city like ours where all the tough kids seem jammed together on the South Side, you either join a gang or get your head knocked off. We're not really fierce guys, not like some of the gangs you read about in other parts of the country. We don't have police records, and we don't go in for mugging or robbery or any of that stuff. We just got together for protection, you might say, and it depends mostly on where a guy lives as to what gang he'll belong to. The toughest gang of all live down on the river flats and call themselves the River Rats. We all stay away from them, much as we can. The River Rats are . . . well, I just wouldn't have wanted to belong to them, not then.

I was walking on the new trail leading to George's place, going slowly so I could look at the sun shining through the trees with a green light. I felt a sudden prickle of cold air on my neck, and the coolness led me like the flow of a little stream falling downhill, right to a small opening that slanted down into the ground. I knew it was the air hole for some cave, a new one, one I'd never been in. You see, the cliffs are made of limestone, and waters trickling down through them for millions of years have cut out many caves. The mouths of the large ones are down at the present river level, and they are mostly all in use as mushroom caves. There are huge steel doors blocking them off, and the mushroom growers have made long beds inside of dirt and manure. Dim electric lights swing down the middle, and the temperature is always a cool 55° which is perfect for mushrooms but chilly for a person.

My gang had been in lots of mushroom caves, but we had to sneak in by the air holes and stand a chance of getting caught by the mushroom growers. They would shout at us, threatening to call the police if they saw us in the shadowy darkness of their stinking caves, thinking we were going to steal their old toadstools. Who wanted them? We never even touched them, except to kick over a few once in a while. The stuff they grew in was too much for us. Outside the caves were big banks of manure, steaming in the cool drafts and smelling like something you'd rather not even get close to.

For a long time now we'd been looking for an unused cave, one we could keep secret for ourselves. We wanted to hold meetings there, safe from the other neighborhood gangs, have initiations, and just sit around in the darkness lit up by a warm fire and chew the fat. We were pretty sure there were a few caves not grabbed off by the mushroom tycoons if we could just find them.

This was it. I knew when I brushed the dirt

---

4. **Jesse James:** U.S. outlaw who lived from 1847 to 1882.

away a little and peered down into the darkness leading into the hillside like a large animal's burrow, that this would be our own cave. I would go tell the gang about it.

I ran all the way back, putting my best into being one of the greatest, Man O'War,[5] and made about as good a time as possible for a horse with only two legs.

The gang was all gathered at the usual place, an abandoned coal shed. They were itchy with restlessness, and it made the perfect announcement.

"You're late, Charley," Pat Dalloway, our leader, said out of the side of his mouth. He likes to act like John Dillinger[6] or the head of the Mafia. He narrowed his eyes while I was giving the details of my discovery.

"What are we waiting for?" Butts yelped. He's a barky type, like a scared dog, and lives on the far side of town. He's only in our Jesse James gang because he's Pat Dalloway's cousin.

"Lead on, boy!" "Let's go!" Chunky and Ted and the others were yelling.

They followed me, a pounding troop at my heels, though we had to stop several times for Chunky to catch his breath.

We clustered round at the spot, and Pat fell on his knees and stuck his head into the hole. He pulled it out again quickly. "It's a good one, Charley," he said with a grin at the gang, "and since you were the finder, to you goes the honor."

I opened my mouth to protest because going into a cave for the first time is always scary. You know such things as saber-toothed tigers and floating ghosts don't really exist, but when you are in total darkness in an unknown place with only a small flashlight, you become suddenly positive they not only do, they are breathing down your neck that instant.

"No, no, we can't have it any other way, can we, boys?" Pat said as he saw my face.

I could only swallow and shrug, but I thought to myself, OK Dalloway, but a couple

more times like this and I'll be ready to take over the gang. It takes guts to be the leader, and Pat seemed to be slacking up a bit.

I took one flashlight in my hand and dropped another inside my shirt. Then I stuck my head in the hole and lay down on my stomach. I was prepared for a gentle, short drop that would end in a small cave from which I'd holler back at the others to "come on in."

Only, after wriggling in till my feet were out of sight of the gang, this little hole took me by surprise and suddenly slanted down at a swift angle. There was nothing to grab at along the way, just the soft sandstone walls worn into smoothness by the ancient waters. I slid down the hole like I was on one of those little tin chutes at a kid's playground, and it occurred to me, sliding like an otter, trying to drag my elbows and toes into the unyielding walls, that I could pop out of this into a really big cave with a nice little drop of maybe a couple hundred feet. I groaned. Why hadn't I had the sense to tie a rope around my waist and have the gang lower me easy? I'd never make a leader because I didn't have any brains, and a voice seemed to tell me I was going to have even fewer in a couple seconds.

I dropped on into what seemed the center of the earth and, when I'd given up hope, rolled out of that chute like a marble and fell about three feet to bounce on soft, cool sand. The flashlight shot out of my hand pointing away from me, its puny beam lost in the vastness of this black cavern. I sat there rubbing my hands and stomach to ease the smarting and feeling myself, but I was OK. However, the thought occurred to me before I even reached for the light, how was I going to get out? That hole was too steep and smooth to

---

5. **Man O' War:** a famous racehorse.

6. **John Dillinger** (dil' in jər): U.S. gangster and bank robber who lived from 1903 to 1934.

climb back up, and something told me the gang wasn't going to follow me in.

I crawled over to the flashlight. When I turned it up towards the ceiling its beam just got lost in the blackness. There was no sound in the cave. It felt as if there had never been a single sound ever in there. I went over to the hole I'd dropped out of and listened up it for the gang. I couldn't hear them. It was so spooky in that huge cave that it felt like I was down among the dead, like in the catacombs[7] I'd read about, and I even looked around a bit, but not too much. I couldn't see anything, just creamy yellow walls and white sand underfoot. I wondered if I was the first person who had ever been in here. It sure looked like it. There wasn't a mark on the walls, and I couldn't see any footprints. My light was wavering around, and I got a <u>desolate</u>[8] feeling that it was going to go out on me.

I knew the guys outside would notify somebody sooner or later, the firemen or police. Even my Dad. Or would they? I began to doubt even that, thinking maybe they might all go on home and be too scared to get themselves into any trouble with the police and might just decide to forget about me. Well, in a place like that, your mind just seems to run away from you.

I had to get out. I turned and started walking, hurrying for what seemed like miles, but there's nothing to judge by, so you don't really know how far. A few steps even seems like a long ways. My flashlight was dimming down, and my fear was growing. I started running, not even watching for anything, just trying to find some new hole, or an end of any kind. The back of my mind kept telling me that most of these big caves had open mouths down on the river level, but I had also heard that some of them emptied out beneath the water. And that would be just great!

The cave was so long and black I felt like Jonah[9] inside his whale. I felt I was going deeper into the earth all the time, but I couldn't tell about that, either. And just when my light was about to go out for good, and I was going to throw myself down and yell in terror for help, I saw a paleness around a bend.

I shot around the corner and found myself in a room about as big as our living room at home. It was still a cave, but someone was living in it. A few scraps of furniture sat around, made-up furniture of boxes and planks and junk. The front of the cave was boarded over with old planks, and a small door swung lazily on leather hinges.

I stopped right in the middle of it and looked around. And then I saw what was really so different from anyone's living room in a house. The walls were covered with statues. Not the kind carved from wood; these statues were cut right out of the walls in what our art teacher calls bas-relief.[10] They seemed almost to be living beings who were growing out of the rock, and all of them were watching me carefully. I was so glad to see the sunlight through the door, I could only sob with relief. But as usual my curiosity was still with me, so I looked around. On one wall I could recognize certain figures. One was Lincoln, surely, with his big nose and sad eyes. Next to him was George Washington, I thought. Another wall held a crucifixion scene with bent-over people seeming to writhe at the foot of it. Next to that was, holy cow, a real masterpiece, I thought in slow admiration. A guy on a horse, both of them wearing armor, was spearing a

---

7. **catacombs** (kat′ ə kōmz′): a series of galleries in an underground burial place.

8. **desolate** (des′ ə lit): miserable; comfortless.

9. **Jonah** (jō′ nə): a Hebrew prophet who was tossed overboard during a storm and was swallowed by a great fish.

10. **bas-relief** (bä′ ri lēf′) *French*: sculpture in which figures are carved in a flat surface so that they project only a little from the background.

dragon who was lashing around with claws and scales all over him. They were all big, more than life-size, and you could see that somebody had put an awful lot of work into them.

As I walked towards the swinging door, it struck me then. I'd seen that door before. I stepped through it, looked around feeling terribly foolish, and found myself staring right into George's startled eyes. I guess he'd never seen anyone walk out of his cave before.

"Hey!" he said.

"Yeah, I know." I waved my hand backwards. "I got lost." I grinned feebly. "A wicked witch changed me into a rabbit, and a dog chased me down a hole, and, well, here I am. . . ."

It was the best I could do, seeing I was so happy I wanted to run over and shake both his hands.

George looked at me a minute, then he laughed. "You're all right, kid," he said. "I told you Charley was a lucky name. Come and sit. You look pretty fagged out."

I stretched out beside him in the sun and squirmed with the pure pleasure of it on my body. Somewhere back in there I had thought I was doomed to wander in darkness for the rest of my life, which in that dry cave didn't seem to be too long to go. It was only when I rolled over on my stomach, wanting to hug the ground, that I felt the extra flashlight biting into me.

"What time is it?" I asked, my face against the dirt.

George squinted at the sun. "Mebbe two o'clock, or so."

I sighed. I'd been in the cave less than half an hour. It had seemed like days.

"That's pretty good stuff in there," I said cautiously. "It looks like . . . well . . . like a regular art gallery."

George looked down at his hands. They were square and blocky with dirt under the nails. "It fills my time," he said. He stared at them for a long time. Finally, gazing down the river, he said quietly, "Look, Charley. I don't pay no rent on that cave, but it's mine just the same. I found it first. I fixed it up. Been here over five years now, and I got a lot more work to do. I'm just beginning to get good." He looked at me, and I could actually see the pleading in his eyes. "If people knew about me, they'd come and drive me out. Against the law, or if it ain't, they'd make one. Now why don't you just go on home and keep your mouth shut. Here. Take this." He handed me a little bit of wood that he had been working on when I'd stepped out of his home. It was a tiny carved fawn, its legs folded under itself and its head bent like it was hiding from dogs who were hunting it.

"Well, gee. Thanks. Thanks a lot." I got up and stood there, tongue-tied. I wanted to say I was sorry I'd intruded, that it was just to save my neck, that I had to come out that way. But he must have known. After all, he knew that cave better than I did, and right then he was welcome to it, all of it. I had no intention of telling anyone; certainly not the gang, but I had to get back to them before they got up a lot of people looking for me.

I plunged down George's hill and onto the trail leading back to where I'd left the others. I ran pretty well. Maybe I'd never beat Man O'War in a straightaway, but I could sure make him blow a little on the curves. If he was still around, that is.

When I got to where I'd left the gang, I slowed down and sauntered up to them. They were all in a knot with serious looks on their faces, and when they turned around, their jaws dropped.

"You lily-livered chickens doing anything to get me out of there?" I blustered at them.

"Hey, Charley! Charley, old boy. We thought you were a goner, sure!" They were all shouting at once and pounding me on the back.

"You been in there before, wise guy, ain't you?" Pat scowled at me. "Tried to be smart. Snuck out another way and let us think you were lost." He was really mad. Some of the guys must have been riding him about getting some help to rescue me. His leadership was toppling, all right. Any day soon, now, Dalloway, I thought, I'm gonna fight you and win. I flexed my arm muscles. They felt good and tight to me.

But at the same time I was thinking desperately. What was I going to tell them to make them stay out of the cave? I had to think up a story, and a good one, quick. "Look," I said. "It ain't even a cave. It's just a kind of tunnel, not big enough for a cat. It goes down a long ways, straight, and then winds around and comes out behind the bend over there, somewhere. I didn't even mark it."

"You were gone too long," Pat said, shoving his face next to mine.

"I was scrabbling along on my belly, the whole way. See?" I showed them the raw marks on my arms and stomach. "It never gets more than two feet high, or wide. It ain't worth beans." I turned. "Come on. Let's go home. I'm starved."

"What you got in your hand, Charley? You must have found something."

I stared at my own hand like I'd never seen it before. I hadn't thought to put the little carving in my pocket. Then I did a stupid thing, which makes me think I'll never be fit to be a leader for a pack of mangy dogs. Instead of blustering it out, I gave a leap downhill and started running hard. With a head start none of them could catch me, and I raced along as fast as I'd ever run in my life before. I could hear them for a while pounding along almost at my back, but one by one, I outran them and got to my home.

I sped up to my bedroom, and in a couple minutes I could hear them all outside, hollering at me, "Charley, hey, come on out. We want to talk to you." But I wouldn't go.

Then I stayed away from the gang for a while. I'd see the fellows in school since we were in the same classes, but I didn't go to the clubhouse nor join them at the drugstore like I always had. And that seemed funny. To me, who had been thinking of taking over the gang any day, and to them, too, because they couldn't figure it out. There was no real reason except I thought I'd try being an individual for a change, instead of just one of a group who all did and thought the same things. And that mostly what Pat Dalloway said to do and think.

I took to visiting old George as often as I had time for it. He was a pretty smart old buzzard, and he seemed to know some secret about life. What I mean is, he had kind of come to terms with life, and he had made all the conditions. He sure didn't work, since every time I ever went there, except once, he was either outside looking at his view, possessing it, kind of, or in his cave doing a carving. He had started a new one of Knute Rockne,[11] which was going to be really great. He let me come into his place now and sit on the bunch of planks and old rags that was his bed. If I just sat and watched him and didn't ask a lot of nosy questions, he ignored me and went on with his work. I usually brought him some tobacco and whatever I could sneak out of the refrigerator behind my Mom's back. I guess she thought I'd suddenly developed a tapeworm because she'd look funny at me and frown once in a while, but never said anything.

At first I pried him a little. "Say, George, what you been doing all your life?"

"My life, boy? I lost it. Laid it down for a little and when I went back looking for it, it was too late. Gone. Just like that." He snapped his fingers.

---

11. **Knute Rockne** (no͞ot räk′ nē): a famous U.S. football player and coach who lived from 1888 to 1931.

"Where were you the other day?"

"Well, occasionally even an old hermit's got to go down into the morass[12] of humanity." He stepped back viewing his work. "If you can find me another picture of Knute here, why, I'd be might obliged."

"Sure." I knew where there was one. In my Dad's picture album. He'd played football when he was in college and was still crazy about the game.

George looked over at me. His beard was only about a half-inch long now because he'd shaved last week. It must have been the day he was gone, I thought. Wonder where he goes and for what? Maybe he's got some money stashed away in a bank and he goes for some every once in a while. I could see he'd bought a few groceries because they stood out in clear sight on a couple orange crates piled up, but I didn't know how he cooked or if he even bothered to. I knew he got his water from the little spring and kept several cans of it in the cave, which he used to throw on his new carving. It softened up the rock a little.

"You ever going to let people see all this some-day?" I asked. "When you're ready, I mean?"

"Maybe I should have done drawings with burnt sticks and red ochre.[13] Of ancient bison and vanished deer. That would have confused a few experts, I'll bet," he answered, almost to himself. If you could call that an answer. That's how George was. I liked being with George. He didn't expect anything of me like my Dad always did, and by now, I was getting pretty fond of the old guy. Oh, I knew he wasn't any Michelangelo,[14] but considering everything, he was pretty good. Lincoln and Washington and St. George and Christ and Knute Rockne and others. I loved the way he mixed them up like they were all friends of each other. Maybe they were.

"You know, Charley boy, " George seemed to be talking to Knute, but I was listening. "I been thinking. That's a big cave in behind there. Lots of beautiful walls. Nothing ever been done to them. My time . . . my grains of sand . . . are running through pretty fast now." He was silent till I thought he'd forgotten what he was talking about. Then he said, "You ever have a hankering to do a little carving?"

I shook my head "no," but his back was turned and he didn't see me.

"Old, old," he was muttering to Knute, "seventy-five, and that's the full allotment. Might not even get to finish this one." He jabbed at Knute's jaw. "It's a way of life, Charley my boy. The only way; creating things. Let others build the cars and roads and wooden houses. You know how long the cave drawings, the ones in southern France, been around?" He whirled on me with a fierce light in his eye.

I shook my head again.

"Fifteen, maybe twenty thousand years." He glared at me. "How do you like that for beating old Mister Time?"

I got up to go. It was getting late, and I didn't have anything to say to him.

"See you, George."

"Yuh," he grunted.

I didn't go back for three weeks. It was late Spring now, and final exams were coming up. Every time it looked like I was going to stick my nose out the door, either my Mom or Dad pounced on me and made me get to studying. The cave was too far to go to after school and still get home in time for supper, and weekends, like I say, I was kept hopping.

Finally school was out. I'd passed everything, and it was a real relief. I couldn't even stay mad at my parents for making me work

---

12. **morass** (mə ras′): swamp or bog: often used figuratively.

13. **ochre** (ō′ kər), also spelled **ocher:** clay used as a pigment.

14. **Michelangelo** (mī′ kəl an′ jə lō′): an Italian sculptor, painter, and architect who lived from 1475 to 1564.

because otherwise I probably wouldn't have made it.

But now I was free for the whole summer. Maybe next year when I'd be sixteen, I'd get a job of some sort, but this summer was still mine, to use as I wanted. I'd been thinking over the last few weeks that I'd spend most of it with old George. Secretly, I'd begun to think about carving. The old boy had something there. I knew he'd teach me. I thought of that long, beautiful, empty cave. We'd haul in firewood and build us a nice, warming fire which would give us light to work by. Maybe someday we could run in an electric line like the mushroom growers. People would come from all around.

My folks would be so surprised they'd be speechless. "Do you mean our boy Charles did this?" they'd say to George, and old George would grin and say, "Yep."

I took a loaf of bread, a half pound of salami from the cupboard, a pocketful of tobacco from my Dad's stock, and slipped off to the cliffs. Over the edge onto the trails and boy, it sure felt good to be running along them again. The trees were solid green now, and the river was running clean like a band of silver far below. Mourning doves were moaning their sad calls, and spiders had flung their lines across the trails overnight.

Coming up to George's cave, I slowed to catch my breath. When I looked up there, something was terribly wrong. The boards hiding the mouth of the cave were all knocked out, though you still couldn't see it from the trail unless you knew it was there. I stopped to listen a minute, and then I heard voices. I knew those voices.

I burst into George's living room, and the shock of it made me sick to my stomach. The whole cave was a mess, completely torn up. The furniture was busted so it was nothing now but old driftwood boards. A fire had been built right in the middle of the cave out of the orange crates. But worse than that, the statues had been destroyed. The delicate ones, the ones that had been carved out almost full, were knocked completely loose and lay on the cave floor as a pile of broken rubbish. The others had heads and arms missing and could never be fixed. "Looey," cross-eyed and stupid, was lounging on what was left of the beautiful horse; St. George had been scraped out of his saddle completely. The place was dirty. And George was nowhere around.

The gang, my gang, was sitting around smoking and looking smug.[15]

"Welcome to our new clubhouse, Charley old boy," Pat Dalloway said.

"Where's George?" My tongue seemed too thick to talk.

"You mean that old bum?" Pat chuckled. "He cleared out after we knocked up the place."

I stepped forward and kicked aside Knute Rockne's face. My fists were cocked.

"You dirty rats," I screamed. "You dirty, filthy no-good rats! Who gave you the right?"

"Aw, come on, Charley," big fat Chunky was saying. "That old bum didn't own this cave. We got as much right to it. We just chased him out and took over, that's all. You helped. We all went in that air hole and found out it ended here."

And that did it. Inside I was all broken up into little pieces. I knew what the outcome would be before I started, but from where I stood, I leaped at Pat and crashed him to the floor. We fought, slugging each other, biting and gouging, rolling over on top of broken statues. Pat was a pretty dirty fighter. He fought to win; no rules. Once I had him on his back and was choking him, but his hand came up with a fistful of sand right into my eyes. From there on he had it all his way. He fin-

---

15. **smug** (smug): self-satisfied; convinced of one's own superiority.

ished me off and for good measure gave me a couple extra kicks. No one else interfered. They knew it was between Pat and me.

"Get out," he panted. "You don't belong no more."

Butts and Jim dragged me out and threw me down the hill. My bread and salami had scattered all over. They tossed it after me. "So long, Charley," they said.

When I could move, I picked myself up and hobbled away. I took the trail going downhill. Tomorrow I would have two black eyes. A pretty way to start summer vacation. And my folks were in for a big surprise, all right, a big, fat dentist bill.

But it isn't over yet. In fact, it's just started.

I been lying up in my bedroom for three days now, thinking. My mother brings me hot soup and cries a little when she looks at me. My father wanted to go to the police and prosecute, but I wouldn't tell him anything. This is between me and my old gang.

To do a thing like that . . . to destroy an old man's dream of immortality[16] . . . to tear up what he called his Passport to Paradise . . . well . . . they're going to pay for it, all right.

Tomorrow I'm getting out of bed. I'm going down to the river flats and join that gang that calls themselves the River Rats. I'm going to fight every guy in it till I'm the leader.

Then I'm going to lead them to that cave.

Pat Dalloway . . . you are going to get what's coming to you!

Bill and Ted and Chunky. Jim and Butts and Looey . . .you are in for a big surprise. . . . When we descend on you . . . when we get through with you . . . you are going to feel just like those statues . . . .

---

16. **immortality** (im′ môr tal′ i tē): living or lasting forever.

# Out of This World: Science Fiction and the Macabre

ALMOST ALL OF the stories in the previous sections show believable characters in lifelike situations. The writers of those stories have chosen to portray the world in a way that readers will accept as realistic. Not all writers portray the world in easily recognizable ways, however. Some writers imagine what lies beyond the everyday.

Science fiction stories offer a universe of possibilities. Time travel, alien beings, war in outer space, incredible advances in technology — anything is possible in a science fiction story. After all, who really knows in what directions science will develop?

Instead of depicting a future or alien world, stories of the macabre reveal a mysterious world behind everyday life — a world filled with bizarre, gruesome, or horrifying events. The dark, the unexplained, the supernatural — these are the dimensions of the macabre.

As you read the stories in this section, expect the unexpected. Some of the stories will lead you into the future. All will lead you into the unknown. No matter what your destination, each story will take you out of this world.

*Belled Cat,* 1935,
HIROAKI TAKAHASHI.
By courtesy of the Trustees of the British Museum, London.

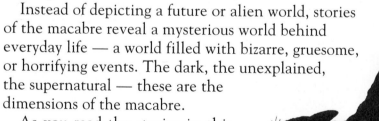

# Literary Vocabulary

## INTRODUCED IN THIS SECTION

**Science Fiction.** Science fiction is prose writing that presents the possibilities of the past or the future, using known scientific data and theories as well as the creative imagination of the writer. Most science fiction comments on present-day society through the writer's fictional conception of a past or future society.

**Tone.** Tone is the attitude a writer takes toward a subject. Style and description in a work of literature help create tone, which might be formal, informal, ironic, angry, serious, or playful. The tone of "The Ransom of Red Chief" is fairly easy to identify as humorous. Sometimes, however, tone is more difficult to identify. For example, the tone of "Two Kinds" might be described as bittersweet, reflecting the complex relationship between mother and daughter.

**Mood.** Mood is the feeling, or atmosphere, that the writer creates for the reader. Descriptive words, setting, and figurative language contribute to the mood of a work, as do the sound and rhythm of the language used. In the following passage from "Marigolds," notice how key descriptive words and long, rhythmic sentences help to create a somber mood of lingering regret.

> Miss Lottie died long ago and many years have passed since I last saw her hut, completely barren at last, for despite my wild contrition she never planted marigolds again. Yet, there are times when the image of those passionate yellow mounds returns with a painful poignancy. For one does not have to be ignorant and poor to find that one's life is barren as the dusty yards of one's town. And I too have planted marigolds.

**Allegory.** An allegory is a narrative in which the characters often stand for abstract ideas. Generally, an allegory teaches a lesson. For example, the parable of the Good Samaritan in the Bible tells of a Jewish man who is attacked by thieves and left for dead by the side of the road. Two religious leaders pass by but do not help him. Finally, a man from Samaria stops to help him, even though Jews and Samaritans generally despised each other. As an allegory, the parable teaches that anyone who needs help has a claim on another's charity, even if the two are enemies. The religious leaders stand for hypocrisy, and the Samaritan represents charity. Often a character's name indicates allegorical meaning, such as the characters named Patience, Purity, and Greed in medieval plays. Modern stories sometimes use elements of allegory. In "The Sniper," the dead gunman at the end might represent universal brotherhood. Interpreted allegorically, the story warns that if you kill any human being, you kill your brother or sister.

# The Feeling of Power

### ISAAC ASIMOV

A biography of Asimov appears on page 636.

## Approaching the Story

Isaac Asimov, one of America's most prolific writers, has written more than three hundred books—including science, science fiction, history, and autobiography. "The Feeling of Power" is one of his most popular science fiction stories. As the story opens, Jehan Shuman is about to introduce a new discovery to two government officials. Do not be confused by the strange names and places of this new earth society, but use these details to piece together an understanding of the world in which the characters function.

## Building Vocabulary

These essential words are footnoted within the story.

**programming** (prō´ gram iŋ): He originated **programming** patterns that resulted in self-directing war computers. (page 169)

**incalculable** (in kal´ kyo͞o lə bəl): I can't predict what the consequences will be in detail, but they will be **incalculable**. (page 172)

**impingement** (im pinj´ mənt): As the human brain takes over, more of our energy can be directed into peacetime pursuits, and the **impingement** of war on the ordinary man will be less. (page 173)

**manipulates** (mə nip´ yo͞o lāts): "The human mind, Computer Loesser, only **manipulates** facts." (page 173)

**skeptically** (skep´ ti kəl lē): Loesser said **skeptically**, "What progress?" (page 174)

**recalcitrant** (ri kal´ si trənt): General Weider . . . addressed his listeners after the fashion of a savage teacher facing a group of **recalcitrant** students. (page 174)

## Connecting Writing and Reading

Predict some of the ways in which computers could change your life in the next fifty years. Make a list of these ways in your journal. Then as you read, jot down the ways in which computers have changed human society in this story.

**J**EHAN SHUMAN WAS used to dealing with the men in authority on long-embattled Earth. He was only a civilian, but he originated programming[1] patterns that resulted in self-directing war computers of the highest sort. Generals consequently listened to him. Heads of congressional committees, too.

There was one of each in the special lounge of New Pentagon. General Weider was space-burnt and had a small mouth puckered almost into a cipher. Congressman Brant was smooth cheeked and cleareyed. He smoked Denebian tobacco with the air of one whose patriotism was so notorious, he could be allowed such liberties.

Shuman, tall, distinguished, and Programmer-first-class, faced them fearlessly.

He said, "This, gentlemen, is Myron Aub."

"The one with the unusual gift that you discovered quite by accident," said Congressman Brant placidly. "Ah." He inspected the little man with the egg-bald head with amiable curiosity.

The little man, in return, twisted the fingers of his hands anxiously. He had never been near such great men before. He was only an aging low-grade Technician who had long ago failed all tests designed to smoke out the gifted ones among mankind and had settled into the rut of unskilled labor. There was just this hobby of his that the great Programmer had found out about and was now making such a frightening fuss over.

General Weider said, "I find this atmosphere of mystery childish."

"You won't in a moment," said Shuman. "This is not something we can leak to the first comer—Aub!" There was something imperative about his manner of biting off that one-syllable name, but then he was a great Programmer speaking to a mere Technician. "Aub! How much is nine times seven?"

Aub hesitated a moment. His pale eyes glimmered with a feeble anxiety. "Sixty-three," he said.

Congressman Brant lifted his eyebrows. "Is that right?"

"Check it for yourself, Congressman."

The congressman took out his pocket computer, nudged the milled edges twice, looked at its face as it lay there in the palm of his hand, and put it back. He said, "Is this the gift you brought us here to demonstrate? An illusionist?"[2]

"More than that, sir. Aub has memorized a few operations, and with them he computes on paper."

"A paper computer?" said the general. He looked pained.

"No, sir," said Shuman patiently. "Not a paper computer. Simply a sheet of paper. General, would you be so kind as to suggest a number?"

"Seventeen," said the general.

"And you, Congressman?"

"Twenty-three."

"Good! Aub, multiply those numbers and please show the gentlemen your manner of doing it."

"Yes, Programmer," said Aub, ducking his head. He fished a small pad out of one shirt pocket and an artist's hairline stylus[3] out of the other. His forehead corrugated as he made painstaking marks on the paper.

General Weider interrupted him sharply. "Let's see that."

Aub passed him the paper, and Weider said, "Well, it looks like the figure seventeen."

Congressman Brant nodded and said, "So it does, but I suppose anyone can copy figures off a computer. I think I could make a passable seventeen myself, even without practice."

---

1. **programming** (prō′ gram iŋ): planning a sequence of computer operations.

2. **illusionist** (i lōō′ zhən ist): magician.

3. **hairline stylus** (her′ līn stī′ ləs): thin-pointed pen.

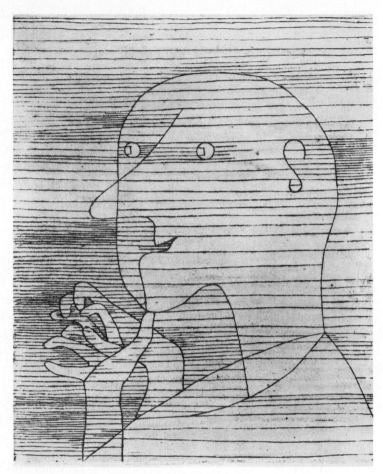

*Old Man Figuring,* 1929, PAUL KLEE.
Etching, printed in brownish black, plate: 11 3/4" x 9 3/8".
Collection, The Museum of Modern Art, New York; purchase.

"If you will let Aub continue, gentlemen," said Shuman without heat.

Aub continued, his hand trembling a little. Finally he said in a low voice, "The answer is three hundred and ninety-one."

Congressman Brant took out his computer a second time and flicked it, "By Godfrey, so it is. How did he guess?"

"No guess, Congressman," said Shuman. "He computed that result. He did it on this sheet of paper."

"Humbug," said the general impatiently. "A computer is one thing, and marks on paper are another."

"Explain, Aub," said Shuman.

"Yes, Programmer. Well, gentlemen, I write down seventeen, and just underneath it, I write twenty-three. Next, I say to myself: seven times three—"

The congressman interrupted smoothly, "Now, Aub, the problem is seventeen times twenty-three."

"Yes, I know," said the little Technician earnestly, "but I *start* by saying seven times three because that's the way it works. Now seven times three is twenty-one."

"And how do you know that?" asked the congressman.

"I just remember it. It's always twenty-one on the computer. I've checked it any number of times."

"That doesn't mean it always will be, though, does it?" said the congressman.

"Maybe not," stammered Aub. "I'm not a mathematician. But I always get the right answers, you see."

"Go on."

"Seven times three is twenty-one, so I write down twenty-one. Then one times three is three, so I write down a three under the two of twenty-one."

"Why under the two?" asked Congressman Brant at once.

"Because—" Aub looked helplessly at his superior for support. "It's difficult to explain."

Shuman said, "If you will accept his work for the moment, we can leave the details for the mathematicians."

*Guide for Interpretation*

Think about how General Weider and Congressman Brant react to Aub's demonstration. Consider what their attitudes reveal about them as individuals and about the society in which they are leaders. Then as you continue the story, notice how the government decides to use the newly rediscovered method of computation.

Brant subsided.

Aub said, "Three plus two makes five, you see, so the twenty-one becomes a fifty-one. Now you let that go for a while and start fresh. You multiply seven and two, that's fourteen, and one and two, that's two. Put them down like this, and it adds up to thirty-four. Now if you put the thirty-four under the fifty-one this way and add them, you get three hundred and ninety-one, and that's the answer."

There was an instant's silence, and then General Weider said, "I don't believe it. He goes through this rigmarole and makes up numbers and multiplies and adds them this way and that, but I don't believe it. It's too complicated to be anything but horn-swoggling."[4]

"Oh no, sir," said Aub in a sweat. "It only *seems* complicated because you're not used to it. Actually, the rules are quite simple and will work for any numbers."

"Any numbers, eh?" said the general. "Come then." He took out his own computer (a severely styled GI model) and struck it at random. Make a five seven three eight on the paper. That's five thousand seven hundred and thirty-eight."

"Yes, sir," said Aub, taking a new sheet of paper.

"Now,"—more punching of his computer— "seven two three nine. Seven thousand two hundred and thirty-nine."

"Yes, sir."

"And now multiply those two."

"It will take some time," quavered Aub.

"Take the time," said the general.

"Go ahead, Aub," said Shuman crisply.

Aub set to work, bending low. He took another sheet of paper and another. The general took out his watch finally and stared at it. "Are you through with your magic making, Technician?"

"I'm almost done, sir. Here it is, sir. Forty-one million, five hundred and thirty-seven thousand, three hundred and eighty-two." He showed the scrawled figures of the result.

General Weider smiled bitterly. He pushed the multiplication contact on his computer and let the numbers whirl to a halt. And then he stared and said in a surprised squeak, "Great Galaxy, the fella's right."

The President of the Terrestrial Federation had grown haggard in office, and, in private, he allowed a look of settled melancholy to appear on his sensitive features. The Denebian war, after its early start of vast movement and great popularity, had trickled down

---

4. **hornswoggling** (hôrn' swäg' liŋ): trickery.

into a sordid matter of maneuver and countermaneuver, with discontent rising steadily on Earth. Possibly, it was rising on Deneb, too.

And now Congressman Brant, head of the important Committee on Military Appropriations, was cheerfully and smoothly spending his half-hour appointment spouting nonsense.

"Computing without a computer," said the president impatiently, "is a contradiction in terms."

"Computing," said the congressman, "is only a system for handling data. A machine might do it, or the human brain might. Let me give you an example." And, using the new skills he had learned, he worked out sums and products until the president, despite himself, grew interested.

"Does this always work?"

"Every time, Mr. President. It is foolproof."

"Is it hard to learn?"

"It took me a week to get the real hang of it. I think you would do better."

"Well," said the president, considering, "it's an interesting parlor game, but what is the use of it?"

"What is the use of a newborn baby, Mr. President? At the moment there is no use, but don't you see that this points the way toward liberation from the machine? Consider, Mr. President," the congressman rose and his deep voice automatically took on some of the cadences he used in public debate, "that the Denebian war is a war of computer against computer. Their computers forge an impenetrable shield of countermissiles against our missiles, and ours forge one against theirs. If we advance the efficiency of our computers, so do they theirs, and for five years a precarious and profitless balance has existed.

"Now we have in our hands a method for going beyond the computer, leapfrogging it, passing through it. We will combine the mechanics of computation with human thought; we will have the equivalent of intelligent computers; billions of them. I can't predict what the consequences will be in detail, but they will be <u>incalculable</u>.[5] And if Deneb beats us to the punch, they may be unimaginably catastrophic."

The president said, troubled, "What would you have me do?"

"Put the power of the administration behind the establishment of a secret project on human computation. Call it Project Number, if you like. I can vouch for my committee, but I will need the administration behind me."

"But how far can human computation go?"

"There is no limit. According to Programmer Shuman, who first introduced me to this discovery—"

"I've heard of Shuman, of course."

"Yes. Well, Dr. Shuman tells me that in theory there is nothing the computer can do that the human mind cannot do. The computer merely takes a finite amount of data and performs a finite number of operations upon them. The human mind can duplicate the process."

The president considered that. He said, "If Shuman says this, I am inclined to believe him—in theory. But, in practice, how can anyone know how a computer works?"

Brant laughed genially. "Well, Mr. President, I asked the same question. It seems that at one time computers were designed directly by human beings. Those were simple computers, of course, this being before the time of the rational use of computers to design more advanced computers."

"Yes, yes. Go on."

"Technician Aub apparently had, as his hobby, the reconstruction of some of these ancient devices, and in so doing he studied the

---

5. **incalculable** (in kal′ kyo͞o lə bəl): too great or uncertain to be figured out or predicted.

details of their workings and found he could imitate them. The multiplication I just performed for you is an imitation of the workings of a computer."

"Amazing!"

The congressman coughed gently, "If I may make another point, Mr. President—the further we can develop this thing, the more we can divert our Federal effort from computer production and computer maintenance. As the human brain takes over, more of our energy can be directed into peacetime pursuits, and the impingement[6] of war on the ordinary man will be less. This will be most advantageous for the party in power, of course."

"Ah," said the president, "I see your point. Well, sit down, Congressman, sit down. I want some time to think about this. But meanwhile, show me that multiplication trick again. Let's see if I can't catch the point of it."

Programmer Shuman did not try to hurry matters. Loesser was conservative, very conservative, and liked to deal with computers as his father and grandfather had. Still, he controlled the West European computer combine, and if he could be persuaded to join Project Number in full enthusiasm, a great deal would be accomplished.

But Loesser was holding back. He said, "I'm not sure I like the idea of relaxing our hold on computers. The human mind is a capricious thing. The computer will give the same answer to the same problem each time. What guarantee have we that the human mind will do the same?"

"The human mind, Computer Loesser, only manipulates[7] facts. It doesn't matter whether the human mind or a machine does it. They are just tools."

"Yes, yes. I've gone over your ingenious demonstration that the mind can duplicate the computer, but it seems to me a little in the air. I'll grant the theory, but what reason have

we for thinking that theory can be converted to practice?"

"I think we have reason, sir. After all, computers have not always existed. The cave men with their triremes,[8] stone axes, and railroads had no computers."

"And possibly they did not compute."

"You know better than that. Even the building of a railroad or a ziggurat[9] called for some computing, and that must have been without computers as we know them."

"Do you suggest they computed in the fashion you demonstrate?"

"Probably not. After all, this method—we call it *graphitics*, by the way, from the old European word *grapho*, meaning 'to write'—is developed from the computers themselves, so it cannot have antedated them. Still, the cave men must have had *some* method, eh?"

"Lost arts! If you're going to talk about lost arts—"

"No, no. I'm not a lost art enthusiast, though I don't say there may not be some. After all, man was eating grain before hydroponics,[10] and if the primitives ate grain they must have grown it in soil. What else could they have done?"

"I don't know, but I'll believe in soil-growing when I see someone grow grain in soil. And I'll believe in making fire by rubbing two pieces of flint together when I see that, too."

Shuman grew placative. "Well, let's stick to graphitics. It's just part of the process of

---

6. **impingement** (im pinj′ mənt): a trespassing or intruding.
7. **manipulates** (mə nip′ yo͞o lāts): works, operates, or treats with skill.
8. **triremes** (trī′ rēms′): warships, used in ancient Greece and Rome.
9. **ziggurat** (zig′ oo rat′): a pryamid-like structure common in ancient Babylonia.
10. **hydroponics** (hī′ drō pän′ iks): the growing of plants in nutrient-rich liquid instead of soil.

etherealization. Transportation by means of bulky contrivances is giving way to direct mass-transference. Communications devices become less massive and more efficient constantly. For that matter, compare your pocket computer with the massive jobs of a thousand years ago. Why not, then, the last step of doing away with computers altogether? Come, sir, Project Number is a going concern; progress is already headlong. But we want your help. If patriotism doesn't move you, consider the intellectual adventure involved."

Loesser said skeptically,[11] "What progress? What can you do beyond multiplication? Can you integrate a transcendental function?"[12]

"In time, sir. In time. In the last month I have learned to handle division. I can determine, and correctly, integral quotients and decimal quotients."

"Decimal quotients? To how many places?"

Programmer Shuman tried to keep his tone casual. "Any number!"

Loesser's lower jaw dropped. "Without a computer?"

"Set me a problem."

"Divide twenty-seven by thirteen. Take it to six places."

Five minutes later, Shuman said, "Two point oh seven six nine two three."

Loesser checked it. "Well now, that's amazing. Multiplication didn't impress me too much because it involved integers after all, and I thought trick manipulation might do it. But decimals—"

"And that is not all. There is a new development that is, so far, top secret and which, strictly speaking, I ought not to mention. Still—we may have made a breakthrough on the square root front."

"Square roots?"

"It involves some tricky points, and we haven't licked the bugs yet, but Technician Aub, the man who invented the science and who has an amazing intuition in connection with it, maintains he has the problem almost solved. And he is only a Technician. A man like yourself, a trained and talented mathematician, ought to have no difficulty."

"Square roots," muttered Loesser, attracted.

"Cube roots, too. Are you with us?"

Loesser's hand thrust out suddenly, "Count me in."

General Weider stumped his way back and forth at the head of the room and addressed his listeners after the fashion of a savage teacher facing a group of recalcitrant[13] students. It made no difference to the general that they were the civilian scientists heading Project Number. The general was the overall head, and he so considered himself at every waking moment.

He said, "Now square roots are all fine. I can't do them myself, and I don't understand the methods, but they're fine. Still, the Project will not be sidetracked into what some of you call the fundamentals. You can play with graphics any way you want to after the war is over, but right now we have specific and very practical problems to solve."

In a far corner, Technician Aub listened with painful attention. He was no longer a Technician, of course, having been relieved of his duties and assigned to the project, with a fine-sounding title and good pay. But, of course, the social distinction remained, and the highly placed scientific leaders could never bring themselves to admit him to their ranks on a footing of equality. Nor, to do Aub justice, did he, himself, wish it. He was as

---

11. **skeptically** (skep′ ti kəl lē): in a doubting manner.

12. **integrate a transcendental function:** a reference to the problems of higher mathematics, a field that quickly embraced, and was greatly enhanced by, computer technology.

13. **recalcitrant** (ri kal′ si trənt): refusing to obey authority or follow rules.

uncomfortable with them as they with him.

The general was saying, "Our goal is a simple one, gentlemen: the replacement of the computer. A ship that can navigate space without a computer on board can be constructed in one fifth the time and at one tenth the expense of a computer-laden ship. We could build fleets five times, ten times, as great as Deneb could if we could but eliminate the computer.

"And I see something even beyond this. It may be fantastic now; a mere dream; but in the future I see the manned missile!"

There was an instant murmur from the audience.

The general drove on. "At the present time, our chief bottleneck is the fact that missiles are limited in intelligence. The computer controlling them can only be so large, and for that reason they can meet the changing nature of antimissile defenses in an unsatisfactory way. Few missiles, if any, accomplish their goal, and missile warfare is coming to a dead end—for the enemy, fortunately, as well as for ourselves.

"On the other hand, a missile with a man or two within, controlling flight by graphitics, would be lighter, more mobile, more intelligent. It would give us a lead that might well mean the margin of victory. Besides which, gentlemen, the exigencies of war compel us to remember one thing. A man is much more dispensable than a computer. Manned missiles could be launched in numbers and under circumstances that no good general would care to undertake as far as computer-directed missiles are concerned—"

He said much more, but Technician Aub did not wait.

Technician Aub, in the privacy of his quarters, labored long over the note he was leaving behind. It read finally as follows:

"When I began the study of what is now called graphitics, it was no more than a hobby. I saw no more in it than an interesting amusement, an exercise of mind.

"When Project Number began, I thought that others were wiser than I; that graphitics might be put to practical use as a benefit to mankind, to aid in the production of really practical mass-transference devices perhaps. But now I see it is to be used only for death and destruction.

"I cannot face the responsibility involved in having invented graphitics."

He then deliberately turned the focus of a protein-depolarizer on himself and fell instantly and painlessly dead.

They stood over the grave of the little Technician while tribute was paid to the greatness of his discovery.

Programmer Shuman bowed his head along with the rest of them but remained unmoved. The Technician had done his share and was no longer needed, after all. He might have started graphitics, but, now that it had started, it would carry on by itself overwhelmingly, triumphantly, until manned missiles were possible with who knew what else.

Nine times seven, thought Shuman with deep satisfaction, is sixty-three, and I don't need a computer to tell me so. The computer is in my own head.

And it was amazing the feeling of power that gave him.

# *Thinking About the Story*

## A PERSONAL RESPONSE

*sharing impressions*

**1.** How did you respond to the vision of the future presented in this story? Write about your response in your journal.

*constructing interpretations*

**2.** Why does knowing how to multiply give Shuman a feeling of power?

**3.** What is revealed about Shuman, General Weider, and Congressman Brant by the way they treat Aub?

### Think about
- how Shuman speaks to Aub during their presentation of graphitics
- how the general and the congressman react to Aub's discovery
- why Shuman and the general decide to use Aub's method of calculation
- how Shuman feels at Aub's grave

**4.** Explain whether you think the negative aspects of this society are caused more by computers or by humans.

## A CREATIVE RESPONSE

**5.** If Myron Aub had gone to the leaders on Deneb and told them the secret of Earth's graphitics, what might have happened?

## A CRITICAL RESPONSE

**6.** Explain some ironies that you see in this story.

### Think about
- situational irony as the contrast between what is expected and what happens
- dramatic irony as the contrast between what the characters know and what the reader knows

**7.** When Isaac Asimov wrote this story in 1957, computers took up entire rooms, and pocket calculators had not been developed yet. If Asimov rewrote this story today, how might it be different?

### Think about
- how the technology of today compares with the technology in the story
- what direction future advances in technology might take
- whether the threat of war is as great now as it was in 1957
- what is the greatest threat in our society today

**8.** How can society encourage scientific development without becoming overly dependent on computers?

# *Analyzing the Writer's Craft*

## THEME AND SCIENCE FICTION

Think of one message in the story that applies to society today, as well as to the future society that is portrayed. Jot down this message in your journal.

**Building a Literary Vocabulary.** Theme is the central idea or message in a story, a perception about life that the author shares with the reader. Most stories contain several themes, one of which usually predominates. Most science fiction comments on present-day society through the writer's conception of a past or future society. In "The Feeling of Power," Myron Aub is an ordinary Technician because he failed the tests designed to identify gifted people—even though, ironically, he was gifted enough to rediscover the art of multiplication. Asimov may be warning readers about the dangers of judging people on the basis of their test scores, a practice that exists today.

**Application: Identifying Themes.** Working in groups of three or four, create a list of two or more messages communicated in the story, including the ones that you already identified. Decide which of these messages is the central theme of the story. Write a slogan to express this theme, display your slogan on a placard, and then stage a demonstration to convince your classmates of the importance of this theme.

# *Connecting Reading and Writing*

**1.** Contrast the characters of Shuman and Aub in a **letter** explaining which man you would recommend for a job.

Option: Create a **wanted poster** published by the Denebian government explaining how to tell the two men apart.

**2.** From Aub's point of view, discuss in a **diary entry** how graphitics might be used to benefit humanity.

Option: Write a **proposal** to Congress to get funding for research on graphitics.

**3.** How would you describe to the government officials in this story what is unique about the power of the human mind? Present your ideas in an **outline** for an editorial.

Option: Write **notes** for a speech on the uniqueness of the human mind.

**4.** Drawing on your prereading predictions, describe what life might be like fifty years from now in an **advertisement** for time travel.

Option: Write a **description** of a setting for a science fiction story that takes place fifty years from now.

# All Cats Are Gray

## ANDRE NORTON

A biography of Norton appears on page 643.

## Approaching the Story

Welcome to the world of the spaceways, where interstellar travel is as common as airplane travel today. This story is a space adventure whose heroine, Steena, is a computer operator and astronaut. A hip narrator tells Steena's story using a kind of space slang, as though he were talking to you at your local hangout.

## Building Vocabulary

These essential words are footnoted within the story.

**derelict** (der´ ə likt): She had been following her bizarre **derelict** orbit through space. (page 180)

**gossamer** (gäs´ ə mər), **expanse** (ek spans´): Right in the middle of the sheer, **gossamer expanse** was a sparkling heap of gems. (page 181).

## Connecting Writing and Reading

What comes to mind when you think of a detective? Make a cluster diagram similar to the one below in which you list qualities that you think make a successful detective. As you read, decide which qualities could be used to describe Steena.

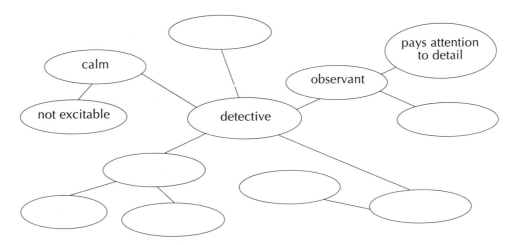

STEENA OF THE Spaceways —that sounds just like the corny title for one of the Stellar-vedo spreads. I ought to know; I've tried my hand at writing enough of them. Only this Steena was no glamorous babe. She was as colorless as a lunar planet—even the hair netted down to her skull had a sort of grayish cast, and I never saw her but once draped in anything but a shapeless and baggy gray spaceall.

Steena was strictly background stuff, and that is where she mostly spent her free hours—in the smelly, smoky background corners of any stellar-port dive frequented by free spacers. If you really looked for her you could spot her—just sitting there listening to the talk—listening and remembering. She didn't open her own mouth often, but when she did, spacers had learned to listen. And the lucky few who heard her rare spoken words—these will never forget Steena.

She drifted from port to port. Being an expert operator on the big calculators, she found jobs wherever she cared to stay for a time. And she came to be something like the masterminded machines she tended—smooth, gray, without much personality of their own.

But it was Steena who told Bub Nelson about the Jovan moon rites—and her warning saved Bub's life six months later. It was Steena who identified the piece of stone Keene Clark was passing around a table one night, rightly calling it unworked Slitite. That started a rush which made ten fortunes overnight for men who were down to their last jets. And, last of all, she cracked the case of the *Empress of Mars*.

All the boys who had profited by her odd store of knowledge and her photographic memory tried at one time or another to balance the scales. But she wouldn't take so much

as a cup of canal water at their expense, let alone the credits they tried to push on her. Bub Nelson was the only one who got around her refusal. It was he who brought her Bat.

About a year after the Jovan affair, he walked into the Free Fall one night and dumped Bat down on her table. Bat looked at Steena and growled. She looked calmly back at him and nodded once. From then on they traveled together—the thin gray woman and the big gray tomcat. Bat learned to know the inside of more stellar bars than even most spacers visit in their lifetimes. He developed a liking for Vernal juice—drank it neat and quick, right out of a glass. And he was always at home on any table where Steena elected to drop him.

This is really the story of Steena, Bat, Cliff Moran, and the *Empress of Mars*, a story which is already a legend of the spaceways. And it's a good story, too. I ought to know, having framed the first version of it myself.

For I was there, right in the Rigel Royal, when it all began on the night that Cliff Moran blew in, looking lower than an antman's belly and twice as nasty. He'd had a spell of luck foul enough to twist a man into a slug snake, and we all knew that there was an attachment out for his ship. Cliff had fought his way up from the back courts of Venaport. Lose his ship and he'd slip back there—to rot. He was at the snarling stage that night when he picked out a table for himself and set out to drink away his troubles.

However, just as the first bottle arrived, so did a visitor. Steena came out of her corner, Bat curled around her shoulders stolewise, his favorite mode of travel. She crossed over and dropped down, without invitation, at Cliff's side. That shook him out of his sulks because Steena never chose company when she could be alone. If one of the man-stones on

Ganymede[1] had come stumping in, it wouldn't have made more of us look out of the corners of our eyes.

She stretched out one long-fingered hand, set aside the bottle he had ordered, and said only one thing, "It's about time for the *Empress of Mars* to appear."

Cliff scowled and bit his lips. He was tough, tough as jet lining—you have to be granite inside and out to struggle up from Venaport to a ship command. But we could guess what was running through his mind at that moment. *The Empress of Mars* was just about the biggest prize a spacer could aim for. But in the fifty years she had been following her bizarre derelict[2] orbit through space, many men had tried to bring her in—and none had succeeded.

A pleasure ship carrying untold wealth, she had been mysteriously abandoned in space by passengers and crew, none of whom had ever been seen or heard of again. At intervals thereafter she had been sighted, even boarded. Those who ventured into her either vanished or returned swiftly without any believable explanation of what they had seen—wanting only to get away from her as quickly as possible. But the man who could bring her in—or even strip her clean in space—that man would win the jackpot.

"All right!" Cliff slammed his fist down on the table. "I'll try even that!"

Steena looked at him, much as she must have looked at Bat the day Bub Nelson brought him to her, and nodded. That was all I saw. The rest of the story came to me in pieces, months later and in another report half the system away.

Cliff took off that night. He was afraid to risk waiting—with a writ out that could pull the ship from under him. And it wasn't until he was in space that he discovered his passengers—Steena and Bat. We'll never know what happened then. I'm betting that Steena made no explanation at all. She wouldn't.

It was the first time she had decided to cash in on her own tip and she was there—that was all. Maybe that point weighed with Cliff; maybe he just didn't care. Anyway, the three were together when they sighted the *Empress* riding, her deadlights gleaming, a ghost ship in night space.

She must have been an eerie sight because her other lights were on too, in addition to the red warnings at her nose. She seemed alive, a Flying Dutchman[3] of space. Cliff worked his ship skillfully alongside and had no trouble in snapping magnetic lines to her lock. Some minutes later the three of them passed into her. There was still air in her cabins and corridors, air that bore a faint corrupt taint which set Bat to sniffing greedily and could be picked up even by the less sensitive human nostrils.

Cliff headed straight for the control cabin, but Steena and Bat went prowling. Closed doors were a challenge to both of them, and Steena opened each as she passed, taking a quick look at what lay within. The fifth door opened on a room which no woman could leave without further investigation.

I don't know who had been housed there when the *Empress* left port on her last lengthy cruise. Anyone really curious can check back on the old photo-reg cards. But there was a lavish display of silk trailing out of two travel kits on the floor, a dressing table crowded with crystal and jeweled containers, along with other lures for the female which drew Steena in. She was standing in front of the dressing table when she glanced into the mirror—glanced into it and froze.

Over her right shoulder she could see the spider-silk cover on the bed. Right in the middle

---

1. **Ganymede** (gan′ i mēd′): the largest of Jupiter's moons.

2. **derelict** (der′ ə likt): abandoned.

3. **Flying Dutchman:** a fabled sailor doomed to sail the seas in his ghostly ship until Judgment Day.

of the sheer, gossamer[4] expanse[5] was a sparkling heap of gems, the dumped contents of some jewel case. Bat had jumped to the foot of the bed and flattened out as cats will, watching those gems, watching them and—something else!

Steena put out her hand blindly and caught up the nearest bottle. As she unstoppered it, she watched the mirrored bed. A gemmed bracelet rose from the pile, rose in the air and tinkled its siren song. It was as if an idle hand played. . . . Bat spat almost noiselessly. But he did not retreat. Bat had not yet decided his course.

She put down the bottle. Then she did something which perhaps few of the men who had listened to her through the years could have done. She moved without hurry or sign of disturbance on a tour about the room. And, although she approached the bed, she did not touch the jewels. She could not force herself to do that. It took her five minutes to play out her innocence and unconcern. Then it was Bat who decided the issue.

He leaped from the bed and escorted something to the door, remaining a careful distance behind. Then he mewed loudly twice. Steena followed him and opened the door wider.

Bat went straight on down the corridor, as intent as a hound on the warmest of scents. Steena strolled behind him, holding her pace to the unhurried gait of an explorer. What sped before them was invisible to her, but Bat was never baffled by it.

They must have gone into the control cabin almost on the heels of the unseen—if the unseen had heels, which there was a good reason to doubt—for Bat crouched just within the doorway and refused to move on. Steena looked down the length of the instrument panels and officers' station seats to where Cliff Moran worked. Her boots made no sound on the heavy carpet, and he did not glance up but sat humming through set teeth, as he tested the tardy and reluctant responses to buttons which had not been pushed in years.

To human eyes they were alone in the cabin. But Bat still followed a moving something, which he had at last made up his mind to distrust and dislike. For now he took a step or two forward and spat—his loathing made plain by every raised hair along his spine. And in that same moment Steena saw a flicker—a flicker of vague outline against Cliff's hunched shoulders, as if the invisible one had crossed the space between them.

But why had it been revealed against Cliff and not against the back of one of the seats or against the panels, the walls of the corridor, or the cover of the bed where it had reclined and played with its loot? What could Bat see?

The storehouse memory that had served Steena so well throughout the years clicked open a half-forgotten door. With one swift motion, she tore loose her spaceall and flung the baggy garment across the back of the nearest seat.

Bat was snarling now, emitting the throaty rising cry that was his hunting song. But he was edging back, back toward Steena's feet, shrinking from something he could not fight but which he faced defiantly. If he could draw it after him, past that dangling spaceall. . . . He had to—it was their only chance!

"What the . . . " Cliff had come out of his seat and was staring at them.

What he saw must have been weird enough: Steena, bare armed and bare shouldered, her usually stiffly netted hair falling wildly down her back; Steena watching empty space with narrowed eyes and set mouth, calculating a single wild chance. Bat, crouched on his belly, was retreating from thin air step by step and wailing like a demon.

---

4. **gossamer** (gäs' ə mər): light, thin, and filmy.
5. **expanse** (ek spans'): a large open area or unbroken surface.

"Toss me your blaster." Steena gave the order calmly—as if they still sat at their table in the Rigel Royal.

And as quietly, Cliff obeyed. She caught the small weapon out of the air with a steady hand—caught and leveled it.

"Stay just where you are!" she warned. "Back, Bat, bring it back!"

With a last throat-splitting screech of rage and hate, Bat twisted to safety between her boots. She pressed with thumb and forefinger, firing at the spacealls. The material turned to powdery flakes of ash—except for certain bits which still flapped from the scorched seat—as if something had protected them from the force of the blast. Bat sprang straight up in the air with a scream that tore their ears.

"What . . . ?" began Cliff again.

Steena made a warning motion with her left hand. *"Wait!"*

She was still tense, still watching Bat. The cat dashed madly around the cabin twice, running crazily with white-ringed eyes and flecks of foam on his muzzle. Then he stopped abruptly in the doorway, stopped and looked back over his shoulder for a long, silent moment. He sniffed delicately.

Steena and Cliff could smell it too now, a thick oily stench which was not the usual odor left by an exploding blaster shell.

Bat came back, treading daintily across the carpet, almost on the tips of his paws. He raised his head as he passed Steena, and then he went confidently beyond to sniff, to sniff and spit twice at the unburned strips of the spaceall. Having thus paid his respects to the late enemy, he sat down calmly and set to washing his fur with deliberation. Steena sighed once and dropped into the navigator's seat.

"Maybe now you'll tell me what's happened?" Cliff exploded as he took the blaster out of her hand.

"Gray," she said dazedly, "it must have been gray—or I couldn't have seen it like that. I'm colorblind, you see. I can see only shades of gray—my whole world is gray. Like Bat's—his world is gray, too—all gray. But he's been compensated, for he can see above and below our range of color vibrations. And apparently, so can I!"

Her voice quavered, and she raised her chin with a new air Cliff had never seen before—a sort of proud acceptance. She pushed back her wandering hair, but she made no move to imprison it under the heavy net again.

"That is why I saw the thing when it crossed between us. Against your spaceall it was another shade of gray—an outline. So I put out mine and waited for it to show against that—it was our only chance, Cliff.

"It was curious at first, I think, and it knew we couldn't see it—which is why it waited to attack. But when Bat's actions gave it away, it moved. So I waited to see that flicker against the spaceall, and then I let him have it. It's really very simple. . . ."

Cliff laughed a bit shakily. "But what *was* this gray thing? I don't get it."

"I think it was what made the *Empress* a derelict. Something out of space, maybe, or from another world somewhere." She waved her hands. "It's invisible because it's a color beyond our range of sight. It must have stayed in here all these years. And it kills—it must—when its curiosity is satisfied." Swiftly she described the scene, the scene in the cabin, and the strange behavior of the gem pile which had betrayed the creature to her.

Cliff did not return his blaster to its holder. "Any more of them on board, d'you think?" He didn't looked pleased at the prospect.

Steena turned to Bat. He was paying particular attention to the space between two front toes in the process of a complete bath. "I don't think so, but Bat will tell us if there are. He can see them clearly, I believe."

But there weren't any more, and two weeks later, Cliff, Steena, and Bat brought the *Empress* into the lunar quarantine station. And that is the end of Steena's story because, as we have been told, happy marriages need no chronicles. Steena had found someone who knew of her gray world and did not find it too hard to share with her—someone besides Bat. It turned out to be a real love match.

The last time I saw her, she was wrapped in a flame-red cloak from the looms of Rigel and wore a fortune in Jovan rubies blazing on her wrists. Cliff was flipping a three-figure credit bill to a waiter. And Bat had a row of Vernal juice glasses set up before him. Just a little family party out on the town.

# Thinking About the Story

## A PERSONAL RESPONSE

*sharing impressions*

**1.** What were your thoughts about Steena as you finished reading? State your thoughts in your journal.

*constructing interpretations*

**2.** Describe how and why Steena changes in the story.

**3.** Why does Steena succeed on the *Empress* when others have failed?
   ***Think about***
   • her qualities as a detective
   • how she differs from other people

**4.** How important do you think Bat is to the story?
   ***Think about***
   • Steena's relationship with Bat
   • Bat's role in destroying the creature on the *Empress*
   • qualities that are common to both Steena and Bat

## A CRITICAL RESPONSE

**5.** What does the narrator add to the story?
   ***Think about***
   • the space slang used
   • the narrator's interpretation of the characters
   • how the story would be different if Steena had narrated it

**6.** The title of this story refers to the saying, "In the dark all cats are gray." Do you think "All Cats Are Gray" is an appropriate title for this story? Why or why not?

**7.** What similarities and differences do you see between this story and "The Feeling of Power"?

# Analyzing the Writer's Craft

## TONE

The way writers think or feel about their subjects is often evident in their work. How do you think Andre Norton feels about Steena and her adventure?

**Building a Literary Vocabulary.** Tone is the attitude a writer takes toward a subject. "The Feeling of Power" has a serious, objective tone. The sinister events are related with the cool detachment of a scientific report. In "All Cats Are Gray," Andre Norton's attitude, or tone, is established primarily by the way the narrator tells the story.

**Application: Analyzing Tone.** Choose several passages from the story and list words or phrases that communicate the tone. Working in a small group, analyze the tone of the story, then experiment with retelling parts of the story using a different tone. Present your retellings to the class.

# Connecting Reading and Writing

**1.** Interpret the meanings of at least eight words coined for places and things in this society of the future. Write definitions in the form of **footnotes** for the story.

Option: Create clues for a **crossword puzzle** using the coined words.

**2.** Try your hand at science fiction by writing a series of **journal entries** describing a trip to another planet.

Option: Add a **scene** to this story.

**3.** Imagine that Cliff and Steena have gone into business as a detective team and write a **help wanted notice** for a case that they could solve together.

Option: Create an **advertisement** for their new detective agency.

**4.** Using your response to question 8, compare on a **chart** the Spaceways society with the world described in "The Feeling of Power."

Option: Present your comparison in an **expository essay** addressed to a student who has read only one of the stories.

# The Masque of the Red Death

## EDGAR ALLAN POE

A biography of Poe appears on page 644.

## *Approaching the Story*

Edgar Allan Poe is considered one of the greatest writers of macabre tales. "The Masque of the Red Death," one of his best-known stories, is set during the late Middle Ages. At that time, before the discovery of antibiotics, infectious diseases spread quickly. In Europe during the fourteenth century, an epidemic of the bubonic plague, or Black Death, killed approximately twenty-five million people, more than one-quarter of the total population. Not surprisingly, people dreaded the plague and avoided its victims. Poe's fictitious plague, the Red Death, is an exaggerated version of this horrible disease.

## *Building Vocabulary*

These essential words are footnoted within the story.

**devastated** (dev´ əs tāt´ ed): The "Red Death" had long **devastated** the country. (page 186)

**pestilence** (pes´ tə ləns): No **pestilence** had ever been so fatal. (page 186)

**dauntless** (dônt´ lis), **sagacious** (sə gā´ shəs): But the Prince Prospero was happy and **dauntless** and **sagacious**. (page 186)

**courtiers** (kôrt´ ē ərz): The **courtiers**, having entered, brought furnaces . . . and welded the bolts. (page 186)

**voluptuous** (və lup´ chōō əs): It was a **voluptuous** scene. (page 186)

**grotesque** (grō tesk´): They were **grotesque**. (page 188)

**untenanted** (un ten´ ənt ed), **tangible** (tan´ jə bəl): The revellers . . . gasped in unutterable horror at finding [the clothes] . . . **untenanted** by any **tangible** form. (page 190)

## *Connecting Writing and Reading*

Think of an infectious disease that does not yet have a cure or a preventive vaccine and write the name down in your journal. Then briefly describe how people respond emotionally to this disease. As you read, note how Prince Prospero responds to the epidemic of his time.

# The Masque of the Red Death

HE "RED DEATH" had long devastated[1] the country. No pestilence[2] had ever been so fatal, or so hideous. Blood was its Avatar[3] and its seal—the redness and horror of blood. There were sharp pains, and sudden dizziness, and then profuse bleeding at the pores, with dissolution. The scarlet stains upon the body, and especially upon the face of the victim, were the pest ban[4] which shut him out from the aid and from the sympathy of his fellow men. And the whole seizure, progress, and termination of the disease were the incidents of half an hour.

But the Prince Prospero was happy and dauntless[5] and sagacious.[6] When his dominions were half depopulated, he summoned to his presence a thousand hale and lighthearted friends from among the knights and dames of his court, and with these retired to the deep seclusion of one of his castellated abbeys.[7] This was an extensive and magnificent structure, the creation of the prince's own eccentric yet august taste. A strong and lofty wall girded it in. The wall had gates of iron. The courtiers,[8] having entered, brought furnaces and massy hammers and welded the bolts. They resolved to leave means neither of ingress or egress[9] to the sudden impulses of despair or of frenzy from within. The abbey was amply provisioned. With such precautions the courtiers might bid defiance to contagion. The external world could take care of itself. It the meantime it was folly to grieve, or to think. The prince had provided all the appliances of pleasure. There were buffoons, there were improvisatori, there were ballet-dancers, there were musicians, there was Beauty, there was wine. All these and security were within. Without was the "Red Death."

It was toward the close of the fifth or sixth month of his seclusion, and while the pestilence raged most furiously abroad, that the Prince Prospero entertained his thousand friends at a masked ball of the most unusual magnificence.

It was a voluptuous[10] scene, that masquerade. But first let me tell of the rooms in which it was held. There were seven—an imperial suite. In many places, however, such suites form a long and straight vista, while

> **Guide for Interpretation**
>
> Notice the contrast between life inside and outside Prince Prospero's abbey. As you read further, consider what the description of the masked ball reveals about the kind of life the prince and his friends have created inside the abbey.

---

1. **devastated** (dev′ əs tāt′ ed): destroyed or demolished.
2. **pestilence** (pes′ tə ləns): a disease that is fatal or very harmful and that spreads rapidly from person to person.
3. **Avatar** (av′ ə tär′): an appearance in physical form of an unseen force, from the Hindu belief in a god's taking of earthly forms.
4. **pest ban:** restrictions placed on plague victims to prevent the disease from spreading.

5. **dauntless** (dônt′ lis): fearless.
6. **sagacious** (sə gā shəs): wise.
7. **castellated abbeys** (kas′ tə lāt′ id ab′ ēz): isolated castlelike structures, usually lived in by people who have taken religious vows.
8. **courtiers** (kôrt′ ē ərz): attendants at a royal court.
9. **ingess or egress** (in′ gres′, ē ′ gres′): entry or exit.
10. **voluptuous** (və lup′ choo əs): sensual; luxurious.

the folding doors slide back nearly to the walls on either hand, so that the view of the whole extent is scarcely impeded. Here the case was very different; as might have been expected from the duke's love of the *bizarre*. The apartments were so irregularly disposed that the vision embraced but little more than one at a time. There was a sharp turn at every twenty or thirty yards, and at each turn a novel effect. To the right and left, in the middle of each wall, a tall and narrow Gothic window looked out upon a closed corridor which pursued the windings of the suite. These windows were of stained glass whose color varied in accordance with the prevailing hue of the decorations of the chambers into which it opened. That at the eastern extremity was hung, for example, in blue— and vividly blue went its windows. The second chamber was purple in its ornaments and tapestries, and here the panes were purple. The third was green throughout, and so were the casements. The fourth was furnished and lighted with orange—the fifth with white—the sixth with violet. The seventh apartment was closely shrouded in black velvet tapestries that hung all over the ceiling and down the walls, falling in heavy folds upon a carpet of the same material and hue. But in this chamber only, the color of the windows failed to correspond with the decorations. The panes here were scarlet—a deep blood color. Now in no one of the seven apartments were there any lamp or candelabrum amid the profusion of golden ornaments that lay scattered to and fro or depended from the roof. There was no light of any kind emanating from lamp or candle within the suite of chambers. But in the corridors that followed the suite, there stood, opposite to each window, a heavy tripod, bearing a brazier[11] of fire that projected its rays through the tinted glass and so glaringly illumined the room. And thus were produced a multitude of gaudy and fantastic appearances. But in the western or black chamber the effect of the firelight that streamed upon the dark hangings through the blood-tinted panes, was ghastly in the extreme, and produced so wild a look upon the countenances of those who entered, that there were few of the company bold enough to set foot within its precincts at all.

It was in this apartment, also, that there stood against the western wall a gigantic clock of ebony.[12] Its pendulum swung to and fro with a dull, heavy, monotonous clang; and when the minute hand made the circuit of the face, and the hour was to be stricken, there came from the brazen lungs of the clock a sound which was clear and loud and deep and exceedingly musical, but of so peculiar a note and emphasis that, at each lapse of an hour, the musicians of the orchestra were constrained to pause, momentarily, in their performance, to hearken to the sound; and thus the waltzers perforce ceased their evolutions; and there was a brief disconcert of the whole gay company; and, while the chimes of the clock yet rang, it was observed that the giddiest turned pale, and the more aged and sedate passed their hands over their brows as if in confused reverie or meditation. But when the echoes had fully ceased, a light laughter at once pervaded the assembly; the musicians looked at each other and smiled as if at their own nervousness and folly, and made whispering vows, each to the other, that the next chiming of the clock should produce in them no similar emotion; and then, after the lapse of sixty minutes (which embrace three thousand and six hundred seconds of the Time that flies), there came yet another chiming of the clock, and then were the same disconcert and tremulousness and meditation as before.

But in spite of these things, it was a gay and magnificent revel. The tastes of the duke were peculiar. He had a fine eye for colors and effects. He disregarded the *decora*[13] of mere

---

11. **brazier** (brā′ zhər): a metal pan for holding burning coals.

12. **ebony** (eb′ ə nē): hard, very dark wood.

13. *decora* (dā kôr′ ə): guidelines.

fashion. His plans were bold and fiery, and his conceptions glowed with barbaric luster. There are some who would have thought him mad. His followers felt that he was not. It was necessary to hear and see and touch him to be *sure* that he was not.

He had directed, in great part, the movable embellishments of the seven chambers, upon occasion of this great *fête;* and it was his own guiding taste which had given character to the masqueraders. Be sure they were <u>grotesque</u>.[14] There were much glare and glitter and piquancy and phantasm—much of what has been seen since in Hernani.[15] There were arabesque figures with unsuited limbs and appointments. There were delirious fancies such as the madman fashions. There was much of the beautiful, much of the wanton, much of the *bizarre,* something of the terrible, and not a little of that which might have excited disgust. To and fro in the seven chambers there stalked, in fact, a multitude of dreams. And these—the dreams—writhed in and about, taking hue from the rooms, and causing the wild music of the orchestra to seem as the echo of their steps. And, anon, there strikes the ebony clock which stands in the hall of velvet. And then, for a moment, all is still, and all is silent save the voice of the clock. The dreams are stiff-frozen as they stand. But the echoes of the chime die away—they have endured but an instant—and a light, half-subdued laughter floats after them as they depart. And now again the music swells, and the dreams live, and writhe to and fro more merrily than ever, taking hue from the many-tinted windows through which stream the rays of the tripods. But to the chamber which lies most westwardly of the seven, there are now none of the maskers who venture; for the night is waning away; and there flows a ruddier light through the blood-colored panes; and the blackness of the sable drapery appalls; and to him whose foot falls upon the sable carpet, there comes

from the near clock of ebony a muffled peal more solemnly emphatic than any which reaches *their* ears who indulge in the more remote gaieties of the other apartments.

But these other apartments were densely crowded, and in them beat feverishly the heart of life. And the revel went whirlingly on, until at length there commenced the sounding of midnight upon the clock. And then the music ceased, as I have told; and the evolutions of the waltzes were quieted; and there was an uneasy cessation of all things as before. But now there were twelve strokes to be sounded by the bell of the clock; and thus it happened, perhaps, that more of thought crept, with more of time, into the meditations of the thoughtful among those who revelled. And thus, too, it happened, perhaps, that before the last echoes of the last chimes had utterly sunk into silence, there were many individuals in the crowd who had found leisure to become aware of the presence of a masked figure which had arrested the attention of no single individual before. And the rumor of this new presence having spread itself whisperingly around, there arose at length from the whole company a buzz, finally of terror, of horror, and of disgust.

In an assembly of phantasms such as I have painted, it may well be supposed that no ordinary appearance could have excited any such sensation. In truth the masquerade license of the night was nearly unlimited; but the figure in question had out-Heroded Herod,[16] and gone beyond the bounds of even the prince's indefinite decorum. There are chords in the

---

14. **grotesque** (grō tesk′): having a twisted, strange, unreal appearance or shape.
15. *Hernani* (er′ nä nē): a play by Victor Hugo, first staged in 1830, that requires very elaborate sets.
16. **out-Heroded Herod** (out′ her′ əd əd her′ əd): been more extreme than the biblical King Herod, who ordered the deaths of all babies in an effort to kill the infant Jesus.

hearts of the most reckless which cannot be touched without emotion. Even with the utterly lost, to whom life and death are equally jests, there are matters of which no jest can be made. The whole company, indeed, seemed now deeply to feel that in the costume and bearing of the stranger neither wit nor propriety existed. The figure was tall and gaunt, and shrouded from head to foot in the habiliments[17] of the grave. The mask which concealed the visage was made so nearly to resemble the countenance of a stiffened corpse that the closest scrutiny must have difficulty in detecting the cheat. And yet all this might have been endured, if not approved, by the mad revellers around. But the mummer[18] had gone so far as to assume the type of the Red Death. His vesture was dabbed in *blood*—and his broad brow, with all the features of the face, was besprinkled with the scarlet horror.

When the eyes of Prince Prospero fell upon this spectral image (which with a slow and solemn movement, as if more fully to sustain its *role*, stalked to and fro among the waltzers), he was seen to be convulsed, in the first moment with a strong shudder either of terror or distaste; but, in the next, his brow reddened with rage.

"Who dares?" he demanded hoarsely of the courtiers who stood near him—"who dares insult us with this blasphemous mockery? Seize him and unmask him—that we may know whom we have to hang at sunrise, from the battlements!"

It was in the eastern or blue chamber in which stood the Prince Prospero as he uttered these words. They rang throughout the seven rooms loudly and clearly—for the prince was a bold and robust man, and the music had become hushed at the waving of his hand.

It was in the blue room where stood the prince, with a group of pale courtiers by his side. At first, as he spoke, there was a slight rushing movement of this group in the direction of the intruder, who at the moment was also near at hand, and now, with deliberate and stately step, made closer approach to the speaker. But from a certain nameless awe with which the mad assumptions of the mummer had inspired the whole party, there were found none who put forth his hand to seize him; so that, unimpeded, he passed within a yard of the prince's person; and, while the vast assembly, as if with one impulse, shrank from the centers of the rooms to the walls, he made his way uninterruptedly, but with the same solemn and measured step which had distinguished him from the first, through the blue chamber to the purple—through the purple to the green —through the green to the orange—through this again to the white—and even thence to the violet, ere a decided movement had been made to arrest him. It was then, however, that the Prince Prospero, maddening with rage and the shame of his own momentary cowardice, rushed hurriedly through the six chambers while none followed him on account of a deadly terror that had seized upon all. He bore aloft a drawn dagger, and had approached, in rapid impetuosity, to within three or four feet of the retreating figure, when the latter, having attained the extremity of the velvet apartment, turned suddenly and confronted his pursuer. There was a sharp cry—and the dagger dropped gleaming upon the sable carpet, upon which, instantly afterwards, fell prostrate in death the Prince Prospero. Then, summoning the wild courage of despair, a throng of the revellers at once threw themselves into the black apartment, and seizing the mummer, whose tall figure stood erect and motionless within the shadow of the ebony clock, gasped in unutterable horror at finding the grave cerements and corpselike mask, which they handled with so violent a

---

17. **habiliments** (hə bil' ə mənts): clothing.
18. **mummer** (mum' ər): a person who wears a mask or disguise and acts out pantomimes; an actor.

rudeness, <u>untenanted</u>[19] by any <u>tangible</u>[20] form.

And now was acknowledged the presence of the Red Death. He had come like a thief in the night. And one by one dropped the revellers in the blood-bedewed halls of their revel, and died each in the despairing posture of his fall. And the life of the ebony clock went out with that of the last of the gay. And the flames of the tripods expired. And Darkness and Decay and the Red Death held illimitable dominion over all.

---

19. **untenanted** (un ten′ ənt ed): not occupied.
20. **tangible** (tan′ jə bəl): that can be touched or felt.

# Thinking About the Story

## A PERSONAL RESPONSE

*sharing impressions*

**1.** What picture lingered in your mind after you read this story? Describe that picture in your journal.

*constructing interpretations*

**2.** At the end of the story, in what sense do Darkness, Decay, and the Red Death have "illimitable dominion," or absolute power, over all?

### Think about
- what literally happens to the revellers
- the final description of the ebony clock and the torches
- what the disease, the Red Death, might represent

**3.** Why do you think the Red Death comes to Prospero's masque, or masked ball, dressed as a victim of the epidemic?

### Think about
- the description of the disease
- the extent to which Prospero and the revellers think they have avoided the epidemic
- the way the revellers, especially Prospero, react to the costume

**4.** What kind of person is Prince Prospero?

### Think about
- the way he responds to the epidemic
- the descriptions of his character and his taste
- the voluptuousness of the masked ball inside the locked castle

**5.** Do you think Prince Prospero and his friends deserve to die? Explain why or why not.

## A CREATIVE RESPONSE

**6.** If the Red Death had chosen to speak to Prince Prospero, what do you think it would have said?

## A CRITICAL RESPONSE

**7.** Compare Prince Prospero's response to the Red Death with the response to a contemporary disease that you described in your journal.

**8.** To understand the mood of this story, reexamine your emotional response and analyze the elements of the story responsible for this response.

**Think about**
- the dominating sounds of the story
- the descriptions of the rooms and of the costumes
- the movements of the characters between rooms

# Analyzing the Writer's Craft

## ALLEGORY AND IRONY

The name *Prospero* is related to the word *prosperous*. Why is Prospero an appropriate name for the prince in this story?

**Building a Literary Vocabulary.** An allegory is a narrative in which characters often stand for abstract ideas. An allegory generally teaches a lesson. Situational irony is a contrast between what a character expects and what actually happens. Prince Prospero's name is ironically allegorical: although he thinks that he prospers in his wealth and his exclusion of the Red Death, in reality the Red Death attends his lavish masquerade and kills everyone. Not all of the allegorical elements in the story are ironic, however. The disease, the Red Death, stands for death itself.

**Application: Interpreting Allegory.** Think about allegorical meanings of other parts of the story. With a partner, determine what you think three of the following elements of the story stand for, indicating which ones are also ironic.

- the castellated abbey
- the arrangement and decoration of the seven rooms
- the fiery torches that illuminate the rooms
- the ebony clock
- the revellers at the masked ball
- the title of the story

Join another pair of students and discuss your interpretations. Then, decide how the allegorical meaning of each element that you discussed relates to the central allegory of the story. Share your conclusions with the class.

**1.** Prince Prospero is said to have a "fine eye for colors and effects" and a "love of the bizarre." Think about the seven colors of his chambers, speculating on why he chose these particular colors and arranged them in the order he did. Include your ideas in a **script** for a guided tour of the abbey.

Option: Write a **parody** of an article on interior decorating in which Prospero's chambers are featured.

**2.** Pretend you are one of the subjects outside the abbey. Write a **eulogy** to be read at the memorial service for Prince Prospero and his thousand guests.

Option: Tell the story of the guests' destruction in a **song.**

**3.** Read another horror story, either by Edgar Allan Poe or by a contemporary writer such as Stephen King. Then compare that story to "The Masque of the Red Death" in a **review** stating which story you think is more horrifying.

Option: Create a **poster** comparing different elements such as conflict, description, and setting as they are exemplified in both stories.

# The Birds

DAPHNE DU MAURIER

A biography of du Maurier apears on page 639.

## *Approaching the Story*

Daphne du Maurier is a well-known writer of popular romance novels that are often tinged with mystery and the macabre. "The Birds" takes place just after World War II in England, on one of the many peninsulas that stretch out into the sea. Because du Maurier lived most of her life on one of these lonely peninsulas in southern England, she was able to write about the sea and the wildlife with great vividness. This story was later turned into a popular movie of the same title, directed by Alfred Hitchcock.

ON DECEMBER THE third the wind changed overnight and it was winter. Until then the autumn had been mellow, soft. The leaves had lingered on the trees, golden red, and the hedgerows were still green. The earth was rich where the plow had turned it.

Nat Hocken, because of a wartime disability, had a pension and did not work full time at the farm. He worked three days a week, and they gave him the lighter jobs: hedging, thatching, repairs to the farm buildings.

Although he was married, with children, his was a solitary disposition; he liked best to work alone. It pleased him when he was given a bank to build up, or a gate to mend at the far end of the peninsula, where the sea surrounded the farmland on either side. Then, at midday, he would pause and eat the pasty[1] that his wife had baked for him and, sitting on the cliff's edge, would watch the birds. Autumn was best for this, better than spring. In spring the birds flew inland, purposeful, intent; they knew where they were bound, the rhythm and ritual of their life brooked no delay. In autumn those that had not migrated overseas but remained to pass the winter were caught up in the same driving urge but, because migration was denied them, followed a pattern of their own. Great flocks of them came to the peninsula, restless, uneasy, spending themselves in motion; now wheeling, circling in the sky, now settling to feed on the rich new-turned soil, but even when they fed it was as though they did so without hunger, without desire. Restlessness drove them to the skies again.

Black and white, jackdaw and gull, mingled in strange partnership, seeking some sort of liberation, never satisfied, never still. Flocks of starlings, rustling like silk, flew to fresh pasture, driven by the same necessity of movement, and the smaller birds, the finches and the larks, scattered from tree to hedge as if compelled.

---

1. **pasty** (pas' tē): a meat pie.

Nat watched them, and he watched the sea birds too. Down in the bay they waited for the tide. They had more patience. Oyster catchers, redshank, sanderling, and curlew watched by the water's edge; as the slow sea sucked at the shore and then withdrew, leaving the strip of seaweed bare and the shingle[2] churned, the sea birds raced and ran upon the beaches. Then that same impulse to flight seized upon them too. Crying, whistling, calling, they skimmed the placid sea and left the shore. Make haste, make speed, hurry, and begone; yet where, and to what purpose? The restless urge of autumn, unsatisfying, sad, had put a spell upon them, and they must flock, and wheel, and cry; they must spill themselves of motion before winter came.

"Perhaps," thought Nat, munching his pasty by the cliff's edge, "a message comes to the birds in autumn, like a warning. Winter is coming. Many of them perish. And like people who, apprehensive[3] of death before their time, drive themselves to work or folly, the birds do likewise."

The birds had been more restless than ever this fall of the year, the agitation more marked because the days were still. As the tractor traced its path up and down the western hills, the figure of the farmer silhouetted on the driving seat, the whole machine and the man upon it would be lost momentarily in the great cloud of wheeling, crying birds. There were many more than usual, Nat was sure of this. Always, in autumn, they followed the plow, but not in great flocks like these, nor with such clamor.

Nat remarked upon it when hedging was finished for the day. "Yes," said the farmer, "there are more birds about than usual; I've noticed it too. And daring, some of them, taking no notice of the tractor. One or two gulls came so close to my head this afternoon I thought they'd knock my cap off! As it was, I could scarcely see what I was doing when they

were overhead and I had the sun in my eyes. I have a notion the weather will change. It will be a hard winter. That's why the birds are restless."

Nat, tramping home across the fields and down the lane to his cottage, saw the birds still flocking over the western hills, in the last glow of the sun. No wind, and the gray sea calm and full. Campion in bloom yet in the hedges, and the air mild. The farmer was right, though, and it was that night the weather turned. Nat's bedroom faced east. He woke just after two and heard the wind in the chimney. Not the storm and bluster of a sou'westerly gale, bringing the rain, but east wind, cold and dry. It sounded hollow in the chimney, and a loose slate rattled on the roof. Nat listened, and he could hear the sea roaring in the bay. Even the air in the small bedroom had turned chill: a draft came under the skirting of the door, blowing upon the bed. Nat drew the blanket round him, leant closer to the back of his sleeping wife, and stayed wakeful, watchful, aware of misgiving without cause.

Then he heard the tapping on the window. There was no creeper on the cottage walls to break loose and scratch upon the pane. He listened, and the tapping continued until, irritated by the sound, Nat got out of bed and went to the window. He opened it, and as he did so something brushed his hand, jabbing at his knuckles, grazing the skin. Then he saw the flutter of the wings and it was gone, over the roof, behind the cottage.

It was a bird; what kind of bird he could not tell. The wind must have driven it to shelter on the sill.

He shut the window and went back to bed but, feeling his knuckles wet, put his mouth to the scratch. The bird had drawn blood. Frightened, he supposed, and bewildered, the

---

2. **shingle:** a beach covered with pebbles and small stones.

3. **apprehensive** (ap′ rē hen′ siv): afraid.

*Bless Our Home and Eagle,* 1962, JERRY N. UELSMANN.
Philadelphia Museum of Art; purchased, Alfred Stieglitz Center Revolving Fund.

bird, seeking shelter, had stabbed at him in the darkness. Once more he settled himself to sleep.

Presently the tapping came again, this time more forceful, more insistent, and now his wife woke at the sound and, turning in the bed said to him, "See to the window, Nat. It's rattling."

"I've already seen to it," he told her. "There's some bird there trying to get in. Can't you hear the wind? It's blowing from the east, driving the birds to shelter."

"Send them away," she said. "I can't sleep with that noise."

He went to the window for the second time, and now when he opened it, there was not one bird upon the sill but half a dozen; they flew straight into his face, attacking him.

He shouted, striking out at them with his arms, scattering them; like the first one, they flew over the roof and disappeared. Quickly he let the window fall and latched it.

"Did you hear that?" he said. "They went for me. Tried to peck my eyes." He stood by the window, peering into the darkness, and could see nothing. His wife, heavy with sleep, murmured from the bed.

"I'm not making it up," he said, angry at her suggestion. "I tell you the birds were on the sill, trying to get into the room."

Suddenly a frightened cry came from the room across the passage where the children slept.

"It's Jill," said his wife, roused at the sound, sitting up in bed. "Go to her. See what's the matter."

Nat lit the candle, but when he opened the bedroom door to cross the passage, the draft blew out the flame.

There came a second cry of terror, this time from both children, and stumbling into their room, he felt the beating of wings about him in the darkness. The window was wide open. Through it came the birds, hitting first the ceiling and the walls, then swerving in mid-flight, turning to the children in their beds.

"It's all right, I'm here," shouted Nat, and the children flung themselves, screaming, upon him, while in darkness the birds rose and dived and came for him again.

"What is it, Nat, what's happened?" his wife called from the further bedroom, and swiftly he pushed the children through the door to the passage and shut it upon them, so that he was alone now in their bedroom with the birds.

He seized a blanket from the nearest bed and, using it as a weapon, flung it to right and left about him in the air. He felt the thud of bodies, heard the fluttering of wings, but they were not yet defeated, for again and again they returned to the assault, jabbing his hands, his head, the little stabbing beaks sharp as a pointed fork. The blanket became a weapon of defense; he wound it about his head and then in greater darkness beat at the birds with his bare hands. He dared not stumble to the door and open it, lest in doing so the birds should follow him.

How long he fought with them in the darkness he could not tell, but at last the beating of the wings about him lessened and then withdrew, and through the density of the blanket he was aware of light. He waited, listened; there was no sound except the fretful crying of one of the children from the bedroom beyond. The fluttering, the whirring of the wings had ceased.

He took the blanket from his head and stared about him. The cold gray morning light exposed the room. Dawn and the open window had called the living birds; the dead lay on the floor. Nat gazed at the little corpses, shocked and horrified. They were all small birds, none of any size; there must have been fifty of them lying there upon the floor. There were robins, finches, sparrows, blue tits, larks, and bramblings, birds that by nature's law kept to their own flock and their own territory and now, joining one with another in their urge for battle, had destroyed themselves against the bedroom walls, or in the strife had been destroyed by him. Some had lost feathers in the fight; others had blood, his blood, upon their beaks.

Sickened, Nat went to the window and stared out across his patch of garden to the fields.

It was bitter cold, and the ground had all the hard black look of frost. Not white frost, to shine in the morning sun, but the black frost that the east wind brings. The sea, fiercer now with the turning tide, white capped and steep, broke harshly in the bay. Of the birds there was no sign. Not a sparrow chattered in the hedge beyond the garden gate, no early missel thrush or blackbird pecked on the grass for worms. There was no sound at all but the east wind and the sea.

Nat shut the window and the door of the small bedroom and went back across the passage to his own. His wife sat up in bed, one child asleep beside her, the smaller in her arms, his face bandaged. The curtains were tightly drawn across the window, the candles lit. Her face looked garish in the yellow light. She shook her head for silence.

"He's sleeping now," she whispered, "but only just. Something must have cut him—there was blood at the corner of his eyes. Jill said it was the birds. She said she woke up, and the birds were in the room."

His wife looked up at Nat, searching his face for confirmation. She looked terrified, bewildered, and he did not want her to know that he was also shaken, dazed almost, by the events of the past few hours.

"There are birds in there," he said, "dead birds, nearly fifty of them. Robins, wrens, all the little birds from hereabouts. It's as though a madness seized them, with the east wind." He sat down on the bed beside his wife and held her hand. "It's the weather," he said. "It must be that, it's the hard weather. They aren't the birds, maybe, from here around. They've been driven down, from upcountry."

"But, Nat," whispered his wife, "it's only this night that the weather turned. There's been no snow to drive them. And they can't be hungry yet. There's food for them out there in the fields."

"It's the weather," repeated Nat. "I tell you, it's the weather."

His face, too, was drawn and tired, like hers. They stared at one another for a while without speaking.

"I'll go downstairs and make a cup of tea," he said.

The sight of the kitchen reassured him. The cups and saucers, neatly stacked upon the dresser, the table and chairs, his wife's roll of knitting on her basket chair, the children's toys in a corner cupboard.

He knelt down, raked out the old embers and relit the fire. The glowing sticks brought normality, the steaming kettle and the brown teapot comfort and security. He drank his tea, carried a cup up to his wife. Then he washed in the scullery and, putting on his boots, opened the back door.

The sky was hard and leaden, and the brown hills that had gleamed in the sun the day before looked dark and bare. The east wind, like a razor, stripped the trees, and the leaves, crackling and dry, shivered and scattered with the wind's blast. Nat stubbed the earth with his boot. It was frozen hard. He had never known a change so swift and sudden. Black winter had descended in a single night.

The children were awake now. Jill was chattering upstairs and young Johnny crying once again. Nat heard his wife's voice, soothing, comforting. Presently they came down. He had breakfast ready for them, and the routine of the day began.

"Did you drive away the birds?" asked Jill, restored to calm because of the kitchen fire, because of day, because of breakfast.

"Yes, they're all gone now," said Nat. "It was the east wind brought them in. They were frightened and lost. They wanted shelter."

"They tried to peck us," said Jill. "They went for Johnny's eyes."

"Fright made them do that," said Nat. "They didn't know where they were in the dark bedroom."

"I hope they won't come again," said Jill. "Perhaps if we put bread for them outside the window they will eat that and fly away."

She finished her breakfast and then went for her coat and hood, her school books and her satchel. Nat said nothing, but his wife looked at him across the table. A silent message passed between them.

"I'll walk with her to the bus," he said. "I don't go to the farm today."

And while the child was washing in the scullery, he said to his wife, "Keep all the windows closed, and the doors too. Just to be on the safe side. I'll go to the farm. Find out if they heard anything in the night." Then he walked with his small daughter up the lane. She seemed to have forgotten her experience of the night before. She danced ahead of him, chasing the leaves, her face whipped with the cold and rosy under the pixie hood.

"Is it going to snow, Dad?" she said. "It's cold enough."

He glanced up at the bleak sky, felt the wind tear at his shoulders.

"No," he said, "it's not going to snow. This is a black winter, not a white one."

All the while he searched the hedgerows for the birds, glanced over the top of them to the fields beyond, looked to the small wood above the farm where the rooks and jackdaws gathered. He saw none.

The other children waited by the bus stop, muffled, hooded like Jill, the faces white and pinched with cold.

Jill ran to them, waving. "My Dad says it won't snow," she called. "It's going to be a black winter."

She said nothing of the birds. She began to push and struggle with another little girl. The bus came ambling up the hill. Nat saw her on to it, then turned and walked back toward the farm. It was not his day for work, but he wanted to satisfy himself that all was well. Jim, the cowman, was clattering in the yard.

"Boss around?" asked Nat.

"Gone to market," said Jim. "It's Tuesday, isn't it?"

He clumped off round the corner of a shed. He had no time for Nat. Nat was said to be superior. Read books, and the like. Nat had forgotten it was Tuesday. This showed how the events of the preceding night had shaken him. He went to the back door of the farmhouse and heard Mrs. Trigg singing in the kitchen, the wireless[4] making a background to her song.

"Are you there, missus?" called out Nat.

She came to the door, beaming, broad, a good-tempered woman.

"Hullo, Mr. Hocken," she said. "Can you tell me where this cold is coming from? Is it Russia? I've never seen such a change. And it's going on, the wireless says. Something to do with the Arctic Circle."

"We didn't turn on the wireless this morning," said Nat. "Fact is, we had trouble last night."

"Kiddies poorly?"

"No . . ." He hardly knew how to explain it. Now, in daylight, the battle of the birds would sound absurd.

He tried to tell Mrs. Trigg what had happened, but he could see from her eyes that she thought his story was the result of a nightmare.

"Sure they were real birds," she said, smiling, "with proper feathers and all? Not the funny-shaped kind that the men see after closing hours on a Saturday night?"

"Mrs. Trigg," he said, "there are fifty dead

---

4. **wireless:** a radio.

birds—robins, wrens, and such—lying low in the floor of the children's bedroom. They went for me; they tried to go for young Johnny's eyes."

Mrs. Trigg stared at him doubtfully.

"Well there, now," she answered. "I suppose the weather brought them. Once in the bedroom, they wouldn't know where they were to. Foreign birds maybe, from that Arctic Circle."

"No," said Nat, "they were the birds you see about here every day."

"Funny thing," said Mrs. Trigg. "No explaining it, really. You ought to write up and ask the *Guardian*. They'd have some answer for it. Well, I must be getting on."

She nodded, smiled, and went back into the kitchen.

Nat, dissatisfied, turned to the farm gate. Had it not been for those corpses on the bedroom floor, which he must now collect and bury somewhere, he would have considered the tale exaggeration too.

Jim was standing by the gate.

"Had any trouble with the birds?" asked Nat.

"Birds? What birds?"

"We got them up our place last night. Scores of them, came in the children's bedroom. Quite savage they were."

"Oh?" It took time for anything to penetrate Jim's head. "Never heard of birds acting savage," he said at length. "They get tame, like, sometimes. I've seen them come to the windows for crumbs."

"These birds last night weren't tame."

"No? Cold, maybe. Hungry. You put out some crumbs."

Jim was no more interested than Mrs. Trigg had been. It was, Nat thought, like air raids in the war. No one down this end of the country knew what the Plymouth folk had seen and suffered. You had to endure something yourself before it touched you. He walked back along the lane and crossed the stile to his cottage.

He found his wife in the kitchen with young Johnny.

"See anyone?" she asked.

"Mrs. Trigg and Jim," he answered. "I don't think they believed me. Anyway, nothing wrong up there."

"You might take the birds away," she said. "I daren't go into the room to make the beds until you do. I'm scared."

"Nothing to scare you now," said Nat. "They're dead, aren't they?"

He went up with a sack and dropped the stiff bodies into it, one by one. Yes, there were fifty of them, all told. Just the ordinary common birds of the hedgerow, nothing as large even as a thrush. It must have been fright that made them act the way they did. Blue tits, wrens—it was incredible to think of the power of their small beaks jabbing at his face and hands the night before. He took the sack out into the garden and was faced now with a fresh problem. The ground was too hard to dig. It was frozen solid, yet no snow had fallen; nothing had happened in the past hours but the coming of the east wind. It was unnatural, queer. The weather prophets must be right. The change was something connected with the Arctic Circle.

The wind seemed to cut him to the bone as he stood there uncertainly, holding the sack. He could see the white capped seas breaking down under in the bay. He decided to take the birds to the shore and bury them.

When he reached the beach below the headland, he could scarcely stand, the force of the east wind was so strong. It hurt to draw breath, and his bare hands were blue. Never had he known such cold, not in all the bad winters he could remember. It was low tide. He crunched his way over the shingle to the softer sand and then, his back to the wind, ground a pit in the sand with his heel. He meant to drop the birds into it, but as he opened up the sack, the force of the wind carried them, lifted them, as though in flight again, and they were blown away from him along the beach, tossed like feathers, spread and scattered, the bodies of the fifty frozen birds. There was something ugly in the sight. He did not like it. The dead birds were swept away from him by the wind.

"The tide will take them when it turns," he said to himself.

He looked out to sea and watched the crested breakers, combing green. They rose stiffly, curled, and broke again, and because it was ebb tide the roar was distant, more remote, lacking the sound and thunder of the flood.

Then he saw them. The gulls. Out there, riding the seas.

What he had thought at first to be the whitecaps of the waves were gulls. Hundreds, thousands, tens of thousands . . . they rose and fell in the trough of the seas, heads to the wind, like a mighty fleet at anchor, waiting on the tide. To eastward, and to the west, the gulls were there. They stretched as far as his eye could reach, in close formation, line upon line. Had the sea been still, they would have covered the bay like a white cloud, head to head, body packed to body. Only the east wind, whipping the sea to breakers, hid them from the shore.

Nat turned and, leaving the beach, climbed the steep path home. Someone should know of this. Someone should be told. Something was happening, because of the east wind and the weather, that he did not understand. He wondered if he should go to the call box by the bus stop and ring up the police. Yet what could they do? What could anyone do? Tens of thousands of gulls riding the sea there, in the bay, because of storm, because of hunger. The police would think him mad, or drunk, or take the statement from him with great calm. "Thank you. Yes, the matter has already been reported. The hard weather is driving the birds inland in great numbers." Nat looked about

him. Still no sign of any other bird. Perhaps the cold had sent them all from upcountry? As he drew near to the cottage, his wife came to meet him at the door. She called to him, excited. "Nat," she said, "it's on the wireless. They've just read out a special news bulletin. I've written it down."

"What's on the wireless?" he said.

"About the birds," she said. "It's not only here—it's everywhere. In London, all over the country. Something has happened to the birds."

Together they went into the kitchen. He read the piece of paper lying on the table.

"Statement from the Home Office[5] at 11 A.M. today. Reports from all over the country are coming in hourly about the vast quantity of birds flocking above towns, villages, and outlying districts, causing obstruction and damage and even attacking individuals. It is thought that the arctic air stream, at present covering the British Isles, is causing birds to migrate south in immense[6] numbers, and that intense hunger may drive these birds to attack human beings. Householders are warned to see to their windows, doors, and chimneys and to take reasonable precautions for the safety of their children. A further statement will be issued later."

A kind of excitement seized Nat; he looked at his wife in triumph.

"There you are," he said. "Let's hope they'll hear that at the farm. Mrs. Trigg will know it wasn't any story. It's true. All over the country. I've been telling myself all morning there's something wrong. And just now, down on the beach, I looked out to sea and there are gulls, thousands of them, tens of thousands—you couldn't put a pin between their heads—and they're all out there, riding on the sea, waiting."

---

5. **Home Office:** the branch of government dealing with the country's domestic affairs.

6. **immense** (im mens′): huge, enormous.

"What are they waiting for, Nat?" she asked.

He stared at her, then looked down again at the piece of paper.

"I don't know," he said slowly. "It says here the birds are hungry."

He went over to the drawer where he kept his hammer and tools.

"What are you going to do, Nat?"

"See to the windows and the chimneys too, like they tell you."

"You think they would break in, with the windows shut? Those sparrows and robins and such? Why, how could they?"

He did not answer. He was not thinking of the robins and the sparrows. He was thinking of the gulls. . . .

He went upstairs and worked there the rest of the morning, boarding the windows of the bedrooms, filling up the chimney bases. Good job it was his free day and he was not working at the farm. It reminded him of the old days, at the beginning of the war. He was not married then, and he had made all the blackout boards[7] for his mother's house in Plymouth. Made the shelter too. Not that it had been of any use when the moment came. He wondered if they would take these precautions up at the farm. He doubted it. Too easygoing, Harry Trigg and his missus. Maybe they'd laugh at the whole thing. Go off to a dance or a whist drive.[8]

"Dinner's ready." She called him, from the kitchen.

"All right. Coming down."

He was pleased with his handiwork. The frames fitted nicely over the little panes and at the base of the chimneys.

When dinner was over and his wife was washing up, Nat switched on the one o'clock news. The same announcement was repeated, the one which she had taken down during the morning, but the news bulletin enlarged upon it. "The flocks of birds have caused dislocation in all areas," read the announcer, "and in London the sky was so dense at ten o'clock this morning that it seemed as if the city were covered by a vast black cloud.

"The birds settled on rooftops, on window ledges, and on chimneys. The species included blackbird, thrush, the common house sparrow, and, as might be expected in the metropolis, a vast quantity of pigeons and starlings, and that frequenter of the London river, the black-headed gull. The sight has been so unusual that traffic came to a standstill in many thoroughfares, work was abandoned in shops and offices, and the streets and pavements were crowded with people standing about to watch the birds."

Various incidents were recounted, the suspected reason of cold and hunger stated again, and warnings to householders repeated. The announcer's voice was smooth and suave. Nat had the impression that this man, in particular, treated the whole business as he would an elaborate joke. There would be others like him, hundreds of them, who did not know what it was to struggle in darkness with a flock of birds. There would be parties tonight in London, like the ones they gave on election nights. People standing about, shouting and laughing, getting drunk. "Come and watch the birds!"

Nat switched off the wireless. He got up and started work on the kitchen windows. His wife watched him, young Johnny at her heels.

"What, boards for down here too?" she said. "Why, I'll have to light up before three o'clock. I see no call for boards down here."

"Better be sure than sorry," answered Nat. "I'm not going to take any chances."

"What they ought to do," she said, "is to call the army out and shoot the birds. That would soon scare them off."

---

7. **blackout boards:** boards used to cover windows during World War II bombing raids.

8. **whist drive** (hwist drīv): a card-playing party.

"Let them try," said Nat. "How'd they set about it?"

"They have the army to the docks," she answered, "when the dockers strike. The soldiers go down and unload the ships."

"Yes," said Nat, "and the population of London is eight million or more. Think of all the buildings, all the flats and houses. Do you think they've enough soldiers to go around shooting birds from every roof?"

"I don't know. But something should be done. They ought to do something."

Nat thought to himself that "they" were no doubt considering the problem at that very moment, but whatever "they" decided to do in London and the big cities would not help the people here, three hundred miles away. Each householder must look after his own.

"How are we off for food?" he said.

"Now, Nat, whatever next?"

"Never mind. What have you got in the larder?"

"It's shopping day tomorrow—you know that. I don't keep uncooked food hanging about—it goes off. Butcher doesn't call till the day after. But I can bring back something when I go in tomorrow."

Nat did not want to scare her. He thought it possible that she might not go to town tomorrow. He looked in the larder for himself and in the cupboard where she kept her tins. They would do for a couple of days. Bread was low.

"What about the baker?"

"He comes tomorrow too."

He saw she had flour. If the baker did not call, she had enough to bake one loaf.

"We'd be better off in the old days," he said, "when the women baked twice a week, and had pilchards[9] salted, and there was food for a family to last a siege, if need be."

"I've tried the children with tinned[10] fish—they don't like it," she said.

Nat went on hammering the boards across the kitchen windows. Candles. They were low in candles too. That must be another thing she meant to buy tomorrow. Well, it could not be helped. They must go early to bed tonight. That was, if . . .

He got up and went out of the back door and stood in the garden, looking down toward the sea. There had been no sun all day, and now, at barely three o'clock, a kind of darkness had already come, the sky sullen, heavy, colorless like salt. He could hear the vicious sea drumming on the rocks. He walked down the path, halfway to the beach. And then he stopped. He could see the tide had turned. The rock that had shown in midmorning was now covered, but it was not the sea that held his eyes. The gulls had risen. They were circling, hundreds of them, thousands of them, lifting their wings against the wind. It was the gulls that made the darkening of the sky. And they were silent. They made not a sound. They just went on soaring and circling, rising, falling, trying their strength against the wind.

Nat turned. He ran up the path, back to the cottage.

"I'm going for Jill," he said. "I'll wait for her at the bus stop."

"What's the matter?" asked his wife. "You've gone quite white."

"Keep Johnny inside," he said. "Keep the door shut. Light up now, and draw the curtains."

"It's only just gone three," she said.

"Never mind. Do what I tell you."

He looked inside the toolshed, outside the back door. Nothing there of much use. A spade was too heavy, and a fork no good. He took the hoe. It was the only possible tool, and light enough to carry.

He started walking up the lane to the bus stop and now and again glanced back over his shoulder.

---

9. **pilchards** (pil′ chərdz): sardines.
10. **tinned:** canned.

The gulls had risen higher now; their circles were broader, wider; they were spreading out in huge formation across the sky.

He hurried on; although he knew the bus would not come to the top of the hill before four o'clock, he had to hurry. He passed no one on the way. He was glad of this. No time to stop and chatter.

At the top of the hill he waited. He was much too soon. There was half an hour still to go. The east wind came whipping across the fields from the higher ground. He stamped his feet and blew upon his hands. In the distance he could see the clay hills, white and clean, against the heavy pallor of the sky. Something black rose from behind them, like a smudge at first, then widening, becoming deeper, and the smudge became a cloud, and the cloud divided again into five other clouds, spreading north, east, south, and west, and they were not clouds at all; they were birds. He watched them travel across the sky, and as one section passed overhead, within two or three hundred feet of him, he knew, from their speed, they were bound inland, upcountry; they had no business with the people here on the peninsula. They were rooks, crows, jackdaws, magpies, jays—all birds that usually preyed upon the smaller species; but this afternoon they were bound on some other mission.

"They've been given the towns," thought Nat. "They know what they have to do. We don't matter so much here. The gulls will serve for us. The others go to the towns."

He went to the call box, stepped inside, and lifted the receiver. The exchange[11] would do. They would pass the message on.

"I'm speaking from the Highway," he said, "by the bus stop. I want to report large formations of birds traveling upcountry. The gulls are also forming in the bay."

"All right," answered the voice, laconic, weary.

"You'll be sure and pass this message on to the proper quarter?"

"Yes . . . yes . . ." Impatient now, fed up. The buzzing note resumed.

"She's another," thought Nat. "She doesn't care. Maybe she's had to answer calls all day. She hopes to go to the pictures tonight. She'll squeeze some fellow's hand and point up at the sky and say 'Look at all them birds!' She doesn't care."

The bus came lumbering up the hill. Jill climbed out and three or four other children. The bus went on toward the town.

"What's the hoe for, Dad?"

They crowded around him, laughing, pointing.

"I just brought it along," he said. "Come on now, let's get home. It's cold, no hanging about. Here, you. I'll watch you across the fields, see how fast you can run."

He was speaking to Jill's companions, who came from different families, living in the council houses.[12] A shortcut would take them to the cottages.

"We want to play a bit in the lane," said one of them.

"No, you don't. You go off home, or I'll tell your mammy."

They whispered to one another, round-eyed, then scuttled off across the fields. Jill stared at her father, her mouth sullen.

"We always play in the lane," she said.

"Not tonight, you don't," he said. "Come on now, no dawdling."

He could see the gulls now, circling the fields, coming in toward the land. Still silent. Still no sound.

"Look, Dad, look over there, look at all the gulls."

"Yes. Hurry, now."

"Where are they flying to? Where are they going?"

---

11. **exchange:** the central office in a telephone system.

12. **council houses:** government housing projects.

"Upcountry, I dare say. Where it's warmer."

He seized her hand and dragged her after him along the lane.

"Don't go so fast. I can't keep up."

The gulls were copying the rooks and crows. They were spreading out in formation across the sky. They headed, in bands of thousands, to the four compass points.

"Dad, what is it? What are the gulls doing?"

They were not intent upon their flight, as the crows, as the jackdaws had been. They still circled overhead. Nor did they fly so high. It was as though they waited upon some signal. As though some decision had yet to be given. The order was not clear.

"Do you want me to carry you, Jill? Here, come pick a back."

This way he might put on speed; but he was wrong. Jill was heavy. She kept slipping. And she was crying too. His sense of urgency, of fear, had communicated itself to the child.

"I wish the gulls would go away. I don't like them. They're coming closer to the lane."

He put her down again. He started running, swinging Jill after him. As they went past the farm turning, he saw the farmer backing his car out of the garage. Nat called to him.

"Can you give us a lift?" he said.

"What's that?"

Mr. Trigg turned in the driving seat and stared at them. Then a smile came to his cheerful, rubicund face.

"It looks as though we're in for some fun," he said. "Have you seen the gulls? Jim and I are going to take a crack at them. Everyone's gone bird crazy, talking of nothing else. I hear you were troubled in the night. Want a gun?"

Nat shook his head.

The small car was packed. There was just room for Jill, if she crouched on top of petrol tins on the back seat.

"I don't want a gun," said Nat, "but I'd be obliged if you'd run Jill home. She's scared of the birds."

He spoke briefly. He did not want to talk in front of Jill.

"OK," said the farmer, "I'll take her home. Why don't you stop behind and join the shooting match? We'll make the feathers fly."

Jill climbed in, and, turning the car, the driver sped up the lane. Nat followed after. Trigg must be crazy. What use was a gun against a sky of birds?

Now that Nat was not responsible for Jill, he had time to look about him. The birds were circling still, above the fields. Mostly herring gull, but the black-backed gull amongst them. Usually they kept apart. Now they were united. Some bond had brought them together. It was the black-backed gull that attacked the smaller birds, and even newborn lambs, so he'd heard. He'd never seen it done. He remembered this now, though, looking above him in the sky. They were coming in toward the farm. They were circling lower in the sky, and the black-backed gulls were to the front, the black-backed gulls were leading. The farm, then, was their target. They were making for the farm.

Nat increased his pace toward his own cottage. He saw the farmer's car turn and come back along the lane. It drew up beside him with a jerk.

"The kid has run inside," said the farmer. "Your wife was watching for her. Well, what do you make of it? They're saying in town the Russians have done it. The Russians have poisoned the birds."

"How could they do that?" asked Nat.

"Don't ask me. You know how stories get around. Will you join my shooting match?"

"No, I'll get along home. The wife will be worried else."

"My missus says if you could eat gull, there'd be some sense in it," said Trigg. "We'd have roast gull, baked gull, and pickle 'em into the bargain. You wait until I let off a few barrels into the brutes. That'll scare 'em."

"Have you boarded your windows?" asked Nat.

"No. Lot of nonsense. They like to scare you on the wireless. I've had more to do today than to go round boarding up my windows."

"I'd board them now, if I were you."

"Garn. You're windy.[13] Like to come to our place to sleep?"

"No, thanks all the same."

"All right. See you in the morning. Give you a gull breakfast."

The farmer grinned and turned his car to the farm entrance.

Nat hurried on. Past the little wood, past the old barn, and then across the stile to the remaining field.

As he jumped the stile, he heard the whirr of wings. A black-backed gull dived down at him from the sky, missed, swerved in flight, and rose to dive again. In a moment it was joined by others, six, seven, a dozen, black-backed and herring mixed. Nat dropped his hoe. The hoe was useless. Covering his head with his arms, he ran toward the cottage. They kept coming at him from the air, silent save for the beating wings. The terrible, fluttering wings. He could feel the blood on his hands, his wrists, his neck. Each stab of a swooping beak tore his flesh. If only he could keep them from his eyes. Nothing else mattered. He must keep them from his eyes. They had not learnt yet how to cling to a shoulder, how to rip clothing, how to dive in mass upon the head, upon the body. But with each dive, with each attack, they became bolder. And they had no thought for themselves. When they dived low and missed, they crashed, bruised and broken, on the ground. As Nat ran, he stumbled, kicking their spent bodies in front of him.

He found the door; he hammered upon it with his bleeding hands. Because of the boarded windows, no light shone. Everything was dark.

"Let me in," he shouted. "It's Nat. Let me in."

He shouted loud to make himself heard above the whirr of the gulls' wings.

Then he saw the gannet, poised for the dive, above him in the sky. The gulls circled, retired, soared, one with another, against the wind. Only the gannet remained. One single gannet, above him in the sky. The wings folded suddenly to its body. It dropped, like a stone. Nat screamed, and the door opened. He stumbled across the threshold, and his wife threw her weight against the door.

They heard the thud of the gannet as it fell.

His wife dressed his wounds. They were not deep. The backs of his hands had suffered most, and his wrists. Had he not worn a cap they would have reached his head. As to the gannet . . . the gannet could have split his skull.

The children were crying, of course. They had seen the blood on their father's hands.

"It's all right now," he told them. "I'm not hurt. Just a few scratches. You play with Johnny, Jill. Mammy will wash these cuts."

He half shut the door to the scullery so that they could not see. His wife was ashen. She began running water from the sink.

"I saw them overhead," she whispered. "They began collecting just as Jill ran in with Mr. Trigg. I shut the door fast, and it jammed. That's why I couldn't open it at once when you came."

"Thank God they waited for me," he said. "Jill would have fallen at once. One bird alone would have done it."

Furtively, so as not to alarm the children, they whispered together as she bandaged his hands and the back of his neck.

"They're flying inland," he said, "thousands of them. Rooks, crows, all the bigger birds. I saw them from the bus stop. They're making for the towns."

"But what can they do, Nat?"

---

13. **windy:** scared; worried about danger.

"They'll attack. Go for everyone out in the streets. Then they'll try the windows, the chimneys."

"Why don't the authorities do something? Why don't they get the army, get machine guns, anything?"

"There's been no time. Nobody's prepared. We'll hear what they have to say on the six o'clock news."

Nat went back into the kitchen, followed by his wife. Johnny was playing quietly on the floor. Only Jill looked anxious.

"I can hear the birds," she said. "Listen, Dad."

Nat listened. Muffled sounds came from the windows, from the door. Wings brushing the surface, sliding, scraping, seeking a way of entry. The sound of many bodies, pressed together, shuffling on the sills. Now and again came a thud, a crash, as some bird dived and fell. "Some of them will kill themselves that way," he thought, "but not enough. Never enough."

"All right," he said aloud. "I've got boards over the windows, Jill. The birds can't get in."

He went and examined all the windows. His work had been thorough. Every gap was closed. He would make extra certain, however. He found wedges, pieces of old tin, strips of wood and metal, and fastened them at the sides to reinforce the boards. His hammering helped to deafen the sound of the birds, the shuffling, the tapping, and more ominous[14]—he did not want his wife or the children to hear it—the splinter of cracked glass.

"Turn on the wireless," he said. "Let's have the wireless."

This would drown the sound also. He went upstairs to the bedrooms and reinforced the windows there. Now he could hear the birds on the roof, the scraping of claws, a sliding, jostling sound.

He decided they must sleep in the kitchen,

keep up the fire, bring down the mattresses and lay them out on the floor. He was afraid of the bedroom chimneys. The boards he had placed at the chimney bases might give way. In the kitchen they would be safe because of the fire. He would have to make a joke of it. Pretend to the children they were playing at camp. If the worst happened, and the birds forced an entry down the bedroom chimneys, it would be hours, days perhaps, before they could break down the doors. The birds would be imprisoned in the bedrooms. They could do no harm there. Crowded together, they would stifle and die.

He began to bring the mattresses downstairs. At sight of them his wife's eyes widened in apprehension. She thought the birds had already broken in upstairs.

"All right," he said cheerfully, "we'll all sleep together in the kitchen tonight. More cosy here by the fire. Then we shan't be worried by those silly old birds tapping at the windows."

He made the children help him rearrange the furniture, and he took the precaution of moving the dresser, with his wife's help, across the window. It fitted well. It was an added safeguard. The mattresses could now be lain, one beside the other, against the wall where the dresser had stood.

"We're safe enough now," he thought. "We're snug and tight, like an air-raid shelter. We can hold out. It's just the food that worries me. Food, and coal for the fire. We've enough for two or three days, not more. By that time…"

No use thinking ahead as far as that. And they'd be giving directions on the wireless. People would be told what to do. And now, in the midst of many problems, he realized that it was dance music only coming over the air. Not *Children's Hour*, as it should have been. He glanced at the dial. Yes, they were on the

---

14. **ominous** (äm′ ə nəs): foretelling evil.

Home Service[15] all right. Dance records. He switched to the Light program. He knew the reason. The usual programs had been abandoned. This only happened at exceptional times. Elections and such. He tried to remember if it had happened in the war, during the heavy raids on London. But of course. The BBC was not stationed in London during the war. The programs were broadcast from other, temporary quarters. "We're better off here," he thought. "We're better off here in the kitchen, with the windows and the doors boarded, than they are up in the towns. Thank God we're not in the towns."

At six o'clock the records ceased. The time signal was given. No matter if it scared the children, he must hear the news. There was pause after the pips. Then the announcer spoke. His voice was solemn, grave. Quite different from midday.

"This is London," he said. "A national emergency was proclaimed at four o'clock this afternoon. Measures are being taken to safeguard the lives and property of the population, but it must be understood that these are not easy to effect immediately, owing to the unforeseen and unparalleled nature of the present crisis. Every householder must take precautions to his own building, and where several people live together, as in flats and apartments, they must unite to do the utmost they can to prevent entry. It is absolutely imperative that every individual stay indoors tonight and that no one at all remain on the streets, or roads, or anywhere without doors. The birds, in vast numbers, are attacking anyone on sight and have already begun an assault upon buildings; but these, with due care, should be impenetrable.[16] The population is asked to remain calm and not to panic. Owing to the exceptional nature of the emergency, there will be no further transmission from any broadcasting station until 7:00 A.M. tomorrow."

They played the national anthem. Nothing more happened. Nat switched off the set. He looked at his wife. She stared back at him.

"What's it mean?" said Jill. "What did the news say?"

"There won't be any more programs tonight," said Nat. "There's been a breakdown at the BBC."

"Is it the birds?" asked Jill. "Have the birds done it?"

"No," said Nat, "it's just that everyone's very busy, and then of course they have to get rid of the birds, messing everything up, in the towns. Well, we can manage without the wireless for one evening."

"I wish we had a gramophone,"[17] said Jill; "that would be better than nothing."

She had her face turned to the dresser, backed against the windows. Try as they did to ignore it, they were all aware of the shuffling, the stabbing, the persistent[18] beating and sweeping of wings.

"We'll have supper early," suggested Nat, "something for a treat. Ask Mammy. Toasted cheese, eh? Something we all like?"

He winked and nodded at his wife. He wanted the look of dread, of apprehension, to go from Jill's face.

He helped with the supper, whistling, singing, making as much clatter as he could, and it seemed to him that the shuffling and the tapping were not so intense as they had been at first. Presently he went up to the bedrooms and listened, and he no longer heard the jostling for place upon the roof.

"They've got reasoning powers," he

---

15. **Home Service:** one of the three radio services offered by the British Broadcasting Corporation (BBC) at this time.

16. **impenetrable** (im pen′ i trə bəl): not capable of being penetrated; able to withstand any attack.

17. **gramophone:** phonograph.

18. **persistent** (pər sist′ ənt): not stopping; determined.

thought; "they know it's hard to break in here. They'll try elsewhere. They won't waste their time with us."

Supper passed without incident, and then, when they were clearing away, they heard a new sound, droning, familiar, a sound they all knew and understood.

His wife looked up at him, her face alight. "It's planes," she said. "They're sending out planes after the birds. That's what I said they ought to do all along. That will get them. Isn't that gunfire? Can't you hear guns?"

It might be gunfire out at sea. Nat could not tell. Big naval guns might have an effect upon the gulls out at sea, but the gulls were inland now. The guns couldn't shell the shore because of the population.

"It's good, isn't it," said his wife, "to hear the planes?" And Jill, catching her enthusiasm, jumped up and down with Johnny. "The planes will get the birds. The planes will shoot them."

Just then they heard a crash about two miles distant, followed by a second, then a third. The droning became more distant, passed away out to sea.

"What was that?" asked his wife. "Were they dropping bombs on the birds?"

"I don't know," answered Nat. "I don't think so."

He did not want to tell her that the sound they had heard was the crashing of aircraft. It was, he had no doubt, a venture on the part of the authorities to send out reconnaissance forces, but they might have known the venture was suicidal. What could aircraft do against birds that flung themselves to death against propeller and fuselage but hurtle to the ground themselves? This was being tried now, he supposed, over the whole country. And at a cost. Someone high up had lost his head.

"Where have the planes gone, Dad?" asked Jill.

"Back to base," he said. "Come on now, time to tuck down for bed."

It kept his wife occupied, undressing the children before the fire, seeing to the bedding, one thing and another, while he went round the cottage again, making sure that nothing had worked loose. There was no further drone of aircraft, and the naval guns had ceased. "Waste of life and effort," Nat said to himself. "We can't destroy enough of them that way. Cost too heavy. There's always gas. Maybe they'll try spraying with gas, mustard gas.[19] We'll be warned first, of course, if they do. There's one thing, the best brains of the country will be on to it tonight."

Somehow the thought reassured him. He had a picture of scientists, naturalists, technicians, and all those chaps they called the back-room boys, summoned to a council; they'd be working on the problem now. This was not a job for the government, for the chiefs of staff—they would merely carry out the orders of the scientists.

"They'll have to be ruthless," he thought. "Where the trouble's worst they'll have to risk more lives if they use gas. All the livestock, too, and the soil—all contaminated. As long as everyone doesn't panic. That's the trouble. People panicking, losing their heads. The BBC was right to warn us of that."

Upstairs in the bedrooms all was quiet. No further scraping and stabbing at the windows. A lull in battle. Forces regrouping. Wasn't that what they called it in the old wartime bulletins? The wind hadn't dropped, though. He could still hear it roaring in the chimneys. And the sea breaking down on the shore. Then he remembered the tide. The tide would be on the turn. Maybe the lull in battle was because of the tide. There was some law the birds obeyed, and it was all to do with the east wind and the tide.

He glanced at his watch. Nearly eight

---

19. **mustard gas:** a poison gas, named for its mustardlike odor.

o'clock. It must have gone high water an hour ago. That explained the lull: the birds attacked with the flood tide. It might not work that way inland, upcountry, but it seemed as if it was so this way on the coast. He reckoned the time limit in his head. They had six hours to go without attack. When the tide turned again, around 1:20 in the morning, the birds would come back. . . .

There were two things he could do. The first to rest with his wife and the children, and all of them snatch what sleep they could until the small hours. The second to go out, see how they were faring at the farm, see if the telephone was still working there so that they might get news from the exchange.

He called softly to his wife, who had just settled the children. She came halfway up the stairs and he whispered to her.

"You're not to go," she said at once; "you're not to go and leave me alone with the children. I can't stand it."

Her voice rose hysterically. He hushed her, calmed her.

"All right," he said, "all right. I'll wait till morning. And we'll get the wireless bulletin then too, at seven. But in the morning, when the tide ebbs again, I'll try for the farm, and they may let us have bread and potatoes, and milk too."

His mind was busy again, planning against emergency. They would not have milked, of course, this evening. The cows would be standing by the gate, waiting in the yard, with the household inside, battened behind boards, as they were here at the cottage. That is, if they had time to take precautions. He thought of the farmer, Trigg, smiling at him from the car. There would have been no shooting party, not tonight.

The children were asleep. His wife, still clothed, was sitting on her mattress. She watched him, her eyes nervous.

"What are you going to do?" she whispered.

He shook his head for silence. Softly, stealthily, he opened the back door and looked outside.

It was pitch dark. The wind was blowing harder than ever, coming in steady gusts, icy, from the sea. He kicked at the step outside the door. It was heaped with birds. There were dead birds everywhere. Under the windows, against the walls. These were the suicides, the divers, the ones with broken necks. Wherever he looked he saw dead birds. No trace of the living. The living had flown seaward with the turn of the tide. The gulls would be riding the seas now, as they had done in the forenoon.

In the far distance, on the hill where the tractor had been two days before, something was burning. One of the aircraft that had crashed; the fire, fanned by the wind, had set light to a stack.

He looked at the bodies of the birds, and he had a notion that if he heaped them, one upon the other, on the windowsills, they would make added protection for the next attack. Not much, perhaps, but something. The bodies would have to be clawed at, pecked, and dragged aside before the living birds could gain purchase[20] on the sills and attack the panes. He set to work in the darkness. It was queer; he hated touching them. The bodies were still warm and bloody. The blood matted their feathers. He felt his stomach turn, but he went on with his work. He noticed grimly that every windowpane was shattered. Only the boards had kept the birds from breaking in. He stuffed the cracked panes with the bleeding bodies of the birds.

When he had finished he went back into the cottage. He barricaded the kitchen door, made it doubly secure. He took off his bandages, sticky with the birds' blood, not with his own cuts, and put on fresh plaster.

His wife had made him cocoa and he drank it thirstily. He was very tired.

---

20. **gain purchase:** get a good hold.

"All right," he said, smiling, "don't worry. We'll get through."

He lay down on his mattress and closed his eyes. He slept at once. He dreamt uneasily, because through his dreams there ran a thread of something forgotten. Some piece of work, neglected, that he should have done. Some precaution that he had known well but had not taken, and he could not put a name to it in his dreams. It was connected in some way with the burning aircraft and the stack upon the hill. He went on sleeping, though; he did not awake. It was his wife shaking his shoulder that awoke him finally.

"They've begun," she sobbed. "They've started this last hour. I can't listen to it any longer alone. There's something smelling bad too, something burning."

Then he remembered. He had forgotten to make up the fire. It was smoldering, nearly out. He got up swiftly and lit the lamp. The hammering had started at the windows and the doors, but it was not that he minded now. It was the smell of singed feathers. The smell filled the kitchen. He knew at once what it was. The birds were coming down the chimney, squeezing their way down to the kitchen range.

He got sticks and paper and put them on the embers, then reached for the can of paraffin.

"Stand back," he shouted to his wife. "We've got to risk this."

He threw the paraffin onto the fire. The flame roared up the pipe, and down upon the fire fell the scorched, blackened bodies of the birds.

The children woke, crying. "What is it?" said Jill. "What's happened?"

Nat had no time to answer. He was raking the bodies from the chimney, clawing them out onto the floor. The flames still roared, and the danger of the chimney catching fire was one he had to take. The flames would send away the living birds from the chimney top.

The lower joint was the difficulty, though. This was choked with the smoldering, helpless bodies of the birds caught by fire. He scarcely heeded the attack on the windows and the door: let them beat their wings, break their beaks, lose their lives in the attempt to force an entry into his home. They would not break in. He thanked God he had one of the old cottages, with small windows, stout walls. Not like the new council houses. Heaven help them up the lane in the new council houses.

"Stop crying," he called to the children. "There's nothing to be afraid of—stop crying."

He went on raking at the burning, smoldering bodies as they fell into the fire.

"This'll fetch them," he said to himself, "the draft and the flames together. We're all right, as long as the chimney doesn't catch. I ought to be shot for this. It's all my fault. Last thing, I should have made up the fire. I knew there was something."

Amid the scratching and tearing at the window boards came the sudden homely striking of the kitchen clock—3:00 A.M. A little more than four hours yet to go. He could not be sure of the exact time of high water. He reckoned it would not turn much before half past seven, twenty to eight.

"Light up the Primus,"[21] he said to his wife. "Make us some tea, and the kids some cocoa. No use sitting around doing nothing."

That was the line. Keep her busy, and the children too. Move about, eat, drink; always best to be on the go.

He waited by the range. The flames were dying. But no more blackened bodies fell from the chimney. He thrust his poker up as far as it could go and found nothing. It was clear. The chimney was clear. He wiped the sweat from his forehead.

"Come on now, Jill," he said, "bring me some more sticks. We'll have a good fire going

---

21. **Primus** (prī′ məs): a portable oil-burning cookstove, similar to a hotplate.

directly." She wouldn't come near him, though. She was staring at the heaped singed bodies of the birds.

"Never mind them," he said. "We'll put those in the passage when I've got the fire steady."

The danger of the chimney was over. It could not happen again, not if the fire was kept burning day and night.

"I'll have to get more fuel from the farm tomorrow," he thought. "This will never last. I'll manage, though. I can do all that with the ebb tide. It can be worked, fetching what we need, when the tide's turned. We've just got to adapt ourselves, that's all."

They drank tea and cocoa and ate slices of bread and Bovril.[22] Only half a loaf left, Nat noticed. Never mind, though, they'd get by.

"Stop it," said young Johnny, pointing to the windows with his spoon, "stop it, you old birds."

"That's right," said Nat, smiling; "we don't want the old beggars, do we? Had enough of 'em."

They began to cheer when they heard the thud of the suicide birds.

"There's another, Dad," cried Jill. "He's done for."

"He's had it," said Nat. "There he goes, the blighter."

This was the way to face up to it. This was the spirit. If they could keep this up, hang on like this until seven, when the first news bulletin came through, they would not have done too badly.

"Give us a cigarette," he said to his wife. "A bit of a smoke will clear away the smell of the scorched feathers."

"There's only two left in the packet," she said. "I was going to buy you some from the co-op."[23]

"I'll have one," he said. "T'other will keep for a rainy day."

No sense trying to make the children rest. There was no rest to be got while the tapping and the scratching went on at the windows. He sat with one arm round his wife and the other round Jill, with Johnny on his mother's lap and the blankets heaped about them on the mattress.

"You can't help admiring the beggars," he said. "They've got persistence. You'd think they'd tire of the game, but not a bit of it."

Admiration was hard to sustain. The tapping went on and on, and a new rasping tone struck Nat's ear, as though a sharper beak than any hitherto had come to take over from its fellows. He tried to remember the names of birds, he tried to think which species would go for this particular job. It was not the tap of the woodpecker. That would be light and frequent. This was more serious because, if it continued long, the wood would splinter as the glass had done. Then he remembered the hawks. Could the hawks have taken over from the gulls? Were there buzzards now upon the sills, using talons as well as beaks? Hawks, buzzards, kestrels, falcons—he had forgotten the birds of prey. He had forgotten the gripping power of the birds of prey. Three hours to go, and while they waited, the sound of the splintering wood, the talons tearing at the wood.

Nat looked about him, seeing what furniture he could destroy to fortify the door. The windows were safe because of the dresser. He was not certain of the door. He went upstairs, but when he reached the landing he paused and listened. There was a soft patter on the floor of the children's bedroom. The birds had broken through. . . . He put his ear to the door. No mistake. He could hear the rustle of wings and the light patter as they searched the floor. The other bedroom was still clear. He went into it and began bringing out the furniture to pile at the head of the stairs should the door of the children's bedroom go. It was a preparation. It might never be needed. He could not

---

22. **Bovril** (bō′ vril): the brand name for a spread to put on toast.

23. **co-op:** a grocery store.

stack the furniture against the door because it opened inward. The only possible thing was to have it at the top of the stairs.

"Come down, Nat. What are you doing?" called his wife.

"I won't be long," he shouted. "Just making everything shipshape up here."

He did not want her to come; he did not want her to hear the pattering of the feet in the children's bedroom, the brushing of those wings against the door.

At five-thirty he suggested breakfast, bacon and fried bread, if only to stop the growing look of panic in his wife's eyes and to calm the fretful children. She did not know about the birds upstairs. The bedroom, luckily, was not over the kitchen. Had it been so, she could not have failed to hear the sound of them up there, tapping the boards. And the silly, sense-less thud of the suicide birds, the death and glory boys, who flew into the bedroom, smash-ing their heads against the walls. He knew them of old, the herring gulls. They had no brains. The black-backs were different; they knew what they were doing. So did the buz-zards, the hawks. . . .

He found himself watching the clock, gaz-ing at the hands that went so slowly round the dial. If his theory was not correct, if the attack did not cease with the turn of the tide, he knew they were beaten. They could not con-tinue through the long day without air, with-out rest, without more fuel, without . . . his mind raced. He knew there were so many things they needed to withstand siege. They were not fully prepared. They were not ready. It might be that it would be safer in the towns after all. If he could get a message through on the farm telephone to his cousin, only a short journey by train upcountry, they might be able to hire a car. That would be quicker—hire a car between tides. . . .

His wife's voice, calling his name, drove away the sudden, desperate desire for sleep.

"What is it? What now?" he said sharply.

"The wireless," said his wife. "I've been watching the clock. It's nearly seven."

"Don't twist the knob," he said, impatient for the first time. "It's on the Home where it is. They'll speak from the Home."

They waited. The kitchen clock struck seven. There was no sound. No chimes, no music. They waited until a quarter past, switching to the Light. The result was the same. No news bulletin came through.

"We've heard wrong," he said. "They won't be broadcasting until eight o'clock."

They left it switched on, and Nat thought of the battery, wondered how much power was left in it. It was generally recharged when his wife went shopping in the town. If the battery failed, they would not hear the instructions.

"It's getting light," whispered his wife. "I can't see it, but I can feel it. And the birds aren't hammering so loud."

She was right. The rasping, tearing sound grew fainter every moment. So did the shuf-fling, the jostling for place upon the step, upon the sills. The tide was on the turn. By eight there was no sound at all. Only the wind. The children, lulled at last by the stillness, fell asleep. At half past eight Nat switched the wireless off.

"What are you doing? We'll miss the news," said his wife.

"There isn't going to be any news," said Nat. "We've got to depend upon ourselves."

He went to the door and slowly pulled away the barricades. He drew the bolts and, kicking the bodies from the step outside the door, breathed the cold air. He had six working hours before him, and he knew he must reserve his strength for the right things, not waste it in any way. Food and light and fuel; these were the necessary things. If he could get them in sufficiency, they could endure another night.

He stepped into the garden, and as he did so

he saw the living birds. The gulls had gone to ride the sea, as they had done before; they sought seafood, and the buoyancy of the tide, before they returned to the attack. Not so the land birds. They waited and watched. Nat saw them, on the hedgerows, on the soil, crowded in the trees, outside in the field, line upon line of birds, all still, doing nothing.

He went to the end of his small garden. The birds did not move. They went on watching him.

"I've got to get food," said Nat to himself. "I've got to go to the farm to find food."

He went back to the cottage. He saw to the windows and the doors. He went upstairs and opened the children's bedroom. It was empty, except for the dead birds on the floor. The living were out there, in the garden, in the fields. He went downstairs.

"I'm going to the farm," he said.

His wife clung to him. She had seen the living birds from the open door.

"Take us with you," she begged. "We can't stay here alone. I'd rather die than stay here alone."

He considered the matter. He nodded.

"Come on, then," he said. "Bring baskets and Johnny's pram.[24] We can load up the pram."

They dressed against the biting wind, wore gloves and scarves. His wife put Johnny in the pram. Nat took Jill's hand.

"The birds," she whimpered, "they're all out there, in the fields."

"They won't hurt us," he said, "not in the light."

They started walking across the field toward the stile, and the birds did not move. They waited, their heads turned to the wind.

When they reached the turning to the farm, Nat stopped and told his wife to wait in the shelter of the hedge with the two children.

"But I want to see Mrs. Trigg," she protested. "There are lots of things we can borrow if they went to market yesterday; not only bread, and . . . "

"Wait here," Nat interrupted. "I'll be back in a moment."

The cows were lowing, moving restlessly in the yard, and he could see a gap in the fence where the sheep had knocked their way through, to roam unchecked in the front garden before the farmhouse. No smoke came from the chimneys. He was filled with misgiving. He did not want his wife or the children to go down to the farm.

"Don't gib now,"[25] said Nat, harshly. "Do what I say."

She withdrew with the pram into the hedge, screening herself and the children from the wind.

He went down alone to the farm. He pushed his way through the herd of bellowing cows, which turned this way and that, distressed, their udders full. He saw the car standing by the gate, not put away in the garage. The windows of the farmhouse were smashed. There were many dead gulls lying in the yard and around the house. The living birds perched on the group of trees behind the farm and on the roof of the house. They were quite still. They watched him.

Jim's body lay in the yard . . . what was left of it. When the birds had finished, the cows had trampled him. His gun was beside him. The door of the house was shut and bolted, but as the windows were smashed it was easy to lift them and climb through. Trigg's body was close to the telephone. He must have been trying to get through to the exchange when the birds came for him. The receiver was

---

24. **pram** (pram): *British,* from *perambulator,* a baby carriage.

25. **gib** (jib): from *gibber,* to speak in a silly, incoherent way.

hanging loose, the instrument torn from the wall. No sign of Mrs. Trigg. She would be upstairs. Was it any use going up? Sickened, Nat knew what he would find.

"Thank God," he said to himself, "there were no children."

He forced himself to climb the stairs, but halfway he turned and descended again. He could see her legs protruding from the open bedroom door. Beside her were the bodies of the black-backed gulls, and an umbrella, broken.

"It's no use," thought Nat, "doing anything. I've only got five hours, less than that. The Triggs would understand. I must load up with what I can find."

He tramped back to his wife and children.

"I'm going to fill up the car with stuff," he said. "I'll put coal in it, and paraffin for the Primus. We'll take it home and return for a fresh load."

"What about the Triggs?" asked his wife.

"They must have gone to friends," he said.

"Shall I come and help you, then?"

"No; there's a mess down there. Cows and sheep all over the place. Wait, I'll get the car. You can sit in it."

Clumsily he backed the car out of the yard and into the lane. His wife and the children could not see Jim's body from there.

"Stay here," he said. "Never mind the pram. The pram can be fetched later. I'm going to load the car."

Her eyes watched his all the time. He believed she understood; otherwise she would have suggested helping him to find the bread and groceries.

They made three journeys altogether, backward and forward between their cottage and the farm, before he was satisfied they had everything they needed. It was surprising, once he started thinking, how many things were necessary. Almost the most important of all was planking for the windows. He had to go round searching for timber. He wanted to renew the boards on all the windows at the cottage. Candles, paraffin, nails, tinned stuff; the list was endless. Besides all that, he milked three of the cows. The rest, poor brutes, would have to go on bellowing.

On the final journey he drove the car to the bus stop, got out, and went to the telephone box. He waited a few minutes, jangling the receiver. No good though. The line was dead. He climbed onto a bank and looked over the countryside, but there was no sign of life at all, nothing in the fields but the waiting, watching birds. Some of them slept—he could see the beaks tucked into the feathers.

"You'd think they'd be feeding," he said to himself, "not just standing in that way."

Then he remembered. They were gorged with food. They had eaten their fill during the night. That was why they did not move this morning. . . .

No smoke came from the chimneys of the council houses. He thought of the children who had run across the fields the night before.

"I should have known," he thought. "I ought to have taken them home with me."

He lifted his face to the sky. It was colorless and gray. The bare trees on the landscape looked bent and blackened by the east wind. The cold did not affect the living birds, waiting out there in the fields.

"This is the time they ought to get them," said Nat. "They're a sitting target now. They must be doing this all over the country. Why don't our aircraft take off now and spray them with mustard gas? What are all our chaps doing? They must know—they must see for themselves."

He went back to the car and got into the driver's seat.

"Go quickly past that second gate," whispered his wife. "The postman's lying there. I don't want Jill to see."

He accelerated. The little Morris bumped

and rattled along the lane. The children shrieked with laughter.

"Up-a-down, up-a-down," shouted young Johnny.

It was a quarter to one by the time they reached the cottage. Only an hour to go.

"Better have cold dinner," said Nat. "Hot up something for yourself and the children, some of that soup. I've no time to eat now. I've got to unload all this stuff."

He got everything inside the cottage. It could be sorted later. Give them all something to do during the long hours ahead. First he must see to the windows and the doors.

He went round the cottage methodically, testing every window, every door. He climbed onto the roof also and fixed boards across every chimney, except the kitchen. The cold was so intense he could hardly bear it, but the job had to be done. Now and again he would look up, searching the sky for aircraft. None came. As he worked he cursed the inefficiency of the authorities.

"It's always the same," he muttered. "They always let us down. Muddle, muddle, from the start. No plan, no real organization. And we don't matter, down here. That's what it is. The people upcountry have priority. They're using gas up there, no doubt, and all the aircraft. We've got to wait and take what comes."

He paused, his work on the bedroom chimney finished, and looked out to sea. Something was moving out there. Something gray and white amongst the breakers.

"Good old Navy," he said. "They never let us down. They're coming down channel—they're turning in the bay."

He waited, straining his eyes, watering in the wind, toward the sea. He was wrong, though. It was not ships. The navy was not there. The gulls were rising from the sea. The massed flocks in the fields, with ruffled feathers, rose in formation from the ground and, wing to wing, soared upward to the sky.

The tide had turned again.

Nat climbed down the ladder and went inside the kitchen. The family were at dinner. It was a little after two. He bolted the door, put up the barricade, and lit the lamp.

"It's nighttime," said young Johnny.

His wife had switched on the wireless once again, but no sound came from it.

"I've been all round the dial," she said, "foreign stations and that lot. I can't get anything."

"Maybe they have the same trouble," he said; "maybe it's the same right through Europe."

She poured out a plateful of the Triggs' soup, cut him a large slice of the Triggs' bread, and spread their dripping upon it.

They ate in silence. A piece of the dripping ran down young Johnny's chin and fell onto the table.

"Manners, Johnny," said Jill. "You should learn to wipe your mouth."

The tapping began at the windows, at the door. The rustling, the jostling, the pushing for position on the sills. The first thud of the suicide gulls upon the step.

"Won't America do something?" said his wife. "They've always been our allies, haven't they? Surely America will do something?"

Nat did not answer. The boards were strong against the windows, and on the chimneys too. The cottage was filled with stores, with fuel, with all they needed for the next few days. When he had finished dinner, he would put the stuff away, stack it neatly, get everything shipshape, handylike. His wife could help him, and the children too. They'd tire themselves out, between now and a quarter to nine, when the tide would ebb; then he'd tuck them down on their mattresses, see that they slept good and sound until three in the morning.

He had a new scheme for the window, which was to fix barbed wire in front of the boards. He had brought a great roll of it from the farm. The nuisance was, he'd have to work at this in the dark, when the lull came between nine and three. Pity he had not thought of it before. Still, as long as the wife slept, and the kids, that was the main thing.

The smaller birds were at the window now. He recognized the light tap-tapping of the beaks and the soft brush of their wings. The hawks ignored the windows. They concentrated their attack upon the door. Nat listened to the tearing sound of splintering wood and wondered how many million years of memory were stored in those little brains, behind the stabbing beaks, the piercing eyes, now giving them this instinct to destroy mankind with all the deft precision of machines.

"I'll smoke that last cigarette," he said to his wife. "Stupid of me—it was the one thing I forgot to bring back from the farm."

He reached for it, switched on the silent wireless. He threw the empty packet on the fire and watched it burn.

# Reviewing Concepts

## CHARACTER AND CONFLICT: MORAL CHOICE

*making
connections*

Many of the short stories in this unit include characters who struggle with inner conflicts. The barber in "Lather and Nothing Else" wrestles with the question of whether to kill Captain Torres while Torres is literally in the barber's hands. The barber's inner conflict is a moral one, and the resolution of his conflict turns out to be a moral choice: he chooses not to kill Torres.

In "The Lady, or the Tiger?" the reader is left wondering what decision the princess will make. In "Initiation" Millicent's moral choice not to join the sorority is clear at the end of the story.

To understand the variety of conflicts and moral choices in the stories in this unit, think back over the characters and situations in those stories. Make a chart similar to the one below. Fill out the chart with information on as many stories as you think involve moral choices.

| Story | Inner conflict | Moral choice |
|-------|----------------|--------------|
| "Lather and Nothing Else" | Barber wonders whether to kill Torres. | decides not to |
| "The Lady, or the Tiger?" | Princess must decide whether to see lover killed or married to a beautiful woman. | ? |

*describing
connections*

Choose three to five stories from your chart and write an **essay** on the moral choices of the characters. Compare and contrast the moral values involved in each choice and the long-term consequences of each choice.

*September Window*, 1970, ANDRÉ KERTÉSZ.
© 1990 Estate of André Kertész.

# Nonfiction

"*Fiction is obliged to
stick to possibilities.
Truth isn't.*"

MARK TWAIN

# Shades of the Past: Childhood Memories

**H**AVE YOU EVER heard the expression "Truth is stranger than fiction"? Sometimes real-life experiences can be stranger—or more interesting—than imaginary ones.

The selections in this section are first-person accounts of actual episodes in the lives of the writers. Each work is an adult's personal recollection of a childhood experience. Some of the selections focus on a person who was important to the writer and may seem to be as much about that person as about the writer.

As you read each selection, think about the writer's purpose in sharing this memory. Perhaps the childhood event or relationship changed the writer's life. Perhaps the writer simply finds the memory amusing or intriguing. You may find a clue to the significance of the memory in the comments the adult writer makes in reflecting upon the experience.

See what you think: Is truth stranger than fiction?

*Girl Under Tree,* 1967,
ANN GRIFALCONI.
Woodblock print.
©1978–1990 Ann Grifalconi,
New York.

# *Literary Vocabulary*

## INTRODUCED IN THIS SECTION

**Autobiography** and **Biography.** An autobiography is the story of a person's life written by that person. Autobiographies can vary in style from impressionistic narratives to straightforward chronological accounts. The selections in this section are examples of different kinds of autobiographical writing.

A biography is a true account of a person's life written by another person. In "A Christmas Memory," Truman Capote's recollection of one holiday from his childhood, there are elements of biography in his portrait of his older cousin.

**Tone.** Tone is the attitude a writer takes toward a subject. Style and description in a work of literature help create tone, which might be formal, informal, ironic, angry, serious, or playful. Often understanding a writer's tone is a key factor in interpreting a work of nonfiction. James Thurber's tone in "The Night the Bed Fell," for example, indicates how seriously the reader should take the events he relates.

**Imagery.** Imagery refers to descriptive words and phrases that re-create sensory experiences for a reader. Images can appeal to any of the five senses: sight, hearing, smell, taste, and touch. The majority of images are visual, stimulating pictures in the reader's mind. For example, in "The Masque of the Red Death," the final description of the courtiers dying and the torches burning out creates a memorable visual image in the reader's mind.

**Irony.** Irony is the contrast between what is expected and what actually exists or happens. **Verbal irony** occurs when a character says one thing and means another, as when someone says, "I certainly am a great cook" after burning dinner. When verbal irony is especially bitter or harsh, it is called sarcasm. **Situational irony** is the contrast between what a character expects and what actually happens, for example, Madame Loisel's discovery that the necklace is false at the end of "The Necklace." **Dramatic irony** refers to the contrast between what a character knows and what the reader knows. In "My Delicate Heart Condition," the dramatic irony centers around Harriet's misunderstanding of *underprivileged,* a word the reader is expected to know.

# Mrs. Flowers

## *from* I Know Why the Caged Bird Sings

MAYA ANGELOU

A biography of Angelou appears on page 636.

## *Approaching the Selection*

The book from which this excerpt is taken tells the story of Maya Angelou's childhood in the rural town of Stamps, Arkansas. The young Angelou, who went by the name of Marguerite Johnson, and her brother Bailey were raised there by their grandmother, whom they called Momma. Momma ran a small grocery store.

The title *I Know Why the Caged Bird Sings* is taken from the poem "Sympathy" by Paul Laurence Dunbar. The last stanza of the poem reads as follows:

I know why the caged bird sings, ah me,
    When his wing is bruised and his bosom sore.—
When he beats his bars and he would be free;
It is not a carol of joy or glee,
    But a prayer that he sends from his heart's deep core.
But a plea, that upward to Heaven he flings—
I know why the caged bird sings!

## *Building Vocabulary*

These essential words are footnoted within the selection.

**inclusively** (in klo͞o´ siv lē), **benign** (bi nīn´): The action was so graceful and **inclusively benign**. (page 223)

**sacrilegious** (sak´ rə lij´ əs): I knew I shouldn't put on a Sunday dress. It might be **sacrilegious**. (page 224)

**infuse** (in fyo͞oz´): "It takes the human voice to **infuse** [words] with the shades of deeper meaning." (page 225)

**aura** (ô´ rə): The essence escapes but its **aura** remains. (page 226)

## *Connecting Writing and Reading*

Think of someone whom you have admired in the past or have wanted to be like. In your journal, give your reasons for admiring this person. As you read this selection, think about why the young Angelou admires Mrs. Flowers.

MRS. BERTHA FLOWERS was the aristocrat of Black Stamps. She had the grace of control to appear warm in the coldest weather, and on the Arkansas summer days it seemed she had a private breeze which swirled around, cooling her. She was thin without the taut look of wiry people, and her printed voile dresses and flowered hats were as right for her as denim overalls for a farmer. She was our side's answer to the richest white woman in town.

Her skin was a rich black that would have peeled like a plum if snagged, but then no one would have thought of getting close enough to Mrs. Flowers to ruffle her dress, let alone snag her skin. She didn't encourage familiarity. She wore gloves too.

I don't think I ever saw Mrs. Flowers laugh, but she smiled often. A slow widening of her thin black lips to show even, small white teeth, then the slow, effortless closing. When she chose to smile on me, I always wanted to thank her. The action was so graceful and inclusively[1] benign.[2]

She was one of the few gentlewomen I have ever known, and has remained throughout my life the measure of what a human being can be.

Momma had a strange relationship with her. Most often when she passed on the road in front of the Store, she spoke to Momma in that soft yet carrying voice, "Good day, Mrs. Henderson." Momma responded with "How you, Sister Flowers?"

Mrs. Flowers didn't belong to our church, nor was she Momma's familiar. Why on earth did she insist on calling her Sister Flowers? Shame made me want to hide my face. Mrs. Flowers deserved better than to be called Sister. Then, Momma left out the verb. Why not ask, "How *are* you, *Mrs.* Flowers?" With the unbalanced passion of the young, I hated her for showing her ignorance to Mrs. Flowers.

It didn't occur to me for many years that they were as alike as sisters, separated only by formal education.

Although I was upset, neither of the women was in the least shaken by what I thought an unceremonious greeting. Mrs. Flowers would continue her easy gait up the hill to her little bungalow, and Momma kept on shelling peas or doing whatever had brought her to the front porch.

Occasionally, though, Mrs. Flowers would drift off the road and down to the Store and Momma would say to me, "Sister, you go on and play." As I left I would hear the beginning of an intimate conversation, Momma persistently using the wrong verb, or none at all.

"Brother and Sister Wilcox is sho'ly the meanest—" "Is," Momma? "Is"? Oh, please, not "is," Momma, for two or more. But they talked, and from the side of the building where I waited for the ground to open up and swallow me, I heard the soft-voiced Mrs. Flowers and the textured voice of my grandmother merging and melting. They were interrupted from time to time by giggles that must have come from Mrs. Flowers (Momma never giggled in her life). Then she was gone.

She appealed to me because she was like people I had never met personally. Like women in English novels who walked the moors (whatever they were) with their loyal dogs racing at a respectful distance. Like the women who sat in front of roaring fireplaces, drinking tea incessantly from silver trays full of scones and crumpets. Women who walked over the "heath" and read morocco-bound books and had two last names divided by a hyphen. It would be safe to say that she made me proud to be Negro, just by being herself.

---

1. **inclusively** (in kloo′ siv lē): in a way that includes, especially in a manner that takes everything into account.
2. **benign** (bi nīn′): good-natured; kindly.

She acted just as refined as whitefolks in the movies and books and she was more beautiful, for none of them could have come near that warm color without looking gray by comparison.

It was fortunate that I never saw her in the company of powhitefolks. For since they tend to think of their whiteness as an evenizer, I'm certain that I would have had to hear her spoken to commonly as Bertha, and my image of her would have been shattered like the unmendable Humpty Dumpty.

One summer afternoon, sweet-milk fresh in my memory, she stopped at the Store to buy provisions. Another Negro woman of her health and age would have been expected to carry the paper sacks home in one hand, but Momma said, "Sister Flowers, I'll send Bailey up to your house with these things."

She smiled that slow dragging smile, "Thank you, Mrs. Henderson. I'd prefer Marguerite, though." My name was beautiful when she said it. "I've been meaning to talk to her, anyway." They gave each other age-group looks.

Momma said, "Well, that's all right then. Sister, go and change your dress. You going to Sister Flowers's."

The chifforobe[3] was a maze. What on earth did one put on to go to Mrs. Flowers's house? I knew I shouldn't put on a Sunday dress. It might be <u>sacrilegious</u>.[4] Certainly not a house dress, since I was already wearing a fresh one. I chose a school dress, naturally. It was formal without suggesting that going to Mrs. Flowers's house was equivalent to attending church.

I trusted myself back into the Store.

"Now, don't you look nice." I had chosen the right thing, for once.

"Mrs. Henderson, you make most of the children's clothes, don't you?"

"Yes, ma'am. Sure do. Store-bought clothes ain't hardly worth the thread it take to stitch them."

"I'll say you do a lovely job, though, so neat. That dress looks professional."

Momma was enjoying the seldom-received compliments. Since everyone we knew (except Mrs. Flowers, of course) could sew competently, praise was rarely handed out for the commonly practiced craft.

"I try, with the help of the Lord, Sister Flowers, to finish the inside just like I does the outside. Come here, Sister."

I had buttoned up the collar and tied the belt, apronlike, in back. Momma told me to turn around. With one hand she pulled the strings and the belt fell free at both sides of my waist. Then her large hands were at my neck, opening the button loops. I was terrified. What was happening?

"Take it off, Sister." She had her hands on the hem of the dress.

"I don't need to see the inside, Mrs. Henderson, I can tell . . ." But the dress was over my head and my arms were stuck in the sleeves. Momma said, "That'll do. See here, Sister Flowers, I French-seams around the armholes." Through the cloth film, I saw the shadow approach. "That makes it last longer. Children these days would bust out of sheet-metal clothes. They so rough."

"That is a very good job, Mrs. Henderson. You should be proud. You can put your dress back on, Marguerite."

"No ma'am. Pride is a sin. And 'cording to the Good Book, it goeth before a fall."

"That's right. So the Bible says. It's a good thing to keep in mind."

I wouldn't look at either of them. Momma hadn't thought that taking off my dress in front of Mrs. Flowers would kill me stone dead. If I had refused, she would have thought I was

---

3. **chifforobe** (shif′ ə rōb′): a combination of a chest of drawers and a small wardrobe, or closet, for storing clothes.
4. **sacrilegious** (sak′ rə lij′ əs): disrespectful of what is thought to be holy.

trying to be "womanish." Mrs. Flowers had known that I would be embarrassed and that was even worse. I picked up the groceries and went out to wait in the hot sunshine. It would be fitting if I got a sunstroke and died before they came outside. Just dropped dead on the slanting porch.

There was a little path beside the rocky road, and Mrs. Flowers walked in front swinging her arms and picking her way over the stones.

She said, without turning her head, to me, "I hear you're doing very good school work, Marguerite, but that it's all written. The teachers report that they have trouble getting you to talk in class." We passed the triangular farm on our left, and the path widened to allow us to walk together. I hung back in the separate unasked and unanswerable questions.

"Come and walk along with me, Marguerite." I couldn't have refused even if I wanted to. She pronounced my name so nicely. Or more correctly, she spoke each word with such clarity that I was certain a foreigner who didn't understand English could have understood her.

"Now no one is going to make you talk—possibly no one can. But bear in mind, language is man's way of communicating with his fellow man, and it is language alone which separates him from the lower animals." That was a totally new idea to me, and I would need time to think about it.

"Your grandmother says you read a lot. Every chance you get. That's good, but not good enough. Words mean more than what is set down on paper. It takes the human voice to infuse[5] them with the shades of deeper meaning."

I memorized the part about the human voice infusing words. It seemed so valid and poetic.

She said she was going to give me some books and that I not only must read them, I must read them aloud. She suggested that I try to make a sentence sound in as many different ways as possible.

"I'll accept no excuse if you return a book to me that has been badly handled." My imagination boggled at the punishment I would deserve if in fact I did abuse a book of Mrs. Flowers's. Death would be too kind and brief.

The odors in the house surprised me. Somehow I had never connected Mrs. Flowers with food or eating or any other common experience of common people. There must have been an outhouse, too, but my mind never recorded it.

The sweet scent of vanilla had met us as she opened the door.

"I made tea cookies this morning. You see, I had planned to invite you for cookies and lemonade so we could have this little chat. The lemonade is in the icebox."

It followed that Mrs. Flowers would have ice on an ordinary day, when most families in our town bought ice late on Saturdays only a few times during the summer to be used in wooden ice-cream freezers.

She took the bags from me and disappeared through the kitchen door. I looked around the room that I had never in my wildest fantasies imagined I would see. Browned photographs leered or threatened from the walls, and the white, freshly done curtains pushed against themselves and against the wind. I wanted to gobble up the room entire and take it to Bailey, who would help me analyze and enjoy it.

"Have a seat, Marguerite. Over there by the table." She carried a platter covered with a tea towel. Although she warned that she hadn't tried her hand at baking sweets for some time, I was certain that like everything else about her the cookies would be perfect.

They were flat, round wafers, slightly browned on the edges and butter yellow in the center. With the cold lemonade they were

---

5. **infuse** (in fyo͞oz′): to fill (with a quality, feeling, etc.).

sufficient for childhood's lifelong diet. Remembering my manners, I took nice little lady-like bites off the edges. She said she had made them expressly for me and that she had a few in the kitchen that I could take home to my brother. So I jammed one whole cake in my mouth, and the rough crumbs scratched the insides of my jaws, and if I hadn't had to swallow, it would have been a dream come true.

As I ate she began the first of what we later called "my lessons in living." She said that I must always be intolerant of ignorance but understanding of illiteracy. That some people, unable to go to school, were more educated and even more intelligent than college professors. She encouraged me to listen carefully to what country people called mother wit. That in those homely sayings was couched the collective wisdom of generations.

When I finished the cookies she brushed off the table and brought a thick, small book from the bookcase. I had read *A Tale of Two Cities* and found it up to my standards as a romantic novel. She opened the first page and I heard poetry for the first time in my life.

"It was the best of times and the worst of times . . ." Her voice slid in and curved down through and over the words. She was nearly singing. I wanted to look at the pages. Were they the same that I had read? Or were there notes, music lined on the pages, as in a hymn book? Her sounds began cascading gently. I knew from listening to a thousand preachers that she was nearing the end of her reading, and I hadn't really heard, heard to understand, a single word.

"How do you like that?"

It occurred to me that she expected a response. The sweet vanilla flavor was still on my tongue, and her reading was a wonder in my ears. I had to speak.

I said, "Yes, ma'am." It was the least I could do, but it was the most also.

"There's one more thing. Take this book of poems and memorize one for me. Next time you pay me a visit, I want you to recite."

I have tried often to search behind the sophistication of years for the enchantment I so easily found in those gifts. The essence escapes but its aura[6] remains. To be allowed, no, invited, into the private lives of strangers, and to share their joys and fears, was a chance to exchange the Southern bitter wormwood for a cup of mead with Beowulf or a hot cup of tea and milk with Oliver Twist.[7] When I said aloud, "It is a far, far better thing that I do, than I have ever done . . ." tears of love filled my eyes at my selflessness.

On the first day, I ran down the hill and into the road (few cars ever came along it) and had the good sense to stop running before I reached the Store.

I was liked, and what a difference it made. I was respected not as Mrs. Henderson's grandchild or Bailey's sister but for just being Marguerite Johnson.

Childhood's logic never asks to be proved (all conclusions are absolute). I didn't question why Mrs. Flowers had singled me out for attention, nor did it occur to me that Momma might have asked her to give me a little talking to. All I cared about was that she had made tea cookies for *me* and read to *me* from her favorite book. It was enough to prove that she liked me.

Momma and Bailey were waiting inside the Store. He said, "My, what did she give you?" He had seen the books, but I held the

---

6. **aura** (ô′ rə): a particular atmosphere or quality that seems to arise from and surround a person or thing.
7. **a chance to exchange . . . with Oliver Twist:** Angelou here compares her existence as a black child in the bigoted South to wormwood, a bitter herb. She hopes to escape this bitterness by turning instead to mead, a sweet drink, or tea with milk, common to such characters as Beowulf and Oliver Twist from English literature.

paper sack with his cookies in my arms shielded by the poems.

Momma said, "Sister, I know you acted like a little lady. That do my heart good to see settled people take to you all. I'm trying my best, the Lord knows, but these days . . ." Her voice trailed off. "Go on in and change your dress."

# Thinking About the Selection

## A PERSONAL RESPONSE

*sharing impressions*

**1.** How would you describe Marguerite's admiration for Mrs. Flowers to a friend? Jot down some descriptive words in your journal.

*constructing interpretations*

**2.** Why do you think Marguerite admires Mrs. Flowers so much?

**3.** How would you answer Bailey's question about what Mrs. Flowers gave Marguerite?

**Think about**
- tangible and intangible gifts that Mrs. Flowers offered

**4.** What do you think motivates Mrs. Flowers to help Marguerite?

**Think about**
- Mrs. Flowers's social and economic position in Stamps
- her relationship with Momma
- Marguerite's performance in school
- what Mrs. Flowers might gain from the relationship

## A CREATIVE RESPONSE

**5.** If Angelou had not met Mrs. Flowers, how might her life have been different?

## A CRITICAL RESPONSE

**6.** If this selection were from a biography of Angelou rather than from her autobiography, how might it be different? Support your answer.

**7.** Select two or three descriptive sentences from the selection and analyze how Angelou uses imagery to enhance her description.

**Think about**
- imagery as descriptive words or phrases that appeal to the senses

**8.** In an essay, Angelou made the following comment about her grandmother's influence on her life: "I was a mute for five years. I wasn't cute and I didn't speak. I don't know what would have happened to me had I been in an integrated school. In another society, I'm sure I would have been ruled out. But my grandma told me all the time, 'Sister, Momma don't care what these people say about you being a moron, being a idiot. Momma don't care. Momma know, Sister, when you and the good Lord get ready, you're gonna be a preacher.'" Compare the encouragement Angelou received from her grandmother to the encouragement she received from Mrs. Flowers. Cite examples from the selection and from the above quotation in explaining your comparison.

 *nalyzing the Writer's Craft*

## AUTOBIOGRAPHY

Recall your answer to question 2, in which you focused on Mrs. Flowers's admirable qualities. Then think about what the young Marguerite overlooks about Mrs. Flowers.

**Building a Literary Vocabulary.** An auto-biography is the story of a person's life written by that person, who generally uses the first-person point of view. In *I Know Why the Caged Bird Sings,* Maya Angelou focuses on the important experiences of her childhood. She does so from an adult perspective, however, often interpreting the feelings she had as a child with the wisdom of an adult. For example, the young Marguerite is so captivated by Mrs. Flowers's aura of refinement that she is surprised by the odors in her house. The adult Angelou writes, "Somehow I had never connected Mrs. Flowers with food or eating or any

other common experience of common people. There must have been an outhouse, too, but my mind never recorded it." One of the challenges of writing a good autobiography is to capture the child's immediate feelings and observations while also expressing the adult's deeper insight, gained through time.

**Application: Interpreting Autobiography.** In a small group, go back through the selection and find sentences that describe Angelou's experiences through the eyes of a child and sentences that express an adult understanding. Then select a long passage to dramatize in a skit showing the child as character and the adult as narrator in this autobiography. For example, actors portraying Marguerite and other characters might act out an episode while a narrator reads the passage.

# Connecting Reading and Writing

**1.** Judging from this chapter on Mrs. Flowers and the stanza from Paul Laurence Dunbar's poem on the prereading page, why do you suppose Maya Angelou titled the first volume of her autobiography *I Know Why the Caged Bird Sings?* Speculate on the meaning of the caged bird and its singing in a **book review.**

Option: Create a **poster** with a picture of a caged bird surrounded by words and phrases offering possible interpretations of this image in the autobiography.

**2.** Interpret a significant childhood memory of your own from your current perspective as a teenager. Bring your memory vividly to life, showing how your perspective has changed, in a **narrative essay** for a teen magazine.

Option: Write a **diary entry** about a childhood memory as you might have written it shortly after the event occurred.

**3.** If Mrs. Flowers read this chapter of Angelou's autobiography, what thoughts and memories do you suppose she would have? Have the older Mrs. Flowers respond in a **letter** to Maya Angelou.

Option: Write a **reminiscence** that Mrs. Flowers could have written about Marguerite's first visit.

**4.** Expand on your answer to question 7 by analyzing how your interpretation of the selection is affected by the images used. Present your conclusion in an **expository essay** addressed to Maya Angelou.

Option: Write your conclusions in the form of **notes** for a lecture to your class.

# A Christmas Memory

## TRUMAN CAPOTE

A biography of Capote appears on page 637.

## *Approaching the Autobiographical Essay*

Truman Capote was a popular—and sometimes controversial— American writer from the time of his literary debut in the 1940's until his death in 1984. Capote grew up in the rural South during the early 1930's. In "A Christmas Memory," he recalls his close relationship with a much older female cousin whom he refers to as "my friend." The adult Capote narrates his story more than twenty years after it happened, focusing on one particular Christmas that represents the kind of experiences he had with his older cousin.

## *Building Vocabulary*

These essential words are footnoted within the selection.

**inaugurating** (in ô′ gyŏŏ rāt′ iŋ), **exhilarates** (eg zil′ ə rāts): My friend, as though officially **inaugurating** the Christmas time of year that **exhilarates** her imagination. . . , announces, "It's fruitcake weather!" (page 231)

**dilapidated** (də lap′ ə dāt′ id): Together, we guide our buggy, a **dilapidated** baby carriage, out to the garden. (page 231)

**conspiracy** (kən spir′ ə sē): Silently, wallowing in the pleasures of **conspiracy**, we take the bead purse from its secret place. (page 233)

**potent** (pōt′ 'nt): **Potent** with eyes that scold, tongues that scald. (page 234)

**severing** (sev′ə r iŋ), **irreplaceable** (ir′ ri plās′ ə bəl): A message . . . confirms a piece of news some secret vein had already received, **severing** from me an **irreplaceable** part of myself. (page 239)

## *Connecting Writing and Reading*

What is your most vivid holiday memory? In your journal, create a cluster diagram of words associated with this particular holiday memory. During your reading, notice what details are memorable to Capote about a Christmas holiday from his past.

*I*MAGINE A MORNING in late November. A coming of winter morning more than twenty years ago. Consider the kitchen of a spreading old house in a country town. A great black stove is its main feature, but there are also a big round table and a fireplace with two rocking chairs placed in front of it. Just today the fireplace commenced its seasonal roar.

A woman with shorn white hair is standing at the kitchen window. She is wearing tennis shoes and a shapeless gray sweater over a summery calico dress. She is small and sprightly, like a bantam hen; but, due to a long youthful illness, her shoulders are pitifully hunched. Her face is remarkable—not unlike Lincoln's, craggy like that, and tinted by sun and wind; but it is delicate too, finely boned; and her eyes are sherry-colored and timid. "Oh, my," she exclaims, her breath smoking the windowpane, "it's fruitcake weather!"

The person to whom she is speaking is myself. I am seven; she is sixty-something. We are cousins, very distant ones, and we have lived together—well, as long as I can remember. Other people inhabit the house, relatives; and though they have power over us, and frequently make us cry, we are not, on the whole, too much aware of them. We are each other's best friend. She calls me Buddy, in memory of a boy who was formerly her best friend. The other Buddy died in the 1880's, when she was still a child. She is still a child.

"I knew it before I got out of bed," she says, turning away from the window with a purposeful excitement in her eyes. "The courthouse bell sounded so cold and clear. And there were no birds singing; they've gone to warmer country, yes, indeed. Oh, Buddy, stop stuffing biscuit and fetch our buggy. Help me find my hat. We've thirty cakes to make."

It's always the same: a morning arrives in November, and my friend, as though officially inaugurating[1] the Christmas time of year that exhilarates[2] her imagination and fuels the blaze of her heart, announces, "It's fruitcake weather! Fetch our buggy. Help me find my hat."

The hat is found, a straw cartwheel corsaged with velvet roses out-of-doors has faded; it once belonged to a more fashionable relative. Together, we guide our buggy, a dilapidated[3] baby carriage, out to the garden and into a grove of pecan trees. The buggy is mine; that is, it was bought for me when I was born. It is made of wicker, rather unraveled, and the wheels wobble like a drunkard's legs. But it is a faithful object; springtimes, we take it to the woods and fill it with flowers, herbs, wild fern for our porch pots. In the summer, we pile it with picnic paraphernalia and sugar-cane fishing poles and roll it down to the edge of a creek. It has its winter uses, too: as a truck for hauling firewood from the yard to the kitchen, as a warm bed for Queenie, our tough little orange and white rat terrier who has survived distemper and two rattlesnake bites. Queenie is trotting beside it now.

Three hours later we are back in the kitchen hulling a heaping buggyload of windfall pecans. Our backs hurt from gathering them. How hard they were to find (the main crop having been shaken off the trees and sold by the orchard's owners, who are not us) among the concealing leaves, the frosted deceiving grass. Caaarackle! A cheery crunch, scraps of miniature thunder sound as the shells collapse and the golden mound of sweet oily ivory meat mounts in the milk-glass bowl. Queenie begs to taste, and now and again my friend sneaks her a mite, though insisting we deprive ourselves. "We mustn't Buddy. If we

---

1. **inaugurating** (in ô′ gyo͞o rāt′ iŋ): making a formal beginning of.
2. **exhilarates** (eg zil′ ə rāts): makes merry or livey.
3. **dilapidated** (də lap′ ə dāt′ id): fallen into partial ruins; decayed.

start, we won't stop. And there's scarcely enough as there is. For thirty cakes." The kitchen is growing dark. Dusk turns the window into a mirror: our reflections mingle with the rising moon as we work by the fireside in the firelight. At last, when the moon is quite high, we toss the final hull into the fire and, with joined sighs, watch it catch flame. The buggy is empty; the bowl is brimful.

We eat our supper (cold biscuits, bacon, blackberry jam) and discuss tomorrow. Tomorrow the kind of work I like best begins: buying. Cherries and citron, ginger and vanilla and canned Hawaiian pineapple, rinds and raisins and walnuts and whiskey and oh, so much flour, butter, so many eggs, spices, flavorings. Why, we'll need a pony to pull the buggy home.

But before these purchases can be made, there is the question of money. Neither of us has any. Except for skinflint sums persons in the house occasionally provide (a dime is considered very big money); or what we earn ourselves from various activities: holding rummage sales; selling buckets of hand-picked blackberries, jars of homemade jam and apple jelly and peach preserves; rounding up flowers for funerals and weddings. Once we won seventy-ninth prize, five dollars, in a national football contest. Not that we know a fool thing about football. It's just that we enter any contest we hear about. At the moment our hopes are centered on the fifty-thousand-dollar Grand Prize being offered to name a new brand of coffee (we suggested "A.M."; and, after some hesitation, for my friend thought it perhaps sacrilegious, the slogan "A.M.! Amen!"). To tell the truth, our only *really* profitable enterprise was the Fun and Freak Museum we conducted in a backyard woodshed two summers ago. The Fun was a stereopticon[4] with slide views of Washington and New York lent us by a relative who had been to those places (she was furious when she discovered why we'd borrowed it); the Freak was

a three-legged biddy chicken hatched by one of our own hens. Everybody hereabouts wanted to see that biddy. We charged grown-ups a nickel, kids two cents, and took in a good twenty dollars before the museum shut down due to the decease of the main attraction.

But one way and another we do each year accumulate Christmas savings, a Fruitcake Fund. These moneys we keep hidden in an ancient bead purse under a loose board under the floor under a chamber pot under my friend's bed. The purse is seldom removed from this safe location except to make a deposit or, as happens every Saturday, a withdrawal; for on Saturdays I am allowed ten cents to go to the picture show. My friend has never been to a picture show, nor does she intend to. "I'd rather hear you tell the story, Buddy. That way I can imagine it more. Besides, a person my age shouldn't squander their eyes. When the Lord comes, let me see him clear." In addition to never having seen a movie, she has never eaten in a restaurant, traveled more than five miles from home, received or sent a telegram, read anything except funny papers and the Bible, worn cosmetics, cursed, wished someone harm, told a lie on purpose, let a hungry dog go hungry. Here are a few things she has done, does do: killed with a hoe the biggest rattlesnake ever seen in this county (sixteen rattles), dip snuff (secretly), tame hummingbirds (just try it) till they balance on her finger, tell ghost stories (we both believe in ghosts) so tingling they chill you in July, talk to herself, take walks in the rain, grow the prettiest japonicas in town, know the recipe for every sort of old-time Indian cure, including a magical wart remover.

Now, with supper finished, we retire to the room in a faraway part of the house where my

---

4. **stereopticon** (ster′ ē äp′ ti kən): a slide projector that allows one picture to fade out as another gradually appears.

friend sleeps in a scrap-quilt-covered iron bed painted rose pink, her favorite color. Silently, wallowing in the pleasures of <u>conspiracy</u>,[5] we take the bead purse from its secret place and spill its contents on the scrap quilt. Dollar bills, tightly rolled and green as May buds. Somber fifty-cent pieces, heavy enough to weight a dead man's eyes.[6] Lovely dimes, the liveliest coin, the one that really jingles. Nickels and quarters, worn smooth as creek pebbles. But mostly a hateful heap of bitter-odored pennies. Last summer, others in the house contracted to pay us a penny for every twenty-five flies we killed. Oh, the carnage of August: the flies that flew to heaven! Yet it was not work in which we took pride. And, as we sit counting pennies, it is as though we were back tabulating dead flies. Neither of us has a head for figures; we count slowly, lose track, start again. According to her calculations, we have $12.73. According to mine, exactly $13. "I do hope you're wrong, Buddy. We can't mess around with thirteen. The cakes will fall. Or put somebody in the cemetery. Why, I wouldn't dream of getting out of bed on the thirteenth." This is true; she always spends thirteenths in bed. So, to be on the safe side, we subtract a penny and toss it out the window.

Of the ingredients that go into our fruit-cakes, whiskey is the most expensive, as well as the hardest to obtain. State laws forbid its sale. But everybody knows you can buy a bottle from Mr. Haha Jones. And the next day, having completed our more prosaic shopping, we set out for Mr. Haha's business address, a "sin-ful" (to quote public opinion) fish-fry and dancing cafe down by the river. We've been there before, and on the same errand; but in previous years our dealings have been with Haha's wife, an iodine-dark Indian woman with brassy, peroxided hair and a dead-tired disposition. Actually, we've never laid eyes on her husband, though we've heard that he's an

Indian too. A giant with razor scars across his cheeks. They call him Haha because he's so gloomy, a man who never laughs. As we approach his cafe (a large log cabin festooned inside and out with chains of garish-gay naked light bulbs and standing by the river's muddy edge under the shade of river trees where moss drifts through the branches like gray mist) our steps slow down. Even Queenie stops prancing and sticks close by. People have been murdered in Haha's cafe. Cut to pieces. Hit on the head. There's a case coming up in court next month. Naturally these goings-on happen at night when the colored lights cast crazy patterns and the Victrola[7] wails. In the daytime, Haha's is shabby and deserted. I knock at the door, Queenie barks, my friend calls, "Mrs. Haha, ma'am? Anyone to home?"

Footsteps. The door opens. Our hearts overturn. It's Mr. Haha Jones himself! And he *is* a giant; he *does* have scars; he *doesn't* smile. No, he glowers at us through Satan-tilted eyes and demands to know, "What you want with Haha?"

For a moment we are too paralyzed to tell. Presently my friend half finds her voice, a whispery voice at best, "If you please, Mr. Haha, we'd like a quart of your finest whiskey."

His eyes tilt more. Would you believe it? Haha is smiling! Laughing, too. "Which one of you is a drinkin' man?"

"It's for making fruitcakes, Mr. Haha. Cooking."

This sobers him. He frowns. "That's no way to waste good whiskey." Nevertheless, he retreats into the shadowed cafe and seconds later appears carrying a bottle of daisy yellow

---

5. **conspiracy** (kən spir′ ə sē): the act of two or more persons plotting together to do something secret or unlawful.

6. **heavy enough to weight a dead man's eyes:** from the custom of putting coins on the eyes of corpses to keep them closed.

7. **Victrola** (vik trō′ lə): *trademark:* phonograph.

unlabeled liquor. He demonstrates its sparkle in the sunlight and says, "Two dollars."

We pay him with nickels and dimes and pennies. Suddenly, jangling the coins in his hand like a fistful of dice, his face softens. "Tell you what," he proposes, pouring the money back into our bead purse, "just send me one of them fruitcakes instead."

"Well," my friend remarks on our way home, "there's a lovely man. We'll put an extra cup of raisins in *his* cake."

The black stove, stoked with coal and firewood, glows like a lighted pumpkin. Eggbeaters whirl, spoons spin round in bowls of butter and sugar, vanilla sweetens the air, ginger spices it; melting, nose-tingling odors saturate the kitchen, suffuse the house, drift out to the world on puffs of chimney smoke. In four days our work is done. Thirty-one cakes, dampened with whiskey, bask on window sills and shelves.

Who are they for?

Friends. Not necessarily neighbor friends; indeed, the larger share are intended for persons we've met maybe once, perhaps not at all. People who've struck our fancy. Like President Roosevelt. Like the Reverend and Mrs. J. C. Lucey, Baptist missionaries to Borneo who lectured here last winter. Or the little knife grinder who comes through town twice a year. Or Abner Packer, the driver of the six o'clock bus from Mobile, who exchanges waves with us every day as he passes in a dust-cloud whoosh. Or the young Wistons, a California couple whose car one afternoon broke down outside the house and who spent a pleasant hour chatting with us on the porch (young Mr. Wiston snapped our picture, the only one we've ever had taken). Is it because my friend is shy with everyone *except* strangers that these strangers, and merest acquaintances, seem to us our truest friends? I think yes. Also, the scrapbooks we keep of thank-you's on White House stationery, time-to-time communica-

tions from California and Borneo, the knife grinder's penny post cards, make us feel connected to eventful worlds beyond the kitchen with its view of a sky that stops.

Now a nude December fig branch grates against the window. The kitchen is empty, the cakes are gone; yesterday we carted the last of them to the post office, where the cost of stamps turned our purse inside out. We're broke. That rather depresses me, but my friend insists on celebrating—with two inches of whiskey left in Haha's bottle. Queenie has a spoonful in a bowl of coffee (she likes her coffee chicory flavored and strong). The rest we divide between a pair of jelly glasses. We're both quite awed at the prospect of drinking straight whiskey; the taste of it brings screwed-up expressions and sour shudders. But by and by we begin to sing, the two of us singing different songs simultaneously. I don't know the words to mine, just, *Come on along, come on along, to the dark-town strutters' ball*. But I can dance; that's what I mean to be, a tap dancer in the movies. My dancing shadow rollicks on the walls; our voices rock the chinaware; we giggle, as if unseen hands were tickling us. Queenie rolls on her back, her paws plow the air, something like a grin stretches her black lips. Inside myself, I feel warm and sparky as those crumbling logs, carefree as the wind in the chimney. My friend waltzes round the stove, the hem of her poor calico skirt pinched between her fingers as though it were a party dress. *Show me the way to go home*, she sings, her tennis shoes squeaking on the floor. *Show me the way to go home*.

Enter: two relatives. Very angry. Potent[8] with eyes that scold, tongues that scald. Listen to what they have to say, the words tumbling together into a wrathful tune: "A child of seven! whiskey on his breath! are you out of your mind? feeding a child of seven! must be

---

8. **potent** (pōt′ 'nt): powerful or forceful.

*Loch Eynort, South Uist, Hebrides,* 1954, PAUL STRAND.
© 1962, Aperture Foundation, Inc., Paul Strand Archive, Millerton, New York.

loony! road to ruination! remember Cousin Kate? Uncle Charlie? Uncle Charlie's brother-in-law? shame! scandal! humiliation! kneel, pray, beg the Lord!"

Queenie sneaks under the stove. My friend gazes at her shoes, her chin quivers, she lifts her skirt and blows her nose and runs to her room. Long after the town has gone to sleep and the house is silent except for the chimings of clocks and the sputter of fading fires, she is weeping into a pillow already as wet as a widow's handkerchief.

"Don't cry," I say, sitting at the bottom of her bed and shivering despite my flannel nightgown that smells of last winter's cough syrup. "Don't cry," I beg, teasing her toes, tickling her feet, "you're too old for that."

"It's because," she hiccups, "I *am* too old. Old and funny."

"Not funny. Fun. More fun than anybody. Listen. If you don't stop crying you'll be so tired tomorrow we can't go cut a tree."

She straightens up. Queenie jumps on the bed (where Queenie is not allowed) to lick her cheeks. "I know where we'll find real pretty trees, Buddy. And holly, too. With berries big as your eyes. It's way off in the woods. Farther than we've ever been. Papa used to bring us Christmas trees from there; carry them on his shoulder. That's fifty years ago. Well, now, I can't wait for morning."

Morning. Frozen rime[9] lusters the grass; the sun, round as an orange and orange as hot-weather moons, balances on the horizon, burnishes the silvered winter woods. A wild turkey calls. A renegade hog grunts in the undergrowth. Soon, by the edge of knee-deep, rapid-running water, we have to abandon the buggy. Queenie wades the stream first, paddles across barking complaints at the swiftness of the current, the pneumonia-making coldness of it. We follow, holding our shoes and equipment (a hatchet, a burlap sack) above our heads. A mile more, of chastising thorns, burrs,

and briers that catch at our clothes; of rusty pine needles brilliant with gaudy fungus and molted feathers. Here, there, a flash, a flutter, an ecstasy of shrillings remind us that not all the birds have flown south. Always, the path unwinds through lemony sun pools and pitch pine tunnels. Another creek to cross; a disturbed armada of speckled trout froths the water round us, and frogs the size of plates practice belly flops; beaver workmen are building a dam. On the farther shore, Queenie shakes herself and trembles. My friend shivers, too: not with cold but enthusiasm. One of her hat's ragged roses sheds a petal as she lifts her head and inhales the pine-heavy air. "We're almost there. Can you smell it, Buddy?" she says, as though we were approaching an ocean.

And, indeed, it is a kind of ocean. Scented acres of holiday trees, prickly-leafed holly. Red berries shiny as Chinese bells; black crows swoop upon them screaming. Having stuffed our burlap sacks with enough greenery and crimson to garland a dozen windows, we set about choosing a tree. "It should be," muses my friend, "twice as tall as a boy. So a boy can't steal the star." The one we pick is twice as tall as me. A brave, handsome brute that survives thirty hatchet strokes before it keels with a creaking, rending cry. Lugging it like a kill, we commence the long trek out. Every few yards we abandon the struggle, sit down and pant. But we have the strength of triumphant huntsmen; that and the tree's virile, icy perfume revive us, goad us on. Many compliments accompany our sunset return along the red clay road to town; but my friend is sly and noncommittal when passers-by praise the treasure perched in our buggy: what a fine tree and where did it come from? "Yonderways," she murmurs vaguely. Once a car stops and the rich mill owner's lazy wife leans out and whines, "Giveya two-bits cash for that ol tree."

9. **rime** (rīm): frost.

Ordinarily my friend is afraid of saying no, but on this occasion she promptly shakes her head. "We wouldn't take a dollar." The mill owner's wife persists. "A dollar, my foot! Fifty cents. That's my last offer. Goodness, woman, you can get another one." In answer, my friend gently reflects, "I doubt it. There's never two of anything."

Home. Queenie slumps by the fire and sleeps till tomorrow, snoring loud as a human.

A trunk in the attic contains a shoebox of ermine tails (off the opera cape of a curious lady who once rented a room in the house), coils of frazzled tinsel gone gold with age, one silver star, a brief rope of dilapidated, undoubtedly dangerous candylike light bulbs. Excellent decorations, as far as they go, which isn't far enough. My friend wants our tree to blaze "like a Baptist window," droop with weighty snows of ornament. But we can't afford the made-in-Japan splendors at the five-and-dime. So we do what we've always done, sit for days at the kitchen table with scissors and crayons and stacks of colored paper. I make sketches and my friend cuts them out: lots of cats, fish too (because they're easy to draw), some apples, some watermelons, a few winged angels devised from saved-up sheets of Hershey-bar tinfoil. We use safety pins to attach these creations to the tree; as a final touch, we sprinkle the branches with shredded cotton (picked in August for this purpose). My friend, surveying the effect, clasps her hands together. "Now honest, Buddy. Doesn't it look good enough to eat?" Queenie tries to eat an angel.

After weaving and ribboning holly wreaths for all the front windows, our next project is the fashioning of family gifts. Tie-dye scarves for the ladies, for the men a home-brewed lemon and licorice and aspirin syrup to be taken "at the first Symptoms of a Cold and after Hunting." But when it comes time for making each other's gift, my friend and I separate to work secretly. I would like to buy her a pearl-handled knife, a radio, a whole pound of chocolate-covered cherries (we tasted some once, and she always swears, "I could live on them, Buddy, Lord yes I could—and that's not taking His name in vain"). Instead, I am building her a kite. She would like to give me a bicycle (she's said so on several million occasions. "If only I could, Buddy. It's bad enough in life to do without something *you* want; but confound it, what gets my goat is not being able to give somebody something you want *them* to have. Only one of these days I will, Buddy. Locate you a bike. Don't ask how. Steal it, maybe"). Instead, I'm fairly certain that she is building me a kite—the same as last year, and the year before; the year before that we exchanged slingshots. All of which is fine by me. For we are champion kite fliers who study the wind like sailors; my friend, more accomplished than I, can get a kite aloft when there isn't enough breeze to carry clouds.

Christmas Eve afternoon we scrape together a nickel and go to the butcher's to buy Queenie's traditional gift, a good, gnawable beef bone. The bone, wrapped in funny paper, is placed high in the tree near the silver star. Queenie knows it's there. She squats at the foot of the tree, staring up in a trance of greed; when bedtime arrives she refuses to budge. Her excitement is equaled by my own. I kick the covers and turn my pillow as though it were a scorching summer's night. Somewhere a rooster crows; falsely, for the sun is still on the other side of the world.

"Buddy, are you awake?" It is my friend, calling from her room, which is next to mine; and an instant later she is sitting on my bed holding a candle. "Well, I can't sleep a hoot," she declares. "My mind's jumping like a jack rabbit. Buddy, do you think Mrs. Roosevelt will serve our cake at dinner?" We huddle in the bed, and she squeezes my hand I-love-you. "Seems like your hand used to be so much smaller. I guess I hate to see you grow up.

When you're grown up, will we still be friends?" I say always. "But I feel so bad, Buddy. I wanted so bad to give you a bike. I tried to sell my cameo Papa gave me. Buddy—" she hesitates, as though embarrassed—"I made you another kite." Then I confess that I made her one, too; and we laugh. The candle burns too short to hold. Out it goes, exposing the starlight, the stars spinning at the window like a visible caroling that slowly, slowly daybreak silences. Possibly we doze; but the beginnings of dawn splash us like cold water. We're up, wide-eyed and wandering while we wait for others to waken. Quite deliberately my friend drops a kettle on the kitchen floor. I tap-dance in front of closed doors. One by one the household emerges looking as though they'd like to kill us both; but it's Christmas, so they can't. First, a gorgeous breakfast; just everything you can imagine—from flapjacks and fried squirrel to hominy grits and honey-in-the-comb. Which puts everyone in a good humor except my friend and I. Frankly, we're so impatient to get at the presents we can't eat a mouthful.

Well, I'm disappointed. Who wouldn't be? With socks, a Sunday school shirt, some handkerchiefs, a hand-me-down sweater, and a year's subscription to a religious magazine for children. *The Little Shepherd*. It makes me boil. It really does.

My friend has a better haul. A sack of Satsumas;[10] that's her best present. She is proudest, however, of a white wool shawl knitted by her married sister. But she *says* her favorite gift is the kite I built her. And it *is* very beautiful; though not as beautiful as the one she made me, which is blue and scattered with gold and green Good Conduct stars; moreover, my name is painted on it, "Buddy."

"Buddy, the wind is blowing."

The wind is blowing, and nothing will do till we've run to a pasture below the house where Queenie had scooted to bury her bone (and where, a winter hence, Queenie will be buried, too). There, plunging through the healthy, waist-high grass, we unreel our kites, feel them twitching at the string like sky fish as they swim into the wind. Satisfied, sun-warmed, we sprawl in the grass and peel Satsumas and watch our kites cavort. Soon I forget the socks and hand-me-down sweater. I'm as happy as if we'd already won the fifty-thousand-dollar Grand Prize in that coffee-naming contest.

"My, how foolish I am!" my friend cries, suddenly alert, like a woman remembering too late she has biscuits in the oven. "You know what I've always thought?" she asks in a tone of discovery, and not smiling at me but a point beyond. "I've always thought a body would have to be sick and dying before they saw the Lord. And I imagined that when He came it would be like looking at the Baptist window: pretty as colored glass with the sun pouring through, such a shine you don't know it's getting dark. And it's been a comfort; to think of that shine taking away all the spooky feeling. But I'll wager it never happens. I'll wager at the very end a body realizes the Lord has already shown Himself. That things as they are"—her hand circles in a gesture that gathers clouds and kites and grass and Queenie pawing earth over her bone—"just what they've always been, was seeing Him. As for me, I could leave the world with today in my eyes."

This is our last Christmas together.

Life separates us. Those who Know Best decide that I belong in a military school. And so follows a miserable succession of bugle-blowing prisons, grim, reveille-ridden summer camps. I have a new home too. But it doesn't count. Home is where my friend is, and there I never go.

And there she remains, puttering around the kitchen. Alone with Queenie. Then

---

10. **Satsumas** (sat′ sə mäs′): small, loose-skinned oranges.

alone. ("Buddy dear," she writes in her wild, hard-to-read script, "yesterday Jim Macy's horse kicked Queenie bad. Be thankful she didn't feel much. I wrapped her in a Fine Linen sheet and rode her in the buggy down to Simpson's pasture where she can be with all her Bones. . . ."). For a few Novembers she continues to bake her fruitcakes single-handed; not as many, but some; and, of course, she always sends me "the best of the batch." Also, in every letter she encloses a dime wadded in toilet paper: "See a picture show and write me the story." But gradually in her letters she tends to confuse me with her other friend, the Buddy who died in the 1880's; more and more, thirteenths are not the only days she stays in bed. A morning arrives in November, a leafless, birdless coming of winter morning, when she cannot rouse herself to exclaim: "Oh, my, it's fruitcake weather!"

And when that happens, I know it. A message saying so merely confirms a piece of news some secret vein had already received, severing[11] from me an irreplaceable[12] part of myself, letting it loose like a kite on a broken string. That is why, walking across a school campus on this particular December morning, I keep searching the sky. As if I expected to see, rather like hearts, a lost pair of kites hurrying toward heaven.

---

11. **severing** (sev′ ər iŋ): separating by cutting apart.
12. **irreplaceable** (ir′ ri plās′ a bəl): not replaceable.

# *Thinking About the Autobiographical Essay*

## A PERSONAL RESPONSE

*sharing impressions*

**1.** What feelings does Capote's holiday memory trigger in you? Describe them briefly in your journal.

*constructing interpretations*

**2.** Why do you think Capote makes two comparisons with kites in the last paragraph?

***Think about***
- what the kites are compared to
- why kites are important to Buddy and his friend

**3.** Why do you suppose Buddy and his older cousin became such good friends?

***Think about***
- their status in the household
- their interests and activities
- the way the cousin treats Buddy

**4.** How would you describe Buddy's friend?

***Think about***
- her feelings about holidays and about Buddy
- the things that give her pleasure
- what she reveals about her religious beliefs and her values

**5.** In what ways does Capote's Christmas memory capture the special quality of his relationship with his friend?

## A CREATIVE RESPONSE

**6.** If "those who Know Best" had not sent Buddy off to a military school, what do you suppose might have happened in the final years of the relationship between Buddy and his friend?

## A CRITICAL RESPONSE

**7.** How does Capote's tone in this selection influence the way you, as a reader, feel about his friend?

> ***Think about***
> • tone as the attitude a writer takes toward a subject
> • the kinds of things Capote says about the friend
> • what you feel about the friend

**8.** Compare what Marguerite learns from Mrs. Flowers in the excerpt from *I Know Why the Caged Bird Sings* to what Buddy learns from his older cousin. Use examples from the selections to support your answer.

# *Analyzing the Writer's Craft*

## IMAGERY

What mental pictures did you imagine as you read this selection? What tastes, smells, sensations, and sounds do you remember imagining?

**Building a Literary Vocabulary.** Imagery refers to words and phrases that re-create sensory experiences for a reader. Images can appeal to any of a reader's senses, sight, hearing, smell, taste, and touch. Truman Capote often creates imagery that engages several senses at the same time. In the following passage from the selection, notice the sights, sounds, and sensations conveyed by the imagery.

Morning. Frozen rime lusters the grass; the sun, round as an orange and orange as hot-weather moons, balances on the horizon, burnishes the silvered winter woods. A wild turkey calls. A renegade hog grunts in the undergrowth. Soon, by the edge of knee-deep, rapid-running water, we have to abandon the buggy. Queenie wades the stream first, paddles across barking complaints at the swiftness of the current, the pneumonia-making coldness of it.

**Application: Analyzing Imagery.** Choose from the selection a descriptive passage that is at least two or three sentences in length. Then create a chart with six columns, similar to the one below. Divide the passage into separate phrases and list each phrase in the first column of the chart. Indicate the kind of image contained in the phrase by putting an **X** in the column for the appropriate sense, as shown in the example. Compare your chart with those of three other classmates and decide as a group which kinds of images predominate in the selection.

| Descriptive phrase | Senses | | | | |
|---|---|---|---|---|---|
| | **Sight** | **Smell** | **Hearing** | **Touch** | **Taste** |
| Frozen rime lusters the grass | X | | | X | |
| | | | | | |

## Connecting Reading and Writing

**1.** Analyze the significance of the many references to kites in this selection. Explain your interpretation in an **expository essay** written for your teacher.

Option: Explain your interpretation in a **review** of the selection.

**2.** Write about a holiday memory of your own, either the one you described in your journal or a different one. Convey your memory in a **poem** for a holiday card.

Option: Write about your holiday memory in a descriptive **essay** that might be published in a holiday issue of a family magazine.

**3.** Buddy's friend remarks to him, "I've always thought a body would have to be sick and dying before they saw the Lord. . . . But I'll wager . . . at the very end a body realizes the Lord has already shown Himself. That things as they are . . . just what they've always been, was seeing Him." Pretend you are a minister and write a **sermon** on the topic that Buddy's friend addresses.

Option: Explain your opinion of his friend's statement in a **diary entry.**

**4.** Imagine that the adult Capote decides to tell his relatives how he feels about their treatment of him and his friend. Write a **dialogue** between Capote and a relative "who Knows Best."

Option: In Capote's voice, write a **letter** to one of his relatives.

# The Night the Bed Fell

## JAMES THURBER

A biography of Thurber appears on page 646.

## *Approaching the Autobiographical Essay*

James Thurber gained widespread popularity as a cartoonist as well as a writer. Until his death in 1961, he was associated with *The New Yorker* magazine, where much of his humorous work first appeared. "The Night the Bed Fell" is taken from *My Life and Hard Times,* Thurber's collection of nonfiction pieces about his youth in Columbus, Ohio. In this selection, the adult Thurber looks back on one riotous night his family experienced.

## *Building Vocabulary*

These essential words are footnoted within the selection.

**ominous** (äm´ ə nəs): We later heard **ominous** creakings as he crawled into bed. (page 243)

**calamity** (kə lam´ ə tē): To avert this **calamity** . . . she always piled her money . . . in a neat stack. (page 243)

**phobia** (fō´ bē ə), **fortitude** (fôrt´ ə tōod): Aunt Gracie Shoaf also had a burglar **phobia**, but she met it with more **fortitude**. (page 243)

**perilous** (per´ ə ləs): It is **perilous** to roll too far toward the edge. (page 244)

## *Connecting Writing and Reading*

Work with a partner to brainstorm a list of silly fears that people sometimes have. Write the list in your journal. As you read this selection, add to your list any silly or irrational fears the characters possess.

I SUPPOSE THAT the high-water mark of my youth in Columbus, Ohio, was the night the bed fell on my father. It makes a better recitation (unless, as some friends of mine have said, one has heard it five or six times) than it does a piece of writing, for it is almost necessary to throw furniture around, shake doors, and bark like a dog, to lend the proper atmosphere and verisimilitude to what is admittedly a somewhat incredible tale. Still, it did take place.

It happened, then, that my father had decided to sleep in the attic one night, to be away where he could think. My mother opposed the notion strongly because, she said, the old wooden bed up there was unsafe; it was wobbly, and the heavy headboard would crash down on Father's head in case the bed fell, and kill him. There was no dissuading him, however, and at a quarter past ten he closed the attic door behind him and went up the narrow, twisting stairs. We later heard <u>ominous</u>[1] creakings as he crawled into bed. Grandfather, who usually slept in the attic bed when he was with us, had disappeared some days before. (On these occasions he was usually gone six or eight days and returned growling and out of temper, with the news that the federal Union was run by a passel of blockheads and that the Army of the Potomac[2] didn't have any more chance than a fiddler's dog.)

We had visiting us at this time a nervous first cousin of mine named Briggs Beall, who believed that he was likely to cease breathing when he was asleep. It was his feeling that if he were not awakened every hour during the night, he might die of suffocation. He had been accustomed to setting an alarm clock to ring at intervals until morning, but I persuaded him to abandon this. He slept in my room, and I told him that I was such a light sleeper that if anybody quit breathing in the same room with me, I would wake instantly. He tested me the first night—which I had suspected he would—by holding his breath after my regular breathing had convinced him I was asleep. I was not asleep, however, and called to him. This seemed to allay his fears a little, but he took the precaution of putting a glass of spirits of camphor on a little table at the head of his bed. In case I didn't arouse him until he was almost gone, he said, he would sniff the camphor, a powerful reviver. Briggs was not the only member of his family who had his crotchets. Old Aunt Melissa Beall (who could whistle like a man, with two fingers in her mouth) suffered under the premonition that she was destined to die on South High Street, because she had been born on South High Street and married on South High Street. Then there was Aunt Sarah Shoaf, who never went to bed at night without the fear that a burglar was going to get in and blow chloroform[3] under her door through a tube. To avert this <u>calamity</u>[4]—for she was in greater dread of anesthetics than of losing her household goods—she always piled her money, silverware, and other valuables in a neat stack just outside her bedroom, with a note reading, "This is all I have. Please take it and do not use your chloroform, as this is all I have." Aunt Gracie Shoaf also had a burglar <u>phobia</u>,[5] but she met it with more <u>fortitude</u>.[6] She was confident that burglars had been getting into her

---

1. **ominous** (äm′ ə nəs): threatening; sinister.
2. **Union . . . Army of the Potomac:** references to the army of the North during the Civil War.
3. **chloroform** (klôr′ ə fôrm′): a colorless, toxic liquid once used as a general anesthetic.
4. **calamity** (kə lam′ ə tē): extreme trouble or misfortune.
5. **phobia** (fō′ bē ə), a strong, unreasonable, continuing fear of something
6. **fortitude** (fôrt′ ə tōōd): the strength to bear pain or misfortune calmly and patiently.

house every night for forty years. The fact that she never missed anything was to her no proof to the contrary. She always claimed that she scared them off before they could take anything, by throwing shoes down the hallway. When she went to bed she piled, where she could get at them handily, all the shoes there were about her house. Five minutes after she had turned off the light, she would sit up in bed and say, "Hark!" Her husband, who had learned to ignore the whole situation as long ago as 1903, would either be sound asleep or pretend to be sound asleep. In either case he would not respond to her tugging and pulling, so that presently she would arise, tiptoe to the door, open it slightly and heave a shoe down the hall in one direction, and its mate down the hall in the other direction. Some nights she threw them all, some nights only a couple of pairs.

But I am straying from the remarkable incidents that took place during the night that the bed fell on Father. By midnight we were all in bed. The layout of the rooms and the disposition of their occupants is important to an understanding of what later occurred. In the front room upstairs (just under Father's attic bedroom) were my mother and my brother Herman, who sometimes sang in his sleep, usually "Marching Through Georgia" or "Onward, Christian Soldiers." Briggs Beall and myself were in a room adjoining this one. My brother Roy was in a room across the hall from ours. Our bull terrier, Rex, slept in the hall.

My bed was an army cot, one of those affairs that are made wide enough to sleep on comfortably only by putting up, flat with the middle section, the two sides which ordinarily hang down like the sideboards of a drop-leaf table. When these sides are up, it is <u>perilous</u>[7] to roll too far toward the edge, for then the cot is likely to tip completely over, bringing the whole bed down on top of one, with a tremen-dous banging crash. This, in fact, is precisely what happened, about two o'clock in the morning. (It was my mother who, in recalling the scene later, first referred to it as "the night the bed fell on your father.")

Always a deep sleeper, slow to arouse (I had lied to Briggs), I was at first unconscious of what had happened when the iron cot rolled me onto the floor and toppled over on me. It left me still warmly bundled up and unhurt, for the bed rested above me like a canopy. Hence I did not wake up, only reached the edge of consciousness and went back. The racket, however, instantly awakened my mother, in the next room, who came to the immediate conclusion that her worst dread was realized: the big wooden bed upstairs had fallen on Father. She therefore screamed, "Let's go to your poor father!" It was this shout, rather than the noise of my cot falling, that awakened Herman, in the same room with her. He thought that mother had become, for no apparent reason, hysterical. "You're all right, Mamma!" he shouted, trying to calm her. They exchanged shout for shout for perhaps ten seconds: "Let's go to your poor father!" and "You're all right!" That woke up Briggs. By this time I was conscious of what was going on, in a vague way, but did not yet realize that I was under my bed instead of on it. Briggs, awakening in the midst of loud shouts of fear and apprehension, came to the quick conclusion that he was suffocating and that we were all trying to "bring him out." With a low moan, he grasped the glass of camphor at the head of his bed and instead of sniffing it, poured it over himself. The room reeked of camphor. "Ugf, ahfg," choked Briggs, like a drowning man, for he had almost succeeded in stopping his breath under the deluge of pungent spirits. He

---

7. **perilous** (per′ ə ləs): involving peril or risk; dangerous.

leaped out of bed and groped toward the open window, but he came up against one that was closed. With his hand, he beat out the glass, and I could hear it crash and tinkle on the alleyway below. It was at this juncture that I, in trying to get up, had the uncanny sensation of feeling my bed above me! Foggy with sleep, I now suspected, in my turn, that the whole uproar was being made in a frantic endeavor to extricate me from what must be an unheard-of and perilous situation. "Get me out of this!" I bawled. "Get me out!" I think I had the nightmarish belief that I was entombed in a mine. "Gugh," gasped Briggs, floundering in his camphor.

By this time my mother, still shouting, pursued by Herman, still shouting, was trying to open the door to the attic, in order to go up and get my father's body out of the wreckage. The door was stuck, however, and wouldn't yield. Her frantic pulls on it only added to the general banging and confusion. Roy and the dog were now up, the one shouting questions, the other barking.

Father, farthest away and soundest sleeper of all, had by this time been awakened by the battering on the attic door. He decided that the house was on fire. "I'm coming, I'm coming!" he wailed in a slow, sleepy voice—it took him many minutes to regain full consciousness. My mother, still believing he was caught under the bed, detected in his "I'm coming!" the mournful, resigned note of one who is preparing to meet his Maker. "He's dying!" she shouted.

"I'm all right!" Briggs yelled to reassure her. "I'm all right!" He still believed that it was his own closeness to death that was worrying Mother. I found at last the light switch in my room, unlocked the door, and Briggs and I joined the others at the attic door. The dog, who never did like Briggs, jumped for him—assuming that he was the culprit in whatever was going on—and Roy had to throw Rex and hold him. We could hear father crawling out of bed upstairs. Roy pulled the attic door open, with a mighty jerk, and father came down the stairs, sleepy and irritable but safe and sound. My mother began to weep when she saw him. Rex began to howl. "What in the name of God is going on here?" asked Father.

The situation was finally put together like a gigantic jigsaw puzzle. Father caught a cold from prowling around in his bare feet, but there were no other bad results. "I'm glad," said Mother, who always looked on the bright side of things, "that your grandfather wasn't here."

# *Thinking About the Autobiographical Essay*

*sharing impressions*

**1.** What do you think of the series of events described in this selection? Jot down your response in your journal.

*constructing interpretations*

**2.** Explain how the situation on the night described by Thurber is "like a gigantic jigsaw puzzle."

**3.** How do the family members' silly or irrational fears create the confusion on that night?

**4.** How would you describe the way that the Thurber family members communicate with one another?

### Think about
- how well they listen to each other
- how their irrational fears influence the way they communicate
- how they express their feelings toward one another

## A CREATIVE RESPONSE

**5.** Thurber's mother says of that night, "I'm glad that your grandfather wasn't here." What might have happened if Grandfather had been present for the action?

## A CRITICAL RESPONSE

**6.** How does irony contribute to the humor in "The Night the Bed Fell"? Support your answer with examples from the selection.

### Think about
- the contrast between what is said and what is meant
- the contrast between what a character expects and what happens
- the contrast between what a character knows and what the reader knows

**7.** Compare the way that humor is created in this selection with the way it is created in O. Henry's "The Ransom of Red Chief." Use details from the selections to illustrate the similarities and differences.

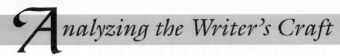

# Analyzing the Writer's Craft

## TONE

How do you think Thurber feels about the members of his family? How do you know his feelings?

**Building a Literary Vocabulary.** Tone is the attitude a writer takes toward a subject. The tone of Thurber's piece is ironic and humorous. Even though he is describing a night when his family experienced a great deal of confusion, Thurber makes it clear from the beginning that he finds the episode amusing. In the opening paragraph, he states that he prefers to retell the story of that night as a recitation with dramatic action and sound effects.

**Application: Understanding Tone.** In a small group pick a passage of two or three paragraphs and identify key words or phrases that illustrate Thurber's ironic humor. Then work up an oral presentation of this passage with sound effects and possibly some dramatic enactment. Preserve Thurber's tone throughout your performance.

# Connecting Reading and Writing

**1.** Relate a comic episode from your own family's experiences, keeping your tone humorous. Create a **script** based on the episode for a television situation comedy.

Option: Create a **comic strip** portraying the episode.

**2.** Read "The Night the Ghost Got In" or "More Alarms at Night" from Thurber's collection *My Life and Hard Times.* Write a **description** praising the selection you chose and "The Night the Bed Fell" to appear on the book jacket of the collection. Be sure to cite interesting examples from each selection to make someone want to buy the book.

Option: Create a **flowchart** tracking the plot of each selection and circle any similarities between the two.

**3.** Thurber recounts this episode in a humorous tone, but think about how one of the other family members might have felt about the same events. Pretend you are one of the other people in Thurber's house that night and write a **monologue** describing what happened.

Option: Imagine talking to a family member other than Thurber about that night and write up your **interview** with that person.

# *from* Dance to the Piper

## AGNES DE MILLE

A biography of de Mille appears on page 639.

### *A*pproaching the Selection

Born in 1909, Agnes de Mille became a well-known dancer, choreographer, director, and author whose influence on the world of dance has extended into the 1990's. Daughter of a playwright and niece of Hollywood director Cecil B. de Mille, Agnes de Mille grew up among artistic people. Her desire to be a dancer, however, came from within. In this selection from the first volume of her autobiography, *Dance to the Piper*, published in 1952, de Mille recalls her beginnings in ballet and the regimen that she followed as a teenager.

THE FIRST LESSON was a private one conducted by Miss Fredova. Miss Fredova was born Winifred Edwards and had received her training in London from Anna Pavlova.[1] She was as slim as a sapling and always wore white, like a trained nurse. She parted her dark hair in the center and drew it to the nape of her neck in glossy wings, Russian style. She was shod in low-heeled sandals. She taught standing erect as a guardsman and beat time with a long pole. First she picked up a watering can and sprinkled water on the floor in a sunny corner by the barre.[2] This, she explained, was so we should not slip. Then she placed our hands on the barre and showed us how to turn our feet ninety degrees from their normal walking stance into first position. Then she told us to plier,[3] or bend our knees deeply, keeping our heels as long as possible on the floor. I naturally stuck out behind. I found the pole placed rigidly against my spine. I naturally pressed forward on my insteps. Her leg and knee planted against my foot curbed this tendency. "I can't move," I said, laughing with winning helplessness.

"Don't talk," she said. "Down-ee, two-ee, three-ee, four-ee. Down the heels, don't rock on your feet."

At the end of ten minutes, the sweat stuck in beads on my forehead. "May I sit down?" I asked.

"You must never sit during practice. It ruins the thigh muscles. If you sit down, you may not continue with class." I, of course, would have submitted to a beating with whips rather

1. **Anna Pavlova** (päv lō′ və): famous Russian ballet dancer who lived from 1885 (?) to 1931.
2. **barre** (bär) *French:* the bar or handrail in a dance studio.
3. **plier** (plē′ ā): *French:* in dance, bending the knees outward while keeping the heels on the floor and the back straight.

than stop. I was taking the first steps into the promised land. The path might be thorny, but it led straight to Paradise. "Down-ee, two-ee, three-ee, four-ee. Nuca.[4] Give me this fourth position. Repeat the exercise."

So she began every lesson. So I have begun every practice period since. It is part of the inviolable[5] ritual of ballet dancing. Every ballet student that has ever trained in the classic technique in any part of the world begins just this way, never any other.

I bent to the discipline. I learned to relax with my head between my knees when I felt sick or faint. I learned how to rest my insteps by lying on my back with my feet vertically up against the wall. I learned how to bind up my toes so that they would not bleed through the satin shoes. But I never sat down. I learned the first and all-important dictate of ballet dancing—never to miss the daily practice, sickness or health, never to miss the barre practice; to miss meals, sleep, rehearsals even but not the practice, not for one day ever under any circumstances, except on Sundays and during childbirth.

I seemed, however, to have little aptitude[6] for the business. What had all this talk about God-given talent amounted to? It was like trying to wiggle my ears. I strained and strained. Nothing perceptible happened. A terrible sense of frustration drove me to striving with masochistic[7] frenzy. Twice I fainted in class. My calves used to ache until tears stuck in my eyes. I learned every possible manipulation of the shoe to ease the aching tendons in my insteps. I used to get abominable stitches[8] in my sides from attempting continuous jumps. But I never sat down. I learned to cool my forehead against the plaster of the walls. I licked the perspiration off from around my mouth. I breathed through my nose though my eyes bugged. But I did not sit and I did not stop.

Ballet technique is arbitrary and very difficult. It never becomes easy; it becomes possible. The effort involved in making a dancer's body is so long and relentless, in many instances so painful, the effort to maintain the technique so grueling that unless a certain satisfaction is derived from the disciplining and punishing, the pace could not be maintained. Most dancers are to an extent masochists. "What a good pain! What a profitable pain!" said Miss Fredova as she stretched her insteps in her two strong hands. "I have practiced for three hours. I am exhausted, and I feel wonderful."

Paradoxically enough, ballet dancing is designed to give the impression of lightness and ease. Nothing in classic dancing should be convulsive or tormented. Derived from the seventeenth- and eighteenth-century court dances, the style is kingly, a series of harmonious and balanced postures linked by serene movement. The style involves a total defiance of gravity, and because this must perforce be an illusion, the effect is achieved first by an enormous strengthening of the legs and feet to produce great, resilient[9] jumps and second by a coordination of arms and head in a rhythm slower than the rhythm of the legs, which have no choice but to take the weight of the body when the body falls. But the slow, relaxed movement of head and arms gives the illusion of sustained flight, gives the sense of effortless ease.

The lungs may be bursting, the heart pounding in the throat, sweat springing from every pore, but hands must float in repose, the head stir gently as though swooning in delight. The diaphragm must be lifted to expand the

---

4. **nuca** (noo′ ka) *Anglicized Russian:* come, now; now then.
5. **inviolable** (in vī′ ō lə bəl): that should not be violated or broken; sacred.
6. **aptitude** (ap′ tə tood′): a natural tendency or ability.
7. **masochistic** (mas′ ə kis′ tik): getting pleasure from being hurt or mistreated by oneself or another.
8. **stitches** (stich iz): sudden sharp pains.
9. **resilient** (ri zil′ yənt): springing back into shape after being stretched, bent, or squeezed.

chest fully, proudly; the abdomen pulled in flat. The knees must be taut and flat to give the extended leg every inch of length. The leg must be turned outward forty-five degrees in the hip socket so that the side of the knee and the long unbroken line of the leg are presented to view and never the lax, droopy line of a bent knee. The leg must look like a sword. The foot arches to prolong the line of extension. The supporting foot turns out forty-five degrees to enhance the line of the supporting leg, to keep the hips even, and to ensure the broadest possible base for the support and balancing of the body.

The ideal ballet body is long limbed with a small, compact torso. This makes for beauty of line; the longer the arms and legs the more exciting the body line. The ideal ballet foot has a high, taut instep and a wide stretch in the Achilles' tendon.[10] This tendon is the spring on which a dancer pushes for his jump, the hinge on which he takes the shock of landing. If there is one tendon in a dancer's body more important than any other, it is this tendon. It is, I should say, the prerequisite[11] for all great technique. When the heel does not stretch easily and softly like a cat's, as mine did not, almost to the point of malformation, the shock of running or jumping must be taken somewhere in the spine by sticking out behind, for instance, in a sitting posture after every jump. I seemed to be all rusty wire and safety pins. My torso was long with unusually broad hips, my legs and arms abnormally short, my hands and feet broad and short. I was fat besides. What I did not know was that I was constructed for endurance and that I developed through effort alone a capacity for outperforming far, far better technicians. Because I was built like a mustang, stocky, mettlesome, and sturdy, I became a good jumper, growing special compensating muscles up the front of my shins for the lack of a helpful heel. But the long, cool, serene classic line was forever denied me.

And at first, of course, the compensations and adjustments were neither present nor indicated. Every dancer makes his own body. He is born only with certain physical tendencies. This making of a ballet leg takes approximately ten years, and the initial stages are almost entirely discouraging, for even the best look awkward and paralyzed at the beginning.

My predicament was intensified by the fact that Mother and Father had no intention of permitting me to slight my other studies for this new enthusiasm. I was allowed one private lesson a week (forty-five minutes) and one class lesson (one hour). In between times I practiced at home alone, something no dancer, pupil or professional, ever does. One needs company to overcome the almost irresistible tendency to flag. One needs someone else's eye on awkward parts impossible to see. It is an unnatural and unprofitable strain for a child to practice without supervision. I practiced in Mother's bathroom, where she had a little barre fitted for me. The floor was slippery and there was no mirror. And I hated to practice there. I flagellated[12] myself into the daily grind.

Since I could not practice long, obviously I must practice harder. I strained and strained. Between the Monday lesson and the Thursday lesson, I developed and matured rigid bad habits. Every week I developed a new bad habit.

The plain truth is I was the worst pupil in the class. Having grown into adolescence feeling that I was remarkably gifted and destined to be great (I remember a friend asking Mother, "But do you want her to be a professional dancer?" and Mother's cool reply, "If she

---

10. **Achilles' tendon** (ə kil′ ēz ten′ dən): the tendon that connects the back of the heel with the calf muscles.
11. **prerequisite** (pri rek′ wə zit): something required beforehand, especially a condition necessary for something to follow.
12. **flagellated** (flaj′ ə lāt′ id): whipped; flogged.

can be a Pavlova—not otherwise"), I now found I could not hold my own with any of the girls standing on the floor beside me. So I crept about at the rear of the group, found matters wrong with my shoes, with my knees, with my hair, resorted to any device to get away from the dreadful exposure.

Only once did I have a small bit of my share of success. On a single occasion Kosloff gave exercises in pantomime. He suddenly stopped the class and called me out from my position in the back of the room. I demonstrated the exercise to a hushed and watching group. I did, of course, the best I could, trembling a little. They applauded. Kosloff beamed on me. He told Uncle Cecil that I showed the finest talent for pantomime of any pupil he had ever taught. This remark was naturally not repeated to me until long after.

My well-filled curriculum—classes, homework, tennis, piano, editing—was ordered with just one thought: to make room for the dance practice. I rose at six-thirty and studied and practiced at breakneck concentration until six in the evening, when I was at last free to put on dancing dress and walk—to Mother's bathroom.

All through the lonely, drab exercises beside Mother's tub, without music or beat, proper floor or mirror, I had the joy of looking forward to dinner with Father, to hearing him talk about his scenarios and what was going on at the studio. Sometimes he talked about music and literature. Once he said he thought I was an artist. Sometimes after dinner he sang and I accompanied him. These evenings my cup ran over. I went to bed early planning next day's practice, praying to do better in class. And as I lay waiting for sleep, breathing in the moist garden smells with my fox terrier slowly pressing me from the comfortable center of the bed, I used to dream about dancing on the stage with Pavlova, dancing until I dropped in a faint at her feet so that she would notice me and say, "That girl has talent."

# Voices of Experience:
## People and Places

*I*S EXPERIENCE THE best teacher? The selections in the previous section were written by adults looking back on memorable childhood experiences. In many of the selections, such as the excerpt from *I Know Why the Caged Bird Sings,* the adult writer comments upon the memory, making it clear that the experience had a strong influence on his or her later life. The selections in the previous section do not, however, reveal much about those later lives. For example, the excerpt from *Dance to the Piper* clearly shows Agnes De Mille's burning desire to be a dancer, but it does not tell whether she realized her dream.

In the selections you are about to read, the writers focus on adult experiences that forced them to assess their lives. Most of the writers present lessons they learned about life. All explain how they achieved—or didn't achieve—their dreams. All explore their interactions with other people and focus on the importance of particular places. In every case, the writer speaks with the voice of experience.

# *Literary Vocabulary*

**Style.**  Style is the particular way that a piece of literature is written. Style refers not so much to what is said but to how it is said. Word choice, lengths of sentences, tone, imagery, and use of dialogue all contribute to a writer's style. In the excerpt from *Dance to the Piper,* de Mille begins with a lighthearted style; her breezy descriptions of the teacher and class convey the wide-eyed enthusiasm of a young girl. Later, the style shifts; the repetition of the phrases "I learned" and "I never sat down" show that de Mille has absorbed the repetitive discipline of a dancer.

**Theme.**  Theme is the central idea or message in a work of literature. It is a writer's perception about life or humanity that is shared with the reader. Theme should not be confused with subject, or what the work is about. Rather, theme is a perception that the writer expresses about a subject. For example, the subject of "A Christmas Memory" is the special relationship between Buddy and his friend. The theme of the selection is that the joy of the holiday season, and of life in general, comes from loving relationships and simple pleasures.

**Conflict    Tone**

# West with the Night

## BERYL MARKHAM

A biography of Markham appears on page 642.

## *Approaching the Selection*

Born in England in 1902, Beryl Markham grew up in East Africa. In her twenties she became an aviator, flying a small plane into remote parts of Africa to deliver passengers, mail, and supplies. In 1936 Markham became the first person to fly westward across the Atlantic Ocean from England to North America, a flight that she describes in this chapter from her autobiography, *West with the Night*. As the selection opens, Markham is awakened from early-morning dreams by a phone call that establishes that night as the time for her flight.

## *Building Vocabulary*

These essential words are footnoted within the selection.

**enigmatic** (en´ ig mat´ ik), **plausible** (plô´ zə bəl): Mine are not **enigmatic** dreams; they are peopled with characters who are **plausible**. (page 255)

**resolute** (rez´ əl lo͞ot): I . . . feel less **resolute** than anxious, much less brave than foolhardy. (page 255)

**inexorable** (in eks´ ə rə bəl): Nothing is so **inexorable** as a promise to your pride. (page 255)

**pedestrian** (pi des´ trē ən): It is too much that with all those **pedestrian** centuries behind us we should, in a few decades, have learned to fly. (page 257)

**abhorrence** (ab hôr´ əns): The **abhorrence** of loneliness is as natural as wanting to live at all. (page 258)

## *Connecting Writing and Reading*

In your journal, make a list of dangerous activities, such as mountain climbing and professional car racing. Then, rate each one according to the degree of danger involved. Circle two or three activities that strike you as the most dangerous, and briefly explain why. As you read, compare the degree of danger in those activities with the degree of danger in Beryl Markham's flight.

I HAVE SELDOM dreamed a dream worth dreaming again, or at least none worth recording. Mine are not enigmatic[1] dreams; they are peopled with characters who are plausible[2] and who do plausible things, and I am the most plausible amongst them. All the characters in my dreams have quiet voices like the voice of the man who telephoned me at Elstree one morning in September of 1936 and told me that there was rain and strong head winds over the west of England and over the Irish Sea, and that there were variable winds and clear skies in mid-Atlantic and fog off the coast of Newfoundland.

"If you are still determined to fly the Atlantic this late in the year," the voice said, "the Air Ministry[3] suggests that the weather it is able to forecast for tonight, and for tomorrow morning, will be about the best you can expect."

The voice had a few other things to say, but not many, and then it was gone, and I lay in bed half-suspecting that the telephone call and the man who made it were only parts of the mediocre dream I had been dreaming. I felt that if I closed my eyes, the unreal quality of the message would be reestablished and that, when I opened them again, this would be another ordinary day with its usual beginning and its usual routine.

But of course I could not close my eyes, nor my mind, nor my memory. I could lie there for a few moments—remembering how it had begun, and telling myself, with senseless repetition, that by tomorrow morning I should either have flown the Atlantic to America—or I should not have flown it. In either case this was the day I would try.

I could stare up at the ceiling of my bedroom in Aldenham House, which was a ceiling undistinguished as ceilings go, and feel less resolute[4] than anxious, much less brave than foolhardy. I could say to myself, "You needn't do it, of course," knowing at the same time that nothing is so inexorable[5] as a promise to your pride.

I could ask, "Why risk it?" as I have been asked since, and I could answer, "Each to his element." By his nature a sailor must sail, by his nature a flyer must fly. I could compute that I had flown a quarter of a million miles; and I could foresee that, so long as I had a plane and the sky was there, I should go on flying more miles.

There was nothing extraordinary in this. I had learned a craft and had worked hard learning it. My hands had been taught to seek the controls of a plane. Usage had taught them. They were at ease clinging to a stick, as a cobbler's fingers are in repose grasping an awl. No human pursuit achieves dignity until it can be called work, and when you can experience a physical loneliness for the tools of your trade, you see that the other things—the experiments, the irrelevant vocations, the vanities you used to hold—were false to you.

Record flights had actually never interested me very much for myself. There were people who thought that such flights were done for admiration and publicity, and worse. But of all the records—from Louis Blériot's first crossing of the English Channel in 1909, through and beyond Kingsford Smith's flight from San Francisco to Sydney, Australia—none had been made by amateurs, nor by novices, nor by men or women less than hardened to failure,

---

1. **enigmatic** (en′ ig mat′ ik): of or like a mystery, riddle, etc.; puzzling; mysterious.
2. **plausible** (plô′ zə bəl): seemingly true, acceptable, reasonable, etc.
3. **Air Ministry:** the British governmental department overseeing air flight.
4. **resolute** (rez′ ə loot′): having or showing a fixed, firm purpose; determined; unwavering.
5. **inexorable** (in eks′ ə rə bəl): that cannot be influenced by a plea; not letting up.

or less than masters of their trade. None of these was false. They were a company that simple respect and simple ambition made it worth more than an effort to follow.

The Carberrys (of Seramai)[6] were in London, and I could remember everything about their dinner party—even the menu. I could remember June Carberry and all her guests, and the man named McCarthy, who lived in Zanzibar, leaning across the table and saying, "J.C., why don't you finance Beryl for a record flight?"

I could lie there staring lazily at the ceiling and recall J.C.'s dry answer: "A number of pilots have flown the North Atlantic, west to east. Only Jim Mollison has done it alone the other way—from Ireland. Nobody has done it alone from England—man or woman. I'd be interested in that, but nothing else. If you want to try it, Burl, I'll back you. I think Edgar Percival could build a plane that would do it, provided you can fly it. Want to chance it?"

"Yes."

I could remember saying that better than I could remember anything—except J.C.'s almost ghoulish grin, and his remark that sealed the agreement: "It's a deal, Burl. I'll furnish the plane and you fly the Atlantic—but, gee, I wouldn't tackle it for a million. Think of all that black water! Think how cold it is!"

And I had thought of both.

I had thought of both for awhile, and then there had been other things to think about. I had moved to Elstree, half-hour's flight from the Percival Aircraft Works at Gravesend, and almost daily for three months now I had flown down to the factory in a hired plane and watched the Vega Gull they were making for me. I had watched her birth and watched her growth. I had watched her wings take shape and seen wood and fabric molded to her ribs to form her long, sleek belly, and I had seen her engine cradled into her frame and made fast.

The Gull had a turquoise blue body and silver wings. Edgar Percival had made her with care, with skill, and with worry—the care of a veteran flyer, the skill of a master designer, and the worry of a friend. Actually the plane was a standard sport model with a range of only 660 miles. But she had a special undercarriage built to carry the weight of her extra oil and petrol tanks. The tanks were fixed into the wings, into the center section, and into the cabin itself. In the cabin they formed a wall around my seat, and each tank had a petcock[7] of its own. The petcocks were important.

"If you open one," said Percival, "without shutting the other first, you may get an airlock. You know the tanks in the cabin have no gauges, so it may be best to let one run completely dry before opening the next. Your motor might go dead in the interval—but she'll start again. She's a De Havilland Gipsy—and Gipsies never stop."

I had talked to Tom.[8] We had spent hours going over the Atlantic chart, and I had realized that the tinker of Molo, now one of England's great pilots, had traded his dreams and had got in return a better thing. Tom had grown older, too; he had jettisoned a dead weight of irrelevant hopes and wonders and had left himself a realistic code that had no room for temporizing or easy sentiment.

"I'm glad you're going to do it, Beryl. It won't be simple. If you can get off the ground in the first place, with such an immense load of fuel, you'll be alone in that place about a night and a day—mostly night. Doing it east to west, the wind's against you. In September,

---

6. **Carberrys (of Seramai):** John (J.C.) and June Carberry were Markham's hosts on their coffee farm in Africa, called Seramai. John Carberry was a flying enthusiast.
7. **petcock** (pet′ käk′): an on/off valve.
8. **Tom:** Tom Black, an experienced aviator and Markham's friend who had taught her how to fly.

so is the weather. You won't have a radio. If you misjudge your course only a few degrees, you'll end up in Labrador or in the sea—so don't misjudge anything."

Tom could still grin. He had grinned; he had said: "Anyway, it ought to amuse you to think that your financial backer lives on a farm called Place of Death and your plane is being built at Gravesend. If you were consistent, you'd christen the Gull *The Flying Tombstone*."

I hadn't been that consistent. I had watched the building of the plane and I had trained for the flight like an athlete. And now, as I lay in bed, fully awake, I could still hear the quiet voice of the man from the Air Ministry intoning, like the voice of a dispassionate court clerk: ". . . the weather for tonight and tomorrow . . . will be about the best you can expect." I should have liked to discuss the flight once more with Tom before I took off, but he was on a special job up north. I got out of bed and bathed and put on my flying clothes and took some cold chicken packed in a cardboard box and flew over to the military field at Abingdon, where the Vega Gull waited for me under the care of the R.A.F.[9] I remember that the weather was clear and still.

Jim Mollison lent me his watch. He said: "This is not a gift. I wouldn't part with it for anything. It got me across the North Atlantic and the South Atlantic, too. Don't lose it—and, for God's sake, don't get it wet. Salt water would ruin the works."

Brian Lewis gave me a lifesaving jacket. Brian owned the plane I had been using between Elstree and Gravesend, and he had thought a long time about a farewell gift. What could be more practical than a pneumatic jacket that could be inflated through a rubber tube?

"You could float around in it for days," said Brian. But I had to decide between the life-saver and warm clothes. I couldn't have both, because of their bulk, and I hate the cold, so I left the jacket.

And Jock Cameron, Brian's mechanic, gave me a sprig of heather. If it had been a whole bush of heather, complete with roots growing in an earthen jar, I think I should have taken it, bulky or not. The blessing of Scotland, bestowed by a Scotsman, is not to be dismissed. Nor is the well-wishing of a ground mechanic to be taken lightly, for these men are the pilot's contact with reality.

It is too much that with all those pedestrian[10] centuries behind us we should, in a few decades, have learned to fly; it is too heady a thought, too proud a boast. Only the dirt on a mechanic's hands, the straining vise, the splintered bolt of steel underfoot on the hangar floor—only these and such anxiety as the face of a Jock Cameron can hold for a pilot and his plane before a flight, serve to remind us that, not unlike the heather, we too are earthbound. We fly, but we have not "conquered" the air. Nature presides in all her dignity, permitting us the study and the use of such of her forces as we may understand. It is when we presume to intimacy, having been granted only tolerance, that the harsh stick falls across our impudent knuckles and we rub the pain, staring upward, startled by our ignorance.

"Here is a sprig of heather," said Jock, and I took it and pinned it into a pocket of my flying jacket.

There were press cars parked outside the field at Abingdon, and several press planes and photographers, but the R.A.F. kept everyone away from the grounds except technicians and a few of my friends.

The Carberrys had sailed for New York a month ago to wait for me there. Tom was still

---

9. **R.A.F.:** the Royal Air Force, Great Britain's air force.
10. **pedestrian** (pi des′ trē ən): going or done on foot.

out of reach with no knowledge of my decision to leave, but that didn't matter so much, I thought. It didn't matter because Tom was unchanging—neither a fairweather pilot nor a fairweather friend. If for a month, or a year, or two years we sometimes had not seen each other, it still hadn't mattered. Nor did this. Tom would never say, "You should have let me know." He assumed that I had learned all that he had tried to teach me, and for my part I thought of him, even then, as the merest student must think of his mentor. I could sit in a cabin overcrowded with petrol tanks and set my course for North America, but the knowledge of my hands on the controls would be Tom's knowledge. His words of caution and words of guidance, spoken so long ago, so many times, on bright mornings over the veld[11] or over a forest, or with a far mountain visible at the tip of our wing, would be spoken again, if I asked.

So it didn't matter, I thought. It was silly to think about.

You can live a lifetime and, at the end of it, know more about other people than you know about yourself. You learn to watch other people, but you never watch yourself because you strive against loneliness. If you read a book, or shuffle a deck of cards, or care for a dog, you are avoiding yourself. The abhorrence[12] of loneliness is as natural as wanting to live at all. If it were otherwise, men would never have bothered to make an alphabet, nor to have fashioned words out of what were only animal sounds, nor to have crossed continents—each man to see what the other looked like.

Being alone in an airplane for even so short a time as a night and a day, irrevocably alone, with nothing to observe but your instruments and your own hands in semidarkness, nothing to contemplate but the size of your small courage, nothing to wonder about but the beliefs, the faces, and the hopes rooted in your mind—such an experience can be as startling as the first awareness of a stranger walking by your side at night. You are the stranger.

It is dark already, and I am over the south of Ireland. There are the lights of Cork, and the lights are wet; they are drenched in Irish rain, and I am above them and dry. I am above them, and the plane roars in a sobbing world, but it imparts no sadness to me. I feel the security of solitude, the exhilaration of escape. So long as I can see the lights and imagine the people walking under them, I feel selfishly triumphant, as if I have eluded care and left even the small sorrow of rain in other hands.

It is a little over an hour now since I left Abingdon. England, Wales, and the Irish Sea are behind me like so much time used up. On a long flight, distance and time are the same. But there had been a moment when Time stopped—and Distance, too. It was the moment I lifted the blue-and-silver Gull from the aerodrome,[13] the moment the photographers aimed their cameras, the moment I felt the craft refuse its burden and strain toward the earth in sullen rebellion, only to listen at last to the persuasion of stick and elevators,[14] the dogmatic argument of blueprints that said she *had* to fly because the figures proved it.

So she had flown, and once airborne, once she had yielded to the sophistry of a draftsman's board, she had said, "There: I have lifted the weight. Now, where are we bound?"—and the question had frightened me.

"We are bound for a place thirty-six hundred miles from here—two thousand miles of it unbroken ocean. Most of the way it will be night. We are flying west with the night."

---

11. **veld:** the open grassland of Africa.
12. **abhorrence** (ab hôr′ əns): hatred.
13. **aerodrome** (er′ ō drōm): a British term for airport.
14. **stick and elevators:** the control lever and moveable tail parts that cause an airplane to go up or down.

So there behind me is Cork; and ahead of me is Berehaven Lighthouse. It is the last light, standing on the last land. I watch it, counting the frequency of its flashes—so many to the minute. Then I pass it and fly out to sea.

The fear is gone now—not overcome nor reasoned away. It is gone because something else has taken its place; the confidence and the trust, the inherent belief in the security of land underfoot—now this faith is transferred to my plane, because the land has vanished and there is no other tangible thing to fix faith upon. Flight is but momentary escape from the eternal custody of earth.

Rain continues to fall, and outside the cabin it is totally dark. My altimeter says that the Atlantic is two thousand feet below me, my Sperry Artificial Horizon says that I am flying level. I judge my drift at three degrees more than my weather chart suggests, and fly accordingly. I am flying blind. A beam to follow would help. So would a radio—but then, so would clear weather. The voice of the man at the Air Ministry had not promised storm.

I feel the wind rising, and the rain falls hard. The smell of petrol in the cabin is so strong and the roar of the plane so loud that my senses are almost deadened. Gradually it becomes unthinkable that existence was ever otherwise.

At 10:00 P.M. I am flying along the Great Circle Course for Harbour Grace, Newfoundland, into a 40-mile headwind at a speed of 130 miles an hour. Because of the weather, I cannot be sure of how many more hours I have to fly, but I think it must be between sixteen and eighteen.

At ten-thirty I am still flying on the large cabin tank of petrol, hoping to use it up and put an end to the liquid swirl that has rocked the plane since my takeoff. The tank has no gauge, but written on its side is the assurance: "This tank is good for four hours."

There is nothing ambiguous about such a guarantee. I believe it, but at twenty-five minutes to eleven, my motor coughs and dies, and the Gull is powerless above the sea.

I realize that the heavy drone of the plane has been, until this moment, complete and comforting silence. It is the actual silence following the last splutter of the engine that stuns me. I can't feel any fear; I can't feel anything. I can only observe with a kind of stupid disinterest that my hands are violently active and know that, while they move, I am being hypnotized by the needle of my altimeter.

I suppose that the denial of natural impulse is what is meant by "keeping calm," but impulse has reason in it. If it is night and you are sitting in an airplane with a stalled motor and there are two thousand feet between you and the sea, nothing can be more reasonable than the impulse to pull back your stick in the hope of adding to that two thousand, if only by a little. The thought, the knowledge, the law that tells you that your hope lies not in this but in a contrary act—the act of directing your impotent craft toward the water—seems a terrifying abandonment not only of reason but of sanity. Your mind and your heart reject it. It is your hands—your stranger's hands—that follow with unfeeling precision the letter of the law.

I sit there and watch my hands push forward on the stick and feel the Gull respond and begin its dive to the sea. Of course it is a simple thing; surely the cabin tank has run dry too soon. I need only to turn another petcock . . .

But it is dark in the cabin. It is easy to see the luminous dial of the altimeter and to note that my height is now eleven hundred feet, but it is not easy to see a petcock that is somewhere near the floor of the plane. A hand gropes and reappears with an electric torch,[15] and fingers, moving with agonizing composure, find the petcock and turn it; and I wait.

At three hundred feet the motor is still dead, and I am conscious that the needle of

_____

15. **electric torch:** a British term for flashlight.

my altimeter seems to whirl like the spoke of a spindle winding up the remaining distance between the plane and the water. There is some lightning, but the quick flash only serves to emphasize the darkness. How high can waves reach—twenty feet, perhaps? Thirty?

It is impossible to avoid the thought that this is the end of my flight, but my reactions are not orthodox; the various incidents of my entire life do not run through my mind like a motion picture film gone mad. I only feel that all this has happened before—and it has. It has all happened a hundred times in my mind, in my sleep, so that now I am not really caught in terror; I recognize a familiar scene, a familiar story with its climax dulled by too much telling.

I do not know how close to the waves I am when the motor explodes to life again. But the sound is almost meaningless. I see my hand easing back on the stick, and I feel the Gull climb up into the storm, and I see the altimeter whirl like a spindle again, paying out the distance between myself and the sea.

The storm is strong. It is comforting. It is like a friend shaking me and saying, "Wake up! You were only dreaming."

But soon I am thinking. By simple calculation I find that my motor had been silent for perhaps an instant more than thirty seconds.

I ought to thank God—and I do, though indirectly. I thank Geoffrey De Havilland, who designed the indomitable Gipsy and who, after all, must have been designed by God in the first place.

A lighted ship—the daybreak—some steep cliffs standing in the sea. The meaning of these will never change for pilots. If one day an ocean can be flown within an hour, if men can build a plane that so masters time, the sight of land will be no less welcome to the steersman of that fantastic craft. He will have cheated laws that the cunning of science has taught him how to cheat, and he will feel his guilt and be eager for the sanctuary of the soil.

I saw the ship and the daybreak, and then I saw the cliffs of Newfoundland wound in ribbons of fog. I felt the elation I had so long imagined, and I felt the happy guilt of having circumvented the stern authority of the weather and the sea. But mine was a minor triumph; my swift Gull was not so swift as to have escaped unnoticed. The night and the storm had caught her, and we had flown blind for nineteen hours.

I was tired now, and cold. Ice began to film the glass of the cabin windows, and the fog played a magician's game with the land. But the land was there. I could not see it, but I had seen it. I could not afford to believe that it was any land but the land I wanted. I could not afford to believe that my navigation was at fault, because there was no time for doubt.

South to Cape Race, west to Sydney on Cape Breton Island. With my protractor, my map, and my compass, I set my new course, humming the ditty that Tom had taught me: "Variation West—magnetic best. Variation East—magnetic least." A silly rhyme, but it served to placate, for the moment, two warring poles—the magnetic and the true. I flew south and found the lighthouse of Cape Race protruding from the fog like a warning finger. I circled twice and went on over the Gulf of St. Lawrence.

After a while there would be New Brunswick, and then Maine—and then New York. I could anticipate. I could almost say, "Well, if you stay awake, you'll find it's only a matter of time now"—but there was no question of staying awake. I was tired and I had not moved an inch since that uncertain moment at Abingdon when the Gull had elected to rise with her load and fly, but I could not have closed my eyes. I could sit there in the cabin, walled in glass and petrol tanks, and be grateful for the sun and the light, and the fact that I could see the water under me. They were almost the last waves I had to pass. Four hundred miles of water, but then the land again—Cape Breton. I would stop at Sydney to refuel and go on. It was easy now. It would be like stopping at Kisumu and going on.

Success breeds confidence. But who has a right to confidence except the gods? I had a following wind, my last tank of petrol was more than three-quarters full, and the world was as bright to me as if it were a new world, never touched. If I had been wiser, I might have known that such moments are, like innocence, short-lived. My engine began to shudder before I saw the land. It died, it spluttered, it started again and limped along. It coughed and spat black exhaust toward the sea.

There are words for everything. There was a word for this—airlock, I thought. This had to be an airlock because there was petrol enough. I thought I might clear it by turning on and turning off all the empty tanks, and so I did that. The handles of the petcocks were sharp little pins of metal, and when I had opened and closed them a dozen times, I saw that my hands were bleeding and that the blood was dropping on my maps and on my clothes, but the effort wasn't any good. I coasted along on a sick and halting engine. The oil pressure and the oil temperature gauges were normal, the magnetos working, and yet I lost altitude slowly while the realization of failure seeped into my heart. If I made the land, I should have been the first to fly the North Atlantic from England, but from my point of view, from a pilot's point of view, a forced landing was failure because New York was my goal. If only I could land and then take off, I would make it still . . . if only, if only . . .

The engine cuts again, and then catches, and each time it spurts to life I climb as high as I can get, and then it splutters and stops and I glide once more toward the water, to rise again and descend again, like a hunting sea bird.

I find the land. Visibility is perfect now, and I see land forty or fifty miles ahead. If I am on my course, that will be Cape Breton. Minute after minute goes by. The minutes almost materialize; they pass before my eyes like links in a long, slow-moving chain, and each time the engine cuts, I see a broken link in the chain and catch my breath until it passes.

The land is under me. I snatch my map and stare at it to confirm my whereabouts. I am, even at my present crippled speed, only twelve minutes from Sydney Airport, where I can land for repairs and then go on.

The engine cuts once more and I begin to glide, but now I am not worried; she will start again, as she has done, and I will gain altitude and fly into Sydney.

But she doesn't start. This time she's dead as death; the Gull settles earthward, and it isn't any earth I know. It is black earth stuck with boulders, and I hang above it, on hope and on a motionless propeller. Only I cannot hang above it long. The earth hurries to meet me; I bank, turn, and sideslip to dodge the boulders; my wheels touch; and I feel them submerge. The nose of the plane is engulfed in mud, and I go forward striking my head on the glass of the cabin front, hearing it shatter, feeling blood pour over my face.

I stumble out of the plane and sink to my knees in muck and stand there foolishly staring, not at the lifeless land, but at my watch.

Twenty-one hours and twenty-five minutes.

Atlantic flight. Abingdon, England, to a nameless swamp—nonstop.

A Cape Breton Islander found me—a fisherman trudging over the bog saw the Gull with her tail in the air and her nose buried, and then he saw me floundering in the embracing soil of his native land. I had been wandering for an hour, and the black mud had got up to my waist, and the blood from the cut in my head had met the mud halfway.

From a distance, the fisherman directed me with his arms and with shouts toward the firm places in the bog, and for another hour I walked on them and came toward him like a

(upper left) AP/Wide World Photos, Inc., New York; (others) UPI/Bettmann, New York.

citizen of Hades blinded by the sun, but it wasn't the sun; I hadn't slept for forty hours.

He took me to his hut on the edge of the coast, and I found that built upon the rocks there was a little cubicle that housed an ancient telephone—put there in case of shipwrecks.

I telephoned to Sydney Airport to say that I was safe and to prevent a needless search being made. On the following morning I did step out of a plane at Floyd Bennett Field, and there was a crowd of people still waiting there to greet me, but the plane I stepped from was not the Gull, and for days while I was in New York I kept thinking about that and wishing over and over again that it had been the Gull, until the wish lost its significance, and time moved on, overcoming many things it met on the way.

# Thinking About the Selection

## A PERSONAL RESPONSE

*sharing impressions*

**1.** How do you feel about the way Markham's flight ends? Write about your feelings in your journal.

*constructing interpretations*

**2.** How does Markham seem to feel about the way her flight ends?

**3.** How well does Markham handle the difficult circumstances of her flight?
### Think about
- the darkness and the storm
- the solitude
- the procedure for changing gas tanks
- the airlock and crash landing

**4.** What seems to be Markham's attitude toward the danger of flying?
### Think about
- her reasons for making the flight
- her comments about other pilots, mechanics, and engineers
- her preparations for the flight, especially the items she takes

**5.** From what you've learned about pilots and flying in this selection, what kind of person do you think would make a good pilot?

## A CRITICAL RESPONSE

**6.** Identify the different sources of conflict Markham experiences before, during, and after her flight. Find examples from the selection to illustrate your analysis.

# Analyzing the Writer's Craft

## STYLE

What strikes you as unusual or interesting in the way this selection is written? Think about how this selection differs from the childhood memories in the last section.

**Building a Literary Vocabulary.** Style is the way in which a piece of literature is written. Many elements contribute to style, such as tone, word choice, sentence length, and imagery. Markham's matter-of-fact tone in this selection—possibly a result of her training as a pilot—is reinforced by her use of technical words, such as *petcock, altimeter,* and *airlock*. This tone, combined with her gritty imagery and philosophical comments, contributes to Markham's unique style of writing: "Only the dirt on a mechanic's hands, the straining vise, the splintered bolt of steel underfoot on the hangar floor . . . serve to remind us that, not unlike the heather, we too are earthbound." Markham's style fits her subject matter. She is not fondly recalling a childhood experience but straightforwardly confronting adult fear, danger, and disappointment.

**Application: Examining Style.** In a small group select three paragraphs from the selection that strike you as vivid or interesting. For each paragraph list a series of observations about its style, such as "interesting imagery" or "effective comparisons" or "philosophical statements." When you have finished, choose the one paragraph that seems to you most typical of Markham's style and share your observations with the class.

# Connecting Reading and Writing

**1.** Was Beryl Markham's flight across the Atlantic a brave or a foolish act? In an **editorial** take a position and use examples to defend it.

Option: Explain your position in an **expository essay** that might be published in an adventure magazine.

**2.** According to Beryl Markham, "You can live a lifetime and, at the end of it, know more about other people than you know about yourself. You learn to watch other people, but you never watch yourself because you strive against loneliness." Decide whether you agree or disagree with Markham's statement and express your opinion in a **letter** to her.

Option: Survey fifteen of your classmates and write a **report** of their opinions about Markham's statement.

**3.** Imagine that you are helping to advertise the film version of this selection. Create a **poster** advertising the movie.

Option: Write a **script** for a preview of the movie, highlighting episodes that would entice an audience.

# Obituary of a Bone Hunter

## LOREN EISELEY

A biography of Eiseley appears on page 639.

## *Approaching the Autobiographical Essay*

As an anthropologist, the late Loren Eiseley paid close attention to archaeology, the scientific study of ancient peoples. Although the search for human origins is difficult at times, a major discovery can lead to fame and fortune. For example, Dutch archaeologist Eugene Dubois won international acclaim by discovering the skull of Pithecanthropus, a primate believed to have existed between human beings and apes. In this selection, Eiseley discusses his early work as an archaeologist, or "bone hunter," and the reasons for his failure to make a big discovery—hence the title obituary, or death notice.

## *Building Vocabulary*

These essential words are footnoted within the selection.

**cavernous** (kav´ ər nəs), **potentialities** (pō ten´ shē al´ ə tēz): And there in a pile of sticks lay an egg, an impressive egg, glimmering palely in the **cavernous** gloom, full of **potentialities.** (page 269)

**desolation** (des´ əl lā´ shən): A feeling of vast loss and **desolation** sweeps over me then. (page 269)

**importuned** (im´ pôr tōōnd´): Should I have followed him? Found where he lived? **Importuned** his relatives? (page 271)

**inscrutable** (in skrōōt´ ə bəl): I think now that in some strange way that old man out of the autumn leaf-fall was the last test of the **inscrutable** gods. (page 271)

## *Connecting Writing and Reading*

How far would you go to achieve fame and fortune? Would you risk your life? endure pain? injure someone? do something illegal? kill an endangered animal? destroy your reputation? In your journal, list what you would and would not do to become rich and famous. While you read, notice what Eiseley will and will not do for fame and fortune.

# Obituary of a Bone Hunter

HE PAPERS AND the magazines reprint the stories endlessly these days—of Sybaris the sin city or, even further back, that skull at Tepexpan.[1] One's ears are filled with chatter about assorted magnetometers[2] and how they are used to pick up the traces of buried objects and no one has to guess at all. They unearth the city, or find the buried skull and bring it home. Then everyone concerned is famous overnight.

I'm the man who didn't find the skull. I'm the man who'd just been looking twenty years for something like it. This isn't sour grapes. It's their skull and welcome to it. What made me sigh was the geophysics[3] equipment. The greatest gambling game in the world—the greatest witsharpener—and now they do it with amplifiers and electronically mapped grids. An effete age, gentlemen, and the fun gone out of it.

There are really two kinds of bone hunters—the big bone hunters and the little bone hunters. The little bone hunters may hunt big bones, but they're little bone hunters just the same. They are the consistent losers in the most difficult game of chance that men can play: the search for human origins. Eugene Dubois, the discoverer of Pithecanthropus, hit the jackpot in a gamble with such stupendous odds that the most devoted numbers enthusiast would have had better sense than to stake his life on them.

I am a little bone hunter. I've played this game for a twenty-year losing streak. I used to think it all lay in the odds—that it was luck that made the difference between the big and little bone hunters. Now I'm not so sure any longer. Maybe it's something else.

Maybe sometimes an uncanny clairvoyance is involved, and if it comes you must act or the time goes by. Anyhow I've thought about it a lot in these later years. You think that way as you begin to get grayer and you see pretty plainly that the game is not going to end as you planned.

With me I think now that there were three chances: the cave of spiders, the matter of the owl's egg, and the old man out of the Golden Age. I muffed them all. And maybe the old man just came to show me I'd sat in the big game for the last time.

In that first incident of the spiders, I was playing a hunch, a long one, but a good one still. I wanted to find Neanderthal man,[4] or

---

1. **Sybaris . . . skull at Tepexpan** (sib′ ə ris, tā′ pās pän′): a reference to two important archaeological finds—the ancient Greek city of Sybaris and the skeletal remains of an early American Indian.
2. **magnetometers** (mag′ nə täm′ ət ərz): instruments for detecting concealed metallic objects. Magnetometers are often used in archaeological expeditions.

3. **geophysics** (je′ ō fiz′ iks): the science that deals with the physical forces that affect the earth.
4. **Neanderthal man** (nē an′ dər thôl): the name given a primitive people that lived in Europe, Africa, and parts of Asia during the early Stone Age. It is presumed, because of the lack of skeletal remains, that they did not live in the Americas.

any kind of ice-age man, in America. One or two important authorities were willing to admit he *might* have got in before the last ice sheet; that he *might* have crossed Bering Strait[5] with the mammoth. He might have, they said, but it wasn't likely. And if he had, it would be like looking for hummingbirds in the Bronx to find him.

Well, the odds were only a hundred to one against me, so I figured I'd look. That was how I landed in the cave of spiders. It was somewhere west out of Carlsbad, New Mexico, in the Guadalupe country. Dry. With sunlight that would blister cactus. We were cave hunting with a dynamiter and a young Harvard assistant. The dynamiter was to blow boulders away from fallen entrances so we could dig what lay underneath.

We found the cave up a side canyon, the entrance blocked with fallen boulders. Even to my youthful eyes it looked old, incredibly old. The waters and the frosts of centuries had eaten at the boulders and gnawed the cave roof. Down by the vanished stream bed a little gleam of worked flints caught our eye.

We stayed there for days, digging where we could and leaving the blasting till the last. We got the Basket Maker remains we had come to get—the earliest people that the scientists of that time would concede had lived in the Southwest. Was there anything more? We tamped a charge under one huge stone that blocked the wall of the cave and scrambled for the outside. A dull boom echoed down the canyon, and the smoke and dust slowly blew away.

Inside the cave mouth the shattered boulder revealed a crack behind it. An opening that ran off beyond our spotlights. The hackles on my neck crawled. This might be the road to—something earlier? There was room for only one man to worm his way in. The dynamiter was busy with his tools. "It's probably nothing," I said to the assistant. "I'll just take a quick look."

As I crawled down that passage on my belly, I thought once or twice about rattlesnakes and what it might be like to meet one on its own level where it could look you in the eye. But after all, I had met snakes before in this country, and besides I had the feeling that there was something worth getting to beyond.

I had it strong—too strong to turn back. I twisted on and suddenly dropped into a little chamber. My light shot across it. It was low and close, and this was the end of the cave. But there was earth on the floor beneath me, the soft earth that must be dug, that might hold something more ancient than the cave entrance. I couldn't stand up; the roof was too low. I would have to dig on hands and knees. I set the light beside me and started to probe the floor with a trench shovel. It was just then that the fear got me.

The light lay beside me shining on the ceiling—a dull, velvety-looking ceiling, different from the stone around. I don't know when I first sensed that something was wrong, that the ceiling was moving, that waves were passing over it like the wind in a stand of wheat. But suddenly I did; suddenly I dropped the shovel and thrust the light closer against the roof. Things began to detach themselves and drop wherever the light touched them. Things with legs. I could hear them plop on the soft earth around me.

---

5. **Bering Strait** (ber′ iŋ strāt): a narrow body of water between Siberia and Alaska. It is believed that early humans first arrived in North America by way of a land bridge that has since been coverd by this body of water.

I shut off the light. The plopping ceased. I sat on my knees in the darkness, listening. My mind was centered on just one thing—escape. I knew what that wavering velvet wall was. Millions upon millions of daddy longlegs —packed in until they hung in layers. Daddy longlegs, the most innocent and familiar of all the spider family. I wish I could say I had seen black widows there among them. It would help now, in telling this.

But I didn't. I didn't really see anything. If I turned on the light that hideous dropping and stirring would commence again. The light woke them. They disliked it.

If I could have stood up it would have been different. If they had not been overhead it would have been different. But they had me on my knees, and they were above and all around. Millions upon millions. How they got there I don't know. All I know is that up out of the instinctive well of my being flowed some ancient, primal fear of the crawler, the walker by night. One clambered over my hand. And above they dangled, dangled. . . . What if they all began to drop at once?

I did not light the light. I had seen enough. I buttoned my jacket close, and my sleeves. I plunged blindly back up the passage down which I had wriggled and which, luckily, was free of them.

Outside the crew looked at me. I was sweating, and a little queer. "Close air," I gasped; "a small hole, nothing there."

We went away then in our trucks. I suppose in due time the dust settled, and the fox found his way in. Probably all that horrible, fecund mass eventually crept, in its single individualities, back into the desert, where it frightened no one. What it was doing there, what evil unknown to mankind it was plotting, I do not know to this day. The evil and the horror, I think now, welled out of my own mind, but somehow that multitude of ancient life in a little, low, dark chamber touched it off. It did not

pass away until I could stand upright again. It was a fear out of the old, four-footed world that sleeps within us still.

Neanderthal man? He might have been there. But I was young, and that was only a first chance gone. Yes, there were things I might have done, but I didn't do them. You don't tell your chief dynamiter that you ran from a daddy longlegs. Not in that country. But do you see, it wasn't one daddy longlegs. That's what I can't seem to make clear to anyone. It wasn't just *one* daddy longlegs. It was millions of them. Enough to bury you. And have you ever thought of being buried under spiders? I thought not. You begin to get the idea?

I had a second chance, and again it was in a cave I found. This time I was alone, tramping up a canyon, watching for bones, and I just happened to glance upward in the one place where the cave could be seen. I studied it a long time—until I could feel the chill crawling down my back. This might be it; this might be the place. . . . This time I would know. This time there would be no spiders.

Through the glasses I could make out a fire-blackened roof, a projecting ledge above the cave mouth, and another one below. It was a small, strange hide-out, difficult to reach, but it commanded the valley on which the canyon opened. And there was the ancient, soot-impregnated cave roof. Ancient man had been there.

I made that climb. Don't ask me how I did it. Probably there had been an easier route ages ago. But I came up a naked chimney of rock down which I lost my knapsack and finally the geologist's pick that had helped me hack out a foothold in the softening rock.

When I flung myself over the ledge where the cave mouth opened, I was shaking from the exhausting muscle tension and fear. No one, I was sure, had come that way for a thousand years, and no one after me would come again. I did not know how I would get down. It was enough momentarily to be safe. In front of me, the cave mouth ran away darkly into the mountain.

I took the flashlight from my belt and loosened my sheath knife. I began to crawl downward and forward, wedging myself over sticks and fallen boulders. It was a clean cave and something was there, I was sure of it. Only, the walls were small and tight. . . .

They were tighter when the voice and the eyes came. I remember the eyes best. I caught them in my flashlight the same instant that I rammed my nose into the dirt and covered my head. They were big eyes and coming my way.

I had never thought at all. I just lay there dazed while a great roaring, buffeting thing beat its way out over my body and went away.

It went out into the silence beyond the cave mouth. A half minute afterward, I peered through my fingers and rolled weakly over. Enough is enough. But this time I wasn't going back empty-handed. Not I. Not on account of a mere bird. Not if I had thought it was a mountain lion, which it could just as well have been. No owl was going to stop me, not even if it was the biggest owl in the Rocky Mountains.

I twitched my ripped shirt into my pants and crawled on. It wasn't much farther. Over the heap of debris down which the great owl had charged at me, I found the last low chamber, the place I was seeking. And there in a pile of sticks lay an egg, an impressive egg, glimmering palely in the <u>cavernous</u>[6] gloom, full of <u>potentialities</u>,[7] and fraught, if I may say so, with destiny.

I affected at first to ignore it. I was after the buried treasures that lay beneath its nest in the cave floor. The egg was simply going to have to look after itself. Its parent had gone, and in a pretty rude fashion, too. I was no vandal, but I was going to be firm. If an owl's egg stood in the path of science—but suddenly the egg seemed very helpless, very much alone. I probed in the earth around the nest. The nest got in the way. This was a time for decision.

I know a primatologist[8] who will lift a rifle and shoot a baby monkey out of its mother's arms for the sake of science. He is a good man, too, and goes home nights to his wife. I tried to focus on this thought as I faced the egg.

I knew it was a rare egg. The race of its great and lonely mother was growing scant in these mountains and would soon be gone. Under it might lie a treasure that would make me famed in the capitals of science, but suppose there was nothing under the nest after all and I destroyed it? Suppose. . . .

Here in this high, sterile silence with the wind crying over frightful precipices, myself and that egg were the only living things. That seemed to me to mean something. At last and quietly I backed out of the cave and slipped down into the chasm out of which I had come. By luck I did not fall.

Sometimes in these later years I think perhaps the skull was there, the skull that could have made me famous. It is not so bad, however, when I think that the egg became an owl. I had had charge of it in the universe's sight for a single hour, and I had done well by life.

It is not the loss of the skull that torments me sometimes on winter evenings. Suppose the big, unutterably frightened bird never came back to its egg? A feeling of vast loss and <u>desolation</u>[9] sweeps over me then. I begin to perceive what it is to doubt.

It was years later that I met the old man. He was waiting in my office when I came in. It

---

6. **cavernous** (kav′ ər nəs): like a large cave.
7. **potentialities** (pō ten′ shē al′ ə tēz): things that can be but are not yet; possibilities.
8. **primatologist** (prī′ mə täl′ ə jist): a scientist who studies primates, the highest order of mammals.
9. **desolation** (des′ ə la′ shən): the state of being lonely, miserable, and comfortless.

was obvious from the timid glances of my secretary that he had been passed from hand to hand and that he had outwitted everybody. Someone in the background made a twisting motion at his forehead.

The old man sat, a colossal ruin, in the reception chair. The squirrel-like twitterings of the office people did not disturb him.

As I came forward he fished in a ragged wallet and produced a clipping. "You made this speech?" he asked.

"Why, yes," I said.

"You said men came here late? A few thousand years ago?"

"Yes, you see—"

"Young man," he interrupted, "you are frightfully wrong."

I was aware that his eyes were contracted to pin points and seemed in some danger of protruding on stalks.

"You have ignored," he rumbled, "the matter of the Miocene period—the Golden Age. A great civilization existed then, far more splendid than this—degenerate time." He struck the floor fiercely with his cane.

"But," I protested, "that period is twenty million years ago. Man wasn't even in existence. Geology shows—"

"Nothing!" said the massive relic. "Geology has nothing to do with it. Sit down. I know all about the Golden Age. I will prove to you that you are wrong."

I collapsed doubtfully into a chair. He told me that he was from some little town in Missouri, but I never believed it for a moment. He smelled bad, and it was obvious that if he brought news of the Golden Age, as he claimed, he had come by devious and dreadful ways from that far era.

"I have here," he said, thrusting his head forward and breathing heavily into my face, "a human jaw. I will unwrap it a little and you can see. It is from a cave I found."

"It is embedded in stalactite[10] drippings," I murmured, hypnotized against my will. "That might represent considerable age. Where did you find it?"

He raised a protesting hand. "Later, son, later. You admit then—?"

I strained forward. "Those teeth," I said, "they are large—they look primitive." The feeling I had had at the mouth of the owl's cave came to me again overpoweringly. "Let me see a little more of the jaw. If the mental eminence should be lacking, you may have something important. Just let me handle it a moment."

With the scuttling alacrity of a crab, the old man drew back and popped the papers over his find. "You admit, then, that it is important? That it proves the Golden Age was real?"

Baffled, I looked at him. He eyed me with an equal wariness.

"Where did you find it?" I asked. "In this light it seemed—it might be—a fossil man. We have been looking a long time. If you would only let me see—"

"I found it in a cave in Missouri," he droned in a rote fashion. "You can never find the cave alone. If you will make a statement to the papers that the Golden Age is true, I will go with you. You have seen the evidence."

Once more I started to protest. "But this has nothing to do with the Golden Age. You may have a rare human fossil there. You are denying science—"

"Science," said the old man with frightening dignity, "is illusion." He arose. "I will not come back. You must make a choice."

For one long moment we looked at each other across the fantastic barriers of our individual minds. Then, on his heavy oakwood cane, he hobbled to the door and was gone. I watched through the window as he crossed the

---

10. **stalactite** (stə lək′ tīt): an icicle-shaped formation hanging from the roof of a cave.

street in a patch of autumn sunlight as phantasmal and unreal as he. Leaves fell raggedly around him until, a tatter among tatters, he passed from sight.

I rubbed a hand over my eyes, and it seemed the secretary looked at me strangely. How was it that I had failed this time? By unbelief? But the man was mad. I could not possibly have made such a statement as he wanted.

Was it pride that cost me that strange jawbone? Was it academic dignity? Should I have followed him? Found where he lived? Importuned[11] his relatives? Stolen, if necessary, that remarkable fragment?

Of course I should! I know that now. Of course I should.

Thirty years have passed since the old man came to see me. I have crawled in many caverns, stooped with infinite aching patience over the bones of many men. I have made no great discoveries.

I think now that in some strange way that old man out of the autumn leaf-fall was the last test of the inscrutable[12] gods. There will be no further chances. The egg and the spiders and the madman—in them is the obituary of a life dedicated to the folly of doubt, the life of a small bone hunter.

---

11. **importuned** (im′ pôr tōōnd′): troubled with requests or demands; urged repeatedly.
12. **inscrutable** (in skrōōt′ ə bəl): that cannot be easily understood.

# Thinking About the Autobiographical Essay

## A PERSONAL RESPONSE

*sharing impressions*

**1.** How did you react to the three experiences described by Eiseley? Jot down some notes in your journal.

*constructing interpretations*

**2.** Do you agree that Eiseley failed to achieve fame and fortune as a bone hunter because he was too "dedicated to the folly of doubt"? Why or why not?

**3.** What would you have done in each of the three situations Eiseley describes?

**4.** How would you describe Eiseley's values?
> ***Think about***
> • the reasons he gives for not pursuing fame and fortune at all costs
> • his purpose in writing this selection

## A CREATIVE RESPONSE

**5.** If Eiseley had made a different choice in any one of the three situations he describes and still not discovered anything, how might this selection be different?

**6.** Unlike the tone of most scientific essays, Eiseley's tone is not always scientific or objective. Go back through the essay and find examples where Eiseley's tone varies from what you would expect to find in a science book.

*Think about*
- places where Eiseley says something that you may doubt he really means
- places where Eiseley's emotions surface

**7.** Compare what Beryl Markham and Loren Eiseley each learn about themselves from their experiences. Use specific details from the selections to make your comparisons.

**8.** In the twentieth century, the illegal excavation and sale of cultural artifacts has become an international problem. How do you think Eiseley would view this problem?

 *nalyzing the Writer's Craft*

## THEME

Do you think Loren Eiseley considers himself a failure because he did not achieve fame and fortune? How do you know how he feels about himself?

**Building a Literary Vocabulary.** Theme is the central idea or message in a work of literature. It is a writer's perception about life or humanity that is shared with the reader. Most selections include several themes, one of which usually predominates.

In the second episode of "Obituary of a Bone Hunter," Eiseley decides not to dig rather than disturb the egg of a rare and endangered owl species and so loses a possible opportunity for a great discovery.

Eiseley writes of the owl egg episode: "Sometimes in these later years I think perhaps the skull was there, the skull that could have made me famous. It is not so bad, however, when I think that the egg became an owl. I had had charge of it in the universe's sight for a single hour, and I had

done well by life." Eiseley does not regret his choice to preserve the owl egg and even seems proud that he did not follow in the footsteps of the primatologist who would "shoot a baby monkey out of its mother's arms for the sake of science."

The episode of the owl's egg illustrates the theme that the preservation of life is more important than possibile scientific advancement.

**Application: Analyzing Theme.** Working in a small group, evaluate how the following themes might be illustrated by the episodes of the cave of spiders and the old man with the skull:

- Fame and fortune, rather than personal integrity, are the standards by which archaeologists are judged successful.
- An important part of life is learning to accept choices you have made, even when some of those choices have resulted in failure.

# Connecting Reading and Writing

**1.** Imagine that you experienced what Eiseley describes in the first two episodes. Describe the situations in **field notes** to be read by other archaeologists.

Option: Write an **outline** for a chapter in your autobiography telling how you handled one of the two situations.

**2.** Decide whether Eiseley's decision not to make the absurd public statement demanded by the old man was foolish or admirable. Argue your opinion in a **persuasive essay** written for an archaeological magazine.

Option: Interview ten of your classmates and present a **report** of their opinions about Eiseley's decision.

**3.** Choose a hero or heroine from an adventure film and speculate about how that person would have responded to any one of the three situations Eiseley describes. Present your ideas as a **script** for a scene from a movie starring that hero or heroine.

Option: Write a **scene** from a story starring that movie hero or heroine.

**4.** Use the *Readers' Guide to Periodical Literature* to identify places in the world where there is intense archaeological excavation for human origins or cultural artifacts. Create a **map** showing the locations of these sites.

Option: Write an **essay** about the excavation process underway at one of the archaeological sites you learned of.

# _from_ Mississippi Solo

## EDDY HARRIS

A biography of Harris appears on page 640.

### _Approaching the Selection_

> _Mississippi Solo_ relates the experiences of writer Eddy Harris as he canoes down the Mississippi River from Lake Itasca, Minnesota, to New Orleans. In the following excerpt, Harris approaches the antebellum town of Natchez, Mississippi, on the last stretch of his journey.

TOO MANY MARVELOUS days in a row and you begin to get used to it, to think that's the way it's supposed to be. Too many good days, too many bad days—you need some break in the monotony of one to appreciate the other. If you only get sunshine, someone said, you end up in a desert.

I guess I'd had enough hard days to last me for a while, enough scary times to be able to appreciate the peaceful, easy, glorious days. On the way to Natchez, I had another one, and I took full advantage of it to do absolutely nothing. No singing, no thinking, no talking to myself. Just feeling. Watching the river, noticing the changes in color, seeing the way it rises and falls depending on the wind and on what lies on the river bed. Each change had something to say, and I listened to the river. The river was talking to me, changing colors from puce to brown to thick, murky green. Saying nothing. The idle chatter you get when you walk with your favorite niece or nephew going no place in particular with nothing special on your minds and the little kid just jabbers away because it's comfortable and he feels like it. The river was like that to me. A comfortable buddy sharing a lazy day.

Nothing else mattered then. Going someplace or not. Arriving in New Orleans or shooting past and landing in Brazil. I didn't care about anything. The river kept me company and kept me satisfied. Nothing else mattered.

Then the river whispered, "Get ready. Get ready."

The day turned gray and strange. Clouds rolled overhead in wild swirls like batter in a bowl. I could see the rainstorm forming off in the distance but swirling rapidly toward me like a dark gray avalanche. I felt the river dip down and up—a shallow dale in the water. I passed from the cool moisture surrounding me and into a pocket of thin air hot and dry. It was as though a gap had opened in the clouds and the sun streamed through to boil the water and heat up this isolated patch of river a scant thirty yards long. My first thought was to shed a shirt and stay cool, but when I passed through the far curtain of the insulated air, I knew I had better do just the opposite. I drifted and donned my yellow rain suit and hood. The sky above grew serious and advanced in my direction with the speed of a hurricane. Looking for a place to land, I scanned the shore. There was no shore. Only trees. Because of the heavy rains and the high water, the shore had disappeared, and the new shoreline of solid earth had been pushed back through the trees and beyond the woods. How far beyond, I couldn't tell. I looked across to the other side of the river half a mile away. No way could I have made it over there. Halfway across and the wind would have kicked up and trapped me in the middle.

The leading edge of the storm came, and the first sprinkles passed over like army scouts. The wooded area lasted only another hundred yards or so, and I thought I could easily get there before the rains arrived. I could then turn left and find ground to pull out and wait out the storm. But the voice of the river came out and spoke to me teasingly but with a chill of seriousness down my spine. I could have ignored it, but as if reading my thoughts and not wanting me to fight it, the river grabbed the end of the canoe and turned me toward the trees. I thought I was looking for land. I wasn't. I was looking for shelter.

The urge to get into the trees came on me quite suddenly and really without thought or effort on my part. Almost an instinct.

No sooner had I ducked into the trees than the sky split open with a loud crash and a splintery crackle of lightning. I was not going to make it through the trees. The wind came in at hurricane strength. The tips of the trees bent way over and aimed toward the ground, like fishing rods hooked on a big one. Water flooded like the tide rushing upstream. The trees swooshed loudly as the leaves and branches brushed hard together. Branches fell. Rains came and poured down bucketfuls.

The trees were tall and no more than three feet around. I maneuvered the canoe as best I could in the wind and rushing water, turned it to face upstream, and kept my back to the rain, which slanted in at a sharp angle. I reached out for the sturdiest tree I could get my arms around and I held on.

Water everywhere. The river sloshed over the side and into the canoe. I tried to keep the stern pointed right into the flow so the canoe could ride the waves, but it didn't work. The canoe was twisted about, and water poured over the side. The rain was heavier than any I had ever been in or seen before. It really was more like a tropical storm. The heavy winds, the amount of water, the warmth of the air, and the cold rain. Only my neck was exposed to the rain. When the rain hit my neck, it ran under the rain suit and very cold down my back.

The wind shifted as the storm came directly overhead. Water streamed straight down. I was drenched, and the canoe was filling up quickly. Anything in the canoe that could float was floating. If the rain continued for long or if the wind kept up strong and the rain kept spilling into the canoe, I would sink. But I was not worried, hardly more than concerned. In fact I enjoyed the feeling of the water all around me and on me, enveloping me like a cocoon, and despite the drama I felt no real threat. I was more amazed than anything, trying to analyze the voice I had heard or whatever instinct or intuition[1] it was that urged me to park in these trees. It had been something so very definite that I could feel it and yet so ethereal[2] that I could not put my finger on it. So I stopped trying and just sat there patiently waiting and hugging my tree. I was one with this river, and nothing could happen to me.

---

1. **intuition** (in' tōō ish' ən): the direct knowing or learning of something without the conscious use of reasoning.
2. **ethereal** (ē thir' ē əl): very light; airy; like the upper regions of space.

The storm slid forward, and the rain slanted in on my face. Then it moved on farther up the river to drench someone else. It was gone as suddenly as it had arisen. Only the trailing edge was left, a light rain that lasted almost until I reached Natchez.

The sky remained gray but lightened, and I paddled from my rain forest and downriver to Natchez. My little boat lumbered through the water. The canoe carried six inches of water and was heavy, and I could find no speed. But I didn't need any. I was relaxed and floating in the mist as thick as the mysteries of the river. It was evening when I reached Natchez.

Natchez, Mississippi, sits high above the river. Green trees and grassy hills rise up from the river to the city. Rising out of the hills and overhanging the river, huge white antebellum mansions guard the approach to the city like statues lining the wide corridor of some great cathedral. The homes stand beautiful and proud, reminders of gentler and nobler times.

The *Delta Queen,* another reminder, was moored at the foot of the old part of town. I went right up to get a closer look. A massive paddle wheeler that takes her voyagers back in time as she carries them up and down the river, stopping for brief glimpses of history at Natchez and St. Francisville and ancient plantations along the route. The captain told me she sails as far up as St. Paul and down to New Orleans, with trips up the Ohio River to Cincinnati. They were on their way shortly to New Orleans, and I asked for a ride.

"You don't want a ride," the captain said. "This is something you want to do all by yourself. You'll feel better if you do, and you'd hate yourself if you didn't."

No, I wouldn't. If he had said OK, I would have hopped quickly on board and ridden down with him. I had already found it, whatever this trip was for; I had done it, even if I didn't understand it yet and probably wouldn't until years from now anyway.

A few great blasts from the steam whistle and she pushed away from shore and set out, lights on the big calliope playing merry music like a circus. It was 1836 all over again. The *Queen* paddled upriver, turned around, and slowly splashed south, the staterooms all lit up and gay. You couldn't see the boat at all in the darkness, only the lights. They seemed to float along with no structure holding them together. Too soon the lights were gone round the bend and the calliope faded into the night and the crowd that had gathered at the riverfront to watch as of old began to disperse.

I bailed out my canoe using a milk carton. It took a while. I had a few passing conversations and then walked up the hill. It was drizzling again, and I must have looked lost.

This was the old town. A little park stretched off to the south—more a promenade than a park—and there were a few quaint shops for the tourists and a bar and a couple of nice-looking restaurants. Three beautiful women were getting out of a car parked along the side of the road when I passed. The three prettiest women in Mississippi. They were going to eat in one of the cute little restaurants. They were all dressed up and hurried because of the rain. They wouldn't want to get their hair and clothes messed up. I asked them quickly if they knew the time, and two of the three ignored me totally and kept walking. I felt like the invisible man. But the third woman had heard me. She looked toward her two friends. She wore a quizzical expression, and it was plain that she was looking for the translation. She must have thought I was speaking a foreign language.

"I won't bite you," I said. "I just want the time."

Then she turned, and the three of them walked purposefully on, and I stood stunned for two seconds; I said nothing else. I chuckled to myself and silently wished for them to slip and fall in the mud. When they didn't, when they had crossed the little gravel parking lot and climbed up the three wooden steps and disappeared into the warmth and dryness of the cozy little eatery, leaving me standing out in the drizzle, I hoped they would order seafood, and I hoped that each one would get a bad oyster or a tainted piece of catfish.

Two steps farther on, I passed a man sitting all alone in his pickup truck. He was killing time, watching the river, and he turned to watch me walk by. When our eyes met, I tapped my wrist and gave the international symbol for "What time is it?" I don't know why I wanted to know; I had no place I had to be and nothing I had to do apart from finding a place to pitch my tent, which I couldn't do until all the shops had closed and everyone had gone home.

Bill invited me to warm up in his truck.

"Do you need to go to the store or anything?" He had a great Southern accent, heavy but cultured and easily understandable.

"Well, I guess I could use some milk and a few things."

He took me on a little tour of Natchez. He was proud of this little place, I could see, and he was happy to drive me around. He even tried to arrange a place for me to sleep for the night and later pointed out the Salvation Army shelter where I could at least be dry all night long. I half expected him to invite me home, put me up in the attic, and then keep me over for Thanksgiving dinner tomorrow night, but that was asking too much. He already had relatives visiting for the holiday.

I told him I'd probably just pitch camp in the little park.

"I wouldn't build a fire or anything if I were you. The police will come down there and make you move. They might even want to lock you up for the night."

Then he fished in his wallet and pulled out a business card.

"If they do come along and throw you in jail, give me a call. You can sleep there for the night, and I can get you out in the morning. I'm the city attorney."

Actually, he was an attorney with a local practice, and he was the acting city attorney whenever the regular city attorney was away, like now.

I had the feeling he wasn't too thrilled to be going home to his wife and the visiting in-laws, that he would rather have stayed down on the levee watching the river and the *Queen* or talking to me or driving me around showing me the beautiful homes of Natchez. Hope Farm. Stanton Hall. Longwood. D'Evereux. Ellicott Hill. Propinquity. Montaigne. Mount Repose. Homes as beautiful and stately and elegant as the names. But Bill had to get on home.

He drove away, and I hung around killing time until late in the evening. When everything had closed and everyone had gone home—about nine o'clock, I'd guess—I pulled my canoe a few yards downriver and put up the tent. It was in a little gully at the edge of the water with the blunt face of a muddy hill behind me. Not one of my more picturesque campsites. A rickety rowboat full of junk was tied up not far away, and later on the owner of it staggered back drunk from town, climbed into the boat, and slept there. I met him in the morning and was shocked to find out who he was—shocked and pleased.

Eleven hundred miles and I don't know how many days ago, Wally at Piasa Harbor had told me about a religious zealot[3] rowing for Jesus down the river in a rickety rowboat of homemade construction. As James White talked the following morning, pieces fell into place and it hit me.

"Hey!" I shouted out of the blue. "I know you."

---

3. **zealot** (zel' ət): person who shows passion and devotion for something, especially to an excessive degree.

"You do?"

"I don't know you, but I heard about you. Back near Alton they were talking about this nut who had taken his bicycle apart and built a contraption for pedaling a boat down the river."

"That's me all right."

How strange to have caught up with him after all this time! I hadn't thought of him once since I left Wally.

We had breakfast together in a fancy hotel restaurant, and they gave us a few funny looks but served us without complaint. Smiles and good-humored politeness instead.

We took our good, sweet time and sat there like millionaires chatting away the morning, talking about the two journeys. Jim had left Idaho on a bicycle pulling a little trailer that held his belongings. He had received the call directly, he said, from Jesus, who had told him to go across the country on this bicycle and spread the good word, get a feeling for this nation, and set the place right. And, I presumed, to report back.

As a man who himself had heard the voice of God, I could not brush his calling aside as fanaticism or lunacy, but I looked askance just the same. The whispers I'd heard never told me directly what to do. Not in simple English, anyway.

When Jim got to Iowa and the river, he was instructed to change his course, get a boat, and go down the river until further notice. He took to rowing down the river until his oars broke apart. He then dismantled the bicycle and set about sawing planks and hammering and putting together until finally he had constructed a paddle wheeler out of his rowboat. Now he could sit on his seat and pedal the crankset of the bicycle, and the wooden planks fashioned into paddle wheels on each side of the boat would propel him.

It was slow but a good idea, except that he got stuck in the rock dam just below Alton,

and Okie, the salvage operator I had met, had to tow him out. Then Jim had to rebuild and repair the damage.

Now, at Natchez, he actually prayed for the boat to fall apart. That would be a sign that his voyage was finished.

"I have to keep going until the voyage is done. Maybe in New Orleans, or maybe I'll have to keep going right on through to the Gulf of Mexico and South America."

"And then what?"

"I'll do whatever He tells me to do. But I'm sure sick of this river."

For a man spreading the good word, he hadn't met with much success, finding the land full of skeptics[4] and godless people not willing to listen. So it would be disaster for them all, he said. Disaster and ruin will strike all those who refused him or who mocked him or who would not turn to God, and I made it a point not to say the wrong thing.

Jim had the look of a monk. Tall and lean, disheveled gray hair and matching stubble on his chin, unconcerned about his appearance, a youthful face that lied about his age, and wild eyes. . . .

"Maybe we could travel together," he offered. "Share Thanksgiving dinner, camp together, keep each other company. It gets lonely, you know."

His boat had everything in the world in it except a television. I don't know how he managed to fit inside and sleep. But he pushed junk aside and squeezed inside and showed me how he slid the plywood platform around that made his bed.

"You could ride inside with me," he said. "We could tie your canoe off and tow it and you could rest."

I declined but did accept the offer for Thanksgiving dinner.

---

4. **skeptics** (skep′ tiks): those who doubt religious teachings.

"You go on ahead. I need to fill up my water bag and take down my tent. I'll catch up with you."

Before he left he pulled a pair of pliers from his junk and repaired the zippers on my tent flaps. Now I wouldn't have to worry about mosquitoes sneaking into the tent at night.

"You learn to fix just about everything out here," he said.

He took off, pedaling down the river, and I watched him go. He looked very silly. Watching him, I felt the arrogance that towboat pilots feel, the contempt for lesser boats, and still the <u>comradery</u>[5] of sharers of the river—rivermen all of us.

I caught up with him after an hour or so, and we built a fire on a sandbar. We boiled rice and heated a big can of beef stew, and Jim prayed over it, and we ate our Thanksgiving meal. It wasn't the finest holiday meal ever, but maybe this time I had so much to be thankful for and was really aware of it for once that this meal of all meals felt most like a Thanksgiving dinner.

---

5. **comradery** (käm' rad rē): loyalty and warm, friendly feeling among companions, associates, fellow workers, etc.

# Meditations:
# Thoughts and Opinions

OPINIONS ARE UNAVOIDABLE. You hear them everywhere—on the bus, at the mall, on radio and television, in the classroom, in the lunchroom. No matter where you go, you are bombarded with opinions.

The selections that follow are all written expressions of opinion. The writers have chosen to share their thoughts and convictions with a wide audience: the reading public. They have points to make about what they think is funny, what they think is important, or what they think is unfair.

You may not agree with everything these writers have to say, but try to understand how they arrived at their opinions. What reasons do the writers give? Do they support their opinions with examples? Have their beliefs been influenced by their past experiences? Ask yourself these questions as you read. The answers may give you something new to think about.

# *Literary Vocabulary*

## INTRODUCED IN THIS SECTION

**Essay.** An essay is a brief nonfiction work that offers an opinion on a subject. The purpose of an essay may be to express ideas and feelings, to analyze, to inform, to entertain, or to persuade. The purpose of James Thurber's autobiographical essay "The Night the Bed Fell" is to entertain. In "Obituary of a Bone Hunter" Loren Eiseley's dual purpose is to analyze why he did not gain fame and fortune and to express his ideas and feelings about the field of archaeology. Essays can be formal or informal. While the formal essay tends to deal objectively with ideas and have a dignified tone, the informal essay is more personal and may have a humorous or conversational tone.

**Figurative Language.** Figurative language is language that communicates ideas beyond the literal meanings of the words. The words in a figurative expression are not literally true; rather, they create impressions in the reader's mind. Two common forms of figurative language are metaphor and extended metaphor. A **metaphor** is a figure of speech that makes a comparison between two things that have something in common. While a simile contains the word *like* or *as,* a metaphor either makes the comparison directly or implies it. In "Obituary of a Bone Hunter" Eiseley describes the wall in the cave of spiders as "that wavering velvet wall." The wall is literally made of rock, but the adjectives wavering and velvet create a metaphor to capture the look and feel of a soft, thick layer of spiders moving on the cave wall. In an **extended metaphor,** two things are compared in various ways. An extended metaphor that compares life to a journey might be expressed in this way: Different ages in a person's life are signposts along life's journey, marked by high points such as graduation, marriage, and childbirth and by obstacles such as illness or divorce.

# How to Tell a Story

## MARK TWAIN

A biography of Twain appears on page 646.

## *Approaching the Essay*

Most people like to laugh—but often what makes them laugh changes over the years. In the last century, Samuel Langhorne Clemens, better known by his pen name, Mark Twain, was considered one of America's great humorists. In addition to writing, he traveled throughout the country entertaining audiences with his clever, well-told stories. In this essay, Twain evaluates the humor of his day by contrasting two ways to tell a joke.

## *Building Vocabulary*

These essential words are footnoted within the selection.

**pathetic** (pə thet´ ik): It is a **pathetic** thing to see. (page 283)

**disjointed** (dis joint´ id): The rambling and **disjointed** humorous story finishes with a nub. (page 283)

**pretense** (prē tens´): The teller will divert attention from that nub . . . with the **pretense** that he does not know it is a nub. (page 283)

**anecdote** (an´ ik dōt´): Let me set down an instance of the comic method, using an **anecdote**. (page 283)

## *Connecting Writing and Reading*

In your journal, record your favorite joke or describe a funny thing that happened to you or a friend. Then briefly explain what makes the joke or the event funny. As you read, evaluate what Twain says makes a story funny.

*I* DO NOT claim that I can tell a story as it ought to be told. I only claim to know how a story ought to be told, for I have been almost daily in the company of the most expert storytellers for many years.

There are several kinds of stories but only one difficult kind—the humorous. I will talk mainly about that one. The humorous story is American; the comic story is English; the witty story is French. The humorous story depends for its effect upon the *manner* of the telling; the comic story and the witty story upon the *matter*.

The humorous story may be spun out to great length and may wander around as much as it pleases and arrive nowhere in particular; but the comic and witty stories must be brief and end with a point. The humorous story bubbles gently along; the others burst.

The humorous story is strictly a work of art—high and delicate art—and only an artist can tell it; but no art is necessary in telling the comic and the witty story; anybody can do it. The art of telling a humorous story—understand, I mean by word of mouth, not print—was created in America and has remained at home.

The humorous story is told gravely; the teller does his best to conceal the fact that he even dimly suspects that there is anything funny about it; but the teller of the comic story tells you beforehand that it is one of the funniest things he has ever heard, then tells it with eager delight and is the first person to laugh when he gets through. And sometimes, if he has had good success, he is so glad and happy that he will repeat the "nub" of it and glance around from face to face, collecting applause, and then repeat it again. It is a pathetic[1] thing to see.

Very often, of course, the rambling and disjointed[2] humorous story finishes with a nub, point, snapper, or whatever you like to call it.

Then the listener must be alert, for in many cases the teller will divert attention from that nub by dropping it in a carefully casual and indifferent way, with the pretense[3] that he does not know it is a nub.

Artemus Ward used that trick a good deal; then, when the belated audience presently caught the joke, he would look up with innocent surprise, as if wondering what they had found to laugh at. Dan Setchell used it before him; Nye and Riley[4] and others use it today.

But the teller of the comic story does not slur the nub; he shouts it at you—every time. And when he prints it, in England, France, Germany, and Italy, he italicizes it, puts some whooping exclamation points after it, and sometimes explains it in a parenthesis. All of which is very depressing and makes one want to renounce joking and lead a better life.

Let me set down an instance of the comic method, using an anecdote[5] which has been popular all over the world for twelve or fifteen hundred years. The teller tells it in this way:

### THE WOUNDED SOLDIER

In the course of a certain battle, a soldier whose leg had been shot off appealed to another soldier who was hurrying by to carry him to the rear, informing him at the same time of the loss which he had sustained; whereupon the generous son of Mars,[6] shouldering the unfortunate, proceeded to carry out his desire. The bullets and cannonballs were flying in all directions, and presently one of the latter took the wounded man's head off—without, however, his deliverer being

---

1. **pathetic** (pə thet′ ik): pitiful; arousing sympathy.
2. **disjointed** (dis jōint′ id): disconnected; not clear or orderly.
3. **pretense** (prē tens′): a claim; often a false claim.
4. **Artemus Ward . . . Dan Setchell . . . Nye and Riley:** noted humorists in Twain's day.
5. **anecdote** (an′ ik dōt′): a short, entertaining story.
6. **Mars** (märz): the Roman god of war.

aware of it. In no long time he was hailed by an officer, who said:

"Where are you going with that carcass?"

"To the rear, sir—he's lost his leg!"

"His leg, forsooth?" responded the astonished officer. "You mean his head, you booby."

Whereupon the soldier dispossessed himself of his burden and stood looking down upon it in great perplexity. At length he said:

"It is true, sir, just as you have said." Then after a pause he added, "*But he* TOLD *me* IT WAS HIS LEG!!!!!"

Here the narrator bursts into explosion after explosion of thunderous horselaughter, repeating that nub from time to time through his gaspings and shriekings and suffocatings.

It takes only a minute and a half to tell that in its comic-story form and isn't worth the telling, after all. Put into the humorous-story form it takes ten minutes and is about the funniest thing I have ever listened to—as James Whitcomb Riley tells it.

He tells it in the character of a dull-witted old farmer who has just heard it for the first time, thinks it is unspeakably funny, and is trying to repeat it to a neighbor. But he can't remember it; so he gets all mixed up and wanders helplessly round and round, putting in tedious details that don't belong in the tale and only retard it; taking them out conscientiously and putting in others that are just as useless; making minor mistakes now and then and stopping to correct them and explain how he came to make them; remembering things which he forgot to put in in their proper place and going back to put them in there; stopping his narrative a good while in order to try to recall the name of the soldier that was hurt, and finally remembering that the soldier's name was not mentioned, and remarking placidly that the name is of no real importance, anyway—better, of course, if one knew it, but not essential, after all—and so on and so on and so on.

The teller is innocent and happy and pleased with himself and has to stop every little while to hold himself in and keep from laughing outright; and does hold in, but his body quakes in a jellylike way with interior chuckles; and at the end of the ten minutes the audience have laughed until they are exhausted, and the tears are running down their faces.

The simplicity and innocence and sincerity and unconsciousness of the old farmer are perfectly simulated, and the result is a performance which is thoroughly charming and delicious. This is art—and fine and beautiful, and only a master can compass it; but a machine could tell the other story.

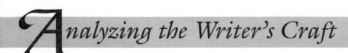
# Thinking About the Essay

## A PERSONAL RESPONSE

*sharing impressions*

**1.** Do you share Twain's preference for the humorous way of telling a story? In your journal, briefly note which kind of story you think is funnier.

*constructing interpretations*

**2.** Explain the "art" involved in what Twain calls a humorous story.

**Think about**
- how Twain differentiates between a humorous story and a comic story
- why Twain thinks a machine could tell a comic story

**3.** How well does Twain's example, "The Wounded Soldier," illustrate his point about what makes a story funny?

**4.** How do you think Twain would judge your favorite joke or TV comedy show?

## A CRITICAL RESPONSE

**5.** To show how humor has changed over the years, compare a contemporary comedian's technique for making people laugh with the techniques described by Twain.

**6.** How do you think Twain would judge the humor in Thurber's "The Night the Bed Fell"? Cite examples from Thurber's story that you think Twain would especially like or criticize.

# Analyzing the Writer's Craft

## ESSAY

What seems to be Twain's main purpose in writing this essay?

**Building a Literary Vocabulary.** An essay is a brief nonfiction work that offers an opinion on a subject. The purpose of an essay may be to express ideas and feelings, to analyze, to inform, to entertain, or to persuade. Twain says at the beginning of his essay, "I do not claim that I can tell a story as it ought to be told. I only claim to know how a story ought to be told." Twain's stated purpose, then, is to analyze storytelling rather than to entertain his readers with storytelling. Twain does not seem to be concerned with persuading or informing his readers either, for he seems confident that they basically agree with him, especially if they are Americans.

Essays can be formal or informal, depending on how objective and serious the tone. Because Twain's essay is sprinkled with humor, anecdotes, and personal comments, it is best classified as informal.

**Application: Understanding an Essay.** To understand the connection among purpose, tone, and style, try rewriting a passage from Twain's essay to change the purpose or the degree of formality. For example, to make the essay more persuasive, you might rewrite the opening in this way: "I hope to convince you of the superiority of the humorous story over the merely comic story." To make the essay more formal, you might begin:

"It is beyond the limits of this essay to relate a humorous narrative in an effective manner. Therefore, the essay will be restricted to a delineation of the proper method of reciting a humorous narrative." Select a passage at least two paragraphs in length to rewrite. Then read your rewritten passage aloud to a classmate and have him or her identify the change in purpose or degree of formality.

# Connecting Reading and Writing

**1.** Using the techniques described by Twain, write **notes** for and then deliver to the class a humorous monologue based on the story or joke you wrote in your journal.

Option: Rewrite the story or joke from your journal as a **humorous anecdote** to be submitted to a literary magazine.

**2.** Create a set of **guidelines** for television writers on how to write a humorous TV script.

Option: Write a **review** of a situation comedy for your school paper, analyzing the humor of the program.

**3.** Read "What Stumped the Bluejays," "The Notorious Jumping Frog of Calaveras County," or another story by Mark Twain. Then pretend you are an editor of a literary magazine and have received the story without Twain's name on it. Write a **review** of the story addressed to your boss, the editor in chief, explaining why you think the story should or should not be published in the magazine.

Option: Express your opinion of what you have read by Mark Twain. Create a **report card** in which you grade Twain as an essayist, humorist, and short story writer.

# The Seeing See Little

## HELEN KELLER

A biography of Keller appears on page 641.

## Approaching the Essay

At nineteen months of age, Helen Keller suffered a disease that left her blind and deaf. For the next five years, she remained cut off from normal human communication. Then, through the efforts of her teacher Anne Sullivan, Keller learned first to communicate using sign language and then to speak, read, and write. Helen Keller went on to graduate from college with honors and to become a successful lecturer and writer.

## Building Vocabulary

These essential words are footnoted within the selection.

**incredulous** (in krej´ oo ləs): I might have been **incredulous** had I not been accustomed to such responses. (page 288)

**intoxicate** (in täks´ i kāt): I should . . . **intoxicate** my eyes on the beauties of the world of Nature. (page 290)

**admonition** (ad´ mə nish´ ən): I who am blind can give . . . one **admonition** to those who would make full use of the gift of sight. (page 290)

## Connecting Writing and Reading

Copy the chart below into your journal. Rank the five senses according to how pleasurable they are for you and, for each sense, write a few words about what you would miss the most if you were to lose that sense.

| Rank | Sense | What I would miss |
|------|-------|-------------------|
| _____ | hearing | _____ |
| _____ | sight | _____ |
| _____ | smell | _____ |
| _____ | taste | _____ |
| _____ | touch | _____ |

While you read, notice which sense Helen Keller thinks is "most delightful," and why.

# The Seeing See Little

ONLY THE DEAF appreciate hearing; only the blind realize the manifold blessings that lie in sight. Particularly does this observation apply to those who have lost sight and hearing in adult life. But those who have never suffered impairment of sight or hearing seldom make the fullest use of these blessed faculties. Their eyes and ears take in all sights and sounds hazily, without concentration, and with little appreciation. It is the same old story of not being grateful for what we have until we lose it, of not being conscious of health until we are ill.

I have often thought it would be a blessing if each human being were stricken blind and deaf for a few days at some time during his or her early adult life. Darkness would make people more appreciative of sight; silence would teach them the joys of sound.

Now and then I have tested my seeing friends to discover what they see. Recently I was visited by a very good friend who had just returned from a long walk in the woods, and I asked her what she had observed. "Nothing in particular," she replied. I might have been incredulous[1] had I not been accustomed to such responses, for long ago I became convinced that the seeing see little.

How was it possible, I asked myself, to walk for an hour through the woods and see nothing worthy of note? I, who cannot see, find hundreds of things to interest me through mere touch. I feel the delicate symmetry of a leaf. I pass my hands lovingly about the smooth skin of a silver birch or the rough, shaggy bark of a pine. In spring I touch the branches of trees hopefully in search of a bud, the first sign of awakening Nature after the winter's sleep. I feel the delightful, velvety texture of a flower and discover its remarkable convolutions, and something of the miracle of Nature is revealed to me. Occasionally, if I am very fortunate, I place my hand gently on a small tree and feel the happy quiver of a bird in full song. I am delighted to have the cool waters of a brook rush through my open fingers. To me, a lush carpet of pine needles or spongy grass is more welcome than the most luxurious Persian rug. To me, the pageant of seasons is a thrilling and unending drama, the action of which streams through my fingertips.

At times my heart cries out with longing to see all these things. If I can get so much pleasure from mere touch, how much more beauty must be revealed by sight? Yet those who have eyes apparently see little. The panorama of color and action that fills the world is taken for granted. It is human, perhaps, to appreciate little of that which we have and to long for that which we have not; but it is a great pity that, in the world of light, the gift of sight is used only as a mere convenience rather than as a means of adding fullness to life.

If I were the president of a university, I should establish a compulsory course in how to use your eyes. The professor would try to show the pupils how they could add joy to their lives by really seeing what passes unnoticed before them. He or she would try to awake their dormant and sluggish faculties.

Perhaps I can best illustrate by imagining what I should most like to see if I were given the use of my eyes, say, for just three days. And while I am imagining, suppose you, too, set

---

1. **incredulous** (in krej′ o͞o ləs): unwilling or unable to believe; doubting.

your mind to work on the problem of how you would use your own eyes if you had only three more days to see. If with the oncoming darkness of the third night you knew that the sun would never rise for you again, how would you spend those three precious, intervening days? What would you most want to let your gaze rest upon?

I, naturally, should want most to see the things that have become dear to me through my years of darkness. You, too, would want to let your eyes rest long on the things that have become dear to you, so that you could take the memory of them with you into the night that loomed before you.

If, by some miracle, I were granted three seeing days, to be followed by a relapse into darkness, I should want to see the people whose kindness and gentleness and companionship have made my life worth living. First I should like to gaze long upon the face of my dear teacher, Mrs. Anne Sullivan Macy, who came to me when I was a child and opened the outer world to me. I should want not merely to see the outline of her face, so that I could cherish it in my memory, but to study that face and find in it the living evidence of the sympathetic tenderness and patience with which she accomplished the difficult task of my education. I should like to see in her eyes that strength of character that has enabled her to stand firm in the face of difficulties, and that compassion for all humanity that she has revealed to me so often.

I do not know what it is to see into the heart of a friend through that "window of the soul," the eye. I can only "see" through my fingertips the outline of a face. I can detect laughter, sorrow, and many other obvious emotions. I know my friends from the feel of their faces. But I cannot really picture their personalities by touch. I know their personalities, of course, through other means, through the thoughts they express to me, through whatever of their

actions are revealed to me. But I am denied that deeper understanding of them that I am sure would come through sight of them, through watching their reactions to various expressed thoughts and circumstances, through noting the immediate and fleeting reactions of their eyes and countenance.

Friends who are near to me I know well, because through the months and years they reveal themselves to me in all their phases; but of casual friends I have only an incomplete impression, an impression gained from a handclasp, from spoken words that I take from their lips with my fingertips or which they tap into the palm of my hand.

How much easier, how much more satisfying it is for you who can see to grasp quickly the essential qualities of another person by watching the subtleties of expression, the quiver of a muscle, the flutter of a hand. But does it ever occur to you to use your sight to see into the inner nature of a friend or acquaintance? Do not most of you seeing people grasp casually the outward features of a face and let it go at that?

For instance, can you describe accurately the faces of five good friends? Some of you can, but many cannot. As an experiment, I have questioned husbands of long standing about the color of their wives' eyes, and often they express embarrassed confusion and admit that they do not know. And, incidentally, it is a chronic complaint of wives that their husbands do not notice new dresses, new hats, and changes in household arrangements.

The eyes of seeing persons soon become accustomed to the routine of their surroundings, and they actually see only the startling and spectacular. But even in viewing the most spectacular sights, the eyes are lazy. Court records reveal every day how inaccurately "eyewitnesses" see. A given event will be "seen" in several different ways by as many witnesses. Some see more than others, but few see everything that is within the range of their vision.

Oh, the things that I should see if I had the power of sight for just three days!

The first day would be a busy one. I should call to me all my dear friends and look long into their faces, imprinting upon my mind the outward evidence of the beauty that is within them. I should let my eyes rest, too, on the face of a baby, so that I could catch a vision of the eager, innocent beauty that precedes the individual's consciousness of the conflicts that life develops.

And I should like to look into the loyal, trusting eyes of my dogs—the grave, canny little Scottie, Darkie, and the stalwart, understanding Great Dane, Helga, whose warm, tender, and playful friendships are comforting to me.

On that busy first day I should also view the small, simple things of my home. I want to see the warm colors in the rugs under my feet, the pictures on the walls, the intimate trifles that transform a house into a home. My eyes would rest respectfully on the books in raised type that I have read, but they would be more eagerly interested in the printed books that seeing people can read; for during the long night of my life, the books I have read and those that have been read to me have built themselves into a great, shining lighthouse, revealing to me the deepest channels of human life and the human spirit.

In the afternoon of that first seeing day, I should take a long walk in the woods and intoxicate[2] my eyes on the beauties of the world of Nature, trying desperately to absorb in a few hours the vast splendor that is con- stantly unfolding itself to those who can see. On the way home from my woodland jaunt, my path would lie near a farm, so that I might see the patient horses plowing in the field (perhaps I should see only a tractor!) and the serene content of people living close to the soil. And I should pray for the glory of a color- ful sunset.

When dusk had fallen, I should experience the double delight of being able to see by arti- ficial light, which the human genius has creat- ed to extend the power of sight when Nature decrees darkness.

In the night of that first day of sight, I should not be able to sleep, so full would be my mind of the memories of the day.

I who am blind can give one hint to those who see—one admonition[3] to those who would make full use of the gift of sight: Use your eyes as if tomorrow you would be stricken blind. And the same method can be applied to the other senses. Hear the music of voices, the song of a bird, the mighty strains of an orches- tra, as if you would be stricken deaf tomorrow. Touch each object you want to touch as if tomorrow your tactile sense would fail. Smell the perfume of flowers, taste with relish each morsel, as if tomorrow you could never smell and taste again. Make the most of every sense; glory in all facets of pleasure and beauty that the world reveals to you through the several means of contact that Nature provides. But of all the senses, I am sure that sight must be the most delightful.

---

2. **intoxicate** (in täks′ i kāt): to make wild with excitement or happiness.

3. **admonition** (ad′ mə nish′ ən): a warning or caution.

*In Glacier National Park,* 1941-42, ANSEL ADAMS.
National Archives, Washington, D.C.

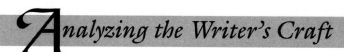

# Thinking About the Essay

## A PERSONAL RESPONSE

*sharing impressions*

**1.** After reading this essay, how did you feel about the way that you use your sense of sight? Describe those feelings in your journal.

*constructing interpretations*

**2.** Explain whether you agree with Helen Keller that sight is the "most delightful" sense.

**3.** How well do you think Helen Keller's sense of touch compensates for her loss of sight?

**Think about**
- what she enjoys about nature
- what she can know about her friends

## A CREATIVE RESPONSE

**4.** If Helen Keller had been presented with the choice of regaining her sight by sacrificing her other senses, what do you think she would have done, and why?

**5.** If this essay had been written by a seeing person, would it have had the same impact on you? Explain why or why not.

## A CRITICAL RESPONSE

**6.** Reread the fourth paragraph, in which Keller describes how she perceives a wooded area through her sense of touch. How does her imagery in the paragraph suggest ways you could better use your sense of sight?

# Analyzing the Writer's Craft

## FIGURATIVE LANGUAGE: METAPHOR

What is Keller referring to when she uses the phrase "the long night of my life"? Why is that an appropriate phrase for her to use?

**Building a Literary Vocabulary.** Figurative language is language that communicates ideas beyond the literal meanings of the words. Keller's phrase "the long night of my life" is a figurative expression called a metaphor. A metaphor makes a comparison between two things that have something in common. While a simile contains the word *like* or *as*, a metaphor either makes the comparison directly or implies it. The implied comparison in Keller's phrase is between night and blindness, both of which bring darkness. The phrase also conveys the feeling of permanence, for Keller's blindness was an unchangeable condition.

**Application: Understanding Metaphor.** With a partner, find at least three additional metaphors in the selection. Copy the chart below and complete it for each metaphor you find. After completing your chart, decide which metaphor you think has the greatest impact in the selection. Share that metaphor with the class and explain what it conveys.

| Metaphor | Two things compared | Idea or emotion conveyed |
|---|---|---|
| "the long night of my life" | night and blindness | permanent darkness |

## Connecting Reading and Writing

**1.** Take a walk through the woods or a park. Write a description of what you observe in an **article** for a conservation magazine. Try to imitate Helen Keller's style by using images that appeal to all of the senses.

Option: Write a **field guide** describing the woods or park where you walked for a science teacher who is conducting a nature tour there.

**2.** With your eyes closed, use only your sense of touch to examine a familiar object. Create a **radio advertisement** promoting the object by describing it in language that appeals primarily to the sense of touch.

Option: Choose several objects and create a **game card** for each, with the name of the object on one side and the description of how it feels on the other. Invent a game to play with the cards, and write the rules.

**3.** If you had only three days to see, what would you do? Write a **list** of people and things you would want to see for the last time during those three days.

Option: Interview ten classmates on what they would want to see and present your findings in a **report.**

**4.** Keller says that she believes there should be a required course on how to use your eyes. Pretend that you are teaching such a course, and create a **calendar of events** for one week's activities.

Option: Write an **instruction manual** for students on how to use their eyes effectively.

# The Knife

## RICHARD SELZER

A biography of Selzer appears on page 645.

## 𝒜pproaching the Essay

Imagine being able to read the thoughts of a surgeon, gowned and masked, standing over the body of a patient. In this essay, surgeon Richard Selzer offers you such an opportunity by re-creating his experience during an operation. While Selzer describes details in the process of surgery and uses medical terms, the emphasis is on his own thoughts and feelings as he wields his knife.

## ℬuilding Vocabulary

These essential words are footnoted within the selection.

**quietude** (kwī´ ə to͞od), **resolve** (ri zalv´): It is the **quietude** of **resolve** layered over fear. (page 295)

**ritual** (rich´ o͞o əl): You turn aside to wash your gloves. It is a **ritual** cleansing. (page 295)

**microcosm** (mī´ krō kä´ zəm): Here is man as **microcosm**, representing in all his parts the earth. (page 295)

**hemorrhage** (hem´ ər ij´): One poke and it might rupture, exploding with sudden **hemorrhage**. (page 296)

**frailty** (frāl´ tē): They are **frailty** itself. (page 296)

**presentiment** (prē zent´ ə mənt): All the night before you have turned with the **presentiment** of death upon you. (page 297)

**carnivore** (kär´ nə vôr): It too is hacked from its bed as the **carnivore** knife lips the blood. (page 298)

## 𝒞onnecting Writing and Reading

Think about something you enjoy doing that is also challenging—for instance, training for athletic competition or creating art or music. In your journal, write about this activity, briefly explaining both its challenges and its rewards. As you read, notice the challenges and rewards that Selzer finds in his work as a surgeon.

ONE HOLDS THE knife as one holds the bow of a cello or a tulip—by the stem. Not palmed or gripped or grasped, but lightly, with the tips of the fingers. The knife is not for pressing. It is for drawing across the field of skin. Like a slender fish, it waits, at the ready, then, go! It darts, followed by a fine wake of red. The flesh parts, falling away to yellow globules of fat. Even now, after so many times, I still marvel at its power—cold, gleaming, silent. More, I am still struck with a kind of dread that it is I in whose hand the blade travels, that my hand is its vehicle, that yet again this terrible steel-bellied thing and I have conspired for a most unnatural purpose, the laying open of the body of a human being.

A stillness settles in my heart and is carried to my hand. It is the quietude[1] of resolve[2] layered over fear. And it is this resolve that lowers us, my knife and me, deeper and deeper into the person beneath. It is an entry into the body that is nothing like a caress; still, it is among the gentlest of acts. Then stroke and stroke again, and we are joined by other instruments, hemostats and forceps, until the wound blooms with strange flowers whose looped handles fall to the sides in steely array.

There is sound, the tight click of clamps fixing teeth into severed blood vessels, the snuffle and gargle of the suction machine clearing the field of blood for the next stroke, the litany of monosyllables with which one prays his way down and in: *clamp*, *sponge*, *suture*[3], tie, cut. And there is color. The green of the cloth, the white of the sponges, the red and yellow of the body. Beneath the fat lies the fascia, the tough, fibrous sheet encasing the muscles. It must be sliced and the red beef of the muscles separated. Now there are retractors to hold apart the wound. Hands move together, part, weave. We are fully engaged, like children absorbed in a game or the craftsmen of some place like Damascus.

Deeper still. The peritoneum, pink and gleaming and membranous, bulges into the wound. It is grasped with forceps and opened. For the first time we can see into the cavity of the abdomen. Such a primitive place. One expects to find drawings of buffalo on the walls. The sense of trespassing is keener now, heightened by the world's light illuminating the organs, their secret colors revealed— maroon and salmon and yellow. The vista is sweetly vulnerable at this moment, a kind of welcoming. An arc of the liver shines high and on the right, like a dark sun. It laps over the pink sweep of the stomach, from whose lower border the gauzy omentum is draped, and through which veil one sees, sinuous, slow as just-fed snakes, the indolent coils of the intestine.

You turn aside to wash your gloves. It is a ritual[4] cleansing. One enters this temple doubly washed. Here is man as microcosm,[5] representing in all his parts the earth, perhaps the universe.

I must confess that the priestliness of my profession has ever been impressed on me. In the beginning there are vows, taken with all solemnity. Then there is the endless harsh novitiate of training, much fatigue, much sacrifice. At last one emerges as celebrant, standing close to the truth lying curtained in the Ark of the body. Not surplice and cassock but mask and gown are your regalia. You hold no chalice, but a knife. There is no wine, no wafer. There are only the facts of blood and flesh.

---

1. **quietude** (kwī′ ə tōōd): a state of being quiet; rest; calmness.
2. **resolve** (ri zälv′): a fixed purpose or intention.
3. **suture** (sōō′ chər): to stitch together the two edges of an incision.
4. **ritual** (rich′ ōō əl): having the nature of a set form or system of formal acts or ceremonies, religious or otherwise.
5. **microcosm** (mī′ krō kä′ zəm): a little world; a miniature universe.

And if the surgeon is like a poet, then the scars you have made on countless bodies are like verses, into the fashioning of which you have poured your soul. I think that if years later I were to see the trace from an old incision of mine, I should know it at once, as one recognizes his pet expressions.

*Guide for Interpretation*

Selzer compares being a surgeon to being a priest and a poet. Consider whether your own ideas about priests and poets help you to imagine what it's like to be a surgeon. Then, as you continue reading the essay, notice the comparison between being a surgeon and being a traveler in a dangerous country.

But mostly you are a traveler in a dangerous country, advancing into the moist and jungly cleft your hands have made. Eyes and ears are shuttered from the land you left behind; mind empties itself of all other thought. You are the root of groping fingers. It is a fine hour for the fingers, their sense of touch so enhanced. The blind must know this feeling. Oh, there is risk everywhere. One goes lightly. The spleen. No! No! Do not touch the spleen that lurks below the left leaf of the diaphragm, a manta ray[6] in a coral cave, its bloody tongue protruding. One poke and it might rupture, exploding with sudden <u>hemorrhage</u>.[7] The filmy omentum must not be torn, the intestine scraped or denuded. The hand finds the liver, palms it, fingers running along its sharp lower edge, admiring. Here are the twin mounds of the kidneys, the apron of the omentum hanging in front of the intestinal coils. One lifts it aside, and the fingers dip among the loops, searching, mapping territory, establishing boundaries. Deeper still, and the womb is touched, then held like a small, muscular bottle—the womb and its earlike appendages, the ovaries. How they do nestle in the cup of a man's hand, their power all dormant. They are <u>frailty</u>[8] itself.

There is a hush in the room. Speech stops. The hands of the others, assistants and nurses,

are still. Only the voice of the patient's respiration remains. It is the rhythm of a quiet sea, the sound of waiting. Then you speak, slowly, the terse entries of a Himalayan climber reporting back.

"The stomach is okay. Greater curvature clean. No sign of ulcer. Pylorus, duodenum fine. Now comes the gallbladder. No stones. Right kidney, left, all right. Liver . . . uh-oh."

Your speech lowers to a whisper, falters, stops for a long, long moment, then picks up again at the end of a sigh that comes through your mask like a last exhalation.

"Three big hard ones in the left lobe, one on the right. Metastatic[9] deposits. Bad, bad. Where's the primary? Got to be coming from somewhere."

The arm shifts direction, and the fingers drop lower and lower into the pelvis—the body impaled now upon the arm of the surgeon to the hilt of the elbow.

"Here it is."

The voice goes flat, all business now.

"Tumor in the sigmoid colon, wrapped all around it, pretty tight. We'll take out a sleeve of the bowel. No colostomy. Not that, anyway. But, God, there's a lot of it down there. Here, you take a feel."

You step back from the table and lean into a sterile basin of water, resting on stiff arms, while the others locate the cancer.

When I was a small boy, I was taken by my

---

6. **manta ray** (man′ tə rā): a broad, flat-bodied fish that has a whiplike tail, frequently with one or more stinging spines.
7. **hemorrhage** (hem′ ər ij′): the escape of large quantities of blood from a blood vessel; heavy bleeding.
8. **frailty** (frāl′ tē): the condition of being delicate and weak.
9. **metastatic** (met′ ə stat′ ik): of or pertaining to the spread of disease from one part of the body to an unrelated part.

father, a general practitioner[10] in Troy, New York, to St. Mary's Hospital, to wait while he made his rounds. The solarium where I sat was all sunlight and large plants. It smelled of soap and starch and clean linen. In the spring, clouds of lilac billowed from the vases; and in the fall, chrysanthemums crowded the magazine tables. At one end of the great high-ceilinged, glass-walled room was a huge cage where colored finches streaked and sang. Even from the first, I sensed the nearness of that other place, the Operating Room, knew that somewhere on these premises was that secret dreadful enclosure where *surgery* was at that moment happening. I sat among the cut flowers, half drunk on the scent, listening to the robes of the nuns brush the walls of the corridor, and felt the awful presence of *surgery*.

Oh, the pageantry! I longed to go there. I feared to go there. I imagined surgeons bent like storks over the body of the patient, a circle of red painted across the abdomen. Silence and dignity and awe enveloped them, these surgeons; it was the bubble in which they bent and straightened. Ah, it was a place I would never see, a place from whose walls the hung and suffering Christ turned his affliction to highest purpose. It is thirty years since I yearned for that old Surgery. And now I merely break the beam of an electric eye, and double doors swing open to let me enter, and as I enter, always, I feel the surging of a force that I feel in no other place. It is as though I am suddenly stronger and larger, heroic. Yes, that's it!

And what of that *other*, the patient, you, who are brought to the operating room on a stretcher, having been washed and purged and dressed in a white gown? Fluid drips from a bottle into your arm, diluting you, leaching your body of its personal brine. As you wait in the corridor, you hear from behind the closed door the angry clang of steel upon steel, as though a battle were being waged. There is the odor of antiseptic and ether, and masked women hurry up and down the halls, in and out of rooms. There is the watery sound of strange machinery, the tinny beeping that is the transmitted heartbeat of yet another *human being*. And all the while the dreadful knowledge that soon you will be taken, laid beneath great lamps that will reveal the secret linings of your body. In the very act of lying down, you have made a declaration of surrender. One lies down gladly for sleep or for love. But to give over one's body and will for surgery, to *lie down* for it, is a yielding of more than we can bear.

Soon a man will stand over you, gowned and hooded. In time the man will take up a knife and crack open your flesh like a ripe melon. Fingers will rummage among your viscera. Parts of you will be cut out. Blood will run free. Your blood. All the night before you have turned with the presentiment[11] of death upon you. You have attended your funeral, wept with your mourners. You think, "I should never have had surgery in the springtime." It is too cruel. Or on a Thursday. It is an unlucky day.

Now it is time. You are wheeled in and moved to the table. An injection is given. "Let yourself go," I say. "It's a pleasant sensation," I say. "Give in," I say.

Let go? Give in? When you know that you are being tricked into the hereafter, that you will end when consciousness ends? As the monstrous silence of anesthesia falls discourteously across your brain, you watch your soul drift off.

Later, in the recovery room, you awaken and gaze through the thickness of drugs at the world returning, and you guess, at first dimly,

10. **general practitioner** (jen′ ər əl prak tish′ ə nər): a doctor who does not specialize in any particular field of medicine.

11. **presentiment** (prē zent′ ə mənt): a feeling that something, especially something of an unfortunate nature, is about to take place.

then surely, that you have not died. In pain and nausea you will know the exultation of death averted, of life restored.

What is it, then, this thing, the knife, whose shape is virtually the same as it was three thousand years ago, but now with its head grown detachable? Before steel, it was bronze. Before bronze, stone—then back into unremembered time. Did man invent it or did the knife precede him here, hidden under ages of vegetation and hoofprints, lying in wait to be discovered, picked up, used?

The scalpel is in two parts, the handle and the blade. Joined, it is six inches from tip to tip. At one end of the handle is a narrow, notched prong upon which the blade is slid, then snapped into place. Without the blade, the handle has a blind, decapitated look. It is helpless as a trussed maniac. But slide on the blade, click it home, and the knife springs instantly to life. It is headed now, edgy, leaping to mount the fingers for the gallop to its feast.

Within the belly a tumor squats, toadish, fungoid.[12] A gray mother and her brood. The only thing it does not do is croak. It too is hacked from its bed as the carnivore[13] knife lips the blood, turning in it in a kind of ecstasy of plenty, a gluttony after the long fast. It is just for this that the knife was created, tempered, heated, its violence beaten into paper-thin force.

At last a little thread is passed into the wound and tied. The monstrous, booming fury is stilled by a tiny thread. The tempest is silenced. The operation is over. On the table, the knife lies spent, on its side, the bloody meal smear-dried upon its flanks. The knife rests.

And waits.

---

12. **fungoid** (fun' goid'): having the characteristics of fungi, such as mushrooms and molds.
13. **carnivore** (kär' nə vôr): any flesh-eating animal.

# Thinking About the Essay

## A PERSONAL RESPONSE

*sharing impressions*

**1.** What impressed you the most about this essay? Jot down a brief description of your impressions in your journal.

*constructing interpretations*

**2.** How does Selzer make the experience of surgery seem real to you?

**3.** Why do you think Selzer interrupts his description of the operation to relate a childhood memory and to speculate about the feelings of the patient?

**4.** What rewards and challenges do you think Selzer finds in his work as a surgeon?

**5.** Why do you think Selzer wrote this essay?
   ***Think about***
   • whom you think he imagines as his audience
   • what you think he wants to accomplish

**6.** If Selzer's purpose had been to explain his surgical procedure to a group of his colleagues, how might this essay be different?

## A CRITICAL RESPONSE

**7.** Why do you think Selzer makes the knife the central focus of this essay?
*Think about*
- the description of the knife as a living thing
- the connection among the knife, the surgeon, and the patient

**8.** Technological developments in modern surgery include the use of lasers instead of knives, and computerized body scans instead of exploratory surgery. How might these developments affect the challenges and rewards Selzer feels as a surgeon?

# *Analyzing the Writer's Craft*

## FIGURATIVE LANGUAGE: METAPHOR AND EXTENDED METAPHOR

Selzer says, "I must confess that the priestliness of my profession has ever been impressed on me." How does the comparison of a surgeon to a priest add to your understanding of what being a surgeon means to Selzer?

**Building a Literary Vocabulary.** A metaphor is a figure of speech that makes a comparison between two things that have something in common. Because Selzer compares surgeon and priest at some length and in several ways, this comparison is called an extended metaphor. The purpose of both metaphor and extended metaphor is to help the reader better understand what the writer describes. Those readers who know something about the special training and work of a priest can understand what Selzer means by the comparison of priest and surgeon. Readers unfamiliar with the priesthood may find the next comparisons, of a surgeon to a poet and to "a traveler in a dangerous country," more helpful.

**Application: Analyzing Metaphors.** Working in a small group, go back through the essay and list five examples of metaphor or extended metaphor. You may include two of those already mentioned. Then jot down on a chart what each example adds to your understanding of what is being described. Finally, select the one metaphor from the chart that your group finds the most interesting or revealing and explain to the class what it reveals for you.

# Connecting Reading and Writing

**1.** What qualities do you think a good surgeon has? Describe these qualities in a **want ad** for the position of surgeon.

Option: Write a **press release** announcing an award being given to a famous surgeon. In the press release highlight the qualities that make that person a success.

**2.** Choose an object that you use every day and describe its form and function, as Selzer does those of his knife. Write a **description** of the object without naming it. Then give your description to a classmate to figure out what the object is.

Option: Create a **cluster diagram** of descriptive phrases about the object.

**3.** Use figurative language to explain your position as a student, ninth grader, son, daughter, sister, brother, athlete, artist—you name it. Write several **metaphors** to capture what being in a certain position or age group is like.

Option: Write one **extended metaphor** about your position.

**4.** Look back at your prereading journal notes on a challenging activity or choose something else that is both challenging and rewarding. Then write an **informal outline** for a speech demonstrating the process of the activity, in a manner similar to the way Selzer demonstrates the process of an operation.

Option: Create a **flowchart** to show how the activity progresses in stages.

# A Dog for All Seasons

## PATRICK McMANUS

A biography of McManus appears on page 643.

## *Approaching the Essay*

Patrick McManus writes about animals and outdoor life for such magazines as *Sports Illustrated* and *Field & Stream.* His work often focuses on the humor in human interactions with nature.

ONE OF THESE days they'll probably come out with a mechanical bird dog that locates pheasants with a special scent detector and radar. A small on-dog computer will record and analyze all available information and give the hunter a report: two roosters and five hens in stubble field—253 feet. A pointer on the dog's back would indicate the exact direction.

There would be luxury models, of course, with built-in stereo and FM sets, a special compartment for lunches, a cooler for beverages. The dog's nose would be a cigarette lighter.

The really high-priced jobs would not only retrieve the bird but pluck it, dress it, wrap it in foil, and quick-freeze it. By the time the bird got back to the hunter, it would be neat and trim as a TV dinner.

Since no self-respecting hunter would want to be seen carrying his dog around by a handle, all but the cheapest models would be designed to look like nifty attache cases.[1] If you passed by some good hunting ground on your way home from work, you could get out and let your attache case nose around in a thicket or two.

There would be minor inconveniences ("We'll have to go back, Harry. I thought I had my bird dog but it's just a bag of briefs"), but on the whole, the mechanical bird dog would have many advantages over the standard makes most of us have now.

Still, I'm something of a traditionalist, and if the mechanical bird dog were to go on the market tomorrow, I'd probably stick with my old ready-made hound, such as he is. His eyes don't light up much any more, let alone his tubes, and you can't light a cigarette on the end of his nose. The sounds that come out of him are not stereo (fortunately), and he has never been much on fidelity[2] any way you look at it. But I would keep him nevertheless. There was a time in my youth, however, when I would have swapped my dog for a mechanical job and thrown in my T-shirt decorated with bottle caps to boot.

Take the flaws of character you find in all dogs and most human beings, roll them up in

---

1. **attache cases** (at ə shā′ kās′ iz): flat, rectangular cases for carrying papers.
2. **fidelity** (fə del′ ə tē): **1** faithful devotion to one's duty; loyalty **2** accuracy of sound reproduction.

the hide of a sickly wart hog, and you would have a reasonable facsimile[3] of my dog Stranger, who was dirty, lazy, bigoted, opinionated, gluttonous, conceited, ill-tempered, and an incorrigible[4] liar.

An old man once summed up Stranger's character succinctly. "He's a prevert!"[5] he said. I didn't know what preverts were but had no doubt Stranger was one of them.

We had called the dog Stranger out of the faint hope he was just passing through. As it turned out, the name was most inappropriate, since he stayed on for nearly a score of years, all the while biting the hands that fed him and making snide remarks about my grandmother's cooking. Eventually the name was abbreviated to "Strange," which was shorter and much more descriptive.

My mother used to say that Strange was like one of the family. Then my grandmother would bawl her out and say that was no way to talk about my uncle George. That was one of Mom's favorite jokes and was probably the reason she allowed the dog to stay on the place. At least, nobody ever thought of another reason.

I used to beg for a decent dog—a Labrador retriever, an Irish setter, or just a regular old mongrel like most of the other guys had—but with no success. We just weren't a two-dog family, and since no one in his right mind would take Strange and Mom wouldn't take advantage of anyone who revealed his low mentality by offering to take Strange, I was stuck with him.

Strange didn't even make good as a criminal. In our part of the country the worst crime a dog can commit is to run deer. As soon as Strange found this out, he rushed out into our clover field and tried to run the deer that grazed there. They would have none of it. They looked at the wildly yapping creature dancing around them and went back to their munching.

Strange had only two chores, but he could never get them straight. He was supposed to attack prowlers, especially those whose character bore the slightest resemblance to his own, and to protect the chickens. He always thought it was the other way around.

Whenever he was caught assaulting a chicken, he would come up with some cock-and-bull story about how the chicken had been about to set fire to the house when he, Strange, happened along and prevented arson. "Bad enough we have a dog that attacks chickens, we have to have one that lies about it besides!" Mom would say. (It should be understood that Strange did not actually speak in words, or at least that anyone ever heard, but with his eyes and gestures with feet, tail, and ears.)

As for prowlers, Strange would go out and invite tramps in off the road for a free meal. While the dog was out in the yard apologizing to the tramp for my grandmother's cooking, the womenfolk would peek out through the curtains and try to determine whether the fellow was dangerous. If so, they would wait until he had just about finished his meal, and then my sister would bellow, "Do you want the gun, Ma? Do you want the gun?" This usually would bring the tramp to his feet and send him at a fast walk toward the nearest cover, the ditch on the far side of the road. Even had the gun been real, which it wasn't, the tramp would have been in no danger—unless, of course, he happened to step between Mom and the dog.

As soon as I was old enough to hunt, I would borrow a shotgun and sneak out to the woods in search of grouse. I had to sneak, not because Mom disapproved of my hunting, but

---

3. **facsimile** (fak sim′ ə lē): an exact reproduction or copy.
4. **incorrigible** (in kôr′ ə jə bəl): that cannot be corrected, improved, or reformed.
5. **prevert** (prē′ vʉrt): mispronunciation of *pervert*.

because Strange would insist upon going along and contributing his advice and services. An army of Cossacks[6] could have bivouacked on our front lawn for the night without his knowing a thing about it, but he could hear the sound of a shotgun shell being dropped into a flannel shirt pocket at a hundred yards.

Just as I would be easing my way out the door, he would come staggering out of the woodshed, his eyes bloodshot and bleary from a night of carousing, and say, "My suggestion is that we try Schultz's woods first and then work our way up Stagg's hill, and if we don't get anything there, we can stop by the Haversteads and shoot some of their chickens."

Strange made slightly less noise going through the woods than an armored division through a bamboo jungle. Nevertheless, we usually managed to get a few birds, apparently because they thought that anything that made that much noise couldn't possibly be hunting.

My dog believed in a mixed bag: grouse, ducks, pheasants, rabbits, squirrels, chipmunks, gophers, skunks, and porcupines. If we saw a cow or horse, he would shout, "There's a big one! Shoot! Shoot!"

Fortunately, Strange tired of hunting after about an hour. "Let's eat the lunch now," he would say. If he had been particularly disgusting that day, I would lie and tell him that I had forgotten to bring a lunch, knowing that it was against his principle—he only had one—to ever be caught more than an hour's distance away from a food supply. He would immediately strike off for home with the look of a man who has suddenly been deposited in the middle of the Mojave Desert.

Thus it went through most of the years of my youth, until finally Strange's years totaled what we supposed to be about a dozen. He sensed death approaching—probably the first thing in his life he ever did sense approaching—and one day staggered to a window, looked out, and said, "A dog like me should live for a thousand years!" Then he died.

Everyone wept and said he hadn't been such a bad dog after all. Everyone except my grandmother, who simply smiled to herself as she stirred the gravy.

That night at dinner I said, "This sure is lumpy gravy" and "This pie crust sure is tough." It seemed the least I could do for Strange.

As I say, there was a time when I would have traded a dog like Strange in an instant for a mechanical bird dog. But now? Well, let me think about that for a while.

---

6. **Cossacks** (käs′ aks′ ): a warlike Russian people, famous for serving in the cavalry.

# Persuasion:
## The Art of Argument

**Y**OU HAVE PROBABLY had strong opinions at some point in your life—it's part of human nature. It's also part of human nature to want the people around you to share your opinions. If you feel strongly about an issue, you probably talk to your friends about it and use all the reasons and examples you can think of to convince your friends to hold the same view. Trying to prove that most of the evidence favors your position is part of the art of argument.

The selections in this section are all expressions of strong personal opinion. More than that, they are attempts by the writers to make you think as they do. In each selection, the writer has marshaled arguments to try to prove a point. As you read, see if the writers succeed in convincing you to share their views.

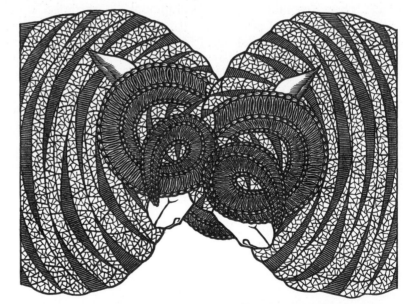

*Two Rams,* 1969,
JACQUES HNIZDOVSKY.
© Stephanie Hnizdovsky.

# *Literary Vocabulary*

## INTRODUCED IN THIS SECTION

**Persuasion.** Persuasion is a technique used by speakers and writers to convince an audience to adopt a particular opinion, perform an action, or both. The most effective persuasion usually appeals to both the reason and the emotions of an audience. Advertisements, newspaper and television editorials, and political speeches all use persuasion.

**Mood.** Mood is the feeling, or atmosphere, that the writer creates for the reader. Descriptive words, setting, and figurative language contribute to the mood of a work, as do the sound and rhythm of the language used. In "West with the Night," Beryl Markham creates a mood of breathless suspense by using the present tense to describe her quick response to an empty gas tank: "A hand gropes and reappears with an electric torch, and fingers, moving with agonizing composure, find the petcock and turn it; and I wait."

## REVIEWED IN THIS SECTION

**Figurative Language**

# I Have a Dream

## MARTIN LUTHER KING, JR.

A biography of King appears on page 642.

### *Approaching the Speech*

Nineteen sixty-three. A century had passed since Lincoln had freed the slaves, but local laws in the South barred most African Americans from registering to vote and from staying in hotels. Public beaches, parks, drinking fountains, restrooms, and lunch counters bore signs reading For Whites Only. The North did not have the same discriminatory laws as the South but shared similar discriminatory attitudes. The civil rights movement emerged in the 1950's to protest discrimination and gained momentum under the inspired leadership of Martin Luther King, Jr., an eloquent minister from Atlanta. King urged African Americans to use nonviolent protest to gain equality, and early in 1963 he helped organize a series of peaceful demonstrations in Birmingham, Alabama. Birmingham police reacted violently to the demonstrations, unleashing attack dogs and aiming fire hoses on the crowds, which included women and children. As television coverage drew national attention to the struggle in the South, President Kennedy proposed a civil rights bill to Congress. King and other leaders organized a mass march on Washington, D.C., to pressure Congress to pass the bill. In the sweltering heat of August 1963, King delivered his impassioned "I Have a Dream" speech on the steps of the Lincoln Memorial, where more than 200,000 demonstrators had gathered.

The following year, Congress passed the Civil Rights Act, and King received the Nobel Prize for peace. King continued to work for justice and equality until he was assassinated in 1968.

Bob Adelman/Magnum Photos, Inc., New York.

## Building Vocabulary

These essential words are footnoted within the selection.

**manacles** (man´ ə kəls), **segregation** (seg´ rə gā´ shən),
**discrimination** (di skrim´ i nā´ shən): The Negro is still sadly crippled by
the **manacles** of **segregation** and the chains of **discrimination**.
(page 308)

**languishing** (laŋ´ gwish iŋ): The Negro is still **languishing** in the corners
of American society. (page 308)

**degenerate** (de jen´ ər āt): We must not allow our creative protests to
**degenerate** into physical violence. (page 309)

**militancy** (mil´ i tənt sē): The marvelous new **militancy**, which has
engulfed the Negro community, must not lead us to a distrust of all
white people. (page 309)

**tribulations** (trib´ yо̄о̄ lā´ shəns): I am not unmindful that some of you
have come here out of great trials and **tribulations**. (page 309)

**discords** (dis´ kôrdz): We will be able to transform the jangling **discords**
of our nation into a beautiful symphony of brotherhood. (page 310)

## Connecting Writing and Reading

What would you identify as the most pressing problems in our country today? In
your journal, list these problems in a chart similar to the one below. As you read
King's speech, jot down the specific problems that King identifies in 1963.

| Problems today | Problems in 1963 |
|----------------|------------------|
|                |                  |

*I* AM HAPPY to join with you today in what will go down in history as the greatest demonstration for freedom in the history of our nation.

Five score years ago, a great American, in whose symbolic shadow we stand today, signed the Emancipation Proclamation.[1] This momentous decree came as a great beacon light of hope to millions of Negro slaves who had been seared in the flames of withering injustice. It came as a joyous daybreak to end the long night of their captivity.

But one hundred years later, the Negro still is not free; one hundred years later, the life of the Negro is still sadly crippled by the manacles[2] of segregation[3] and the chains of discrimination;[4] one hundred years later, the Negro lives on a lonely island of poverty in the midst of a vast ocean of material prosperity; one hundred years later, the Negro is still languishing[5] in the corners of American society and finds himself in exile in his own land.

So we've come here today to dramatize a shameful condition. In a sense we've come to our nation's capital to cash a check. When the architects of our republic wrote the magnificent words of the Constitution and the Declaration of Independence, they were signing a promissory note[6] to which every American was to fall heir. This note was the promise that all men, yes, black men as well as white men, would be guaranteed the unalienable rights of life, liberty, and the pursuit of happiness.

It is obvious today that America has defaulted on this promissory note insofar as her citizens of color are concerned. Instead of honoring this sacred obligation, America has given the Negro people a bad check, a check which has come back marked "insufficient funds." But we refuse to believe that the bank of justice is bankrupt. We refuse to believe that there are insufficient funds in the great vaults of opportunity of this nation. And so we've come to cash this check, a check that will give us upon demand the riches of freedom and the security of justice.

We have also come to this hallowed spot to remind America of the fierce urgency of now. This is no time to engage in the luxury of cooling off or to take the tranquilizing drug of gradualism. Now is the time to make real the promises of democracy; now is the time to rise from the dark and desolate valley of segregation to the sunlit path of racial justice; now is the time to lift our nation from the quicksands of racial injustice to the solid rock of brother-

> **Guide for Interpretation**
> Think about King's references to "check," "promissory note," and "the bank of justice." King states that the Constitution and the Declaration of Independence serve as promises of freedom and equality to future generations of Americans, much as a check or promissory note from a bank serves as a promise of financial payment. King's extended metaphor emphasizes the fact that the United States owes all its citizens equal rights under the law. As you continue to read the speech, notice the additional reasons King gives for the marchers' presence in Washington.

---

1. **Emancipation Proclamation** (ē man′ sə pā′ shən präk′ lə mā′ shən): document signed by President Lincoln during the Civil War, freeing slaves in the Confederate states.
2. **manacles** (man′ ə kəls): handcuffs.
3. **segregation** (seg′ rə gā′ shən): the policy of forcing racial groups to live apart from each other, go to separate schools, and so on.

4. **discrimination** (di skrim′ i nā′ shən): a showing of favoritism or prejudice in treatment.
5. **languishing** (laŋ′ gwish iŋ): living under distressing conditions or in a state of suffering.
6. **promissory note** (präm′ i sôr′ ē): a written promise to repay a debt.

hood; now is the time to make justice a reality for all of God's children. It would be fatal for the nation to overlook the urgency of the moment. This sweltering summer of the Negro's legitimate discontent will not pass until there is an invigorating autumn of freedom and equality.

Nineteen sixty-three is not an end, but a beginning. And those who hope that the Negro needed to blow off steam and will now be content will have a rude awakening if the nation returns to business as usual. There will be neither rest nor tranquility in America until the Negro is granted his citizenship rights. The whirlwinds of revolt will continue to shake the foundations of our nation until the bright day of justice emerges.

But there is something that I must say to my people, who stand on the worn threshold which leads into the palace of justice. In the process of gaining our rightful place, we must not be guilty of wrongful deeds. Let us not seek to satisfy our thirst for freedom by drinking from the cup of bitterness and hatred. We must forever conduct our struggle on the high plain of dignity and discipline. We must not allow our creative protests to degenerate[7] into physical violence. Again and again we must rise to the majestic heights of meeting physical force with soul force. The marvelous new militancy,[8] which has engulfed the Negro community, must not lead us to a distrust of all white people. For many of our white brothers, as evidenced by their presence here today, have come to realize that their destiny is tied up with our destiny. And they have come to realize that their freedom is inextricably bound to our freedom. We cannot walk alone. And as we walk, we must make the pledge that we shall always march ahead. We cannot turn back.

There are those who are asking the devotees of civil rights, "When will you be satisfed?" We can never be satisfied as long as the Negro is the victim of the unspeakable horrors of police brutality; we can never be satisfied as long as our bodies, heavy with the fatigue of travel, cannot gain lodging in the motels of the highways and the hotels of the cities; we cannot be satisfied as long as the Negro's basic mobility is from a smaller ghetto to a larger one; we can never be satisfied as long as our children are stripped of their selfhood and robbed of their dignity by signs stating For Whites Only; we cannot be satisfied as long as the Negro in Mississippi cannot vote and a Negro in New York believes he has nothing for which to vote. No! No, we are not satisfied, and we will not be satisfied until "justice rolls down like waters and righteousness like a mighty stream."

I am not unmindful that some of you have come here out of great trials and tribulations.[9] Some of you have come fresh from narrow jail cells. Some of you have come from areas where your quest for freedom left you battered by the storms of persecution and staggered by the winds of police brutality. You have been the veterans of creative suffering. Continue to work with the faith that unearned suffering is redemptive.[10] Go back to Mississippi. Go back to Alabama. Go back to South Carolina. Go back to Georgia. Go back to Louisiana. Go back to the slums and ghettos of our Northern cities, knowing that somehow this situation can and will be changed. Let us not wallow in the valley of despair.

I say to you today, my friends, even though we face the difficulties of today and tomorrow,

---

7. **degenerate** (dē jen′ ər āt): to become less moral, cultured, and so on.
8. **militancy** (mil′ i tənt sē): the state of being ready and willing to fight, especially, aggressively active in support of a cause.
9. **tribulations** (trib′ yo͞o lā′ shəns): the causes of great misery and distress; deep sorrows.
10. **redemptive** (ri demp′ tiv): having the power to restore one by making up for wrongdoing.

I still have a dream. It is a dream deeply rooted in the American dream. I have a dream that one day this nation will rise up and live out the true meaning of its creed, "We hold these truths to be self-evident; that all men are created equal." I have a dream that one day on the red hills of Georgia, sons of former slaves and the sons of former slave owners will be able to sit down together at the table of brotherhood. I have a dream that one day even the state of Mississippi, a state sweltering with the heat of injustice, sweltering with the heat of oppression, will be transformed into an oasis of freedom and justice. I have a dream that my four little children will one day live in a nation where they will not be judged by the color of their skin, but by the content of their character.

I have a dream today!

I have a dream that one day down in Alabama—with its vicious racists, with its Governor having his lips dripping with the words of interposition and nullification[11]—one day right there in Alabama, little black boys and black girls will be able to join hands with little white boys and white girls as sisters and brothers.

I have a dream today!

I have a dream that one day every valley shall be exalted, and every hill and mountain shall be made low. The rough places will be plain and the crooked places will be made straight, "and the glory of the Lord shall be revealed, and all flesh shall see it together."

This is our hope. This is the faith that I go back to the South with. With this faith we will be able to hew out of the mountain of despair a stone of hope. With this faith we will be able to transform the jangling <u>discords</u>[12] of our nation into a beautiful symphony of brotherhood. With this faith we will be able to work together, to pray together, to struggle together, to go to jail together, to stand up for freedom together, knowing that we will be free one day. And this will be the day. This will be the day when all of God's children will be able to sing with new meaning, "My country 'tis of thee, sweet land of liberty, of thee I sing. Land where my fathers died, land of the pilgrims' pride, from every mountainside, let freedom ring." And if America is to be a great nation, this must become true.

So let freedom ring from the prodigious hill-tops of New Hampshire; let freedom ring from the mighty mountains of New York; let freedom ring from the heightening Alleghenies of Pennsylvania; let freedom ring from the snow-capped Rockies of Colorado; let freedom ring from the curvaceous slopes of California. But not only that. Let freedom ring from Stone Mountain of Georgia; let freedom ring from Lookout Mountain of Tennessee; let freedom ring from every hill and molehill of Mississippi. "From every mountainside, let freedom ring."

And when this happens, and when we allow freedom to ring, when we let it ring from every village and every hamlet, from every state and every city, we will be able to speed up that day when all of God's children—black men and white men, Jews and Gentiles, Protestants and Catholics—will be able to join hands and sing in the words of the old Negro spiritual, "Free at last. Free at last. Thank God Almighty, we are free at last."

---

11. **interposition** (in′ tər pə zish′ ən) and **nullification** (nul′ ə fi kā′ shən): acts taken by state officials to undermine the enforcement of federal laws.

12. **discords** (dis′ kôrdz): tones sounded together that lack harmony.

# Thinking About the Speech

## A PERSONAL RESPONSE

*sharing impressions*

**1.** What sentences and phrases from this speech stand out in your mind? Jot these down in your journal.

*constructing interpretations*

**2.** How does King's dream at the end of this speech offer a solution to the problems he identifies?

### Think about
- specific examples of discrimination he gives
- the groups of people that he wants to join hands together

**3.** Why do you think King quotes from the Declaration of Independence, the United States Constitution, the national anthem, and an old spiritual in his speech?

**4.** What do you think the words *freedom* and *justice* mean to King?

## A CREATIVE RESPONSE

**5.** If this speech were delivered today, what problems might it address?

## A CRITICAL RESPONSE

**6.** To what extent do you think this speech is specific to the problems of a single time and place and to what extent is it not limited to any one time or place? Go back to the speech and find passages that support your answer.

**7.** This speech is King's most famous and is considered by critics to be one of the great speeches of the twentieth century. Tell whether you agree with this view and give examples from the speech that influence your opinion.

# Analyzing the Writer's Craft

## PERSUASION

Think about King's audience for this speech—the 200,000 marchers gathered to hear him, the legislators in the Capitol, and the rest of the country who learned of the speech through the news media. What do you think King wanted to accomplish with this speech?

**Building a Literary Vocabulary.** Persuasion is a technique used by speakers and writers to convince an audience to adopt a particular opinion, perform an action, or both. King probably has several persuasive aims for his speech. First, he is trying to persuade Congress to pass the civil rights bill to end injustice and discrimination. Second, he wants to convince the marchers to persist in nonviolent action to put the spotlight on inequality. Finally, King eloquently unfolds his dream in order to inspire all Americans to end injustice and racial discrimination.

**Application: Identifying Persuasion.** Working in a small group, choose a passage that you think is particularly persuasive. Make a tape recording of one of your group members reading this passage. Then, from your school or public library, obtain a recording of King delivering the speech. As a class, listen to and compare the two recordings. Discuss how delivery affects the persuasiveness of a speech.

# Connecting Reading and Writing

**1.** Read media accounts of the march on Washington in August 1963. Create **cue cards** for a television news report about that day.

Option: Write an **editorial** expressing your opinion about the events of that day.

**2.** Using your prereading notes that describe a national problem, write your own "I Have a Dream" **speech** that expresses your hopes for the future of the country.

Option: Draw pictures or find magazine pictures that represent your hopes for the future of the country. Write **captions** that explain the pictures.

**3.** Analyze how King's use of metaphor adds to the impact of the speech. Using examples from King's speech, write **instructions** teaching a classmate how to use figurative language in a speech.

Option: Present your analysis in a **review** of the speech for a literary magazine.

**4.** Imagine that you are at the Lincoln Memorial listening to King's speech. Write a **letter** to your family describing your reactions.

Option: Think of a national law that should be changed or passed. Using persuasive language similar to King's, write a **petition** calling for that change and circulate the petition among your classmates.

# _from_ A Whale for the Killing

## FARLEY MOWAT

A biography of Mowat appears on page 643.

## _Approaching the Selection_

Farley Mowat is a Canadian writer, naturalist, and environmentalist whose book _A Whale for the Killing_ expresses his concern over the destruction of the natural world. This excerpt begins with a reference to a community that lives in harmony with the local whales. Mowat then goes on to recount an incident that occurred when he was visiting the port of St. Pierre off the east coast of Canada.

## _Building Vocabulary_

These essential words are footnoted with the selection.

**appalled** (ə pôld´), **wanton** (wän´ tən): I was **appalled** and infuriated, but there seemed to be nothing I could do to end this exhibition of **wanton** bloodlust. (page 315)

**derision** (di rizh´ ən): They had responded to my anger with **derision**. (page 315)

**sibilant** (sib´ əl ənt): The strange, **sibilant** breathing of the whales kept me company. (page 315)

**empathy** (em´ pə thē): I began to experience an indescribable sense of **empathy** with them. (page 316)

**ingenious** (in jēn´ yəs): The **ingenious** sportsmen of St. Pierre had set the stage for a massacre. (page 316)

**ensanguined** (en saŋ´ gwind), **delirium** (di lir´ ē əm): Men flung up their **ensanguined** faces, wiped the blood away, and laughed and shouted in the **delirium** of dealing death. (pages 316–317)

## _Connecting Writing and Reading_

Under what circumstances do you believe it is acceptable to kill an animal? Would you kill one for food? for clothing? for medical research? for sport? if the animal were suffering? if it is a danger to people or property? In your journal, write down any reasons that you would find acceptable. As you read this essay, consider how Mowat responds to this issue.

# from A Whale for the Killing

THE TRANQUIL acceptance of the fin whales at Burgeo[1] was in sharp contrast to an incident I witnessed at about this time at St. Pierre, the capital and only port for the French islands of St. Pierre-Miquelon, which lie a few miles off the south coast of Newfoundland.[2] Most of the inhabitants there are fishermen too, but St. Pierre itself is full of shops, tourist establishments, ship repair facilities, and people whose loyalties lie with the modern industrial society.

On a moonless night in August 1961, my schooner lay moored to a rotting dock in St. Pierre harbor. About midnight I went on deck to smoke a pipe and enjoy the silence, but the quiet was soon broken by what sounded like a gust of heavy breathing in the waters almost alongside. Startled, I grabbed a flashlight and played its beam over the dark waters. The calm surface was mysteriously roiled in great, spreading rings. As I puzzled over the meaning of this phenomenon, there came another burst of heavy exhalations. I swung the light to port and was in time to see one, three, then a dozen broad black backs smoothly break the oily surface, blow, then slip away into the depths again.

I was seeing a school of potheads who had made their way into the sewage-laden waters of the inner harbor. They must have had a pressing reason, for no free-swimming animal in its right mind would have entered that cesspool willingly. The skipper of a local dragger later told me he had met a small group of killer whales close to the harbor channel on the day the potheads entered. Killer whales have been given a ferocious reputation by men, one not at all deserved; but it is true that they will occasionally make a meal of a pothead calf, and the potheads in St. Pierre harbor were accompanied by several calves.

When I went to bed, the whales were still circling leisurely. I slept late, to be awakened by the snarl of outboard engines, by excited shouting, and by the sound of feet pounding on my deck. When I thrust my head out of the hatch, I found what appeared to be about half the male population of St. Pierre, accompanied by a good many women and children, closely clustered along the waterfront.

There was a slight fog lying over the harbor. In and out of it wove two overpowered launches, roaring along at full throttle. In the bow of one stood a young man wielding a homemade lance, which he had made by lashing a hunting knife to the end of an oar. In the second boat was another young man, balancing a rifle across his knees. Both boats were in furious pursuit of the potheads, which numbered some fifteen adults and six or seven calves.

The whales were very frightened. The moment one of them surfaced, the boats tore down upon it, while gunners on the shore poured out a fusillade of shots. The big animals had no time to ventilate their lungs properly but were forced to submerge after snatching a single breath. The calves, choking for oxygen, were often slow in diving. Time after time the harpooner got close enough to ram his hunting knife into the back of one of them, so that long streamers of crimson began to appear on

---

1. **Burgeo:** a coastal village in southwest Newfoundland.
2. **Newfoundland:** (noo' fənd land): an island of Canada, located off the east coast.

the filthy surface of the harbor. It was obvious that neither the gunfire—mostly from .22 caliber rifles—nor the lance were capable of killing the whales outright; but it did not appear that killing them was the object. In truth, what I was watching was a sporting event.

I was appalled[3] and infuriated, but there seemed to be nothing I could do to end this exhibition of wanton[4] bloodlust. A fisherman friend of mine, Theophille Detcheverey, came aboard, and I poured out my distress to him. He shrugged.

"That one in the big speedboat, he is the son of the biggest merchant here. The other, with the spear, he is from France. He came here two years ago to start a raft voyage across the Atlantic. But he don't get out of the bars until today, I think. They are pigs, eh? But we are not all pigs. You see, there is no fisherman helping them with their dirty work."

This was true enough, if of small comfort to the whales. The fishermen of St. Pierre had left for the cod grounds at dawn. When they returned in their laden dories late in the afternoon, the excitement in the harbor had reached a crescendo. All the fast pleasure craft available had joined in the game. The onlookers crowding around the harbor became so densely packed it was hard to push one's way through. I had chased scores of them off my decks where they sought a better vantage point, and they had responded to my anger with derision.[5] For ten hours, relays of boats had chased the whales. Clusters of men with rifles stood at the pierhead at the harbor entrance, and every time the potheads tried to escape in that direction, they were met with a barrage of bullets which now included heavy-caliber slugs. Unable to run that gauntlet, the whales were forced to give up their attempts to escape in the only direction open to them.

Toward evening the whales, most of them now bleeding profusely, had become so exhausted they began to crowd up into the dangerous shoal[6] water at the head of the harbor where the boats could not follow. Here they lay, gasping and rolling, until they had recovered enough strength to return to deeper water. Many times they swam directly under my boat, and they were beautiful . . . superb masters of the seas, now at the mercy of the bifurcated killer of the land.[7]

At dusk the sportsmen called it a day and went home to dinner. The audience departed. The fog rolled in thickly and silence returned. Again I sat on deck, and again the strange, sibilant[8] breathing of the whales kept me company. I could not go to my berth, knowing what must await them with the dawn. Finally I untied my little dinghy and rowed out into the darkness of the fog shroud. I had a vague hope that I might be able to drive the herd out of the harbor before daylight brought a renewal of their ordeal.

It was an uncanny experience, and a nerve-wracking one, to row my little cockleshell silently through that dense and dripping fog, not knowing where the whales might be. The size of them—the largest must have been nearly twenty feet long—and their mysterious and unseen presence intimidated me. I felt extraordinarily vulnerable, detached from my own world, adrift on the lip of a world that was utterly alien. I thought, as a man would think, that if there was the capacity of vengeance in these beasts, surely I would experience it.

---

3. **appalled** (ə pôld′): filled with horror or dismay.

4. **wanton** (wän′ tən): without sense or mercy.

5. **derision** (di rizh′ ən): contempt, ridicule.

6. **shoal** (shōl): a shallow place in a river or sea.

7. **bifurcated** (bī′ fər kāt′ id) **killer of the land:** humankind. *Bifurcated* means "having two branches" or "forked."

8. **sibilant** (sib′ əl ənt): having or making a hissing sound.

Then, with heart-stopping suddenness, the entire pod surfaced all around me. A calf blew directly under one upraised oar, and my little boat rocked lightly in its wash. It should have been a terrifying moment, but it was not. Inexplicably, I was no longer afraid. I began talking to the beasts in a quiet way, warning them that they must leave. They stayed at or near the surface, swimming very slowly—perhaps still exhausted—and I had no difficulty staying with them. Time after time they surfaced all around me, and although any one of them, even the smallest calf, could have easily overturned the dinghy, they avoided touching it. I began to experience an indescribable sense of empathy[9] with them . . . and a mounting frustration. How could I help them to escape from what the morrow held?

We slowly circled the harbor—this strange flotilla of man and whales—but they would not go near the harbor mouth, either because they knew the killer whales were still in the vicinity or because of the vicious barrage of bullets with which men had greeted their every attempt to escape during the daylight hours.

Eventually I decided to try desperate measures. At the closest point to the harbor entrance to which they would go, I suddenly began howling at them and wildly flailing my oars against the water. Instantly they sounded, diving deep and long. I heard them blow once more at the far side of the harbor, but they never came close to me again. I had done the wrong thing—the human thing—and my action had brought an end to their acceptance of me.

The whales were still in the harbor when dawn broke. During the long evening in the bars, the ingenious[10] sportsmen of St. Pierre had set the stage for a massacre.

Early in the morning, just as the tide was beginning to ebb, half a dozen boats came out and formed a line abreast at the harbor mouth.

Slowly, they began to sweep the harbor, driving the herd closer and closer to the shoals. When the whales sounded and doubled back, they were again met with rifle fire from the breakwater as on the day before. One of the largest beasts seemed to be leading these attempts to escape, with the rest following close in its wake. It looked like a stalemate until three small whales became momentarily separated from the pod as it came under the fusillade from the breakwater. They gave way to panic. Fleeing at full speed on the surface, and close-harried by a fast speedboat, they torpedoed across the harbor and into the shoals where the tide was dropping fast. Within minutes they were hopelessly aground.

Howling like the veriest banshees, men and boys armed with axes and carving knives leaped into the knee-deep shallows. Blood began to swirl thickly about them. The apparent leader of the pod, responding to what impulse I shall never know, charged toward the three stranded and mutilated whales. There was a wild melee of running, falling, yelling people; then the big whale stranded too. The rest of the herd, following close behind, were soon ashore as well. Only one calf remained afloat. It swam aimlessly back and forth just beyond the fatal shoals and for a few minutes was ignored as the boats crowded in upon the herd and men leapt overboard, jostling one another in their lust to have a hand in the slaughter. Blood from one impaled whale spouted high over their heads—a red and drenching rain. Men flung up their ensanguined[11] faces, wiped the blood away, and

---

9. **empathy** (em′ pə thē): the ability to share in another's emotions, thoughts, or feeling.

10. **ingenious** (in jēn′ yəs): clever, resourceful, inventive.

11. **ensanguined** (en saŋ′ gwind): stained with blood; bloody.

laughed and shouted in the delirium[12] of dealing death.

Finally someone noticed the calf. Arms, red and savage, pointed urgently. A man leapt into his speedboat. The engine roared. He circled once at top speed then bore straight at the calf, which was in such shoal water it could not sound. The boat almost ran up on its back. The calf swerved frantically, beat its flukes wildly, and was aground.

The slashing and the hacking on that bloody foreshore continued long after all the whales had bled to death. A crowd of four or five hundred people drank in the spectacle with eager appetite. It was a great fiesta in St. Pierre. Throughout the remainder of the day there was a crowd standing and staring at the monstrous corpses. I particularly remember a small boy, who could not have been more than eight years of age, straddling a dead calf and repeatedly striking into its flesh with a pocket knife, while his father stood by and encouraged him.

Nor were the "townies" of St. Pierre the only ones to enjoy the spectacle. Many American and Canadian tourists had witnessed the show and now were busy taking pictures of one another posing beside the dead behemoths. Something to show the folks back home.

It was a grand exhibition . . . but the aftermath was not so grand. Those many tons of putrefying flesh could not be left lying where they were. So, on the following day, several big trucks appeared at the shore where lay the carcasses of twenty-three pothead whales. One by one the whales were hauled up by a mobile derrick and either loaded aboard the trucks or, if they were too big, chained behind. Then the trucks carried and dragged the bodies across the island to a cliff, where, one by one, they were rolled over the steep slopes . . . and returned to the freedom of the seas.

---

12. **delirium** (di lir′ ē əm): uncontrollably wild excitement.

## A PERSONAL RESPONSE

*sharing impressions*

**1.** What words describe your feelings as you read about the attack on the whales? Record these words in your journal.

*constructing interpretations*

**2.** What do you think motivates the people who kill the whales?

**3.** Compare the qualities exhibited by humans and whales in this essay.
### Think about
- how both the sports enthusiasts and Mowat treat the whales
- how the whales behave in their school compared to the way humans behave in a crowd
- the father and eight-year-old son compared to the whales and their calves

**4.** Do you share Mowat's response to the killing of the whales? Why or why not?

## A CREATIVE RESPONSE

**5.** If Mowat had used the same impassioned language to describe a group of rats that were trapped and killed, how would the impact of the essay be different?

## A CRITICAL RESPONSE

**6.** How effective is Mowat's emotional language in persuading you to share his opinion about the killing of animals? Go back through the essay and find examples of emotional language that influenced your opinion.

**7.** In the late 1980's, worldwide media attention focused on a joint effort by the United States and the Soviet Union to save three whales trapped by ice floes in Alaska. Do you think that this incident or the one described in the essay is more typical of the human response to endangered species? Give reasons for your answer.

# Analyzing the Writer's Craft

## MOOD

Reread the passage in which Mowat rows his dinghy among the whales on the night after the first attack. What feelings do you get from the description of that experience?

**Building a Literary Vocabulary.** Mood is the feeling, or atmosphere, that the writer creates for the reader. Descriptive words, setting, and figurative language contribute to the mood of a work, as do the sound and rhythm of the language used. The passage in which Mowat rows his dinghy among the whales contains several subtle, shifting moods. His description of rowing through fog while being uncertain of the location of the whales creates an eerie mood that builds in intensity until the moment of "heart-stopping suddenness" when the whales surface around his dinghy. The mood then shifts to one of calm as Mowat recounts how the whales unexpectedly accept him. Finally, Mowat relates his desperate

attempt to drive the whales from the harbor, an action that terrifies them and causes them to reject him. His sadness, expressed in the words, "I had done the wrong thing—the human thing," helps create a mood of regret for the lost bond with the whales that might have enabled him to help them.

**Application: Identifying Mood.** In groups of four, go back through the selection and find at least three other passages that have moods you can identify. Once you have named the moods, decide what colors would best represent those moods. For the example already given, dark gray could represent eeriness, light blue could show calm, and violet could stand for regret. As a group decide on a way to use color in a class presentation about mood. For example, one group member could read the passages your group chose while the other group members could unfurl banners of the appropriate colors.

# Connecting Reading and Writing

**1.** Imagine that you were the eight-year-old boy who stabbed the dead calf and that you are now a teenager reading Mowat's essay in school. Write a **letter** to Mowat expressing your feelings about the killing of the whales and about his essay.

Option: Imagining you are the teenage boy, write an **eyewitness account** of the attack on the whales to be shared with your classmates, who have read Mowat's essay.

**2.** Research Greenpeace, the Nature Conservancy, the World Wildlife Fund, or some other organization that tries to protect animals throughout the world. List the goals and activities of the organization in an **advertisement** persuading your classmates to donate to the organization.

Option: Create a **pamphlet** that the organization might mail to the subscribers of a hunting magazine.

**3.** Even though Mowat failed to prevent the slaughter of the whales, he at least tried to help them after the first attack. What do you think could have been done to prevent the killing? Explain your plan in a **proposal** addressed to the mayor of St. Pierre.

Option: Write a **persuasive speech** to be delivered at the harbor on the day after the first attack.

**4.** Research endangered species. Create a **poster** with descriptions of the current status of endangered animals to help educate younger students.

Option: Create a **crossword puzzle** for which the answers are the names of endangered species. As a class, choose the best puzzle and submit it to a nature magazine.

# Primal Screen

## ELLEN GOODMAN

A biography of Goodman appears on page 640.

*Approaching the Essay*

Ellen Goodman is a journalist whose newspaper columns are published throughout the United States. She writes about issues that are central to the everyday lives of her readers. The title of this selection is a pun on *Primal Scream,* the title of a book describing a therapeutic treatment for people who find it difficult to face reality.

SOMEDAY, I WOULD like to see a television series about a family that sits around the set watching a series about a family that sits around the set.

It might not make the Nielsen top ten,[1] but it isn't such a strange idea. Especially when you think about what's going on now.

Night after night, inside the tube, warm and wiggly families spend their prime time "communicating" like crazy and "solving problems" together like mad. Meanwhile, outside the tube, real families sit and wait for a commercial break just to talk to each other.

About the only subject that never comes up before our glazed eyes is what the medium[2] does to our family life. But, I suppose we already know that.

According to a recent Gallup Poll, television comes out as a major heavy in our family lives. On the scale of problems, TV didn't rate as bad as inflation, but it ran neck and neck with unemployment.

According to a recent Roper Poll, it even causes fights. When people were asked what husbands and wives argued about, money was the champion. But television was a strong contender. Considering how much time we spend in front of the tube, that may not be such a shock.

To a certain extent, we blame the programs. In the Gallup Poll, for example, people worried most about the overemphasis on sex and violence. Surely half of those fights between husbands and wives must be about the more fundamental issue of turning it off.

Deep down below our poll-taking consciousness, we know that the worst aspect of our addiction isn't what's on TV, but how long the TV is on. We can't help but be aware of what happens when we spend more time facing the screen than facing each other.

In that same Gallup Poll, a large number of us said that the way to improve family life is by sharing—sharing family needs, recreational

---

1. **Nielsen top ten:** the ten most-watched television shows, as determined by the Nielsen rating service.
2. **medium** (mē′ dē əm): a means of communication, in this case television.

activities, and chores. But when you are watching, you aren't doing. The only experience you share is a <u>vicarious</u>[3] one.

I am absolutely convinced that the average wife feels tuned out by the twelfth consecutive weekend sports event because she is being tuned out. The average kid develops that distant, slack-jawed, hypnotic stare because he or she is hooked.

In the same way, the people who spend night after night in front of the tube should not worry about it. They've become an audience and not a family. Television simply presents us with one model of family life. Watching it makes us fit another model.

But the striking thing in all of this research about how we feel and behave is the role of choice. On the one hand, we have real anxiety about what TV is doing to us. On the other hand, we let it happen.

We choose to turn it on and each other off. We choose peace and quiet when we let the kids watch TV instead of running around the living room. We choose to "relax" in the semicomatose slump.

The average viewing time of the American child between six and sixteen years of age is twenty to twenty-four hours a week. A large percentage of parents place no restrictions on either the number of hours watched or the type of program viewed.

At the very least, we behave as if we were powerless to wrench each other away.

I grant you that there are a lot of things that touch on our families that are totally out of our individual control. We can't regulate foreign affairs. We can't set the price for oil. We have about as great a chance of controlling inflation as we do of capping Mount St. Helens.[4]

But a television set has a dial and a plug. And we have hands. It is absurd to let our feelings of helplessness in the world start creeping into our private lives.

Just once, we ought to create a private show about a real-life family that kicked the habit.

---

3. **vicarious** (vi ker′ ē əs): felt by one as if he or she were actually taking part in another's experience.
4. **Mount St. Helens:** volcano in Washington state that erupted in 1980.

# Reviewing Concepts

## AUTOBIOGRAPHY AND ESSAY: SOME COMMON CONCERNS

*making connections*

Much like fiction, nonfiction can address personal feelings and relationships as well as comment on society and moral values. The bar graph below shows the extent to which five subject areas are covered in the excerpt from *I Know Why the Caged Bird Sings.*

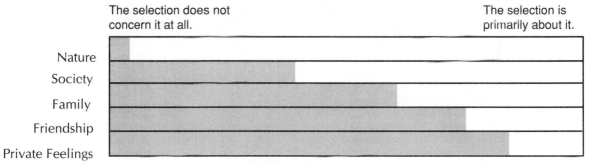

The selection does not concern it at all.

The selection is primarily about it.

Nature
Society
Family
Friendship
Private Feelings

Most readers would agree that the selection primarily concerns Angelou's private feelings as revealed in her relationship with her grandmother and her friendship with Mrs. Flowers. References to the segregation of Angelou's hometown provide the social commentary of the selection. Nature is mentioned hardly at all.

To get a sense of the similarities and differences between different kinds of nonfiction, create a bar graph for each of the selections in the unit. On each bar graph show how much of each of the five subject areas is revealed in the selection.

*describing connections*

Draw some conclusions from the information on your bar graphs. Write **notes** for an oral presentation in which you state some generalizations about the selections in this unit.

### Think about

- similarities between the autobiographical accounts and the essays
- selections that are most alike
- selections that stand out as different from the others, and why

*Flower and Water,* 1982, REIKA IWAMI.
Woodcut on paper. National Museum of Women in the Arts, Washington, D.C.; gift of Kappy Hendricks.

# Poetry

"I look at a poem as a performance. I look on the poet as being . . . just like an athlete."

ROBERT FROST

# Observations: Ideas in Poetry

**E**SSAYS OFTEN COMMUNICATE a writer's observations about life. For example, in "The Seeing See Little," Helen Keller states her observation that sighted people too often take their senses for granted, and then she uses examples to support her observation.

Poems can also express a writer's observations and ideas. Poets usually do not state their observations directly but convey them through the use of contrasts, comparisons, and descriptions. Often the observations in a poem are made by someone who is not necessarily the poet, just as the narrator in a short story is not necessarily the writer.

Each of the poems in this section conveys an observation about life. As you read, ask yourself who is speaking in the poem. How does that person feel about the situation he or she is describing? Are there any comparisons or contrasts in the poem? Answering these questions will help you to understand the ideas the poet is trying to express.

*Na K'in,* 1951, RAUL ANGUIANO. Artist's proof, collection of Tamara J. Whitzl and René H. Arceo.

# *Literary Vocabulary*

## INTRODUCED IN THIS SECTION

**Speaker.** The speaker in a poem is the voice that talks to the reader, similar to the narrator in fiction. In the first poem of this section, "Sunset Colors," the speaker uses the pronoun I and takes part in the action of the poem. In the second poem in the section, "The Bean Eaters," the speaker makes no references at all to himself or herself.

**Tone.** Tone is the attitude a writer takes toward a subject. In the excerpt from *A Whale for the Killing,* Mowat's outrage over the slaughter of the whales is conveyed by the words he chooses to describe the event, such as "I was appalled and infuriated, but there seemed to be nothing I could do to end this exhibition of wanton bloodlust." In poetry, the speaker's comments often provide clues to the tone.

**Theme.** Theme is the central idea or message in a work of literature. Theme should not be confused with subject, or what the work is about. Rather, theme is a perception about life or humanity that a writer expresses about a subject. For example, the subject of "Primal Screen" is television; the theme is that Americans spend so much time watching television that they neglect their family life.

**Alliteration.** Alliteration is the repetition of consonant sounds at the beginnings of words. The tongue twister "Peter Piper picked a peck of pickled peppers" is an example of alliteration.

# Sunset Colors YOSHINO HIROSHI

# The Bean Eaters GWENDOLYN BROOKS

A biography of Brooks appears on page 637.

## Approaching the Poems

Because of declining birth rates and increasing life expectancies, the United States is becoming a society with more and more elderly citizens. Both of the following poems show elderly citizens in everyday situations. The first poem tells about a young girl's encounter with three elderly people on a train. The second portrays an elderly couple in their home.

## Connecting Writing and Reading

Consider what you know about elderly people. Then in your journal make a chart in which you compare yourself to elderly people in each of the following areas: activities, interests, attitudes, friends and acquaintances, and goals. As you read, compare your ideas about the elderly with those expressed in the poems.

*The Woman Who Lives in the Sun,* 1960, KENOJUAK.
West Baffin Eskimo Co-Operative, Ltd., Toronto, Canada.

# Sunset Colors

As usual the train was crowded.
The young were sitting
and the old were standing.
A girl who'd had her head down
5   stood up and gave her seat to an old man
who sat down quickly
and then got off at the next station
without thanking her.
The girl sat down again.
10   An old woman got pushed in front of her.
The girl had her head down.
But, standing up once more,
she offered her seat to the old woman.
Who got off at the next station
15   but did say thank you.
The girl sat down again.
Things always go in threes.
Another old man got pushed in front of her.
The poor girl kept her head down
20   and this time
she didn't stand up.
The next station came
and the one after that.
She kept gnawing on her lip
25   tensing her body.
I got off.
I wonder how far she was going,
sitting so stiffly, keeping her head down.
Soft-hearted people
30   always, anywhere,
feel the pain of others
like their own.

# Thinking About the Poem

## A PERSONAL RESPONSE

*sharing
impressions*

**1.** What are your impressions of the girl in this poem? Describe your impressions in your journal.

*constructing
interpretations*

**2.** How do the last four lines relate to the rest of the poem?

**3.** Why do you think the girl in the poem gives up her seat twice to old people but then keeps her seat the third time?

**4.** How do the descriptions of old people compare with what you know about old people?

**5.** Why do you think this poem is called "Sunset Colors"?
### Think about
- the phrase "sunset years," which refers to old age
- what the word *colors* may refer to

## A CREATIVE RESPONSE

**6.** How would the poem be different if the last four lines were not included?

## A CRITICAL RESPONSE

**7.** Some readers think that the crowded train with its old and young passengers represents life. Explain why you agree or disagree with this interpretation of the poem.
### Think about
- why the young are sitting and the old are standing
- why the old people are the ones who get off the train
- whether the girl's offering her seat makes a difference to the older people

**8.** What do you think is the speaker's attitude toward the people and situation described in this poem?
### Think about
- places in the poem where the speaker interprets the situation
- places where he or she draws conclusions about the girl

# The Bean Eaters

They eat beans mostly, this old yellow pair.
Dinner is a casual affair.
Plain chipware on a plain and creaking wood,
Tin flatware.

5    Two who are Mostly Good.
Two who have lived their day,
But keep on putting on their clothes
And putting things away.

And remembering...
10   Remembering, with twinklings and twinges,
As they lean over the beans in their rented back room
      that is full of beads and receipts and dolls and cloths,
      tobacco crumbs, vases and fringes.

# Thinking About the Poem

## A PERSONAL RESPONSE

*sharing impressions*

**1.** How do you feel about the old couple described in this poem?

**2.** How does the old couple seem to feel about their past life together?

*constructing interpretations*

**Think about**
- the phrase "twinklings and twinges" to describe the way they remember
- the list of details in the last two lines

**3.** What can you tell about the present life of the old couple from the details in the first two stanzas?

**4.** Compare what you find out about the old couple in this poem with what you wrote about elderly people on your prereading chart.

**5.** Do you think your feelings about the old couple in this poem would be different if the poet had not written the last stanza?

**6.** During a poetry reading, Gwendolyn Brooks explained that as she wrote "The Bean Eaters," she tried to keep in mind two people who looked like beans. Why might she have chosen beans for this particular mental image?

**Think about**
- beans as inexpensive but nutritious food
- what the old couple and a pair of beans might have in common

# *Analyzing the Writer's Craft*

## TONE AND THEME

How would you describe Gwendolyn Brooks's attitude toward the old couple in the poem?

**Building a Literary Vocabulary.** Tone is the attitude a writer, a poet in this case, takes toward a subject. Style and description help create tone. Brooks's attitude toward the old couple can be inferred by studying each stanza of the poem. Even though Brooks portrays a poverty-stricken old couple in shabby surroundings in the first stanza, she emphasizes two important things about them in the second stanza: first, they are "Mostly Good" people, and second, they show admirable persistence in continuing to live a neat and orderly life, "putting on their clothes/And putting things away."

In the last stanza, Brooks more openly reveals her attitude toward the old couple when she shows the pleasures they take ("twinklings and twinges") in their memories and the fullness of their life together. Despite the poverty of the old couple's surroundings, Brooks does not seem to feel sorry for them; her tone is respectful, even celebratory.

Brooks's tone is closely related to the theme of the poem. Theme is the central idea or message in a work of literature. Theme should not be confused with subject, or what the work is about. Rather, theme is a perception about life or humanity that a writer expresses about a subject.

**Application: Expressing Theme and Tone.** Now that you have examined Brooks's attitude toward the old couple, consider what she wants her readers to think and feel about them. Get together in a group of three and discuss the message that Brooks communicates through her portrait of the old couple. Then paraphrase the poem in one or two paragraphs. Include the same descriptions as Brooks's but add direct statements to make her message and tone more obvious. Then compare your paraphrase with the paraphrases of two other groups so that you may see the variety of ways theme and tone can be expressed directly.

# Lineage  MARGARET WALKER

# Women  ALICE WALKER

Biographies of Margaret Walker and Alice Walker appear on page 647.

## Approaching the Poems

Some people are proud of their lineage—the people they descended from—because of rich or famous ancestors. In these two poems, the speakers are proud of their ancestors for more personal reasons. Both of the poets, Margaret Walker and Alice Walker, have published books of poetry, but they are more famous for writing fiction. Alice Walker's novel *The Color Purple* won the Pulitzer Prize and was made into a popular movie.

## Connecting Writing and Reading

In your journal draw a family tree, filling in as many of your family members' names as you can. Use the chart below as a model.

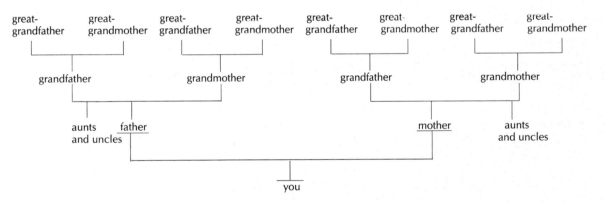

Once your family tree is complete, write a few sentences about the relative or ancestor you most admire. What similarities are there between you and this person? As you read, compare your feelings toward your relative or ancestor with the feelings expressed in the poems.

# Lineage

My grandmothers were strong.
They followed plows and bent to toil.
They moved through fields sowing seed.
They touched earth and grain grew.
5     They were full of sturdiness and singing.
My grandmothers were strong.

My grandmothers are full of memories
Smelling of soap and onions and wet clay
With veins rolling roughly over quick hands
10    They have many clean words to say.
My grandmothers were strong.
Why am I not as they?

## *Thinking About the Poem*

### A PERSONAL RESPONSE

*sharing impressions*

**1.** What feelings or thoughts about your ancestors does the poem awaken in you? Write about these in your journal.

*constructing interpretations*

**2.** What effect does the last line have on your interpretation of the poem?

**3.** What do you think the speaker in the poem means by the word *strong?*
   **Think about**
   • the activities of the grandmothers
   • the outstanding qualities of the grandmothers

**4.** Why do you think the speaker's grandmothers were so strong?

**5.** How do the speaker's feelings about her ancestors compare with your feelings about the relative or ancestor you most admire?

### A CREATIVE RESPONSE

**6.** How might the speaker feel if she knew nothing about her lineage?

**7.** Find several examples of alliteration and repetition in the poem and speculate about why Margaret Walker chose to use these techniques.

### *Think about*
- alliteration as the repetition of initial consonant sounds
- the ideas emphasized by the repeated initial sounds, words, and lines
- the effect of the alliterative phrases and repetitions

*Negress*, 1946, ELIZABETH CATLETT.

# Women

They were women then
My mama's generation
Husky of voice—Stout of
Step
5   With fists as well as
Hands
How they battered down
Doors
And ironed
10   Starched white
Shirts
How they led
Armies
Headragged Generals

15   Across mined
Fields
Booby-trapped
Ditches
To discover books
20   Desks
A place for us
How they knew what we
*Must* know
Without knowing a page
25   Of it
Themselves.

## Thinking About the Poem

### A PERSONAL RESPONSE

*sharing impressions*

**1.** Write a few words in your journal that tell how you picture the women described in the poem.

*constructing interpretations*

**2.** What do you think the speaker admires most about his or her mother's generation?

**3.** Why do you think the mothers are described as generals crossing "mined fields" and "booby-trapped ditches"?

**Think about**
- what the mothers were fighting for
- what obstacles they might have had to overcome

**4.** If this poem were about fathers instead of mothers, what kinds of battles do you think would be described?

**5.** Compare "Lineage" and "Women" as tributes to past generations of women.
   ***Think about***
   • what the women described in each poem have in common
   • how the speaker in each poem views the differences between his or her own generation and a past generation

# Connecting Reading and Writing

**1.** Imagine what one of the ancestors in "Lineage" or one of the mothers in "Women" would say to the speaker in the poem. Write her reply as a **poem** directed to the speaker.

Option: Write the ancestor's or the mother's reply as a **letter** to the speaker.

**2.** Choose the ancestor or relative whom you described in your journal or a historical character whom you wish were an ancestor. Create a **storyboard** for a short documentary film showing scenes that reveal the person's admirable qualities.

Option: Write a **character sketch** for a children's magazine showing that person as someone to imitate.

**3.** Research your lineage by interviewing family members. Take notes for an **oral history** to be written about your family.

Option: Compare yourself to your ancestors in an **autobiographical sketch** to be given to your future children.

**4.** Imagine that you are an editor who must cut one of the four poems: "Sunset Colors," "The Bean Eaters," "Lineage," or "Women." Make a chart listing pluses and minuses for each poem and then write your **recommendation** of which poem to cut.

Option: Write a **memo** to your boss explaining which poem you would cut and why.

# Ape BABETTE DEUTSCH

# Moco Limping DAVID NAVA MONREAL

Biographies of Deutsch and Monreal appear on pages 639 and 643.

## Approaching the Poems

These two poems present perceptive observations about animals. The first poem starts with an objective description of an ape in a zoo and shifts to a speculation about the ape's emotions. In the second poem, the speaker describes his crippled dog, comparing the animal to the type of dog he once wanted to own.

## Ape

His eyes are mournful, but the long lined palm
He thrusts between the bars expects the best.
His old man's face as innocent as calm,
The beggar puts compassion[1] to the test
5 And fails. He grips the bars; his pained state grows
To a brown study[2] framed in dusty fur.
He has a cold. He sneezes, cleans his nose,
Then gravely licks a flexile forefinger.

A pause; the bald mauve hand from which men shrink,
10 The fingers, strong to clutch, quick to explore,
Again extended, are again refused.
The eyes, poor sorrow's jewels, seldom wink,
But to his grinning public, as before,
Show endless patience, endlessly abused.

**1. compassion** (kəm pash' ən): sympathy, pity, or sorrow for the trouble of another.

**2. brown study:** a state of gloomy thoughtfulness, from the association of the color brown with gloominess.

# Moco Limping

My dog hobbles
with a stick
of a leg that
he drags behind
5     him as he moves.
And I was a man
that wanted a
beautiful, noble
animal as a pet.
10    I wanted him
to be strong and
capture all the
attention by
the savage grace
15    of his gait.
I wanted him to
be the first
dog howling in
the pack.
20    The leader,
the brutal hunter
that broke through
the woods with
thunder.
25    But, instead he's
this rickety

little canine
that leaves trails
in the dirt
30    with his club foot.
He's the stumbler
that trips while
chasing lethargic
bees and butterflies.
35    It hurts me to
see him so
abnormal,
so clumsy and
stupid.
40    My vain heart weeps
knowing he
is mine.
But then he turns
my way and
45    looks at me with
eyes that cry out
with life.
He jumps at me with
his feeble paws.
50    I feel his warm fur
and his imperfection is
     forgotten.

# Shape and Sound: Music and Movement in Poetry

THINK ABOUT THE differences between a jazz dancer and a ballet dancer. The rhythmic, inventive movements of a jazz dancer directly contrast with the patterned steps and poses of a classically trained ballet dancer. Both types of dancing are forms of creative expression. One is a free-form response to music; the other is defined by formal rules.

Like jazz dancers moving freely to music, some poets choose to express their thoughts and feelings in a loosely structured form. For example, Yoshino Hiroshi chose an informal structure for "Sunset Colors," one that allowed him more freedom of expression. Other poets are like ballet dancers in that they create within the bounds of a formal structure.

The music and movement of the poems in this section come through traditional verse forms. As you read these poems, notice how the poets have structured language to create certain shapes and sounds.

*Boy Playing Marimba,* 1974, CHRISTINE PRICE.
From *Singing Tales of Africa,* retold by Adjai Robinson, Scribner's, 1974.

# Literary Vocabulary

INTRODUCED IN THIS SECTION

**Rhyme.** Rhyme is the occurrence of a similar or identical sound at the ends of words, for example *explore* and *before*. Rhyme that occurs at the ends of lines of poetry is called **end rhyme.** End rhymes that are not exact but approximate are called **off rhymes,** for example *sun* and *gone.* A **rhyme scheme** is the pattern of end rhyme in a poem. The pattern is charted by assigning a letter of the alphabet, beginning with the letter *a*, to each line. Lines that rhyme are given the same letter. The first stanza of "Ape" has the following rhyme scheme: *ababcdcd.*

**Rhythm** and **Meter.** Rhythm refers to the pattern of stressed and unstressed syllables in a line of poetry. Meter is the repetition of a regular rhythmic unit in a line of poetry. The meter of a poem emphasizes the musical quality of the language. Although all poems have rhythm, not all of them have a regular meter. Of the poems in the previous section, only "Ape" has a regular meter.

Each unit of meter is known as a foot, with each foot having one stressed and one or two unstressed syllables. Examining a line of poetry to determine the number and kind of feet is called **scanning.** An unstressed syllable is marked by this sign ĕ ; a stressed syllable is indicated by this sign / . Straight lines divide the poetic line into feet. The first two lines of "Ape" can be scanned as follows:

Hĭs ey'es │ are mournful, but the long lined palm

He thrusts between the bars expects the best.

Many poets experiment with combinations of stressed and unstressed syllables to achieve desired effects in their poems.

**Ballad.** A ballad is a narrative poem that was originally meant to be sung. Ballads are usually about ordinary people who have unusual adventures, with a single tragic incident as the central focus. Traditional ballads are written in four-line stanzas with regular rhythm and rhyme. Both "Barbara Allen's Cruelty" and "The Shooting of John Dillinger" in this section are ballads.

REVIEWED IN THIS SECTION

**Alliteration**

# A Poison Tree — WILLIAM BLAKE

# Velvet Shoes — ELINOR WYLIE

Biographies of Blake and Wylie appear on pages 637 and 647.

## Approaching the Poems

The English poet William Blake at times disturbed readers of the early 1800's with the force and passion of his ideas. "A Poison Tree," like many of Blake's short poems, presents a complex, symbolic idea in deceptively simple rhyme and meter. In contrast, the modern American poet Elinor Wylie refrains from expressing ideas in "Velvet Shoes," preferring instead to let the images and the sound and rhythm of the language create a unique experience for the reader.

## Building Vocabulary

These essential words are defined alongside "A Poison Tree."

**wrath** (rath): I told my **wrath**, my **wrath** did end. (line 2)

**deceitful** (dē sēt′ fəl), **wiles** (wīlz):  And I sunned it with smiles,/
And with soft **deceitful wiles.** (lines 7-8)

## Connecting Writing and Reading

If you were a poet, what kinds of ideas and experiences would you choose to write about? Copy the following list of topics in your journal and place pluses beside items you might choose to write about and minuses beside items that you would not.

| | |
|---|---|
| love | joy |
| hate | anger |
| friendship | silence |
| conflict | music |

As you read each of these poems, notice which of the above ideas or experiences are expressed through traditional rhyme and meter.

# A Poison Tree

I was angry with my friend:
I told my wrath,[1] my wrath did end.
I was angry with my foe:
I told it not, my wrath did grow.

5    And I water'd it in fears,
Night and morning with my tears;
And I sunned it with smiles,
And with soft deceitful[2] wiles.[3]

And it grew both day and night,
10   Till it bore an apple bright;
And my foe beheld it shine,
And he knew that it was mine,

And into my garden stole
When the night had veil'd the pole:
15   In the morning glad I see
My foe outstretch'd beneath the tree.

**1.** **wrath** (rath): intense
anger; rage.

**2.** **deceitful** (dē sēt′ fəl):
untruthful; false.

**3.** **wiles** (wīlz): sly or clever
tricks used to fool or lure
someone

*Tree Trunk,* 1958, JACQUES HNIZDOVSKY.
© Stephanie Hnizdovsky.

# Thinking About the Poem

## A PERSONAL RESPONSE

*sharing impressions*

**1.** In your journal, write a few words describing the way you see the speaker in this poem.

*constructing interpretations*

**2.** Why do you think the speaker's foe dies?
**Think about**
- what is implied by the way the speaker "water'd" and "sunned" the anger
- what the "apple bright" might be
- why the foe stole into the garden

**3.** Why do you think the speaker expresses anger to a friend but not to a foe?

**4.** What would you say are the pros and cons of the two ways of dealing with anger depicted in the poem?

## A CREATIVE RESPONSE

**5.** If the speaker had decided to reveal his or her anger to the foe, how would the ideas in the poem have been different?

## A CRITICAL RESPONSE

**6.** Do you think the comparison of repressed anger to a poison tree is an effective way to convey the ideas in the poem? Use details of the comparison to support your answer.

**7.** "A Poison Tree" was originally titled "Christian Forbearance." In Blake's time, it was commonly taught that forbearance—or self-control and restraint —was a virtue. Based on your interpretation of the poem, why do you think Blake changed the title?

# Velvet Shoes

Let us walk in the white snow *a*
In a soundless space; *b*
With footsteps quiet and slow, *a*
At a tranquil pace, *b*
5  Under veils of white lace. *b*

I shall go shod in silk, *c*
And you in wool, *d*
White as a white cow's milk, *c*
More beautiful *d*
10  Than the breast of a gull. *d*

We shall walk through the still town *e*
In a windless peace; *f*
We shall step upon white down, *e*
Upon silver fleece, *f*
15  Upon softer than these. *f*

We shall walk in velvet shoes; *g*
Wherever we go *a*
Silence will fall like dews *g*
On white silence below. *a*
20  We shall walk in the snow. *a*

abab b c d c d d e f e f f g a g a a

# *T*hinking About the Poem

## A PERSONAL RESPONSE

*sharing
impressions*

**1.** What feelings does this poem leave you with? Describe those feelings in your journal.

*constructing
interpretations*

**2.** What kind of experience do you think the speaker wants the walk in the snow to be?

### Think about
- feelings you have as you read
- words that relate to sound
- words that relate to sights and sensations

**3.** Whom do you imagine the speaker is inviting to walk in the snow? Why?

## A CREATIVE RESPONSE

**4.** If the speaker were suggesting a walk in a meadow or forest, how would the feeling of the poem be different?

## A CRITICAL RESPONSE

**5.** Look at the many alliterative words in the poem and analyze their effect in creating an experience for you.

### Think about
- which initial consonant sounds are repeated in the poem
- which sounds predominate
- the feelings conveyed by those sounds

RHYME AND METER

Think about which words rhyme in "Velvet Shoes." Try tapping out the rhythm of the poem on your desk as you read.

**Building a Literary Vocabulary.** Rhyme is the occurrence of a similar or identical sound at the ends of words, for example *snow* and *slow* in the first stanza of "Velvet Shoes." Rhyme that occurs at the ends of lines of poetry is called end rhyme. End rhymes that are not exact but approximate are called off rhymes, for example *wool, beautiful,* and *gull* in the second stanza.

The pattern of end rhyme in a poem is called the rhyme scheme. The rhyme scheme is charted by assigning a letter of the alphabet to each line of the poem. The last word in the first line is assigned the letter *a*. End words that rhyme with this word are also assigned the letter *a*. The next new sound to appear at the end of a line is given the letter *b*. This process is followed throughout the poem, as in this example:

| | |
|---|---|
| Let us walk in the white snow | a |
| In a soundless space; | b |
| With footsteps quiet and slow, | a |
| At a tranquil pace, | b |
| Under veils of white lace. | b |
| | |
| I shall go shod in silk, | c |
| And you in wool, | d |
| White as a white cow's milk, | c |
| More beautiful | d |
| Than the breast of a gull. | d |

The rhyme scheme for these two stanzas of "Velvet Shoes" is *ababb cdcdd.*

Meter is the repetition of a regular rhythmic unit in a line of poetry. Each unit is known as a foot, with each foot having one accented and one or two unaccented syllables. Modern poets frequently use a combination of metrical feet in their poems. In the poem, for example, some of the lines contain three accented syllables, and some lines have only two. In all the lines there is an irregular number of unaccented syllables. The meter, therefore, is a combination of two- and three-foot lines. Both rhyme and meter in "Velvet Shoes" contribute to the musical quality of the language.

**Application: Identifying Rhyme and Meter.** In a group of four or five, reread "A Poison Tree" by William Blake and identify the regular pattern of rhyme and meter in the poem. Then, experiment with ways to set the poem to music: create a tune for the poem, set the words to an existing tune that has similar meter, or perform the poem as a rap song. Share your presentation with the class.

# Barbara Allen's Cruelty ANONYMOUS

## The Shooting of John Dillinger
### Outside the Biograph Theater, July 22, 1934 DAVID WAGONER

A biography of Wagoner appears on page 647.

## *Approaching the Ballads*

Tragic love affairs and criminal exploits have been the subjects of ballads for hundreds of years. "Barbara Allen's Cruelty" is an old Scottish ballad that tells the fate of two unhappy lovers. "The Shooting of John Dillinger" is a contemporary ballad about the death of one of the most famous criminals in United States history. During 1933 and 1934, Dillinger's daring bank robberies and prison escapes captured national headlines and placed Dillinger on the FBI's most-wanted list.

## *Building Vocabulary*

These essential words are defined alongside "Barbara Allen's Cruelty."
**slighted:** And **slighted** Barbara Allen? (line 24)
**shun** (shun)**:** And **shun** the fault I fell in: (line 38)

## *Connecting Writing and Reading*

In your journal, copy the following list of errors and crimes. Then, next to each item write what you think would be a just punishment.
- ignoring someone you love
- rejecting someone who loves you
- stealing from people's houses
- stealing from a bank
- shooting a bank robber
- shooting a police officer

As you read these ballads, decide whether the characters deserve their fates, that is, what happens to them. A good way to use the Guide for Interpretation is to read each ballad through once, then go back and use the side notes to study the ballad more carefully.

# Barbara Allen's Cruelty

In Scarlet town, where I was born,
    There was a fair maid dwellin',
Made every youth cry *Well-a-way!*
    Her name was Barbara Allen.

5  All in the merry month of May,
    When green buds they were swellin',
Young Jemmy Grove on his deathbed lay,
    For love of Barbara Allen.

He sent his man in to her then,
10    To the town where she was dwellin';
"O haste and come to my master dear,
    If your name be Barbara Allen."

So slowly, slowly rase she up,
    And slowly she came nigh him,
15  And when she drew the curtain by—
    "Young man, I think you're dyin'."

"O it's I am sick and very very sick,
    And it's all for Barbara Allen."—
"O the better for me ye'se never be,
20    Tho' your heart's blood were a-spillin'!"

"O dinna ye mind, young man," says she,
    "When the red wine ye were fillin',
That ye made the healths[1] go round and round,
    And <u>slighted</u>[2] Barbara Allen?"

25  He turn'd his face unto the wall,
    And death was with him dealin':
"Adieu, adieu, my dear friends all,
    And be kind to Barbara Allen!"

As she was walking o'er the fields,
30    She heard the dead-bell knellin';
And every jow[3] the dead-bell gave
    Cried "Woe to Barbara Allen."

*Guide for Interpretation*

◆ **Lines 5-8:** Notice the contrast between "the merry month of May," a time of rebirth, and Jemmy Grove's fatal love sickness.

◆ **Lines 17-20:** Jemmy Grove and Barbara Allen accuse each other in this dialogue. He says he's dying because of his love for her; she replies that it would have been better for her if she had never met him.

**1. healths:** toasts to good health.

**2. slighted:** treated with disrespect or indifference.

◆ **Lines 21-24:** At this time, Jimmy Grove's toast to Barbara Allen's health would be the same as bragging about being intimate with her. Thus, he slights her by jeopardizing her reputation.

**3. jow** (jou): a single stroke in the ringing or tolling of a bell.

"O mother, mother, make my bed,
 O make it saft and narrow:
35 My love has died for me today,
 I'll die for him tomorrow."

"Farewell," she said, "ye virgins all,
 And shun⁴ the fault I fell in:
Henceforth take warning by the fall
40 Of cruel Barbara Allen."

**4. shun** (shun): keep away from.

# *Thinking About the Ballad*

## A PERSONAL RESPONSE

*sharing impressions*

**1.** In your journal jot down your reaction to Barbara Allen as she is portrayed in this ballad.

*constructing interpretations*

**2.** What do you think Barbara Allen means by her "fault" and her "fall" in the last stanza?

**3.** Do you think Barbara Allen deserves to be called "cruel" in this poem? Explain why or why not.
 ***Think about***
  • the way all the young men respond to her
  • what she accuses Jemmy Grove of doing
  • why she refers to herself as "cruel" at the end

**4.** How would you explain the reasons for the failure of the lovers' relationship?

**Think about**

• how they treat each other
• why they each seem fated to die
• why Barbara Allen warns other young women at the end

## A CREATIVE RESPONSE

**5.** If Barbara Allen and Jemmy Grove lived today, how might their fates be different?

## A CRITICAL RESPONSE

**6.** Through the centuries this ballad has spread to several countries, including the United States, and has developed into more than ninety versions. What qualities do you think account for its long-term popularity?

**7.** In several versions of the poem, the deaths take place at Martinmas time, which is November 11, instead of in "the merry month of May." How might the change in season affect the overall feeling of the poem? Explain your answer.

# The Shooting of **John Dillinger**
## Outside the Biograph Theater,
## July 22, 1934

*Guide for Interpretation*

Chicago ran a fever of a hundred and one that groggy
    Sunday.
A reporter fried an egg on a sidewalk; the air looked shaky.
And a hundred thousand people were in the lake[1] like
    shirts in a laundry.
Why was Johnny lonely?

5   Not because two dozen solid citizens, heat-struck, had
    keeled over backward.
Not because those lawful souls had fallen out of their
    sockets and melted.
But because the sun went down like a lump in a furnace or
    a bull in the Stockyards.
Where was Johnny headed?
Under the Biograph Theater sign that said, "Our Air Is
    Refrigerated."

10  Past seventeen FBI men and four policemen who stood in
    doorways and sweated.
Johnny sat down in a cold seat to watch Clark Gable get
    electrocuted.[2]
Had Johnny been mistreated?
Yes, but Gable told the D.A.[3] he'd rather fry than be shut
    up forever.
Two women sat by Johnny. One looked sweet, one looked
    like J. Edgar Hoover.[4]

15  Polly Hamilton made him feel hot, but Anna Sage made
    him shiver.
Was Johnny a good lover?
Yes, but he passed out his share of squeezes and pokes like
    a jittery masher
While Agent Purvis sneaked up and down the aisle like an
    extra usher,
Trying to make sure they wouldn't slip out till the show
    was over.

20  Was Johnny a fourflusher?[5]
No, not if he knew the game. He got it up or got it back.
But he liked to take snapshots of policemen with his own
    Kodak,
And once in a while he liked to take them with an
    automatic.[6]

**1. lake:** Chicago borders Lake Michigan, a cool place to go on a hot day.

**Lines 1-15:** Notice the references to death and killing and to heat and cold in these opening lines.

**2. Clark . . . electrocuted:** a reference to the movie *Manhattan Melodrama,* in which Clark Gable plays a gangster who is executed.

**3. D.A.:** District Attorney, one who prosecutes accused criminals.

**4. J. Edgar Hoover:** director of the Federal Bureau of Investigation from 1924 to 1972.

**5. fourflusher:** a bluffer; one who pretends to be something in order to deceive.

**6. automatic:** a reference to a submachine gun.

Why was Johnny frantic?
25 Because he couldn't take a walk or sit down in a movie
Without being afraid he'd run smack into somebody
Who'd point at his rearranged face and holler, "Johnny!"
Was Johnny ugly?
Yes, because Dr. Wilhelm Loeser had given him a new
profile
30 With a baggy jawline and squint eyes and an erased dimple,
With kangaroo-tendon cheekbones and a gigolo's mustache
that should've been illegal.
Did Johnny love a girl?
Yes, a good-looking, hard-headed Indian named Billie
Frechette.
He wanted to marry her and lie down and try to get over it,
35 But she was locked in jail for giving him first-aid and
comfort.
Did Johnny feel hurt?
He felt like breaking a bank or jumping over a railing
Into some panicky teller's cage to shout, "Reach for the
ceiling!"
Or like kicking some vice president in the bum checks and
smiling.
40 What was he really doing?
Going up the aisle with the crowd and into the lobby
With Polly saying, "Would *you* do what Clark done?" And
Johnny saying, "Maybe."
And Anna saying, "If he'd been smart, he'd of acted like
Bing Crosby."
Did Johnny look flashy?
45 Yes, his white-on-white shirt and tie were luminous.
His trousers were creased like knives to the tops of his
shoes,
And his yellow straw hat came down to his dark glasses.
Was Johnny suspicious?
Yes, and when Agent Purvis signalled with a trembling
cigar,
50 Johnny ducked left and ran out of the theater,
And innocent Polly and squealing Anna were left nowhere.
Was Johnny a fast runner?
No, but he crouched and scurried past a friendly liquor
store
Under the coupled arms of double-daters, under awnings,
under stars,
55 To the curb at the mouth of an alley. He hunched there.
Was Johnny a thinker?

**Lines 24-27:** John Dillinger became quite a celebrity as a bank robber and was recognized widely before having plastic surgery.

**Lines 29-47:** Think about the portrait of Dillinger that these details about his life create for you.

No, but he was thinking more or less of Billie Frechette
Who was lost in prison for longer than he could possibly
    wait,
And then it was suddenly too hard to think around a
    bullet.
60  Did anyone shoot straight?
Yes, but Mrs. Etta Natalsky fell out from under her picture
    hat.
Theresa Paulus sprawled on the sidewalk, clutching her
    left foot.
And both of them groaned loud and long under the
    streetlight.
Did Johnny like that?
65  No, but he lay down with those strange women, his face in
    the alley,
One shoe off, cinders in his mouth, his eyelids heavy.
When they shouted questions at him, he talked back to
    nobody.
Did Johnny lie easy?
Yes, holding his gun and holding his breath as a last trick,
70  He waited, but when the Agents came close, his breath
    wouldn't work.
Clark Gable walked his last mile; Johnny ran half a block.
Did he run out of luck?
Yes, before he was cool, they had him spread out on
    dished-in marble
In the Cook County Morgue, surrounded by babbling
    people
75  With a crime reporter presiding over the head of the table.
Did Johnny have a soul?
Yes, and it was climbing his slippery wind-pipe like a
    trapped burglar.
It was beating the inside of his ribcage, hollering, "Let me
    out of here!"
Maybe it got out, and maybe it just stayed there.
80  Was Johnny a money-maker?
Yes, and thousands paid 25¢ to see him, mostly women,
And one said, "I wouldn't have come, except he's a moral
    lesson,"
And another, "I'm disappointed. He feels like a dead man."
Did Johnny have a brain?
85  Yes, and it always worked best through the worst of
    dangers,
Through flat-footed hammerlocks,[7] through guarded doors,
    around corners,

**Line 71:** Consider why the speaker makes this connection between Dillinger's last moments and the movie he had just seen.

**Line 81:** Notice the many references to Dillinger's celebrity throughout the rest of the poem.

**7. hammerlock:** a wrestling hold.

But it got taken out in the morgue and sold to some
    doctors.
Could Johnny take orders?
No, but he stayed in the wicker basket carried by six men
90   Through the bulging crowd to the hearse and let himself
    be locked in,
And he stayed put as it went driving south in a driving
    rain.
And he didn't get stolen?
No, not even after his old hard-nosed dad refused to sell
The quick-drawing corpse for $10,000 to somebody in a
    carnival.
95   He figured he'd let *Johnny* decide how to get to Hell.
Did anyone wish him well?
Yes, half of Indiana[8] camped in the family pasture,
And the minister said, "With luck, he could have been a
    minister."
And up the sleeve of his oversized gray suit, Johnny
    twitched a finger.
100  Does anyone remember?
Everyone still alive. And some dead ones. It was a new
    kind of holiday
With hot and cold drinks and hot and cold tears. They
    planted him in a cemetery
With three unknown vice presidents, Benjamin Harrison[9],
    and James Whitcomb Riley,[10]
Who never held up anybody.

**8. Indiana:** Dillinger was originally from Indiana.

◆ **Line 102:** Notice how heat and cold are referred to again at the end of the poem.

**9. Benjamin Harrison:** the twenty-third President of the United States.

**10. James Whitcomb Riley:** an American poet.

# Thinking About the Ballad

## A PERSONAL RESPONSE

*sharing impressions*

**1.** How do you feel about what happens to John Dillinger? In your journal write words and phrases that describe your feelings.

*constructing interpretations*

**2.** Why do you think the speaker links John Dillinger with Clark Gable, Benjamin Harrison, and James Whitcomb Riley?

**3.** What do you think is the speaker's attitude toward Dillinger's celebrity status?
### Think about
- why the speaker speculates about Dillinger's soul
- ways that Dillinger is considered a "money-maker"
- why the speaker includes the fact that doctors wanted Dillinger's brain
- why Dillinger's burial is called "a new kind of holiday"

**4.** What picture of Dillinger do you form from this poem?
### Think about
- his physical appearance
- his relationships with women
- his attitude toward criminal activity
- the way he dies

**5.** Do you think Dillinger deserves his fate? Why or why not?

## A CREATIVE RESPONSE

**6.** If Dillinger had started a shootout with the FBI instead of running away, how might this poem have been different?

## A CRITICAL RESPONSE

**7.** Anna Sage betrayed Dillinger to the FBI. She told agents she would accompany Dillinger to the Biograph and would wear a red dress. Find clues in the poem to Sage's role in Dillinger's capture.

**8.** Compare "Barbara Allen's Cruelty" and "The Shooting of John Dillinger" as ballads and explain which one you like better.
### Think about
- words that are repeated as refrains
- the use of rhyme or off-rhyme and meter
- the subject matter

# Connecting Reading and Writing

**1.** Imagine how today's news media would report the tragic fates of Barbara Allen and Jemmy Grove or the death of John Dillinger. Retell one of the stories in the way that an **article** in *People* magazine might present it.

Option: Report the news of the lovers' deaths or Dillinger's shooting as it might appear in a **gossip column.**

**2.** Research newspaper accounts of Dillinger's death and burial and compare that information with Wagoner's depiction in the poem. Make a **chart** comparing the information in the two accounts in terms of detail, depth, and drama to accompany an oral presentation of the information to the class.

Option: Write an **essay** for your teacher explaining which account you think gives a better version of Dillinger's fate and why.

**3.** Give a voice to a character other than the speaker in one of these four poems. Let the foe in "A Poison Tree" speak his mind, or respond as the one spoken to in "Velvet Shoes." Have Jemmy Grove confess his fault or John Dillinger talk back to David Wagoner. Rewrite the poem as a **parody** in which the character you have chosen is the speaker. Imagine that your parody will be printed next to the original poem in a ninth-grade literature textbook.

Option: Expand the role of another character by adding **lines** or another **stanza** to one of the poems: imagine that the longer version will be published with the original in a literary magazine.

**4.** Pretend that you have agreed to help a friend who, because of illness, missed the class discussion of these four poems. However, you also want to attend baseball practice on the same afternoon. Write your classmate a **summary** of what the poems are about, highlighting interesting observations you remember from other classmates.

Option: Write a **recommendation** to your teacher suggesting two of the poems your friend should study and why.

# Haiku

## MATSUO BASHŌ, YOSA BUSON, WALLACE STEVENS, JACK KEROUAC

Biographies of Bashō, Buson, Stevens, and Kerouac appear on pages 636, 637, 645, and 641.

## *Approaching the Poems*

Haiku is a highly expressive kind of Japanese poetry in which form is of primary importance. A traditional haiku contains a total of seventeen syllables arranged in three lines with a pattern of five, seven, and five syllables per line. However, translations of haiku often cannot conform to that pattern. Originally haiku described an experience in nature, but contemporary haiku deals with a variety of subjects. Haiku presents a single, clear picture designed to evoke a specific emotional response in the reader. Both Bashō and Buson are considered among the best of the Japanese haiku poets. Wallace Stevens and Jack Kerouac are two modern American writers who have experimented with the haiku form.

---

The temple bell stops—
   but the sound keeps coming
      out of the flowers.
            —Matsuo Bashō

The sea in springtime—
   all the warm day in breathing swells,
      in breathing swells.
            —Yosa Buson

Among twenty snowy mountains
The only moving thing
Was the eye of the blackbird.
            —Wallace Stevens

Nodding against
the walls, the flowers
sneeze.
            —Jack Kerouac

# Transformations: The Magic of Language

I N "A POISON TREE" the speaker describes his repressed anger by comparing it to a tree whose fruit fatally poisons his foe. Through that comparison Blake transforms something abstract and difficult to understand—a dangerous emotion— into a picture of something tangible and familiar.

Poets often use language not only to express ideas and emotions but also to make their subject matter more concrete and understandable to the reader. For example, in "Moco Limping" the speaker describes his dog's "stick of a leg," a comparison to help the reader picture a withered, weak leg. To convey the difficulty and intensity of life in the past, the speaker in "Women" describes her forebears as "Headragged Generals" fighting battles for their children.

As you read the poems that follow, think about the nature of the comparisons that are made—and watch for the transformations of ideas into images.

*Swan,* 1990,
PAUL HOFFMAN.
Collection of the artist, Memphis, Tennessee.

# Literary Vocabulary

**Figurative Language.** Figurative language is language that communicates ideas beyond the literal meanings of the words. The words in a figurative expression are not literally true; rather, they create impressions in the reader's mind. Three common forms of figurative language are simile, metaphor, and hyperbole. A **simile** is a comparison between two things that are actually unlike yet have something in common. A simile usually contains the word *like* or *as*. For example, in "Velvet Shoes" "White as a white cow's milk" is a simile comparing the whiteness of snow to the whiteness of milk. A **metaphor** also makes a comparison between two things that have something in common, but it either makes the comparison directly or implies it. The phrase "We shall step upon white down" in "Velvet Shoes" is a metaphor comparing snow to the soft white feathers of a young bird. In an **extended metaphor,** two things are compared at length and in various ways. William Blake's comparison of repressed anger to a poison tree is an extended metaphor. **Hyperbole** is a figure of speech in which the truth is exaggerated for emphasis or for a humorous effect. For example, in "Moco Limping" the speaker imagines the dog he desired as "the brutal hunter/that broke through/the woods with/thunder." The description of the imaginary dog is exaggerated to emphasize its strength.

**Symbol.** A symbol is a person, place, activity, or object that stands for something beyond itself. Cultural symbols are those whose meanings can be understood by people in the same culture. For example, white is a symbol of mourning in Asian cultures, whereas black symbolizes mourning in European cultures. Literary symbols take on meaning within the context of a literary work. For example, the fake necklace in "The Necklace" symbolizes the falseness of Madame Loisel's materialistic values.

**Theme**

# The Way It Is  GLORIA ODEN

# Mother to Son  LANGSTON HUGHES

Biographies of Oden and Hughes appear on pages 644 and 641.

## Approaching the Poems

One of the most important influences on a child growing up is the role model provided by a parent. The following poems are portraits of two mothers. The speaker in "The Way It Is" is a daughter talking about her mother, while the speaker in "Mother to Son" is a mother addressing her son.

## Building Vocabulary

These essential words are defined alongside "The Way It Is."

**commercial** (kə mur′ shəl): such **commercial** virtues (line 7)

**inaudible** (in ôd′ ə bəl): an **inaudible** allegiance (line 37)

**dominant** (däm′ ə nənt): these are the **dominant** measures of / my sense of beauty (lines 41 and 42)

## Connecting Writing and Reading

Choose one of your parents or another adult in your life whom you consider a role model. Think about how much you resemble that person—for example, in physical appearance and sense of humor. Then consider ways in which you would like to resemble that person more. Copy the following chart in your journal and fill it out with information about you and the person you resemble.

| Ways I resemble _____ | Ways I'd like to resemble _____ |
|------------------------------|-----------------------------------------|
|                              |                                         |

As you read, look for ways in which the two mothers in these poems provide role models for their children.

# The Way It Is

I have always known
that had I been blonde
blue-eyed
with skin fabled white as the unicorn's
5   with cheeks tinted and pearled
as May morning on the lips of a rose
such <u>commercial</u>[1] virtues
could never have led me to assume myself
anywhere near as beautiful as
10  my mother
whose willow fall of black hair
—now pirate silver—
I brushed as a child
(earning five cents)
15  when shaken free from the bun
as wrapped round and pinned
it billowed in a fine mist
from her proud shoulders
to her waist.

20  Brown as I am, she is browner.
Walnut
like the satin leaves of the oak
that fallen overwinter in woods
where night comes quickly
25  and whose wind-peaked piles
deepen the shadows of
such seizure.

Moreover, she is tall.
At her side standing
30  I feel I am still
the scarecrow child of
yesteryear:
owl-eyed
toothed, boned, and angled
35  opposite to her
soft southern presence—
an <u>inaudible</u>[2] allegiance
but sweetening her attendance
upon strangers and friends.

**1. commercial** (kə mʉr′ shəl):
designed to have wide
popular appeal.

**2. inaudible** (in ôd′ ə bəl):
that cannot be heard.

40    Dark hair, dark skin
      these are the <u>dominant</u>[3] measures of
      my sense of beauty
      which explains possibly
      why being a black girl
45    in a country of white strangers
      I am so pleased with myself.

**3. dominant** (däm′ ə nənt): having superior force or influence; ruling.

# Thinking About the Poem

## A PERSONAL RESPONSE

*sharing impressions*

**1.** Does this poem remind you of any emotions you have experienced? Write about those emotions in your journal.

*constructing interpretations*

**2.** Why do you think the speaker is pleased with herself?
   ***Think about***
   - the "commercial virtues" expressed in lines 1-6
   - the sense of beauty the speaker gets from her mother

**3.** In what ways does the speaker compare herself to her mother?
   ***Think about***
   - the physical aspects of each that the speaker chooses to highlight
   - how she feels standing by her mother's side in lines 28-36

**4.** Evaluate the mother in this poem as a model for her daughter.

## A CRITICAL RESPONSE

**5.** How do the similes in lines 4-6 and lines 21-23 add to the contrast between the two standards of beauty?
   ***Think about***
   - simile as a comparison, usually containing *like* or *as*
   - the objects that skin color is compared to
   - your associations with those objects

**6.** What message do you suppose this poet wants to communicate to society about role models?

# Mother to Son

Well, Son, I'll tell you
Life for me ain't been no crystal stair
It's had tacks in it,
And splinters,
5    And boards torn up,
And places with no carpets on the floor,
Bare.
But all the time
I'se been climbin' on
10    And reachin' landin's
And turnin' corners
And sometimes goin' on in the dark
Where there ain't been no light.
So, Boy, don't you turn back.
15    Don't you set down on the steps
'Cause you find it's kinder hard.
Don't you fall now—
For I'se still goin', Honey,
I'se still climbin'
20    And life for me ain't been
               no crystal stair.

*The Mother*, 1952, CHARLES WHITE.
Hirshhorn Museum and Sculpture Garden, Smithsonian Institution, Washington, D.C.
Gift of Joseph H. Hirshhorn, 1966.

# *Thinking About the Poem*

*sharing*
*impressions*

**1.** How do you feel about the speaker's observations about life? Describe your feelings in your journal.

*constructing*
*interpretations*

**2.** What do you think the speaker means by saying that her life has not been a "crystal stair"?

> **Think about**
> - the comparison of life to a stairway
> - the characteristics of crystal

**3.** What can you learn about the speaker from the way she refers to the stairway?

> **Think about**
> - what the descriptions in lines 3–7 reveal about her life
> - what the descriptions in lines 8–13 indicate about how she has dealt with life
> - what her advice to her son reveals about her character

**4.** What kind of role model do you think the speaker is for her son?

## A CRITICAL RESPONSE

**5.** Why do you think Hughes created this particular mother as the speaker in his poem?

> **Think about**
> - how your feelings about her affect your acceptance of her message
> - how her dialect relates to her message

**6.** Examine the portraits of the mothers in "The Way It Is" and "Mother to Son." Identify qualities of these mothers that you would like to imitate in your own life.

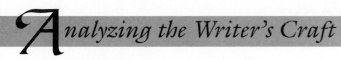

# *Analyzing the Writer's Craft*

## FIGURATIVE LANGUAGE: EXTENDED METAPHOR

What picture of the speaker's life can you imagine from the first seven lines of the poem?

**Building a Literary Vocabulary.** A metaphor makes a comparison between two things that have something in common. A metaphor either makes the comparison directly or implies it. An extended metaphor draws that comparison out and compares the two things in many ways. The extended metaphor in this poem reveals the obstacles and difficulties of the speaker's life. In the first seven lines, Langston Hughes includes realistic details—tacks, splinters, missing boards and carpets—that the speaker could have literally encountered while she was going up a flight of stairs to her apartment. In this way, Hughes builds on the idea of the speaker's struggle while at the same time realistically illustrating her life of poverty.

**Application: Interpreting Extended Metaphor.** In the remainder of the extended metaphor, the speaker explains how she has persevered through life and gives advice to her son. With a partner, make a chart similar to the one below and on it list an interpretation for each part of the extended metaphor. Two examples are provided for you. Then share the interpretations on your chart with another pair of students.

| Part of the metaphor | Interpretation |
|---|---|
| 1. "climbin' on" | keeping going, not giving up |
| 2. "reachin' landin's" | reaching parts of life that have been restful, peaceful, or easy |

Mother to Son 367

# Rhinoceros     ADRIEN STOUTENBURG

# The Sharks     DENISE LEVERTOV

Biographies of Stoutenburg and Levertov appear on pages 646 and 642.

## Approaching the Poems

Some readers expect poetry to be about springtime, flowers, or love, but these two poems were inspired by seemingly unromantic subjects. In "Rhinoceros" the speaker's thoughts turn from a contemplation of the rhino to a commentary on humankind. "The Sharks" explores the speaker's response to the arrival of sharks in a public swimming area.

## Building Vocabulary

This essential word is defined alongside "The Sharks."

**sinister** (sin′ is tər):  The sea becomes / **sinister,** are they everywhere? (lines 3 and 4)

## Connecting Writing and Reading

What do you know about rhinos and sharks? Copy the following chart in your journal and mark X's in the appropriate columns to show the characteristics of each animal.

| Characteristics | Rhinos | | | Sharks | | |
|---|---|---|---|---|---|---|
| | No | Somewhat | Very | No | Somewhat | Very |
| friendly | | | | | | |
| intelligent | | | | | | |
| graceful | | | | | | |
| powerful | | | | | | |
| dangerous | | | | | | |
| mysterious | | | | | | |

As you read the poems, notice how each speaker describes the characteristics of the animal.

# Rhinoceros

I have never seen that beast
with his snout bearing a pagoda[1]
and his eyes like little fragments
and his haunches carrying hills
5   with them.  His teeth, I have read,
are monuments, and his heart colder
than a key in winter
though he sweats from pores round as goblets
full of swamps.
10  The white hunters have killed him
a thousand times over.

I think of myself walking toward him
and preaching a love of creatures,
leaves in my palm, or a loaf of sugar,
15  and his great horn still,
the knees waiting,
and between us, like birds,
a twittering hope,
or merely the pause
20  between monster and monster.

**1. pagoda** (pə gō′ də): a
towerlike structure, usually
a temple, commonly found
in India, China, and Japan.

# *Thinking About the Poem*

## A PERSONAL RESPONSE

*sharing impressions*

**1.** What descriptions of the rhinoceros stand out in your mind? Write a few descriptive words or phrases in your journal.

*constructing interpretations*

**2.** Explain why you think the speaker uses the term *monster* at the end of the poem.

> ### Think about
> - who the monsters are
> - the characteristics that make them monsters

**3.** Do you share the speaker's hopes and fears about the relationship between humans and wild animals? Why or why not?

## A CREATIVE RESPONSE

**4.** How might this poem be different if it were about an actual encounter between the speaker and a rhinoceros?

## A CRITICAL RESPONSE

**5.** How does the figurative language in the first stanza transform the rhino's physical appearance and set up the imaginary meeting of the speaker and rhino in the second stanza?

> ### Think about
> - characteristics of the rhino that are emphasized by the similes and metaphors
> - the effect of hyperbole, or exaggeration, in the description
> - the speaker's hopes and fears in the second stanza

**6.** Because rhinos are hunted for their horns, the rhinoceros population has dwindled so rapidly that all species currently are listed as endangered. Captive-breeding programs offer the only hope for the survival of some species. How does this information affect your interpretation of the poem?

# The Sharks

Well, then, the last day the sharks appeared.
Dark fins appear, innocent
as if in fair warning. The sea becomes
sinister,[1] are they everywhere?
5  I tell you, they break six feet of water.[2]
Isn't it the same sea, and won't we
play in it any more?
I like it clear and not
too calm, enough waves
10  to fly in on. For the first time
I dared to swim out of my depth.
It was sundown when they came, the time
when a sheen of copper stills the sea,
not dark enough for moonlight, clear enough
15  to see them easily. Dark
the sharp lift of the fins.

**1. sinister** (sin′ is tər): threatening harm, evil, or misfortune.

**2. they . . . water:** the sharks can enter water as shallow as six feet, posing a danger to swimmers.

## *T*hinking About the Poem

### A PERSONAL RESPONSE

*sharing impressions*

**1.** Jot down a few words in your journal that describe your impressions of the sharks in the poem.

*constructing interpretations*

**2.** Who do you picture the speaker to be?

**3.** How does the presence of the sharks change the way the speaker perceives the sea?

> **Think about**
> * the description of the speaker's activities in lines 6–10
> * the words used to describe the sea when the sharks are sighted

**4.** How does the portrayal of sharks in this poem compare to your own notions about sharks? Review the characteristics you marked on your prereading chart.

## A CREATIVE RESPONSE

**5.** If the sharks had come at noon and not at sundown, how would the effect of the poem be different?

## A CRITICAL RESPONSE

**6.** What do you think the sharks represent in this poem?

### Think about

- the repetition of the word *dark*
- the description in lines 2-4
- the speaker's reaction to them
- the time of day when they arrive

**7.** Of the four poems in this section, which do you like best, and why? Give examples from the poem to illustrate why that poem is your preference.

# Connecting Reading and Writing

**1.** Think about what "Rhinoceros" and "The Sharks" would be like if they were written in a different genre. Rewrite "The Sharks" as it might appear as a **first-person narrative** in a teen magazine. You may add details and clarification to your narrative according to your interpretation of the poem; but be sure to be consistent with the idea and feeling of the poem.

Option: Argue the ideas expressed in "Rhinoceros" as a **letter to the editor** of an environmental magazine.

**2.** Imagine that the officers of the PTA have asked you to contribute to a special magazine they are creating to help parents understand teenagers.

Write an **extended metaphor** similar to the one in "Mother to Son," expressing your ideas about what life is like for a teenager.

Option: For the magazine, write a **comparison/ contrast essay** in which you explain how teenagers' lives differ from their parents' lives.

**3.** Summarize the use of hyperbole, simile, and metaphor in "The Way It Is," "Mother to Son," "Rhinoceros," and "The Sharks" on a **chart** that could be used by a study group reviewing for a test.

Option: Write a **literary evaluation** ranking the four poems according to how effective you think the figurative language is.

# Dandelions Deborah Austin

# Training Demetrio Herrera

## *Approaching the Poems*

Each of these poems focuses on an extreme in the natural world—the lowly weeds in "Dandelions" and the great sea in "Training." Both poems use extended metaphors in a similar way to emphasize the power of the subjects. In "Dandelions," the battle against these common weeds is compared to a battle against enemy troops. The metaphor is developed through the use of such words as *beleaguered, batteries, barrage, concussion,* and *battalions,* military terms concerning the troop movements and explosions of war. In "Training," the sea is compared to a boxer training for a big fight.

# Dandelions

under cover of night and rain
the troops took over.
waking to total war in beleaguered houses
over breakfast we faced the batteries
5    marshalled by wall and stone, deployed
with a master strategy no one had suspected
and now all
firing

pow

10  all day, all yesterday
and all today
the barrage continued
deafening sight.
reeling now, eyes ringing from noise, from walking
15  gingerly over the mined lawns
exploded at every second
rocked back by the starshellfire
concussion of gold on green
bringing battle-fatigue

20  pow by lionface firefur pow by
goldburst shellshock pow by
whoosh splat splinteryellow pow by
pow  by  pow
tomorrow smoke drifts up
25  from the wrecked battalions,
all the ammunition, firegold fury, gone.
smoke
drifts
thistle-blown
30  over the war-zone, only
here and there, in the shade by the
peartree
pow  in the crack by the
curbstone pow and back of the

35    ashcan, lonely
      guerrilla snipers, hoarding

      their fire shrewdly
      never

      pow

40    surrender

# Training

The sea—quick pugilist[1]—
uses for a pun
          ching
             ball
5    the restless little boats.

With the towel of the wind,
even rubs down the boxer's
sweaty body.

The buildings—
10   ringside fans—
crowd close to watch
the big training.

(The dock is whispering
with a smoking ship . . .)

15   And the surf's applause
makes the tower stand on tiptoe
With its watch in hand
to keep the time.
Stray kids,
20   the sea-birds
sneak in through the roof.

**1. pugilist** (py$\overline{oo}$′ ji ləst): a boxer.

# Sensations: Poetry as Experience

CAMERA MANUFACTURERS continually urge the public to capture the moment. Using language instead of film, poets also try to capture the moment. They do so by choosing words and phrases that convey the sights, sounds, and other sensations of an experience.

*Man with Raised Arms,* 1919, FRANS MASEREEL. From *Passionate Journey* by Frans Masereel. © Europa Verlag, Zurich, Switzerland.

Like photographs, many poems create visual images through details of size, shape, and color. Poems also appeal to the other senses. For example, the poem "Dandelions" humorously creates the sounds of a battle with the weeds in lines such as "whoosh splat splinteryellow pow by / pow by pow." Some images in this poem appeal to more than one sense, such as the lines "rocked back by the starshellfire / concussion of gold on green." These lines evoke the sights and sounds of a battle.

As you read the poems that follow, notice the ways in which the language appeals to your senses. See how the writing captures a moment and re-creates it for you.

# Literary Vocabulary

## INTRODUCED IN THIS SECTION

**Imagery.** Imagery refers to words and phrases that re-create sensory experiences for a reader. Images can appeal to any of the five senses: sight, hearing, smell, taste, and touch. The majority of images are visual, stimulating pictures in the reader's mind. In "The Sharks," for example, the phrase "the time when a sheen of copper stills the sea" is a strong visual image of a sunset reflected in water.

## REVIEWED IN THIS SECTION

**Simile    Metaphor    Rhyme**

# Jazz Fantasia CARL SANDBURG

# My Papa's Waltz THEODORE ROETHKE

Biographies of Sandburg and Roethke appear on page 645.

## Approaching the Poems

Carl Sandburg and Theodore Roethke could be said to represent opposite trends in American poetry. Interested in history and folklore, Sandburg celebrated common people and the vitality of American life. Roethke, on the other hand, was influenced by the insights and approaches of psychology. His poems are personal explorations of his own identity and search for meaning. Although the poems that follow illustrate some of the differences between Sandburg and Roethke, the poems are similar in the use of words and phrases that appeal to the senses. A fantasia, referred to in the title "Jazz Fantasia," is a musical composition that has no fixed form but depends largely on the composer's fancy.

## Connecting Writing and Reading

Imagine that you are attending a rock concert. Which of your senses, in addition to hearing, would be affected? In your journal, jot down words and phrases that describe the sensory experiences you are likely to have at a rock concert. Then, as you read the poems that follow, notice the words and phrases that re-create the sensory experiences associated with music and dancing.

# Jazz Fantasia

Drum on your drums, batter on your banjoes,
sob on the long cool winding saxophones.
Go to it, O jazzmen.

Sling your knuckles on the bottoms of the happy
5   tin pans, let your trombones ooze, and go husha-
husha-hush with the slippery sand-paper.

Moan like an autumn wind high in the lonesome treetops, moan soft
like you wanted somebody terrible, cry like a racing car slipping away
from a motorcycle cop, bang-bang! you jazzmen, bang altogether
10   drums, traps, banjoes, horns, tin cans—make two people fight on the
top of a stairway and scratch each other's eyes in a clinch tumbling
down the stairs.

Can the rough stuff . . . now a Mississippi steamboat pushes up the
night river with a hoo-hoo-hoo-oo . . . and the green lanterns calling
15   to the high soft stars . . . a red moon rides on the humps of the low
river hills . . . go to it, O jazzmen.

*Gut Bucket Trombonist,* TOMI UNGERER.
From *Esquire's World of Jazz,* Thos. Y. Crowell, 1975.

# *Thinking About the Poem*

*sharing
impressions*

**1.** What sights and sounds do you remember most from the poem? Record them in your journal.

*constructing
interpretations*

**2.** How does the jazz music affect the speaker?

**Think about**
- the emotions that the speaker imagines the music creating
- the scenes that the speaker visualizes
- the specific sounds made by the jazz instruments

**3.** How do the sensory experiences of the jazz musicians compare to those of the speaker in the poem?

## A CREATIVE RESPONSE

**4.** If this poem were about rock music, what verbs and descriptive words might be used?

## A CRITICAL RESPONSE

**5.** In "Jazz Fantasia" Sandburg captures the sounds and rhythms as well as the joyous spontaneity of improvised jazz. How is the poem itself also a fantasia in terms of its form? Find specific examples in the poem to support your answer.

**6.** How does the figurative language in the poem help create the sensory experiences? Use specific examples of similes and metaphors to support your answer.

# My Papa's Waltz

The whiskey on your breath
Could make a small boy dizzy;
But I held on like death:
Such waltzing was not easy.

5     We romped until the pans
Slid from the kitchen shelf;
My mother's countenance
Could not unfrown itself.

The hand that held my wrist
10     Was battered on one knuckle;
At every step I missed
My right ear scraped a buckle.

You beat time on my head
With a palm caked hard by dirt,
15     Then waltzed me off to bed
Still clinging to your shirt.

## *T*hinking About the Poem

### A PERSONAL RESPONSE

*sharing impressions*

**1.** Who are you left thinking about at the end of this poem? Write about that person in your journal.

*constructing interpretations*

**2.** How do you think the speaker as a young boy feels about being waltzed by his father?

**Think about**
- phrases that re-create the boy's sensory experiences
- phrases that describe the way he holds on to his father
- the title of the poem

**3.** Why, do you think, is the mother frowning in the poem?

## A CREATIVE RESPONSE

**4.** How might the mother and son in this poem respond if the father were reading a bedtime story to his son instead of waltzing?

## A CRITICAL RESPONSE

**5.** One of Roethke's collections of poetry is titled *The Lost Son.* In it, he explores his mixed feelings about his relationship with his strict father. How does this information about Roethke influence your interpretation of the poem?

# Connecting Reading and Writing

**1.** Using the mother's point of view, write a **description** of the waltz between father and son that might help one of your classmates understand "My Papa's Waltz."

Option: Create a **dialogue** between the mother and father discussing the incident after the son has been put to bed. Then get together with a partner to perform your dialogue for the class.

**2.** Get together with a partner and play a detective game with "My Papa's Waltz." On a sheet of paper, list the sensory details you think are clues to important things that are left unsaid about the incident. Then write down your guesses about what the clues indicate. Write a **detective's report** summarizing the conclusions you have made about the poem.

Option: Imagine that the poem has been published in a new anthology. Create a **book jacket** for the anthology, choosing a quotation from the poem and praising the sensory details.

**3.** Create a cluster diagram of words and phrases that describe how your favorite type of music affects you. Write a **poem,** modeled on "Jazz Fantasia," describing that type of music. Think about submitting your poem to a magazine about music.

Option: Write a **letter** to your favorite musician or musical group explaining why you enjoy their music.

**4.** Imagine that students in your class are taking turns explaining literary concepts. You have been assigned the task of explaining how sensory experiences can be re-created in poetry. Choose examples from "Jazz Fantasia" and "My Papa's Waltz" to use in notes for an **oral presentation** on this topic.

Option: Create a **chart** identifying images selected from the poems and the experiences those images describe to accompany a class lecture.

# Spring is like a perhaps hand E. E. CUMMINGS

# A Bird Came Down the Walk EMILY DICKINSON

Biographies of cummings and Dickinson appear on pages 638 and 639.

## *Approaching the Poems*

Emily Dickinson spent most of her life as a recluse, rarely venturing beyond her father's house and garden in Amherst, Massachusetts. In contrast, e.e. cummings volunteered as an ambulance driver during World War I, studied art in Paris, and gave public lectures criticizing modern society. Yet, despite their vast personality differences, Dickinson and cummings share the distinction of being two of the most experimental poets in American literature. Each of them consistently broke the rules of punctuation and capitalization—cummings went so far as to have his name legally changed to all lowercase letters. Each of the poets coined new words and used existing words in unexpected ways. Dickinson experimented with off-rhymes; cummings rearranged the usual order of words in sentences. The poems that follow illustrate how these two poets played with language, shaping it to fit their ideas.

## *Connecting Writing and Reading*

What would you emphasize if you had to describe spring? In your journal, list ten qualities that you associate with spring. Then, as you read the poems that follow, notice what qualities cummings emphasizes about spring and what Dickinson emphasizes about a bird. Use the Guide for Interpretation to help you understand the poems.

# Spring is like a perhaps hand

Spring is like a perhaps hand
(which comes carefully
out of Nowhere) arranging
a window, into which people look (while
5   people stare
arranging and changing placing
carefully there a strange
thing and a known thing here) and

changing everything carefully

10   spring is like a perhaps
Hand in a window
(carefully to
and fro moving New and
Old things, while
15   people stare carefully
moving a perhaps
fraction of flower here placing
an inch of air there) and

without breaking anything.

# *T*hinking About the Poem

## A PERSONAL RESPONSE

*sharing*
*impressions*

**1.** What words and phrases from the poem stand out in your mind? Jot these in your journal.

*constructing*
*interpretations*

**2.** How do you think the description of a hand in a window relates to the coming of spring?

> **Think about**
> * why the hand is called a "perhaps hand"
> * what kind of window it might be
> * what the hand is doing in lines 6-8 and in lines 16-18

**3.** Why, do you imagine, are the people in the poem staring?

**4.** Compare the items in your prereading list with the qualities of spring emphasized in this poem.

## A CREATIVE RESPONSE

**5.** If this poem were written with standard punctuation and capitalization, how would the effect be different?

## A CRITICAL RESPONSE

**6.** Evaluate whether the way cummings experiments with language helps or hinders the reader in understanding his ideas.

> **Think about**
> * unusual word order in the poem
> * use of parentheses
> * unusual capitalization

**7.** In what ways do you think that cummings's training as a painter influenced his writing of this poem? Go back through the poem and find details that support your opinion.

# A Bird Came Down the Walk

A Bird came down the Walk—
He did not know I saw—
He bit an Angleworm in halves
And ate the fellow, raw,

5   And then he drank a Dew
From a convenient Grass—
And then hopped sidewise to the Wall
To let a Beetle pass—

He glanced with rapid eyes
10  That hurried all around—
They looked like frightened Beads, I thought—
He stirred his Velvet Head

Like one in danger, Cautious,
I offered him a Crumb
15  And he unrolled his feathers
And rowed him softer home—

Than Oars divide the Ocean,
Too silver for a seam—
Or Butterflies, off Banks of Noon
20  Leap, plashless as they swim.

*Guide for Interpretation*

♦ **Lines 1-8:** In these two stanzas the speaker gives a literal description of the bird's actions.

♦ **Lines 9-11:** The speaker begins to make comparisons in this stanza and interprets the bird's feelings as "frightened."

♦ **Lines 15-18:** Instead of stating that the bird flew away, the speaker uses a metaphor. Think about how the motion of rowing is like a bird in flight. Also consider how the image of oars parting the ocean without making "a seam" describes a bird flying in the sky.

♦ **Lines 19-20:** The bird's flight is also compared to butterflies leaping off "Banks of Noon." A bank is the land rising at the edge of a river or stream. Speculate about the meaning of *plashless,* and try to visualize the fanciful image Dickinson creates in these two lines.

# Thinking About the Poem

## A PERSONAL RESPONSE

*sharing impressions*

**1.** What details do you remember most from the poem? Record them in your journal.

*constructing interpretations*

**2.** What do the last six lines convey to you about the bird's flight?

**3.** What qualities do you think the speaker wants to emphasize about the bird?

**4.** What do you think this encounter with the bird means to the speaker?
   ***Think about***
   - why the speaker goes from being a silent observer to offering the bird a crumb
   - why the speaker's descriptions of the bird change from literal observations to pure imagination

## A CREATIVE RESPONSE

**5.** If the speaker had not inserted his or her thoughts and actions, how would the poem be different?

## A CRITICAL RESPONSE

**6.** What do you think Dickinson might have wanted to accomplish with her use of dashes and unusual capitalization? Go back through the poem and choose specific examples to speculate about.

**7.** Which of the four poems—"Jazz Fantasia," "My Papa's Waltz," "Spring is like a perhaps hand," or "A Bird Came Down the Walk"—is the most vivid re-creation of an experience for you? Explain why and give examples from the poem as support.

# Analyzing the Writer's Craft

## IMAGERY

In line 12, the bird "stirred his Velvet Head." What does the word *velvet* make you think about or feel?

**Building a Literary Vocabulary.** Imagery refers to words and phrases that re-create sensory experiences for a reader. Images can appeal to any of the five senses—sight, hearing, smell, taste, and touch. For example, the image "Velvet Head" appeals to the senses of sight and touch. Because *velvet* has connotations of richness, beauty, and softness, the image helps the reader share the speaker's feelings of attraction to the bird.

**Application: Analyzing Images.** With a partner, go back through the four poems "Jazz Fantasia," "My Papa's Waltz," "Spring is like a perhaps hand," and "A Bird Came Down the Walk." Identify at least two images from each poem and create a diagram for each image showing the senses appealed to and the feelings evoked in you as a reader. Two images have already been diagrammed for you. When you have finished, share your diagrams with the class.

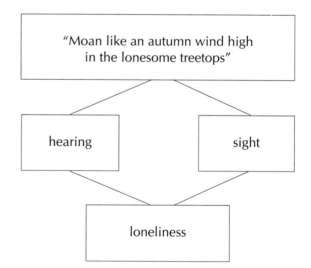

"A Bird Came Down the Walk"

"Velvet Head"

sight — touch

attraction

"Jazz Fantasia"

"Moan like an autumn wind high in the lonesome treetops"

hearing — sight

loneliness

# Ode to the Watermelon

PABLO NERUDA

Translated from the Spanish by Robert Bly

A biography of Neruda appears on page 643.

## *Approaching the Poem*

Close your eyes and imagine heat so overpowering that the air seems to shimmer. Thirst becomes an obsession. Now imagine how you would feel about something that has the power to rescue you from such torment, and you may understand why Pablo Neruda wrote a poem glorifying the watermelon. Born in Chile, Neruda is one of the most original poets to write in the Spanish language. He called this poem an ode, a kind of poem written, usually in a dignified style, to commemorate a person, event, or thing—in this case, a watermelon.

The tree of intense
summer,
hard,
is all blue sky,
5   yellow sun,
fatigue in drops,
a sword
above the highways,
a scorched shoe
10   in the cities:
the brightness and the world
weigh us down,
hit us
in the eyes
15   with clouds of dust,
with sudden golden blows,
they torture
our feet
with tiny thorns,

20 with hot stones,
and the mouth
suffers
more than all the toes:
the throat
25 becomes thirsty,
the teeth,
the lips, the tongue:
we want to drink
waterfalls,
30 the dark blue night,
the South Pole,
and then
the coolest of all
the planets crosses
35 the sky,
the round, magnificent,
star-filled watermelon.
It's a fruit from the thirst-tree.
It's the green whale of the summer.
40 The dry universe
all at once
given dark stars
by this firmament of coolness
lets the swelling
45 fruit
come down:
its hemispheres open
showing a flag
green, white, red,
50 that dissolves into
wild rivers, sugar,
delight!

Jewel box of water, <u>phlegmatic</u>[1]
queen
55 of the fruitshops,
warehouse
of <u>profundity</u>,[2] moon
on earth!
You are pure,
60 rubies fall apart

*Watermelon*, 1990, ZHOU PING.

1. **phlegmatic** (fleg mat′ ik):
calm and composed.

2. **profundity** (prō fun′ də tē):
depth, especially great depth.

in your abundance,
and we
want
to bite into you,
65    to bury our
face
in you, and
our hair, and
the soul!
70    When we're thirsty
we glimpse you
like
a mine or a mountain
of fantastic food,
75    but
among our longings and our teeth
you change
simply
into cool light
80    that slips in turn into
spring water
that touched us once
singing.
And that is why
85    you don't weigh us down
in the siesta hour[3]
that's like an oven,
you don't weigh us down,
you just
90    go by
and your heart, some cold ember,
turned itself into a single
drop of water.

**3. siesta hour** (sē es′ tə): a time period after lunch used for napping, especially in Latin America and southern Europe.

*Poems by* ROBERT FROST

# Fire and Ice

# Nothing Gold Can Stay

# Birches

A biography of Frost appears on page 640.

## *A*pproaching the Poems

Reading several poems by the same poet gives the reader an opportunity to observe the poet's development, to follow the treatment of a particular theme or idea, and to detect subtle variations in tone. The close readings of individual poems can lead to broader conclusions about the poet and his or her work.

The poems you are about to read are all by Robert Frost, considered one of the most important American poets of the twentieth century. Much of Frost's work reflects his New England heritage and the images and values of rural life. Though Frost's verse appears to be simple, almost rough and "unpoetic," the ideas conveyed are frequently complex. Frost himself once said that poetry is a way of "saying one thing and meaning another."

## *B*uilding Vocabulary

These essential words are defined alongside the first two poems.

**suffice** (sə fīs′): for destruction ice / Is also great / And would **suffice.** ("Fire and Ice," lines 7-9)

**hue** (hyo͞o): Nature's first green is gold, / Her hardest **hue** to hold. ("Nothing Gold Can Stay," lines 1-2)

**subsides** (səb sīdz′): Then leaf **subsides** to leaf. ("Nothing Gold Can Stay," line 5)

Think about parallels between the natural world and human life: for example, the struggle between a spider and a fly may suggest a struggle for survival in the human world. Look over the following list of common occurrences or events in nature.

- an ant struggling to carry a crumb
- a bear protecting her cubs
- two dogs fighting over territory
- a violent thunderstorm
- a blizzard of ice and snow
- a forest fire

Choose one occurrence from the list or think of one on your own. In your journal, jot down ideas about human life suggested by the natural events. As you read these poems, notice the parallels that Frost draws between human life and the natural world. Use the Guide for Interpretation to help you with a careful reading of the poems.

# Fire and Ice

Some say the world will end in fire,
Some say in ice.
From what I've tasted of desire
I hold with those who favor fire.
5  But if it had to perish twice,
I think I know enough of hate
To say that for destruction ice
Is also great
And would suffice.[1]

*Guide for Interpretation*

◆ **Lines 3-4:** Notice the connection Frost draws between human desire and natural fire. Think about how the two things are similar.

**1. suffice** (sə fīs′): be enough.

# Nothing Gold Can Stay

Nature's first green² is gold,
Her hardest <u>hue</u>³ to hold.
Her early leaf's a flower;
But only so an hour.
5    Then leaf <u>subsides</u>⁴ to leaf.
So Eden sank to grief,
So dawn goes down to day.
Nothing gold can stay.

*Guide for Interpretation*

◆ **Lines 1-4:** Here, Frost describes early spring, a brief time when the color yellow predominates.

**2. green:** a reference to growth.

**3. hue** (hyo͞o): a particular shade or tint of a given color.

**4. subsides** (səb sīdz′): sinks or falls; descends.

◆ **Line 6:** With this reference to the lost Garden of Eden, Frost draws a parallel between changes in nature and human loss.

## *T*hinking About the Poems

### A PERSONAL RESPONSE

*sharing impressions*

**1.** What feelings are you left with after reading these two poems? Jot some ideas in your journal.

*constructing interpretations*

**2.** Why do you think the speaker in the second poem concludes that "nothing gold can stay"?

**Think about**
- possible meanings of the word *gold*
- the kinds of changes described in the poem

**3.** Do you agree with the speaker in "Fire and Ice" about what will destroy the world? Why or why not?

**4.** What parallels can you find between the natural world and human life in these two poems?

***Think about***
- what fire and ice represent in the first poem
- how Eden relates to the natural changes in "Nothing Gold Can Stay"
- how the causes of destruction in "Fire and Ice" relate to the causes of loss in "Nothing Gold Can Stay"

## A CREATIVE RESPONSE

**5.** If Frost had not chosen to draw parallels between human life and the natural world, what other ways could he have used to say the same things?

## A CRITICAL RESPONSE

**6.** In another one of Frost's poems, the speaker says that "courage in the heart" is needed "To overcome the fear within the soul/And go ahead to any accomplishment." Do you think that the speakers in these two poems would agree with this attitude toward courage? Why or why not? Find details in the poems to support your opinion.

# Connecting Reading and Writing

**1.** Re-examine what "Fire and Ice" says about desire and hate. Consider how desire and hate are alike and different, and whether they are equally destructive. Compare and contrast the two emotions in an **essay** for your teacher.

Option: Write at least four **proverbs** for your classmates about the nature of desire and hate and the consequences of taking these emotions to an extreme.

**2.** Decide whether you agree with the speaker of "Nothing Gold Can Stay" that nothing in life is permanent. Write a **letter** to the speaker in which you express your opinion and support it with examples.

Option: Express the idea that nothing is permanent—or the idea that some things are—in three T-shirt **slogans** using metaphors or similes that appeal to contemporary teenagers.

# Birches

When I see birches bend to left and right
Across the lines of straighter darker trees,
I like to think some boy's been swinging them.
But swinging doesn't bend them down to stay

5    As ice-storms do. Often you must have seen them
Loaded with ice a sunny winter morning
After a rain. They click upon themselves
As the breeze rises, and turn many-colored
As the stir cracks and crazes their enamel.

10  Soon the sun's warmth makes them shed crystal shells
Shattering and avalanching on the snow-crust—
Such heaps of broken glass to sweep away
You'd think the inner dome of heaven had fallen.
They are dragged to the withered bracken[1] by the load,

15  And they seem not to break; though once they are bowed
So low for long, they never right themselves:
You may see their trunks arching in the woods
Years afterwards, trailing their leaves on the ground
Like girls on hands and knees that throw their hair

20  Before them over their heads to dry in the sun.
But I was going to say when Truth broke in
With all her matter-of-fact about the ice-storm
I should prefer to have some boy bend them
As he went out and in to fetch the cows—

25  Some boy too far from town to learn baseball,
Whose only play was what he found himself,
Summer or winter, and could play alone.
One by one he subdued his father's trees
By riding them down over and over again

30  Until he took the stiffness out of them,
And not one but hung limp, not one was left
For him to conquer. He learned all there was
To learn about not launching out too soon
And so not carrying the tree away

35  Clear to the ground. He always kept his poise
To the top branches, climbing carefully
With the same pains you use to fill a cup
Up to the brim, and even above the brim.
Then he flung outward, feet first, with a swish,

40  Kicking his way down through the air to the ground.

**Lines 4–5:** Notice the speaker's transition from imagining a boy swinging on birch trees to recalling the effect of ice storms on the trees.

**Lines 10–20:** Think about senses appealed to in this description of the trees after the ice storm.

**1. bracken:** (brak′ ′n): a growth of large, coarse ferns.

**Lines 21–24:** The speaker now returns to imagining a boy bending the trees as he swings. Notice how the speaker seems to feel about the intrusion of "Truth."

**Lines 32–35:** Consider possible meanings of the phrase "not launching out too soon."

So was I once myself a swinger of birches.
And so I dream of going back to be.
It's when I'm weary of considerations,
And life is too much like a pathless wood
45   Where your face burns and tickles with the cobwebs
Broken across it, and one eye is weeping
From a twig's having lashed across it open.
I'd like to get away from earth awhile
And then come back to it and begin over.
50   May no fate willfully misunderstand me
And half grant what I wish and snatch me away
Not to return. Earth's the right place for love:
I don't know where it's likely to go better.
I'd like to go by climbing a birch tree,
55   And climb black branches up a snow-white trunk
*Toward* heaven, till the tree could bear no more,
But dipped its top and set me down again.
That would be good both going and coming back.
One could do worse than be a swinger of birches.

◆ **Lines 41-42:** Here it becomes clear that the speaker is not just imagining a boy swinging on the trees but also recalling similar childhood joys.

◆ **Lines 43-47:** Think about the contrast between the speaker's description of a childhood pleasure and the comparison of human life to a "pathless wood." Note the images of physical pain.

◆ **Lines 52-53:** Speculate about what kind of love the speaker means here.

# Thinking About the Poem

## A PERSONAL RESPONSE

*sharing impressions*

**1.** What images from nature remain in your mind after reading this poem? Briefly describe them in your journal.

*constructing interpretations*

**2.** What do you think being a "swinger of birches" means to the speaker?
   ***Think about***
   - why going up to heaven and coming back to earth are both considered
   - why the speaker "dreams" of again becoming a swinger of birches in lines 42-47
   - why swinging on birches is important to the boy in lines 25-40

**3.** What kind of person do you imagine the speaker to be?

**4.** How do you think the statement "Earth's the right place for love: / I don't know where it's likely to go better" relates to the rest of the poem?

**5.** Why do you think the speaker interrupts the description of the boy swinging on birches at the beginning of the poem to discuss ice storms?

   ***Think about***
   - the different effects of the natural ice storms and the human boy on the birches
   - possible meanings of the references to heaven in line 13 and again in line 56
   - what the boy and the ice storms might represent in terms of the speaker's life

## A CRITICAL RESPONSE

**6.** How do the feelings evoked by the images of the ice storm in lines 10-20 compare with the feelings evoked by the image of the boy's effect on the trees in lines 28-35? Go back to the poem and find details to support your response.

**7.** Think about the themes of these three poems—"Fire and Ice," "Nothing Gold Can Stay," and "Birches." What, if any, common theme do you think Frost might have wanted to convey?

## *Connecting Reading and Writing*

**1.** Using what you have learned from this poem about swinging on birches, write a list of **instructions** describing the process for someone who would like to be a "swinger of birches."

Option: Pretend that you are the boy described in the poem and write an **invitation** to your cousin in the city. Describe the pleasures of swinging on birches in an effort to convince your cousin to spend the summer with you.

**2.** Imagine that you are organizing a public reading of Frost's poetry and that you want to hire dramatic readers who are similar in personality to the speakers of the poems. Write a **help-wanted ad** that describes the three people you want to hire.

Option: Write a brief **character sketch** of each of the three speakers to accompany each poem in a collection of Frost's poetry. You may have to infer some details, such as age and gender, but you should also include all the characteristics evident in the poems.

**3.** Think about the subject matter, the kinds of images, the ideas, the tone, and the form of all three poems—"Fire and Ice," "Nothing Gold Can Stay," and "Birches." Make a **chart** with a column for each of these five areas and fill in each column with information from the poems. Use your chart as a basis for reviewing these poems for a test.

Option: Look for similarities among the three poems. Then, draw some conclusions about the characteristics of Frost's poetry in an **expository essay** that could help other students understand Robert Frost.

*POETRY*

# Reviewing Concepts

## IMAGERY: TOUCHING THE SENSES AND EMOTIONS

*making connections*

Images appeal to the five senses: sight, hearing, touch, smell, and taste. Usually, images also stir the emotions. That is, an image will make the reader feel a certain way, even though it may be difficult or impossible for the reader to explain why. For example, in "The Sharks" the image of the dark shark fins above the water appeals to the sense of sight. It also evokes a feeling of fear or an apprehension of danger. Other feelings evoked by imagery may include wonder, respect, disgust, pity, sadness, cheerfulness, affection, humility, scorn, anger, and amusement.

Think back over the poems in the unit. Make a chart similar to the one below. Choose about ten poems that you think contain interesting images and for each poem fill out the columns on the chart. You do not need to write down all the images in each poem, just the ones that evoke the strongest feelings in you. An example has been done for you.

| Poem | Image(s) | Sense(s) appealed to | Feeling(s) evoked |
|---|---|---|---|
| "The Sharks" | "a sheen of copper stills the sea" | sight | peacefulness |
| | "dark/the sharp lift of fins" | sight | fear or sense of danger |

*describing connections*

Draw some conclusions about yourself from the information on your chart. Write an **essay** in which you discuss the kinds of images that you like best and why.

### Think about
- what many images on your chart seem to have in common
- senses that the images primarily appeal to
- similar feelings that occur frequently

*Odysseus,* 1961, HANS ERNI.
From *The Odyssey,* translated by Robert Fitzgerald, Doubleday & Co./ Random House, New York.

# The Homeric Epic

*"Where shall a man find sweetness to surpass
his own home and his parents?
In far lands he shall not, though he find a
house of gold."*

HOMER

# Stories by Firelight: Homer and His Audience

THE TIME IS 1000 B.C. Imagine sitting in a great banquet hall, feasting on meat, cheese, olives, and wine. The room is dark except for sputtering torches and the reflection of firelight on bronze shields and spears lining the walls. Amidst the clinking of goblets and the rumble of conversation, you suddenly hear the melodious strains of a harp. The whole room stills. Down at the end of the smoke-filled hall, seated before the massive stone hearth, a blind poet is about to recite from memory a long tale of battles and adventures, love and revenge. The poet is Homer and the tale is *The Odyssey*.

As you read the excerpts from *The Odyssey*, try to immerse yourself in the atmosphere and action of the epic, just as Homer's audience did three thousand years ago.

The Bettmann Archive, New York.

# Literary Vocabulary

**Epic.** An epic is a long narrative poem on a serious subject presented in an elevated or formal style. An epic traces the adventures of a hero whose actions represent the ideals and values of a nation or race. Many countries have epics that celebrate their national heroes. For example, *Cid* is the epic of Spain; *The Song of Roland* is the epic of France. The oldest recorded work of literature is a Babylonian epic called *Gilgamesh.* The epic as a type of literature was perfected by the ancient Greeks with *The Iliad* and *The Odyssey* of Homer. The plot of an epic usually involves a long and dangerous journey complicated by supernatural events and beings; the setting is large in scale and ranges over many locales. An epic addresses universal concerns, such as good and evil, life and death, and sin and redemption. Some epics are mythological or fictional, while others, like *The Odyssey,* may have some factual basis.

**Epic Hero.** An epic hero is a larger-than-life figure who represents a nation or race. The epic hero takes part in dangerous adventures, accomplishes great deeds, and shows superhuman qualities, such as great courage and strength. The epic hero usually must complete a long, difficult journey. Odysseus is an epic hero whose victories over enemies both human and supernatural are recounted in *The Odyssey.*

**Epic Simile.** A simile is a comparison between two things that are actually unlike yet have something in common. An epic simile, also called a Homeric simile, is an elaborate comparison that is more involved and ornate. Sometimes an epic simile compares a character to an impressive element in nature. Epic similes contain the words *like, as, so, just as,* or *just so.* At one point in *The Odyssey,* Odysseus is impatiently waiting for sunset because he will sail for home at day's end. His feelings are described in the following epic simile:

> Just as a farmer's hunger grows, behind
> the bolted plow and share, all day afield,
> drawn by his team of winedark oxen: sundown
> is benison for him, sending him homeward
> stiff in the knees from weariness, to dine;
> just so the light on the sea rim gladdened Odysseus.

**Epithet.** An epithet is a brief descriptive phrase that points out traits associated with a particular person or thing. An epithet is often an aid to characterization. For example, Odysseus is often called "the master strategist."

# The Odyssey

## THE TROJAN WAR

To historians, the Trojan War was a struggle for control of a crucial waterway in the Aegean Sea. To the poet Homer and to the millions who have read *The Iliad* and *The Odyssey*, the war was fought for the most beautiful woman in the world, the legendary Helen. For all we know, this conflict saw no more courage, drama, and valor than any other in the world's long history. However, as described by Homer, the Trojan War set the standards of heroism for centuries to come.

Homer based his two great epics on a group of legends about the war. He created a two-level structure. On one level, human beings battle each other on earth. The Trojan prince Paris runs off with Helen, the wife of a Greek leader. The Greeks band together and sail to Troy to seek revenge. Because the Greeks are unable to break through the walls of the city, however, the war bogs down for ten long years. Finally victorious, many of the Greek leaders suffer misfortune on their way home from Troy.

On the other level, the gods and goddesses battle on Mount Olympus (ō lim′ pəs), using their influence on human actions to best each other in trivial quarrels and petty jealousies. For example, Athena (ə the′ nə), goddess of war and of practical wisdom, takes up the Greek cause; Aphrodite (af rō dī′ tē), goddess of love, sides with the Trojans.

## HOMER'S EPICS

In *The Iliad* and *The Odyssey*, Homer presents plots and characters and deals with themes that echo through all of Western literature, from other epic poems to today's action-packed adventure movies. The heroes of *The Iliad* are warriors: the fierce, merciless Achilles (ə kil′ ēz) on the Greek side and the courageous, noble Hector of Troy. *The Odyssey* focuses on the actions and character of Odysseus (ō dis′ ē əs), "the master strategist." Unlike other warrior heroes, Odysseus is a trickster—intelligent, clever, and some would say sneaky. In the war with Troy, he wins fame not through ferocity, as Achilles does, or through courage, as Hector does, but through trickery. The ultimate defeat of Troy results from one of Odysseus' tricks. He orders a huge wooden horse built and left at the gates of Troy at night. The Trojans, waking to find it there—and not a Greek in sight—assume that their enemy has fled, leaving them a peace offering. They take the horse inside the walled city only to discover, too late, that it is filled with Greek soldiers and Troy is doomed.

Odysseus' heroic feat at Troy is recounted early in *The Odyssey*. The events in the rest of the epic are set after the war and concern the adventures and struggles of "the master strategist" as he makes his journey home to the island of Ithaca (ith′ ə kə). Instead of military opponents, Odysseus most often encounters monsters who try to devour him and beautiful women who try to keep him from his wife, Penelope.

Penelope, in the meantime, waits loyally at home for him. Her life is made miserable by suitors who believe that Odysseus is dead. They hope to marry her and gain, with her hand, Odysseus' wealth and property. Odysseus' son, Telemachus (te lem′ ə kəs), must dodge the suitors' attempts to have him killed. Athena protects him and educates him in the ways of the world.

To Homer's audience, the strange, often mythical lands through which Odysseus travels had all the mystery and danger of the interplanetary landscapes of *Star Trek* and *Star Wars*. The ancient Greeks could imagine monsters living just beyond the boundaries of the known world, as we today imagine aliens in the next galaxy. It was not necessary for them to believe that a one-eyed giant did exist, only that it could exist. After all, no one actually knew what lay beyond the farthest horizon.

Homer's epics were first told orally. He composed them in verse, partly because the rhyme and rhythm made them easier to memorize. After his death, the two epics were recited every four years at the Greek festival of Athena.

Generations after *The Iliad* and *The Odyssey* were first created, they were put into written form in the language of ancient Greece. Robert Fitzgerald has translated the two epics into modern English, also using poetry. Though the epics were originally spoken, they are far from conversational in tone and feeling. Rather, they are more like songs, full of carefully refined images and language that can be best appreciated when read aloud.

# *from* The Odyssey
# The Cyclops

HOMER    Translated from the Greek by ROBERT FITZGERALD

## *Approaching the Epic*

In *The Odyssey,* the story of Odysseus' adventures is told by Odysseus himself. Toward the end of his ten-year journey, Odysseus is washed up, naked and alone, on the island of Phaeacia (fē āsh' ə). To repay the Phaeacians' hospitality toward him, Odysseus relates the story of his long journey from Troy. The following excerpt is a flashback to one of Odysseus' first adventures, soon after he and his men have sailed from the battlefields of Troy.

Odysseus begins the episode by telling how he and his men have landed on a small island to rest and get resuppiled for their journey. The island lies very close to the mainland—so close that Odysseus can see the smoke from campfires and hear the bleating of sheep. The next morning, Odysseus decides to explore the mainland, which, unbeknownst to him at the time, is the Land of the Cyclopes (sī klō' pēz), a race of one-eyed giants.

## *Building Vocabulary*

These essential words are defined alongside the epic.

**prodigious** (prō dij' əs): A **prodigious** man/slept in this cave alone. (page 408, lines 19-20)

**rogues** (rōgz), **ravage** (rav' ij): "Or are you wandering **rogues**, who . . ./**ravage** other folk by sea?" (page 410, lines 91-92)

**avenge** (ə venj'): Zeus will **avenge**/the unoffending guest. (page 410, lines 107-108)

**sage:** To this rough shout they made a **sage** reply. (page 414, line 251)

**tactics:** I drew on all my wits, and ran through **tactics**. (page 414, line 265)

**adversary** (ad' vər ser ē): I sent a few [words] back to the **adversary**. (page 416, line 322)

**titanic** (tī tan' ik): He laid hands upon a bigger stone/ . . . **titanic** for the cast. (page 418, lines 387-388)

**disdained** (dis dānd'): Zeus **disdained** my offering. (page 418, line 404)

Who is your favorite monster? What creature from horror movies and stories do you think is the most frightening? In your journal, make a chart similar to the one below and list characteristics of your favorite monster. Then, briefly explain why he or she qualifies as the best monster ever created. As you read about Odysseus' encounter with the Cyclops, fill out the chart with characteristics of the Cyclops.

| Monster | Physical Appearance | Actions | Attitudes |
| --- | --- | --- | --- |
| | | | |

*Cyclops,* 1961, HANS ERNI.
From *The Odyssey,* translated by Robert Fitzgerald,
Doubleday & Co./ Random House, New York.

# Book Nine:
# New Coasts and Poseidon's Son

"When the young Dawn with fingertips of rose
came in the east, I called my men together
and made a speech to them:

                        'Old shipmates, friends,
the rest of you stand by; I'll make the crossing
5    in my own ship, with my own company,
and find out what the mainland natives are—
for they may be wild savages, and lawless,
or hospitable and god-fearing men.'

At this I went aboard, and gave the word
10  to cast off by the stern. My oarsmen followed,
filing in to their benches by the rowlocks,
and all in line dipped oars in the gray sea.

As we rowed on, and nearer to the mainland,
at one end of the bay, we saw a cavern
15  yawning above the water, screened with laurel,
and many rams and goats about the place
inside a sheepfold—made from slabs of stone
earthfast between tall trunks of pine and rugged
towering oak trees.

                        A prodigious[1] man
20  slept in this cave alone, and took his flocks
to graze afield—remote from all companions,
knowing none but savage ways, a brute
so huge, he seemed no man at all of those
who eat good wheaten bread; but he seemed rather
25  a shaggy mountain reared in solitude.
We beached there, and I told the crew
to stand by and keep watch over the ship;
as for myself I took my twelve best fighters
and went ahead. I had a goatskin full
30  of that sweet liquor that Euanthes'[2] son,
Maron, had given me. He kept Apollo's
holy grove at Ismarus; for kindness
we showed him there, and showed his wife and child,
he gave me seven shining golden talents[3]

**Guide for Interpretation**

♦ **Line 1:** "Dawn with fingertips of rose" is an example of an epithet, a brief descriptive phrase that points out traits associated with a particular person or thing. You will find other epithets throughout these excerpts from *The Odyssey*.

♦ **Lines 3-8:** Odysseus sets off to explore the mainland with one ship and a crew of men.

1. **prodigious** (prō dij′ əs): amazing; of great size or power.

♦ **Lines 19-25:** Note the description of this savage character.

2. **Euanthes** (yо̄о̄ an′ thēz).

3. **talents:** large units of money used in ancient Greece.

35    perfectly formed, a solid silver winebowl,
and then this liquor—twelve two-handled jars
of brandy, pure and fiery. Not a slave
in Maron's household knew this drink; only
he, his wife and the storeroom mistress knew;
40    and they would put one cupful—ruby-colored,
honey-smooth—in twenty more of water,
but still the sweet scent hovered like a fume
over the winebowl. No man turned away
when cups of this came round.

                                A wineskin full
45    I brought along, and victuals[4] in a bag,
for in my bones I knew some towering brute
would be upon us soon—all outward power,
a wild man, ignorant of civility.

We climbed, then, briskly to the cave. But Cyclops
50    had gone afield, to pasture his fat sheep,
so we looked round at everything inside:
a drying rack that sagged with cheeses, pens
crowded with lambs and kids, each in its class:
firstlings apart from middlings, and the 'dewdrops,'
55    or newborn lambkins, penned apart from both.
And vessels full of whey[5] were brimming there—
bowls of earthenware and pails for milking.
My men came pressing round me, pleading:

                                'Why not
take these cheeses, get them stowed, come back,
60    throw open all the pens, and make a run for it?
We'll drive the kids and lambs aboard. We say
put out again on good salt water!'

                                    Ah,
how sound that was! Yet I refused. I wished
to see the caveman, what he had to offer—
65    no pretty sight, it turned out, for my friends.
We lit a fire, burnt an offering,
and took some cheese to eat; then sat in silence
around the embers, waiting. When he came
he had a load of dry boughs on his shoulder
70    to stoke his fire at suppertime. He dumped it
with a great crash into that hollow cave,
and we all scattered fast to the far wall.

**4. victuals** (vit′ 'ls): food.

♦ **Lines 29-31 and 44-48:** Note what Odysseus takes with him on land and why.

**5. whey** (hwā): the watery part of milk that separates from the thicker part in cheese making.

♦ **Lines 58-64:** Think about why Odysseus refuses his men's "sound" suggestion to rob the Cyclops, leave the cave, and sail away.

♦ **Line 66:** Odysseus and his men burn a portion of food as an offering to the gods to secure the gods' goodwill. Such sacrifices are frequently performed by the sailors during their difficult journey home.

Then over the broad cavern floor he ushered
the ewes he meant to milk. He left his rams
75 and he-goats in the yard outside, and swung
high overhead a slab of solid rock
to close the cave. Two dozen four-wheeled wagons,
with heaving wagon teams, could not have stirred
the tonnage of that rock from where he wedged it
80 over the doorsill. Next he took his seat
and milked his bleating ewes. A practiced job
he made of it, giving each ewe her suckling;
thickened his milk, then, into curds and whey,
sieved out the curds to drip in withy baskets,
85 and poured the whey to stand in bowls
cooling until he drank it for his supper.
When all these chores were done, he poked the fire,
heaping on brushwood. In the glare he saw us.
'Strangers,' he said, 'who are you? And where from?
90 What brings you here by sea ways—a fair traffic?
Or are you wandering <u>rogues</u>,[6] who cast your lives
like dice, and <u>ravage</u>[7] other folk by sea?'

We felt a pressure on our hearts, in dread
of that deep rumble and that mighty man.
95 But all the same I spoke up in reply:

'We are from Troy, Achaeans,[8] blown off course
by shifting gales on the Great South Sea;
homeward bound, but taking routes and ways
uncommon; so the will of Zeus would have it.
100 We served under Agamemnon,[9] son of Atreus—
the whole world knows what city
he laid waste, what armies he destroyed.
It was our luck to come here; here we stand,
beholden for your help, or any gifts
105 you give—as custom is to honor strangers.
We would entreat you, great Sir, have a care
for the gods' courtesy; Zeus will <u>avenge</u>[10]
the unoffending guest.'

He answered this
from his brute chest, unmoved:
'You are a ninny,
110 or else you come from the other end of nowhere,
telling me, mind the gods! We Cyclopes
care not a whistle for your thundering Zeus

---

♦ **Lines 77-80:** Notice the size of the rock closing the entrance to the Cyclops' cave.

**6. rogues** (rōgz): rascals; scoundrels.

**7. ravage** (rav' ij): destroy or ruin.

**8. Achaeans** (ə kē' ənz): another name for Greeks; a reference to Odysseus' men.

**9. Agamemnon** (ag ə mem' nän'): chief of the Greek forces during the Trojan War.

♦ **Lines 103-108:** Here Odysseus appeals to the Cyclops' hospitality. Kindness and hospitality to strangers were very important values in ancient Greece. For the Greeks, mistreating a guest was the same as dishonoring the gods.

**10. avenge** (ə venj'): get revenge for an injury or wrong.

---

or all the gods in bliss; we have more force by far.
I would not let you go for fear of Zeus—
115 you or your friends—unless I had a whim to.
Tell me, where was it, now, you left your ship—
around the point, or down the shore, I wonder?'

He thought he'd find out, but I saw through this,
and answered with a ready lie:

                                        'My ship?
120 Poseidon[11] Lord, who sets the earth a-tremble,
broke it up on the rocks at your land's end.
A wind from seaward served him, drove us there.
We are survivors, these good men and I.'

Neither reply nor pity came from him,
125 but in one stride he clutched at my companions
and caught two in his hands like squirming puppies
to beat their brains out, spattering the floor.
Then he dismembered them and made his meal,
gaping and crunching like a mountain lion—
130 everything: innards, flesh, and marrow bones.
We cried aloud, lifting our hands to Zeus,
powerless, looking on at this, appalled;
but Cyclops went on filling up his belly
with manflesh and great gulps of whey,
135 then lay down like a mast among his sheep.
My heart beat high now at the chance of action,
and drawing the sharp sword from my hip I went
along his flank to stab him where the midriff
holds the liver. I had touched the spot
140 when sudden fear stayed me: if I killed him
we perished there as well, for we could never
move his ponderous doorway slab aside.
So we were left to groan and wait for morning.

When the young Dawn with fingertips of rose
145 lit up the world, the Cyclops built a fire
and milked his handsome ewes, all in due order,
putting the sucklings to the mothers. Then,
his chores being all dispatched, he caught
another brace[12] of men to make his breakfast,
150 and whisked away his great door slab
to let his sheep go through—but he, behind,
reset the stone as one would cap a quiver.

**Lines 111-115:** Note that the Cyclopes do not respect or fear the gods.

**Lines 118-123:** Speculate about why Odysseus lies about his ship.

**11. Poseidon** (pō sī′ d′n): god of the seas and of earthquakes.

**Lines 124-130:** The two similes in this passage emphasize the helplessness of the men ("like squirming puppies") and the savagery of the Cyclops ("gaping and crunching like a mountain lion").

**Lines 139-142:** Notice why Odysseus does not kill the Cyclops at this time.

**12. brace:** a pair.

There was a din of whistling as the Cyclops
rounded his flock to higher ground, then stillness.
155 And now I pondered how to hurt him worst,
if but Athena[13] granted what I prayed for.
Here are the means I thought would serve my turn:

a club, or staff, lay there along the fold—
an olive tree, felled green and left to season
160 for Cyclops' hand. And it was like a mast
a lugger[14] of twenty oars, broad in the beam—
a deep-sea-going craft—might carry:
so long, so big around, it seemed. Now I
chopped out a six-foot section of this pole
165 and set it down before my men, who scraped it;
and when they had it smooth, I hewed again
to make a stake with pointed end. I held this
in the fire's heart and turned it, toughening it,
then hid it, well back in the cavern, under
170 one of the dung piles in profusion there.
Now came the time to toss for it: who ventured
along with me? whose hand could bear to thrust
and grind that spike in Cyclops' eye, when mild
sleep had mastered him? As luck would have it,
175 the men I would have chosen won the toss—
four strong men, and I made five as captain.

At evening came the shepherd with his flock,
his woolly flock. The rams as well, this time,
entered the cave: by some sheep-herding whim—
180 or a god's bidding—none were left outside.
He hefted his great boulder into place
and sat him down to milk the bleating ewes
in proper order, put the lambs to suck,
and swiftly ran through all his evening chores.
185 Then he caught two more men and feasted on them.
My moment was at hand, and I went forward
holding an ivy bowl of my dark drink,
looking up, saying:

                              'Cyclops, try some wine.
Here's liquor to wash down your scraps of men.
190 Taste it, and see the kind of drink we carried
under our planks. I meant it for an offering
if you would help us home. But you are mad,
unbearable, a bloody monster! After this,

**13. Athena** (ə thē′ nə):
goddess of wisdom and of
warfare, who gives special
help and protection to
Odysseus.

**14. lugger** (lug′ ər): small
vessel.

◆ **Lines 172-174:** Notice what
Odysseus plans to do to the
Cyclops.

will any other traveler come to see you?'

195 He seized and drained the bowl, and it went down
so fiery and smooth he called for more:

'Give me another, thank you kindly. Tell me,
how are you called? I'll make a gift will please you.
Even Cyclopes know the wine-grapes grow

200 out of grassland and loam in heaven's rain,
but here's a bit of nectar and ambrosia!'[15]

Three bowls I brought him, and he poured them down.
I saw the fuddle and flush come over him,
then I sang out in cordial tones:

                'Cyclops,

205 you ask my honorable name? Remember
the gift you promised me, and I shall tell you.
My name is Nohbdy: mother, father, and friends,
everyone calls me Nohbdy.'

                And he said:
'Nohbdy's my meat, then, after I eat his friends.

210 Others come first. There's a noble gift, now.'

Even as he spoke, he reeled and tumbled backward,
his great head lolling to one side; and sleep
took him like any creature. Drunk, hiccuping,
he dribbled streams of liquor and bits of men.

215 Now, by the gods, I drove my big hand spike
deep in the embers, charring it again,
and cheered my men along with battle talk
to keep their courage up: no quitting now.
The pike of olive, green though it had been,

220 reddened and glowed as if about to catch.
I drew it from the coals and my four fellows
gave me a hand, lugging it near the Cyclops
as more than natural force nerved them; straight
forward they sprinted, lifted it, and rammed it

225 deep in his crater eye, and I leaned on it
turning it as a shipwright turns a drill
in planking, having men below to swing
the two-handled strap that spins it in the groove.
So with our brand we bored that great eye socket

230 while blood ran out around the red hot bar.

**15. nectar and ambrosia**
(nek′ tər, am brō′ zhə): drink
and food of the gods in
classical mythology.

◆ **Line 207:** Say the name
Nohbdy out loud and
speculate about Odysseus'
reasons for giving this name.

◆ **Lines 197-198 and 209-210:**
Compare the Cyclops' crude
trick with what Odysseus has
planned.

◆ **Lines 215-218:** Odysseus not
only shows great courage and
cunning in this episode but
also proves himself a kind
and able leader of his men.

Eyelid and lash were seared; the pierced ball
hissed broiling, and the roots popped.

                                 In a smithy
one sees a white-hot axehead or an adze
plunged and wrung in a cold tub, screeching steam—

235   the way they make soft iron hale and hard—:
just so that eyeball hissed around the spike.
The Cyclops bellowed and the rock roared round him,
and we fell back in fear. Clawing his face
he tugged the bloody spike out of his eye,

240   threw it away, and his wild hands went groping;
then he set up a howl for Cyclopes
who lived in caves on windy peaks nearby.
Some heard him; and they came by divers ways
to clump around outside and call:

                           'What ails you,

245   Polyphemus?[16] Why do you cry so sore
in the starry night? You will not let us sleep.
Sure no man's driving off your flock? No man
has tricked you, ruined you?'
                      Out of the cave
the mammoth Polyphemus roared in answer:

250   'Nohbdy, Nohbdy's tricked me, Nohbdy's ruined me!'

To this rough shout they made a <u>sage</u>[17] reply:

'Ah well, if nobody has played you foul
there in your lonely bed, we are no use in pain
given by great Zeus. Let it be your father,

255   Poseidon Lord, to whom you pray.'
                         So saying
they trailed away. And I was filled with laughter
to see how like a charm the name deceived them.
Now Cyclops, wheezing as the pain came on him,
fumbled to wrench away the great doorstone

260   and squatted in the breach with arms thrown wide
for any silly beast or man who bolted—
hoping somehow I might be such a fool.
But I kept thinking how to win the game:
death sat there huge; how could we slip away?

265   I drew on all my wits, and ran through <u>tactics</u>,[18]
reasoning as a man will for dear life,
until a trick came—and it pleased me well.

---

♦ **Lines 232-236:** In this epic simile, Odysseus compares the hissing sound created when he and his men stab the Cyclops' eye to the sound made by a hot iron just taken from a fire being plunged into cold water—"screeching steam."

**16. Polyphemus** (päl i fē′ məs): the name of the Cyclops.

**17. sage:** showing wisdom and good judgment.

♦ **Lines 254-255:** Polyphemus is the son of the god Poseidon.

**18. tactics:** any methods used to gain an end; skillful strategies or procedures.

The Cyclops' rams were handsome, fat, with heavy
fleeces, a dark violet.

◆ Lines 263-279: Odysseus
thinks of a new strategy on
the spot.

                                    Three abreast
270 I tied them silently together, twining
    cords of willow from the ogre's bed;
    then slung a man under each middle one
    to ride there safely, shielded left and right.
    So three sheep could convey each man. I took
275 the woolliest ram, the choicest of the flock,
    and hung myself under his kinky belly,
    pulled up tight, with fingers twisted deep
    in sheepskin ringlets for an iron grip.
    So, breathing hard, we waited until morning.

280 When Dawn spread out her fingertips of rose
    the rams began to stir, moving for pasture,
    and peals of bleating echoed round the pens
    where dams with udders full called for a milking.
    Blinded, and sick with pain from his head wound,
285 the master stroked each ram, then let it pass,
    but my men riding on the pectoral[19] fleece
    the giant's blind hands blundering never found.
    Last of them all my ram, the leader, came,
    weighted by wool and me with my meditations.
290 The Cyclops patted him, and then he said:

    'Sweet cousin ram, why lag behind the rest
    in the night cave? You never linger so,
    but graze before them all, and go afar
    to crop sweet grass, and take your stately way
295 leading along the streams, until at evening
    you run to be the first one in the fold.
    Why, now, so far behind? Can you be grieving
    over your Master's eye? That carrion rogue
    and his accurst companions burnt it out
300 when he had conquered all my wits with wine.
    Nohbdy will not get out alive, I swear.
    Oh, had you brain and voice to tell
    where he may be now, dodging all my fury!
    Bashed by this hand and bashed on this rock wall
305 his brains would strew the floor, and I should have
    rest from the outrage Nohbdy worked upon me.'

    He sent us into the open, then. Close by,

**19. pectoral** (pek′ tə rəl):
having to do with the chest
or breast, in this case the
underbelly.

I dropped and rolled clear of the ram's belly,
going this way and that to untie the men.
310 With many glances back, we rounded up
his fat, stiff-legged sheep to take aboard,
and drove them down to where the good ship lay.
We saw, as we came near, our fellows' faces
shining; then we saw them turn to grief
315 tallying those who had not fled from death.
I hushed them, jerking head and eyebrows up,
and in a low voice told them: 'Load this herd;
move fast, and put the ship's head toward the breakers.'
They all pitched in at loading, then embarked
320 and struck their oars into the sea. Far out,
as far off shore as shouted words would carry,
I sent a few back to the adversary:[20]

'O Cyclops! Would you feast on my companions?
Puny, am I, in a Caveman's hands?
325 How do you like the beating that we gave you,
you damned cannibal? Eater of guests
under your roof! Zeus and the gods have paid you!'

The blind thing in his doubled fury broke
a hilltop in his hands and heaved it after us.
330 Ahead of our black prow it struck and sank
whelmed in a spuming geyser, a giant wave
that washed the ship stern foremost back to shore.
I got the longest boathook out and stood
fending us off, with furious nods to all
335 to put their backs into a racing stroke—
row, row, or perish. So the long oars bent
kicking the foam sternward, making head
until we drew away, and twice as far.
Now when I cupped my hands I heard the crew
340 in low voices protesting:

                              'Godsake, Captain!
Why bait the beast again? Let him alone!'
'That tidal wave he made on the first throw
all but beached us.'

                              'All but stove us in!'
'Give him our bearing with your trumpeting,
345 he'll get the range and lob a boulder.'

'Aye,

He'll smash our timbers and our heads together!'

I would not heed them in my glorying spirit,
but let my anger flare and yelled:

'Cyclops,

if ever mortal man inquire
350  how you were put to shame and blinded, tell him
Odysseus, raider of cities, took your eye:
Laertes'[21] son, whose home's on Ithaca!'

At this he gave a mighty sob and rumbled:

'Now comes the weird[22] upon me, spoken of old.
355  A wizard, grand and wondrous, lived here—Telemus,
a son of Eurymus; great length of days
he had in a wizardry among the Cyclopes,
and these things he foretold for time to come:
my great eye lost, and at Odysseus' hands.
360  Always I had in mind some giant, armed
in giant force, would come against me here.
But this, but you—small, pitiful and twiggy—
you put me down with wine, you blinded me.
Come back, Odysseus, and I'll treat you well,
365  praying the god of earthquake[23] to befriend you—
his son I am, for he by his avowal
fathered me, and, if he will, he may
heal me of this black wound—he and no other
of all the happy gods or mortal men.'

370  Few words I shouted in reply to him:
'If I could take your life I would and take
your time away, and hurl you down to hell!
The god of earthquake could not heal you there!'

At this he stretched his hands out in his darkness
375  toward the sky of stars, and prayed Poseidon:

'O hear me, lord, blue girdler of the islands,
if I am thine indeed, and thou art father:
grant that Odysseus, raider of cities, never
see his home: Laertes' son, I mean,
380  who kept his hall on Ithaca. Should destiny
intend that he shall see his roof again

◆ **Line 351:** Odysseus uses the epithet "raider of cities" to emphasize his warlike characteristics in this boast to the Cyclops.

**21. Laertes** (lā er' tēz): Odysseus' father.

**22. weird:** in its original usage, weird meant "fate."

◆ **Lines 360-363:** Polyphemus is not blind to the irony of being beaten by someone at most one-eighth his size.

**23. god of earthquake:** Poseidon.

among his family in his father land,
far be that day, and dark the years between.
Let him lose all companions, and return
385  under strange sail to bitter days at home,'

In these words he prayed, and the god heard him.
Now he laid hands upon a bigger stone
and wheeled around, titanic[24] for the cast,
to let it fly in the black-prowed vessel's track.
390  But it fell short, just aft the steering oar,
and whelming seas rose giant above the stone
to bear us onward toward the island.

There

as we ran in we saw the squadron waiting,
the trim ships drawn up side by side, and all
395  our troubled friends who waited, looking seaward.
We beached her, grinding keel in the soft sand,
and waded in, ourselves, on the sandy beach.
Then we unloaded all the Cyclops' flock
to make division, share and share alike,
400  only my fighters voted that my ram,
the prize of all, should go to me. I slew him
by the seaside and burnt his long thighbones
to Zeus beyond the stormcloud, Cronus' son,
who rules the world. But Zeus disdained[25] my offering;
405  destruction for my ships he had in store
and death for those who sailed them, my companions.
Now all day long until the sun went down
we made our feast on mutton and sweet wine,
till after sunset in the gathering dark
410  we went to sleep above the wash of ripples.

When the young Dawn with fingertips of rose
touched the world, I roused the men, gave orders
to man the ships, cast off the mooring lines;
and filing in to sit beside the rowlocks
415  oarsmen in line dipped oars in the gray sea.
So we moved out, sad in the vast offing,
having our precious lives, but not our friends."

◆ **Lines 378-385:** Note the details of Polyphemus' curse on Odysseus. Poseidon grants his son's desire for revenge, causing Odysseus such hardship that his return home is delayed ten years and his ships and men are ultimately destroyed

**24. titanic** (ti tan' ik): of great size, strength, or power

◆ **Lines 401-404:** Consider why Odysseus sacrifices the ram that saved him in honor of Zeus.

**25. disdained** (dis dānd'): refused or rejected with scorn.

◆ **Lines 404-406:** Zeus is the king of all the gods, but his brother Poseidon has considerable influence over Zeus' decisions.

Epic

# Thinking About the Epic

## A PERSONAL RESPONSE

*sharing*
*impressions*

**1.** What is your reaction to Odysseus' encounter with Polyphemus? Jot down your response in your journal.

*constructing*
*interpretations*

**2.** Think back over events in this episode and explain where things go smoothly and where things go wrong for Odysseus and his men.

**3.** What positive and negative qualities of Odysseus' character are revealed in his encounter with Polyphemus?

### Think about
- why he wants to see Polyphemus in the first place
- how he defeats Polyphemus
- how effective a leader he is
- why he baits Polyphemus at the end and tells his real name

**4.** How does Polyphemus compare with your prereading description of your favorite monster?

## A CREATIVE RESPONSE

**5.** If Polyphemus had not brought the rams into the cave, how might Odysseus and his men have escaped?

## A CRITICAL RESPONSE

**6.** Explain how the epic simile in lines 232-236 and other similes in this episode help make this epic more dramatic.

**7.** From the characterization of Polyphemus, what conclusions can you draw about the qualities that ancient Greek society considered barbaric or monstrous? Use specific examples from the excerpt to support your ideas.

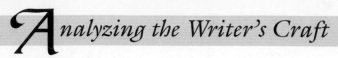
# Analyzing the Writer's Craft

## EPIC HERO

Think about the character of Odysseus. What qualities and actions do you think make him a hero?

**Building a Literary Vocabulary.** An epic hero is a larger-than-life figure who represents a nation or a race. The epic hero takes part in dangerous adventures, accomplishes great deeds, and often shows superhuman qualities such as great courage and strength. The epic hero usually must complete a long, difficult journey. Odysseus was a hero from Greek legend, famous both for his role in the Trojan War and his arduous, ten-year journey home afterward. The positive qualities that he displays were ideals in Greek society.

**Application: Analyzing an Epic Hero.** With a partner, evaluate to what extent Odysseus acts like an epic hero in this episode with Polyphemus. Create a two-column chart. In the first column list the larger-than-life qualities and actions that show Odysseus to be an epic hero. In the second column, list Odysseus' more human qualities and actions that do not seem to fit the definition of an epic hero—for example, faults he exhibits or unwise choices he makes. After you have completed your chart, jot down anything about Odysseus' character that you think needs improvement. Then as you read the next excerpt from *The Odyssey,* you will be able to decide whether Odysseus changes for the better.

# _from_ The Odyssey
## The Homecoming

### *A*pproaching the Epic

After Odysseus arrives on the shore of his homeland, the goddess Athena approaches. She warns him that his palace is overrun by more than one hundred suitors who, believing that Odysseus is dead, want to marry his wife and take over his fortune. Following Athena's advice, Odysseus disguises himself as an old beggar and visits the palace. There he notices that two suitors in particular, Antinous (an tin′ ō əs) and Eurymachus (yōō rim′ ə kəs), are rude and demanding. With Athena's help, Odysseus has a tearful reunion with Telemachus, and together they discuss how to avenge their family honor. In the meantime, Penelope—who does not know that Odysseus has returned—gets out Odysseus' old bow and declares a contest for the suitors, with marriage to her as the prize.

### *B*uilding Vocabulary

These essential words are defined alongside the epic.

**commandeered** (käm′ ən dird′): "Suitors indeed, you **commandeered** this house/to feast and drink in, day and night" (page 423, lines 14-15)

**plundered** (plun′ dərd): Antinous/. . . had mocked and **plundered** [Odysseus]. (page 424, lines 45-49)

**adversities** (ad vʉr′ sə tēz): "I bore **adversities,** but in the twentieth year/I am ashore in my own land." (page 425, lines 70-71)

**contempt** (kən tempt′): "**Contempt** was all you had for the gods who rule wide heaven." (page 431, line 269)

**restitution** (res′ tə tōō′ shən): "We'll make/**restitution** of wine and meat consumed." (page 432, lines 286-287)

### *C*onnecting Writing and Reading

How do you think that Odysseus will be able to kill all the suitors, most of whom are young, strong, armed, and dangerous? Write your prediction in your journal. As you read, watch for details of how Odysseus takes revenge.

*Testing the Bow,* 1961, HANS ERNI.
From *The Odyssey,* translated by Robert Fitzgerald, Doubleday & Co./ Random House, New York.

# Book Twenty-One:
## The Test of the Bow

*Finally giving up hope that Odysseus will return, Penelope devises an archery contest to determine which of the suitors she will marry. She enters the storeroom and takes down the heavy bow that Odysseus left behind when he went to war.*

*Guide for Interpretation*

                           Now Penelope
sank down, holding the weapon on her knees,
and drew her husband's great bow out, and sobbed
and bit her lip and let the salt tears flow.
Then back she went to face the crowded hall

5     tremendous bow in hand, and on her shoulder hung
the quiver[1] spiked with coughing death. Behind her
maids bore a basket full of axeheads, bronze
and iron implements for the master's game.
Thus in her beauty she approached the suitors,

10   and near a pillar of the solid roof
she paused, her shining veil across her cheeks,
her maids on either hand and still,
then spoke to the banqueters:

                          "My lords, hear me:
suitors indeed, you <u>commandeered</u>[2] this house

15   to feast and drink in, day and night, my husband
being long gone, long out of mind. You found
no justification for yourselves—none
except your lust to marry me. Stand up, then:
we now declare a contest for that prize.

20   Here is my lord Odysseus' hunting bow.
Bend and string it if you can. Who sends an arrow
through iron axe-helve sockets, twelve in line?
I join my life with his, and leave this place, my home,
my rich and beautiful bridal house, forever

25   to be remembered, though I dream it only."

Then to Eumaeus:[3]

                       "Carry the bow forward.
Carry the blades."

◆ **Lines 1-3:** Notice that Penelope still grieves for Odysseus even after twenty years.

**1. quiver** (kwiv′ ər): a portable case for arrows.

**2. commandeered** (käm ən dird′): took by force.

◆ **Lines 20-22:** Note that the contest has two parts: First, the suitors must bend the heavy bow and string it— a task that could be accomplished only by someone as strong as Odysseus. Second, they must shoot an arrow accurately enough to go through the holes of twelve axeheads set up in a row.

**3. Eumaeus** (yo͞o mē′ əs): the faithful swineherd of Odysseus.

Tears came to the swineherd's eyes
as he reached out for the big bow. He laid it
down at the suitors' feet. Across the room
30   the cowherd sobbed, knowing the master's weapon.
Antinous growled, with a glance at both:

                                        "Clods.
They go to pieces over nothing.

                              You two, there,
why are you sniveling? To upset the woman
even more? Has she not pain enough
35   over her lost husband? *Sit down.*
Get on with dinner quietly, or cry about it
outside, if you must. Leave us the bow.
A clean-cut game, it looks to me.
Nobody bends that bowstave easily
40   in this company. Is there a man here
made like Odysseus? I remember him
from childhood: I can see him even now."

That was the way he played it, hoping inwardly
to span the great horn bow with corded gut
45   and drill the iron with his shot—he, Antinous,
destined to be the first of all to savor
blood from a biting arrow at his throat,
a shaft drawn by the fingers of Odysseus
whom he had mocked and <u>plundered</u>,[4] leading on
50   the rest, his boon companions. . . .

*Despite heating and greasing the bow, the lesser suitors prove*
*unable to string it. The most able suitors, Antinous and*
*Eurymachus, hold off. While the suitors are busy with the bow,*
*Odysseus—still disguised as an old beggar—goes to enlist the*
*aid of two of his trusted servants, Eumaeus the swineherd and*
*Philoetius (fil ē′ shi əs) the cowherd.*

Two men had meanwhile left the hall:
swineherd and cowherd, in companionship,
one downcast as the other. But Odysseus
followed them outdoors, outside the court,
55   and coming up said gently:

                              "You, herdsman,
and you, too, swineherd, I could say a thing to you,
or should I keep it dark?

**Lines 27-30:** Notice the emotion expressed by the two servants when they are reminded of their master.

**Lines 31-37:** Notice the arrogant way in which Antinous speaks and how he treats Odysseus' servants.

**Lines 45-50:** Note in these lines the foreshadowing of Antinous' death.

**4. plundered** (plun′ dərd): forcibly taken the goods from.

No, no; speak,
my heart tells me. Would you be men enough
to stand by Odysseus if he came back?
60 Suppose he dropped out of a clear sky, as I did?
Suppose some god should bring him?
Would you bear arms for him, or for the suitors?"

The cowherd said:
"Ah, let the master come!
Father Zeus, grant our old wish! Some courier
65 guide him back! Then judge what stuff is in me
and how I manage arms!"

Likewise Eumaeus
fell to praying all heaven for his return,
so that Odysseus, sure at least of these,
told them:
"I am at home, for I am he.
70 I bore adversities,[5] but in the twentieth year
I am ashore in my own land. I find
the two of you, alone among my people,
longed for my coming. Prayers I never heard
except your own that I might come again.
75 So now what is in store for you I'll tell you:
If Zeus brings down the suitors by my hand
I promise marriages to both, and cattle,
and houses built near mine. And you shall be
brothers-in-arms of my Telemachus.
80 Here, let me show you something else, a sign
that I am he, that you can trust me, look:
this old scar from the tusk wound that I got
boar hunting on Parnassus—
Autolycus' sons and I."

Shifting his rags
85 he bared the long gash. Both men looked, and knew,
and threw their arms around the old soldier, weeping,
kissing his head and shoulders. He as well
took each man's head and hands to kiss, then said—
to cut it short, else they might weep till dark—

90 "Break off, no more of this.
Anyone at the door could see and tell them.
Drift back in, but separately at intervals
after me.

**5. adversities** (ad vʉr′ sə tēz): misfortunes or troubles.

♦ **Lines 71-74:** Think about why Odysseus values the loyalty of these two servants so much.

Now listen to your orders:
when the time comes, those gentlemen, to a man,
95  will be dead against giving me bow or quiver.
Defy them. Eumaeus, bring the bow
and put it in my hands there at the door.
Tell the women to lock their own door tight.
Tell them if someone hears the shock of arms
100  or groans of men, in hall or court, not one
must show her face, but keep still at her weaving.
Philoetius, run to the outer gate and lock it.
Throw the cross bar and lash it."

He turned back
into the courtyard and the beautiful house
105  and took the stool he had before. They followed
one by one, the two hands loyal to him.

Eurymachus had now picked up the bow.
He turned it round, and turned it round
before the licking flame to warm it up,
110  but could not, even so, put stress upon it
to jam the loop over the tip
though his heart groaned to bursting.
Then he said grimly:

"Curse this day.
What gloom I feel, not for myself alone,
and not only because we lose that bride.
115  Women are not lacking in Achaea,[6]
in other towns, or on Ithaca. No, the worst
is humiliation—to be shown up for children
measured against Odysseus—we who cannot
even hitch the string over his bow.
120  What shame to be repeated of us, after us!"

Then spoke Odysseus, all craft and gall:
"My lords, contenders for the queen, permit me:
a passion in me moves me to speak out.
I put it to Eurymachus above all
125  and to that brilliant prince, Antinous. . . .
But let me try my hand at the smooth bow!
Let me test my fingers and my pull
to see if any of the oldtime kick is there,
or if thin fare and roving took it out of me."

♦ **Lines 93-103:** Note the details of Odysseus' plan.

6. **Achaea** (ə kē′ ə): a region in Greece.

♦ **Lines 112-120:** In expressing his shame and humiliation, Eurymachus speaks here for all the suitors. Think about the importance of having a reputation for physical strength—both in our own time as well as in ancient Greece.

♦ **Lines 121-129:** With this suggestion, Odysseus begins to put his plan into action.

130 Now irritation beyond reason swept them all,
since they were nagged by fear that he could string it.
Antinous answered, coldly and at length:

"You bleary vagabond, no rag of sense is left you.
Are you not coddled here enough, at table
135 taking meat with gentlemen, your betters,
denied nothing, and listening to our talk?
When have we let a tramp hear all our talk?
The sweet goad of wine has made you rave! . . . "

At this the watchful queen Penelope
140 interposed:
                              "Antinous, discourtesy
to a guest of Telemachus—whatever guest—
that is not handsome. What are you afraid of?
Suppose this exile put his back into it
and drew the great bow of Odysseus—
145 could he then take me home to be his bride?
You know he does not imagine that! No one
need let that prospect weigh upon his dinner!
How very, very improbable it seems."

*At Telemachus' request, Penelope leaves the men to settle
the question of the bow among themselves.*

The swineherd had the horned bow in his hands
150 moving toward Odysseus, when the crowd
in the banquet hall broke into an ugly din,
shouts rising from the flushed young men:
                              "Ho! Where
do you think you are taking that, you smutty slave?"

"What is this dithering?"

                              "We'll toss you back alone
155 among the pigs, for your own dogs to eat,
if bright Apollo nods and the gods are kind!"

He faltered, all at once put down the bow, and stood
in panic, buffeted by waves of cries,
hearing Telemachus from another quarter
160 shout:

"Go on, take him the bow!

**♦ Lines 133-138:** Notice the
way Antinous treats the man
he believes to be an old
beggar.

**♦ Lines 139-148:** The phrase
"the watchful queen" is an
epithet that characterizes
Penelope as patient and
observant. Here she asserts
the values of courtesy and
hospitality so important to the
ancient Greeks—values that
the suitors consistently abuse.

Do you obey this pack?
You will be stoned back to your hills! Young as I am
my power is over you! I wish to God
I had as much the upper hand of these!
165 There would be suitors pitched like dead rats
through our gate, for the evil plotted here!"

Telemachus' frenzy struck someone as funny,
and soon the whole room roared with laughter at him,
so that all tension passed. Eumaeus picked up
170 bow and quiver, making for the door,
and there he placed them in Odysseus' hands.
Calling Eurycleia[7] to his side he said:

"Telemachus
trusts you to take care of the women's doorway.
Lock it tight. If anyone inside
175 should hear the shock of arms or groans of men
in hall or court, not one must show her face,
but go on with her weaving."

The old woman
nodded and kept still. She disappeared
into the women's hall, bolting the door behind her.
180 Philoetius left the house now at one bound,
catlike, running to bolt the courtyard gate.
A coil of deck-rope of papyrus fiber
lay in the gateway; this he used for lashing,
and ran back to the same stool as before,
185 fastening his eyes upon Odysseus.

And Odysseus took his time,
turning the bow, tapping it, every inch,
for borings that termites might have made
while the master of the weapon was abroad.
The suitors were now watching him, and some
190 jested among themselves:

"A bow lover!"
"Dealer in old bows!"

"Maybe he has one like it
at home!"

"Or has an itch to make one for himself."

Lines 159-171: As Penelope did earlier, Telemachus stands up to the suitors. Even though the suitors just laugh at him, Telemachus' attempt creates enough of a diversion for Eumaeus to deliver the bow safely to Odysseus.

7. Eurycleia (yoo ri klē′ ə): Odysseus' old female servant, who has remained loyal to him.

Lines 172-177: Eumaeus repeats Odysseus' orders to lock the women's quarters, but he tells Eurycleia that they are Telemachus' commands in order to protect Odysseus' disguise.

"See how he handles it, the sly old buzzard!"

And one disdainful suitor added this:

195 "May his fortune grow an inch for every inch he
      bends it!"

But the man skilled in all ways of contending,
satisfied by the great bow's look and heft,
like a musician, like a harper, when
with quiet hand upon his instrument
200 he draws between his thumb and forefinger
a sweet new string upon a peg: so effortlessly
Odysseus in one motion strung the bow.
Then slid his right hand down the cord and plucked it,
so the taut gut vibrating hummed and sang
205 a swallow's note.

                    In the hushed hall it smote the suitors
and all their faces changed. Then Zeus thundered
overhead, one loud crack for a sign.
And Odysseus laughed within him that the son
of crooked-minded Cronus had flung that omen down.
210 He picked one ready arrow from his table
where it lay bare: the rest were waiting still
in the quiver for the young men's turn to come.
He nocked it, let it rest across the handgrip,
and drew the string and grooved butt of the arrow,
215 aiming from where he sat upon the stool.

                              Now flashed
arrow from twanging bow clean as a whistle
through every socket ring, and grazed not one,
to thud with heavy brazen head beyond.

                              Then quietly
Odysseus said:

                    "Telemachus, the stranger
220 you welcomed in your hall has not disgraced you.
I did not miss, neither did I take all day
stringing the bow. My hand and eye are sound,
not so contemptible as the young men say.
The hour has come to cook their lordships' mutton—
225 supper by daylight. Other amusements later,

♦ **Lines 198-205:** The epic simile comparing Odysseus to a musician stringing his harp emphasizes Odysseus' grace and skill.

♦ **Lines 206-209:** The thunder, as a sign from Zeus, indicates that the gods are on Odysseus' side.

with song and harping that adorn a feast."
He dropped his eyes and nodded, and the prince
Telemachus, true son of King Odysseus,
belted his sword on, clapped hand to his spear,
230 and with a clink and glitter of keen bronze
stood by his chair, in the forefront near his father.

◆ **Lines 227-231:** Note that this book ends with the image of father and son standing side by side facing more than one hundred enemies.

# Book Twenty-Two:
## Death in the Great Hall

Now shrugging off his rags the wiliest fighter of the
        islands
leapt and stood on the broad door sill, his own bow in his
        hand.
He poured out at his feet a rain of arrows from the quiver
235 and spoke to the crowd:

◆ **Line 232:** The epithet "the wiliest fighter of the islands" emphasizes Odysseus' cleverness at this important point in the story.

    "So much for that. Your clean-cut game is over.
Now watch me hit a target that no man has hit before,
if I can make this shot. Help me, Apollo."[8]

**8. Apollo:** the god Apollo was the patron of archers.

He drew to his fist the cruel head of an arrow for Antinous
just as the young man leaned to lift his beautiful drinking
        cup,
240 embossed, two-handled, golden: the cup was in his fingers:
the wine was even at his lips: and did he dream of death?
How could he? In that revelry amid his throng of friends
who would imagine a single foe—though a strong foe
        indeed—
could dare to bring death's pain on him and darkness on
        his eyes?
245 Odysseus' arrow hit him under the chin
and punched up to the feathers through his throat.

Backward and down he went, letting the winecup fall
from his shocked hand. Like pipes his nostrils jetted
crimson runnels, a river of mortal red,
250 and one last kick upset his table
knocking the bread and meat to soak in dusty blood.

Now as they craned to see their champion where he lay
the suitors jostled in uproar down the hall,

◆**Lines 238-251:** Think about why Odysseus kills Antinous first.

everyone on his feet. Wildly they turned and scanned
255  the walls in the long room for arms; but not a shield,
not a good ashen spear was there for a man to take and
    throw.
All they could do was yell in outrage at Odysseus:

"Foul! to shoot at a man! That was your last shot!"

"Your own throat will be slit for this!"
                        "Our finest lad is down!
260  You killed the best on Ithaca."
                    "Buzzards will tear your eyes out!"

For they imagined as they wished—that it was a
    wild shot,
an unintended killing—fools, not to comprehend
they were already in the grip of death.
But glaring under his brows Odysseus answered:

265  "You yellow dogs, you thought I'd never make it
home from the land of Troy. You took my house to
    plunder,
twisted my maids to serve your beds. You dared
bid for my wife while I was still alive.
Contempt[9] was all you had for the gods who rule wide
    heaven,
270  contempt for what men say of you hereafter.
Your last hour has come. You die in blood."

As they all took this in, sickly green fear
pulled at their entrails, and their eyes flickered
looking for some hatch or hideaway from death.
275  Eurymachus alone could speak. He said:

"If you are Odysseus of Ithaca come back,
all that you say these men have done is true.
Rash actions, many here, more in the countryside.
But here he lies, the man who caused them all.
280  Antinous was the ringleader, he whipped us on
to do these things. He cared less for a marriage
than for the power Croneon has denied him
as king of Ithaca. For that
he tried to trap your son and would have killed him.
285  He is dead now and has his portion. Spare
your own people. As for ourselves, we'll make

**Lines 254-256:** In preparation for this confrontation, Odysseus and Telemachus earlier removed all the weapons and shields that were hanging on the walls.

**Lines 264-271:** In this speech, Odysseus reveals his identity.

**9. contempt** (kən tempt′): scorn; disrespect.

**Lines 275-290:** Note Eurymachus' strategy here.

restitution[10] of wine and meat consumed, and add, each one, a tithe of twenty oxen
with gifts of bronze and gold to warm your heart.
290 Meanwhile we cannot blame you for your anger."

10. **restitution** (res′ tə to͞o′ shən): repayment.

Odysseus glowered under his black brows
and said:
                         "Not for the whole treasure of your fathers,
all you enjoy, lands, flocks, or any gold
put up by others, would I hold my hand.
295 There will be killing till the score is paid.
You forced yourselves upon this house. Fight your way
     out,
or run for it, if you think you'll escape death.
I doubt one man of you skins by."

**♦Lines 291–298:** Consider why Odysseus rejects Eurymachus' offer of restitution.

They felt their knees fail, and their hearts—but heard
300 Eurymachus for the last time rallying them.

"Friends," he said, "the man is implacable.
Now that he's got his hands on bow and quiver
he'll shoot from the big door stone there
until he kills us to the last man.
                                        Fight, I say,
305 let's remember the joy of it. Swords out!
Hold up your tables to deflect his arrows.
After me, everyone: rush him where he stands.
If we can budge him from the door, if we can pass
into the town, we'll call out men to chase him.
310 This fellow with his bow will shoot no more."

**♦Lines 304–310:** Eurymachus urges the group of suitors to gang up on Odysseus, who is blocking the only exit from the banquet hall.

He drew his own sword as he spoke, a broadsword of
     fine bronze,
honed like a razor on either edge. Then crying hoarse
     and loud
he hurled himself at Odysseus. But the kingly man let fly
an arrow at that instant, and the quivering feathered butt
315 sprang to the nipple of his breast as the barb stuck in his
     liver.
The bright broadsword clanged down. He lurched and
     fell aside,
pitching across his table. His cup, his bread and meat,
were spilt and scattered far and wide, and his head slammed
     on the ground.

Revulsion, anguish in his heart, with both feet kicking out,
320  he downed his chair, while the shrouding wave of mist
    closed on his eyes.
    Amphinomus[11] now came running at Odysseus,
broadsword naked in his hand. He thought to make
the great soldier give way at the door.
But with a spear throw from behind Telemachus hit him
325  between the shoulders, and the lancehead drove
clear through his chest. He left his feet and fell
forward, thudding, forehead against the ground.
Telemachus swerved around him, leaving the long dark
    spear
planted in Amphinomus. If he paused to yank it out
330  someone might jump him from behind or cut him down
    with a sword
at the moment he bent over. So he ran—ran from the
    tables
to his father's side and halted, panting, saying:

"Father let me bring you a shield and spear,
a pair of spears, a helmet.
335  I can arm on the run myself; I'll give
outfits to Eumaeus and this cowherd.
Better to have equipment."

                       Said Odysseus:
"Run then, while I hold them off with arrows
as long as the arrows last. When all are gone
340  if I'm alone they can dislodge me."

                             Quick
upon his father's word Telemachus
ran to the room where spears and armor lay.
He caught up four light shields, four pairs of spears,
four helms of war high-plumed with flowing manes,
345  and ran back, loaded down, to his father's side.
He was the first to pull a helmet on
and slide his bare arm in a buckler strap.
The servants armed themselves, and all three took their
    stand
beside the master of battle.
                       While he had arrows
350  he aimed and shot, and every shot brought down
one of his huddling enemies.
But when all barbs had flown from the bowman's fist,

**11. Amphinomus** (am fin′ ə
məs)

◆ **Lines 321-337:** Telemachus
proves to be a valuable help
to his father.

he leaned his bow in the bright entry way
beside the door, and armed: a four-ply shield
355      hard on his shoulder, and a crested helm,
horsetailed, nodding stormy upon his head,
then took his tough and bronze-shod spears.

*The suitors make various unsuccessful attempts to expel
Odysseus from his post at the door. Athena urges Odysseus on
to battle, yet holds back her fullest aid, waiting for Odysseus
and Telemachus to prove themselves. Six of the suitors attempt
an attack on Odysseus, but Athena deflects their arrows.
Odysseus and his men seize this opportunity to launch their
own attack, and the suitors begin to fall. At last Athena's
presence becomes known to all, as the shape of her shield
becomes visible above the hall. The suitors, recognizing the
intervention of the gods on Odysseus' behalf, are frantic to
escape but to no avail. Odysseus and his men are compared to
falcons who show no mercy to the flocks of birds they pursue
and capture. Soon the room is reeking with blood. Thus the
battle with the suitors comes to an end, and Odysseus
prepares himself to meet Penelope.*

# Book Twenty-Three:
## The Trunk of the Olive Tree

Greathearted Odysseus, home at last,
was being bathed now by Eurynome[12]
360      and rubbed with golden oil, and clothed again
in a fresh tunic and a cloak. Athena
lent him beauty, head to foot. She made him
taller, and massive, too, with crisping hair
in curls like petals of wild hyacinth
365      but all red-golden. Think of gold infused
on silver by a craftsman, whose fine art
Hephaestus[13] taught him, or Athena; one
whose work moves to delight: just so she lavished
beauty over Odysseus' head and shoulders.
370      He sat then in the same chair by the pillar,
facing his silent wife, and said:

**12. Eurynome** (yo͞o rin′ ə mē): a servant.

◆ **Lines 361-369:** Notice that Athena enhances Odysseus' physical appearance before his reunion with his wife.

**13. Hephaestus** (hē fes′ təs): the god of fire; also armorer and craftsman, who made weapons and gold furnishings for the other gods.

"Strange woman,
the immortals of Olympus made you hard,
harder than any. Who else in the world
would keep aloof as you do from her husband
375 if he returned to her from years of trouble,
cast on his own land in the twentieth year?

Nurse, make up a bed for me to sleep on.
Her heart is iron in her breast."

Penelope
spoke to Odysseus now. She said:

"Strange man,
380 if man you are . . . This is no pride on my part
nor scorn for you—not even wonder, merely.
I know so well how you—how he—appeared
boarding the ship for Troy. But all the same . . .

Make up his bed for him, Eurycleia.
385 Place it outside the bedchamber my lord
built with his own hands. Pile the big bed
with fleeces, rugs, and sheets of purest linen."

With this she tried him to the breaking point,
and he turned on her in a flash raging:

390 "Woman, by heaven you've stung me now!
Who dared to move my bed?
No builder had the skill for that—unless
a god came down to turn the trick. No mortal
in his best days could budge it with a crowbar.
395 There is our pact and pledge, our secret sign,
built into that bed—my handiwork
and no one else's!
An old trunk of olive
grew like a pillar on the building plot,
and I laid out our bedroom round that tree,
400 lined up the stone walls, built the walls and roof,
gave it a doorway and smooth-fitting doors.
Then I lopped off the silver leaves and branches,
hewed and shaped that stump from the roots up
into a bedpost, drilled it, let it serve
405 as model for the rest. I planed them all,
inlaid them all with silver, gold and ivory,

◆ **Lines 371-383:** Think about why Penelope might hold herself aloof from a man who claims to be her husband from twenty years before and who has just killed one hundred men in her banquet hall.

◆ **Lines 397-410:** One of the four posts of the bed is the trunk of an olive tree still rooted in the ground, which only Odysseus is supposed to know about. The bed symbolizes Odysseus' and Penelope's lasting relationship.

*from* The Odyssey **435**

and stretched a bed between—a pliant web
of oxhide thongs dyed crimson.

                        There's our sign!
I know no more. Could someone else's hand
410  have sawn that trunk and dragged the frame away?"

Their secret! as she heard it told, her knees
grew tremulous and weak, her heart failed her.
With eyes brimming tears she ran to him,
throwing her arms around his neck and kissed him,
415  murmuring:

                         "Do not rage at me, Odysseus!
No one ever matched your caution! Think
what difficulty the gods gave: they denied us
life together in our prime and flowering years,
kept us from crossing into age together.
420  Forgive me, don't be angry. I could not
welcome you with love on sight! I armed myself
long ago against the frauds of men,
impostors who might come—and all those many
whose underhanded ways bring evil on!
425  Helen of Argos, daughter of Zeus and Leda,
would she have joined the stranger, lain with him,
if she had known her destiny? known the Achaeans
in arms would bring her back to her own country?
Surely a goddess moved her to adultery,
430  her blood unchilled by war and evil coming,
the years, the desolation; ours, too.
But here and now, what sign could be so clear
as this of our own bed?
No other man has ever laid eyes on it—
435  only my own slave, Actoris,[14] that my father
sent with me as a gift—she kept our door.
You make my stiff heart know that I am yours."

Now from his breast into his eyes the ache
of longing mounted, and he wept at last,
440  his dear wife, clear and faithful, in his arms,
longed for
    as the sunwarmed earth is longed for by a swimmer
spent in rough water where his ship went down
under Poseidon's blow, gale winds and tons of sea.
Few men can keep alive through a big surf

◆ **Lines 411-412:** Notice that Penelope's order to move the bed in lines 384-386 is a deliberate test to see if the man who claims to be her husband knows their secret sign. Penelope thus proves to be a shrewd trickster herself, the perfect match for Odysseus.

◆ **Lines 420-424:** These lines give insight into the battle that Penelope has had to fight during Odysseus' absence.

◆ **Lines 425-431:** Penelope contrasts her faithfulness with Helen's adultery, which was the cause of the Trojan War and therefore the cause of Penelope's and Odysseus' long separation.

**14. Actoris** (ak tō′ rəs).

445   to crawl, clotted with brine, on kindly beaches
     in joy, in joy, knowing the abyss behind:
     and so she too rejoiced, her gaze upon her husband,
     her white arms round him pressed as though forever.

◆ **Lines 441-446:** In this epic simile, Odysseus is compared to a swimmer who has survived a shipwreck and is battling rough seas to arrive finally and "in joy" on the warm beach—in this case, Penelope's "white arms."

# Thinking About the Epic

## A PERSONAL RESPONSE

*sharing impressions*

**1.** How did you feel about the reunion between Odysseus and Penelope after their twenty years apart? Jot down some impressions in your journal.

*constructing interpretations*

**2.** From what you know about Odysseus and Penelope, think of possible reasons why they stayed faithful to each other for so long.

**3.** How does Odysseus involve others in his plot to take revenge on the suitors?

**4.** Explain what new feelings or deeper understandings you have about Odysseus after reading the account of his homecoming.

    ***Think about***
- new aspects of his character revealed in this excerpt
- whether you like him more or less than before

**5.** Do you think Odysseus was right to take violent revenge on the suitors? Explain why or why not.

    ***Think about***
- why he scorns Eurymachus' offer of restitution
- whether the suitors deserve to die
- why the gods might be on Odysseus' side

## A CREATIVE RESPONSE

**6.** If Odysseus had accepted Eurymachus' offer of restitution, how might your feelings about him be different?

**7.** How does Odysseus' way of getting out of the Cyclops' cave compare to the way he takes revenge on the suitors?

> ***Think about***
> * the difficulty and complexity of each situation
> * the need for help from others
> * the amount of skill and strength needed
> * the amount of intelligence and cunning needed

**8.** Loyalty and faithfulness are major concerns throughout *The Odyssey.* Compare the ancient Greek views on these two values as they are illustrated in the excerpts with the views of Americans today.

# Connecting Reading and Writing

**1.** Think of a modern-day equivalent of the suitors—a serious one, such as a group of terrorists or a gang, or a humorous one, such as a carload of unwelcome relatives. Write a **story** of epic proportions—in prose or verse—relating how you, as epic hero or heroine, get rid of the scoundrels.

Option: Pretend you are going to stage the modern reenactment of Odysseus' revenge on the suitors. What actors would you cast to play Odysseus, Telemachus, Antinous, Eurymachus, and Penelope? Write a **proposal** to a Hollywood producer in which you give the plot summary of your production and list the actors you would cast.

**2.** What do you think it would be like for Odysseus to be home after twenty years of adventures at Troy and at sea? Imagine Odysseus' thoughts a year after his arrival home as he might express them in a **letter** to the king who was his host on Phaeacia.

Option: Have Odysseus reminisce about his life as though he were giving an **interview** on a television talk show.

**3.** Do you think Odysseus is an admirable character? Review his positive and negative qualities as shown in these two excerpts. Present your opinions, with some supporting examples, in **notes** to be used in a debate with your classmates.

Option: Imagine that Odysseus is running for political office. Write a **speech** highlighting his leadership qualities in order to persuade voters that he is the best candidate.

**4.** Speculate about why *The Odyssey* is still considered a classic more than twenty-five hundred years after it was written. Examine such aspects of the work as character, suspense, description, and theme. Present your analysis of the epic's appeal in a **book review** for a school literary magazine.

Option: Interview ten of your classmates to gather their opinions about why *The Odyssey* has endured. Write a **summary** of their comments to be shared with next year's freshman class.

# An Ancient Gesture

EDNA ST. VINCENT MILLAY

# Penelope

DOROTHY PARKER

Biographies of Millay and Parker appear on pages 643 and 644.

## Approaching the Poems

For centuries Odysseus and Penelope have so captivated the imagination of readers and writers that many other works of literature have been written about these two characters. In both of the poems that follow, twentieth-century poets explore Penelope's perspective. In "An Ancient Gesture" Odysseus is called by his Latin name, Ulysses. This poem refers to a famous episode in *The Odyssey* in which Penelope delays the suitors by claiming that she must weave a burial cloth for Odysseus' father before she can remarry. Unbeknownst to the suitors, Penelope rips out her weaving each night, thus continually postponing completion of the cloth and her own decision to marry one of the suitors. The speaker in the poem "Penelope" is Penelope herself, and she refers to Odysseus simply as "he."

# An Ancient Gesture

I thought, as I wiped my eyes on the corner of my apron:
Penelope did this too.
And more than once: you can't keep weaving all day
And undoing it all through the night;
5    Your arms get tired, and the back of your neck gets tight;
And along towards morning, when you think it will never be light,
And your husband has been gone, and you don't know where, for years,
Suddenly you burst into tears;
There is simply nothing else to do.

10   And I thought, as I wiped my eyes on the corner of my apron:
This is an ancient gesture, authentic, antique,
In the very best tradition, classic, Greek;
Ulysses did this too.
But only as a gesture,—a gesture which implied
15   To the assembled throng that he was much too moved to speak.
He learned it from Penelope. . . .
Penelope, who really cried.

# Penelope

In the pathway of the sun,
   In the footsteps of the breeze,
Where the world and sky are one,
   He shall ride the silver seas,
5       He shall cut the glittering wave,
I shall sit at home, and rock;
Rise, to heed a neighbor's knock;
Brew my tea, and snip my thread;
Bleach the linen for my bed.
10       They will call him brave.

*Audience,* 1990, TOM DUCKWORTH.

# Modern Drama

"*An artist must not be the judge of his characters or of what they say, but only an impartial witness.*"

ANTON CHEKHOV

# Setting the Stage: Understanding Drama

THE HOUSE LIGHTS DIM. Members of the audience grow quiet and settle in their seats. Backstage, an actress paces back and forth reciting her opening lines. Finally, the curtain rises.

Like fiction, drama has setting, characters, and plot. Unlike fiction, drama is meant to be performed. You see the setting. You hear the characters speak and watch them move across the stage. For a brief time, you actually witness an unfolding story—and it seems almost real, thanks to the costumes, scenery, lighting, and sound effects that create the illusion of another world.

Reading the script of a play is a different experience from watching a play, but the experience can be just as enjoyable if you take the right approach. The skills you used in reading fiction will aid you in reading drama. Look for changes in the characters and try to understand their relationships. Pay attention to the events of the plot, especially those that create suspense or bring the action to a climax. Visualize the sets, the characters' movements on stage, and the characters' expressions as they are described. As you read, see if you can imagine yourself sitting in an audience, watching these plays performed.

*Mask,* 1949,
HENRI MATISSE.
Bibliothèque Nationale, Paris.

# *Literary Vocabulary*

## INTRODUCED IN THIS UNIT

**Drama.** Drama is literature in which plot and character are developed through dialogue and action; in other words, drama is literature in play form. Dramas are intended to be performed by actors who appear on a stage or before cameras or microphones. Most plays are divided into acts, with each act having a climax. Sometimes the acts of a play are subdivided into scenes. *The Miracle Worker* is a three-act play. Each act contains several scenes, which flow into one another rather than shift abruptly. Some plays, like *A Marriage Proposal,* have only one act.

**Character.** Characters are the people (and occasionally animals or fantasy creatures) who participate in the action of a literary work. Characters are either **main** or **minor,** depending upon the extent of their development and on their importance in the work. In a script of a play, the complete cast of characters is listed at the beginning.

**Dialogue.** Dialogue is written conversation between two or more characters. Dialogue is used in all forms of literature but is most important in drama.

**Stage Directions.** Stage directions are notes included in the script of a play to help performers and directors put on the play or to help readers picture the action. Stage directions can describe setting, lighting, sound effects, the movement of actors, or the way in which dialogue is spoken.

**Flashback.** A flashback is a conversation, an episode, or an event that happened before the beginning of a play. Sometimes a flashback interrupts the chronological flow of a play to give information helpful in understanding a character's present situation.

## REVIEWED IN THIS UNIT

**Conflict    Symbol**

# The Miracle Worker

## WILLIAM GIBSON

A biography of Gibson appears on page 640.

## Approaching the Play

*The Miracle Worker* presents an important incident from the early childhood of Helen Keller, a woman who gained worldwide fame for her courage and determination in overcoming her disabilities. The play is set in the South, approximately twenty years after the Civil War. The first scene opens with a discussion between a doctor and Helen's parents—Captain Arthur Keller and his second wife, Kate. The baby, Helen, has been gravely ill.

## Building Vocabulary

These essential words are footnoted in the play.

**indulgent** (in dul′ jənt): Keller **(indulgent).** I've brought up two of them, but this is my wife's first. (page 448)

**impudence** (im′ py$\overline{oo}$ dəns): I'm badgered enough here by females without your **impudence.** (page 451)

**presumes** (prē z$\overline{oo}$mz ): This girl, this—cub of a girl—**presumes!** (page 475)

**wary** (wer′ ē): *Helen...becomes puzzled and suddenly very **wary.*** (page 487)

**compassion** (kəm pash′ ən): *She bends in **compassion** to touch her lips to Helen's temple.* (page 498)

**aversion** (ə vʉr′ zhən): Most of us take some **aversion** to our teachers. (page 504)

## Connecting Writing and Reading

In your journal, list several everyday tasks that you think would be difficult or impossible to accomplish if you could neither see, hear, nor speak. Then, as you read this play notice how difficult Helen Keller's disabilities make ordinary life for her and her family.

# CHARACTERS

| | | | |
|---|---|---|---|
| A Doctor | James | Martha | Blind Girls |
| Kate | Anagnos | Percy | A Servant |
| Keller | Annie Sullivan | Aunt Ev | Offstage Voices |
| Helen | Viney | | |

**Time.** *The 1880's.*

**Place.** *In and around the Keller homestead in Tuscumbia, Alabama; also, briefly, the Perkins Institution for the Blind, in Boston.*

*The playing space is divided into two areas by a more or less diagonal line, which runs from downstage right to upstage[1] left.*

*The area behind this diagonal is on platforms and represents the Keller house. Inside we see, down right, a family room; and up center, elevated, a bedroom. On stage level near center, outside a porch, there is a water pump.*

*The other area, in front of the diagonal, is neutral ground. It accommodates various places as designated at various times—the yard before the Keller home, the Perkins Institution for the Blind, the garden house, and so forth.*

*The convention of the staging is one of cutting through time and place, and its essential qualities are fluidity and spatial counterpoint.[2] To this end, the less set there is, the better; in a literal set, the fluidity will seem merely episodic. The stage therefore should be free, airy, unencumbered by walls. Apart from certain practical items—such as the pump, a window to climb out of, doors to be locked—locales should be only skeletal suggestions, and the movement from one to another should be accomplishable by little more than lights.*

# ACT ONE

*It is night over the Keller homestead.*

*Inside, three adults in the bedroom are grouped around a crib, in lamplight. They have been through a long vigil, and it shows in their tired bearing and disarranged clothing. One is a young gentlewoman with a sweet girlish face, Kate Keller; the second is an elderly Doctor, stethoscope at neck, thermometer in fingers; the third is a hearty gentleman in his forties with chin whiskers, Captain Arthur Keller.*

**Doctor.** She'll live.

**Kate.** Thank God.

*(The Doctor leaves them together over the crib, packs his bag.)*

**Doctor.** You're a pair of lucky parents. I can tell you now, I thought she wouldn't.

**Keller.** Nonsense, the child's a Keller; she has the constitution of a goat. She'll outlive us all.

**Doctor** *(amiably).* Yes, especially if some of

---

1. **downstage...upstage:** *downstage* refers to the area toward the front of the stage and is sometimes abbreviated *down*. *Upstage* refers to the area at the back of the stage and is abbreviated *up*.
2. **spatial counterpoint:** in drama, action that creates a visual balance by using different parts of the stage, perhaps at the same time.

you Kellers don't get a night's sleep. I mean you, Mrs. Keller.

**Keller.** You hear, Katie?

**Kate.** I hear.

**Keller** (*indulgent*).[3] I've brought up two of them, but this is my wife's first; she isn't battle-scarred yet.

**Kate.** Doctor, don't be merely considerate. Will my girl be all right?

**Doctor.** Oh, by morning she'll be knocking down Captain Keller's fences again.

**Kate.** And isn't there anything we should do?

**Keller** (*jovial*). Put up stronger fencing, ha?

**Doctor.** Just let her get well; she knows how to do it better than we do.

(*He is packed, ready to leave.*)

Main thing is the fever's gone. These things come and go in infants; never know why. Call it acute congestion of the stomach and brain.

**Keller.** I'll see you to your buggy, Doctor.

**Doctor.** I've never seen a baby with more vitality, that's the truth.

(*He beams a good night at the baby and Kate, and Keller leads him downstairs with a lamp. They go down the porch steps, and across the yard, where the Doctor goes off left; Keller stands with the lamp aloft. Kate, meanwhile, is bent lovingly over the crib, which emits a bleat; her finger is playful with the baby's face.*)

**Kate.** Hush. Don't you cry now; you've been trouble enough. Call it acute congestion, indeed. I don't see what's so cute about a congestion, just because it's yours. We'll have your father run an editorial in his paper, the wonders of modern medicine. They don't know what they're curing even when they cure it. Men, men and their battle scars; we women will have to—

(*But she breaks off, puzzled, moves her finger before the baby's eyes.*)

Will have to—Helen?

(*Now she moves her hand, quickly.*)

Helen.

(*She snaps her fingers at the baby's eyes twice, and her hand falters; after a moment she calls out, loudly.*)

Captain. Captain, will you come—

(*But she stares at the baby, and her next call is directly at her ears.*)

Captain!

(*And now, still staring, Kate screams. Keller in the yard hears it, and runs with the lamp back to the house. Kate screams again, her look intent on the baby and terrible. Keller hurries in and up.*)

**Keller.** Katie? What's wrong?

**Kate.** Look.

(*She makes a pass with her hand in the crib, at the baby's eyes.*)

**Keller.** What, Katie? She's well; she needs only time to—

**Kate.** She can't see. Look at her eyes.

(*She takes the lamp from him, moves it before the child's face.*)

She can't *see!*

**Keller** (*hoarsely*). Helen.

**Kate.** Or hear. When I screamed, she didn't

---

3. **indulgent** (in dul′ jənt): kind or too kind; not strict.

blink. Not an eyelash—

**Keller.** Helen. Helen!

**Kate.** She can't *hear* you!

**Keller.** *Helen!*

(*His face has something like fury in it, crying the child's name. Kate, almost fainting, presses her knuckles to her mouth, to stop her own cry. The room dims out quickly.*

*Time, in the form of a slow tune of distant belfry chimes that approaches in a crescendo and then fades, passes; the light comes up again on a day five years later, on three kneeling children and an old dog outside around the pump.*

*The dog is a setter named Belle, and she is sleeping. Two of the children are black, Martha and Percy. The third child is Helen, six and a half years old, quite unkempt, in body a vivacious little person with a fine head; attractive, but noticeably blind, one eye larger and protruding. Her gestures are abrupt, insistent, lacking in human restraint, and her face never smiles. She is flanked by the other two, in a litter of paper-doll cutouts; and while they speak, Helen's hands thrust at their faces in turn, feeling baffledly at the movements of their lips.*)

**Martha** (*snipping*). First I'm gonna cut off this doctor's legs, one, two, now then—

**Percy.** Why you cuttin' off that doctor's legs?

**Martha.** I'm gonna give him a operation. Now I'm gonna cut off his arms, one, two. Now I'm gonna fix up—

(*She pushes* Helen's *hand away from her mouth.*)

You stop that.

**Percy.** Cut off his stomach; that's a good operation.

**Martha.** No, I'm gonna cut off his head first; he got a bad cold.

**Percy.** Ain't gonna be much of that doctor left to fix up, time you finish all them opera—

(*But Helen is poking her fingers inside his mouth, to feel his tongue; he bites at them, annoyed, and she jerks them away. Helen now fingers her own lips, moving them in imitation, but soundlessly.*)

**Martha.** What you do, bite her hand?

**Percy.** That's how I do. She keep pokin' her fingers in my mouth; I just bite 'em off.

**Martha.** What she tryin' do now?

**Percy.** She tryin' *talk.* She gonna get mad. Looka her tryin' talk.

(Helen *is scowling, the lips under her fingers moving in ghostly silence, growing more and more frantic; until in a bizarre rage, she bites at her own fingers. This sends Percy off into laughter, but alarms Martha.*)

**Martha.** Hey, you stop now.

(*She pulls* Helen's *hand down.*)

You just sit quiet and—

(*But at once Helen topples Martha on her back, knees pinning her shoulders down, and grabs the scissors. Martha screams. Percy darts to the bell string on the porch, yanks it, and the bell rings.*

*Inside, the lights have been gradually coming up on the main room, where we see the family informally gathered, talking, but in pantomime; Kate sits darning socks near a cradle, occasionally rocking it. Captain Keller in spectacles is working over newspaper pages at a table. A benign visitor in a hat, Aunt Ev, is sharing the sewing basket, putting the finishing touches on a big, shapeless doll made out of towels. An indolent young man,* James Keller, *is at the window watching the children.*

*With the ring of the bell,* Kate *is instantly on her feet and out the door onto the porch, to take in the scene. Now we see what these five years have done to her. The girlish playfulness is gone; she is a woman steeled in grief.*)

**Kate** (*for the thousandth time*). Helen.

(*She is down the steps at once to them, seizing* Helen's *wrists and lifting her off* Martha. Martha *runs off in tears and screams for momma, with* Percy *after her.*)

Let me have those scissors.

(*Meanwhile the family inside is alerted,* Aunt Ev *joining* James *at the window.* Captain Keller *resumes work.*)

**James** (*blandly*). She only dug Martha's eyes out. Almost dug. It's always almost. No point worrying till it happens, is there?

(*They gaze out, while* Kate *reaches for the scissors in* Helen's *hand. But* Helen *pulls the scissors back. They struggle for them for a moment; then* Kate *gives up, lets* Helen *keep them. She tries to draw* Helen *into the house.* Helen *jerks away.* Kate *next goes down on her knees, takes* Helen's *hands gently, and using the scissors like a doll, makes* Helen *caress and cradle them; she points* Helen's *finger housewards.* Helen's *whole body now becomes eager; she surrenders the scissors.* Kate *turns her toward the door and gives her a little push.* Helen *scrambles up and toward the house, and* Kate, *rising, follows her.*)

**Aunt Ev.** How does she stand it? Why haven't you seen this Baltimore man? It's not a thing you can let go on and on, like the weather.

**James.** The weather here doesn't ask permission of me, Aunt Ev. Speak to my father.

**Aunt Ev.** Arthur. Something ought to be done for that child.

**Keller.** A refreshing suggestion. What?

(Kate *entering turns* Helen *to* Aunt Ev, *who gives her the towel doll.*)

**Aunt Ev.** Why, this very famous oculist in Baltimore I wrote you about. What was his name?

**Kate.** Dr. Chisholm.

**Aunt Ev.** Yes, I heard lots of cases of blindness that people thought couldn't be cured, he's cured. He just does wonders. Why don't you write to him?

**Keller.** I've stopped believing in wonders.

**Kate** (*rocks the cradle*). I think the Captain will write to him soon. Won't you Captain?

**Keller.** No.

**James** (*lightly*). Good money after bad, or bad after good. Or bad after bad—

**Aunt Ev.** Well, if it's just a question of money, Arthur, now you're marshal you have this Yankee money. Might as well—

**Keller.** Not money. The child's been to specialists all over Alabama and Tennessee. If I thought it would do good, I'd have her to every fool doctor in the country.

**Kate.** I think the Captain will write to him soon.

**Keller.** Katie, how many times can you let them break your heart?

**Kate.** Any number of times.

(Helen, *meanwhile, sits on the floor to explore the doll with her fingers, and her hand pauses over the face. This is no face, a blank area of towel, and it troubles her. Her hand searches for features, and taps questioningly for eyes, but no one notices. She then yanks at her Aunt's dress, and taps again vigorously for eyes.)*

**Aunt Ev.** What, child?

*(Obviously not hearing, Helen commences to go around, from person to person, tapping for eyes, but no one attends or understands.)*

**Kate** *(no break).* As long as there's the least chance. For her to see. Or hear, or—

**Keller.** There isn't. Now I must finish here.

**Kate.** I think, with your permission, Captain, I'd like to write.

**Keller.** I said no, Katie.

**Aunt Ev.** Why, writing does no harm, Arthur, only a little bitty letter. To see if he can help her.

**Keller.** He can't.

**Kate.** We won't know that to be a fact, Captain, until after you write.

**Keller** *(rising, emphatic).* Katie, he can't. *(He collects his papers.)*

**James** *(facetiously).* Father stands up; that makes it a fact.

**Keller.** You be quiet! I'm badgered enough here by females without your impudence.[4]

*(James shuts up, makes himself scarce. Helen now is groping among things on Keller's desk, and paws his papers to the floor. Keller is exasperated.)*

Katie.

*(Kate quickly turns Helen away, and retrieves the papers.)*

I might as well try to work in a henyard as in this house—

**James** *(placating).* You really ought to put her away, Father.

**Kate** *(staring up).* What?

**James.** Some asylum. It's the kindest thing.

**Aunt Ev.** Why, she's your sister, James, not a nobody—

**James.** Half sister, and half-mentally defective; she can't even keep herself clean. It's not pleasant to see her about all the time.

**Kate.** Do you dare? Complain of what you *can* see?

**Keller** *(very annoyed).* This discussion is at an end! I'll thank you not to broach it again, Ev.

*(Silence descends at once. Helen gropes her way with the doll, and Keller turns back for a final word, explosive.)*

I've done as much as I can bear; I can't give my whole life to it! The house is at sixes and sevens from morning till night over the child. It's time some attention was paid to Mildred here instead!

**Kate** *(gently dry).* You'll wake her up, Captain.

**Keller.** I want some peace in the house. I don't care how, but one way we won't have it is by rushing up and down the country every time someone hears of a new quack.[5] I'm as sensible to this affliction as anyone else; it hurts me to look at the girl.

**Kate.** It was not our affliction I meant you to write about, Captain.

*(Helen is back at Aunt Ev, fingering her dress, and yanks two buttons from it.)*

---

4. **impudence** (im′ pyo͞o dəns): shameless boldness and disrespect.

5. **quack:** a person without proper training or skill who pretends to be a doctor, often falsely claiming to be able to perform wonder cures.

**Aunt Ev.** Helen! My buttons.

(Helen *pushes the buttons into the doll's face. Kate now sees, comes swiftly to kneel, lifts Helen's hands to her own eyes in question.*)

**Kate.** Eyes?

(Helen *nods energetically.*)

She wants the doll to have eyes.

(*Another kind of silence now, while Kate takes pins and buttons from the sewing basket and attaches them to the doll as eyes. Keller stands, caught, and watches morosely. Aunt Ev blinks, and conceals her emotions by inspecting her dress.*)

**Aunt Ev.** My goodness me, I'm not decent.

**Kate.** She doesn't know better, Aunt Ev. I'll sew them on again.

**James.** Never learn with everyone letting her do anything she takes it into her mind to—

**Keller.** You be quiet!

**James.** What did I say now?

**Keller.** You talk too much.

**James.** I was agreeing with you!

**Keller.** Whatever it was. Deprived child, the least she can have are the little things she wants.

(James, *very wounded, stalks out of the room onto the porch; he remains here, sulking.*)

**Aunt Ev** (*indulgently*). It's worth a couple of buttons. Kate, look.

(Helen *now has the doll with eyes, and cannot contain herself for joy; she rocks the doll, pats it vigorously, kisses it.*)

This child has more sense than all these

men Kellers, if there's ever any way to reach that mind of hers.

(*But Helen suddenly has come upon the cradle, and unhesitatingly overturns it; the swaddled baby tumbles out, and Captain Keller barely manages to dive and catch it in time.*)

**Keller.** Helen!

(*All are in commotion. The baby screams, but Helen, unperturbed, is laying her doll in its place. Kate, on her knees, pulls her hands off the cradle, wringing them. Helen is bewildered.*)

**Kate.** Helen, Helen, you're not to do such things; how can I make you understand—

**Keller** (*hoarsely*). Katie.

**Kate.** How can I get it into your head, my darling, my poor—

**Keller.** Katie, some way of teaching her an iota of discipline has to be—

**Kate** (*flaring*). How can you discipline an afflicted child? Is it her fault?

(Helen's *fingers have fluttered to her* Mother's *lips, vainly trying to comprehend their movements.*)

**Keller.** I didn't say it was her fault.

**Kate.** Then whose? I don't know what to do! How can I teach her, beat her—until she's black and blue?

**Keller.** It's not safe to let her run around loose. Now there must be a way of confining her, somehow, so she can't—

**Kate.** Where, in a cage? She's a growing child; she has to use her limbs!

**Keller.** Answer me one thing. Is it fair to Mildred here?

**Kate** (*inexorably*). Are you willing to put her away?

(*Now* Helen's *face darkens in the same rage as at herself earlier, and her hand strikes at* Kate's *lips.* Kate *catches her hand again, and* Helen *begins to kick, struggle, twist.*)

**Keller.** Now what?

**Kate.** She wants to talk, like—be like you and me.

(*She holds* Helen, *struggling, until we hear from the child her first sound so far, an inarticulate, weird noise in her throat such as an animal in a trap might make; and* Kate *releases her. The second she is free,* Helen *blunders away, collides violently with a chair, falls, and sits weeping.* Kate *comes to her, embraces, caresses, soothes her, and buries her own face in her hair, until she can control her voice.*)

Every day she slips further away. And I don't know how to call her back.

**Aunt Ev.** Oh, I've a mind to take her up to Baltimore myself. If that doctor can't help her, maybe he'll know who can.

**Keller** (*presently, heavily*). I'll write the man, Katie.

(*He stands with the baby in his clasp, staring at* Helen's *head, hanging down on* Kate's *arm.*

*The lights dim out, except the one on* Kate *and* Helen. *In the twilight,* James, Aunt Ev, *and* Keller *move off slowly, formally, in separate directions;* Kate, *with* Helen *in her arms, remains, motionless, in an image that overlaps into the next scene and fades only when it is well under way.*

*Without pause, from the dark down left we hear a man's voice with a Greek accent speaking.*)

**Anagnos.** —who could do nothing for the girl, of course. It was Dr. Bell who thought she might somehow be taught. I have written the family only that a suitable governess, Miss Annie Sullivan, has been found here in Boston—

(*The lights begin to come up, down left, on a long table and chair. The table contains equipment for teaching the blind by touch—a small replica of the human skeleton, stuffed animals, models of flowers and plants, piles of books. The chair contains a girl of twenty,* Annie Sullivan, *with a face that in repose is grave and rather obstinate; and when active is impudent, combative, twinkling with all the life that is lacking in* Helen's, *and handsome. There is a crude vitality to her. Her suitcase is at her knee.* Anagnos, *a stocky, bearded man, comes into the light only toward the end of his speech.*)

**Anagnos.** —and will come. It will no doubt be difficult for you there, Annie. But it has been difficult for you at our school too, hm? Gratifying, yes, when you came to us and could not spell your name, to accomplish so much here in a few years, but always an Irish battle. For independence.

(*He studies* Annie, *humorously; she does not open her eyes.*)

This is my last time to counsel you, Annie, and you do lack some—by some I mean all—what, tact or talent to bend. To others. And what has saved you on more than one occasion here at Perkins is that there was nowhere to expel you to. Your eyes hurt?

**Annie.** My ears, Mr. Anagnos.

(*And now she has opened her eyes. They are inflamed, vague, slightly crossed, clouded by the granular growth of trachoma;[6] and she often keeps them closed to shut out the pain of light.*)

**Anagnos** (*severely*). Nowhere but back to Tewksbury, where children learn to be saucy. Annie, I know how dreadful it was there, but that battle is dead and done with. Why not let it stay buried?

**Annie** (*cheerily*). I think God must owe me a resurrection.

**Anagnos** (*a bit shocked*). What?

**Annie** (*taps her brow*). Well, he keeps digging up that battle!

**Anagnos.** That is not a proper thing to say, Annie. It is what I mean.

**Annie** (*meekly*). Yes. I know what I'm like. What's this child like?

**Anagnos.** Like?

**Annie.** Well—bright or dull, to start off.

**Anagnos.** No one knows. And if she is dull, you have no patience with this?

**Annie.** Oh, in grownups you have to, Mr. Anagnos. I mean in children it just seems a little—precocious. Can I use that word?

**Anagnos.** Only if you can spell it.

**Annie.** Premature. So I hope at least she's a bright one.

**Anagnos.** Deaf, blind, mute—who knows? She is like a little safe, locked, that no one can open. Perhaps there is a treasure inside.

**Annie.** Maybe it's empty, too?

**Anagnos.** Possible. I should warn you; she is much given to tantrums.

**Annie.** Means something is inside. Well, so am I, if I believe all I hear. Maybe you should warn *them*.

**Anagnos** (*frowns*). Annie, I wrote them no word of your history. You will find yourself among strangers now, who know nothing of it.

**Annie.** Well, we'll keep them in a state of blessed ignorance.

**Anagnos.** Perhaps *you* should tell it?

**Annie** (*bristling*). Why? I have enough trouble with people who don't know.

**Anagnos.** So they will understand. When you have trouble.

**Annie.** The only time I have trouble is when I'm right.

(*But she is amused at herself, as is Anagnos.*)

Is it my fault it's so often? I won't give them trouble, Mr. Anagnos. I'll be so ladylike they won't notice I've come.

**Anagnos.** Annie, be—humble. It is not as if you have so many offers to pick and choose. You will need their affection, working with this child.

**Annie** (*humorously*). I hope I won't need their pity.

**Anagnos.** Oh, we can all use some pity.

(*crisply*)

So. You are no longer our pupil; we throw you into the world, a teacher. *If the child can be taught.* No one expects you to work miracles, even for twenty-five dollars a month. Now, in this envelope a loan, for the railroad, which you will repay me when you have a bank account. But in this box, a gift. With our love.

---

6. **trachoma** (trə kō′ mə): a contagious eye infection.

(Annie *opens the small box he extends, and sees a garnet ring. She looks up, blinking, and down.*)

I think other friends are ready to say goodbye.

(*He moves as though to open doors.*)

**Annie.** Mr. Anagnos.

(*Her voice is trembling.*)

Dear Mr. Anagnos, I—

(*But she swallows while getting the ring on her finger, and cannot continue until she finds a woebegone joke.*)

Well, what should I say? I'm an ignorant, opinionated girl, and everything I am I owe to you?

**Anagnos** (*smiles*). That is only half true, Annie.

**Annie.** Which half? I crawled in here like a drowned rat. I thought I died when Jimmie died, that I'd never again—come alive. Well, you say with love so easy, and I haven't *loved* a soul since, and I never will, I suppose; but this place gave me more than my eyes back. Or taught me how to spell, which I'll never learn anyway; but with all the fights and the trouble I've been here, it taught me what help is, and how to live again; and I don't want to say goodbye. Don't open the door; I'm crying.

**Anagnos** (*gently*). They will not see.

(*He moves again as though opening doors, and in comes a group of girls, eight-year-olds to seventeen-year-olds; as they walk, we see they are blind. Anagnos shepherds them in with a hand.*)

**A Child.** Annie?

**Annie** (*her voice cheerful*). Here, Beatrice.

(*As soon as they locate her voice, they throng joyfully to her, speaking all at once. Annie is down on her knees to the smallest, and the following are the more intelligible fragments in the general hubbub.*)

**Children.** There's a present. We bought you a going-away present, Annie!

**Annie.** Oh, now, you shouldn't have—

**Children.** We did, we did. Where's the present?

**Smallest Child** (*mournfully*). Don't go, Annie, away.

**Children.** Alice has it. Alice! Where's Alice? Here I am! Where? Here!

(*An arm is aloft of the group, waving a present; Annie reaches for it.*)

**Annie.** I have it. I have it, everybody. Should I open it?

**Children.** Open it; everyone be quiet! Do, Annie! She's opening it. Ssh!

(*A setting of silence while Annie unwraps it. The present is a pair of smoked glasses, and she stands still.*)

Is it open, Annie?

**Annie.** It's open.

**Children.** It's for your eyes, Annie. Put them on, Annie! 'Cause Mrs. Hopkins said your eyes hurt since the operation. And she said you're going where the sun is *fierce*.

**Annie.** I'm putting them on now.

**Smallest Child** (*mournfully*). Don't go, Annie, where the sun is fierce.

**Children.** Do they fit all right?

**Annie.** Oh, they fit just fine.

**Children.** Did you put them on? Are

they pretty, Annie?

**Annie.**  Oh, my eyes feel hundreds of percent better already, and pretty. Why, do you know how I look in them? Splendiloquent. Like a race horse!

**Children** (*delighted*).  There's another present! Beatrice! We have a present for Helen, too! Give it to her, Beatrice. Here Annie!

(*This present is an elegant doll, with movable eyelids and a momma sound.*)

It's for Helen. And we took up a collection to buy it. And Laura dressed it.

**Annie.**  It's beautiful!

**Children.**  So don't forget; you be sure to give it to Helen from us, Annie!

**Annie.**  I promise it will be the first thing I give her. If I don't keep it for myself, that is; you know I can't be trusted with dolls!

**Smallest Child** (*mournfully*).  Don't go, Annie, to her.

**Annie** (*her arm around her*).  Sarah, dear. I don't *want* to go.

**Smallest Child.**  Then why are you going?

**Annie** (*gently*).  Because I'm a big girl now, and big girls have to earn a living. It's the only way I can. But if you don't smile for me first, what I'll just have to do is—

(*She pauses, inviting it.*)

**Smallest Child.**  What?

**Annie.**  Put *you* in my suitcase, instead of this doll. And take *you* to Helen in Alabama!

(*This strikes the children as very funny, and they begin to laugh and tease the smallest child, who after a moment does smile for Annie.*)

**Anagnos** (*then*).  Come, children. We must get the trunk into the carriage and Annie into her train, or no one will go to Alabama. Come, come.

(*He shepherds them out, and Annie is left alone on her knees with the doll in her lap. She reaches for her suitcase, and by a subtle change in the color of the light, we go with her thoughts into another time. We hear a boy's voice whispering; perhaps we see shadowy intimations of these speakers in the background.*)

**Boy's Voice.**  Where we goin', Annie?

**Annie** (*in dread*).  Jimmie.

**Boy's Voice.**  Where we goin'?

**Annie.**  I said—I'm takin' care of you—

**Boy's Voice.**  Forever and ever?

**Man's Voice** (*impersonal*).  Annie Sullivan, aged nine, virtually blind. James Sullivan, aged seven—What's the matter with your leg, Sonny?

**Annie.**  Forever and ever.

**Man's Voice.**  Can't he walk without that crutch?

(*Annie shakes her head, and does not stop shaking it.*)

Girl goes to the women's ward. Boy to the men's.

**Boy's Voice** (*in terror*).  Annie! Annie, don't let them take me—Annie!

**Anagnos** (*offstage*).  Annie! Annie?

(*But this voice is real, in the present, and Annie comes up out of her horror, clearing her head with a final shake. The lights begin to pick out Kate in the Keller house, as Annie in a bright tone calls back.*)

**Annie.**  Coming!

*(This word catches* Kate, *who stands half turned and attentive to it, almost as though hearing it. Meanwhile,* Annie *turns and hurries out, lugging the suitcase.*

*The room dims out; the sound of railroad wheels begins from off left, and maintains itself in a constant rhythm underneath the following scenes; the remaining lights have come up on the Keller homestead.* James *is lounging on the porch, waiting. In the upper bedroom which is to be* Annie's, Helen *is alone, puzzledly exploring, fingering and smelling things, the curtains, empty drawers in the bureau, water in the pitcher by the washbasin, fresh towels on the bedstead. Downstairs in the family room,* Kate, *turning to a mirror, hastily adjusts her bonnet, watched by a black servant in an apron,* Viney.)

**Viney.** Let Mr. Jimmy go by hisself. You been pokin' that garden all day; you ought to rest your feet.

**Kate.** I can't wait to see her, Viney.

**Viney.** Maybe she ain't gone be on this train neither.

**Kate.** Maybe she is.

**Viney.** And maybe she ain't.

**Kate.** And maybe she is. Where's Helen?

**Viney.** She upstairs, smellin' around. She know somethin' funny's goin' on.

**Kate.** Let her have her supper as soon as Mildred's in bed, and tell Captain Keller when he comes that we'll be delayed tonight.

**Viney.** Again?

**Kate.** I don't think we need say *again.* Simply delayed will do.

*(She runs upstairs to* Annie's *room,* Viney *speaking after her.)*

**Viney.** I mean that's what he gone say. "What, again?"

*(*Viney *works at setting the table. Upstairs* Kate *stands in the doorway, watching* Helen's *groping explorations.)*

**Kate.** Yes, we're expecting someone. Someone for my Helen.

*(*Helen *happens upon her skirt, clutches her leg.* Kate *in a tired dismay, kneels to tidy her hair and soiled pinafore.)*

Oh, dear, this was clean not an hour ago.

*(*Helen *feels her bonnet, shakes her head darkly, and tugs to get it off.* Kate *retains it with one hand, diverts* Helen *by opening her other hand under her nose.)*

Here. For while I'm gone.

*(*Helen *sniffs, reaches, and pops something into her mouth, while* Kate *speaks a bit guiltily.)*

I don't think one peppermint drop will spoil your supper.

*(She gives* Helen *a quick kiss, and hurries downstairs again. Meanwhile* Captain Keller *has entered the yard from around the rear of the house, newspaper under arm, cleaning off and munching on some radishes. He sees* James *lounging at the porch post.)*

**Keller.** Jimmie?

**James** *(unmoving).* Sir?

**Keller** *(eyes him).* You don't look dressed for anything useful, boy.

**James.** I'm not. It's for Miss Sullivan.

**Keller.** Needn't keep holding up that porch; we have wooden posts for that. I asked you to see that those strawberry plants were moved this evening.

**James.** I'm moving your—Mrs. Keller, instead. To the station.

**Keller** (*heavily*). Mrs. Keller. Must you always speak of her as though you haven't met the lady?

(*Kate comes out on the porch, and James inclines his head.*)

**James** (*ironic*). Mother.

(*He starts off the porch, but sidesteps Keller's glare like a blow.*)

I said mother!

**Kate.** Captain.

**Keller.** Evening, my dear.

**Kate.** We're off to meet the train, Captain. Supper will be a trifle delayed tonight.

**Keller.** What, again?

**Kate** (*backing out*). With your permission, Captain?

(*And they are gone, Keller watches them offstage, morosely.*

*Upstairs, Helen meanwhile has groped for her mother, touched her cheek in a meaningful gesture, waited, touched her cheek, waited, then found the open door, and made her way down. Now she comes into the family room, touches her cheek again; Viney regards her.*)

**Viney.** What you want, honey, your momma?

(*Helen touches her cheek again. Viney goes to the sideboard, gets a tea-cake, gives it into Helen's hand; Helen pops it into her mouth.*)

Guess one little tea-cake ain't gone ruin your appetite.

(*She turns Helen toward the door. Helen wanders out onto the porch, as Keller comes up the steps. Her hands encounter him, and she touches her cheek again, waits.*)

**Keller.** She's gone.

(*He is awkward with her. When he puts his hand on her head, she pulls away. Keller stands regarding her, heavily.*)

She's gone; my son and I don't get along; you don't know I'm your father; no one likes me; and supper's delayed.

(*Helen touches her cheek, waits. Keller fishes in his pocket.*)

Here, I brought you some stick candy; one nibble of sweets can't do any harm.

(*He gives her a large stick candy; Helen falls to it. Viney peers out the window.*)

**Viney** (*reproachfully*). Cap'n Keller, now how'm I gone get her to eat her supper you fill her up with that trash?

**Keller** (*roars*). Tend to your work!

(*Viney beats a rapid retreat. Keller thinks better of it, and tries to get the candy away from Helen, but Helen hangs on to it; and when Keller pulls, she gives his leg a kick. Keller hops about. Helen takes refuge with the candy down behind the pump, and Keller then irately flings his newspaper on the porch floor, stamps into the house past Viney, and disappears.*

*The lights half dim on the homestead, where Viney and Helen, going about their business, soon find their way off. Meanwhile, the railroad sounds off left have mounted in a crescendo to a climax typical of a depot at arrival time. The lights come up on stage left, and we see a suggestion of a station. Here Annie in her smoked glasses and disarrayed by travel is waiting with her suitcase, while James walks to* meet her. *She has a battered paperbound book, which is a Perkins report,[7] under her arm.*)

**James** (*coolly*). Miss Sullivan?

**Annie** (*cheerily*). Here! At last. I've been on trains so many days I thought they must be backing up every time I dozed off—

**James.** I'm James Keller.

**Annie.** James?

(*The name stops her.*)

I had a brother Jimmie. Are you Helen's?

**James.** I'm only half a brother. You're to be her governess?

**Annie** (*lightly*). Well. Try!

**James** (*eyeing her*). You look like half a governess.

(Kate *enters.* Annie *stands moveless, while* James *takes her suitcase.* Kate's *gaze on her is doubtful, troubled.*)

Mrs. Keller, Miss Sullivan.

(Kate *takes her hand.*)

**Kate** (*simply*). We've met every train for two days.

(Annie *looks at* Kate's *face, and her good humor comes back.*)

**Annie.** I changed trains every time they stopped. The man who sold me that ticket ought to be tied to the tracks—

**James.** You have a trunk, Miss Sullivan?

**Annie.** Yes.

(*She passes* James *a claim check, and he bears the suitcase out behind them.* Annie *holds the battered book.* Kate *is studying her face, and* Annie *returns the gaze. This is a mutual appraisal, southern gentlewoman and working-class Irish girl, and* Annie *is not*

quite comfortable under it.*)

You didn't bring Helen. I was hoping you would.

**Kate.** No, she's home.

(*A pause.* Annie *tries to make ladylike small talk, though her energy now and then erupts. She catches herself up, whenever she hears it.*)

**Annie.** You—live far from town, Mrs. Keller?

**Kate.** Only a mile.

**Annie.** Well, I suppose I can wait one more mile. But don't be surprised if I get out to push the horse!

**Kate.** Helen's waiting for you, too. There's been such a bustle in the house; she expects something, heaven knows what.

(*Now she voices part of her doubt, not as such, but* Annie *understands it.*)

I expected—a desiccated spinster. You're very young.

**Annie** (*resolutely*). Oh, you should have seen me when I left Boston. I got much older on this trip.

**Kate.** I mean, to teach anyone as difficult as Helen.

**Annie.** I mean to try. They can't put you in jail for trying!

**Kate.** Is it possible, even? To teach a deaf-blind child *half* of what an ordinary child learns—has that ever been done?

**Annie.** Half?

---

7. **Perkins report:** This is a reference to a report written by a Dr. Howe of the Perkins Institution for the Blind about the education of a woman who is, like Helen, deaf and blind.

**Kate.** A tenth.

**Annie** (*reluctantly*). No.

(*Kate's face loses its remaining hope, still appraising her youth.*)

Dr. Howe did wonders, but—an ordinary child? No, never. But then I thought when I was going over his reports—

(*She indicates the one in her hand.*)

—he never treated them like ordinary children. More like—eggs everyone was afraid would break.

**Kate** (*a pause*). May I ask how old you are?

**Annie.** Well, I'm not in my teens, you know! I'm twenty.

**Kate.** All of twenty.

(*Annie takes the bull by the horns, valiantly.*)

**Annie.** Mrs. Keller, don't lose heart just because I'm not on my last legs. I have three big advantages over Dr. Howe that money couldn't buy for you. One is his work behind me. I've read every word he wrote about it and he wasn't exactly what you'd call a man of few words. Another is *be* young; why, I've got energy to do anything. The third is, I've been blind.

(*But it costs her something to say this.*)

**Kate** (*quietly*). Advantages.

**Annie** (*wry*). Well, some have the luck of the Irish; some do not.

(*Kate smiles; she likes her.*)

**Kate.** What will you try to teach her first?

**Annie.** First, last, and—in between, language.

**Kate.** Language.

**Annie.** Language is to the mind more than light is to the eye. Dr. Howe said that.

**Kate.** Language.

(*She shakes her head.*)

We can't get through to teach her to sit still. You *are* young, despite your years, to have such— confidence. Do you, inside?

(*Annie studies her face; she likes her, too.*)

**Annie.** No, to tell you the truth, I'm as shaky inside as a baby's rattle!

(*They smile at each other, and Kate pats her hand.*)

**Kate.** Don't be.

(*James returns to usher them off.*)

We'll do all we can to help, and to make you feel at home. Don't think of us as strangers, Miss Annie.

**Annie**(*cheerily*). Oh, strangers aren't so strange to me. I've known them all my life!

(*Kate smiles again, Annie smiles back, and they precede James offstage.*

*The lights dim on them, having simultaneously risen full on the house. Viney has already entered the family room, taken a water pitcher, and come out and down to the pump. She pumps real water. As she looks offstage, we hear the clop of hoofs, a carriage stopping, and voices.*)

**Viney.** Cap'n Keller! Cap'n Keller, they comin'!

(*She goes back into the house, as Keller comes out on the porch to gaze.*)

She sure 'nuff came, Cap'n.

(*Keller descends, and crosses toward the carriage; this conversation begins offstage and moves on.*)

**Keller** (*very courtly*). Welcome to Ivy Green, Miss Sullivan. I take it you are Miss Sullivan—

**Kate.** My husband, Miss Annie, Captain Keller.

**Annie** (*her best behavior*). Captain, how do you do.

**Keller.** A pleasure to see you, at last. I trust you had an agreeable journey?

**Annie.** Oh, I had several! When did this country get so big?

**James.** Where would you like the trunk, Father?

**Keller.** Where Miss Sullivan can get at it, I imagine.

**Annie.** Yes, please. Where's Helen?

**Keller.** In the hall, Jimmie—

**Kate.** We've put you in the upstairs corner room, Miss Annie. If there's any breeze at all this summer, you'll feel it—

(*In the house, the setter* Belle *flees into the family room, pursued by* Helen *with groping hands. The dog doubles back out the same door, and* Helen, *still groping for her, makes her way out to the porch. She is messy; her hair tumbled, her pinafore now ripped, her shoelaces untied.* Keller *acquires the suitcase, and* Annie *gets her hands on it too, though still endeavoring to live up to the general air of propertied manners.*)

**Keller.** And the suitcase—

**Annie** (*pleasantly*). I'll take the suitcase, thanks.

**Keller.** Not at all, I have it, Miss Sullivan.

**Annie.** I'd like it.

**Keller** (*gallantly*). I couldn't think of it, Miss Sullivan. You'll find in the South we—

**Annie.** Let me.

**Keller.** —view women as the flowers of civiliza—

**Annie** (*impatiently*). I've got something in it for Helen!

(*She tugs it free;* Keller *stares.*)

Thank you. When do I see her?

**Kate.** There. There is Helen.

(Annie *turns, and sees* Helen *on the porch. A moment of silence. Then* Annie *begins across the yard to her, lugging her suitcase.*)

**Keller** (*sotto voce*[8]). Katie—

(Kate *silences him with a hand on his arm. When* Annie *finally reaches the porch steps, she stops, contemplating* Helen *for a last moment before entering her world. Then she drops the suitcase on the porch with intentional heaviness.* Helen *starts with the jar, and comes to grope over it.* Annie *puts forth her hand, and touches* Helen's. Helen *at once grasps it, and commences to explore it, like reading a face. She moves her hand on to* Annie's *forearm, and dress; and* Annie *brings her face within reach of* Helen's *fingers, which travel over it, quite without timidity, until they encounter and push aside the smoked glasses.* Annie's *gaze is grave, unpitying, very attentive. She puts her hands on* Helen's *arms, but* Helen *at once pulls away, and they confront each other with a distance between. Then* Helen *returns to the suitcase, tries to open it, cannot.* Annie *points* Helen's *hand overhead.* Helen *pulls away, tries to open the suitcase again;* Annie *points her hand overhead again.* Helen *points overhead, a question; and* Annie, *drawing* Helen's *hand to her own face, nods.* Helen *now begins tugging the suitcase toward the*

---

8. **sotto voce** (sät′ ō vō′ chē): in a low tone of voice, so as not to be overheard.

*door. When Annie tries to take it from her, she fights her off and backs through the door-way with it. Annie stands a moment, then follows her in, and together they get the suit-case up the steps into Annie's room.)*

**Kate.** Well?

**Keller.** She's very rough, Katie.

**Kate.** I like her, Captain.

**Keller.** Certainly rear a peculiar kind of young woman in the North. How old is she?

**Kate** (*vaguely*). Ohh—Well, she's not in her teens, you know.

**Keller.** She's only a child. What's her family like, shipping her off alone this far?

**Kate.** I couldn't learn. She's very close-mouthed about some things.

**Keller.** Why does she wear those glasses? I like to see a person's eyes when I talk to—

**Kate.** For the sun. She was blind.

**Keller.** Blind.

**Kate.** She's had nine operations on her eyes. One just before she left.

**Keller.** Blind, good heavens, do they expect one blind child to teach another? Has she experience at least? How long did she teach there?

**Kate.** She was a pupil.

**Keller** (*heavily*). Katie, Katie. This is her first position?

**Kate** (*bright voice*). She was valedictorian—

**Keller.** Here's a houseful of grownups can't cope with the child. How can an inexperienced, half-blind Yankee schoolgirl manage her?

*(James moves in with the trunk on his shoulder.)*

**James** (*easily*). Great improvement. Now we have two of them to look after.

**Keller.** You look after those strawberry plants!

*(James stops with the trunk. Keller turns from him without another word, and marches off.)*

**James.** Nothing I say is right.

**Kate.** Why say anything?

*(She calls.)*

Don't be long, Captain. We'll have supper right away—

*(She goes into the house, and through the rear door of the family room. James trudges in with the trunk, takes it up the steps to Annie's room, and sets it down outside the door. The lights elsewhere dim somewhat.*

*Meanwhile, inside, Annie has given Helen a key. While Annie removes her bonnet, Helen unlocks and opens the suitcase. The first thing she pulls out is a voluminous shawl. She fingers it until she perceives what it is; then she wraps it around her, and acquiring Annie's bonnet and smoked glasses as well, dons the lot. The shawl swamps her, and the bonnet settles down upon the glasses, but she stands before a mirror cocking her head to one side, then to the other, in a mockery of adult action. Annie is amused, and talks to her as one might to a kitten, with no trace of company manners.)*

**Annie.** All the trouble I went to, and that's how I look?

*(Helen then comes back to the suitcase, gropes for more, lifts out a pair of female drawers.[9])*

---

9. **drawers:** underpants.

Oh, no. Not the drawers!

(*But* Helen, *discarding them, comes to the elegant doll. Her fingers explore its features, and when she raises it and finds its eyes open and close, she is at first startled, then delighted. She picks it up, taps its head vigorously, taps her own chest, and nods questioningly.* Annie *takes her finger, points it to the doll, points it to* Helen, *and touching it to her own face, also nods.* Helen *sits back on her heels, clasps the doll to herself and rocks it.* Annie *studies her, still in bonnet and smoked glasses like a caricature of herself, and addresses her humorously.*)

All right, Miss O'Sullivan. Let's begin with doll.

(*She takes* Helen's *hand. In her palm,* Annie's *forefinger points, thumb holding her other fingers clenched.*)

D.

(*Her thumb next holds all her fingers clenched, touching* Helen's *palm.*)

O.

(*Her thumb and forefinger extend.*)

L.

(*Same contact repeated.*)

L.

(*She puts* Helen's *hand to the doll.*)

Doll.

**James.** You spell pretty well.

(Annie, *in one hurried move, gets the drawers swiftly back into the suitcase, the lid banged shut, and her head turned, to see* James *leaning in the doorway.*)

Finding out if she's ticklish? She is.

(Annie *regards him stonily, but after a scowling moment,* Helen *tugs at her hand again, imperious.* Annie *repeats the letters, and* Helen *interrupts her fingers in the middle, feeling each of them, puzzled.* Annie *touches* Helen's *hand to the doll, and begins spelling into it again.*)

**James.** What is it, a game?

**Annie** (*curtly*). An alphabet.

**James.** Alphabet?

**Annie.** For the deaf.

(Helen *now repeats the finger movements in air, exactly, her head cocked to her own hand, and* Annie's *eyes suddenly gleam.*)

Ho. How *bright* she is!

**James.** You think she knows what she's doing?

(*He takes* Helen's *hand, to throw a meaningless gesture into it; she repeats this one too.*)

She imitates everything; she's a monkey.

**Annie** (*very pleased*). Yes, she's a bright little monkey, all right.

(*She takes the doll from* Helen *and reaches for her hand;* Helen *instantly grabs the doll back.* Annie *takes it again, and* Helen's *hand next, but* Helen *is incensed now. When* Annie *draws her hand to her face to shake her head no, then tries to spell to her,* Helen *slaps at* Annie's *face.* Annie *grasps* Helen *by both arms, and swings her into a chair, holding her pinned there, kicking, while glasses, doll, bonnet fly in various directions.* James *laughs.*)

**James.** She wants her doll back.

**Annie.** When she spells it.

**James.** Spell, she doesn't know the thing has a name, even.

**Annie.** Of course not. Who expects her to, now? All I want is her fingers to learn the letters.

**James.** Won't mean anything to her.

(*Annie gives him a look. She then tries to form Helen's fingers into the letters, but Helen swings a haymaker instead, which Annie barely ducks, at once pinning her down again.*)

Doesn't like that alphabet, Miss Sullivan. You invent it yourself?

(*Helen is now in a rage, fighting tooth and nail to get out of the chair, and Annie answers while struggling and dodging her kicks.*)

**Annie.** Spanish monks under a—vow of silence. Which I wish *you'd* take!

(*And suddenly releasing Helen's hands, she comes and shuts the door in James's face. Helen drops to the floor, groping around for the doll. Annie looks around desperately, sees her purse on the bed, rummages in it, and comes up with a battered piece of cake wrapped in newspaper. With her foot she moves the doll deftly out of the way of Helen's groping; and going on her knee, she lets Helen smell the cake. When Helen grabs for it, Annie removes the cake and spells quickly into the reaching hand.*)

Cake. From Washington, up north; it's the best I can do.

(*Helen's hand waits, baffled. Annie repeats it.*)

C, a, k, e. Do what my fingers do; never mind what it means.

(*She touches the cake briefly to Helen's nose, pats her hand, presents her own hand. Helen spells the letters rapidly back. Annie pats her hand enthusiastically, and gives her the cake.*)

Helen *crams it into her mouth with both hands. Annie watches her, with humor.*)

Get it down fast; maybe I'll steal that back, too. Now.

(*She takes the doll, touches it to Helen's nose, and spells again into her hand.*)

D, o, l, l. Think it over.

(*Helen thinks it over, while Annie presents her own hand. Then Helen spells three letters. Annie waits a second, then completes the word for Helen in her palm.*)

L.

(*She hands over the doll, and Helen gets a good grip on its leg.*)

Imitate now, understand later. End of the first les—

(*She never finishes, because Helen swings the doll with a furious energy. It hits Annie squarely in the face, and she falls back with a cry of pain, her knuckles up to her mouth. Helen waits, tensed for further combat. When Annie lowers her knuckles, she looks at blood on them. She works her lips, gets to her feet, finds the mirror, and bares her teeth at herself. Now she is furious herself.*)

You little wretch, no one's taught you any manners? I'll—

(*But rounding from the mirror, she sees the door slam. Helen and the doll are on the outside, and Helen is turning the key in the lock. Annie darts over, to pull the knob; the door is locked fast. She yanks it again.*)

Helen! Helen, let me out of—

(*She bats her brow at the folly of speaking but James, now downstairs, hears her and turns to see Helen with the key and doll groping her way down the steps. James takes in the whole situation, makes a move to intercept but then changes his mind, lets her pass, and amusedly follows her out onto the porch. Upstairs,Annie meanwhile rattles the knob, kneels, peers through the keyhole, gets up. She goes to the window, looks down, frowns. James from the yard sings gaily up to her,)*

**James.** *Buffalo girl, are you coming out tonight,*

*Coming out tonight,*

*Coming out—*

*(He drifts back into the house. Annie takes a handkerchief, nurses her mouth, stands in the middle of the room, staring at door and window in turn; and so catches sight of herself in the mirror, her cheek scratched, her hair dishevelled, her handkerchief bloody, her face disgusted with herself. She addresses the mirror, with some irony.)*

**Annie.** Don't worry. They'll find you; you're not lost. Only out of place.

*(But she coughs, spits something into her palm, and stares at it, outraged.)*

And toothless.

*(She winces.)*

Oo! It hurts.

*(She pours some water into the basin, dips the handkerchief, and presses it to her mouth. Standing there, bent over the basin in pain—with the rest of the set dim and unreal, and the lights upon her taking on the subtle color of the past—she hears again, as do we, the faraway voices; and slowly she lifts her head to them. The boy's voice is the same; the others are cracked old crones[10] in a nightmare, and perhaps we see their shadows.)*

**Boy's Voice.** It hurts, Annie, it hurts.

**First Crone's Voice.** Keep that brat shut up, can't you, girlie. How's a body to get

any sleep in this darn ward?

**Boy's Voice.** It hurts. It hurts.

**Second Crone's Voice.** Shut up, you!

**Boy's Voice.** Annie, when are we goin' home? You promised!

**Annie.** Jimmie—

**Boy's Voice.** Forever and ever, you said forever—

*(Annie drops the handkerchief, averts to the window, and is arrested there by the next cry.)*

Annie, Annie, you there? Annie! It *hurts!*

**Third Crone's Voice.** Grab him; he's fallin'![11]

**Boy's Voice.** *Annie!*

**Doctor's Voice** *(a pause, slowly).* Little girl. Little girl, I must tell you your brother will be going on a—

*(But Annie claps her hands to her ears, to shut this out; there is instant silence.)*

*As the lights bring the other areas in again, James goes to the steps to listen for any sound from upstairs. Keller, reentering from left, crosses toward the house; he passes Helen en route to her retreat under the pump. Kate reenters the rear door of the family room, with flowers for the table.)*

**Kate.** Supper is ready, Jimmie. Will you call your father?

**James.** Certainly.

*(But he calls up the stairs, for Annie's benefit.)*

---

10. **old crones:** old women.
11. **Grab him; he's fallin'!:** Annie Sullivan's brother, Jimmie, had a bad hip and needed crutches to stand. He eventually died while they were in the poorhouse.

Father! Supper!

**Keller** (*at the door*). No need to shout; I've been cooling my heels for an hour. Sit down.

**James.** Certainly.

**Keller.** Viney!

(*Viney backs in with a roast, while they get settled around the table.*)

**Viney.** Yes, Cap'n, right here.

**Kate.** Mildred went directly to sleep, Viney?

**Viney.** Oh, yes, that babe's an angel.

**Kate.** And Helen had a good supper?

**Viney** (*vaguely*). I dunno, Miss Kate, somehow she didn't have much of a appetite tonight—

**Kate** (*a bit guiltily*). Oh, dear.

**Keller** (*hastily*). Well, now. Couldn't say the same for my part. I'm famished. Katie, your plate.

**Kate** (*looking*). But where is Miss Annie?

(*a silence*)

**James** (*pleasantly*). In her room.

**Keller.** In her room? Doesn't she know hot food must be eaten hot? Go bring her down at once, Jimmie.

**James** (*rises*). Certainly. I'll get a ladder.

**Keller** (*stares*). What?

**James.** I'll need a ladder. Shouldn't take me long.

**Kate** (*stares*). What shouldn't take you—

**Keller.** Jimmie, do as I say! Go upstairs at once and tell Miss Sullivan supper is getting cold—

**James.** She's locked in her room.

**Keller.** Locked in her—

**Kate.** What on earth are you—

**James.** Helen locked her in and made off with the key.

**Kate** (*rising*). And you sit here and say nothing?

**James.** Well, everybody's been telling me not to say anything.

(*He goes serenely out and across the yard whistling. Keller, thrusting up from his chair, makes for the stairs.*)

**Kate.** Viney, look out in back for Helen. See if she has that key.

**Viney.** Yes, Miss Kate.

(*Viney goes out the rear door.*)

**Keller** (*calling down*). She's out by the pump!

(*Kate goes out on the porch after Helen, while Keller knocks on Annie's door, then rattles the knob, imperiously.*)

Miss Sullivan! Are you in there?

**Annie.** Oh, I'm here, all right.

**Keller.** Is there no key on your side?

**Annie** (*with some asperity*). Well, if there was a key in here, I wouldn't be in here. Helen took it; the only thing on my side is me.

**Keller.** Miss Sullivan. I—

(*He tries, but cannot hold it back.*)

Not in the house ten minutes, I don't see *how* you managed it!

(*He stomps downstairs again, while Annie mutters to herself.*)

**Annie.** And even I'm not on my side.

**Keller** (*roaring*). Viney!

**Viney** (*reappearing*). Yes, Cap'n?

**Keller.** Put that meat back in the oven!

(Viney *bears the roast off again, while Keller strides out onto the porch. Kate is with* Helen *at the pump, opening her hands.*)

**Kate.** She has no key.

**Keller.** Nonsense, she must have the key. Have you searched in her pockets?

**Kate.** Yes. She doesn't have it.

**Keller.** Katie, she must have the key.

**Kate.** Would you prefer to search her yourself, Captain?

**Keller.** No, I would not prefer to search her! She almost took my kneecap off this evening, when I tried merely to—

(James *reappears carrying a long ladder, with* Percy *running after him to be in on things.*)

Take that ladder back!

**James.** Certainly.

(*He turns around with it.* Martha *comes skipping around the upstage corner of the house to be in on things, accompanied by the setter,* Belle.)

**Kate.** She could have hidden the key.

**Keller.** Where?

**Kate.** Anywhere. Under a stone. In the flower beds. In the grass—

**Keller.** Well, I can't plow up the entire grounds to find a missing key! Jimmie!

**James.** Sir!

**Keller.** Bring me a ladder!

**James.** Certainly.

(Viney *comes around the downstage side of the house to be in on things; she has* Mildred *over her shoulder, bleating.* Keller *places the*

ladder against Annie's *window and mounts.* Annie, *meanwhile, is running about making herself presentable, washing the blood off her mouth, straightening her clothes, tidying her hair. Another black servant enters to gaze in wonder, increasing the gathering ring of spectators.*)

**Kate** (*sharply*). What is Mildred doing up?

**Viney.** Cap'n woke her, ma'am, all that hollerin'.

**Keller.** Miss Sullivan!

(Annie *comes to the window, with as much air of gracious normality as she can manage;* Keller *is at the window.*)

**Annie** (*brightly*). Yes, Captain Keller?

**Keller.** Come out!

**Annie.** I don't see how I can. There isn't room.

**Keller.** I intend to carry you. Climb onto my shoulder and hold tight.

**Annie.** Oh, no. It's—very chivalrous of you, but I'd really prefer to—

**Keller.** Miss Sullivan, follow instructions! I will not have you also tumbling out of our windows.

(Annie *obeys, with some misgivings.*)

I hope this is not a sample of what we may expect from you. In the way of simplifying the work of looking after Helen.

**Annie.** Captain Keller, I'm perfectly able to go down a ladder under my own—

**Keller.** I doubt it, Miss Sullivan. Simply hold onto my neck.

(*He begins down with her, while the spectators stand in a wide and somewhat awestricken circle, watching.* Keller *half-misses a rung, and* Annie *grabs at his whiskers.*)

My neck, Miss Sullivan!

**Annie.** I'm sorry to inconvenience you this way—

**Keller.** No inconvenience, other than having that door taken down and the lock replaced, if we fail to find that key.

**Annie.** Oh, I'll look everywhere for it.

**Keller.** Thank you. Do not look in any rooms that can be locked. There.

(*He stands her on the ground.* James *applauds.*)

**Annie.** Thank you very much.

(*She smooths her skirt, looking as composed and ladylike as possible.* Keller *stares around at the spectators.*)

**Keller.** Go, go, back to your work. What are you looking at here? There's nothing here to look at.

(*They break up, move off.*)

Now would it be possible for us to have supper, like other people?

(*He marches into the house.*)

**Kate.** Viney, serve supper. I'll put Mildred to sleep.

(*They all go in.* James *is the last to leave, murmuring to* Annie *with a gesture.*)

**James.** Might as well leave the l, a, d, d, e, r, hm?

(Annie *ignores him, looking at* Helen; James *goes in too. Imperceptibly the lights commence to narrow down.* Annie *and* Helen *are now alone in the yard, seated at the pump, where she has been oblivious to it all, a battered little savage, playing with her doll in a picture of innocent contentment.* Annie *comes near, leans against the house, and taking off her smoked glasses, studies her, not without awe. Presently* Helen *rises, gropes around to see if anyone is present;* Annie *evades her hand, and when* Helen *is satisfied she is alone, the key suddenly protrudes out of her mouth. She takes it in her fingers, stands thinking, gropes to the pump, lifts a loose board, drops the key into the well, and hugs herself gleefully.* Annie *stares. But after a moment she shakes her head to herself; she cannot keep the smile from her lips.*)

**Annie.** You *devil.*(*Her tone is one of great respect, humor, and acceptance of challenge.*)

You think I'm so easily gotten rid of? You have a thing or two to learn first. I have nothing else to do.

(*She goes up the steps to the porch, but turns for a final word, almost of warning.*)

And nowhere to go.

(*And presently she moves into the house to the others, as the lights dim down and out, except for the small circle upon* Helen *solitary at the pump, which ends the act.*)

# Thinking About Act One

## A PERSONAL RESPONSE

*sharing impressions*

**1.** In your journal, jot down a few words that describe your thoughts about the first encounter between Helen and Annie.

*constructing interpretations*

**2.** How does Annie Sullivan's attitude toward Helen and her disabilities compare with the Keller family's attitude?

### Think about
- what Annie and the family think about Helen's intelligence
- what they expect her to be able to learn
- why the family members give Helen sweet things to eat

**3.** From what you find out about Helen in this act, what challenges, other than her disabilities, does she present to Annie Sullivan?

**4.** What reason is there to hope that Annie Sullivan will be able to teach Helen anything?

### Think about
- the strong points of Annie's character
- the potential for learning that Helen shows

## A CREATIVE RESPONSE

**5.** If this act did not include Annie Sullivan's background as revealed in her conversation with Mr. Anagnos and by the voices from the past, how might your understanding of her character be different?

## A CRITICAL RESPONSE

**6.** How important are the stage directions to this play?

**7.** Based on your understanding of Act One, predict what is likely to happen in the rest of the play.

### Think about
- Annie Sullivan's statement that she will try to teach Helen "first, last, and—in between, language"
- Helen's anger when Annie tries to make her spell "doll"
- the family conflict indicated by the bickering between Captain Keller and James
- Annie's feelings toward Helen when she sees Helen drop the key down the well

# ACT TWO

*It is evening.*

*The only room visible in the Keller house is Annie's, where by lamplight, Annie is at a desk writing a letter. At her bureau, Helen in her customary unkempt state is tucking her doll in the bottom drawer as a cradle, the contents of which she has dumped out, creating as usual a fine disorder.*

*Annie mutters each word as she writes her letter, slowly, her eyes close to and almost touching the page, to follow with difficulty her penwork.*

**Annie.** " . . . and, nobody, here, has, attempted, to, control, her. The, greatest, problem, I, have, is, how, to, discipline, her, without, breaking, her, spirit."

*(resolute voice)*

"But, I, shall, insist, on, reasonable, obedience, from, the, start—"

*(At which point Helen, groping about on the desk, knocks over the inkwell. Annie jumps up, rescues her letter, rights the inkwell, grabs a towel to stem the spillage, and then wipes at Helen's hands; as always Helen pulls free, but not until Annie first gets three letters into her palm.)*

Ink.

*(Helen is enough interested in and puzzled by this spelling that she proffers her hand again; so Annie spells, and impassively dunks it back in the spillage.)*

Ink. It has a name.

*(She wipes the hand clean, and leads Helen to her bureau, where she looks for something to engage her. She finds a sewing card, with needle and thread, and going to her knees, shows Helen's hand how to connect one row of holes.)*

Down. Under. Up. And be careful of the needle—

*(Helen gets it, and Annie rises.)*

Fine. You keep out of the ink, and perhaps I can keep out of—the soup.

*(She returns to the desk, tidies it, and resumes writing her letter, bent close to the page.)*

"These, blots, are, her, handiwork. I—"

*(She is interrupted by a gasp; Helen has stuck her finger, and sits sucking at it, darkly. Then with vengeful resolve she seizes her doll, and is about to dash its brains out on the floor when Annie, diving, catches it in one hand, which she at once shakes with hopping pain but otherwise ignores, patiently.)*

All right, let's try temperance.

*(Taking the doll, she kneels, goes through the motion of knocking its head on the floor, spells into Helen's hand.)*

Bad, girl.

*(She lets Helen feel the grieved expression on her face. Helen imitates it. Next, she makes Helen caress the doll and kiss the hurt spot and hold it gently in her arms, then spells into her hands,)*

Good, girl.

*(She lets Helen feel the smile on her face. Helen sits with a scowl, which suddenly clears. She pats the doll, kisses it, wreathes her face in a large, artificial smile, and bears the doll to the washstand, where she carefully sits it. Annie watches, pleased.)*

Very good girl—

*(Whereupon Helen elevates the pitcher and dashes it on the floor instead. Annie leaps to her feet, and stands inarticulate; Helen calmly gropes back to sit by the sewing card and needle.*

Annie *manages to achieve self-control. She picks up a fragment or two of the pitcher, sees Helen is puzzling over the card, and resolutely kneels to demonstrate it again. She spells into Helen's hand.*

Kate, *meanwhile, coming around the corner with folded sheets on her arm, halts at the doorway and watches them for a moment in silence; she is moved, but level.)*

**Kate** *(presently)*. What are you saying to her?

(Annie, *glancing up, is a bit embarrassed, and rises from the spelling, to find her company manners.)*

**Annie.** Oh, I was just making conversation. Saying it was a sewing card.

**Kate.** But does that—

(*She imitates with her fingers.)*

—mean that to her?

**Annie.** No. No, she won't know what spelling is till she knows what a word is.

**Kate.** Yet you keep spelling to her? Why?

**Annie** *(cheerily)*. I like to hear myself talk!

**Kate.** The Captain says it's like spelling to the fence post.

**Annie** *(a pause)*. Does he, now.

**Kate.** Is it?

**Annie.** No, it's how I watch you talk to Mildred.

**Kate.** Mildred.

**Annie.** Any baby. Gibberish, grown-up gibberish, baby-talk gibberish, do they understand one word of it to start? Somehow they begin to. If they hear it. I'm letting Helen hear it.

**Kate.** Other children are not—impaired.

**Annie.** Ho, there's nothing impaired in that head; it works like a mousetrap!

**Kate** *(smiles)*. But after a child hears how many words, Miss Annie, a million?

**Annie.** I guess no mother's ever minded enough to count.

(*She drops her eyes to spell into Helen's hand, again indicating the card; Helen spells back, and Annie is amused.)*

**Kate** *(too quickly)*. What did she spell?

**Annie.** I spelt card. She spelt cake!

(*She takes in Kate's quickness, and shakes her head, gently.)*

No, it's only a finger-game to her, Mrs. Keller. What she has to learn first is that things have names.

**Kate.** And when will she learn?

**Annie.** Maybe after a million and one words.

(*They hold each other's gaze; Kate then speaks quietly.)*

**Kate.** I should like to learn those letters, Miss Annie.

**Annie** *(pleased)*. I'll teach you tomorrow morning. That makes only half a million each!

**Kate** *(then)*. It's her bedtime.

(Annie *reaches for the sewing card. Helen objects; Annie insists, and Helen gets rid of Annie's hand by jabbing it with the needle. Annie gasps, and moves to grip Helen's wrist; but Kate intervenes with a proffered sweet, and Helen drops the card, crams the sweet into her mouth, and scrambles up to search her mother's hands for more. Annie nurses her wound, staring after the sweet.)*

I'm sorry, Miss Annie.

**Annie** (*indignantly*). Why does she get a reward? For stabbing me?

**Kate.** Well—

(*then tiredly*)

We catch our flies with honey, I'm afraid. We haven't the heart for much else, and so many times she simply cannot be compelled.

**Annie** (*ominous*). Yes. I'm the same way myself.

(Kate *smiles and leads* Helen *off around the corner.* Annie, *alone in her room, picks up things; and in the act of removing* Helen's *doll, gives way to unmannerly temptation. She throttles it. She drops it on her bed, and stands pondering. Then she turns back, sits decisively, and writes again, as the lights dim on her.*)

(*grimly*)

"The, more, I, think, the, more, certain, I, am, that, obedience, is, the, gateway, through, which, knowledge, enters, the, mind, of, the, child—"

(On the word "obedience" *a shaft of sunlight hits the water pump outside, while* Annie's *voice ends in the dark, followed by a distant cockcrow. Daylight comes up over another corner of the sky, with* Viney's *voice heard at once.*)

**Viney.** Breakfast ready!

(Viney *comes down into the sunlight beam, and pumps a pitcherful of water. While the pitcher is brimming, we hear conversation from the dark. The light grows to the family room of the house, where all are either entering or already seated at breakfast, with* Keller *and* James *arguing the war.* Helen *is wandering around the table to explore the contents of the other plates. When* Annie *is in her chair, she watches* Helen. Viney

re-enters, sets the pitcher on the table; Kate *lifts the almost empty biscuit plate with an inquiring look;* Viney *nods and bears it off back, neither of them interrupting the men.* Annie, *meanwhile, sits with fork quiet, watching* Helen, *who at her mother's plate, pokes her hand among some scrambled eggs.* Kate *catches* Annie's *eyes on her, smiles with wry gesture.* Helen *moves on to* James's *plate, the male talk continuing,* James *deferential and* Keller *overriding.*)

**James.** —no, but shouldn't we give the devil his due, Father? The fact is we lost the South two years earlier when he out-thought us behind Vicksburg.[1]

**Keller.** Out-thought is a peculiar word for a butcher.

**James.** Harness maker, wasn't he?

**Keller.** I said butcher; his only virtue as a soldier was numbers, and he led them to slaughter with no more regard than for so many sheep.

**James.** But even if in that sense he was a butcher, the fact is he—

**Keller.** And a drunken one, half the war.

**James.** Agreed, Father. If his own people said he was, I can't argue he—

**Keller.** Well, what is it you find to admire in such a man, Jimmie, the butchery or the drunkenness?

**James.** Neither, Father, only the fact that he beat us.

**Keller.** He didn't.

---

1. **The fact is . . . Vicksburg:** James and Keller are discussing General Ulysses S. Grant, the commander of the Union army during the Civil War. Vicksburg, a city on the Mississippi, was captured by Grant in 1863.

**James.** Is it your contention we won the war, sir?

**Keller.** He didn't beat us at Vicksburg. We lost Vicksburg because Pemberton gave Bragg five thousand of his cavalry; and Loring, whom I knew personally for a nincompoop before you were born, marched away from Champion's Hill with enough men to have held them. We lost Vicksburg by stupidity verging on treason.

**James.** I would have said we lost Vicksburg because Grant was one thing no Yankee general was before him—

**Keller.** Drunk? I doubt it.

**James.** Obstinate.

**Keller.** Obstinate. Could any of them compare even in that with old Stonewall? If he'd been there, we would still have Vicksburg.

**James.** Well, the butcher simply wouldn't give up; he tried four ways of getting around Vicksburg, and on the fifth try he got around. Anyone else would have pulled north and—

**Keller.** He wouldn't have got around if we'd had a Southerner in command, instead of a half-breed Yankee traitor like Pemberton—

*(While this background talk is in progress, Helen is working around the table, ultimately toward Annie's plate. She messes with her hands in James's plate, then in Keller's, both men taking it so for granted they hardly notice. Then Helen comes groping with soiled hands past her own plate, to Annie's; her hand goes to it, and Annie, who has been waiting, deliberately lifts and removes her hand. Helen gropes again. Annie firmly pins her by the wrist, and removes her hand from the table. Helen thrusts her hands again; Annie catches them; and Helen begins to flail and make noises. The interruption brings Keller's gaze upon them.)*
What's the matter there?

**Kate.** Miss Annie. You see, she's accustomed to helping herself from our plates to anything she—

**Annie** *(evenly)*. Yes, but *I'm* not accustomed to it.

**Keller.** No, of course not. Viney!

**Kate.** Give her something, Jimmie, to quiet her.

**James** *(blandly)*. But her table manners are the best she has. Well.

*(He pokes across with a chunk of bacon at Helen's hand, which Annie releases; but Helen knocks the bacon away and stubbornly thrusts at Annie's plate. Annie grips her wrists again; the struggle mounts.)*

**Keller.** Let her this time, Miss Sullivan; it's the only way we get any adult conversation. If my son's half merits that description.

*(He rises.)*

I'll get you another plate.

**Annie** *(gripping Helen)*. I have a plate, thank you.

**Kate** *(calling)*. Viney! I'm afraid what Captain Keller says is only too true; she'll persist in this until she gets her own way.

**Keller** *(at the door)*. Viney, bring Miss Sullivan another plate—

**Annie** *(stonily)*. I have a plate; nothing's wrong with the plate. I intend to keep it.

*(Silence for a moment, except for Helen's noises as she struggles to get loose. The Kellers' are a bit nonplussed, and Annie is too darkly intent on Helen's manners to have any thoughts now of her own.)*

**James.** Ha. You see why they took Vicksburg?

**Keller** (*uncertainly*). Miss Sullivan. One plate or another is hardly a matter to struggle with a deprived child about.

**Annie.** Oh, I'd sooner have a more—

(Helen *begins to kick,* Annie *moves her ankles to the opposite side of the chair.*)

—heroic issue myself, I—

**Keller.** No, I really must insist you—

(Helen *bangs her toe on the chair and sinks to the floor, crying with rage and feigned injury.* Annie *keeps hold of her wrists, gazing down, while* Kate *rises.*)

Now she's hurt herself.

**Annie** (*grimly*). No, she hasn't.

**Keller.** Will you please let her hands go?

**Kate.** Miss Annie, you don't know the child well enough yet, she'll keep—

**Annie.** I know an ordinary tantrum well enough, when I see one, and a badly spoiled child—

**James.** Hear, hear.

**Keller** (*very annoyed*). Miss Sullivan! You would have more understanding of your pupil if you had some pity in you. Now kindly do as I—

**Annie.** Pity?

(She *releases* Helen *to turn equally annoyed on* Keller *across the table. Instantly* Helen *scrambles up and dives at* Annie's *plate. This time* Annie *intercepts her by pouncing on her wrists like a hawk, and her temper boils.*)

For this *tyrant?* The whole house turns on her whims. Is there anything she wants she doesn't get? I'll tell you what I pity, that the sun won't rise and set for her all her life, and

every day you're telling her it will. What good will your pity do her when you're under the strawberries, Captain Keller?

**Keller** (*outraged*). Kate, for the love of heaven will you—

**Kate.** Miss Annie, please, I don't think it serves to lose our—

**Annie.** It does you good, that's all. It's less trouble to feel sorry for her than to teach her anything better, isn't it?

**Keller.** I fail to see where you have taught her anything yet, Miss Sullivan!

**Annie.** I'll begin this minute, if you'll leave the room, Captain Keller!

**Keller** (*astonished*). Leave the—

**Annie.** Everyone, please.

(She *struggles with* Helen, *while* Keller *endeavors to control his voice.*)

**Keller.** Miss Sullivan, you are here only as a paid teacher. Nothing more, and not to lecture—

**Annie.** I can't *un*teach her six years of pity if you can't stand up to one tantrum! Old Stonewall, indeed. Mrs. Keller, you promised me help.

**Kate.** Indeed I did, we truly want to—

**Annie.** Then leave me alone with her. Now!

**Keller** (*in a wrath*). Katie, will you come outside with me? At once, please.

(He *marches to the front door.* Kate *and* James *follow him. Simultaneously* Annie *releases* Helen's *wrists, and the child again sinks to the floor, kicking and crying her weird noises.* Annie *steps over her to meet* Viney *coming in the rear doorway with biscuits and a clean plate, surprised at the general commotion.)*

**Viney.** Heaven sakes—

**Annie.** Out, please.

*(She backs Viney out with one hand, closes the door on her astonished mouth, locks it, and removes the key. Keller, meanwhile, snatches his hat from a rack, and Kate follows him down the porch steps. James lingers in the doorway to address Annie across the room with a bow.)*

**James.** If it takes all summer, general.

*(Annie comes over to his door in turn, removing her glasses grimly. As Keller outside begins speaking, Annie closes the door on James, locks it, removes the key, and turns with her back against the door to stare ominously at Helen, kicking on the floor.*

*James takes his hat from the rack, and going down the porch steps, joins Kate and Keller talking in the yard, Keller in a sputter of ire.)*

**Keller.** This girl, this—cub of a girl—*pre-sumes!*[2] I tell you, I'm of half a mind to ship her back to Boston before the week is out. You can inform her so from me!

**Kate** *(eyebrows up)*. I, Captain?

**Keller.** She's a *hireling!* Now I want it clear, unless there's an apology and complete change of manner, she goes back on the next train! Will you make that quite clear?

**Kate.** Where will you be, Captain, while I am making it quite—

**Keller.** At the office!

*(He begins off left, finds his napkin still in his irate hand, is uncertain with it, dabs his lips with dignity, gets rid of it in a toss to James, and marches off. James turns to eye Kate.)*

**James.** Will you?

*(Kate's mouth is set, and James studies it lightly.)*

I thought what she said was exceptionally intelligent. I've been saying it for years.

**Kate** *(not without scorn)*. To his face?

*(She comes to relieve him of the white napkin, but reverts again with it.)*

Or will you take it, Jimmie? As a flag?

*(James stalks out, much offended; and Kate, turning, stares across the yard at the house. The lights narrowing down to the following pantomime in the family room, leave her motionless in the dark.*

*Annie, meanwhile, has begun by slapping both keys down on a shelf out of Helen's reach. She returns to the table, upstage. Helen's kicking has subsided, and when from the floor her hand finds Annie's chair empty, she pauses. Annie clears the table of Kate's, James's, and Keller's plates. She gets back to her own across the table just in time to slide it deftly away from Helen's pouncing hand. She lifts the hand and moves it to Helen's plate, and after an instant's exploration, Helen sits again on the floor and drums her heels. Annie comes around the table and resumes her chair. When Helen feels her skirt again, she ceases kicking, waits for whatever is to come, renews some kicking, waits again. Annie, retrieving her plate, takes up a forkful of food, stops it halfway to her mouth, gazes at it devoid of appetite, and half-lowers it; but after a look at Helen she sighs, dips the forkful toward Helen in a for-your-sake toast, and puts it in her own mouth to chew, not without an effort.*

Helen *now gets hold of the chair leg, and*

---

2. **presumes** (prē zo͞omz′): takes (something) upon oneself without permission or authority; dares (to say or do something).

half succeeds in pulling the chair out from under her. Annie *bangs it down with her rear, heavily, and sits with all her weight.* Helen's *next attempt to topple it is unavailing, so her fingers dive in a pinch at* Annie's *flank.* Annie, *in the middle of her mouthful, almost loses it with startle, and she slaps down her fork to round on* Helen. *The child comes up with curiosity to feel what* Annie *is doing, so* Annie *resumes eating, letting* Helen's *hand follow the movement of her fork to her mouth; whereupon* Helen *at once reaches into* Annie's *plate.* Annie *firmly removes her hand to her own plate.* Helen *in reply pinches* Annie's *thigh, a good, mean pinchful that makes* Annie *jump.* Annie *sets the fork down, and sits with her mouth tight.* Helen *digs another pinch into her thigh, and this time* Annie *slaps her hand smartly away.* Helen *retaliates with a roundhouse fist that catches* Annie *on the ear, and* Annie's *hand leaps at once in a forceful slap across* Helen's *cheek.* Helen *is the startled one now.* Annie's *hand in compunction falters to her own face, but when* Helen *hits at her again,* Annie *deliberately slaps her again.* Helen *lifts her fist irresolute for another roundhouse;* Annie *lifts her hand resolute for another slap; and they freeze in this posture, while* Helen *mulls it over. She thinks better of it, drops her fist, and giving* Annie *a wide berth, gropes around to her mother's chair, to find it empty. She blunders her way along the table upstage, and encountering the empty chairs and missing plates, she looks bewildered. She gropes back to her mother's chair, again touches her cheek and indicates the chair, and waits for the world to answer.*

Annie *now reaches over to spell into her hand, but* Helen *yanks it away. She gropes to the front door, tries the knob, and finds the door locked, with no key. She gropes to the rear door, and finds it locked, with no key.*

*She commences to bang on it.* Annie *rises, crosses, takes her wrists, draws her resisting back to the table, seats her, and releases her hands upon her plate. As* Annie *herself begins to sit,* Helen *writhes out of her chair, runs to the front door, and tugs and kicks at it.* Annie *rises again, crosses, draws her by one wrist back to the table, seats her, and sits.* Helen *escapes back to the door, knocking over her mother's chair en route.* Annie *rises again in pursuit, and this time lifts* Helen *bodily from behind and bears her kicking to her chair. She deposits her, and once more turns to sit.* Helen *scrambles out, but as she passes,* Annie *catches her up again from behind and deposits her in the chair.* Helen *scrambles out on the other side, for the rear door, but* Annie *at her heels catches her up and deposits her again in the chair. She stands behind it.* Helen *scrambles out to her right, and the instant her feet hit the floor,* Annie *lifts and deposits her back. She scrambles out to her left, and is at once lifted and deposited back. She tries right again and is deposited back, and tries left again and is deposited back; and now feints* Annie *to the right but is off to her left, and is promptly deposited back. She sits a moment, and then starts straight over the tabletop, dishware notwithstanding.* Annie *hauls her in and deposits her back, with her plate spilling in her lap, and she melts to the floor and crawls under the table, laborious among its legs and chairs; but* Annie *is swift around the table and waiting on the other side when she surfaces, immediately bearing her aloft.* Helen *clutches at* James's *chair for anchorage, but it comes with her, and halfway back she abandons it to the floor.* Annie *deposits her in her chair and waits.* Helen *sits tensed motionless. Then she tentatively puts out her left foot and hand,* Annie *interposes her own hand, and at the contact* Helen *jerks hers in. She tries her right foot;* Annie *blocks it with* her own, and Helen jerks hers in. Finally, leaning back, she slumps down in her chair, in a sullen biding.

Annie backs off a step, and watches; Helen offers no move. Annie takes a deep breath. Both of them and the room are in considerable disorder, two chairs down and the table a mess, but Annie makes no effort to tidy it; she only sits on her own chair, and lets her energy refill. Then she takes up knife and fork, and resolutely addresses her food. Helen's hand comes out to explore, and seeing it, Annie sits without moving. The child's hand goes over her hand and fork, pauses—Annie still does not move—and withdraws. Presently it moves for her own plate, slaps about for it, and stops, thwarted. At this, Annie again rises, recovers Helen's plate from the floor and a handful of scattered food from the deranged tablecloth, drops it on the plate, and pushes the plate into contact with Helen's fist. Neither of them now moves for a pregnant moment—until Helen suddenly takes a grab of food and wolfs it down. Annie permits herself the humor of a minor bow and warming her hands together; she wanders off a step or two, watching. Helen cleans up the plate.

After a glower of indecision, she holds the empty plate out for more. Annie accepts it, and crossing to the removed plates, spoons food from them onto it. She stands debating the spoon, tapping it a few times on Helen's plate; and when she returns with the plate, she brings the spoon, too. She puts the spoon first into Helen's hand, then sets the plate down. Helen, discarding the spoon, reaches with her hand, and Annie stops it by the wrist; she replaces the spoon in it. Helen impatiently discards it again, and again Annie stops her hand, to replace the spoon in it. This time Helen throws the spoon on the floor. Annie, after considering it, lifts

Helen bodily out of the chair; and in a wrestling match on the floor, closes her fingers upon the spoon, and returns her with it to the chair. Helen again throws the spoon on the floor. Annie lifts her out of the chair again; but in the struggle over the spoon Helen, with Annie on her back, sends her sliding over her head. Helen flees back to her chair and scrambles into it. When Annie comes after her, she clutches it for dear life. Annie pries one hand loose, then the other, then the first again, then the other again, and then lifts Helen by the waist, chair and all, and shakes the chair loose. Helen wrestles to get free, but Annie pins her to the floor, closes her fingers upon the spoon, and lifts her kicking under one arm. With her other hand, she gets the chair in place again, and plunks Helen back on it. When she releases her hand, Helen throws the spoon at her.

Annie now removes the plate of food. Helen, grabbing, finds it missing, and commences to bang with her fists on the table. Annie collects a fistful of spoons and descends with them and the plate on Helen; she lets her smell the plate, at which Helen ceases banging, and Annie puts the plate down and a spoon in Helen's hand. Helen throws it on the floor. Annie puts another spoon in her hand. Helen throws it on the floor. Annie puts another spoon in her hand. Helen throws it on the floor. When Annie comes to her last spoon she sits next to Helen, and gripping the spoon in Helen's hand compels her to take food in it up to her mouth. Helen sits with lips shut. Annie waits a stolid moment, then lowers Helen's hand. She tries again; Helen's lips remain shut. Annie waits, lowers Helen's hand. She tries again; this time Helen suddenly opens her mouth and accepts the food. Annie lowers the spoon with a sigh of relief, and Helen spews the mouthful out at her face. Annie sits a moment with eyes closed, then takes the pitcher and dashes its water into Helen's face, who gasps astonished. Annie, with Helen's hand, takes up another spoonful, and shoves it into her open mouth. Helen swallows involuntarily, and while she is catching her breath, Annie forces her palm open, throws four swift letters into it, then another four, and bows toward her with devastating pleasantness.)*

**Annie.** Good girl.

*(Annie lifts Helen's hand to feel her face, nodding; Helen grabs a fistful of her hair, and yanks. The pain brings Annie to her knees, and Helen pummels her. They roll under the table, and the lights commence to dim out on them.*

*Simultaneously the light at left has been rising, slowly, so slowly that it seems at first we only imagine what is intimated in the yard: a few ghostlike figures, in silence, motionless, waiting. Now the distant belfry chimes commence to toll the hour, also very slowly, almost—it is twelve—interminably; the sense is that of a long time passing. We can identify the figures before the twelfth stroke, all facing the house in a kind of watch; Kate is standing exactly as before, but now with the baby Mildred sleeping in her arms; and placed here and there, unmoving, are Aunt Ev in her hat with a hanky to her nose, and the two black children, Percy and Martha, with necks outstretched eagerly, and Viney with a knotted kerchief on her head and a feather duster in her hand.*

*The chimes cease, and there is silence. For a long moment, none of the group moves.)*

**Viney** *(presently).* What am I gone do, Miss Kate? It's noontime; dinner's comin'; I didn't get them breakfast dishes out of there yet.

*(Kate says nothing, stares at the house, Martha shifts Helen's doll in her clutch, and it plaintively says momma.)*

**Kate** *(presently).* You run along, Martha.

*(Aunt Ev blows her nose.)*

**Aunt Ev** *(wretchedly).* I can't wait out here a minute longer, Kate. Why, this could go on all afternoon, too.

**Kate.** I'll tell the captain you called.

**Viney** *(to the children).* You hear what Miss Kate say? Never you mind what's going on here.

*(Still no one moves.)*

You run along, tend your own bizness.

*(Finally Viney turns on the children with the feather duster.)*

Shoo!

*(The two children divide before her. She chases them off. Aunt Ev comes to Kate, in her dignity.)*

**Aunt Ev.** Say what you like, Kate, but that child is a *Keller.*

*(She opens her parasol, preparatory to leaving.)*

I needn't remind you that all the Kellers are cousins to General Robert E. Lee.[3] I don't know *who* that girl is.

*(She waits, but Kate, staring at the house, is without response.)*

The only Sullivan I've heard of—from Boston too, and I'd think twice before locking her up with that kind—is that man John L.[4]

---

3. **General Robert E. Lee:** the commander of the Confederate army during the Civil War.
4. **John L. Sullivan:** world heavyweight boxing champion during the 1880's.

(*And Aunt Ev departs, with head high. Presently Viney to Kate, her arms out for the baby.*)

**Viney.** You give me her, Miss Kate; I'll sneak her in back, to her crib.

(*But Kate is moveless, until Viney starts to take the baby; Kate looks down at her before relinquishing her.*)

**Kate** (*slowly*). This child never gives me a minute's worry.

**Viney.** Oh, yes, this one's the angel of the family, no question bout *that*.

(*She begins off rear with the baby, heading around the house; and Kate now turns her back on it, her hand to her eyes. At this moment there is the slamming of a door, and when Kate wheels, Helen is blundering down the porch steps into the light, like a ruined bat. Viney halts, and Kate runs in. Helen collides with her mother's knees, and reels off and back to clutch them as her savior. Annie, with smoked glasses in hand, stands on the porch, also much undone, looking as though she had indeed just taken Vicksburg. Kate, taking in Helen's ravaged state, becomes steely in her gaze up at Annie.*)

**Kate.** What happened?

(*Annie meets Kate's gaze, and gives a factual report, too exhausted for anything but a flat voice.*)

**Annie.** She ate from her own plate.

(*She thinks a moment.*)

She ate with a spoon. Herself.

(*Kate frowns, uncertain with thought, and glances down at Helen.*)

And she folded her napkin.

(*Kate's gaze now wavers, from Helen to Annie, and back.*)

**Kate** (*softly*). Folded—her napkin?

**Annie.** The room's a wreck, but her napkin is folded.

(*She pauses, then,*)

I'll be in my room, Mrs. Keller.

(*She moves to re-enter the house; but she stops at Viney's voice.*)

**Viney** (*cheery*). Don't be long, Miss Annie. Dinner will be ready right away!

(*Viney carries Mildred around the back of the house. Annie stands unmoving, takes a deep breath, stares over her shoulder at Kate and Helen; then inclines her head graciously, and goes with a slight stagger into the house. The lights in her room above steal up in readiness for her.*

*Kate remains alone with Helen in the yard, standing protectively over her, in a kind of wonder.*)

**Kate.** (*slowly*). Folded her napkin.

(*She contemplates the wild head in her thighs; and moves her fingertips over it, with such a tenderness, and something like a fear of its strangeness, that her own eyes close. She whispers, bending to it,*)

My Helen—folded her napkin—

(*And still erect, with only her head in surrender, Kate for the first time that we see, loses her protracted war with grief; but she will not let a sound escape her, only the grimace of tears comes, and sobs that shake her in a grip of silence. But Helen feels them, and her hand comes up in its own wondering, to interrogate her mother's face, until Kate buries her lips in the child's palm.*

*Upstairs, Annie enters her room, closes the door, and stands back against it. The lights, growing on her with their special color, commence to fade on Kate and Helen. Then Annie goes wearily to her suitcase, and lifts it to take it toward the bed. But it knocks an object to the floor, and she turns back to regard it. A new voice comes in a cultured murmur, hesitant as with the effort of remembering a text,)*

**Man's Voice.** This—soul—

*(Annie puts the suitcase down, and kneels to the object. It is the battered Perkins report, and she stands with it in her hand, letting memory try to speak,)*

This—blind, deaf, mute—woman—

*(Annie sits on her bed, opens the book, and finding the passage, brings it up an inch from her eyes to read, her face and lips following the overheard words, the voice quite factual now.)*

Can nothing be done to disinter this human soul? The whole neighborhood would rush to save this woman if she were buried alive by the caving in of a pit, and labor with zeal until she were dug out. Now, if there were one who had as much patience as zeal, he might awaken her to a consciousness of her immortal—

*(When the boy's voice comes, Annie closes her eyes, in pain.)*

**Boy's Voice.** Annie? Annie, you there?

**Annie.** Hush.

**Boy's Voice.** Annie, what's that noise?

*(Annie tries not to answer; her own voice is drawn out of her, unwilling.)*

**Annie.** Just a cot, Jimmie.

**Boy's Voice.** Where they pushin' it?

**Annie.** To the deadhouse.

**Boy's Voice.** Annie. Does it hurt, to be dead?

*(Annie escapes by opening her eyes; her hand works restlessly over her cheek. She retreats into the book again, but the cracked old crones interrupt, whispering. Annie slowly lowers the book.)*

**First Crone's Voice.** There is schools.

**Second Crone's Voice.** There is schools outside—

**Third Crone's Voice.** —schools where they teach blind ones, worse'n you—

**First Crone's Voice.** To read—

**Second Crone's Voice.** To read and write—

**Third Crone's Voice.** There is schools outside where they—

**First Crone's Voice.** There is schools—

*(Silence. Annie sits with her eyes shining, her hand almost in a caress over the book. Then,)*

**Boy's Voice.** You ain't going to school, are you, Annie?

**Annie** *(whispering)*. When I grow up.

**Boy's Voice.** You ain't either, Annie. You're goin' to stay here take care of me.

**Annie.** I'm goin' to school when I grow up.

**Boy's Voice.** You said we'll be together, forever and ever and ever—

**Annie** *(fierce)*. I'm goin' to school when I grow up!

**Doctor's Voice** *(slowly)*. Little girl. Little girl, I must tell you. Your brother will be going on a journey, soon.

*(Annie sits rigid, in silence. Then the boy's voice pierces it, a shriek of terror.)*

**Boy's Voice.** *Annie!*

*(It goes into Annie like a sword; she doubles onto it. The book falls to the floor. It takes her a racked moment to find herself and what she was engaged in here. When she sees the suitcase she remembers, and lifts it once again toward the bed. But the voices are with her, and she halts with suitcase in hand.)*

**First Crone's Voice.**  Goodbye, Annie.

**Doctor's Voice.**  Write me when you learn how.

**Second Crone's Voice.**  Don't tell anyone you came from here. Don't tell anyone—

**Third Crone's Voice.**  Yeah, don't tell anyone you come from—

**First Crone's Voice.**  Yeah, don't tell anyone—

**Second Crone's Voice.**  Don't tell any—

*(The echoing voices fade. After a moment, Annie lays the suitcase on the bed; and the last voice comes faintly, from far away.)*

**Boy's Voice.**  Annie. It hurts, to be dead. Forever.

*(Annie falls to her knees by the bed, stifling her mouth in it. When at last she rolls blindly away from it, her palm comes down on the open report. She opens her eyes, regards it dully, and then, still on her knees, takes in the print.)*

**Man's Voice** *(factual)*.  —might awaken her to a consciousness of her immortal nature. The chance is small indeed; but with a smaller chance they would have dug desperately for her in the pit; and is the life of the soul of less importance than that of the body?

*(Annie gets to her feet. She drops the book on the bed, and pauses over her suitcase; after a moment, she unclasps and opens it.*

*Standing before it, she comes to her decision. She at once turns to the bureau, and taking her things out of its drawers, commences to throw them into the open suitcase.*

*In the darkness down left, a hand strikes a match, and lights a hanging oil lamp. It is Keller's hand, and his voice accompanies it, very angry. The lights, rising here before they fade on Annie, show Keller and Kate inside a suggestion of a garden house, with a bay-window seat toward center and a door at back.)*

**Keller.**  Katie, I will not *have* it! Now you did not see when that girl after supper tonight went to look for Helen in her room—

**Kate.**  No.

**Keller.**  The child practically climbed out of her window to escape from her! What kind of teacher *is* she? I thought I had seen her at her worst this morning, shouting at me, but I come home to find the entire house disorganized by her—Helen won't stay one second in the same room, won't come to the table with her, won't let herself be bathed or undressed or put to bed by her, or even by Viney now; and the end result is that *you* have to do more for the child than before we hired this girl's services! From the moment she stepped off the train, she's been nothing but a burden, incompetent, impertinent, ineffectual, immodest—

**Kate.**  She folded her napkin, Captain.

**Keller.**  What?

**Kate.**  Not ineffectual. Helen did fold her napkin.

**Keller.**  What in heaven's name is so extraordinary about folding a napkin?

**Kate** *(with some humor)*.  Well. It's more than you did, Captain.

**Keller.** Katie, I did not bring you all the way out here to the garden house to be frivolous. Now, how does Miss Sullivan propose to teach a deaf-blind pupil who won't let her even touch her?

**Kate** (*a pause*). I don't know.

**Keller.** The fact is, today she scuttled any chance she ever had of getting along with the child. If you can see any point or purpose to her staying on here longer, it's more than—

**Kate.** What do you wish me to do?

**Keller.** I want you to give her notice.

**Kate.** I can't.

**Keller.** Then if you won't, I must. I simply will not—

(*He is interrupted by a knock at the back door. Keller, after a glance at Kate, moves to open the door. Annie, in her smoked glasses, is standing outside. Keller contemplates her heavily.*)

Miss Sullivan.

**Annie.** Captain Keller.

(*She is nervous, keyed up to seizing the bull by the horns again, and she assumes a cheeriness which is not unshaky.*)

Viney said I'd find you both over here in the garden house. I thought we should—have a talk?

**Keller** (*reluctantly*). Yes, I—Well, come in.

(*Annie enters, and is interested in this room; she rounds on her heel, anxiously, studying it. Keller turns the matter over to Kate, sotto voce.*)

Katie.

**Kate** (*turning it back, courteously*). Captain.

(*Keller clears his throat, makes ready.*)

**Keller.** I, ah—wanted first to make my position clear to Mrs. Keller, in private. I have decided I—am not satisfied—in fact, am deeply dissatisfied—with the manner in which—

**Annie** (*intent*). Excuse me, is this little house ever in use?

**Keller** (*with patience*). In the hunting season. If you will give me your attention, Miss Sullivan.

(*Annie turns her smoked glasses upon him; they hold his unwilling stare.*)

I have tried to make allowances for you because you come from a part of the country where people are—women, I should say—come from who—well, for whom—

(*It begins to elude him.*)

allowances must—be made. I have decided, nevertheless, to—that is, decided I—

(*vexedly*)

Miss Sullivan, I find it difficult to talk through those glasses.

**Annie** (*eagerly, removing them*). Oh, of course.

**Keller** (*dourly*). Why do you wear them, the sun has been down for an hour.

**Annie** (*pleasantly, at the lamp*). Any kind of light hurts my eyes.

(*A silence; Keller ponders her, heavily.*)

**Keller.** Put them on. Miss Sullivan, I have decided to—give you another chance.

**Annie** (*cheerfully*). To do what?

**Keller.** To—remain in our employ.

(*Annie's eyes widen.*)

But on two conditions. I am not accustomed to rudeness in servants or women, and that is the first. If you are to stay, there must be a radical change of manner.

**Annie** (*a pause*). Whose?

**Keller** (*exploding*). Yours, young lady, isn't it obvious? And the second is that you persuade me there's the slightest hope of your teaching a child who flees from you now like the plague, to anyone else she can find in this house.

**Annie** (*a pause*). There isn't.

(Kate *stops sewing, and fixes her eyes upon* Annie.)

**Kate.** What, Miss Annie?

**Annie.** It's hopeless here. I can't teach a child who runs away.

**Keller** (*nonplussed*). Then—do I understand you—propose—

**Annie.** Well, if we all agree it's hopeless, the next question is what—

**Kate.** Miss Annie.

(*She is leaning toward* Annie, *in deadly earnest; it commands both* Annie *and* Keller.)

I am not agreed. I think perhaps you—underestimate Helen.

**Annie.** I think everyone else here does.

**Kate.** She did fold her napkin. She learns, she learns. Do you know she began talking when she was six months old? She could say "water." Not really—"wahwah." "Wahwah," but she meant water. She knew what it meant, and only six months old; I never saw a child so—bright, or outgoing—

(*Her voice is unsteady, but she gets it level.*)

It's still in her, somewhere, isn't it? You should have seen her before her illness, such a good-tempered child—

**Annie** (*agreeably*). She's changed.

(A *pause,* Kate *not letting her eyes go; her appeal at last is unconditional, and very quiet.*)

**Kate.** Miss Annie, put up with it. And with us.

**Keller.** Us!

**Kate.** Please? Like the lost lamb in the parable, I love her all the more.

**Annie.** Mrs. Keller, I don't think Helen's worst handicap is deafness or blindness. I think it's your love. And pity.

**Keller.** Now what does that mean?

**Annie.** All of you here are so sorry for her you've kept her—like a pet, why, even a dog you housebreak. No wonder she won't let me come near her. It's useless for me to try to teach her language or anything else here. I might as well—

**Kate** (*cuts in*). Miss Annie, before you came we spoke of putting her in an asylum.

(Annie *turns back to regard her. A pause.*)

**Annie.** What kind of asylum?

**Keller.** For mental defectives.

**Kate.** I visited there. I can't tell you what I saw, people like—animals, with—*rats* in the halls, and—

(*She shakes her head on her vision.*)

What else are we to do, if you give up?

**Annie.** Give up?

**Kate.** You said it was hopeless.

**Annie.** Here. Give up, why, I only today saw what has to be done, to begin!

(*She glances from* Kate *to* Keller, *who stare, waiting; and she makes it as plain and simple as her nervousness permits.*)

I—want complete charge of her.

**Keller.** You already have that. It has resulted in—

**Annie.** No, I mean day and night. She has to be dependent on me.

**Kate.** For what?

**Annie.** Everything. The food she eats, the clothes she wears, fresh—

(*She is amused at herself, though very serious.*)

—air, yes, the air she breathes, whatever her body needs is a—primer, to teach her out of. It's the only way; the one who lets her have it should be her teacher.

(*She considers them in turn; they digest it,* Keller *frowning,* Kate *perplexed.*)

Not anyone who *loves* her. You have so many feelings they fall over each other like feet. You won't use your chances and you won't let me.

**Kate.** But if she runs from you—*to us*—

**Annie.** Yes, that's the point. I'll have to live with her somewhere else.

**Keller.** What!

**Annie.** Till she learns to depend on and listen to me.

**Kate** (*not without alarm*). For how long?

**Annie.** As long as it takes.

(*A pause. She takes a breath.*)

I packed half my things already.

**Keller.** Miss—Sullivan!

(*But when* Annie *attends upon him, he is speechless, and she is merely earnest.*)

**Annie.** Captain Keller, it meets both your conditions. It's the one way I can get back in touch with Helen, and I don't see how I can be rude to you again if you're not around to interfere with me.

**Keller** (*red-faced*). And what is your intention if I say no? Pack the other half, for home, and abandon your charge to—to—

**Annie.** The asylum?

(*She waits, appraises* Keller's *glare and* Kate's *uncertainty, and decides to use her weapons.*)

I grew up in such an asylum. The state almshouse.[5]

(Kate's *head comes up on this, and* Keller *stares hard;* Annie's *tone is cheerful enough, albeit level as gunfire.*)

Rats—why, my brother Jimmie and I used to play with the rats because we didn't have toys. Maybe you'd like to know what Helen will find there, not on visiting days? One ward was full of the—old women, crippled, blind, most of them dying; but even if what they had was catching, there was nowhere else to move them; and that's where they put us. There were younger ones across the hall, with T.B., and epileptic fits, and some insane. The youngest were in another ward to have babies they didn't want; they started at thirteen, fourteen. They'd leave afterwards, but the babies stayed, and we played with them, too, but not many of them lived. The first year we had eighty; seventy died. The room Jimmie and I played in was the deadhouse, where they kept the bodies till they could dig—

**Kate** (*closes her eyes*). Oh, my dear—

**Annie.** —the graves.

(*She is immune to* Kate's *compassion.*)

---

5. **almshouse:** formerly, a home for people too poor to support themselves.

No, it made me strong. But I don't think you need send Helen there. She's strong enough.

(*She waits again; but when neither offers her a word, she simply concludes.*)

No, I have no conditions, Captain Keller.

**Kate** (*not looking up*). Miss Annie.

**Annie.** Yes.

**Kate** (*a pause*). Where would you—take Helen?

**Annie.** Ohh—

(*brightly*) Italy?

**Keller** (*wheeling*). What?

**Annie.** Can't have everything. How would this garden house do? Furnish it, bring Helen here after a long ride so she won't recognize it, and you can see her every day. If she doesn't know. Well?

**Kate** (*a sigh of relief*). Is that all?

**Annie.** That's all.

**Kate.** Captain.

(Keller *turns his head; and* Kate's *request is quiet but firm.*)

With your permission?

**Keller** (*teeth in cigar*). Why must she depend on you for the food she eats?

**Annie** (*a pause*). I want control of it.

**Keller.** Why?

**Annie.** It's a way to reach her.

**Keller** (*stares*). You intend to *starve* her into letting you touch her?

**Annie.** She won't starve; she'll learn. All's fair in love and war. Captain Keller, you never cut supplies?

**Keller.** This is hardly a war!

**Annie.** Well, it's not love. A siege is a siege.

**Keller** (*heavily*). Miss Sullivan. Do you *like* the child?

**Annie** (*straight in his eyes*). Do you?

(*a long pause*)

**Kate.** You could have a servant here—

**Annie** (*amused*). I'll have enough work without looking after a servant! But the boy Percy could sleep here, run errands—

**Kate** (*also amused*). We can let Percy sleep here, I think, Captain?

**Annie** (*eagerly*). And some old furniture, all our own—

**Kate** (*also eager*). Captain? Do you think that walnut bedstead in the barn would be too—

**Keller.** I have not yet consented to Percy! Or to the house, or to the proposal! Or to Miss Sullivan's—staying on when I—

(*But he erupts in an irate surrender.*)

Very well, I consent to everything!

(*He shakes his cigar at* Annie.)

For two weeks. I'll give you two weeks in this place, and it will be a miracle if you get the child to tolerate you.

**Kate.** Two weeks? Miss Annie, can you accomplish anything in two weeks?

**Keller.** Anything or not, two weeks; then the child comes back to us. Make up your mind, Miss Sullivan, yes or no?

**Annie.** Two weeks. For only one miracle?

(*She nods at him, nervously.*)

I'll get her to tolerate me.

(Keller *marches out, and slams the door.*

Kate *on her feet regards* Annie, *who is facing the door.*)

**Kate** (*then*). You can't think as little of love as you said.

(Annie *glances questioning.*)

Or you wouldn't stay.

**Annie** (*a pause*). I didn't come here for love. I came for money!

(Kate *shakes her head to this, with a smile; after a moment, she extends her open hand.* Annie *looks at it, but when she puts hers out it is not to shake hands, it is to set her fist in* Kate's *palm.*)

**Kate** (*puzzled*). Hm?

**Annie.** A. It's the first of many. Twenty-six!

(Kate *squeezes her fist, squeezes it hard, and hastens out after Keller.* Annie *stands as the door closes behind her, her manner so apprehensive that finally she slaps her brow, holds it, sighs, and, with her eyes closed, crosses herself for luck.*

*The lights dim into a cool silhouette scene around her, the lamp paling out, and now, in formal entrances, persons appear around* Annie *with furniture for the room.* Percy *crosses the stage with a rocking chair and waits.* Martha, *from another direction, bears in a stool.* Viney *bears in a small table, and the other black servant rolls in a bed partway from left; and* Annie, *opening her eyes to put her glasses back on, sees them. She turns around in the room once, and goes into action, pointing out locations for each article. The servants place them and leave, and then* Annie *darts around, interchanging them. In the midst of this—while* Percy *and* Martha *reappear with a tray of food and a chair, respectively—*James *comes down from the house with* Annie's *suitcase, and stands viewing the room and her quizzically;* Annie *halts abruptly under his eyes, embarrassed, then seizes the suitcase from his hand, explaining herself brightly.*)

**Annie.** I always wanted to live in a doll's house!

(*She sets the suitcase out of the way, and continues.* Viney *at left appears to position a rod with drapes for a doorway, and the other servant at center pushes in a wheelbarrow loaded with a couple of boxes of* Helen's *toys and clothes.* Annie *helps lift them into the room, and the servant pushes the wheelbarrow off. In none of this is any heed taken of the imaginary walls of the garden house. The furniture is moved in from every side, and itself defines the walls.*

Annie *now drags the box of toys into center, props up the doll conspicuously on top. With the people melted away, except for* James, *all is again still. The lights turn again without pause, rising warmer.*)

**James.** You don't let go of things easily, do you? How will you—win her hand now, in this place?

**Annie** (*curtly*). Do I know? I lost my temper, and here we are!

**James** (*lightly*). No touching, no teaching. Of course, you *are* bigger—

**Annie.** I'm not counting on force; I'm counting on her. That little imp is dying to know.

**James.** Know what?

**Annie.** Anything. Any and every crumb in God's creation. I'll have to use that appetite too.

(*She gives the room a final survey, straightens the bed, arranges the curtains.*)

**James** (*a pause*). Maybe she'll teach you.

**Annie.** Of course.

**James.** That she isn't. That there's such a thing as—dullness of heart. Acceptance. And letting go. Sooner or later we all give up, don't we?

**Annie.** Maybe you all do. It's my idea of the original sin.

**James.** What is?

**Annie** (*witheringly*). Giving up.

**James** (*nettled*). You won't open her. Why can't you let her be? Have some—pity on her, for being what she is—

**Annie.** If I'd ever once thought like that, I'd be dead!

**James** (*pleasantly*). You will be. Why trouble?

(*Annie turns to glare at him; he is mocking.*)

Or will you teach me?

(*And with a bow, he drifts off.*

*Now in the distance there comes the clopping of hoofs, drawing near, and nearer, up to the door; and they halt. Annie wheels to face the door. When it opens this time, the Kellers—Kate in traveling bonnet, Keller also hatted—are standing there with Helen between them; she is in a cloak. Kate gently cues her into the room. Helen comes in groping, baffled but interested in the new surroundings; Annie evades her exploring hand, her gaze not leaving the child.*)

**Annie.** Does she know where she is?

**Kate** (*shakes her head*). We rode her out in the country for two hours.

**Keller.** For all she knows, she could be in another town—

(*Helen stumbles over the box on the floor, and in it discovers her doll and other battered toys, is pleased, sits by them, then becomes puzzled and suddenly very <u>wary</u>.[6] She scrambles up and back to her mother's thighs; but Annie steps in, and it is hers that Helen embraces. Helen recoils, gropes, and touches her cheek instantly.*)

**Kate.** That's her sign for me.

**Annie.** I know.

(*Helen waits, then recommences her groping, more urgently. Kate stands indecisive, and takes an abrupt step toward her, but Annie's hand is a barrier.*)

In two weeks.

**Kate.** Miss Annie, I—Please be good to her. These two weeks, try to be very good to her—

**Annie.** I will.

(*Kate, turning then, hurries out. The Kellers cross back to the main house.*

*Annie closes the door. Helen starts at the door jar, and rushes it. Annie holds her off. Helen kicks her, breaks free, and careens around the room like an imprisoned bird, colliding with furniture, groping wildly, repeatedly touching her cheek in a growing panic. When she has covered the room, she commences her weird screaming. Annie moves to comfort her, but her touch sends Helen into a paroxysm of rage. She tears away, falls over her box of toys, flings its contents in handfuls in Annie's direction, flings the box too, reels to her feet, rips curtains from the window, bangs and kicks at the door, sweeps objects off the mantlepiece and shelf, a little tornado incarnate, all destruction, until she comes upon her doll and, in the act of hurling it, freezes. Then she clutches it to herself, and in exhaustion sinks sobbing to the floor. Annie stands contemplating her, in some awe.*)

---

6. **wary** (wer′ ē): cautious.

Two weeks.

(*She shakes her head, not without a touch of disgusted bewilderment.*)

What did I get into now?

(*The lights have been dimming throughout, and the garden house is lit only by moonlight now, with Annie lost in the patches of dark.*

Kate, *now hatless and coatless, enters the family room by the rear door, carrying a lamp.* Keller, *also hatless, wanders simultaneously around the back of the main house to where* James *has been waiting, in the rising moonlight, on the porch.*)

**Keller.**  I can't understand it. I had every intention of dismissing that girl, not setting her up like an empress.

**James.**  Yes, what's her secret, sir?

**Keller.**  Secret?

**James** (*pleasantly*).  That enables her to get anything she wants out of you? When I can't.

(*James turns to go into the house, but* Keller *grasps his wrist, twisting him half to his knees.* Kate *comes from the porch.*)

**Keller.**  (*angrily*).  She does *not* get anything she—

**James** (*in pain*).  Don't—don't—

**Kate.**  Captain.

**Keller.**  He's afraid.

(*He throws* James *away from him, with contempt.*)

What *does* he want out of me?

**James** (*an outcry*).  My God, don't you know?

(*He gazes from* Keller *to* Kate.)

Everything you forgot, when you forgot my mother.

**Keller.**  What!

(*James wheels into the house.* Keller *takes a stride to the porch, to roar after him.*)

One thing that girl's secret is not; she doesn't fire one shot and disappear!

(*Kate stands rigid, and* Keller *comes back to her.*)

Katie. Don't mind what he—

**Kate.**  Captain, I am proud of you.

**Keller.**  For what?

**Kate.**  For letting this girl have what she needs.

**Keller.**  Why can't my son be? He can't bear me; you'd think I treat him as hard as this girl does Helen—

(*He breaks off, as it dawns in him.*)

**Kate** (*gently*).  Perhaps you do.

**Keller.**  But he has to learn some respect!

**Kate** (*a pause wryly*).  Do you like the child?

(*She turns again to the porch, but pauses, reluctant.*)

How empty the house is, tonight.

(*After a moment she continues on in.* Keller *stands moveless, as the moonlight dies on him.*

*The distant belfry chimes toll, two o'clock, and with them, a moment later, comes the boy's voice on the wind, in a whisper.*)

**Boy's Voice.**  Annie. Annie.

(*In her patch of dark* Annie, *now in her nightgown, hurls a cup into a corner as though it were her grief, getting rid of its taste through her teeth.*)

**Annie.**  No! No pity, I won't have it.

*(She comes to Helen, prone on the floor.)*

On either of us.

*(She goes to her knees, but when she touches Helen's hand, the child starts up awake, recoils, and scrambles away from her under the bed. Annie stares after her. She strikes her palm on the floor, with passion.)*

I *will* touch you!

*(She gets to her feet, and paces in a kind of anger around the bed, her hand in her hair, and confronting Helen at each turn.)*

How, how? How do I—

*(Annie stops. Then she calls out urgently, loudly.)*

Percy! Percy!

*(She moves swiftly to the drapes, at left.)*

Percy, wake up!

*(Percy's voice comes in a thick sleepy mumble, unintelligible.)*

Get out of bed and come in here. I need you.

*(Annie darts away, finds and strikes a match, and touches it to the hanging lamp. The lights come up dimly in the room, and Percy stands bare to the waist in torn overalls, between the drapes, with eyes closed, swaying. Annie goes to him, pats his cheeks vigorously.)*

Percy. You awake?

**Percy.** No'm.

**Annie.** How would you like to play a nice game?

**Percy.** Whah?

**Annie.** With Helen. She's under the bed. Touch her hand.

*(She kneels Percy down at the bed, thrusting*

his hand under it to contact Helen's. Helen emits an animal sound and crawls to the opposite side, but commences sniffing. Annie rounds the bed with Percy and thrusts his hand again at Helen. This time Helen clutches it, sniffs in recognition, and comes scrambling out after Percy to hug him with delight. Percy, alarmed, struggles, and Helen's fingers go to his mouth.)*

**Percy.** Lemme go. Lemme go—

*(Helen fingers her own lips, as before, moving them in dumb imitation.)*

She tryin' talk. She gonna hit me—

**Annie** *(grimly).* She can talk. If she only knew. I'll show you how. She makes letters.

*(She opens Percy's other hand, and spells into it.)*

This one is C. C.

*(She hits his palm with it a couple of times, her eyes upon Helen across him. Helen gropes to feel what Percy's hand is doing, and when she encounters Annie's, she falls back from them.)*

She's mad at me now, though, she won't play. But she knows lots of letters. Here's another, A. C, a. C, a.

*(But she is watching Helen, who comes groping, consumed with curiosity. Annie makes the letters in Percy's hand, and Helen pokes to question what they are up to. Then Helen snatches Percy's other hand, and quickly spells four letters into it. Annie follows them aloud.)*

C, a, k, e! She spells cake; she gets cake.

*(She is swiftly over to the tray of food, to fetch cake and a jug of milk.)*

She doesn't know yet it means this. Isn't it funny. She knows how to spell it and doesn't *know* she knows?

(*She breaks the cake into two pieces, and extends one to each; Helen rolls away from her offer.*)

Well, if she won't play it with me, I'll play with you. Would you like to learn one she doesn't know?

**Percy.** No'm.

(*But Annie seizes his wrist, and spells to him.*)

**Annie.** M, i, l, k. M is this. I, that's an easy one, just the little finger. L is this—

(*And Helen comes back with her hand, to feel the new word. Annie brushes her away, and continues spelling aloud to Percy. Helen's hand comes back again, and tries to get in. Annie brushes it away again. Helen's hand insists, and Annie puts it away rudely.*)

No, why should I talk to you? I'm teaching Percy a new word. L. K is this—

(*Helen now yanks their hands apart. She butts Percy away, and thrusts her palm insistently. Annie's eyes are bright, with glee.*)

Ho, you're jealous, are you!

(*Helen's hand waits, intractably waits.*)

All right.

(*Annie spells into it, milk; and Helen after a moment spells it back to Annie. Annie takes her hand, with her whole face shining. She gives a great sigh.*)

Good! So I'm finally back to where I can touch you, hm? Touch and go! No love lost, but here we go.

(*She puts the jug of milk into Helen's hand and squeezes Percy's shoulder.*)

You can go to bed now; you've earned your

sleep. Thank you.

(*Percy, stumbling up, weaves his way out through the drapes. Helen finishes drinking, and holds the jug out, for Annie. When Annie takes it, Helen crawls onto the bed, and makes for sleep. Annie stands, looks down at her.*)

Now all I have to teach you is—one word. Everything.

(*She sets the jug down. Now Annie spies the doll on the floor, stoops to pick it up, and with it dangling in her hand, turns off the lamp. A shaft of moonlight is left on Helen in the bed, and a second shaft on the rocking chair; and Annie, after putting off her smoked glasses, sits in the rocker with the doll. She is rather happy, and dangles the doll on her knee, and it makes its momma sound. Annie whispers to it in mock solicitude.*)

Hush, little baby. Don't—say a word—

(*She lays it against her shoulder, and begins rocking with it, patting its diminutive behind; she talks the lullaby to it, humorously at first.*)

Momma's gonna buy you—a mockingbird;

If that—mockingbird don't sing—

(*The rhythm of the rocking takes her into the tune, softly, and more tenderly.*)

Momma's gonna buy you a diamond ring;

If that diamond ring turns to brass—

(*A third shaft of moonlight outside now rises to pick out James at the main house, with one foot on the porch step; he turns his body, as if hearing the song.*)

Momma's gonna buy you a looking glass;

If that looking glass gets broke—

(*In the family room, a fourth shaft picks out

Keller *seated at the table, in thought; and he, too, lifts his head, as if hearing.)*

*Momma's gonna buy you a billy goat;*

*If that billy goat won't pull—*

*(The fifth shaft is upstairs in Annie's room, and picks out Kate, pacing there; and she halts, turning her head, too, as if hearing.)*

*Momma's gonna buy you a cart and bull;*

*If that cart and bull turns over,*

*Momma's gonna buy you a dog named Rover;*

*If that dog named Rover won't bark—*

*(With the shafts of moonlight on Helen, and James, and Keller, and Kate, all moveless, and Annie rocking the doll, the curtain ends the act.)*

# Thinking About Act Two

## A PERSONAL RESPONSE

*sharing impressions*

**1.** What do you think about Annie's idea to take Helen to the garden house? Describe your response in your journal.

*constructing interpretations*

**2.** Explain whether you think Annie Sullivan's treatment of Helen is justified.

**Think about**
- her belief that "obedience is the gateway through which knowledge enters the mind of the child"
- the positive and negative results of her long struggle with Helen at the breakfast table
- why James compares her to General Grant at Vicksburg
- her strategy for getting Helen to accept her touch again

**3.** Do you agree with Annie Sullivan that Helen's worst handicap, or disability, is her family's love and pity? Explain why or why not.

**4.** Which member of the Keller household, including Annie, do you think has the most influence on family decisions, and why?

## A CREATIVE RESPONSE

**5.** If Annie had never suffered the hardships and horrors of her childhood, how do you think her approach to Helen might differ?

**6.** What do the flashbacks to Annie Sullivan's past add to the play so far?
**Think about**
- what key information they give about Annie's relationship to her brother and about the decisions she has made
- what feeling they would create in an audience
- why they always occur in relation to Helen, usually right after Annie has a fight with her
- why they cause Annie such emotional pain

**7.** Compare Annie's approach to Helen with the narrator's approach to his brother Doodle in the short story "The Scarlet Ibis." Support your ideas with examples.

 *nalyzing the Writer's Craft*

## CONFLICT

Act Two ends with the major characters lit by shafts of light on separate areas of the stage. Keller, James, and Kate are all alert "as if hearing" the lullaby Annie sings. What do you think William Gibson wanted to emphasize by staging the final moments of the act in this way?

**Building a Literary Vocabulary.** Conflict is a struggle between opposing forces. An external conflict involves a character pitted against an outside force—nature, a physical obstacle, or another character. An internal conflict is one that occurs within a character. The central conflict of this play is the contest of wills between Annie and Helen. William Gibson also dramatizes other external conflicts: tensions within the Keller family, for example, as well as conflicts between men and women, between North and South, and between the genteel, upper-class Kellers and the independent, working-class Annie Sullivan. In addition, several characters in the play suffer inner conflicts. For example, Annie is haunted by the losses and hard-

ships of the past as she faces the difficult challenges of the present. By showing all the characters separated at the end of Act Two, Gibson illustrates the isolation that conflict often brings. And yet, the characters are all attentive to Annie's song, suggesting that the conflicts will be resolved in the next act.

**Application: Identifying Conflict.** Working with a partner, explore external conflicts that exist between characters. On a sheet of paper write the names of the characters in a wide circle. Indicate the intensity of the conflict that exists between two characters by the kind of line you draw between them—use a straight line to indicate little or no conflict, a wavy line to indicate some conflict, and a heavy, jagged line to indicate serious conflict. Then circle the names of the characters that you think experience an internal conflict and jot down a few words next to each name to identify the inner struggle.

# ACT THREE

*The stage is totally dark, until we see Annie and Helen silhouetted on the bed in the garden house. Annie's voice is audible, very patient, and worn; it has been saying this for a long time.*

**Annie.**  Water, Helen. This is water. W, a, t, e, r. It has a *name*.

*(A silence. Then,)*

Egg, e, g, g. It has a *name*, the name stands for the thing. Oh, it's so simple, simple as birth, to explain.

*(The lights have commenced to rise, not on the garden house but on the homestead. Then,)*

Helen, Helen, the chick *has* to come out of its shell, sometime. You come out, too.

*(In the bedroom upstairs, we see Viney unhurriedly washing the window, dusting, turning the mattress, readying the room for use again; then in the family room a diminished group at one end of the table—Kate, Keller, James—finishing up a quiet breakfast; then outside, down right, the other black servant on his knees, assisted by Martha, working with a trowel around a new trellis and wheelbarrow. The scene is one of everyday calm, and all are oblivious to Annie's voice.)*

There's only one way out, for you, and it's language. To learn that your fingers can talk. And say anything, anything you can name. This is a mug. Mug, m, u, g. Helen, it has a name. It—has—a—*name*—

*(Kate rises from the table.)*

**Keller** *(gently)*.  You haven't eaten, Katie.

**Kate** *(smiles, shakes her head)*.  I haven't the appetite. I'm too—restless, I can't sit to it.

**Keller.**  You should eat, my dear. It will be a long day, waiting.

**James** *(lightly)*.  But it's been a short two weeks. I never thought life could be so—noiseless, went much too quickly for me.

*(Kate and Keller gaze at him, in silence. James becomes uncomfortable.)*

**Annie.**  C, a, r, d. Card. C, a—

**James.**  Well, the house has been practically normal, hasn't it?

**Keller** *(harshly)*.  Jimmie.

**James.**  Is it wrong to enjoy a quiet breakfast, after five years? And you two even seem to enjoy each other—

**Keller.**  It could be even more noiseless, Jimmie, without your tongue running every minute. Haven't you enough feeling to imagine what Katie has been undergoing, ever since—

*(Kate stops him, with her hand on his arm.)*

**Kate.**  Captain.

*(to James)*

It's true. The two weeks have been normal, quiet, all you say. But not short. Interminable.

*(She rises, and wanders out; she pauses on the porch steps, gazing toward the garden house.)*

**Annie** *(fading)*.  W, a, t, e, r. But it means this. W, a, t, e, r. This. W, a, t—

**James.**  I only meant that Miss Sullivan is a boon. Of contention,[1] though, it seems.

---

1. **boon . . . contention:** Boon means benefit or blessing; contention means controversy or dispute. James makes a pun here on the phrase *bone of contention,* meaning a matter for argument.

**Keller** (*heavily*). If and when you're a parent, Jimmie, you will understand what separation means. A mother loses a—protector.

**James** (*baffled*). Hm?

**Keller.** You'll learn; we don't just keep our children safe. They keep us safe.

(*He rises, with his empty coffee cup and saucer.*)

There are, of course, all kinds of separation. Katie has lived with one kind for five years. And another is disappointment. In a child.

(*He goes with the cup out the rear door. James sits for a long moment of stillness. In the garden house, the lights commence to come up. Annie, haggard at the table, is writing a letter, her face again almost in contact with the stationery. Helen, apart on the stool, and for the first time as clean and neat as a button, is quietly crocheting an endless chain of wool, which snakes all around the room.*)

**Annie.** "I, feel, every, day, more, and, more, in—"

(*She pauses, and turns the pages of a dictionary open before her; her finger descends the words to a full stop. She elevates her eyebrows, then copies the word.*)

"—adequate."

(*In the main house James pushes up, and goes to the front doorway, after Kate.*)

**James.** Kate?

(*Kate turns her glance. James is rather weary.*)

I'm sorry. Open my mouth, like that fairy tale, frogs jump out.

**Kate.** No. It has been better. For everyone.

(*She starts away, up center.*)

**Annie** (*writing*). "If, only, there, were, someone, to, help, me, I, need, a, teacher, as, much, as, Helen—"

**James.** Kate.

(*Kate halts, waits.*)

What does he want from me?

**Kate.** That's not the question. Stand up to the world, Jimmie; that comes first.

**James** (*a pause, wryly*). But the world is him.

**Kate.** Yes. And no one can do it for you.

**James.** Kate.

(*His voice is humble.*)

At least we—Could you—be my friend?

**Kate.** I am.

(*Kate turns to wander, up back of the garden house. Annie's murmur comes at once; the lights begin to die on the main house.*)

**Annie.** "—my, mind, is, undisiplined, full, of, skips, and, jumps, and—"

(*She halts, rereads, frowns.*)

Hm.

(*Annie puts her nose again in the dictionary, flips back to an earlier page, and fingers down the words; Kate presently comes down toward the bay window with a trayful of food.*)

Disinter—disinterested—disjoin—dis—

(*She backtracks, indignant.*)

Disinterested, disjoin—Where's disipline?

(*She goes a page or two back, searching with her finger, muttering.*)

What a dictionary; have to know how to spell it before you can look up how to spell it; disciple, discipline! Diskipline.

(*She corrects the word in her letter.*)

(*But her eyes are bothering her; she closes them in exhaustion and gently fingers the eyelids. Kate watches her through the window.*)

**Kate.** What are you doing to your eyes?

(*Annie glances around; she puts her smoked glasses on, and gets up to come over, assuming a cheerful energy.*)

**Annie.** It's worse on my vanity! I'm learning to spell. It's like a surprise party; the most unexpected characters turn up.

**Kate.** You're not to overwork your eyes, Miss Annie.

**Annie.** Well.

(*She takes the tray, sets it on her chair, and carries chair and tray to* Helen.)

Whatever I spell to Helen I'd better spell right.

**Kate** (*almost wistful*). How—serene she is.

**Annie.** She learned this stitch yesterday. Now I can't get her to stop!

(*She disentangles one foot from the wool chain, and sets the chair before* Helen. Helen, *at its contact with her knee, feels the plate, promptly sets her crocheting down, and tucks the napkin in at her neck; but* Annie *withholds the spoon. When* Helen *finds it missing, she folds her hands in her lap, and quietly waits.* Annie *twinkles at* Kate *with mock devoutness.*)

Such a little lady; she'd sooner starve than eat with her fingers.

(*She gives* Helen *the spoon, and* Helen *begins to eat, neatly.*)

**Kate.** You've taught her so much, these two weeks. I would never have—

**Annie.** Not enough.

(*She is suddenly gloomy; shakes her head.*)

Obedience isn't enough. Well, she learned two nouns this morning, *key* and *water*, brings her up to eighteen nouns and three verbs.

**Kate** (*hesitant*). But—not—

**Annie.** No. Not that they mean things. It's still a finger game, no meaning.

(*She turns to* Kate, *abruptly.*)

Mrs. Keller—

(*But she defers it; she comes back, to sit in the bay and lift her hand.*)

Shall we play our finger game?

**Kate.** How will she learn it?

**Annie.** It will come.

(*She spells a word;* Kate *does not respond.*)

**Kate.** How?

**Annie** (*a pause*). How does a bird learn to fly?

(*She spells again.*)

We're born to use words, like wings; it has to come.

**Kate.** How?

**Annie** (*another pause, wearily*). All right. I don't know how.

(*She pushes up her glasses, to rub her eyes.*)

I've done everything I could think of. Whatever she's learned here—keeping herself clean, knitting, stringing beads, meals, setting-up exercises each morning; we climb trees; hunt eggs; yesterday a chick was born in her hands—all of it I spell; everything we do, we never stop spelling. I go to bed with—writer's cramp from talking so much!

**Kate.** I worry about you, Miss Annie. You must rest.

**Annie.** Now? She spells back in her *sleep*; her fingers make letters when she doesn't know! In her bones, those five fingers know; that hand aches to—speak out, and something in her mind is asleep. How do I—nudge that awake? That's the one question.

**Kate.** With no answer.

**Annie** (*long pause*). Except keep at it. Like this.

(*She again begins spelling—I, need—and* Kate's *brows gather, following the words.*)

**Kate.** More—time?

(*She glances at* Annie, *who looks her in the eyes, silent.*)

Here.

**Annie.** Spell it.

(Kate *spells a word—no—shaking her head;* Annie *spells two words—why, not—back, with an impatient question in her eyes; and* Kate *moves her head in pain to answer it.*)

**Kate.** Because I can't—

**Annie.** Spell it! If she ever learns, you'll have a lot to tell each other. Start now.

(Kate *painstakingly spells in air. In the midst of this the rear door opens, and* Keller *enters with the setter, Belle, in tow.*)

**Keller.** Miss Sullivan? On my way to the office, I brought Helen a playmate—

**Annie.** Outside please, Captain Keller.

**Keller.** My dear child, the two weeks are up today; surely you don't object to—

**Annie** (*rising*). They're not up till six o'clock.

**Keller** (*indulgent*). Oh, now. What differ-

ence can a fraction of one day—

**Annie.** An agreement is an agreement. Now you've been very good, I'm sure you can keep it up for a few more hours.

(*She escorts* Keller *by the arm over the threshold; he obeys, leaving Belle.*)

**Keller.** Miss Sullivan, you are a tyrant.

**Annie.** Likewise, I'm sure. You can stand there, and close the door if she comes.

**Kate.** I don't think you know how eager we are to have her back in our arms—

**Annie.** I do know; it's my main worry.

**Keller.** It's like expecting a new child in the house. Well, she *is*, so—composed, so—

(*gently*)

Attractive. You've done wonders for her, Miss Sullivan.

**Annie** (*not a question*) Have I.

**Keller.** If there's anything you want from us in repayment, tell us; it will be a privilege to—

**Annie.** I just told Mrs. Keller. I want more time.

**Kate.** Miss Annie—

**Annie.** Another week.

(Helen *lifts her head, and begins to sniff.*)

**Keller.** We miss the child. *I* miss her, I'm glad to say, that's a different debt I owe you—

**Annie.** Pay it to Helen. Give *her* another week.

**Kate** (*gently*). Doesn't she miss us?

**Keller.** Of course she does. What a wrench this unexplainable—exile must be to her. Can you say it's not?

**Annie.**  No. But I—

(Helen *is off the stool, to grope about the room; when she encounters Belle, she throws her arms around the dog's neck in delight.*)

**Kate.**  Doesn't she need affection too, Miss Annie?

**Annie** (*wavering*).  She—never shows me she needs it. She won't have any—caressing or—

**Kate.**  But you're not her mother.

**Keller.**  And what would another week accomplish? We are more than satisfied. You've done more than we ever thought possible, taught her constructive—

**Annie.**  I can't promise anything. All I can—

**Keller** (*no break*).  —things to do, to behave like—even look like—a human child, so manageable, contented, cleaner, more—

**Annie** (*withering*).  Cleaner.

**Keller.**  Well. We say cleanliness is next to godliness, Miss—

**Annie.**  Cleanliness is next to nothing. She has to learn that everything has its name! That words can be her *eyes*, to everything in the world outside her, and inside too. What is she without words? With them, she can think, have ideas, be reached; there's not a thought or fact in the world that can't be hers. You publish a newspaper, Captain Keller. Do I have to tell you what words are? And she has them already—

**Keller.**  Miss Sullivan.

**Annie.**  —eighteen nouns and three verbs. They're in her fingers now. I need only time to push *one* of them into her mind! One, and everything under the sun will follow.

Don't you see what she's learned here is only clearing the way for that? I can't risk her unlearning it. Give me more time alone with her, another week to—

**Keller.**  Look.

(*He points, and Annie turns. Helen is playing with Belle's claws; she makes letters with her fingers, shows them to Belle, waits with her palm, then manipulates the dog's claws.*)

What is she spelling?

(*a silence*)

**Kate.**  Water?

(*Annie nods.*)

**Keller.**  Teaching a dog to spell.

(*a pause*)

The dog doesn't know what she means, any more than she knows what you mean, Miss Sullivan. I think you ask too much, of her and yourself. God may not have meant Helen to have the—eyes you speak of.

**Annie** (*toneless*).  I mean her to.

**Keller** (*curiously*).  What is it to you?

(*Annie's head comes slowly up.*)

You make us see how we indulge her for our sake. Is the opposite true, for you?

**Annie** (*then*).  Half a week?

**Keller.**  An agreement *is* an agreement.

**Annie.**  Mrs. Keller?

**Kate** (*simply*).  I want her back.

(*A wait; Annie then lets her hands drop in surrender, and nods.*)

**Keller.**  I'll send Viney over to help you pack.

**Annie.**  Not until six o'clock. I have

her till six o'clock.

**Keller** (*consenting*). Six o'clock. Come, Katie.

(Kate, *leaving the window, joins him around back, while* Keller *closes the door; they are shut out.*

*Only the garden house is daylit now, and the light on it is narrowing down.* Annie *stands watching* Helen *work* Belle's *claws. Then she settles beside them on her knees, and stops* Helen's *hand.*)

**Annie** (*gently*). No.

(*She shakes her head, with* Helen's *hand to her face, then spells.*)

Dog. D, o, g. Dog.

(*She touches* Helen's *hand to* Belle. Helen *dutifully pats the dog's head, and resumes spelling to its paw.*)

Not water.

(Annie *rolls to her feet, brings a tumbler of water back from the tray, and kneels with it, to seize* Helen's *hand and spell.*)

Here, Water. *Water.*

(*She thrusts* Helen's *hand into the tumbler.* Helen *lifts her hand out dripping, wipes it daintily on* Belle's *hide; and taking the tumbler from* Annie, *endeavors to thrust* Belle's *paw into it.* Annie *sits watching, wearily.*)

I don't know how to tell you. Not a soul in the world knows how to tell you. Helen, Helen.

(*She bends in* compassion[2] *to touch her lips to* Helen's *temple, and instantly* Helen *pauses, her hands off the dog, her head slightly averted. The lights are still narrowing, and* Belle *slinks off. After a moment,* Annie *sits back.*)

Yes, what's it to me? They're satisfied. Give them back their child and dog, both housebroken; everyone's satisfied. But me, and you.

(Helen's *hand comes out into the light, groping.*)

Reach. *Reach!*

(Annie, *extending her own hand, grips* Helen's; *the two hands are clasped, tense in the light, the rest of the room changing in shadow.*)

I wanted to teach you—oh, everything the earth is full of, Helen, everything on it that's ours for a wink, and it's gone; and what we are on it, the—light we bring to it and leave behind in—words. Why, you can see five thousand years back in a light of words, everything we feel, think, know—and share, in words, so not a soul is in darkness, or done with, even in the grave. And I know, I *know*, one word and I can—put the world in your hand—and whatever it is to me, I won't take less! How, how, how do I tell you that *this*—

(*She spells.*)

—means a *word*, and the word means this *thing*, wool?

(*She thrusts the wool at* Helen's *hand;* Helen *sits, puzzled.* Annie *puts the crocheting aside.*)

Or this—s, t, o, o, l—means this *thing*, stool?

(*She claps* Helen's *palm to the stool.* Helen *waits, uncomprehending.* Annie *snatches up her napkin, spells,*)

*Napkin!*

---

2. **compassion** (kəm pash′ ən): sympathy, pity, or sorrow for the trouble of another.

*(She forces it in Helen's hand, waits, discards it, lifts a fold of the child's dress, spells,)*

*Dress!*

*(She lets it drop, spells,)*

*F, a, c, e, face!*

*(She draws Helen's hand to her cheek, and pressing it there, staring into the child's responseless eyes, hears the distant belfry begin to toll, slowly: one, two, three, four, five, six.*

*On the third stroke, the lights stealing in around the garden house show us figures waiting: Viney, the other servant, Martha, Percy at the drapes, and James on the dim porch. Annie and Helen remain, frozen. The chimes die away. Silently Percy moves the drape rod back out of sight; Viney steps into the room—not using the door—and unmakes the bed; the other servant brings the wheelbarrow over, leaves it handy, rolls the bed off; Viney puts the bed linens on the top of a waiting boxful of Helen's toys, and loads the box on the wheelbarrow; Martha and Percy take out the chairs, with the trayful, then the table; and James, coming down and into the room, lifts Annie's suitcase from its corner. Viney and the other servant load the remaining odds and ends on the wheelbarrow, and the servant wheels it off. Viney and the children departing leave only James in the room with Annie and Helen. James studies the two of them, without mockery, and then, quietly going to the door and opening it, bears the suitcase out, and housewards. He leaves the door open.*

*Kate steps into the doorway, and stands. Annie, lifting her gaze from Helen, sees her; she takes Helen's hand from her cheek, and returns it to the child's own, stroking it there twice, in her mother-sign, before spelling slowly into it,)*

*M, o, t, h, e, r. Mother.*

*(Helen, with her hand free, strokes her cheek, suddenly forlorn. Annie takes her hand again.)*

*M, o, t, h—*

*(But Kate is trembling with such impatience that her voice breaks from her, harsh.)*

**Kate.** Let her *come!*

*(Annie lifts Helen to her feet, with a turn, and gives her a little push. Now Helen begins groping, sensing something, trembling herself; and Kate, falling one step in onto her knees, clasps her, kissing her. Helen clutches her, tight as she can. Kate is inarticulate, choked, repeating Helen's name again and again. She wheels with her in her arms, to stumble away out the doorway. Annie stands unmoving, while Kate in a blind walk carries Helen like a baby behind the main house, out of view.*

*Annie is now alone on the stage. She turns, gazing around at the stripped room, bidding it silently farewell, impassively, like a defeated general on the deserted battlefield. All that remains is a stand with a basin of water; and here Annie takes up an eyecup, bathes each of her eyes, empties the eyecup, drops it in her purse, and tiredly locates her smoked glasses on the floor. The lights alter subtly; in the act of putting on the glasses, Annie hears something that stops her, with head lifted. We hear it too, the voices out of the past, including her own now, in a whisper,)*

**Boy's Voice.** You said we'd be together, forever—You promised, forever and—Annie!

**Anagnos's Voice.** But that battle is dead and done with. Why not let it stay buried?

**Annie's Voice** *(whispering)*. I think God

must owe me a resurrection.

**Anagnos's Voice.** What?

(*A pause, and Annie answers it herself, heavily.*)

**Annie.** And I owe God one.

**Boy's Voice.** Forever and ever—

(*Annie shakes her head.*)

—forever, and ever, and—

(*Annie covers her ears.*)

—forever, and ever, and ever—

(*It pursues Annie; she flees to snatch up her purse, wheels to the doorway, and Keller is standing in it. The lights have lost their special color.*)

**Keller.** Miss—Annie.

(*He has an envelope in his fingers.*)

I've been waiting to give you this.

**Annie** (*after a breath*). What?

**Keller.** Your first month's salary.

(*He puts it in her hand.*)

With many more to come, I trust. It doesn't express what we feel; it doesn't pay our debt. For what you've done.

**Annie.** What have I done?

**Keller.** Taken a wild thing, and given us back a child.

**Annie** (*presently*). I taught her one thing, no. Don't do this, don't do that—

**Keller.** It's more than all of us could, in all the years we—

**Annie.** I wanted to teach her what language is. I wanted to teach her yes.

**Keller.** You will have time.

**Annie.** I don't know how. I know without it to do nothing but obey is—no gift. Obedience without understanding is a—blindness, too. Is that all I've wished on her?

**Keller** (*gently*). No, no—

**Annie.** Maybe. I don't know what else to do. Simply go on, keep doing what I've done, and have—faith that inside she's—That inside it's waiting. Like water, underground. All I can do is keep on.

**Keller.** It's enough. For us.

**Annie.** You can help, Captain Keller.

**Keller.** How?

**Annie.** Even learning no has been at a cost. Of much trouble and pain. Don't undo it.

**Keller.** Why should we wish to—

**Annie** (*abruptly*). The world isn't an easy place for anyone. I don't want her just to obey, but to let her have her way in everything is a lie, to *her*. I can't—

(*Her eyes fill; it takes her by surprise, and she laughs through it.*)

And I don't even love her. She's not my child! Well. You've got to stand between that lie and her.

**Keller.** We'll try.

**Annie.** Because *I* will. As long as you let me stay, that's one promise I'll keep.

**Keller.** Agreed. We've learned something too, I hope.

(*a pause*)

Won't you come now, to supper?

**Annie.** Yes.

(*She wags the envelope, ruefully.*)

Why doesn't God pay His debts each month?

**Keller.** Beg your pardon?

**Annie.** Nothing. I used to wonder how I could—

(*The lights are fading on them, simultaneously rising on the family room of the main house, where Viney is polishing glassware at the table set for dinner.*)

—earn a living.

**Keller.** Oh, you do.

**Annie.** I really do. Now the question is, can I survive it!

(Keller *smiles, offers his arm.*)

**Keller.** May I?

(Annie *takes it, and the lights lose them as he escorts her out.*

*Now in the family room the rear door opens, and Helen steps in. She stands a moment, then sniffs in one deep, grateful breath; and her hands go out vigorously to familiar things, over the door panels, and to the chairs around the table, and over the silverware on the table, until she meets Viney; she pats her flank approvingly.*)

**Viney.** Oh, we glad to have you back too, prob'ly.

(Helen *hurries groping to the front door, opens and closes it, removes its key, opens and closes it again to be sure it is unlocked, gropes back to the rear door and repeats the procedure, removing its key and hugging herself gleefully.*

*Aunt Ev is next in by the rear door, with a relish tray; she bends to kiss Helen's cheek. Helen finds Kate behind her, and thrusts the keys at her.*)

**Kate.** What? Oh.

(*to* Ev)

Keys.

(*She pockets them; lets Helen feel them.*)

Yes, I'll keep the keys. I think we've had enough of locked doors, too.

(James, *having earlier put Annie's suitcase inside her door upstairs and taken himself out of view around the corner, now reappears and comes down the stairs as Annie and Keller mount the porch steps. Following them into the family room, he pats Annie's hair in passing, rather to her surprise.*)

**James.** Evening, General.

(*He takes his own chair opposite.*

Viney *bears the empty water pitcher out to the porch. The remaining suggestion of garden house is gone now, and the water pump is unobstructed.* Viney *pumps water into the pitcher.*

Kate, *surveying the table, breaks the silence.*)

**Kate.** Will you say grace, Jimmie?

(*They bow their heads, except for Helen, who palms her empty plate and then reaches to be sure her mother is there. James considers a moment, glances across at Annie, lowers his head again, and obliges.*)

**James** (*lightly*). And Jacob was left alone, and wrestled with an angel until the breaking of the day; and the hollow of Jacob's thigh was out of joint, as he wrestled with him; and the angel said, Let me go, for the day breaketh. And Jacob said, I will not let thee go, except thou bless me. Amen.

(Annie *has lifted her eyes suspiciously at James, who winks expressionlessly and inclines his head to Helen.*)

Oh, you angel.

(*The others lift their faces;* Viney *returns with the pitcher, setting it down near* Kate; *then goes out the rear door; and* Annie *puts a napkin around* Helen.)

**Aunt Ev.**  That's a very strange grace, James.

**Keller.**  Will you start the muffins, Ev?

**James.**  It's from the Good Book, isn't it?

**Aunt Ev** (*passing a plate*).  Well, of course it is. Didn't you know?

**James.**  Yes, I knew.

**Keller** (*serving*).  Ham, Miss Annie?

**Annie.**  Please.

**Aunt Ev.**  Then why ask?

**James.**  I meant it *is* from the Good Book, and therefore a fitting grace.

**Aunt Ev.**  Well. I don't know about *that*.

**Kate** (*with the pitcher*).  Miss Annie?

**Annie.**  Thank you.

**Aunt Ev.**  There's an awful *lot* of things in the Good Book that I wouldn't care to hear just before eating.

(*When* Annie *reaches for the pitcher,* Helen *removes her napkin and drops it to the floor.* Annie *is filling* Helen's *glass when she notices it. She considers* Helen's *bland expression a moment, then bends, retrieves it, and tucks it around* Helen's *neck again.*)

**James.**  Well, fitting in the sense that Jacob's thigh was out of joint, and so is this piggie's.

**Aunt Ev.**  I declare, James—

**Kate.**  Pickles, Aunt Ev?

**Aunt Ev.**  Oh, I should say so; you know

my opinion of your pickles—

**Kate.**  This is the end of them, I'm afraid. I didn't put up nearly enough last summer; this year I intend to—

(*She interrupts herself, seeing* Helen *deliberately lift off her napkin and drop it again to the floor. She bends to retrieve it, but* Annie *stops her arm.*)

**Keller** (*not noticing*).  Reverend looked in at the office today to complain his hens have stopped laying. Poor fellow, *he* was out of joint; all he could—

(*He stops too, to frown down the table at* Kate, Helen, *and* Annie *in turn, all suspended in midmotion.*)

**James** (*not noticing*).  I've always suspected those hens.

**Aunt Ev.**  Of what?

**James.**  I think they're Papist.[3] Has he tried—

(*He stops, too, following* Keller's *eyes.* Annie *now stoops to pick the napkin up.*)

**Aunt Ev.**  James, now you're pulling my—lower extremity, the first thing you know we'll be—

(*She stops, too, hearing herself in the silence.* Annie, *with everyone now watching, for the third time puts the napkin on* Helen. Helen *yanks it off, and throws it down.* Annie *rises, lifts* Helen's *plate, and bears it away.* Helen, *feeling it gone, slides down and commences to kick up under the table; the dishes jump.* Annie *contemplates this for a moment; then, coming back, takes* Helen's *wrists firmly and swings her off the chair.* Helen, *struggling, gets one hand free, and catches at her mother's skirt. When* Kate

---

3. **Papist** (pā′ pist): Roman Catholic.

*takes her by the shoulders,* Helen *hangs quiet.*)

**Kate.** Miss Annie.

**Annie.** No.

**Kate** (*a pause*). It's a very special day.

**Annie** (*grimly*). It will be, when I give in to that.

(*She tries to disengage* Helen's *hand;* Kate *lays hers on* Annie's)

**Kate.** Please. I've hardly had a chance to welcome her home—

**Annie.** Captain Keller.

**Keller** (*embarrassed*). Oh. Katie, we—had a little talk, Miss Annie feels that if we indulge Helen in these—

**Aunt Ev.** But what's the child done?

**Annie.** She's learned not to throw things on the floor and kick. It took us the best part of two weeks and—

**Aunt Ev.** But only a napkin; it's not as if it were breakable!

**Annie.** And everything she's learned *is*? Mrs. Keller, I don't think we should—play tug-of-war for her. Either give her to me or you keep her from kicking.

**Kate.** What do you wish to do?

**Annie.** Let me take her from the table.

**Aunt Ev.** Oh, let her stay. My goodness, she's only a child; she doesn't have to wear a napkin if she doesn't want to her first evening—

**Annie** (*level*). And ask outsiders not to interfere.

**Aunt Ev** (*astonished*). Out—outsi—I'm the child's *aunt*!

**Kate** (*distressed*). Will once hurt so much, Miss Annie? I've—made all Helen's favorite foods, tonight.

(*a pause*)

**Keller** (*gently*). It's a homecoming party, Miss Annie.

(Annie *after a moment releases* Helen. *But she cannot accept it. At her own chair, she shakes her head and turns back, intent on* Kate.)

**Annie.** She's testing you. You realize?

**James** (*to* Annie). She's testing *you*.

**Keller.** Jimmie, be quiet.

(James *sits, tense.*)

Now she's home, naturally she—

**Annie.** And wants to see what will happen. At your hands. I said it was my main worry. Is this what you promised me not half an hour ago?

**Keller** (*reasonably*). But she's *not* kicking, now—

**Annie.** And not learning not to. Mrs. Keller, teaching her is bound to be painful, to everyone. I know it hurts to watch, but she'll live up to just what you demand of her, and no more.

**James** (*palely*). She's testing *you*.

**Keller** (*testily*). Jimmie.

**James.** I have an opinion. I think I should—

**Keller.** No one's interested in hearing your opinion.

**Annie.** *I'm* interested. Of course she's testing me. Let me keep her to what she's learned, and she'll go on learning from me.

Take her out of my hands, and it all comes apart.

(Kate *closes her eyes, digesting it;* Annie *sits again, with a brief comment for her.*)

Be bountiful; it's at her expense.

(*She turns to* James, *flatly.*)

Please pass me more of—her favorite foods.

(*Then* Kate *lifts* Helen's *hand, and turning her toward* Annie, *surrenders her;* Helen *makes for her own chair.*)

**Kate** (*low*). Take her, Miss Annie.

**Annie** (*then*). Thank you.

(*But the moment* Annie, *rising, reaches for her hand,* Helen *begins to fight and kick, clutching to the tablecloth, and uttering laments.* Annie *again tries to loosen her hand, and* Keller *rises.*)

**Keller** (*tolerant*). I'm afraid you're the difficulty, Miss Annie. Now I'll keep her to what she's learned; you're quite right there—

(*He takes* Helen's *hands from* Annie, *pats them;* Helen *quiets down.*)

—but I don't see that we need send her from the table; after all, she's the guest of honor. Bring her plate back.

**Annie.** If she was a seeing child, none of you would tolerate one—

**Keller.** Well, she's not. I think some compromise is called for. Bring her plate, please.

(Annie's *jaw sets, but she restores the plate, while* Keller *fastens the napkin around* Helen's *neck; she permits it.*)

There. It's not unnatural. Most of us take some aversion[4] to our teachers, and occasionally another hand can smooth things out.

(*He puts a fork in* Helen's *hand;* Helen *takes it. Genially,*)

Now. Shall we start all over?

(*He goes back around the table, and sits.* Annie *stands watching.* Helen *is motionless, thinking things through, until with a wicked glee she deliberately flings the fork on the floor. After another moment, she plunges her hand into her food, and crams a fistful into her mouth.*)

**James** (*wearily*). I think we've started all over—

(Keller *shoots a glare at him, as* Helen *plunges her other hand into* Annie's *plate.* Annie *at once moves in, to grasp her wrist; and* Helen, *flinging out a hand, encounters the pitcher. She swings with it at* Annie. Annie, *falling back, blocks it with an elbow, but the water flies over her dress.* Annie *gets her breath, then snatches the pitcher away in one hand, hoists* Helen *up bodily under the other arm, and starts to carry her out, kicking.* Keller *stands.*)

**Annie** (*savagely polite*). Don't get up!

**Keller.** Where are you going?

**Annie.** Don't smooth anything else out for me; don't interfere in any way! I treat her like a seeing child because I *ask* her to see. I *expect* her to see. Don't undo what I do!

**Keller.** Where are you taking her?

**Annie.** To make her fill this pitcher again!

(*She thrusts out with* Helen *under her arm, but* Helen *escapes up the stairs and* Annie *runs after her.* Keller *stands rigid.* Aunt Ev *is astounded.*)

**Aunt Ev.** You let her speak to you like that, Arthur? A creature who *works* for you?

---

4. **aversion** (ə vʉr′ zhən): a strong or definite dislike.

**Keller** (*angrily*). No. I don't.

(*He is starting after Annie when James, on his feet with shaky resolve, interposes his chair between them in Keller's path.*)

**James.** Let her go.

**Keller.** What!

**James** (*a swallow*). I said—let her go. She's right.

(*Keller glares at the chair and him. James takes a deep breath, then headlong,*)

She's right, Kate's right, I'm right, and you're wrong. If you drive her away from here, it will be over my dead—chair. Has it never occurred to you that on one occasion you might be consummately wrong?

(*Keller's stare is unbelieving, even a little fascinated. Kate rises in trepidation, to mediate.*)

**Kate.** Captain.

(*Keller stops her with his raised hand; his eyes stay on James's pale face, for a long hold. When he finally finds his voice, it is gruff.*)

**Keller.** Sit down, everyone.

(*He sits. Kate sits. James holds onto his chair. Keller speaks mildly.*)

Please sit down, Jimmie.

(*James sits, and a moveless silence prevails; Keller's eyes do not leave him.*

Annie *has pulled* Helen *downstairs again by one hand, the pitcher in her other hand, down the porch steps, and across the yard to the pump. She puts* Helen's *hand on the pump handle, grimly.*)

**Annie.** All right. Pump.

(*Helen touches her cheek, waits uncertainly.*)

No, she's not here. Pump!

(*She forces Helen's hand to work the handle, then lets go. And Helen obeys. She pumps till the water comes. Then Annie puts the pitcher in her other hand and guides it under the spout, and the water tumbling half into and half around the pitcher douses Helen's hand. Annie takes over the handle to keep water coming, and does automatically what she has done so many times before, spells into Helen's free palm,*)

Water. W, a, t, e, r. Water. It has a—name—

(*And now the miracle happens. Helen drops the pitcher on the slab under the spout. It shatters. She stands transfixed. Annie freezes on the pump handle. There is a change in the sundown light, and with it a change in Helen's face, some light coming into it we have never seen there, some struggle in the depths behind it; and her lips tremble, trying to remember something the muscles around them once knew, till at last it finds its way out, painfully, a baby sound buried under the debris of years of dumbness.*)

**Helen.** Wah. Wah.

(*and again, with great effort*)

Wah. Wah.

(*Helen plunges her hand into the dwindling water, spells into her own palm. Then she gropes frantically. Annie reaches for her hand, and Helen spells into Annie's hand.*)

**Annie** (*whispering*). Yes.

(*Helen spells into it again.*)

Yes!

(*Helen grabs at the handle, pumps for more water, plunges her hand into its spurt, and grabs Annie's to spell it again.*)

From the film *The Miracle Worker,* 1962, starring Anne Bancroft and Patty Duke.
Photofest, New York.

Yes! Oh, my dear—

(*She falls to her knees to clasp* Helen's *hand, but* Helen *pulls it free, stands almost bewildered, then drops to the ground, pats it swiftly, holds up her palm, imperious.* Annie *spells into it,*)

Ground.

(Helen *spells it back.*)

Yes!

(Helen *whirls to the pump, pats it, holds up her palm, and* Annie *spells into it.*)

Pump.

(Helen *spells it back.*)

Yes! Yes!

(*Now* Helen *is in such an excitement she is possessed, wild, trembling, cannot be still, turns, runs, falls on the porch steps, claps it, reaches out her palm, and* Annie *is at it instantly to spell,*)

Step.

(Helen *has no time to spell back now. She whirls, groping, to touch anything, encounters the trellis, shakes it, thrusts out her palm, and* Annie, *while spelling to her, cries wildly at the house.*)

Trellis. Mrs. Keller! Mrs. Keller!

(*Inside,* Kate *starts to her feet.* Helen *scrambles back onto the porch, groping, and finds the bell string, tugs it. The bell rings; the distant chimes begin tolling the hour; all the bells in town seem to break into speech, while* Helen *reaches out and* Annie *spells feverishly into her hand.* Kate *hurries out, with* Keller *after her.* Aunt Ev *is on her feet, to peer out the window. Only* James *remains at the table, and with a napkin wipes his damp brow. From up right and left the servants—*Viney, *the two black children, the*

other servant—*run in, and stand watching from a distance as* Helen, *ringing the bell, with her other hand encounters her mother's skirt. When she throws a hand out,* Annie *spells into it,*)

Mother.

(Keller *now seizes* Helen's *hand. She touches him, gestures a hand, and* Annie *again spells,*)

Papa—She *knows!*

(Kate *and* Keller *go to their knees, stammering, clutching* Helen *to them; and* Annie *steps unsteadily back to watch the threesome,* Helen *spelling wildly into* Kate's *hand, then into* Keller's, Kate *spelling back into* Helen's. *They cannot keep their hands off her, and rock her in their clasp.*

Then Helen *gropes, feels nothing, turns all around, pulls free, and comes with both hands groping to find* Annie. *She encounters* Annie's *thighs.* Annie *kneels to her,* Helen's *hand pats* Annie's *cheek impatiently, points a finger, and waits; and* Annie *spells into it,*)

Teacher.

(Helen *spells back, slowly;* Annie *nods.*)

Teacher.

(*She holds* Helen's *hand to her cheek. Presently* Helen *withdraws it, not jerkily, only with reserve, and retreats a step. She stands thinking it over, then turns again and stumbles back to her parents. They try to embrace her, but she has something else in mind. It is to get the keys, and she hits* Kate's *pocket until* Kate *digs them out for her.*

Annie, *with her own load of emotion, has retreated, her back turned, toward the pump, to sit.* Kate *moves to* Helen, *touches her hand questioningly, and* Helen *spells a word* to her. Kate *comprehends it, their first act of verbal communication, and she can hardly utter the word aloud, in wonder, gratitude, and deprivation. It is a moment in which she simultaneously finds and loses a child.)*

**Kate.** Teacher?

*(Annie turns; and Kate, facing Helen in her direction by the shoulders, holds her back, holds her back, and then relinquishes her. Helen feels her way across the yard, rather shyly, and when her moving hands touch Annie's skirt, she stops. Then she holds out the keys and places them in Annie's hand. For a moment neither of them moves. Then Helen slides into Annie's arms, and lifting away her smoked glasses, kisses her on the cheek. Annie gathers her in.*

*Kate, torn both ways, turns from this, gestures the servants off, and makes her way into the house, on Keller's arm. The servants go, in separate directions.*

*The lights are half down now, except over the pump. Annie and Helen are here, alone in the yard. Annie has found Helen's hand, almost without knowing it, and she spells slowly into it, her voice unsteady, whispering,)*

**Annie.** I, love, Helen.

*(She clutches the child to her, tight this time, not spelling, whispering into her hair.)*

Forever, and—

*(She stops. The lights over the pump are taking on the color of the past, and it brings Annie's head up, her eyes opening, in fear; and as slowly as though drawn she rises, to listen, with her hand on Helen's shoulders. She waits, waits, listening with ears and eyes both, slowly here, slowly there; and hears only silence. There are no voices. The color passes on, and when her eyes come back to Helen, she can breathe the end of her phrase without fear,)*

—ever.

*(In the family room, Kate has stood over the table, staring at Helen's plate, with Keller at her shoulder. Now James takes a step to move her chair in, and Kate sits, with head erect, and Keller inclines his head to James; so it is Aunt Ev, hesitant, and rather humble, who moves to the door.*

*Outside, Helen tugs at Annie's hand, and Annie comes with it. Helen pulls her toward the house; and hand in hand, they cross the yard, and ascend the porch steps, in the rising lights, to where Aunt Ev is holding the door open for them.*

*The curtain ends the play.)*

# Thinking About Act Three

## A PERSONAL RESPONSE

*sharing impressions*

**1.** What words come to mind to describe your feelings at the end of the play? Jot down these words in your journal.

*constructing interpretations*

**2.** What might Annie Sullivan mean by saying that she owes God a resurrection?

### Think about
- why she says to Anagnos in both Act One and Act Three that God owes her a resurrection
- how the statement relates to the death of her brother
- how the statement might apply to both Helen and Annie

**3.** If Helen had not remembered the word *water,* which she knew before she was disabled, do you think she would have been able to make the breakthrough toward understanding language? Why or why not?

**4.** Which of the Keller family relationships do you think have changed the most by the end of the play? Explain.

### Think about
- why James asks Kate to be his friend
- how Kate "simultaneously finds and loses a child"
- how Keller reacts when James tells him he is wrong

## A CREATIVE RESPONSE

**5.** If James had not stopped his father from going after Annie and Helen, what do you think might have happened?

## A CRITICAL RESPONSE

**6.** What do you think keys and locks represent in this play?

### Think about
- why Helen locks Annie in her room in Act One
- why Annie locks Helen in the dining room in Act Two
- why Helen gives the keys to her mother as soon as she comes home from the garden house
- why Helen gives Annie the keys at the end of the play

**7.** In her autobiography, *The Story of My Life,* Helen Keller writes, "Have you ever been at sea in a dense fog, when it seemed as if a tangible white darkness shut you in, and the great ship, tense and anxious, groped her way toward the shore with plummet and sounding-line, and you waited with beating heart for something to happen? I was like that ship before my education began, only I was without compass or sounding-line, and had no way of knowing how near the harbor was." What does Helen Keller's description of her life before education reveal about the significance of Annie Sullivan in her life?

**8.** What do you think that you, as a reader, have gained or lost from reading this play instead of seeing it performed?

# Connecting Reading and Writing

**1.** How would you train yourself if you were going to play the part of Helen Keller or Annie Sullivan in this play? Write an **agenda** for a two-week training session.

Option: Write a **diary** for an imaginary one-week training period that you experienced.

**2.** Do you agree with Annie Sullivan that a person must be taught discipline before he or she can learn anything else? Write an **editorial** for your school newspaper stating your opinion and supporting it with examples from the play and from real life.

Option: Write a **petition** to be submitted to the school board asking for more or less discipline to help the students at your school learn better. Have classmates sign your petition if they agree with it.

**3.** Choose the character in the play whom you thought was the most interesting. Write a description of that character to be included in the **stage bill** passed out at a performance of the play.

Option: Write **director's notes** to yourself about what kind of actor you would cast in the part and how you would tell him or her to play it.

**4.** Read Chapter IV from *The Story of My Life* by Helen Keller. In a **literary evaluation** to be published along with the play, compare and contrast Keller's version of how she first learned language with Gibson's version.

Option: Based on the information in the two versions, write a **problem-solution essay** that Helen Keller might write for teachers of deaf-blind children.

# A Marriage Proposal

## ANTON CHEKHOV
Translated from the Russian

A biography of Chekhov appears on page 638.

## *Approaching the Play*

Anton Chekhov, a Russian author who lived in the late 1800's, is considered one of the world's major playwrights. *A Marriage Proposal* is a one-act farce, a play that uses exaggeration for a humorous effect. During the time period in which the play is set, land ownership was essential to the standing of aristocratic Russian families. One way aristocrats increased their estates —and their power—was by making marriages that were good from an economic viewpoint. Marriage often had little to do with love. A spouse was chosen for his or her social standing and wealth. An excellent match was one that joined the vast estates of two already important families.

## CHARACTERS

Stepan Stepanovitch Tschubukov (ste pän′ step pä′ nô vich chŏŏ bŏŏ kôf′),
*a country farmer*
Natalia Stepanovna (nä täl′ yə ste pä nôv′ nə), *his daughter*
*(aged twenty-five)*
Ivan Vassiliyitch Lomov (i vän′ vä sil′ ē yich lô′ môf), *Tschubukov's*
*neighbor*

**Time.** *The present [1890's].*

**Scene.** *The reception room in Tschubukov's country home in Russia. Tschubukov discovered as the curtain rises. Enter Lomov, wearing a dress suit.*

**Tschubukov** (*going toward him and greeting him*). Who is this I see? My dear fellow! Ivan Vassiliyitch! I'm so glad to see you! (*shakes hands*) But this is a surprise! How are you?

**Lomov.** Thank you! And how are you?

**Tschubukov.** Oh, so-so, my friend. Please sit down. It isn't right to forget one's neighbor. But tell me, why all this ceremony? Dress clothes, white gloves, and all? Are you on your way to some engagement, my good fellow?

**Lomov.** No, I have no engagement except with you, Stepan Stepanovitch.

**Tschubukov.** But why in evening clothes, my friend? This isn't New Year's!

**Lomov.** You see, it's simply this, that — (*composing himself*) I have come to you, Stepan Stepanovitch, to trouble you with a request. It is not the first time I have had the honor of turning to you for assistance, and you have always, that is — I beg your pardon, I am a bit excited! I'll take a drink of water first, dear Stepan Stepanovitch. (*He drinks.*)

**Tschubukov** (*aside*). He's come to borrow money! I won't give him any! (*to* Lomov) What is it, then, dear Lomov?

**Lomov.** You see — dear — Stepanovitch, pardon me, Stepan — Stepan — dearvitch — I mean — I am terribly nervous, as you will be so good as to see! What I mean to say— you are the only one who can help me, though I don't deserve it, and — I have no right whatever to make this request of you.

**Tschubukov.** Oh, don't beat about the bush, my dear fellow. Tell me!

**Lomov.** Immediately — in a moment. Here it is, then: I have come to ask for the hand of your daughter, Natalia Stepanovna.

**Tschubukov** (*joyfully*). Angel! Ivan Vassiliyitch! Say that once again! I didn't quite hear it!

**Lomov.** I have the honor to beg —

**Tschubukov** (*interrupting*). My dear, dear man! I am so happy that everything is so — everything! (*embraces and kisses him*) I have wanted this to happen for so long. It has been my dearest wish! (*He represses a tear.*) And I have always loved you, my dear fellow, as my own son! May God give you His blessings and his grace and — I always wanted it to happen. But why am I standing here like a blockhead? I am completely dumbfounded with pleasure, completely dumbfounded. My whole being — ! I'll call Natalia ——

**Lomov.** Dear Stepan Stepanovitch, what do you think? May I hope for Natalia Stepanovna's acceptance?

**Tschubukov.** Really! A fine boy like you — and you think she won't accept on the minute? Lovesick as a cat and all that —! (*He goes out, right.*)

**Lomov.** I'm cold. My whole body is trembling as though I was going to take my examination! But the chief thing is to settle matters! If a person meditates too much, or hesitates, or talks about it, waits for an ideal or for true love, he never gets it. Brrr! It's cold! Natalia is an excellent housekeeper, not at all bad-looking, well educated — what more could I ask? I'm so excited my ears are roaring! (*He drinks water.*) And not marry, that won't do! In the first place, I'm thirty-five — a critical age, you might say. In the second place, I must live a well-regulated life. I have a weak heart, continual palpitation, and I am very sensitive and always getting excited. My lips begin to tremble and the pulse in my right temple throbs terribly. But the worst of it all is sleep! I hardly lie down and begin to doze before something in my left side begins to pull and tug, and something begins to hammer in my left shoulder — and in my head, too! I jump up like a madman, walk about a little, lie down again, but the moment I fall asleep I have a terrible cramp in the side. And so it is all night long!

(*Enter* Natalia Stepanovna.)

**Natalia.** Ah! It's you. Papa said to go in: there was a dealer in there who'd come to buy something. Good afternoon, Ivan Vassiliyitch.

**Lomov.** Good day, my dear Natalia Stepanovna.

**Natalia.** You must pardon me for wearing my apron and this old dress: we are working today. Why haven't you come to see us oftener? You've not been here for so long! Sit down. (*They sit down.*) Won't you have something to eat?

**Lomov.** Thank you, I have just had lunch.

**Natalia.** Smoke, do, there are the matches. Today it is beautiful and only yesterday it rained so hard that the workmen couldn't do a stroke of work. How many bricks have you cut? Think of it! I was so anxious that I had the whole field mowed, and now I'm sorry I did it, because I'm afraid the hay will rot. It would have been better if I had waited. But what on earth is this? You are in evening clothes! The latest cut! Are you on your way to a ball? And you seem to be looking better, too—really. Why are you dressed up so gorgeously?

**Lomov** (*excited*). You see, my dear Natalia Stepanovna—it's simply this: I have decided to ask you to listen to me—of course it will be a surprise, and indeed you'll be angry, but I—(*aside*) How fearfully cold it is!

**Natalia.** What is it? (*a pause*) Well?

**Lomov.** I'll try to be brief. My dear Natalia Stepanovna, as you know, for many years, since my childhood, I have had the honor to know your family. My poor aunt and her husband, from whom, as you know, I inherited the estate, always had the greatest respect for your father and your poor mother. The Lomovs and the Tschubukovs have been for decades on the friendliest, indeed the closest, terms with each other, and furthermore my property, as you know, adjoins your own. If you will be so good as to remember, my meadows touch your birch woods.

**Natalia.** Pardon the interruption. You said "my meadows"—but are they yours?

**Lomov.** Yes, they belong to me.

**Natalia.** What nonsense! The meadows belong to us—not to you!

**Lomov.** No, to me! Now, my dear Natalia Stepanovna!

**Natalia.** Well, that is certainly news to me. How do they belong to you?

**Lomov.** How? I am speaking of the meadows lying between your birch woods and my brick-earth.

**Natalia.** Yes, exactly. They belong to us.

**Lomov.** No, you are mistaken, my dear Natalia Stepanovna, they belong to me.

**Natalia.** Try to remember exactly, Ivan Vassiliyitch. Is it so long ago that you inherited them?

**Lomov.** Long ago! As far back as I can remember they have always belonged to us.

**Natalia.** But that isn't true! You'll pardon my saying so.

**Lomov.** It is all a matter of record, my dear

Natalia Stepanovna. It is true that at one time the title to the meadows was disputed, but now everyone knows they belong to me. There is no room for discussion. Be so good as to listen: my aunt's grandmother put these meadows, free from all costs, into the hands of your father's grandfather's peasants for a certain time while they were making bricks for my grandmother. These people used the meadows free of cost for about forty years, living there as they would on their own property. Later, however, when—

**Natalia.** There's not a word of truth in that! My grandfather, and my great-grandfather, too, knew that their estate reached back to the swamp, so that the meadows belong to us. What further discussion can there be? I can't understand it. It is really most annoying.

**Lomov.** I'll show you the papers, Natalia Stepanovna.

**Natalia.** No, either you are joking, or trying to lead me into a discussion. That's not at all nice! We have owned this property for nearly three hundred years, and now all at once we hear that it doesn't belong to us. Ivan Vassiliyitch, you will pardon me, but I really can't believe my ears. So far as I am concerned, the meadows are worth very little. In all they don't contain more than five acres and they are worth only a few hundred rubles,[1] say three hundred, but the injustice of the thing is what affects me. Say what you will, I can't bear injustice.

**Lomov.** Only listen until I have finished, please! The peasants of your respected father's grandfather, as I have already had the honor to tell you, baked bricks for my grandmother. My aunt's grandmother wished to do them a favor—

**Natalia.** Grandfather! Grandmother! Aunt! I know nothing about them. All I know is that the meadows belong to us, and that ends the matter.

**Lomov.** No, they belong to me!

**Natalia.** And if you keep on explaining it for two days, and put on five suits of evening clothes, the meadows are still ours, ours, ours! I don't want to take your property, but I refuse to give up what belongs to us!

**Lomov.** Natalia Stepanovna, I don't need the meadows, I am only concerned with the principle. If you are agreeable, I beg of you, accept them as a gift from me!

**Natalia.** But I can give them to you, because they belong to me! That is very peculiar, Ivan Vassiliyitch! Until now we have considered you as a good neighbor and a good friend; only last year we lent you our threshing machine so that we couldn't thresh until November, and now you treat us like thieves! You offer to give me my own land. Excuse me, but neighbors don't treat each other that way. In my opinion, it's a very low trick—to speak frankly—

**Lomov.** According to you I'm a usurper, then, am I? My dear lady, I have never appropriated[2] other people's property, and I shall permit no one to accuse me of such a thing! (*He goes quickly to the bottle and drinks water.*) The meadows are mine!

**Natalia.** That's not the truth! They are mine!

**Lomov.** Mine!

**Natalia.** Eh? I'll prove it to you! This afternoon I'll send my reapers into the meadows.

**Lomov.** W—h—a—t?

---

1. **rubles** (rōō′ bəlz): units of Russian money.
2. **appropriated** (ə prō′ prē′ āt id): taken for one's own use, especially in an improper manner.

**Natalia.** My reapers will be there today!

**Lomov.** And I'll chase them off!

**Natalia.** If you dare!

**Lomov.** The meadows are mine, you understand? Mine!

**Natalia.** Really, you needn't scream so! If you want to scream and snort and rage you may do it at home, but here please keep yourself within the limits of common decency.

**Lomov.** My dear lady, if it weren't that I were suffering from palpitation of the heart and hammering of the arteries in my temples, I would deal with you very differently! (*in a loud voice*) The meadows belong to me!

**Natalia.** Us!

**Lomov.** Me!
(*enter* Tschubukov, *right*)

**Tschubukov.** What's going on here? What is he yelling about?

**Natalia.** Papa, please tell this gentleman to whom the meadows belong, to us or to him?

**Tschubukov** (*to* Lomov). My dear fellow, the meadows are ours.

**Lomov.** But, merciful heavens, Stepan Stepanovitch, how do you make that out? You at least might be reasonable. My aunt's grandmother gave the use of the meadows free of cost to your grandfather's peasants; the peasants lived on the land for forty years and used it as their own, but later when—

**Tschubukov.** Permit me, my dear friend. You forget that your grandmother's peasants never paid, because there had been a lawsuit over the meadows, and everyone knows that the meadows belong to us. You haven't looked at the map.

**Lomov.** I'll prove to you that they belong to me!

**Tschubukov.** Don't try to prove it, my dear fellow.

**Lomov.** I will!

**Tschubukov.** My good fellow, what are you shrieking about? You can't prove anything by yelling, you know. I don't ask for anything that belongs to you, nor do I intend to give up anything of my own. Why should I? If it has gone so far, my dear man, that you really intend to claim the meadows, I'd rather give them to the peasants than you, and I certainly shall!

**Lomov.** I can't believe it! By what right can you give away property that doesn't belong to you?

**Tschubukov.** Really, you must allow me to decide what I am to do with my own land! I'm not accustomed, young man, to have people address me in that tone of voice. I, young man, am twice your age, and I beg you to address me respectfully.

**Lomov.** No! No! You think I'm a fool! You're making fun of me! You call my property yours and then expect me to stand quietly by and talk to you like a human being. That isn't the way a good neighbor behaves, Stepan Stepanovitch! You are no neighbor, you're no better than a land-grabber. That's what you are!

**Tschubukov.** Wh—at? What did he say?

**Natalia.** Papa, send the reapers into the meadows this minute!

**Tschubukov** (*to* Lomov). What was that you said, sir?

**Natalia.** The meadows belong to us and I won't give them up! I won't give them up! I won't give them up!

**Lomov.** We'll see about that! I'll prove in court that they belong to me.

**Tschubukov.** In court! You may sue in court, sir, if you like! Oh, I know you, you are only waiting to find an excuse to go to law! You're an intriguer,[3] that's what you are! Your whole family were always looking for quarrels. The whole lot!

**Lomov.** Kindly refrain from insulting my family. The entire race of Lomov has always been honorable! And never has one been brought to trial for embezzlement, as your dear uncle was!

**Tschubukov.** And the whole Lomov family were insane!

**Natalia.** Every one of them!

**Tschubukov.** Your grandmother was a dipsomaniac,[4] and the younger aunt, Nastasia Michailovna, ran off with an architect.

**Lomov.** And your mother limped. (*He puts his hand over his heart.*) Oh, my side pains! My temples are bursting! Lord in Heaven! Water!

**Tschubukov.** And your dear father was a gambler—and a glutton!

**Natalia.** And your aunt was a gossip like few others!

**Lomov.** And you are an intriguer. Oh, my heart! And it's an open secret that you cheated at the elections—my eyes are blurred! Where is my hat?

**Natalia.** Oh, how low! Liar! Disgusting thing!

**Lomov.** Where's the hat? My heart! Where shall I go? Where is the door? Oh—it seems—as though I were dying! I can't—my legs won't hold me—(*goes to the door*)

**Tschubukov** (*following him*). May you never darken my door again!

**Natalia.** Bring your suit to court! We'll see! (Lomov *staggers out, center.*)

**Tschubukov** (*angrily*). The devil!

**Natalia.** Such a good-for-nothing! And then they talk about being good neighbors!

**Tschubukov.** Loafer! Scarecrow! Monster!

**Natalia.** A swindler like that takes over a piece of property that doesn't belong to him and then dares to argue about it!

**Tschubukov.** And to think that this fool dares to make a proposal of marriage!

**Natalia.** What? A proposal of marriage?

**Tschubukov.** Why, yes! He came here to make you a proposal of marriage.

**Natalia.** Why didn't you tell me that before?

**Tschubukov.** That's why he had on his evening clothes! The poor fool!

**Natalia.** Proposal for me? Oh! (*falls into an armchair and groans*) Bring him back! Bring him back!

**Tschubukov.** Bring whom back?

**Natalia.** Faster, faster, I'm sinking! Bring him back! (*She becomes hysterical.*)

**Tschubukov.** What is it? What's wrong with you? (*his hands to his head*) I'm cursed with bad luck! I'll shoot myself! I'll hang myself!

**Natalia.** I'm dying! Bring him back!

**Tschubukov.** Bah! In a minute! Don't bawl! (*He rushes out, center.*)

---

3. **intriguer** (in trēg′ ər): a schemer.
4. **dipsomaniac** (dip′ sə mā′ nē′ ak′): a drunk.

**Natalia** (*groaning*). What have they done to me? Bring him back! Bring him back!

**Tschubukov** (*comes running in*). He's coming at once! The devil take him! Ugh! Talk to him yourself, I can't.

**Natalia** (*groaning*). Bring him back!

**Tschubukov.** He's coming, I tell you! "Oh, Lord! What a task it is to be the father of a grown daughter!" I'll cut my throat! I really will cut my throat! We've argued with the fellow, insulted him, and now we've thrown him out!—and you did it all, you!

**Natalia.** No you! You haven't any manners, you are brutal! If it weren't for you, he wouldn't have gone!

**Tschubukov.** Oh, yes, I'm to blame! If I shoot or hang myself, remember *you'll* be to blame. You forced me to it! You! (Lomov *appears in the doorway.*) There, talk to him yourself! (*He goes out.*)

**Lomov.** Terrible palpitation! My leg is lamed! My side hurts me—

**Natalia.** Pardon us, we were angry, Ivan Vassiliyitch. I remember now—the meadows really belong to you.

**Lomov.** My heart is beating terribly! My meadows—my eyelids tremble—(*They sit down.*) We were wrong. It was only the principle of the thing—the property isn't worth much to me, but the principle is worth a great deal.

**Natalia.** Exactly, the principle! Let us talk about something else.

**Lomov.** Because I have proofs that my aunt's grandmother had, with the peasants of your good father—

**Natalia.** Enough, enough. (*aside*) I don't know how to begin. (*to* Lomov) Are you going hunting soon?

**Lomov.** Yes, heath-cock shooting, respected Natalia Stepanovna. I expect to begin after the harvest. Oh, did you hear? My dog, Ugadi, you know him—limps!

**Natalia.** What a shame! How did that happen?

**Lomov.** I don't know. Perhaps it's a dislocation, or maybe he was bitten by some other dog. (*He sighs.*) The best dog I ever had—to say nothing of his price! I paid Mironov a hundred and twenty-five rubles for him.

**Natalia.** That was too much to pay, Ivan Vassiliyitch.

**Lomov.** In my opinion it was very cheap. A wonderful dog!

**Natalia.** Papa paid eighty-five rubles for his Otkatai, and Otkatai is much better than your Ugadi!

**Lomov.** Really? Otkatai is better than Ugadi? What an idea! (*He laughs.*) Otkatai better then Ugadi!

**Natalia.** Of course he is better. It is true Otkatai is still young; he isn't full-grown yet, but in the pack or on the leash with two or three, there is no better than he, even—

**Lomov.** I really beg your pardon, Natalia Stepanovna, but you quite overlooked the fact that he has a short lower jaw, and a dog with a short lower jaw can't snap.

**Natalia.** Short lower jaw? That's the first time I ever heard that!

**Lomov.** I assure you, his lower jaw is shorter than the upper.

**Natalia.** Have you measured it?

**Lomov.** I have measured it. He is good at running, though.

**Natalia.** In the first place, our Otkatai is

purebred, a full-blooded son of Sapragavas and Stameskis, and as for your mongrel, nobody could ever figure out his pedigree;[5] he's old and ugly, and as skinny as an old hag.

**Lomov.** Old, certainly! I wouldn't take five of your Otkatais for him! Ugadi is a dog, and Otkatai is—it is laughable to argue about it! Dogs like your Otkatai can be found by the dozens at any dog dealer's, a whole pound full!

**Natalia.** Ivan Vassiliyitch, you are very contrary today. First our meadows belong to you, and then Ugadi is better than Otkatai. I don't like it when a person doesn't say what he really thinks. You know perfectly well that Otkatai is a hundred times better than your silly Ugadi. What makes you keep on saying he isn't?

**Lomov.** I can see, Natalia Stepanovna, that you consider me either a blind man or a fool. But at least you may as well admit that Otkatai has a short lower jaw!

**Natalia.** It isn't so!

**Lomov.** Yes, a short lower jaw!

**Natalia** (*loudly*). It's not so!

**Lomov.** What makes you scream, my dear lady?

**Natalia.** What makes you talk such nonsense? It's disgusting! It is high time that Ugadi was shot, and yet you compare him with Otkatai!

**Lomov.** Pardon me, but I can't carry on this argument any longer. I have palpitation of the heart!

**Natalia.** I have always noticed that the hunters who do the most talking know the least about hunting.

**Lomov.** My dear lady, I beg of you to be still. My heart is bursting! (*He shouts.*)

Be still!

**Natalia.** I won't be still until you admit that Otkatai is better! (*enter Tschubukov*)

**Tschubukov.** Well, has it begun again?

**Natalia.** Papa, say frankly, on your honor, which dog is better: Otkatai or Ugadi?

**Lomov.** Stepan Stepanovitch, I beg of you, just answer this: has your dog a short lower jaw or not? Yes or no?

**Tschubukov.** And what if he has? Is it of such importance? There is no better dog in the whole country.

**Lomov.** My Ugadi is better. Tell the truth, now!

**Tschubukov.** Don't get so excited, my dear fellow! Permit me. Your Ugadi certainly has his good points. He is from a good breed, has a good stride, strong haunches, and so forth. But the dog, if you really want to know it, has two faults; he is old and has a short lower jaw.

**Lomov.** Pardon me, I have palpitation of the heart!—Let us keep to facts—just remember in Maruskins's meadows, my Ugadi kept ear to ear with the Count Rasvachai and your dog.

**Tschubukov.** He was behind, because the Count struck him with his whip.

**Lomov.** Quite right. All the other dogs were on the fox's scent, but Otkatai found it necessary to bite a sheep.

**Tschubukov.** That isn't so!—I am sensitive about that and beg you to stop this argument. He struck him because everybody looks on a strange dog of good blood with envy. Even you, sir, aren't free from the sin.

5. **pedigree:** (ped′ i grē′): a recorded list of ancestors, essential in establishing an animal as a purebred.

No sooner do you find a dog better than Ugadi than you begin to—this, that—his, mine—and so forth! I remember distinctly.

**Lomov.** I remember something, too!

**Tschubukov** (*mimicking him*). I remember something, too! What do you remember?

**Lomov.** Palpitation! My leg is lame—I can't—

**Natalia.** Palpitation! What kind of hunter are you? You ought to stay in the kitchen by the stove and wrestle with the potato peelings, and not go fox-hunting! Palpitation!

**Tschubukov.** And what kind of hunter are you? A man with your diseases ought to stay at home and not jolt around in the saddle. If you were a hunter! But you only ride around in order to find out about other people's dogs, and make trouble for everyone. I am sensitive! Let's drop the subject. Besides, you're no hunter.

**Lomov.** You only ride around to flatter the Count! My heart! You intriguer! Swindler!

**Tschubukov.** And what of it? (*shouting*) Be still!

**Lomov.** Intriguer!

**Tschubukov.** Baby! Puppy! Walking drugstore!

**Lomov.** Old rat! Jesuit![6] Oh, I know you!

**Tschubukov.** Be still! Or I'll shoot you—with my worst gun, like a partridge! Fool! Loafer!

**Lomov.** Everyone knows that—oh, my heart!—that your poor late wife beat you. My leg—my temples—Heavens—I'm dying—I—

**Tschubukov.** And your housekeeper wears the trousers in your house!

**Lomov.** Here—here—there—there—my heart has burst! My shoulder is torn apart. Where is my shoulder? I'm dying! (*He falls into a chair.*) The doctor! (*faints*)

**Tschubukov.** Baby! Half-baked clam! Fool!

**Natalia.** Nice sort of hunter you are! You can't even sit on a horse. (*to Tschubukov*) Papa, what's the matter with him? (*She screams.*) Ivan Vassiliyitch! He is dead!

**Lomov.** I'm ill! I can't breathe! Air!

**Natalia.** He is dead! (*She shakes Lomov in the chair.*) Ivan Vassiliyitch! What have we done! He is dead! (*She sinks into a chair.*) The doctor—doctor! (*She goes into hysterics.*)

**Tschubukov.** Ahh! What is it? What's the matter with you?

**Natalia** (*groaning*). He's dead! Dead!

**Tschubukov.** Who is dead? Who? (*looking at Lomov*) Yes, he is dead! Good God! Water! The doctor! (*holding the glass to Lomov's lips*) Drink! No, he won't drink! He's dead! What a terrible situation! Why didn't I shoot myself? Why have I never cut my throat? What am I waiting for now? Only give me a knife! Give me a pistol! (*Lomov moves.*) He's coming to! Drink some water—there!

**Lomov.** Sparks! Mists! Where am I?

**Tschubukov.** Get married! Quick, and then go to the devil! She's willing! (*He joins the hands of Lomov and Natalia.*) She's

---

6. **Jesuit** (jezh′ ōō it): a member of a Catholic religious order that was suppressed in Russia because of its resistance to the authority of the czar, the ruler of Russia. At the time, the term had the negative meaning of "one who schemes or plots."

agreed! Only leave me in peace!

**Lomov.** Wh—what? (*getting up*) Whom?

**Tschubukov.** She's willing! Well? Kiss each other and—the devil take you both!

**Natalia** (*groans*). He lives! Yes, yes, I'm willing!

**Tschubukov.** Kiss each other!

**Lomov.** Eh? Whom? (Natalia *and* Lomov *kiss.*) Very nice! Pardon me, but what is this for? Oh, yes, I understand! My heart—sparks—I am happy. Natalia Stepanovna. (*He kisses her hand.*) My leg is lame!

**Natalia.** I'm happy, too!

**Tschubukov.** Ahh! A load off my shoulders! Ahh!

**Natalia.** And now at least you'll admit that Ugadi is worse than Otkatai!

**Lomov.** Better!

**Natalia.** Worse!

**Tschubukov.** Now the domestic joys have begun. Champagne!

**Lomov.** Better!

**Natalia.** Worse, worse, worse!

**Tschubukov** (*trying to drown them out*). Champagne, champagne!

# Reviewing Concepts

---

STAGE DIRECTIONS AND DIALOGUE: THE COMPONENTS OF DRAMA ──────

*making
connections*

The stage directions and the dialogue in a play work together to reveal important aspects of character and plot. To better understand the plays in this unit, review both the dialogue and the stage directions, looking for details of character and plot. On a chart similar to the one below, list important traits for each of the main characters in *The Miracle Worker*. Then list important events of the plot for each of the three acts. Fill out another chart with information from *A Marriage Proposal*.

Play: *The Miracle Worker*

| Characters | Important Traits |
|---|---|
| Annie Sullivan | |
| Helen Keller | |
| Captain Keller | |
| Kate Keller | |
| James Keller | |
| **Acts** | **Important Events** |
| Act One | |
| Act Two | |
| Act Three | |

*describing
connections*

Create a **brochure** advertising a drama festival in which both of these plays are to be performed at different times on the same evening. Try to entice an audience into seeing both plays by pointing out what an interesting contrast they make. Use the information on your charts as a source of specific details from each play.

### Think about
- striking traits of interesting characters
- the most suspenseful, touching, or humorous events of the plots
- aspects of the plays that are different

Compare your brochures with those of three classmates.

Temple

Black freyars

The Globe

# Shakespearean Drama

"*All the world's a stage,*
*And all the men and women*
*merely players.*"

WILLIAM SHAKESPEARE

# All the World's a Stage: Shakespearean Drama

THE BIGGEST DIFFERENCE between Shakespearean and modern drama is the difference in language. English continually changes, in part because everyday life continually changes. Shakespeare's references to fencing, horseback riding, and herbal medicines made sense to sixteenth-century audiences but often confuse readers today.

Popular expressions also change. Think about the difference between slang expressions that you use and the ones your parents use. Slang changes drastically from generation to generation, until it is almost unrecognizable after four hundred years. To Shakespeare, "Marry!" was a mild oath and "Soft" meant "Wait a minute."

Although the English language has changed in four hundred years, people today are not that much different from the characters in Shakespeare's plays. Romeo and his friends act like teenage boys today—they enjoy telling jokes, teasing each other, trying to decide which girl is the prettiest, and boasting about whom they could beat in a fight. Juliet is a thirteen-year-old girl in love for the first time; so it follows that she and her parents do not always agree.

As you read Shakespeare's *Romeo and Juliet,* look for the main traits of the characters, the main events of the plot, and the conflicts that develop. Try to identify when characters are being offensive, affectionate, or witty in their speeches, but do not get bogged down in the details of an insult or a joke. The farther you read in the play, the more comfortable you will be with Shakespeare's language and characters.

# Literary Vocabulary

INTRODUCED IN THIS UNIT

**Tragedy.** In drama, tragedy refers to a play in which events turn out disastrously for the main character or characters. Usually, the tragic hero or heroine dies at the end of the play, after facing death with courage and nobility of spirit. Readers or viewers generally feel both pity and fear for a tragic character: pity because they feel sorry for the character, and fear because they realize that the problems and struggles faced by the character are perhaps an inevitable part of human life.

**Plot.** Plot refers to the actions and events in a literary work. The plot in a classic, five-act tragedy such as *Romeo and Juliet* follows a general pattern: First comes the **exposition,** an introduction that sets the tone, provides the setting, introduces the characters, and gives other important information. Next follows the **rising action,** in which complications of the conflict build to a climax, or turning point. In a tragedy the **climax** is the moment when the fortunes of the main characters are at their peak, usually in the third act. The **falling action** comes after the climax and shows forces acting against the main characters. The falling action leads to the final **catastrophe** in the last act, usually the deaths of the main characters.

**Soliloquy.** In drama a soliloquy is a speech in which a character utters thoughts aloud. Generally, the character is on the stage alone, not speaking to other characters and perhaps not even consciously addressing the audience.

**Paradox.** A paradox is a statement that seems to contradict itself but is, nevertheless, true. At the beginning of *Romeo and Juliet*, Romeo is in love with a girl named Rosaline, who does not return his affections. He describes his love in a series of paradoxes, which capture his mixed feelings. For example, "cold fire" signifies the passion that warms his heart yet has brought him cold rejection.

**Foil.** A foil is a character whose qualities contrast with those of another character. A writer might use a foil to emphasize a character's traits or to make those traits look more or less important. In *The Odyssey*, Helen of Troy is a foil for Penelope because Helen's adultery makes Penelope's faithfulness even more admirable.

**Comic Relief.** Comic relief is the inclusion of humorous scenes or characters in serious drama to relieve the emotional intensity and, by contrast, to heighten the seriousness of the story.

REVIEWED IN THIS UNIT

**Irony    Imagery**

# The Tragedy of
# Romeo and Juliet

## THE EARLY YEARS OF WILLIAM SHAKESPEARE

Born in 1564, William Shakespeare was raised in Stratford-on-Avon, an attractive market town in southwest England. His father, who made gloves for a living, was an important person in the town, serving as alderman and later as mayor. The town of Stratford remained important to Shakespeare his entire life. While other theater people invested their money in London, Shakespeare invested in Stratford, and he always owned a house there.

As a child Shakespeare attended the local grammar school in Stratford. Then, when he was about thirteen, his father's business ran into problems. As the family's financial situation worsened, Shakespeare probably had to leave school. He may have been apprenticed at that time to a tradesman.

When he was eighteen, Shakespeare married Anne Hathaway. By the time he was twenty-one, he was the father of three children. Because he could not hope for financial help from his father, Shakespeare tried teaching school for a while. According to some accounts, he was arrested about this time for poaching deer from the nearby forests of a nobleman. When he was twenty-three, Shakespeare decided to leave Stratford for London, a bustling center of art, commerce, and theater.

## SHAKESPEARE IN LONDON

When Shakespeare arrived in London, Elizabeth I was on the throne. During her reign from 1558 to 1603, now called the Elizabethan Age, literature and theater thrived. The young Shakespeare could not have chosen a better time to make his mark.

Shakespeare first entered the theater as an actor. He traveled with touring companies from town to town, acting mostly in public buildings, in the open air, or in the back rooms of inns. However, by the time he was twenty-seven, he had begun to find success as a playwright.

Then, shortly thereafter, the theaters of London were closed for almost two years because of the plague. People were afraid to get together in public places, where they might catch the fatal disease. The theaters did not reopen until 1594.

Shakespeare,
PABLO PICASSO.
©1990 ARS, New York,
/SPADEM, Paris.

In that year Shakespeare became part of a theatrical group called Lord Chamberlain's Company or the Chamberlain's Men. He was one of the leading actors of the group as well as its most popular playwright. In 1599 this group had a theater built called the Globe, and Shakespeare was a shareholder, or part owner, of the theater. James I took over sponsorship of the theater group when he became king after Elizabeth I.

Shakespeare continued to spend most of his time in London until 1610, when he retired from the theater. He was only forty-six years old, but he left London to live the life of a gentleman in Stratford. He had already invested a large amount of his earnings in Stratford and owned one of the largest houses in the town. Shakespeare's plays, however, were still produced at the Globe, and he frequently traveled to the city.

William Shakespeare died in April of 1616, just one month after he had made his will. Judging by this document, he was a generous man who had many friends.

## THEATER IN THE ELIZABETHAN AGE

The theater of Shakespeare's time was different in many ways from the modern theater. Plays were a major form of popular entertainment, attracting all kinds of people, who played an active role in the performances. Elizabethan audiences did not sit quietly and then applaud at the end of an act. They cheered, hissed, and sometimes threw rotten eggs and vegetables onto the stage. Playwrights had to make sure that they gave the people plenty of excitement and laughs and romance. If they failed to provide such entertainment, their plays might get booed off the stage.

The Globe, the theater where most of Shakespeare's plays were performed, was three stories high. It was octagon shaped with an open-air court in the center. The stage reached out into this central area and was surrounded by tiers of seats that had a roof over them. The middle- and upper-class members of the audience sat in the covered seats. People who were too poor to buy seats paid one penny to stand in the uncovered courtyard.

Although plays were staged without sets, elaborate costumes and props enhanced the action and provided spectacle. For example, a death scene in which an actor was stabbed was gory because the actor wore a pig bladder full of red liquid inside his costume. Elizabethan playwrights provided numerous stabbings and ghosts and sword fights to please the audience.

In those days, women were not allowed to act in plays. All the female roles were played by young male actors. Shakespeare liked to have fun with this convention by having the female characters in his comedies dress up as boys, so that there were boys playing women pretending to be boys. When *Romeo and Juliet* was first performed, the part of Juliet was played by a young man.

## THE TRAGEDY OF ROMEO AND JULIET

*Romeo and Juliet* is one of Shakespeare's three most popular plays, along with *Hamlet* and *Richard III*. It has romance, sword fights, comedy, and tragic death—everything an Elizabethan or modern audience could ask for. In the centuries following its first production, the play has inspired paintings, operas, ballets, and other plays. It was the basis of the Broadway musical and later the movie *West Side Story*, in which the two feuding families are represented by Latino and Anglo gangs in New York City.

At the time Shakespeare decided to write *Romeo and Juliet*, one of his friends was the Earl of Southampton. Southampton, in turn, was close friends with his neighbors, Sir Charles and Sir Henry Danvers. The Danvers brothers were fiery swordsmen, and their family was involved in a feud with a family named Long. One night the Danvers brothers and their followers broke into the Long family's house and started a fight. After Henry Danvers killed Henry Long, Shakespeare's friend Southampton hid the Danvers brothers and helped them get away.

The Danvers family feud has many similarities to the feud in *Romeo and Juliet*. The love story in the play came from a poem by Arthur Brooke titled "The Tragicall Historye of Romeus and Juliet." One character who did not appear in Brooke's version of the story is Mercutio. This wild and quarrelsome but faithful friend of Romeo's is one of Shakespeare's most appealing characters. He may have been based on Shakespeare's close friend Christopher Marlowe. Marlowe, another great Elizabethan playwright, was killed in a fight in a tavern.

Most of Shakespeare's plays can be traced in this way to various literary sources and to incidents in his life and in the world around him. He drew from everything he knew to create the rich, colorful, and truthful pictures of life found in his work. His language, his sense of theater, and his insight into human nature—these are the qualities that make his plays great.

# The Tragedy of
# Romeo and Juliet

## WILLIAM SHAKESPEARE

### *Approaching the Play*

Almost four hundred years old, *Romeo and Juliet* still moves audiences because of Shakespeare's dramatic portrayal of young lovers caught between destructive forces beyond their control. The play is set in northern Italy in the fourteenth century, during a time when Italian cities were not unified into a nation but were each governed by an independent ruler. Sometimes the peace of a city was disturbed by violent feuds between powerful families. In such cases not only the family members but also all the servants of the household actively participated in the feud. The head of a family had absolute control over his wife, children, and servants. For example, it was customary for a father to arrange marriages for his daughters without consulting them. This play takes place in the month of July, a time when hot weather sets "the mad blood stirring." The first speech of the play is provided by the Chorus, an actor or group of actors that speaks to the audience directly to comment on the action.

### *Building Vocabulary*

These essential words are defined alongside the play.

**pernicious** (pər nish′ əs): That quench the fire of your **pernicious** rage (page 536, line 84)

**adversary** (ad′ vər ser′ ē): Here were the servants of your **adversary** (page 537, line 107)

**portentous** (pôr ten′ təs): Black and **portentous** must this humor prove (page 538, line 142)

**enmity** (en′ mə tē): And I am proof against their **enmity**. (page 559, line 73)

**feign** (fān): But old folks, many **feign** as they were dead—(page 572, line 16)

**dirges** (dʉrj′ əz): Our solemn hymns to sullen **dirges** change (page 616, line 88)

**redress** (ri dres′ ): "With speedy help doth lend **redress**." (page 618, line 139)

**inexorable** (in eks' ə rə bəl): More fierce and more **inexorable** far (page 624, line 38)

**scourge** (skʉrj): See what a **scourge** is laid upon your hate (page 632, line 292)

## *Connecting Writing and Reading*

Which do you think is the more powerful force in human lives—love or hate? In your journal, list several actions—such as getting married—that people generally do because of love. Make a second list of actions—such as murder—that people generally do because of hate. Go back through your lists and circle any actions that you think could be based on either motive. As you read *Romeo and Juliet,* notice the extent to which love and hate motivate the characters in the play.

From the film *Romeo and Juliet,* 1967, starring Leonard Whiting and Olivia Hussey. Photofest, New York.

# Romeo and Juliet

## CHARACTERS

### THE MONTAGUES

Lord Montague (män′ tə gyo͞o′)
Lady Montague
Romeo, *son of Montague*
Benvolio, *nephew of Montague*
  *and friend of Romeo*
Balthasar (bäl′ thə sär),
  *servant to Romeo*
Abram, *servant to Montague*

*[handwritten note in left margin: R-cousin]*

### THE CAPULETS

Lord Capulet (kap′ yo͞o let′)
Lady Capulet
Juliet, *daughter of Capulet*
Tybalt (tib′ əlt) *nephew of Lady Capulet*
Nurse to Juliet
Peter, *servant to Juliet's Nurse*
Sampson
Gregory    } *servants to Capulet*
An old man of the Capulet family

Prince Escalus (es′ kə ləs), *ruler of Verona*
Mercutio (mer kyo͞o′ shē ō), *kinsman of the*
  *Prince and friend of Romeo*
Friar Laurence, *a Franciscan priest*
Friar John, *another Franciscan priest*
Count Paris, *a young nobleman, kinsman*
  *of the Prince*
Apothecary
Page to Paris
Chief Watchman
Three Musicians
An Officer
Citizens of Verona; Gentlemen and
  Gentlewomen of both houses; Maskers,
  Torchbearers, Pages, Guards,
  Watchmen, Servants, and Attendants

———

**Place:** *Verona* (ve ro′ nə); *and Mantua* (man′ cho͞o wə), *in northern Italy*

## PROLOGUE

*[The Chorus enters from the back of the stage to introduce and explain the theme of the play.]*

**Chorus.** Two households, both alike in dignity,[1]
In fair Verona, where we lay our scene,
From ancient grudge break to new mutiny,[2]
Where civil blood makes civil hands unclean.

5 From forth the fatal loins of these two foes,
A pair of star-crossed[3] lovers take their life,
Whose misadventured piteous overthrows
Doth with their death bury their parents' strife.
The fearful passage of their death-marked love,

10 And the continuance of their parents' rage,
Which, but their children's end, naught could remove,
Is now the two hours' traffic[4] of our stage,
The which if you with patient ears attend,
What here shall miss, our toil shall strive to mend.[5]

*[Exit.]*

1. **dignity:** rank.

2. **mutiny:** quarrel.

◆ **Line 4:** Citizens' hands are soiled with another citizen's blood.

3. **star-crossed:** unlucky because of the position of the stars.

◆ **Lines 6-8:** The Chorus outlines the plot of the play in this exposition.

4. **traffic:** action.

5. **mend:** make clear.

# ACT ONE

**SCENE 1** *[A public square in Verona.]*

*[Enter Sampson and Gregory, servants of the house of Capulet, armed with swords and bucklers (shields).]*

**Sampson.** Gregory, on my word, we'll not carry coals.[1]

**Gregory.** No, for then we should be colliers.[2]

**Sampson.** I mean, an[3] we be in choler,[4] we'll draw.

**Gregory.** Ay, while you live, draw your neck out of collar.

5 **Sampson.** I strike quickly, being moved.

**Gregory.** But thou art not quickly moved to strike.

**Sampson.** A dog of that house of Montague moves me.

**Gregory.** To move is to stir, and to be valiant is to stand. Therefore, if thou art moved, thou runnest away.

10 **Sampson.** A dog of that house shall move me to stand. I will take the wall of any man or maid of Montague's.

1. **carry coals:** endure insults.

2. **colliers:** coal dealers.

3. **an:** if.

4. **in choler** (käl′ ər): angry.

◆ **Lines 1-4:** *Collar,* which in line 4 refers to a hangman's noose, sounds like *collier* and *choler.* The servants are punning, playing with words that have similar sounds but different meanings.

◆ **Lines 10-11:** To take the wall means to go to the inside of the sidewalk, where the ground was higher and less muddy, and thus show superiority. Sampson intends to provoke the Montague servants by assuming the more honorable place on the sidewalk.

**Gregory.** That shows thee a weak slave, for the weakest goes to the wall.[5]

15 **Sampson.** 'Tis true; and therefore women, being the weaker vessels, are ever thrust to the wall. Therefore I will push Montague's men from the wall and thrust his maids to the wall. ~~house~~ (rape the women)

**Gregory.** The quarrel is between our masters and us their men.

20 **Sampson.** 'Tis all one. I will show myself a tyrant. When I have fought with the men, I will be cruel with the maids: I will cut off their heads.

**Gregory.** The heads of the maids?

**Sampson.** Ay, the heads of the maids, or their
25 maidenheads. Take it in what sense thou wilt.

**Gregory.** They must take it in sense that feel it.

**Sampson.** Me they shall feel while I am able to stand; and 'tis known I am a pretty piece of flesh.

**Gregory.** 'Tis well thou art not fish; if thou hadst, thou
30 hadst been poor-John.[6] Draw thy tool! Here comes two of the house of Montagues.

*[Enter* Abram *and* Balthasar, *servants to the* Montagues.*]*

**Sampson.** My naked weapon is out. Quarrel! I will back thee.

**Gregory.** How? turn thy back and run?

35 **Sampson.** Fear me not.

**Gregory.** No, marry.[7] I fear thee!

**Sampson.** Let us take the law of our sides; let them begin.

40 **Gregory.** I will frown as I pass by, and let them take it as they list.[8]

**Sampson.** Nay, as they dare. I will bite my thumb at them; which is disgrace to them, if they bear it.

**Abram.** Do you bite your thumb at us, sir?

**Sampson.** I do bite my thumb, sir.

**Abram.** Do you bite your thumb at us, sir?

**5. weakest . . . wall:** The weakest must yield; Gregory is quoting a proverb.

♦ **Lines 18-19:** Notice how eager the servants are to participate in the quarrel of their master.

**6. poor-John:** dried hake, a cheap kind of fish.

**7. marry:** by the Virgin Mary; a mild oath.

♦ **Lines 37-50:** Sampson warns Gregory that if they start the quarrel they will not be legally in the right. Instead Sampson tries to provoke the Montague servants with insulting gestures, in this case by biting his thumb at them.

**8. list:** please.

45 **Sampson.** [*Aside to Gregory*] Is the law of our side if I say ay?

**Gregory.** [*Aside to Sampson*] No.

**Sampson.** No, sir, I do not bite my thumb at you, sir; but I bite my thumb, sir.

50 **Gregory.** Do you quarrel, sir?

**Abram.** Quarrel, sir? No, sir.

**Sampson.** But if you do, sir, I am for you. I serve as good a man as you.

**Abram.** No better.

55 **Sampson.** Well, sir.

[*Enter Benvolio, nephew of Montague and first cousin of Romeo.*]

**Gregory.** [*Aside to Sampson*] Say "better." Here comes one of my master's kinsmen.

*master's better*

**Sampson.** Yes, better, sir.

**Abram.** You lie.

60 **Sampson.** Draw, if you be men. Gregory, remember thy swashing blow.

[*They fight.*]

**Benvolio.** Part, fools! [*Beats down their swords.*] Put up your swords. You know not what you do.

[*Enter Tybalt, hot-headed nephew of Lady Capulet and first cousin of Juliet.*]

(Lightning)

**Tybalt.** What, art thou drawn among these heartless *loves to* 
65 hinds? Turn thee, Benvolio! look upon thy death. *fight*

(Peace)

**Benvolio.** I do but keep the peace. Put up thy sword, Or manage it to part these men with me.

**Tybalt.** What, drawn, and talk of peace? I hate the word As I hate hell, all Montagues, and thee.
70 Have at thee, coward!

[*They fight.*]

[*Enter several of both houses, who join the fray; then enter Citizens and Peace Officers, with clubs.*]

◆ **Lines 45–47:** Think of an aside as a whisper that the audience is intended to overhear.

◆ **Lines 64–65:** Tybalt plays on the words hart—a male deer—and hinds—female deer. This pun is intended to be an insult to the servants and to Benvolio. Notice that "hot-headed" Tybalt assumes that Benvolio has drawn his sword in order to fight with the servants.

◆ **Lines 66–70:** Notice the contrast between Benvolio, who wants to make peace, and Tybalt, who seems to be looking for an excuse to fight.

**Officer.** Clubs, bills, and partisans![9] Strike! beat them down!

**Citizens.** Down with the Capulets! Down with the Montagues!

*[Enter old* Capulet *and Lady Capulet.]*

75 **Capulet.** What noise is this? Give me my long sword, ho!

**Lady Capulet.** A crutch, a crutch! Why call you for a sword?

**Capulet.** My sword, I say! Old Montague is come
And flourishes his blade in spite[10] of me.

*[Enter old* Montague *and Lady Montague.]*

**Montague.** Thou villain Capulet!—Hold me not, let
80 me go.

**Lady Montague.** Thou shalt not stir one foot to seek a foe.

*[Enter* Prince Escalus, *with attendants. At first no one hears him.]*

**Prince.** Rebellious subjects, enemies to peace,
Profaners of this neighbor-stained steel—[11]
Will they not hear? What, ho! you men, you beasts,
That quench the fire of your pernicious[12] rage
85 With purple fountains issuing from your veins!
On pain of torture, from those bloody hands
Throw your mistempered weapons to the ground
And hear the sentence of your moved prince.
Three civil brawls, bred of an airy word
90 By thee, old Capulet, and Montague,
Have thrice disturbed the quiet of our streets
And made Verona's ancient citizens
Cast by their grave beseeming ornaments
To wield old partisans, in hands as old,
90 Cankered with peace, to part your cankered hate.[13]
If ever you disturb our streets again,
Your lives shall pay the forfeit of the peace.
For this time all the rest depart away.
You, Capulet, shall go along with me;
100 And, Montague, come you this afternoon,

*trying to discipline them* (handwritten margin note)

**9. bills . . . partisans:** kinds of long-handled spears with sharp blades.

◆ **Lines 76-78:** Note that the heads of the two families eagerly participate in the feud.
**10. spite:** contempt.

**11. neighbor-stained steel:** swords stained with neighbors' blood.

**12. pernicious** (pər nish′ əs): destructive.

◆ **Lines 84-86:** Notice the metaphor in these lines. The anger of the feuding men is compared to a fire that can only be extinguished with a fountain of their own blood.

**13. Cankered . . . cankered:** rusted . . . corroded.

◆ **Lines 97-98.** Having lost patience with the feuding families, the prince decrees that if the feud causes another brawl to break out in Verona, Capulet and Montague will pay for the disturbance of the peace with their lives.

To know our farther pleasure in this case,
To old Freetown, our common judgment place.
Once more, on pain of death, all men depart.

*[Exeunt all but Montague, Lady Montague, and
Benvolio.]*

105 **Montague.** Who set this ancient quarrel new abroach?[14]
Speak, nephew, were you by when it began?

**Benvolio.** Here were the servants of your adversary[15]
And yours, close fighting ere I did approach.
I drew to part them. In the instant came
110 The fiery Tybalt, with his sword prepared;
Which, as he breathed defiance to my ears,
He swung about his head and cut the winds,
Who, nothing hurt withal,[16] hissed him in scorn.
While we were interchanging thrusts and blows,
115 Came more and more, and fought on part and part,
Till the Prince came, who parted either part.

**Lady Montague.** O, where is Romeo? Saw you him
today?
Right glad I am he was not at this fray.

**Benvolio.** Madam, an hour before the worshiped sun
120 Peered forth the golden window of the East,
A troubled mind drave me to walk abroad,
Where, underneath the grove of sycamore
That westward rooteth from the city's side,
So early walking did I see your son.
125 Towards him I made, but he was ware of me
And stole into the covert of the wood.
I—measuring his affections by my own,
Which then most sought where most might not be
found,
Being one too many by my weary self—
130 Pursued my humor,[17] not pursuing his,
And gladly shunned who gladly fled from me.

**Montague.** Many a morning hath he there been seen,
With tears augmenting the fresh morning's dew,
Adding to clouds more clouds with his deep sighs;
135 But all so soon as the all-cheering sun
Should in the farthest East begin to draw
The shady curtains from Aurora's[18] bed,
Away from light steals home my heavy[19] son

**14. set . . . abroach:** reopened this old quarrel.

**15. adversary** (ad′ vər ser′ ē): enemy.

**16. withal:** by this.

♦ **Lines 117–126:** Notice that Romeo is discussed before he appears on stage. Think about the impression of Romeo that you get from Benvolio's comments.

*Romeo's very sad doesn't want to talk to his friend*

**17. humor:** mood.

**18. Aurora** (ô rôr′ə ): goddess of the dawn.
**19. heavy:** depressed.

140 And private in his chamber pens himself,
Shuts up his windows, locks fair daylight out,
And makes himself an artificial night.
Black and <u>portentous</u>[20] must this humor prove
Unless good counsel may the cause remove.

**Benvolio.** My noble uncle, do you know the cause?

145 **Montague.** I neither know it nor can learn of him.

**Benvolio.** Have you importuned[21] him by any means?

**Montague.** Both by myself and many other friends;
But he, his own affections' counselor,
Is to himself—I will not say how true—
150 But to himself so secret and so close,
So far from sounding and discovery,[22]
As is the bud bit with an envious worm
Ere he can spread his sweet leaves to the air
Or dedicate his beauty to the sun.
155 Could we but learn from whence his sorrows grow,
We would as willingly give cure as know.

[*Enter* Romeo *lost in thought.*]

**Benvolio.** See, where he comes. So please you step aside,
I'll know his grievance, or be much denied.

**Montague.** I would thou wert so happy by thy stay[23]
160 To hear true shrift.[24] Come, madam, let's away.

[*Exeunt* Montague *and* Lady.]

**Benvolio.** Good morrow, cousin.

**Romeo.** Is the day so young?

**Benvolio.** But new struck nine.

**Romeo.** Ay me! sad hours seem long.
Was that my father that went hence so fast?

**Benvolio.** It was. What sadness lengthens Romeo's
hours?

165 **Romeo.** Not having that which having makes them
short.

**Benvolio.** In love?

**Romeo.** Out—

**Benvolio.** Of love?

---

**20. portentous:** (pôr ten′ təs): promising something bad or harmful.

♦ **Lines 132-143:** In his conversation with Benvolio, Montague reveals that Romeo is sad and has been avoiding his friends and family. Images of light and dark are used here to portray Romeo's sad mood. When the sun appears, Romeo seeks darkness.

**21. importuned:** continued to ask.

**22. sounding and discovery:** responding to efforts to understand his problem.

♦ **Lines 148-154:** In this simile, Romeo, secretive and isolated at his young age, is compared to a bud that is destroyed by a worm before even opening its leaves.

♦ **Lines 155-156:** Note that no one knows why Romeo has been acting strangely.

**23. happy . . . stay:** fortunate in your waiting.
**24. shrift:** confession.

**Romeo.** Out of her favor where I am in love.

170 **Benvolio.** Alas that love,[25] so gentle in his view,
Should be so tyrannous and rough in proof![26]

**Romeo.** Alas that love, whose view is muffled still,[27] *is Rosalyn*
Should without eyes see pathways to his will!
Where shall we dine?—O me! What fray was here?—
175 Yet tell me not, for I have heard it all.
Here's much to do with hate, but more with love.
Why then, O brawling love! O loving hate!
O anything, of nothing first create!
O heavy lightness! serious vanity![28]
180 Misshapen chaos of well-seeming forms!
Feather of lead, bright smoke, cold fire, sick health!
Still-waking[29] sleep, that is not what it is!
This love feel I, that feel no love in this.[30]
Dost thou not laugh?

**Benvolio.**                    No, coz,[31] I rather weep.

185 **Romeo.** Good heart, at what?

**Benvolio.**                    At thy good heart's oppression.

**Romeo.** Why, such is love's transgression.
Griefs of mine own lie heavy in my breast,
Which thou wilt propagate, to have it prest
With more of thine. This love that thou hast shown
190 Doth add more grief to too much of mine own.
Love is a smoke raised with the fume of sighs;
Being purged, a fire sparkling in lovers' eyes;
Being vexed, a sea nourished with lovers' tears.
What is it else? A madness most discreet,
195 A choking gall, and a preserving sweet.
Farewell, my coz.

**Benvolio.**                    Soft![32] I will go along.
An if you leave me so, you do me wrong.

**Romeo.** Tut! I have lost myself; I am not here:
This is not Romeo, he's some other where.

200 **Benvolio.** Tell me in sadness,[33] who is that you love?

**Romeo.** What, shall I groan and tell thee?

**Benvolio.**                    Groan? Why, no;
But sadly tell me who.

*all oxymorons*
*hate/passion*

*making fun of*
*him*

---

**25. love:** a reference to Cupid, god of love.

**26. proof:** experience.

**27. view . . . still:** always blindfolded.

**28. vanity:** frivolity.

**29. still-waking:** always watchful.

**30. that feel . . . in this:** who can take no pleasure in this love.

◆ **Lines 174-183:** Romeo notices the signs of the earlier fight and comments that it springs from hate, but also from love: hatred between the Capulets and Montagues and love of family and fighting. This reflection leads Romeo back to the subject of love, his sole preoccupation. Note that Romeo speaks in a series of paradoxes.

**31. coz:** cousin.

◆ **Lines 186-195:** In a series of rhyming couplets, Romeo continues his elaborate description of love. The couplet form is frequently used in love poems; as used in these lines, the couplets suggest that Romeo may be in love with the idea of love.

**32. Soft:** Wait a minute.

**33. sadness:** seriousness.

**Romeo.** Bid a sick man in sadness make his will.
Ah, word ill urged to one that is so ill!
205 In sadness, cousin, I do love a woman.

**Benvolio.** I aimed so near when I supposed you loved.

**Romeo.** A right good markman! And she's fair I love.

**Benvolio.** A right fair mark, fair coz, is soonest hit.

**Romeo.** Well, in that hit you miss. She'll not be hit
210 With Cupid's arrow. She hath Dian's wit,[34]
And, in strong proof of chastity well armed,
From Love's weak childish bow she lives unharmed.
She will not stay the siege of loving terms,
Nor bide the encounter of assailing eyes,
215 Nor ope her lap to saint-seducing gold.
O, she is rich in beauty; only poor
That, when she dies, with beauty dies her store.

**Benvolio.** Then she hath sworn that she will still[35] live chaste?

**Romeo.** She hath, and in that sparing makes huge waste;
220 For beauty, starved with her severity,
Cuts beauty off from all posterity.
She is too fair, too wise, wisely too fair,
To merit bliss by making me despair.
She hath forsworn to[36] love, and in that vow
225 Do I live dead that live to tell it now.

**Benvolio.** Be ruled by me: forget to think of her.

**Romeo.** O, teach me how I should forget to think!

**Benvolio.** By giving liberty unto thine eyes:
Examine other beauties.

**Romeo.**                    'Tis the way
230 To call hers (exquisite) in question more.[37]
These happy masks[38] that kiss fair ladies' brows,
Being black, puts us in mind they hide the fair.
He that is strucken blind cannot forget
The precious treasure of his eyesight lost.
235 Show me a mistress that is passing[39] fair,
What doth her beauty serve but as a note
Where I may read who passed[40] that passing fair?
Farewell. Thou canst not teach me to forget.

**Benvolio.** I'll pay that doctrine, or else die in debt.[41]

**Lines 203-205:** Romeo says that it is not kind to advise a sick person to make a will, and so it is not kind to ask him to identify his love.

**34. Dian's wit:** a reference to Diana, goddess of chastity, the moon, and the hunt. She shunned love and marriage.

**Lines 209-217:** The woman Romeo loves is not moved by his declarations of love, his adoring gaze, or his wealth. Romeo fears she will die without passing on her beauty to children.

**35. still:** forever.

**36. forsworn to:** sworn not to.

**Lines 245-225:** This paradox—"live dead"—is humorous because it is so exaggerated. Think about what this statement suggests about the nature of Romeo's love.

**Lines 226-229:** In contrast to Romeo's poetic views of love, Benvolio's approach is more down-to-earth.

**37. 'Tis the way . . . more:** to examine others' beauty is the way to realize the greater beauty of the woman Romeo loves.

**38. masks:** worn to protect faces from the sun.

**39. passing:** exceedingly.

**40. passed:** surpassed.

**41. pay . . . debt:** convince you that you are wrong.

**SCENE 2** [*A street near the* Capulet *house.*]

[*Enter* Capulet *with* Paris, *a kinsman of the* Prince, *and* Servant.]

**Capulet.** But Montague is bound as well as I,
    In penalty alike; and 'tis not hard, I think,
    For men so old as we to keep the peace.

**Paris.** Of honorable reckoning[1] are you both,
5    And pity 'tis you lived at odds so long.
    But now, my lord, what say you to my suit?[2]

**Capulet.** But saying o'er what I have said before:
    My child is yet a stranger in the world,
    She hath not seen the change of fourteen years;
10    Let two more summers wither in their pride
    Ere we may think her ripe to be a bride.

**Paris.** Younger than she are happy mothers made.

**Capulet.** And too soon marred are those so early made.
    The earth hath swallowed all my hopes but she;
15    She is the hopeful lady of my earth.[3]
    But woo her, gentle Paris, get her heart;
    My will to her consent is but a part.
    An she agree, within her scope of choice
    Lies my consent and fair according[4] voice.
20    This night I hold an old accustomed feast,
    Whereto I have invited many a guest,
    Such as I love, and you among the store,
    One more, most welcome, makes my number more.
    At my poor house look to behold this night
25    Earth-treading stars that make dark heaven light.
    Such comfort as do lusty young men feel
    When well-appareled April on the heel
    Of limping Winter treads, even such delight
    Among fresh female buds shall you this night
30    Inherit[5] at my house. Hear all, all see,
    And like her most whose merit most shall be;
    Which, on more view of many, mine, being one,
    May stand in number, though in reck'ning none.
    Come, go with me. [*To* Servant, *giving him a paper.*] Go,
      sirrah,[6] trudge about
35    Through fair Verona; find those persons out
    Whose names are written there, and to them say,

*[handwritten note: Paris i solder, capulet is arranging a marriage]*

**1. reckoning:** reputation.

**2. suit:** courtship.

**3. hopeful . . . earth:** center of my universe.

**4. according:** agreeing.

♦ **Lines 13-19:** Capulet believes that early motherhood is damaging to a young woman's health. Juliet is his only living child, so he is reluctant for her to marry young. However, Capulet says that if Paris can win Juliet's love, then he will agree to the marriage. Think about the kind of father Capulet seems to be.

**5. inherit:** have.

♦ **Lines 24-33:** Capulet tells Paris to look at other women at the feast to be sure that Juliet is his choice. Capulet declares that, though Juliet will be just one among many beauties that Paris will see at the feast, none will be worth more than she.

**6. sirrah:** a term used in addressing servants.

My house and welcome on their pleasure stay.[7]

[*Exeunt* Capulet *and Paris.*]

**Servant.** Find them out whose names are written here! It
is written that the shoemaker should meddle with his
40    yard and the tailor with his last, the fisher with his
pencil and the painter with his nets; but I am sent to
find those persons whose names are here writ, and can
never find what names the writing person hath here
writ. I must to the learned. In good time![8]

[*Enter* Benvolio *and Romeo.*]

45    **Benvolio.** Tut, man, one fire burns out another's
    burning;
One pain is lessened by another's anguish;
Turn giddy, and be holp[9] by backward turning;
One desperate grief cures with another's languish.
Take thou some new infection to thy eye,
50    And the rank poison of the old will die.

**Romeo.** Your plantain leaf[10] is excellent for that.

**Benvolio.** For what, I pray thee?

**Romeo.**                For your broken shin.

**Benvolio.** Why, Romeo, art thou mad?

**Romeo.** Not mad, but bound more than a madman is;
55    Shut up in prison, kept without my food,
Whipped and tormented and—God-den,[11] good fellow.

**Servant.** God gi'go-den. I pray, sir, can you read?

**Romeo.** Ay, mine own fortune in my misery.

**Servant.** Perhaps you have learned it without book. But
60    I pray, can you read anything you see?

**Romeo.** Ay, if I know the letters and the language.

**Servant.** Ye say honestly. Rest you merry![12]

[*Romeo's joking goes over the clown's head. He concludes
that* Romeo *cannot read and prepares to seek someone who
can.*]

**Romeo.** Stay, fellow; I can read.

[*He reads.*]

**7. on their . . . stay:** await
the pleasure of their
company.

◆ **Lines 38-44:** Shakespeare
often created humor through
the servant characters in his
plays. This servant reveals
that he is unable to read and
cannot fulfill his errand
without assistance from
someone more learned.

**8. In good time:** What luck;
an exclamation on seeing
Romeo and Benvolio
approach.

◆ **Lines 45-50:** Benvolio tries
to convince Romeo that he
can cure his lovesickness by
substituting another woman
in his heart. Notice Benvolio's
description of love in terms of
bad health, as a "new
infection" and "rank poison."

**9. holp:** helped.

**10. plantain leaf:** a weed
used to stop bleeding.

**11. God-den:** Good
afternoon or good evening; a
greeting intended for the
servant he has just seen.

◆ **Lines 54-56:** Romeo likens
his suffering over Rosaline to
being mad. In Shakespeare's
time the mentally ill were
commonly bound, starved,
and sometimes physically
abused. Romeo feels that, like
a madman, he is bound by
his feelings for Rosaline.

**12. Rest you merry:** May
you continue happy; a way
of saying goodbye.

"Signior Martino and his wife and daughters;
65 County[13] Anselmo and his beauteous sisters;
The lady widow of Vitruvio;
Signior Placentio and his lovely nieces;
Mercutio and his brother Valentine;
Mine uncle Capulet, his wife, and daughters;
70 My fair niece Rosaline and Livia;
Signior Valentio and his cousin Tybalt;
Lucio and the lively Helena."

[*Gives back the paper.*] A fair assembly. Whither should
   they come?

**Servant.** Up.

75 **Romeo.** Whither?

**Servant.** To supper, to our house.

**Romeo.** Whose house?

**Servant.** My master's.

**Romeo.** Indeed I should have asked you that before.

80 **Servant.** Now I'll tell you without asking. My master is
   the great rich Capulet; and if you be not of the house of
   Montagues, I pray come and crush[14] a cup of wine.
   Rest you merry!

[*Exit.*]

**Benvolio.** At this same ancient[15] feast of Capulet's
85 Sups the fair Rosaline[16] whom thou so lovest,
   With all the admired beauties of Verona.
   Go thither, and with unattainted[17] eye
   Compare her face with some that I shall show,
   And I will make thee think thy swan a crow.

90 **Romeo.** When the devout religion of mine eye
   Maintains such falsehood, then turn tears to fires;
   And these, who, often drowned, could never die,
   Transparent[18] heretics, be burnt for liars!
   One fairer than my love? The all-seeing sun
95 Ne'er saw her match since first the world begun.

**Benvolio.** Tut! you saw her fair, none else being by,
   Herself poised[19] with herself in either eye;
   But in that crystal scales[20] let there be weighed
   Your lady's love against some other maid

**13. County:** Count.

**14. crush:** slang for drink.

**15. ancient:** traditional.
**16. Rosaline** (rōz' ə līn): the woman Romeo has been brooding over.
**17. unattainted:** unbiased.

◆ **Lines 90-93:** Romeo says that if he ever perceives someone else as more beautiful than Rosaline, his tears will turn to fire and his eyes will be like heretics, who are burned for holding false religious beliefs.
**18. transparent:** bright, clear.
**19. poised:** balanced.
**20. crystal scales:** a reference to Romeo's eyes.

100  That I will show you shining at this feast,
And she shall scant show well that now shows best.

**Romeo.** I'll go along, no such sight to be shown,
But to rejoice in splendor of mine own.

[Exeunt.]

◆ **Lines 102-103:** Romeo agrees to go to the Capulet feast only to observe Rosaline's "splendor."

**SCENE 3**  [*A room in* Capulet's *house.*]

[*Enter* Lady Capulet *and* Nurse.]

**Lady Capulet.** Nurse, where's my daughter? Call her
forth to me.
**Nurse.** Now, by my maidenhead at twelve year old,
I bade her come. What, lamb! what, ladybird!
God forbid! Where's this girl? What, Juliet!

[*Enter* Juliet.]

5  **Juliet.** How now? Who calls?

**Nurse.** Your mother.

**Juliet.** Madam, I am here. What is your will?

**Lady Capulet.** This is the matter—Nurse, give leave
awhile,[1]
We must talk in secret. Nurse, come back again;
10  I have remembered me, thou's[2] hear our counsel.
Thou knowest my daughter's of a pretty age.

**Nurse.** Faith, I can tell her age unto an hour.

**Lady Capulet.** She's not fourteen.

**Nurse.**                          I'll lay fourteen of my teeth—
And yet, to my teen[3] be it spoken, I have but four—
15  She's not fourteen. How long is it now
To Lammastide?[4]

**Lady Capulet.** A fortnight and odd days.

**Nurse.** Even or odd, of all days in the year,
Come Lammas Eve at night shall she be fourteen.
Susan and she (God rest all Christian souls!)
20  Were of an age. Well, Susan is with God;
She was too good for me. But, as I said,
On Lammas Eve at night shall she be fourteen;
That shall she, marry;[5] I remember it well.
'Tis since the earthquake[6] now eleven years;
25  And she was weaned (I never shall forget it),

*Juliet's B'day July 31st*

1. **give leave awhile:** leave us for a while.

2. **thou's:** thou shalt (you shall).

◆ **Lines 9-10:** Note that the nurse is included in confidential family discussions.

3. **teen:** sorrow.

4. **Lammastide:** August 1, a holy feast day.

◆ **Lines 19-21:** The nurse remembers Juliet's age because Juliet was born at the same time as the nurse's daughter Susan, who has died.

5. **marry:** indeed.

6. earthquake occurred in England.

Of all the days of the year, upon that day.
For I had then laid wormwood to my dug,
Sitting in the sun under the dovehouse wall.
My lord and you were then at Mantua—
30 Nay, I do bear a brain[7]—But, as I said,
When it did taste the wormwood on the nipple
Of my dug and felt it bitter, pretty fool,
To see it tetchy[8] and fall out with the dug!
Shake, quoth the dovehouse![9] 'Twas no need, I trow,[10]
35 To bid me trudge.
And since that time it is eleven years,
For then she could stand alone; nay, by the rood,[11]
She could have run and waddled all about;
For even the day before, she broke her brow;
40 And then my husband (God be with his soul!
'A was a merry man) took up the child.
"Yea," quoth he, "dost thou fall upon thy face?
Thou wilt fall backward when thou has more wit,
Wilt thou not, Jule?" And, by my holidam,[12]
45 The pretty wretch left crying, and said "Ay."
To see now how a jest shall come about!
I warrant, an I should live a thousand years,
I never should forget it. "Wilt thou not, Jule?" quoth he,
And, pretty fool, it stinted,[13] and said "Ay."

50 **Lady Capulet.** Enough of this. I pray thee hold thy
    peace.
**Nurse.** Yes, madam. Yet I cannot choose but laugh
    To think it should leave crying and say "Ay."
    And yet, I warrant, it had upon its brow
    A bump as big as a young cock'rel's stone;
55 A perilous knock; and it cried bitterly.
    "Yea," quoth my husband, "fallst upon thy face?
    Thou wilt fall backward when thou comest to age,
    Wilt thou not, Jule?" It stinted, and said "Ay."

**Juliet.** And stint thou too, I pray thee, nurse, say I.

60 **Nurse.** Peace, I have done. God mark thee to his grace!
    Thou wast the prettiest babe that e'er I nursed.
    An I might live to see thee married once,
    I have my wish.

**Lady Capulet.** Marry, that "marry" is the very theme
65 I came to talk of. Tell me, daughter Juliet,
    How stands your disposition to be married?

7. **I . . . brain:** I have a good memory.

8. **tetchy:** fretful, peevish.

9. **shake . . . dovehouse:** that is, the earthquake shook the dovehouse.

10. **trow:** guess.

11. **rood:** cross.

◆ **Lines 39–45:** The nurse recalls a time when Juliet, as a young child, fell and cut her forehead. The nurse's late husband teased the child by referring to a future time when she would lose her virginity upon marriage.

12. **holidam:** a holy relic.

◆ **Lines 17–49:** The nurse, who likes to ramble on at great length to anyone who will listen, adds another comic element to the play. Compare the nurse's relationship with Juliet to Lady Capulet's relationship with her daughter.

13. **stinted:** stopped (crying).

**Juliet.** It is an honor that I dream not of.

**Nurse.** An honor? Were not I thine only nurse,
  I would say thou hadst sucked wisdom from thy teat.

70 **Lady Capulet.** Well, think of marriage now. Younger
    than you,
  Here in Verona, ladies of esteem,
  Are made already mothers. By my count,
  I was your mother much upon these years[14]
  That you are now a maid. Thus then in brief:
75   The valiant Paris seeks you for his love.

**Nurse.** A man, young lady! lady, such a man
  As all the world—why he's a man of wax.[15]

**Lady Capulet.** Verona's summer hath not such a flower.

**Nurse.** Nay, he's a flower, in faith—a very flower.

80 **Lady Capulet.** What say you? Can you love the
    gentleman?
  This night you shall behold him at our feast.
  Read o'er the volume of young Paris' face,
  And find delight writ there with beauty's pen;
  Examine every several[16] lineament,
85   And see how one another lends content;[17]
  And what obscured in this fair volume lies
  Find written in the margent of his eyes.
  This precious book of love, this unbound lover,
  To beautify him only lacks a cover.
90   The fish lives in the sea, and 'tis much pride
  For fair without the fair within to hide.[18]
  That book in many's eyes doth share the glory,
  That in gold clasps locks in the golden story;
  So shall you share all that he doth possess,
95   By having him making yourself no less.

**Nurse.** No less? Nay, bigger! Women grow by men.

**Lady Capulet.** Speak briefly, can you like of Paris' love?

**Juliet.** I'll look to like, if looking liking move;
  But no more deep will I endart mine eye
100   Than your consent gives strength to make it fly.

[*Enter a* Servingman.]

**Servingman.** Madam, the guests are come, supper served
  up, you called, my young lady asked for, the nurse cursed

---

◆ **Line 67:** Juliet, at just under the age of fourteen, has not even begun to think of marriage.

**14. much . . . years:** at much the same age.

**15. man of wax:** a perfect model of a man.

◆ **Lines 76-79:** Notice that the nurse cannot keep from adding her comments and opinions to the conversation between Lady Capulet and Juliet.

**16. several:** separate.

**17. one . . . content:** each feature enhances the others.

**18. for . . . hide:** for fair outside to cover a fair inside.

◆ **Lines 82-93:** In this extended metaphor Lady Capulet compares Paris' face to a book. She says that what Juliet cannot learn of Paris' character from his features, his eyes will make clear. The *margent* (margin) in books of the time was used for explanatory notes. Contrast Lady Capulet's statement with the expression "You can't judge a book by its cover."

◆ **Lines 98-100:** Juliet means that she is ready to look upon Paris favorably if that is enough to make her love him. Notice Juliet's formality with her mother and her obedience as a daughter.

in the pantry, and everything in extremity.[19] I must hence to wait. I beseech you follow straight.[20]

105 **Lady Capulet.** We follow thee. [*Exit* Servingman.]<br>
Juliet, the County stays.[21]

**Nurse.** Go, girl, seek happy nights to happy days.

[Exeunt.]

SCENE 4 [*A street near the* Capulet *house.*]

[*Enter* Romeo, Mercutio, Benvolio, *with five or six other* Maskers; Torchbearers.]

**Romeo.** What, shall this speech be spoke for our excuse? Or shall we on without apology?

**Benvolio.** The date is out of such prolixity.
We'll have no Cupid hoodwinked[1] with a scarf,
5 Bearing a Tartar's painted bow of lath,[2]
Scaring the ladies like a crowkeeper;[3]
Nor no without-book prologue, faintly spoke
After the prompter, for our entrance;
But let them measure us by what they will,
10 We'll measure them a measure,[4] and be gone.

**Romeo.** Give me a torch. I am not for this ambling;
Being but heavy,[5] I will bear the light.

**Mercutio.** Nay, gentle Romeo, we must have you dance.

**Romeo.** Not I, believe me. You have dancing shoes
15 With nimble soles; I have a soul of lead
So stakes me to the ground I cannot move.

**Mercutio.** You are a lover. Borrow Cupid's wings
And soar with them above a common bound.

**Romeo.** I am too sore enpierced with his shaft
20 To soar with his light feathers, and so bound
I cannot bound a pitch[6] above dull woe.
Under love's heavy burden do I sink.

**Mercutio.** And, to sink in it, should you burden love—
Too great oppression for a tender thing.

25 **Romeo.** Is love a tender thing? It is too rough,
Too rude, too boist'rous, and it pricks like thorn.

**Mercutio.** If love be rough with you, be rough with love.

---

**19. extremity:** confusion.

**20. straight:** at once.

**21. County stays:** Count Paris waits for you.

◆ **Lines 1-10:** When uninvited people wanted to attend an Elizabethan feast, they simply wore masks and sent in a costumed messenger to announce their coming. Benvolio says that this custom of sending a messenger is out of date, and goes on to list the devices they will not use to announce their presence.

**1. We'll . . . hoodwinked:** We will not provide someone dressed up as Cupid blindfolded.

**2. Tartar's . . . lath:** The shorter bow carried by the Tartars more closely resembled Cupid's bow.

**3. crowkeeper:** scarecrow.

**4. measure . . . measure:** perform a dance.

**5. heavy:** sad.

◆ **Lines 14-16:** Romeo puns on the words *soles* and *soul* and compares the condition of his soul with the heaviness of lead. In contrast to Benvolio and Mercutio, Romeo believes himself too burdened with lovesickness to dance.

◆ **Lines 19-22:** Romeo plays with the two meanings of the word *bound*—"to be tied" and "to leap." His repeated word play shows that he is preoccupied with being lovesick.

**6. pitch:** height or distance.

Prick love for pricking, and you beat love down.
Give me a case[7] to put my visage in.
30 A visor for a visor![8] What care I
What curious eye doth quote[9] deformities?
Here are the beetle brows shall blush for me.

**Benvolio.** Come, knock and enter, and no sooner in
But every man betake him to his legs.[10]

35 **Romeo.** A torch for me! Let wantons[11] light of heart
Tickle the senseless rushes[12] with their heels;
For I am proverbed with a grandsire phrase,[13]
I'll be a candle-holder[14] and look on;
The game was ne'er so fair, and I am done.

40 **Mercutio.** Tut, dun's the mouse, the constable's own
word![15]
If thou art Dun, we'll draw thee from the mire[16]
Of, save your reverence, love, wherein thou stickst
Up to the ears. Come, we burn daylight,[17] ho!

**Romeo.** Nay, that's not so.

**Mercutio.**                    I mean, sir, in delay
45 We waste our lights in vain, like lamps by day.
Take our good meaning, for our judgment sits
Five times in that ere once in our five wits.[18]

**Romeo.** And we mean well in going to this masque;
But 'tis no wit[19] to go.

**Mercutio.**                    Why, may one ask?

50 **Romeo.** I dreamt a dream tonight.[20]

**Mercutio.**                    And so did I.

**Romeo.** Well, what was yours?

**Mercutio.**                    That dreamers often lie.

**Romeo.** In bed asleep, while they do dream things true.

**Mercutio.** O, then I see Queen Mab[21] hath been with
you.
She is the fairies' midwife, and she comes
55 In shape no bigger than an agate stone
On the forefinger of an alderman,
Drawn with a team of little atomies[22]
Athwart men's noses as they lie asleep;

**7. case:** mask.

**8. visor . . . visor:** a mask for an ugly face.

**9. quote:** notice.

**10. betake . . . legs:** join the dancing.

**11. wantons:** playful or frolicsome ones.

**12. rushes:** dried plants of the bulrush family, which often covered Elizabethan floors.

**13. grandsire phrase:** old saying.

**14. candle-holder:** spectator.

**15. dun's . . . word:** a pun on Romeo's *done* and a proverb meaning "Be still as a mouse," as a constable might.

**16. Dun . . . mire:** In the Christmas game "Dun is in the mire," a log representing a horse stuck in the mud was hauled out by the players.

**17. burn daylight:** waste time.

**18. for . . . wits:** for others value the good meaning, rather than the intelligent wording, of what we say.

**19. wit:** wisdom.

**20. tonight:** last night.

**21. Queen Mab:** In Celtic mythology, Queen Mab, the fairy queen, was thought to ride across the faces of sleepers, bringing dreams. She was also thought to enjoy mischief and practical jokes.

◆ **Lines 53-95:** This is known as the "Queen Mab" speech. It begins as Mercutio's attempt to distract Romeo from his problems, but Mercutio's highly imaginative nature causes him to lose himself in his story.

**22. atomies:** tiny creatures.

Her wagon spokes made of long spinners'[23] legs,
The cover, of the wings of grasshoppers;
60  Her traces,[24] of the smallest spider's web;
Her collars, of the moonshine's wat'ry beams;
Her whip, of cricket's bone; the lash, of film;[25]
Her wagoner,[26] a small grey-coated gnat,
Not half so big as a round little worm
65  Pricked from the lazy finger of a maid;
Her chariot is an empty hazelnut,
Made by the joiner[27] squirrel or old grub,
Time out o' mind the fairies' coachmakers.
And in this state she gallops night by night
70  Through lovers' brains, and then they dream of love;
O'er courtiers' knees, that dream on curtsies straight;
O'er lawyers' fingers, who straight dream on fees;
O'er ladies' lips, who straight on kisses dream,
Which oft the angry Mab with blisters plagues,
75  Because their breaths with sweetmeats tainted are.
Sometime she gallops o'er a courtier's nose,
And then dreams he of smelling out a suit,[28]
And sometime comes she with a tithe-pig's tail
Tickling a parson's nose as 'a lies asleep,
80  Then dreams he of another benefice.[29]
Sometime she driveth o'er a soldier's neck,
And then dreams he of cutting foreign throats,
Of breaches, ambuscadoes,[30] Spanish blades,
Of healths[31] five fathom deep; and then anon
85  Drums in his ear, at which he starts and wakes,
And being thus frighted, swears a prayer or two
And sleeps again. This is that very Mab
That plaits the manes of horses in the night
And bakes the elflocks in foul sluttish hairs,
90  Which once untangled much misfortune bodes.
This is the hag,[32] when maids lie on their backs,
That presses them and learns them first to bear,
Making them women of good carriage.
This is she—

95  **Romeo.**        Peace, peace, Mercutio, peace!
Thou talkst of nothing.

**Mercutio.**                True, I talk of dreams;
Which are the children of an idle brain,
Begot of nothing but vain fantasy;
Which is as thin of substance as the air,

---

**23. spinners':** spiders'.

**24. traces:** harness.

**25. film:** delicate thread.

**26. wagoner:** coachman.

◆ **Lines 65-66:** This is a reference to the popular belief that worms bred in the fingers of the idle.

**27. joiner:** carpenter.

**28. suit:** a petition to the monarch for some favor.

◆ **Lines 79-80:** The parson in Elizabethan England was entitled to a tithe, or tenth, of his parishioners' produce.

**29. benefice:** a well-paying position.

**30. ambuscadoes:** ambushes.

**31. healths:** toasts to one's health.

◆ **Lines 88-91:** The knots in the manes of horses and uncombed human hair were sometimes attributed to mischievous fairies.

**32. hag:** nightmare.

◆ **Lines 95-96:** Romeo recognizes that Mercutio is losing control and attempts to calm him down and bring him back to reality.

And more inconstant than the wind, who woos
100 Even now the frozen bosom of the North
And, being angered, puffs away from thence,
Turning his face to the dew-dropping South.[33]

**Benvolio.** This wind you talk of blows us from ourselves.
Supper is done, and we shall come too late.

105 **Romeo.** I fear, too early; for my mind misgives[34]
Some consequence, yet hanging in the stars,
Shall bitterly begin his fearful date
With this night's revels and expire the term
Of a despised life, closed in my breast,
110 By some vile forfeit of untimely death.
But he that hath the steerage of my course
Direct my sail! On, lusty gentlemen!

**Benvolio.** Strike, drum.

*[Exeunt.]*

**SCENE 5** *[A spacious hall in* Capulet's *house. Musicians waiting.]*

*[Servingmen come forth with napkins.]*

**First Servingman.** Where's Potpan, that he helps not to take away? He shift a trencher![1] he scrape a trencher!

**Second Servingman.** When good manners shall lie all in one or two men's hands, and they unwashed too, 'tis a foul thing.

5 **First Servingman.** Away with the joint-stools, remove the court-cupboard, look to the plate. Good thou, save me a piece of marchpane[2] and, as thou lovest me, let the porter let in Susan Grindstone and Nell. Anthony, and Potpan!

10 **Second Servingman.** Ay, boy, ready.

**First Servingman.** You are looked for and called for, asked for and sought for, in the great chamber.

**Third Servingman.** We cannot be here and there too. Cheerly, boys! Be brisk awhile, and the longer liver take
15 all.

*[Exeunt.]*

*[Maskers appear with* Capulet, Lady Capulet, Juliet, *all the* Guests, *and Servants.]*

**33. dew-dropping South:** south wind bringing rain.

**34. misgives:** fears.

♦ **Lines 106-113:** Romeo has a feeling of foreboding about the evening and calls upon a higher power—"he that hath the steerage of my course"—for guidance. Romeo reflects the fourteenth-century belief that fate or the movement of the stars controlled human affairs. This speech echoes the phrase "star-crossed lovers" from the Prologue.

**1. trencher:** wooden platter.

**2. marchpane:** marzipan, a sweet made of almond paste.

**Capulet.** Welcome, gentlemen! Ladies that have their toes
    Unplagued with corns will have a bout³ with you.
    Ah ha, my mistresses! which of you all

20     Will now deny to dance? She that makes dainty,⁴
    She I'll swear hath corns. Am I come near ye now?
    Welcome, gentlemen! I have seen the day
    That I have worn a visor⁵ and could tell
    A whispering tale in a fair lady's ear,

25     Such as would please. 'Tis gone, 'tis gone, 'tis gone!
    You are welcome, gentlemen! Come, musicians, play.
    A hall, a hall!⁶ give room! and foot it, girls.

*[Music plays and they dance.]*

    More light, you knaves! and turn the tables up,
    And quench the fire, the room is grown too hot.

30     Ah, sirrah, this unlooked-for sport⁷ comes well.
    Nay, sit, nay, sit, good cousin⁸ Capulet,
    For you and I are past our dancing days.
    How long is't now since last yourself and I
    Were in a mask?

**Second Capulet.** By'r Lady, thirty years.

35 **Capulet.** What, man? 'Tis not so much, 'tis not so much!
    'Tis since the nuptial of Lucentio,
    Come Pentecost⁹ as quickly as it will,
    Some five-and-twenty years, and then we masked.

**Second Capulet.** 'Tis more, 'tis more! His son is elder, sir;
40     His son is thirty.

**Capulet.**       Will you tell me that?
    His son was but a ward¹⁰ two years ago.

**Romeo.** *[To a Servingman]* What lady's that, which doth enrich the hand
    Of yonder knight?

**Servant.** I know not, sir.

45 **Romeo.** O, she doth teach the torches to burn bright!
    It seems she hangs upon the cheek of night
    Like a rich jewel in an Ethiop's ear—
    Beauty too rich for use, for earth too dear!¹¹
    So shows a snowy dove trooping with crows
50     As yonder lady o'er her fellows shows.
    The measure done, I'll watch her place of stand
    And, touching hers, make blessed my rude hand.

**3. bout:** dance.

**4. makes dainty:** pretends to be shy.

◆ **Lines 17–21:** As Capulet greets the dancers, he good-humoredly tries to shame the ladies into dancing by suggesting that those who hang back must have corns on their toes.

**5. worn a visor:** worn a mask.

**6. a hall:** Clear the hall for dancing.

**7. this unlooked-for sport:** a reference to the appearance of the uninvited maskers.

**8. cousin:** a term used for any relative less close in blood than brother or sister of the speaker.

**9. Pentecost:** the seventh Sunday after Easter.

**10. ward:** minor.

◆ **Lines 42–43:** Romeo sees Juliet for the first time.

**11. dear:** precious.

◆ **Lines 49–50:** Benvolio's plan has worked. Romeo now thinks of Rosaline and the other women present as crows in comparison to Juliet, "a snowy dove."

Did my heart love till now? Forswear[12] it, sight!
For I ne'er saw true beauty till this night.

55 **Tybalt.** This, by his voice, should be a Montague.
Fetch me my rapier, boy. What, dares the slave
Come hither, covered with an antic face,
To fleer[13] and scorn at our solemnity?[14]
Now, by the stock and honor of my kin,
60 To strike him dead I hold it not a sin.

**Capulet.** Why, how now, kinsman? Wherefore storm you
so?

**Tybalt.** Uncle, this is a Montague, our foe;
A villain, that is hither come in spite
To scorn at our solemnity this night.

65 **Capulet.** Young Romeo is it?

**Tybalt.** 'Tis he, that villain Romeo.

**Capulet.** Content thee, gentle coz, let him alone.
'A bears him like a portly[15] gentleman,
And, to say truth, Verona brags of him
To be a virtuous and well-governed youth.
70 I would not for the wealth of all this town
Here in my house do him disparagement.[16]
Therefore be patient, take no note of him.
It is my will; the which if thou respect,
Show a fair presence and put off these frowns,
75 An ill-beseeming semblance[17] for a feast.

**Tybalt.** It fits when such a villain is a guest.
I'll not endure him.

**Capulet.** He shall be endured.
What, goodman boy?[18] I say he shall. Go to![19]
Am I the master here, or you? Go to!
80 You'll not endure him? God shall mend my soul![20]
You'll make a mutiny among my guests!
You will set cock-a-hoop![21] You'll be the man.

**Tybalt.** Why, uncle, 'tis a shame.

**Capulet.** Go to, go to!
You are a saucy boy. Is't so, indeed?
85 This trick[22] may chance to scathe you. I know what.[23]
You must contrary me! Marry, 'tis time.—
Well said, my hearts![24]—You are a princox[25]—go!
Be quiet, or—More light, more light!—For shame!

---

**12. forswear:** to promise
earnestly to give up.

♦ **Lines 53-54:** Notice how
quickly Romeo forgets his
feelings for Rosaline now
that he has seen Juliet.

**13. fleer:** sneer.

**14. solemnity:** celebration.

♦ **Lines 55-60:** When Tybalt
recognizes Romeo, he
instantly calls for his sword
(rapier). Note that he does not
consider it wrong to kill
someone for family honor.

**15. portly:** dignified.

**16. disparagement:** discredit.

♦ **Lines 66-75:** Contrast
Capulet's reaction to Romeo's
presence with that of Tybalt.

**17. ill-beseeming semblance**:
unbecoming appearance.

**18. goodman boy:**
*Goodman* indicated a man
under the rank of gentleman.
*Boy* is an insulting term.

**19. Go to:** Be off.

**20. God . . . soul:** an
exclamation.

**21. set cock-a-hoop:** act
recklessly, without restraint.

**22. trick:** habit.

**23. what:** what I'm doing.

**24. hearts:** good fellows; an
admiring reference to the skill
of the dancers.

**25. princox:** a saucy,
conceited youngster.

♦ **Lines 83-89:** Capulet is
carrying on two conversations
at the same time, encouraging
the dancers while scolding
Tybalt.

I'll make you quiet; what!—Cheerly, my hearts!

90 **Tybalt.** Patience perforce[26] with willful choler[27] meeting
Makes my flesh tremble in their different greeting.[28]
I will withdraw; but this intrusion shall,
Now seeming sweet, convert to bitter gall.

[Exit.]

**Romeo.** If I profane with my unworthiest hand
95 This holy shrine, the gentle fine is this:
My lips, two blushing pilgrims,[29] ready stand
To smooth that rough touch with a tender kiss.

**Juliet.** Good pilgrim, you do wrong your hand too much,
Which mannerly devotion shows in this;
100 For saints have hands that pilgrims' hands do touch,
And palm to palm is holy palmers'[30] kiss.

**Romeo.** Have not saints lips, and holy palmers too?

**Juliet.** Ay, pilgrim, lips that they must use in prayer.

**Romeo.** O, then, dear saint, let lips do what hands do!
105 They pray; grant thou, lest faith turn to despair.

**Juliet.** Saints do not move, though grant for prayers'
sake.

**Romeo.** Then move not while my prayer's effect I take.
Thus from my lips, by thine my sin is purged.

[Kisses her.]

**Juliet.** Then have my lips the sin that they have took.

110 **Romeo.** Sin from my lips? O trespass sweetly urged!
Give me my sin again.

[Kisses her.]

**Juliet.**                   You kiss by the book.[31]

**Nurse.** Madam, your mother craves a word with you.

**Romeo.** What is her mother?

**Nurse.**                   Marry, bachelor,
Her mother is the lady of the house.
115 And a good lady, and a wise and virtuous.
I nursed her daughter that you talked withal.
I tell you, he that can lay hold of her
Shall have the chinks.

**26. patience perforce:** imposed restraint.

**27. choler:** anger.

**28. different greeting:** opposition.

♦ **Lines 94-97:** Romeo is holding Juliet's hand as he talks to her for the first time.

**29. pilgrims:** people who travel to a holy place as a religious act.

**30. palmers:** pilgrims to the Holy Land; a pun on palm.

♦ **Lines 98-101:** When Juliet realizes that Romeo is about to kiss her hand, she places their hands palm to palm and refers to that as a "holy palmers' kiss."

♦ **Lines 94-107:** These lines form a Shakespearean sonnet, a love poem characterized by three four-line stanzas followed by a couplet. The lines also contain a complicated extended metaphor, in which Romeo shrewdly gets Juliet to kiss him by comparing himself to a worshiping pilgrim and Juliet to a shrine. Note that Juliet does not discourage him but continues the religious comparison.

**31. by the book:** according to the book of instructions on gallantry.

♦ **Lines 117-118:** The nurse tells Romeo, a stranger to her, that the man who marries Juliet will become rich.

**Romeo.**                    Is she a Capulet?
O dear³² account! my life is my foe's debt.

120 **Benvolio.**  Away, be gone, the sport is at the best.

**Romeo.**  Ay, so I fear; the more is my unrest.

**Capulet.**  Nay, gentlemen, prepare not to be gone;
We have a trifling foolish banquet towards.³³

*[They whisper in his ear.]*

Is it e'en so? Why then, I thank you all.
125 I thank you, honest gentlemen. Good night.
More torches here! *[Exeunt* Maskers.*]* Come on then,
   let's to bed.
Ah, sirrah, by my fay, it waxes late;
I'll to my rest.

*[Exeunt all but* Juliet *and* Nurse.*]*

**Juliet.**  Come hither, nurse. What is yond gentleman?

130 **Nurse.**  The son and heir of old Tiberio.

**Juliet.**  What's he that now is going out of door?

**Nurse.**  Marry, that, I think, be young Petruchio.

**Juliet.**  What's he that follows there, that would not dance?

**Nurse.**  I know not.

135 **Juliet.**  Go ask his name.—If he be married,
My grave is like to be my wedding bed.

**Nurse.**  His name is Romeo, and a Montague,
The only son of your great enemy.

**Juliet.**  My only love, sprung from my only hate!
140 Too early seen unknown, and known too late!
Prodigious³⁴ birth of love it is to me
That I must love a loathed enemy.

**Nurse.**  What's this? what's this?

**Juliet.**                    A rhyme I learnt even now
Of one I danced withal.

*[One calls within,* "Juliet."*]*

**Nurse.**                    Anon, anon!
145 Come, let's away; the strangers all are gone.

*[Exeunt.]*

---

**32. dear:** costly.

**33. towards:** in preparation.

♦ **Lines 135-136:** Notice how quickly Juliet's attitude toward love and marriage has changed from what she revealed in her conversation with her mother earlier.

**34. prodigious:** unnatural, thus promising bad luck.

♦ **Lines 139-142:** Note the paradox of Juliet's "only love," Romeo, springing from her "only hate," the Montagues as her family enemies. She realizes that in her first experience with love she has unwittingly made the worst possible choice but believes it is too late to end her feelings for Romeo.

# *Thinking About Act One*

## A PERSONAL RESPONSE

*sharing impressions*

**1.** How do you feel about the love at first sight between Romeo and Juliet? Describe your reaction in your journal.

*constructing interpretations*

**2.** In your opinion, how might Juliet be changed by meeting Romeo?

### Think about
- her reaction when Lady Capulet tells her of Paris's proposal
- her response to Romeo at the party
- what the speech beginning "My only love, sprung from my only hate!" indicates about her understanding of the circumstances

**3.** Explain whether you think there are any differences between Romeo's old feelings for Rosaline and his new love for Juliet.

### Think about
- why he constantly talks about his lovesickness for Rosaline before meeting Juliet
- why he falls in love with each one
- how Rosaline and Juliet each respond to him

**4.** Under the circumstances, what actions do you think Romeo and Juliet can take now that they have fallen in love?

**5.** Which characters in Act One do you think are most motivated by love, and which are most motivated by hate? Explain your answer.

## A CREATIVE RESPONSE

**6.** If Romeo and Juliet had learned each other's identity before speaking to each other, how might their meeting have been different?

## A CRITICAL RESPONSE

**7.** How do the paradoxes uttered by Romeo and by Juliet reflect the dilemmas that those characters are caught in?

### Think about
- Romeo's descriptions of love in Scene 1
- Juliet's reaction after learning Romeo's identity

**8.** What effect does it have on you as a reader that Shakespeare reveals the ending of the play in the Prologue?

**9.** What conflicts in contemporary American society do you think are similar to the feud between the Montagues and the Capulets? Use specific details from the play to make the comparison.

# ACT TWO

## PROLOGUE

*[Enter Chorus.]*

**Chorus.** Now old desire¹ doth in his deathbed lie,
    And young affection gapes² to be his heir;
    That fair³ for which love groaned for and would die,
    With tender Juliet matched, is now not fair.
5    Now Romeo is beloved, and loves again,
    Alike⁴ bewitched by the charm of looks;
    But to his foe supposed he must complain,
    And she steal love's sweet bait from fearful hooks.
    Being held a foe, he may not have access
10    To breathe such vows as lovers use to swear,
    And she as much in love, her means much less
    To meet her new beloved anywhere;
    But passion lends them power, time means, to meet,
    Temp'ring extremities⁵ with extreme sweet.

                                    *[Exit.]*

**1. old desire:** Romeo's love for Rosaline.

**2. gapes:** longs.

**3. fair:** beautiful woman (Rosaline).

**4. alike:** both.

**5. temp'ring extremities:** moderating difficulties.

## SCENE 1 *[A lane by the wall of Capulet's orchard.]*

*[Enter Romeo alone.]*

**Romeo.** Can I go forward when my heart is here?
    Turn back, dull earth,¹ and find thy center² out.

        *[Climbs the wall and leaps down within it.]*

*[Enter Benvolio with Mercutio.]*

**Benvolio.** Romeo! my cousin Romeo! Romeo!

**Mercutio.**                      He is wise,
    And, on my life, hath stol'n him home to bed.

5  **Benvolio.** He ran this way, and leapt this orchard wall.
    Call, good Mercutio.

**Mercutio.**              Nay, I'll conjure too.
    Romeo! humors! madman! passion! lover!
    Appear thou in the likeness of a sigh;
    Speak but one rhyme, and I am satisfied!
10    Cry but "Ay me!" pronounce but "love" and "dove";
    Speak to my gossip³ Venus one fair word,
    One nickname for her purblind⁴ son and heir,

**1. earth:** body.

**2. center:** center of the universe; that is, Juliet.

◆ **Lines 6-7:** Mercutio intends to lure Romeo to appear with talk of love just as the right magic words "conjure" a spirit.

**3. gossip:** crony, friend.

**4. purblind:** weak-sighted.

Young Adam Cupid, he that shot so trim[5]
When King Cophetua[6] loved the beggar maid!
15 He heareth not, he stirreth not, he moveth not;
The ape is dead, and I must conjure him.
I conjure thee by Rosaline's bright eyes,
By her high forehead and her scarlet lip,
By her fine foot, straight leg, and quivering thigh,
20 And the demesnes[7] that there adjacent lie,
That in thy likeness thou appear to us!

**Benvolio.** An if he hear thee, thou wilt anger him.

**Mercutio.** This cannot anger him. 'Twould anger him
To raise a spirit in his mistress' circle
25 Of some strange nature, letting it there stand
Till she had laid it and conjured it down.
That were some spite; my invocation
Is fair and honest[8] and in his mistress' name
I conjure only but to raise up him.

30 **Benvolio.** Come, he hath hid himself among these trees
To be consorted with the humorous night.
Blind is his love, and best befits the dark.

**Mercutio.** If love be blind, love cannot hit the mark.
Now will he sit under a medlar tree
35 And wish his mistress were that kind of fruit
As maids call medlars when they laugh alone.
Oh, Romeo, that she were, O, that she were
An open et cetera, thou a pop'rin pear!
Romeo, good night. I'll to my truckle bed;[9]
40 This field-bed is too cold for me to sleep.
Come, shall we go?

**Benvolio.**                    Go then, for 'tis in vain
To seek him here that means not to be found.

*[Exeunt.]*

**SCENE 2** *[Capulet's orchard.]*

*[Enter Romeo.]*

**Romeo.** He jests at scars that never felt a wound.

*[Enter Juliet above at a window.]*

But soft! What light through yonder window breaks?
It is the East, and Juliet is the sun!
Arise, fair sun, and kill the envious moon,

**5. trim:** accurately.

**6. King Cophetua:** the hero of a popular ballad.

◆ **Line 16:** Mercutio compares Romeo, who refuses to heed his call, to a trained ape who plays dead until his master gives the word.

**7. demesnes:** regions.

**8. fair and honest:** proper and honorable.

◆ **Lines 34-36:** A medlar was an apple-like fruit. This is a pun on the word *meddler,* one who interferes.

**9. truckle bed:** trundle bed, a small bed on casters, pushed under the great bed in the daytime.

◆ **Lines 3-41:** Mercutio's joking in this passage provides comic relief from the tension created at the end of Act One, when Romeo and Juliet each realize they have fallen in love with one of their enemies.

◆ **Line 1:** Romeo feels his friends are making jokes about his passion because they have not experienced the intensity of love.

5    Who is already sick and pale with grief
That thou her maid art far more fair than she.
Be not her maid, since she is envious;
Her vestal livery[1] is but sick and green,
And none but fools do wear it; cast it off.
10    It is my lady; O, it is my love!
O that she knew she were!
She speaks, yet she says nothing. What of that?
Her eye discourses;[2] I will answer it.
I am too bold; 'tis not to me she speaks.
15    Two of the fairest stars in all the heaven,
Having some business, do entreat her eyes
To twinkle in their spheres till they return.
What if her eyes were there, they in her head?
The brightness of her cheek would shame those stars
20    As daylight doth a lamp; her eyes in heaven
Would through the airy region stream so bright
That birds would sing and think it were not night.
See how she leans her cheek upon her hand!
O that I were a glove upon that hand,
25    That I might touch that cheek!

**Juliet.**                         Ay me!

**Romeo.**                     She speaks.
O, speak again, bright angel! for thou art
As glorious to this night, being o'er my head,
As is a winged messenger of heaven
Unto the white-upturned wond'ring eyes
30    Of mortals that fall back to gaze on him
When he bestrides the lazy-pacing clouds
And sails upon the bosom of the air.

**Juliet.** O Romeo, Romeo! wherefore[3] art thou Romeo?
Deny thy father and refuse thy name!
35    Or, if thou wilt not, be but sworn my love,
And I'll no longer be a Capulet.

**Romeo.** *[Aside]* Shall I hear more, or shall I speak at this?

**Juliet.** 'Tis but thy name that is my enemy.
Thou art thyself, though not[4] a Montague.
40    What's Montague? It is nor hand, nor foot,
Nor arm, nor face, nor any other part
Belonging to a man. O, be some other name!
What's in a name? That which we call a rose
By any other name would smell as sweet.

---

♦ **Lines 3-6:** Note that Romeo compares Juliet to the sun. Remember that Romeo earlier had compared Rosaline to Diana, goddess of the moon.

**1. vestal livery:** maiden's dress.

**2. discourses:** speaks.

♦ **Lines 15-22:** Romeo compares Juliet's eyes to two bright stars that could light up the sky and transform night into day. If the stars were in place of her eyes, Romeo says, the brightness of her complexion would make them look dull.

♦ **Lines 26-32:** Notice the simile comparing Juliet's radiance as Romeo looks up at her to that of an angel in the eyes of mortals.

**3. wherefore:** why.

♦ **Lines 33-36:** Juliet is lamenting that the man she loves is a Montague, a name she is supposed to hate.

**4. though not:** even if you were not.

45 So Romeo would, were he not Romeo called,
Retain that dear perfection which he owes[5]
Without that title. Romeo, doff thy name;
And for that name, which is no part of thee,
Take all myself.

**Romeo.**            I take thee at thy word.
50 Call me but love, and I'll be new baptized;
Henceforth I never will be Romeo.

**Juliet.** What man art thou that, thus bescreened in night,
So stumblest on my counsel?[6]

**Romeo.**                By a name
I know not how to tell thee who I am.
55 My name, dear saint, is hateful to myself,
Because it is an enemy to thee.
Had I it written, I would tear the word.

**Juliet.** My ears have yet not drunk a hundred words
Of that tongue's utterance, yet I know the sound.
60 Art thou not Romeo, and a Montague?

**Romeo.** Neither, fair saint, if either thee dislike.

**Juliet.** How camest thou hither, tell me, and wherefore?
The orchard walls are high and hard to climb,
And the place death, considering who thou art,
65 If any of my kinsmen find thee here.

**Romeo.** With love's light wings did I o'erperch[7] these
walls;
For stony limits cannot hold love out,
And what love can do, that dares love attempt.
Therefore thy kinsmen are no let[8] to me.

70 **Juliet.** If they do see thee, they will murder thee.

**Romeo.** Alack, there lies more peril in thine eye
Than twenty of their swords! Look thou but sweet,
And I am proof[9] against their enmity.[10]

**Juliet.** I would not for the world they saw thee here.

75 **Romeo.** I have night's cloak to hide me from their sight;
And but[11] thou love me, let them find me here.
My life were better ended by their hate
Than death prorogued,[12] wanting of thy love.

**Juliet.** By whose direction foundst thou out this place?

**5. owes:** owns.

**6. counsel:** private thoughts.

◆ **Lines 49-53:** Romeo startles Juliet by revealing his presence to her.

**7. o'erperch:** climb over.

**8. let:** hindrance.

**9. proof:** armored.
**10. enmity** (en' mə tē): the bitter attitude or feelings of an enemy.

**11. and but:** unless.
◆ **Line 76:** If Juliet does not love him, Romeo prefers to have her kinsmen discover him and put an end to his misery.
**12. prorogued:** postponed.

80 **Romeo.** By love, that first did prompt me to enquire.
He lent me counsel, and I lent him eyes.
I am no pilot, yet, wert thou as far
As that vast shore washed with the farthest sea,
I would adventure for such merchandise.

85 **Juliet.** Thou knowest the mask of night is on my face;
Else would a maiden blush bepaint my cheek
For that which thou hast heard me speak tonight.
Fain would I dwell on form[13]—fain, fain deny
What I have spoke; but farewell compliment![14]
90 Dost thou love me? I know thou wilt say "Ay";
And I will take thy word. Yet, if thou swearst,
Thou mayst prove false. At lovers' perjuries,
They say Jove[15] laughs. O gentle Romeo,
If thou dost love, pronounce it faithfully.
95 Or if thou thinkst I am too quickly won,
I'll frown, and be perverse, and say thee nay,
So thou wilt woo; but else, not for the world.
In truth, fair Montague, I am too fond,[16]
And therefore thou mayst think my 'havior light;[17]
100 But trust me, gentleman, I'll prove more true
Than those that have more cunning to be strange.[18]
I should have been more strange, I must confess,
But that thou overheardst, ere I was ware,
My true love's passion. Therefore pardon me,
105 And not impute this yielding to light love,
Which the dark night hath so discovered.[19]

**Romeo.** Lady, by yonder blessed moon I swear,
That tips with silver all these fruit-tree tops—

**Juliet.** O, swear not by the moon, the inconstant moon,
110 That monthly changes in her circled orb,[20]
Lest that thy love prove likewise variable.

**Romeo.** What shall I swear by?

**Juliet.** Do not swear at all;
Or if thou wilt, swear by thy gracious self,
Which is the god of my idolatry,
115 And I'll believe thee.

**Romeo.** If my heart's dear love—

**Juliet.** Well, do not swear. Although I joy in thee,
I have no joy of this contract[21] tonight.
It is too rash, too unadvised,[22] too sudden;

---

**13. Fain . . . form:** Gladly would I behave according to convention.

**14. compliment:** polite behavior.

◆ **Lines 85-89:** Juliet is embarrassed that Romeo has overheard her because it was considered improper for a woman to declare her feelings before the man declared his. However, she decides to disregard such rules of behavior ("farewell compliment").

**15. Jove:** in classical mythology, ruler of the gods and humans.

**16. fond:** foolishly affectionate.

**17. light:** improper.

**18. strange:** cold, distant.

**19. discovered:** revealed.

**20. orb:** orbit.

**21. contract:** vow of love.

**22. unadvised:** heedless.

◆ **Lines 117-120:** Juliet compares their sudden love to lightning that quickly disappears. She is worried that their passion is growing too quickly.

120　Too like the lightning, which doth cease to be
　　Ere one can say "It lightens." Sweet, good night!
　　This bud of love, by summer's ripening breath,
　　May prove a beauteous flow'r when next we meet.
　　Good night, good night! As sweet repose and rest
　　Come to thy heart as that within my breast!

125　**Romeo.** O, wilt thou leave me so unsatisfied?

**Juliet.** What satisfaction canst thou have tonight?

**Romeo.** The exchange of thy love's faithful vow for
　　mine.

**Juliet.** I gave thee mine before thou didst request it;
　　And yet I would it were to give again.

130　**Romeo.** Wouldst thou withdraw it? For what purpose,
　　love?

**Juliet.** But to be frank[23] and give it thee again.
　　And yet I wish but for the thing I have.
　　My bounty is as boundless as the sea,
　　My love as deep; the more I give to thee,
135　The more I have, for both are infinite.
　　I hear some noise within. Dear love, adieu!

　　　　　　　　　　　　　　　[Nurse *calls within.*]

Anon,[24] good nurse! Sweet Montague, be true.
Stay but a little, I will come again.

　　　　　　　　　　　　　　　　　　　[*Exit.*]

**Romeo.** O blessed, blessed night! I am afeard,
140　Being in night, all this is but a dream,
　　Too flattering-sweet to be substantial.[25]

[*Re-enter* Juliet, *above.*]

**Juliet.** Three words, dear Romeo, and good night indeed.
　　If that thy bent of love[26] be honorable,
　　Thy purpose marriage, send me word tomorrow,
145　By one that I'll procure[27] to come to thee,
　　Where and what time thou wilt perform the rite;
　　And all my fortunes at thy foot I'll lay
　　And follow thee my lord throughout the world.

**Nurse.** [*Within*] Madam!

150　**Juliet.** I come, anon.—But if thou meanst not well,

**23. frank:** generous.

◆ **Lines 133-135:** In this paradox Juliet says that the more love she gives to Romeo, the more she has to give. Think about what this paradox conveys about Juliet's love for Romeo, and about the nature of love itself.

**24. anon:** in a minute.

**25. substantial:** real.

**26. thy bent of love:** the intention of your love.

**27. procure:** provide.

Act Two, Scene 2  561

I do beseech thee—

**Nurse.** *[Within]*        Madam!

**Juliet.**                                By-and-by²⁸ I come.—
To cease thy suit and leave me to my grief.
Tomorrow will I send.

**Romeo.**                        So thrive my soul—

**Juliet.** A thousand times good night!

*[Exit.]*

155  **Romeo.** A thousand times the worse, to want thy light!
Love goes toward love as schoolboys from their books;
But love from love, towards school with heavy looks.

*[Enter* Juliet *again, above.]*

**Juliet.** Hist! Romeo, hist! O for a falc'ner's voice
To lure this tassel-gentle²⁹ back again!
160  Bondage is hoarse and may not speak aloud;
Else would I tear the cave where Echo³⁰ lies,
And make her airy tongue more hoarse than mine
With repetition of my Romeo's name.
Romeo!

165  **Romeo.** It is my soul that calls upon my name.
How silver-sweet sound lovers' tongues by night,
Like softest music to attending ears!

**Juliet.** Romeo!

**Romeo.**        My sweet?

**Juliet.**                        What o'clock tomorrow
Shall I send to thee?

**Romeo.**                        By the hour of nine.

170  **Juliet.** I will not fail. 'Tis twenty years till then.
I have forgot why I did call thee back.

**Romeo.** Let me stand here till thou remember it.

**Juliet.** I shall forget, to have thee still stand there,
Rememb'ring how I love thy company.

175  **Romeo.** And I'll still stay, to have thee still forget,
Forgetting any other home but this.

**Juliet.** 'Tis almost morning. I would have thee gone—

**28. by-and-by:** at once.

◆ **Lines 143-152:** Juliet asks that Romeo arrange to marry her or cease his wooing of her.

◆ **Lines 156-157:** In this simile, Romeo compares the eagerness of lovers to be with each other to the eagerness with which students flee from schoolwork, and the sorrow of lovers parting to the reluctance of students to go to school.

**29. tassel-gentle:** male falcon.

**30. Echo:** a nymph who pined away for the man she loved until only her voice was left.

◆ **Lines 160-163:** Being under the control of her parents ("bondage"), Juliet must be careful not to be overheard when she calls Romeo back to her.

◆ **Lines 171-176:** Notice the playing with the words *forget* and *remember* in these lines. This light banter between Romeo and Juliet captures the delight the lovers feel.

And yet no farther than a wanton's[31] bird,
That lets it hop a little from her hand,
180 Like a poor prisoner in his twisted gyves,[32]
And with a silk thread plucks it back again,
So loving-jealous of his liberty.

**Romeo.** I would I were thy bird.

**Juliet.**                              Sweet, so would I.
Yet I should kill thee with much cherishing.
185 Good night, good night! Parting is such sweet sorrow,
That I shall say good night till it be morrow.

                                                    [Exit.]

**Romeo.** Sleep dwell upon thine eyes, peace in thy breast!
Would I were sleep and peace, so sweet to rest!
Hence will I to my ghostly father's[33] cell,
190 His help to crave and my dear hap[34] to tell.

                                                    [Exit.]

SCENE 3 [Friar Laurence's cell.]

[Enter Friar Laurence alone, with a basket.]

**Friar Laurence.** The grey-eyed morn smiles on the
     frowning night,
Chequ'ring the Eastern clouds with streaks of light;
And flecked darkness like a drunkard reels
From forth day's path and Titan's[1] fiery wheels.
5 Now, ere the sun advance his burning eye
The day to cheer and night's dank dew to dry,
I must upfill this osier cage[2] of ours
With baleful[3] weeds and precious-juiced flowers.
The earth that's nature's mother is her tomb,
10 What is her burying grave, that is her womb;
And from her womb children of divers kind
We sucking on her natural bosom find;
Many for many virtues excellent,
None but for some, and yet all different.
15 O, mickle[4] is the powerful grace[5] that lies
In plants, herbs, stones, and their true qualities;
For naught so vile that on the earth doth live
But to the earth some special good doth give;
Nor aught so good but, strained[6] from that fair use,
20 Revolts from true birth,[7] stumbling on abuse.
Virtue itself turns vice, being misapplied,

**31. wanton's:** spoiled child's.

**32. gyves** (jīvs)**:** chains.

**33. ghostly father's cell:** the small room belonging to Romeo's spiritual advisor, Friar Laurence.

**34. dear hap:** great good fortune.

◆ **Lines 1-6:** Friar Laurence begins his soliloquy by describing what the sky looks like as night turns into day.

**1. Titan:** the sun god.

◆ **Lines 7-8:** Friar Laurence is an herbalist, one who knows which plants can be used for medicines and poisons.

**2. osier cage:** wicker basket.

**3. baleful:** poisonous.

**4. mickle:** great.

**5. grace:** goodness.

**6. strained:** turned aside.

**7. revolts from true birth:** is corrupted from its own special purpose.

And vice sometime's by action dignified.
Within the infant rind of this small flower
Poison hath residence, and medicine power;
25 For this, being smelt, with that part cheers each part;[8]
Being tasted, slays all senses with the heart.[9]
Two such opposed kings encamp them still
In man as well as herbs—grace and rude will;[10]
And where the worser is predominant,
30 Full soon the canker[11] death eats up that plant.

[*Enter* Romeo.]

**Romeo.** Good morrow, father.

**Friar Laurence.** Benedicite![12]
What early tongue so sweet saluteth me?
Young son, it argues a distempered[13] head
So soon to bid good morrow to thy bed.
35 Care keeps his watch in every old man's eye,
And where care lodges sleep will never lie;
But where unbruised youth with unstuffed brain
Doth couch his limbs, there golden sleep doth reign.
Therefore thy earliness doth me assure
40 Thou art uproused with some distemp'rature;[14]
Or if not so, then here I hit it right—
Our Romeo hath not been in bed tonight.

**Romeo.** That last is true, the sweeter rest was mine.

**Friar Laurence.** God pardon sin! Wast thou with
Rosaline?

45 **Romeo.** With Rosaline, my ghostly father? No.
I have forgot that name, and that name's woe.

**Friar Laurence.** That's my good son! But where hast thou
been then?

**Romeo.** I'll tell thee ere thou ask it me again.
I have been feasting with mine enemy,
50 Where on a sudden one hath wounded me
That's by me wounded. Both our remedies
Within thy help and holy physic[15] lies.
I bear no hatred, blessed man, for, lo,
My intercession[16] likewise steads[17] my foe.

55 **Friar Laurence.** Be plain, good son, and homely in thy
drift.[18]
Riddling[19] confession finds but riddling shrift.[20]

♦ **Lines 15-30:** Friar Laurence likens the potential of plants both to heal and to kill to the mixture of good and evil in humans.

**8. that part cheers each part:** its odor refreshes all parts of the body.

**9. with the heart:** by stopping the heart.

**10. rude will:** desire for evil.

**11. canker:** cankerworm, which destroys plants.

**12. Benedicite:** Latin for "God bless you."

**13. distempered:** troubled.

**14. distemp'rature:** sickness.

♦ **Lines 49-51:** Note that Romeo uses a violent image of wounds and wounding to describe his and Juliet's falling in love.

**15. physic:** remedy.

**16. intercession:** plea.

**17. steads:** helps.

**18. Be plain . . . drift:** Tell your story in simple speech.

**19. riddling:** speaking in riddles.

**20. shrift:** forgiveness.

**Romeo.** Then plainly know my heart's dear love is set
    On the fair daughter of rich Capulet;
    As mine on hers, so hers is set on mine,
60    And all combined,[21] save what thou must combine
    By holy marriage. When, and where, and how
    We met, we wooed, and made exchange of vow,
    I'll tell thee as we pass; but this I pray,
    That thou consent to marry us today.

65  **Friar Laurence.** Holy Saint Francis! What a change is
      here!
    Is Rosaline, that thou didst love so dear,
    So soon forsaken? Young men's love then lies
    Not truly in their hearts, but in their eyes.
    Jesu Maria! What a deal of brine
70    Hath washed thy sallow cheeks for Rosaline!
    How much salt water thrown away in waste,
    To season love, that of it doth not taste![22]
    The sun not yet thy sighs from heaven clears,[23]
    Thy old groans ring yet in mine ancient ears.
75    Lo, here upon thy cheek the stain doth sit
    Of an old tear that is not washed off yet.
    If e'er thou wast thyself, and these woes thine,
    Thou and these woes were all for Rosaline.
    And art thou changed? Pronounce this sentence then:
80    Women may fall when there's no strength in men.

**Romeo.** Thou chidst[24] me oft for loving Rosaline.

**Friar Laurence.** For doting, not for loving, pupil mine.

**Romeo.** And badest me bury love.

**Friar Laurence.**                 Not in a grave
    To lay one in, another ought to have.

85  **Romeo.** I pray thee chide not. She whom I love now
    Doth grace for grace and love for love allow.
    The other did not so.

**Friar Laurence.**         O, she knew well
    Thy love did read by rote, that could not spell.
    But come, young waverer, come go with me.
90    In one respect I'll thy assistant be;
    For this alliance may so happy prove
    To turn your households' rancor to pure love.

**Romeo.** O, let us hence! I stand on[25] sudden haste.

---

**21. combined:** united spiritually.

**22. season . . . taste:** preserve love, that does not seem to have been affected by it.

**23. The sun . . . clears:** The heat of the sun has not yet cleared the air of Romeo's sighs over Rosaline.

◆ **Lines 65-79:** Friar Laurence questions the sincerity of Romeo's love for Juliet when he has so recently been grieving over Rosaline.

**24. chidst:** scolded.

◆ **Lines 85-87:** Note the important distinction that Romeo makes between Rosaline and Juliet.

◆ **Lines 90-92:** Friar Laurence agrees to marry Romeo and Juliet because he hopes the marriage will end the feud between the two families.

**25. stand on:** demand.

**Friar Laurence.** Wisely, and slow. They stumble that run fast.

*[Exeunt.]*

◆ **Line 94:** Note Friar Laurence's caution to slow down.

**SCENE 4** *[A street.]*

*[Enter Benvolio and Mercutio.]*

**Mercutio.** Where the devil should this Romeo be?
   Came he not home tonight?

**Benvolio.** Not to his father's. I spoke with his man.[1]

1. **man:** servant.

**Mercutio.** Why, that same pale hard-hearted wench, that Rosaline,
5   Torments him so that he will sure run mad.

**Benvolio.** Tybalt, the kinsman to old Capulet,
   Hath sent a letter to his father's house.

**Mercutio.** A challenge, on my life.

**Benvolio.** Romeo will answer it.

◆ **Lines 6-12:** Tybalt, the hot-headed nephew of Capulet, has sent a letter to Romeo challenging him to a duel. Benvolio believes Romeo will accept Tybalt's challenge.

10   **Mercutio.** Any man that can write may answer a letter.

**Benvolio.** Nay, he will answer the letter's master, how he dares, being dared.

2. **pin:** center of a target.

3. **butt-shaft:** unpointed arrow.

**Mercutio.** Alas, poor Romeo, he is already dead! stabbed with a white wench's black eye; shot through the ear
15   with a love song; the very pin[2] of his heart cleft with the blind bow-boy's butt-shaft;[3] and is he a man to encounter Tybalt?

4. **Prince of Cats:** In the medieval tale of Reynard the Fox, Tibert (whose name is similar to Tybalt's) is Prince of Cats.

**Benvolio.** Why, what is Tybalt?

5. **compliments:** fashionable behavior.

**Mercutio.** More than Prince of Cats,[4] I can tell you. O,
20   he's the courageous captain of compliments.[5] He fights as you sing pricksong[6]—keeps time, distance, and proportion; rests me his minim rest,[7] one, two, and the third in your bosom! the very butcher of a silk button, a duelist, a duelist! a gentleman of the very first house,[8] of
25   the first and second cause.[9] Ah, the immortal *passado!* the *punto reverso!* the *hay!*[10]

6. **as you sing pricksong:** by following sheet music; in other words, by following strict form.

7. **minim rest:** the shortest pause in music.

8. **of the very first house:** of the finest school of fencing; expert.

9. **cause:** cause for dueling.

**Benvolio.** The what?

10. *passado . . . hay:* dueling terms.

**Mercutio.** The pox of such antic, lisping, affecting fantasticoes[11]—these new tuners of accent! "By Jesu, a
30   very good blade! a very tall[12] man! a very good whore!"

11. **fantasticoes:** fantastical fellows, dandies.

12. **tall:** brave.

Why, is not this a lamentable thing, grandsire, that we should be thus afflicted with these strange flies, these fashion-mongers, these perdona-mi's,[13] who stand so much on the new form that they cannot sit at ease on
35  the old bench? O, their bones, their bones![14]

*[Enter* Romeo, *no longer moody.]*

**Benvolio.** Here comes Romeo! here comes Romeo!

**Mercutio.** Without his roe, like a dried herring. O, flesh, flesh, how art thou fishified! Now is he for the numbers[15] that Petrarch flowed in. Laura,[16] to his lady,
40  was but a kitchen wench (marry, she had a better love to berhyme her) Dido a dowdy, Cleopatra a gypsy, Helen and Hero hildings[17] and harlots, Thisbe a grey eye or so, but not to the purpose. Signior Romeo, *bon jour!* There's a French salutation to your French slop.[18] You
45  gave us the counterfeit[19] fairly last night.

**Romeo.** Good morrow to you both. What counterfeit did I give you?

**Mercutio.** The slip, sir, the slip. Can you not conceive?[20]

**Romeo.** Pardon, good Mercutio. My business was great,
50  and in such a case as mine a man may strain courtesy.

**Mercutio.** That's as much as to say, such a case as yours constrains a man to bow in the hams.

**Romeo.** Meaning, to curtsy.

**Mercutio.** Thou hast most kindly hit it.

55  **Romeo.** A most courteous exposition.

**Mercutio.** Nay, I am the very pink of courtesy.[21]

**Romeo.** Pink for flower.

**Mercutio.** Right.

**Romeo.** Why, then is my pump well-flowered.[22]

60  **Mercutio.** Well said! Follow me this jest now till thou hast worn out thy pump, that, when the single sole of it is worn, the jest may remain, after the wearing, solely singular.

**Romeo.** Oh, single-soled[23] jest, solely singular for the
65  singleness![24]

---

♦ **Lines 19-35:** Mercutio gets carried away in making fun of Tybalt's following of proper fencing form and etiquette. Mercutio regards Tybalt as a dandy.

**13. perdona-mi's:** fellows of affected manners, who use foreign phrases to appear sophisticated.

**14. bones:** a pun on the French *bon,* "good."

**15. numbers:** verses.

**16. Laura:** Petrarch's beloved, for whom he wrote his sonnets.

**17. hildings:** good-for-nothings.

**18. French slop:** baggy breeches.

**19. counterfeit:** a piece of counterfeit money was called a slip.

**20. conceive:** understand.

♦ **Lines 55-85:** Romeo and Mercutio match wits in these lines.

**21. very pink of courtesy:** the height of polite behavior.

**22. then is . . . flowered:** then my shoe is pinked—that is, perforated in a decorative floral pattern.

**23. single-soled:** feeble.
**24. solely . . . singleness:** in a class by itself for silliness.

**Mercutio.** Come between us, good Benvolio! My wits faint.

**Romeo.** Switch and spurs,[25] switch and spurs! or I'll cry a match.[26]

70 **Mercutio.** Nay, if our wits run the wild-goose chase,[27] I am done; for thou hast more of the wild goose in one of thy wits than, I am sure, I have in my whole five. Was I with you there for the goose?[28]

**Romeo.** Thou wast never with me for anything when 75 thou wast not there for the goose.

**Mercutio.** I will bite thee by the ear for that jest.

**Romeo.** Nay, good goose, bite not!

**Mercutio.** Thy wit is a very bitter sweeting; it is a most sharp sauce.

80 **Romeo.** And is it not, then, well served in to a sweet goose?

**Mercutio.** O, here's a wit of cheveril,[29] that stretches from an inch narrow to an ell[30] broad!

**Romeo.** I stretch it out for that word "broad," which, 85 added to the goose, proves thee far and wide a broad goose.

**Mercutio.** Why, is not this better now than groaning for love? Now art thou sociable, now art thou Romeo; now art thou what thou art, by art as well as by nature. For this driveling love is like a great natural[31] that runs lolling up and down to hide his bauble[32] in a hole.

90 **Benvolio.** Stop there, stop there!

**Mercutio.** Thou desirest me to stop in my tale against the hair.[33]

**Benvolio.** Thou wouldst else have made thy tale large.[34]

95 **Mercutio.** O, thou art deceived! I would have made it short; for I was come to the whole depth of my tale, and meant indeed to occupy the argument no longer.

*[Enter Nurse and Peter, her servant. He is carrying a large fan.]*

**Romeo.** Here's goodly gear![35]

**25. switch and spurs:** keep up the pace (at full gallop).
**26. cry a match:** claim the victory.
**27. wild-goose chase:** a follow-the-leader race on horseback.
**28. Was . . . goose:** Did I score off you with the word *goose*?

**29. cheveril:** kid leather.
**30. ell:** forty-five inches.

♦ **Lines 86-90:** Mercutio is glad that Romeo seems to be lighthearted and sharp-witted again. He assumes that Romeo is no longer in love.
**31. natural:** fool.
**32. bauble:** the stick, ornamented with a doll's head, that was carried by a court jester or "natural."
**33. against the hair:** against the natural direction of the hair; that is, against my wish.
**34. large:** improper.

**35. goodly gear:** handsome stuff (joking).

**Mercutio.** A sail, a sail!

**Benvolio.** Two, two! a shirt and a smock.[36]

**Nurse.** Peter!

**Peter.** Anon.

**Nurse.** My fan, Peter.

**Mercutio.** Good Peter, to hide her face; for her fan's the fairer of the two.

**Nurse.** God ye good morrow, gentlemen.

**Mercutio.** God ye good-den,[37] fair gentlewoman.

**Nurse.** Is it good-den?

**Mercutio.** 'Tis no less, I tell ye, for the bawdy hand of the dial is now upon the prick of noon.

**Nurse.** Out upon you! What a man are you!

**Romeo.** One, gentlewoman, that God hath made himself to mar.

**Nurse.** By my troth, it is well said. "For himself to mar," quoth'a? Gentlemen, can any of you tell me where I may find the young Romeo?

**Romeo.** I can tell you; but young Romeo will be older when you have found him than he was when you sought him. I am the youngest of that name, for fault[38] of a worse.

**Nurse.** You say well.

**Mercutio.** Yea, is the worst well? Very well took,[39] i' faith! wisely, wisely.

**Nurse.** If you be he, sir, I desire some confidence with you.

**Benvolio.** She will endite him to some supper.

**Mercutio.** A bawd, a bawd, a bawd! So ho![40]

**Romeo.** What hast thou found?

**Mercutio.** No hare,[41] sir; unless a hare, sir, in a lenten pie, that is something stale and hoar[42] ere it be spent.

*[Sings.]*

100

105

110

115

120

125

**36. a shirt and a smock:** a man and a woman.

**37. God ye good-den:** Good afternoon.

**38. fault:** lack.

**39. took:** understood.

◆ **Lines 124-125:** The nurse says *confidence* but means *conference.* Benvolio mocks her by using the word *endite* rather than *invite.*

**40. So ho:** a hunter's cry when sighting a hare.

**41. hare:** slang for prostitute.

**42. hoar:** moldy.

130                "An old hare hoar,
                   And an old hare hoar,
                   Is very good meat in Lent;
                   But a hare that is hoar
                   Is too much for a score
135                  When it hoars ere it be spent."
Romeo, will you come to your father's? We'll to dinner thither.

**Romeo.** I will follow you.

**Mercutio.** Farewell, ancient lady. Farewell, [*sings*] lady,
140    lady, lady.

                        [*Exeunt* Mercutio *and* Benvolio.]

**Nurse.** Marry, farewell! I pray you, sir, what saucy merchant was this that was so full of his ropery?[43]

**Romeo.** A gentleman, nurse, that loves to hear himself talk and will speak more in a minute than he will stand
145    to in a month.

**Nurse.** An 'a speak anything against me, I'll take him down, an 'a were lustier than he is, and twenty such Jacks;[44] and if I cannot, I'll find those that shall. Scurvy[45] knave! I am none of his flirt-gills;[46] I am none
150    of his skainsmates.[47] [*Turning to* Peter.] And thou must stand by too, and suffer every knave to use me at his pleasure!

**Peter.** I saw no man use you at his pleasure. If I had, my weapon should quickly have been out, I warrant you. I
155    dare draw as soon as another man, if I see occasion in a good quarrel, and the law on my side.

**Nurse.** Now, afore God, I am so vexed that every part about me quivers. Scurvy knave! Pray you, sir, a word; and as I told you, my young lady bade me enquire you
160    out. What she bid me say, I will keep to myself; but first let me tell ye, if ye should lead her into a fool's paradise, as they say, it were a very gross kind of behavior, as they say; for the gentlewoman is young; and therefore, if you should deal double with her, truly it were an ill thing to
165    be offered to any gentlewoman, and very weak dealing.

**Romeo.** Nurse, commend me[48] to thy lady and mistress. I protest[49] unto thee—

◆ **Lines 126-142:** Mercutio mocks the nurse by implying that she is a woman of loose morals. The nurse manages to maintain her dignity, but her outrage erupts after Mercutio leaves.

**43. ropery:** nurse's mistake for *roguery,* "the talk and behavior of a scoundrel."

**44. Jacks:** rascals.
**45. scurvy:** contemptible.
**46. flirt-gills:** loose women.
**47. skainsmates:** gangsters.

**48. commend me:** give my respectful greetings.
**49. protest:** declare.

**Nurse.** Good heart, and i' faith I will tell her as much. Lord, Lord! she will be a joyful woman.

170 **Romeo.** What wilt thou tell her, nurse? Thou dost not mark[50] me.

**Nurse.** I will tell her, sir, that you do protest, which, as I take it, is a gentlemanlike offer.

**Romeo.** Bid her devise
175 Some means to come to shrift[51] this afternoon;
And there she shall at Friar Laurence' cell
Be shrived[52] and married. Here is for thy pains.

**51. shrift:** confession.

**52. shrived:** forgiven of sins.

**Nurse.** No, truly, sir; not a penny.

**Romeo.** Go to![53] I say you shall.

**53. Go to:** Say no more.

180 **Nurse.** This afternoon, sir? Well, she shall be there.

**Romeo.** And stay, good nurse, behind the abbey wall.
Within this hour my man shall be with thee
And bring thee cords made like a tackled stair,[54]
Which to the high topgallant[55] of my joy
185 Must be my convoy in the secret night.
Farewell. Be trusty, and I'll quit[56] thy pains.
Farewell. Commend me to thy mistress.

**54. tackled stair:** rope ladder.
**55. topgallant:** topmost.
**56. quit:** reward.

**Nurse.** Now God in heaven bless thee! Hark you, sir.

**Romeo.** What sayst thou, my dear nurse?

190 **Nurse.** Is your man secret? Did you ne'er hear say,
Two may keep counsel, putting one away?[57]

**57. Two . . . away:** Two can keep a secret if only one of them knows it.

**Romeo.** I warrant thee my man's as true as steel.

**Nurse.** Well, sir, my mistress is the sweetest lady. Lord, Lord! when 'twas a little prating thing—O, there is a
195 nobleman in town, one Paris, that would fain lay knife aboard;[58] but she, good soul, had as lief see a toad, a very toad, as see him. I anger her sometimes, and tell her that Paris is the properer[59] man; but I'll warrant you, when I say so, she looks as pale as any clout[60] in the versal
200 world.[61] Doth not rosemary and Romeo begin both with a letter?

**58. would fain . . . aboard:** is eager to get her for himself.
**59. properer:** more handsome.
**60. clout:** cloth.
**61. versal world** universe.

**Romeo.** Ay, nurse, what of that? Both with an R.

◆ **Line 203:** The letter R was called the dog's letter because it sounds like the growling of a dog.

**Nurse.** Ah, mocker! that's the dog's name. R is for the—No; I know it begins with some other letter; and

205　she hath the prettiest sententious[62] of it, of you and
　　rosemary, that it would do you good to hear it.

**Romeo.** Commend me to thy lady.

**Nurse.** Ay, a thousand times. [*Exit* Romeo.] Peter!

**Peter.** Anon.

210　**Nurse.** Peter, take my fan, and go before, and apace.[63]

　　　　　　　　　　　　　　　　　　　　[*Exeunt.*]

**SCENE 5** [*Capulet's orchard.*]

[*Enter* Juliet.]

**Juliet.** The clock struck nine when I did send the nurse;
　　In half an hour she promised to return.
　　Perchance she cannot meet him. That's not so.
　　O, she is lame! Love's heralds should be thoughts,
5　Which ten times faster glide than the sun's beams
　　Driving back shadows over lowering hills.
　　Therefore do nimble-pinioned doves draw Love,
　　And therefore hath the wind-swift Cupid wings.
　　Now is the sun upon the highmost hill
10　Of this day's journey, and from nine till twelve
　　Is three long hours; yet she is not come.
　　Had she affections and warm youthful blood,
　　She would be as swift in motion as a ball;
　　My words would bandy[1] her to my sweet love,
15　And his to me.
　　But old folks, many <u>feign</u>[2] as they were dead—
　　Unwieldy, slow, heavy, and pale as lead.

[*Enter* Nurse *and* Peter.]

　　O God, she comes! O honey nurse, what news?
　　Hast thou met with him? Send thy man away.

20　**Nurse.** Peter, stay at the gate.

　　　　　　　　　　　　　　　　　　　　[*Exit* Peter.]

**Juliet.** Now, good sweet nurse—O Lord, why lookst thou
　　sad?
　　Though news be sad, yet tell them merrily;
　　If good, thou shamest the music of sweet news
　　By playing it to me with so sour a face.

25　**Nurse.** I am aweary, give me leave[3] awhile.

**62. sententious:** nurse's mistake for *sentence,* which also means "proverb."

**63. apace:** quickly.

◆ **Line 7:** Venus, the goddess of love, rode in a chariot drawn by swift-winged doves.

**1. bandy:** hit back.

**2. feign** (fān): pretend or act.

◆ **Lines 1-17:** In this soliloquy, Juliet describes her impatience while waiting for the slow-footed nurse, who has been gone three hours. Juliet contrasts the slowness and heaviness of "old folks" with her own "affections and warm youthful blood."

**3. give me leave:** let me alone.

Fie, how my bones ache! What a jaunce[4] have I had!

**Juliet.** I would thou hadst my bones, and I thy news.
Nay, come, I pray thee speak. Good, good nurse, speak.

**Nurse.** Jesu, what haste! Can you not stay awhile?
30    Do you not see that I am out of breath?

**Juliet.** How art thou out of breath when thou hast breath
To say to me that thou art out of breath?
The excuse that thou dost make in this delay
Is longer than the tale thou dost excuse.
35    Is thy news good or bad? Answer to that.
Say either, and I'll stay the circumstance.[5]
Let me be satisfied, is't good or bad?

**Nurse.** Well, you have made a simple[6] choice; you know
not how to choose a man. Romeo? No, not he. Though
40    his face be better than any man's, yet his leg excels all
men's; and for a hand and a foot, and a body, though
they be not to be talked on, yet they are past compare.
He is not the flower of courtesy, but, I'll warrant him, as
gentle as a lamb. Go thy ways, wench; serve God. What,
have you dined at home?

45  **Juliet.** No, no. But all this did I know before.
What say he of our marriage? What of that?

**Nurse.** Lord, how my head aches! What a head have I!
It beats as it would fall in twenty pieces.
My back o' t'other side—ah, my back, my back!
50    Beshrew[7] your heart for sending me about
To catch my death with jauncing up and down!

**Juliet.** I' faith, I am sorry that thou art not well.
Sweet, sweet, sweet nurse, tell me, what says my love?

**Nurse.** Your love says, like an honest gentleman, and a
55    courteous, and a kind, and a handsome, and, I warrant, a
virtuous—Where is your mother?

**Juliet.** Where is my mother? Why, she is within.
Where should she be? How oddly thou repliest!
"Your love says, like an honest gentleman,
60    'Where is your mother?'"

**Nurse.**             O God's Lady dear!
Are you so hot?[8] Marry come up, I trow.[9]
Is this the poultice for my aching bones?

---

**4. jaunce:** running to and fro.

**5. stay the circumstance:** wait for details.

**6. simple:** foolish.

**7. beshrew:** a plague on.

◆ **Lines 38-56:** The nurse teases Juliet by deliberately holding back the news from Romeo. Her slowness provides a contrast to the fiery speed of the two lovers.

**8. hot:** impatient.
**9. Marry . . . trow:** Really, you are too impatient, I declare.

Henceforward do your messages yourself.

**Juliet.** Here's such a coil!¹⁰ Come, what says Romeo?

10. **coil:** fuss.

65 **Nurse.** Have you got leave to go to shrift today?

**Juliet.** I have.

**Nurse.** Then hie you hence to Friar Laurence' cell;
There stays a husband to make you a wife.
Now comes the wanton blood up in your cheeks:
70 They'll be in scarlet straight at any news.
Hie you to church; I must another way,
To fetch a ladder, by the which your love
Must climb a bird's nest soon when it is dark.
I am the drudge, and toil in your delight;
75 But you shall bear the burden soon at night.
Go; I'll to dinner; hie you to the cell.

**Juliet.** Hie to high fortune! Honest nurse, farewell.

*[Exeunt.]*

**SCENE 6** *[Friar Laurence's cell.]*

*[Enter Friar Laurence and Romeo.]*

**Friar Laurence.** So smile the heavens upon this holy act
That after-hours with sorrow chide us not!

**Romeo.** Amen, amen! But come what sorrow can,
It cannot countervail¹ the exchange of joy
5 That one short minute gives me in her sight.
Do thou but close our hands with holy words,
Then love-devouring death do what he dare—
It is enough I may but call her mine.

1. **countervail:** outweigh.

**Friar Laurence.** These violent delights have violent ends
10 And in their triumph die, like fire and powder,
Which, as they kiss, consume. The sweetest honey
Is loathsome in his own deliciousness
And in the taste confounds the appetite.
Therefore love moderately: long love doth so;
15 Too swift arrives as tardy as too slow.

*[Enter Juliet.]*

Here comes the lady. O, so light a foot
Will ne'er wear out the everlasting flint.²
A lover may bestride the gossamer³
That idles in the wanton summer air,

◆ **Lines 9-15:** Friar Laurence compares the intensity of Romeo's and Juliet's "violent" love to the destruction that results when fire and gunpowder combine. He also compares their love to honey, which is unpleasant if overindulged in. He advises Romeo that a reasonable love is better and longer-lasting than an extreme and hasty love. Consider whether you agree with the priest's advice.

2. **flint:** hard stone.
3. **gossamer:** cobweb.

20    And yet not fall; so light is vanity.[4]

**Juliet.** Good even to my ghostly confessor.

**Friar Laurence.** Romeo shall thank thee, daughter, for us
      both.

**Juliet.** As much[5] to him, else is his thanks too much.

**Romeo.** Ah, Juliet, if the measure of thy joy
25    Be heaped like mine, and that[6] thy skill be more
      To blazon[7] it, then sweeten with thy breath
      This neighbor air, and let rich music's tongue
      Unfold the imagined happiness that both
      Receive in either by this dear encounter.

30    **Juliet.** Conceit,[8] more rich in matter than in words,
      Brags of his substance, not of ornament.
      They are but beggars that can count their worth;
      But my true love is grown to such excess
      I cannot sum up sum of half my wealth.

35    **Friar Laurence.** Come, come with me, and we will make
            short work;
      For, by your leaves, you shall not stay alone
      Till Holy Church incorporate two in one.

                                        *[Exeunt.]*

4. **vanity:** the unreality of
love's illusions.

5. **as much:** the same
greeting.

6. **that:** if.
7. **blazon:** describe.

8. **conceit:** understanding

# Thinking About Act Two

## A PERSONAL RESPONSE

*sharing impressions*

**1.** Which character made the strongest impression on you in Act Two? In your journal, jot down words and phrases to describe that character.

*constructing interpretations*

**2.** Do you think that Romeo and Juliet get married too soon? Why or why not?

**Think about**
- how long they have known each other
- how they describe their feelings for each other in the balcony scene
- possible reasons why Juliet is the one to suggest marriage
- what might happen if their families discover that they have fallen in love

**3.** Evaluate whether Friar Laurence acts responsibly in performing the secret marriage.

**Think about**
- how young Romeo and Juliet are
- the friar's own caution to act "wisely, and slow"
- how realistic the friar's hope is that Romeo and Juliet's love will overcome their families' hate

**4.** Why do you think the nurse helps Juliet marry Romeo even though she knows the Capulets want Juliet to marry Paris?

**5.** Do you think Mercutio is a good friend to Romeo? Why or why not?

**Think about**
- Mercutio's attitude toward Romeo's interest in love
- why they talk to each other with puns and plays on words
- how Mercutio compares to Benvolio as Romeo's friend

## A CREATIVE RESPONSE

**6.** If Friar Laurence had acted differently—for instance, if he had informed both the Montagues and the Capulets about Romeo and Juliet—what do you think would have happened?

**7.** What do you think the soliloquies reveal about character that cannot be revealed by dialogue? Go back through the act and find specific soliloquies to illustrate your response.

**8.** How much do you think the relationship between Romeo and Juliet resembles modern love and courtship?

### Think about
- Juliet's feelings of embarrassment when Romeo overhears her declaration of love for him
- why they keep the relationship a secret from their parents
- their decision to get married immediately

**9.** Compare the joking among Romeo, Mercutio, and Benvolio to the way contemporary teens talk to one another. What similarities and differences do you find?

# ACT THREE

**SCENE 1** *[A public place.]*

*Guide for Interpretation*

*[Enter Mercutio, Benvolio, Page and Servants.]*

**Benvolio.** I pray thee, good Mercutio, let's retire.
The day is hot, the Capulets abroad,
And if we meet, we shall not scape a brawl,
For now, these hot days, is the mad blood stirring.

5 **Mercutio.** Thou art like one of those fellows that, when
he enters the confines of a tavern, claps me his sword
upon the table and says "God send me no need of thee!"
and by the operation of the second cup[1] draws him on
the drawer,[2] when indeed there is no need.

10 **Benvolio.** Am I like such a fellow?

**Mercutio.** Come, come, thou art as hot a Jack in thy
mood as any in Italy; and as soon moved to be moody,[3]
and as soon moody to be moved.[4]

**Benvolio.** And what to?

15 **Mercutio.** Nay an there were two such, we should have
none shortly, for one would kill the other. Thou! why,
thou wilt quarrel with a man that hath a hair more or a
hair less in his beard than thou hast. Thou wilt quarrel
with a man for cracking nuts, having no other reason
20 but because thou hast hazel eyes. What eye but such an
eye would spy out such a quarrel? Thy head is as full of
quarrels as an egg is full of meat; and yet thy head hath
been beaten as addle as an egg for quarreling. Thou hast
quarreled with a man for coughing in the street, because
25 he hath wakened thy dog that hath lain asleep in the
sun. Didst thou not fall out with a tailor for wearing his
new doublet[5] before Easter? with another for tying his
new shoes with old riband?[6] And yet thou wilt tutor me
from quarreling!

30 **Benvolio.** An I were so apt to quarrel as thou art, any
man should buy the fee simple[7] of my life for an hour
and a quarter.[8]

**Mercutio.** The fee simple? O simple!

*[Enter Tybalt and others.]*

---

**Lines 1–4:** Benvolio suggests that he and Mercutio go inside to avoid a fight with the Capulets, who are in the streets ("abroad").

**1. by the operation . . . cup:** as the second drink begins to affect him.

**2. drawer:** waiter.

**Lines 5–9:** Note the irony of Mercutio describing Benvolio, who is a peaceful person, as a tavern brawler.

**3. moved to be moody:** inclined to anger.

**4. moody to be moved:** quarrelsome.

**Line 15:** Mercutio pretends to misunderstand Benvolio's *to* in the preceding line.

**Lines 15–29:** Again being ironic, Mercutio teases Benvolio by giving examples to show that Benvolio is quick to start fights with people.

**5. doublet:** short, close-fitting jacket.

**6. riband:** ribbon.

**7. fee simple:** absolute ownership.

**8. an hour and a quarter:** the brief period of time that someone so ready to fight would remain alive.

**Benvolio.** By my head, here come the Capulets.

35 **Mercutio.** By my heel, I care not.

**Tybalt.** Follow me close, for I will speak to them.
Gentlemen, good den. A word with one of you.

**Mercutio.** And but one word with one of us?
Couple it with something; make it a word and a blow.

40 **Tybalt.** You shall find me apt enough to that, sir, an you
will give me occasion.[9]

**Mercutio.** Could you not take some occasion without
giving?

**Tybalt.** Mercutio, thou consortest[10] with Romeo.

45 **Mercutio.** Consort? What, dost thou make us minstrels?
An thou make minstrels of us, look to hear nothing but
discords. Here's my fiddlestick;[11] here's that shall make
you dance. Zounds,[12] consort!

**Benvolio.** We talk here in the public haunt of men.
50 Either withdraw unto some private place
And reason coldly of your grievances,
Or else depart. Here all eyes gaze on us.

**Mercutio.** Men's eyes were made to look, and let them
gaze. I will not budge for no man's pleasure, I.

[*Enter* Romeo.]

55 **Tybalt.** Well, peace be with you, sir. Here comes my
man.

**Mercutio.** But I'll be hanged, sir, if he wear your livery.[13]
Marry, go before to field,[14] he'll be your follower!
Your worship in that sense may call him man.

**Tybalt.** Romeo, the love I bear thee can afford
60 No better term than this: thou art a villain.[15]

**Romeo.** Tybalt, the reason that I have to love thee
Doth much excuse the appertaining rage[16]
To such a greeting. Villain am I none.
Therefore farewell. I see thou knowst me not.

65 **Tybalt.** Boy, this shall not excuse the injuries
That thou hast done me; therefore turn and draw.

**Romeo.** I do protest I never injured thee,

**9. occasion:** cause, reason.

**10. consortest:** are friendly with.

◆ **Lines 45-48:** A consort was a group of traveling musicians, or minstrels. Mercutio deliberately misunderstands Tybalt.

**11. fiddlestick:** sword.

**12. Zounds:** By God's wounds, an exclamation of anger.

◆ **Lines 49-52:** Mercutio and Benvolio are foils for each other. Mercutio antagonizes Tybalt, while Benvolio tries to placate both Mercutio and Tybalt by suggesting that they discuss their disagreement in private.

**13. livery:** servant's uniform.

◆ **Lines 55-56:** Mercutio takes the most insulting meaning of Tybalt's words by interpreting his use of *man* as "servant."

**14. field:** dueling place.

**15. villain:** a form of address to a servant.

**16. appertaining rage:** anger suitable.

◆ **Lines 61-64:** Romeo forgives Tybalt's insult. He realizes that Tybalt does not know they are kinsmen as a result of Romeo's marriage to Juliet.

But love thee better than thou canst devise
Till thou shalt know the reason of my love;
70 And so, good Capulet, which name I tender[17]
As dearly as mine own, be satisfied.

**Mercutio.**  O calm, dishonorable, vile submission!
*Alla stoccata*[18] carries it away.

[Draws.]

Tybalt, you ratcatcher, will you walk?[19]

75 **Tybalt.**  What wouldst thou have with me?

**Mercutio.**  Good King of Cats, nothing but one of your
nine lives. That I mean to make bold withal, and, as you
shall use me hereafter, dry-beat the rest of the eight.
Will you pluck your sword out of his pilcher[20] by the
80 ears?[21] Make haste, lest mine be about your ears ere it be
out.

**Tybalt.**  I am for you.

[Draws.]

**Romeo.**  Gentle Mercutio, put thy rapier up.

**Mercutio.**  Come, sir, your *passado!*

[They fight.]

85 **Romeo.**  Draw, Benvolio; beat down their weapons.
Gentlemen, for shame! forbear this outrage!
Tybalt, Mercutio, the Prince expressly hath
Forbid this bandying[22] in Verona streets.
Hold, Tybalt! Good Mercutio!

[Tybalt, *under* Romeo's *arm, thrusts* Mercutio *in, and flies
with his* Men.]

**Mercutio.**                                        I am hurt.
A plague o' both your houses! I am sped.[23]
90 Is he gone and hath nothing?

**Benvolio.**                        What, art thou hurt?

**Mercutio.**  Ay, ay, a scratch, a scratch. Marry, 'tis
enough.
Where is my page? Go, villain, fetch a surgeon.

[Exit Page.]

---

17. **tender:** cherish.

18. *alla stoccata:* a thrust in fencing.

◆ **Lines 72-74:** Mercutio, irritated at Romeo's calm response to Tybalt, challenges Tybalt to a fight.
19. **will you walk:** step aside with me.

20. **his pilcher:** its scabbard.
21. **ears:** hilt.

22. **bandying:** quarreling.

23. **sped:** done for.

**Romeo.** Courage, man. The hurt cannot be much.

95 **Mercutio.** No, 'tis not so deep as a well, nor so wide as a church door; but 'tis enough, 'twill serve. Ask for me tomorrow, and you shall find me a grave man. I am peppered,[24] I warrant, for this world. A plague o' both your houses! Zounds, a dog, a rat, a mouse, a cat, to
100 scratch a man to death! A braggart, a rogue, a villain, that fights by the book of arithmetic![25] Why the devil came you between us? I was hurt under your arm.

**Romeo.** I thought all for the best.

**Mercutio.** Help me into some house, Benvolio,
105 Or I shall faint. A plague o' both your houses! They have made worms' meat of me. I have it, And soundly too. Your houses!

*[Exit, supported by Benvolio.]*

**Romeo.** This gentleman, the Prince's near ally,[26]
My very friend, hath got this mortal hurt
110 In my behalf—my reputation stained With Tybalt's slander—Tybalt, that an hour Hath been my kinsman, O sweet Juliet, Thy beauty hath made me effeminate And in my temper softened valor's steel!

*[Re-enter Benvolio.]*

115 **Benvolio.** O Romeo, Romeo, brave Mercutio's dead! That gallant spirit hath aspired[27] the clouds, Which too untimely here did scorn the earth.

**Romeo.** This day's black fate on mo[28] days doth depend; This but begins the woe others must end.

*[Re-enter Tybalt.]*

120 **Benvolio.** Here comes the furious Tybalt back again.

**Romeo.** Alive in triumph, and Mercutio slain? Away to heaven respective lenity,[29] And fire-eyed fury be my conduct now! Now, Tybalt, take the "villain" back again
125 That late thou gavest me, for Mercutio's soul Is but a little way above our heads, Staying for thine to keep him company. Either thou or I, or both, must go with him.

**24. peppered:** completely destroyed.

**25. by the book of arithmetic:** by the textbook on fencing; by exact rules.

◆ **Lines 90-107:** Mercutio's wit and punning continue although he is mortally wounded. He curses both the Montagues and the Capulets. Think about how much Mercutio's injury is due to a web of circumstances and how much responsibility he bears for events.

**26. ally:** kinsman.

◆ **Lines 108-114:** Romeo believes that his love for Juliet has made him weak.

**27. aspired:** soared to.

**28. mo:** more.

◆ **Lines 118-119:** Romeo predicts that Mercutio's death will cost other lives.

**29. respective lenity:** considerate mercy.

◆ **Lines 124-128:** Notice the challenge Romeo directs at Tybalt: one or both of them will die unless Tybalt withdraws his insult of "villain."

**Tybalt.** Thou, wretched boy, that didst consort him here,
130    Shalt with him hence.

**Romeo.**                    This shall determine that.

*[They fight. Tybalt falls.]*

**Benvolio.** Romeo, away, be gone!
    The citizens are up, and Tybalt slain.
    Stand not amazed. The Prince will doom thee death
    If thou art taken. Hence, be gone, away!

135 **Romeo.** O, I am fortune's fool!

**Benvolio.**                    Why dost thou stay?

*[Exit Romeo.]*

*[Enter Citizens.]*

**Citizen.** Which way ran he that killed Mercutio?
    Tybalt, that murderer, which way ran he?

**Benvolio.** There lies that Tybalt.

**Citizen.**                    Up, sir, go with me.
    I charge thee in the Prince's name obey.

*[Enter Prince with his Attendants, Montague, Capulet, their Wives, and others.]*

140 **Prince.** Where are the vile beginners of this fray?

**Benvolio.** O noble Prince, I can discover[30] all
    The unlucky manage[31] of this fatal brawl.
    There lies the man, slain by young Romeo,
    That slew thy kinsman, brave Mercutio.

145 **Lady Capulet.** Tybalt, my cousin! O my brother's child!
    O Prince! O cousin! O husband! O, the blood is spilled
    Of my dear kinsman! Prince, as thou art true,
    For blood of ours shed blood of Montague.
    O cousin, cousin!

150 **Prince.** Benvolio, who began this bloody fray?

**Benvolio.** Tybalt, here slain, whom Romeo's hand did
        slay.
    Romeo, that spoke him fair, bid him bethink
    How nice[32] the quarrel was, and urged withal
    Your high displeasure. All this—uttered
155    With gentle breath, calm look, knees humbly bowed—

**30. discover:** reveal.
**31. manage:** circumstances.

◆ **Lines 151-174:** At the Prince's request, Benvolio recounts the events of the fight. Think about the accuracy of Benvolio's retelling.
**32. nice:** trivial.

Could not take truce with the unruly spleen[33]
Of Tybalt deaf to peace, but that he tilts
With piercing steel at bold Mercutio's breast;
Who, all as hot, turns deadly point to point,
160 And, with a martial scorn, with one hand beats
Cold death aside and with the other sends
It back to Tybalt, whose dexterity
Retorts[34] it. Romeo he cries aloud,
"Hold, friends! friends, part!" and swifter than his
        tongue,
165 His agile arm beats down their fatal points,
And 'twixt them rushes; underneath whose arm
An envious[35] thrust from Tybalt hit the life
Of stout Mercutio, and then Tybalt fled,
But by-and-by comes back to Romeo,
170 Who had but newly entertained revenge,
And to't they go like lightning; for, ere I
Could draw to part them, was stout[36] Tybalt slain;
And, as he fell, did Romeo turn and fly.
This is the truth, or let Benvolio die.

175 **Lady Capulet.** He is a kinsman to the Montague;
Affection makes him false, he speaks not true.
Some twenty of them fought in this black strife,
And all those twenty could but kill one life.
I beg for justice, which thou, Prince, must give.
180 Romeo slew Tybalt; Romeo must not live.

**Prince.** Romeo slew him; he slew Mercutio.
Who now the price of his dear blood doth owe?

**Montague.** Not Romeo, Prince; he was Mercutio's
        friend;
His fault concludes but what the law should end,
185 The life of Tybalt.

**Prince.**                And for that offense
Immediately we do exile him hence.
I have an interest in your hate's proceeding,
My blood for your rude brawls doth lie a-bleeding;
But I'll amerce[37] you with so strong a fine
190 That you shall all repent the loss of mine.
I will be deaf to pleading and excuses;
Nor tears nor prayers shall purchase out[38] abuses.
Therefore use none. Let Romeo hence in haste,
Else, when he is found, that hour is his last.

---

33. **spleen:** fiery temper.

34. **retorts:** returns.

35. **envious:** hateful.

36. **stout:** valiant.

◆ **Lines 183-185:** Lord Montague claims that Romeo is guilty only of avenging Mercutio's death, which the law would have done anyway.

37. **amerce:** punish.
38. **purchase out:** pay for.

◆ **Lines 193-194:** The Prince banishes Romeo from Verona. If Romeo is ever found in that city, he will be killed.

195 Bear hence this body, and attend our will.
  Mercy but murders, pardoning those that kill.

             *[Exeunt.]*

## SCENE 2 *[Capulet's orchard.]*

*[Enter* Juliet *alone.]*

**Juliet.** Gallop apace, you fiery-footed steeds,
  Toward Phoebus'[1] lodging! Such a wagoner
  As Phaëton[2] would whip you to the West,
  And bring in cloudy night immediately.
5 Spread thy close curtain, love-performing night,
  That runaways' eyes may wink, and Romeo
  Leap to these arms, untalked of and unseen.
  Lovers can see to do their amorous rites
  By their own beauties; or, if love be blind,
10 It best agrees with night. Come, civil[3] night,
  Thou sober-suited matron, all in black,
  And learn me how to lose a winning match,
  Played for a pair of stainless maidenhoods.
  Hood my unmanned[4] blood bating[5] in my cheeks.
15 With thy black mantle; till strange[6] love, grown bold,
  Think true love acted simple modesty.[7]
  Come, night; come, Romeo; come, thou day in night;
  For thou wilt lie upon the wings of night
  Whiter than new snow on a raven's back.
20 Come, gentle night; come, loving, black-browed night;
  Give me my Romeo; and, when he shall die,
  Take him and cut him out in little stars,
  And he will make the face of heaven so fine
  That all the world will be in love with night
25 And pay no worship to the garish sun.
  O, I have bought the mansion of a love,
  But not possessed it; and though I am sold,
  Not yet enjoyed. So tedious is this day
  As is the night before some festival
30 To an impatient child that hath new robes
  And may not wear them. Oh, here comes my nurse,

*[Enter* Nurse, *wringing her hands, with the ladder of cords in her lap.]*

  And she brings news; and every tongue that speaks
  But Romeo's name speaks heavenly eloquence.
  Now, nurse, what news? What hast thou there? the cords

**1. Phoebus:** another name for Apollo, the sun god in Greek mythology.

**2. Phaëton:** the son of Phoebus, who tried to drive his father's chariot but could not control the horses. They galloped toward the west too fast, thus bringing early night.

◆ **Lines 1-7:** Juliet wants the night to come quickly so that she can be with Romeo.

**3. civil:** respectable.

**4. unmanned:** untamed.

**5. bating:** fluttering.

**6. strange:** diffident, reserved.

**7. modesty:** chastity.

◆ **Lines 17-25:** Notice the images of light and dark in this soliloquy. Night and day have been given new meaning: night is now desirable and day is disparaged.

◆ **Lines 26-28:** Juliet says that though she has gone through the marriage ceremony—"bought the mansion"—she has yet had no experience of being married.

35   That Romeo bid thee fetch?

**Nurse.**                    Ay, ay, the cords.

**Juliet.** Ay me! what news? Why dost thou wring thy
      hands?

**Nurse.** Ah, well-a-day![8] he's dead, he's dead, he's dead!
      We are undone, lady, we are undone!
      Alack the day! he's gone, he's killed, he's dead!

40   **Juliet.** Can heaven be so envious?

**Nurse.**                    Romeo can,
      Though heaven cannot. O Romeo, Romeo!
      Who ever would have thought it? Romeo!

**Juliet.** What devil art thou that dost torment me thus?
      This torture should be roared in dismal hell.
45   Hath Romeo slain himself? Say thou but "I,"[9]
      And that bare vowel "I" shall poison more
      Than the death-darting eye of a cockatrice.[10]
      I am not I, if there be such an "I,"
      Or those eyes shut, that make thee answer "I."
50   If he be slain, say "I," or if not, "no."
      Brief sounds determine of my weal or woe.[11]

**Nurse.** I saw the wound, I saw it with mine eyes,
      (God save the mark!)[12] here on his manly breast.
      A piteous corse,[13] a bloody piteous corse;
55   Pale, pale as ashes, all bedaubed in blood,
      All in gore blood. I swounded[14] at the sight.

**Juliet.** O, break, my heart! poor bankrout,[15] break at
      once!
      To prison, eyes; ne'er look on liberty!
      Vile earth, to earth resign;[16] end motion here,
60   And thou and Romeo press one heavy bier!

**Nurse.** O Tybalt, Tybalt, the best friend I had!
      O courteous Tybalt! honest gentleman!
      That ever I should live to see thee dead!

**Juliet.** What storm is this that blows so contrary?
65   Is Romeo slaughtered, and is Tybalt dead?
      My dear-loved cousin, and my dearer lord?
      Then, dreadful trumpet,[17] sound the general doom!
      For who is living, if those two are gone?

**Nurse.** Tybalt is gone, and Romeo banished;

8. **well-a-day:** alas.

◆ **Line 43:** Note Juliet's frustration that the Nurse takes so long to explain what happened.

9. **Say . . . "I":** a pun on *aye* ("yes").

10. **cockatrice:** fabulous serpent that killed by its glance.

11. **determine . . . woe:** decide my well-being or my grief.

12. **God . . . mark:** a phrase uttered to turn aside the bad luck that might result from seeing such a disaster.

13. **corse:** corpse.

14. **swounded:** fainted.

15. **bankrout:** bankrupt.

16. **Vile . . . resign:** Miserable body, resign yourself to death.

◆ **Lines 57-60:** The nurse has misled Juliet into thinking that Romeo has been killed. Juliet exclaims that she and Romeo will share one bier, or burial place.

17. **dreadful trumpet:** the trumpet that proclaims doomsday.

70 Romeo that killed him, he is banished.

**Juliet.** O God! Did Romeo's hand shed Tybalt's blood?

**Nurse.** It did! it did! alas the day, it did!

**Juliet.** O serpent heart, hid with a flow'ring face!
Did ever dragon keep[18] so fair a cave?

18. **keep:** guard.

75 Beautiful tyrant! fiend angelical!
Dove-feathered raven! wolvish-ravening lamb!
Despised substance of divinest show!
Just opposite to what thou justly seemst,
A damned saint, an honorable villain!

♦ **Lines 73-85:** Juliet's paradoxes here express the violent conflict between her attraction to Romeo and her horror that he has killed Tybalt, her "dear-loved cousin."

80 O nature, what hadst thou to do in hell
When thou didst bower the spirit of a fiend
In mortal paradise of such sweet flesh?
Was ever book containing such vile matter
So fairly bound? O, that deceit should dwell
85 In such a gorgeous palace!

**Nurse.**                            There's no trust,
No faith, no honesty in men; all perjured,
All forsworn, all naught, all dissemblers.[19]
Ah, where's my man? Give me some aqua vitae.[20]
These griefs, these woes, these sorrows make me old.

19. **All forsworn . . .**
**dissemblers:** all faithless, all wicked, all pretenders.
20. **aqua vitae:** brandy.

90 Shame come to Romeo!

**Juliet.**                            Blistered be thy tongue
For such a wish! He was not born to shame.
Upon his brow shame is ashamed to sit;
For 'tis a throne where honor may be crowned
Sole monarch of the universal earth.
95 O, what a beast was I to chide at him!

**Nurse.** Will you speak well of him that killed your
cousin?

**Juliet.** Shall I speak ill of him that is my husband?
Ah, poor my lord, what tongue shall smooth thy name
When I, thy three-hours' wife, have mangled it?
100 But wherefore, villain, didst thou kill my cousin?
That villain cousin would have killed my husband.
Back, foolish tears, back to your native spring!
Your tributary drops belong to woe,
Which you, mistaking, offer up to joy.

♦ **Lines 100-102:** Juliet's only comfort for Tybalt's death is the knowledge that he wanted to kill Romeo but was unsuccessful.

105 My husband lives, that Tybalt would have slain;
And Tybalt's dead, that would have slain my husband.
All this is comfort; wherefore weep I then?

Some word there was, worser than Tybalt's death,
That murdered me. I would forget it fain;[21]
110    But O, it presses to my memory
Like damned guilty deeds to sinners' minds!
"Tybalt is dead, and Romeo—banished."
That "banished," that one word "banished,"
Hath slain ten thousand Tybalts. Tybalt's death
115    Was woe enough, if it had ended there;
Or, if sour woe delights in fellowship
And needly[22] will be ranked with other griefs,
Why followed not, when she said "Tybalt's dead,"
Thy father, or thy mother, nay, or both,
120    Which modern[23] lamentation might have moved?
But with a rearward[24] following Tybalt's death,
"Romeo is banished"—to speak that word
Is father, mother, Tybalt, Romeo, Juliet,
All slain, all dead. "Romeo is banished"—
125    There is no end, no limit, measure, bound,
In that word's death; no words can that woe sound.
Where is my father and my mother, nurse?

**Nurse.** Weeping and wailing over Tybalt's corse.
Will you go to them? I will bring you thither.

130    **Juliet.** Wash they his wounds with tears? Mine shall be
       spent,
When theirs are dry, for Romeo's banishment.
Take up those cords. Poor ropes, you are beguiled,
Both you and I, for Romeo is exiled.
He made you for a highway to my bed;
135    But I, a maid, die maiden-widowed.
Come, cords; come, nurse. I'll to my wedding bed;
And death, not Romeo, take my maidenhead!

**Nurse.** Hie to your chamber. I'll find Romeo
To comfort you. I wot[25] well where he is.
140    Hark ye, your Romeo will be here at night.
I'll to him; he is hid at Laurence' cell.

**Juliet.** O, find him! give this ring to my true knight
And bid him come to take his last farewell.

                          *[Exeunt.]*

**SCENE 3** *[Friar Laurence's cell.]*

*[Enter Friar Laurence.]*

**21. fain:** willingly.

**22. needly:** of necessity.

**23. modern:** ordinary.
**24. rearward:** a guard bringing up the rear; a follow-up.

◆ **Lines 112-126:** The full impact of the nurse's statement and Romeo's banishment is beginning to hit Juliet. Though she exaggerates in order to express the depth of her feelings, she is right in suggesting that all will suffer in the aftermath of Romeo's banishment.

◆ **Lines 135-137:** Juliet says she will die a widow without ever really having been a wife. Her husband, she says, will be death, not Romeo.
**25. wot:** know.

**Friar Laurence.**  Romeo, come forth; come forth, thou
    fearful man.
    Affliction is enamored of thy parts,
    And thou art wedded to calamity.

*[Enter Romeo.]*

**Romeo.**  Father, what news? What is the Prince's doom?
5    What sorrow craves acquaintance at my hand
    That I yet know not?

**Friar Laurence.**       Too familiar
    Is my dear son with such sour company.
    I bring thee tidings of the Prince's doom.

**Romeo.**  What less than doomsday is the Prince's doom?

10  **Friar Laurence.**  A gentler judgment vanished[1] from his
    lips—
    Not body's death, but body's banishment.

1. **vanished:** issued.

**Romeo.**  Ha, banishment? Be merciful, say "death";
    For exile hath more terror in his look,
    Much more than death. Do not say "banishment."

15  **Friar Laurence.**  Hence from Verona art thou banished.
    Be patient,[2] for the world is broad and wide.

2. **patient:** calm.

**Romeo.**  There is no world without Verona walls,
    But purgatory, torture, hell itself.
    Hence banished is banisht from the world,
20    And world's exile[3] is death. Then "banishment,"
    Is death mistermed. Calling death "banishment,"
    Thou cuttst my head off with a golden axe
    And smilest upon the stroke that murders me.

3. **world's exile:** exile from
the world of Juliet.

**Friar Laurence.**  O deadly sin! O rude unthankfulness!
25    Thy fault our law calls death; but the kind Prince,
    Taking thy part, hath rushed[4] aside the law,
    And turned that black word death to banishment.
    This is dear[5] mercy, and thou seest it not.

4. **rushed:** brushed.

◆ **Lines 24-28:** Friar Laurence
believes that Romeo is
fortunate to be merely
banished when, according to
Verona's law, Romeo's crime
deserves a penalty of death.

5. **dear:** precious.

**Romeo.**  'Tis torture, and not mercy. Heaven is here,
30    Where Juliet lives; and every cat and dog
    And little mouse, every unworthy thing,
    Live here in heaven and may look on her;
    But Romeo may not. More validity,[6]
    More honorable state, more courtship lives
35    In carrion flies than Romeo. They may seize

6. **validity:** worth.

On the white wonder of dear Juliet's hand
And steal immortal blessing from her lips,
Who, even in pure and vestal modesty,
Still blush, as thinking their own kisses sin;
40 But Romeo may not—he is banished.
This may flies do, when I from this must fly;
They are free men, but I am banished.
And sayst thou yet that exile is not death?
Hadst thou no poison mixed, no sharp-ground knife,
45 No sudden mean of death, though ne'er so mean,
But "banished" to kill me—"banished"?
O friar, the damned use that word in hell;
Howling attends it! How hast thou the heart,
Being a divine, a ghostly confessor,
50 A sin-absolver, and my friend professed,
To mangle me with that word "banished"?

**Friar Laurence.** Thou fond[7] mad man, hear me a little
speak.

**Romeo.** O, thou wilt speak again of banishment.

**Friar Laurence.** I'll give thee armor to keep off that
word;
55 Adversity's sweet milk, philosophy,
To comfort thee, though thou art banished.

**Romeo.** Yet "banished"? Hang up philosophy!
Unless philosophy can make a Juliet,
Displant a town, reverse a prince's doom,
60 It helps not, it prevails not. Talk no more.

**Friar Laurence.** O, then I see that madmen have no
ears.

**Romeo.** How should they, when that wise men have no
eyes?

**Friar Laurence.** Let me dispute with thee of thy
estate.[8]

**Romeo.** Thou canst not speak of that thou dost not feel.
65 Wert thou as young as I, Juliet thy love,
An hour but married, Tybalt murdered,
Doting like me, and like me banished,
Then mightst thou speak, then mightst thou tear thy
hair,
And fall upon the ground, as I do now,

◆ **Lines 29-51:** Contrast
Romeo's reaction to his
banishment with Friar
Laurence's reaction.

**7. fond:** foolish.

**8. dispute . . . estate:** discuss
your circumstances.

◆ **Lines 64-70:** Think about
how Romeo explains the
difference between the
priest's optimism and his own
despair. Consider whether
you agree with Romeo.

*he'd rather die than live w/o Juliet*

*you're too old to understand me*

70    Taking the measure of an unmade grave.

*[Nurse knocks within.]*

**Friar Laurence.** Arise; one knocks. Good Romeo, hide
    thyself.

**Romeo.** Not I; unless the breath of heartsick groans
    Mist-like infold me from the search of eyes.

*[Knock.]*

**Friar Laurence.** Hark, how they knock! Who's there?
    Romeo, arise;
75    Thou wilt be taken.—Stay awhile!—Stand up;

*[Knock.]*

Run to my study.—By-and-by![9]—God's will,
What simpleness is this.—I come, I come!

*[Knock.]*

Who knocks so hard? Whence come you? What's your
    will?

**Nurse.** *[Within.]* Let me come in, and you shall know my
    errand.
80    I come from Lady Juliet.

**Friar Laurence.**          Welcome then.

*[Enter Nurse.]*

**Nurse.** O holy friar, O, tell me, holy friar,
    Where is my lady's lord, where's Romeo?

**Friar Laurence.** There on the ground, with his own tears
    made drunk.

**Nurse.** O, he is even[10] in my mistress' case,
85    Just in her case! O woeful sympathy!
Piteous predicament! Even so lies she,
Blubb'ring and weeping, weeping and blubbering.
Stand up, stand up! Stand, an you be a man.
For Juliet's sake, for her sake, rise and stand!
90    Why should you fall into so deep an O?[11]

**Romeo.** *[Rises]* Nurse—

**Nurse.** Ah sir! ah sir! Well, death's the end of all.

9. **By-and-by:** Wait a
moment.

10. **even:** exactly.

11. **O:** cry of grief.

**Romeo.** Spakest thou of Juliet? How is it with her?
Doth not she think me an old[12] murderer,
95    Now I have stained the childhood of our joy
With blood removed but little from her own?
Where is she? and how doth she? and what says
My concealed lady[13] to our canceled love?

**Nurse.** O, she says nothing, sir, but weeps and weeps;
100   And now falls on her bed, and then starts up,
And Tybalt calls; and then on Romeo cries,
And then down falls again.

**Romeo.**                    As if that name,
Shot from the deadly level[14] of a gun,
Did murder her; as that name's cursed hand
105   Murdered her kinsman. O tell me, friar, tell me,
In what vile part of this anatomy
Doth my name lodge? Tell me, that I may sack
The hateful mansion.

                              [*Draws his dagger.*]

**Friar Laurence.**              Hold thy desperate hand.
Art thou a man? Thy form cries out thou art;
110   Thy tears are womanish, thy wild acts denote
The unreasonable fury of a beast.
Unseemly woman in a seeming man!
Or ill-beseeming[15] beast in seeming both!
Thou hast amazed me. By my holy order,
115   I thought thy disposition better tempered.
Hast thou slain Tybalt? Wilt thou slay thyself?
And slay thy lady too that lives in thee,
By doing damned hate upon thyself?
Why railst thou on[16] thy birth, the heaven, and earth?
120   Since birth and heaven and earth, all three do meet
In thee at once; which thou at once wouldst lose.
Fie, fie, thou shamest thy shape, thy love, thy wit,
Which, like a usurer,[17] aboundst in all,
And usest none in that true use indeed
125   Which should bedeck thy shape, thy love, thy wit.
Thy noble shape is but a form of wax,[18]
Digressing[19] from the valor of a man;
Thy dear love sworn but hollow perjury,
Killing that love which thou hast vowed to cherish;
130   Thy wit, that ornament to shape and love,
Misshapen in the conduct of them both,

**12. old:** experienced.

**13. concealed lady:** secret bride.

**14. level:** aim.

◆ **Lines 105–108:** Notice how quickly Romeo thinks of suicide as a solution to his problems. Romeo's question about where his name lodges relates to Juliet's lines in Act Two, Scene 2: "What's Montague? It is nor hand, nor foot,/Nor arm, nor face, nor any other part/Belonging to a man."

**15. ill-beseeming:** unsuitable.

**16. railst thou on:** complain about.

◆ **Lines 116–121:** Suicide was considered to be such a serious sin that it would cause the victim's soul to be damned eternally.

**17. usurer:** miser.

**18. form of wax:** waxwork figure.

**19. digressing:** differing.

Like powder in a skilless soldier's flask,[20]
Is set afire by thine own ignorance,
And thou dismembered with thine own defense.[21]

135　　What, rouse thee, man! Thy Juliet is alive,
For whose dear sake thou wast but lately dead.
There art thou happy. Tybalt would kill thee,
But thou slewest Tybalt. There art thou happy.
The law, that threatened death, becomes thy friend

140　　And turns it to exile. There art thou happy.
A pack of blessings light upon thy back;
Happiness courts thee in her best array;
But, like a misbehaved and sullen wench,
Thou poutst upon thy fortune and thy love.

145　　Take heed, take heed, for such die miserable.
Go get thee to thy love, as was decreed,
Ascend her chamber, hence and comfort her.
But look thou stay not till the watch be set,[22]
For then thou canst not pass to Mantua,

150　　Where thou shalt live till we can find a time
To blaze[23] your marriage, reconcile your friends,
Beg pardon of the Prince, and call thee back
With twenty hundred thousand times more joy
Than thou wentst forth in lamentation.

155　　Go before, nurse. Commend me to thy lady,
And bid her hasten all the house to bed,
Which heavy sorrow makes them apt[24] unto.
Romeo is coming.

**Nurse.**　O Lord, I could have stayed here all the night
160　　To hear good counsel. O, what learning is!
My lord, I'll tell my lady you will come.

**Romeo.**　Do so, and bid my sweet prepare to chide.

[Nurse *offers to go and turns again.*]

**Nurse.**　Here is a ring she bid me give you, sir.
Hie you, make haste, for it grows very late.

　　　　　　　　　　　　　　　　　　　　　　　　[*Exit.*]

165　　**Romeo.**　How well my comfort is revived by this!

**Friar Laurence.**　Go hence; good night; and here stands
　　all your state:[25]
Either be gone before the watch be set,
Or by the break of day disguised from hence.
Sojourn in Mantua. I'll find out your man,

---

**20. flask:** powder horn.

**21. dismembered . . . defense:** destroyed by your own weapon.

♦ **Lines 135-144:** Notice the reasons that Friar Laurence gives for Romeo to be happy. Consider whether you agree with the priest's assessment of Romeo's situation.

♦ **Lines 146-154:** Note the priest's plan for Romeo and Juliet.

**22. watch be set:** the night watchmen go on duty at the gates.

**23. blaze:** announce.

**24. apt:** inclined.

**25. here . . . state:** on this depends your fortune

<table>
<tr><td>170</td><td>And he shall signify from time to time<br>Every good hap[26] to you that chances here.<br>Give me thy hand. 'Tis late. Farewell; good night.</td><td>**26. hap:** happening.</td></tr>
</table>

**Romeo.** But that a joy past joy calls out on me,
It were a grief so brief to part with thee.
175    Farewell.

*[Exeunt.]*

### SCENE 4 *[Capulet's house.]*

*[Enter Capulet, Lady Capulet, and Paris.]*

**Capulet.** Things have fall'n out,[1] sir, so unluckily
That we have had no time to move[2] our daughter.
Look you, she loved her kinsman Tybalt dearly,
And so did I. Well, we were born to die.
5    'Tis very late; she'll not come down tonight.
I promise you, but for your company,
I would have been abed an hour ago.

**1. fall'n out:** worked out.
**2. move:** make your proposal to.

◆ **Lines 1-11:** Notice the dramatic irony created by the fact that the audience knows Juliet is grief-stricken about both Tybalt's death and Romeo's banishment, but her parents believe her sadness is due only to Tybalt's death.

**Paris.** These times of woe afford no time to woo.
Madam, good night. Commend me to your daughter.

10 **Lady Capulet.** I will, and know her mind early
     tomorrow;
Tonight she's mewed up to her heaviness.[3]

**3. mewed . . . heaviness:** confined with her sorrow.

*[Paris offers to go and Capulet calls him again.]*

**Capulet.** Sir Paris, I will make a desperate tender[4]
Of my child's love. I think she will be ruled
In all respects by me; nay more, I doubt it not.
15    Wife, go you to her ere you go to bed;
Acquaint her here of my son[5] Paris' love
And bid her (mark you me?) on Wednesday next—
But, soft! what day is this?

**4. desperate tender:** bold offer.

**5. son:** future son-in-law.

**Paris.**                 Monday, my lord.

**Capulet.** Monday! ha, ha! Well, Wednesday is too soon.
20    A[6] Thursday let it be—a Thursday, tell her,
She shall be married to this noble earl.
Will you be ready? Do you like this haste?
We'll keep no great ado[7]—a friend or two;
For hark you, Tybalt being slain so late,[8]
25    It may be thought we held him carelessly,[9]
Being our kinsman, if we revel much.
Therefore we'll have some half a dozen friends,

**6. a:** on.

**7. ado:** formality.
**8. late:** recently.
**9. held him carelessly:** did not care about him.

And there an end. But what say you to Thursday?

**Paris.** My lord, I would that Thursday were tomorrow.

30 **Capulet.** Well, get you gone. A Thursday be it then.
Go you to Juliet ere you go to bed;
Prepare her, wife, against[10] this wedding day.
Farewell, my lord.—Light to my chamber, ho!
Afore me,[11] it is so very very late
35 That we may call it early by-and-by.
Good night.

*[Exeunt.]*

**SCENE 5** *[Capulet's orchard.]*

*[Enter* Romeo *and* Juliet *above, at the window.]*

**Juliet.** Wilt thou be gone? It is not yet near day.
It was the nightingale, and not the lark,
That pierced the fearful hollow of thine ear.
Nightly she sings on yond pomegranate tree.
5 Believe me, love, it was the nightingale.

**Romeo.** It was the lark, the herald of the morn;
No nightingale. Look, love, what envious streaks
Do lace[1] the severing[2] clouds in yonder East.
Night's candles[3] are burnt out, and jocund day
10 Stands tiptoe on the misty mountain tops.
I must be gone and live, or stay and die.

**Juliet.** Yond light is not daylight; I know it, I.
It is some meteor that the sun exhales
To be to thee this night a torchbearer
15 And light thee on thy way to Mantua.
Therefore stay yet; thou needst not to be gone.

**Romeo.** Let me be ta'en, let me be put to death.
I am content, so thou wilt have it so.
I'll say yon grey is not the morning's eye,
20 'Tis but the pale reflex[4] of Cynthia's[5] brow;
Nor that is not the lark whose notes do beat
The vaulty heaven so high above our heads.
I have more care[6] to stay than will to go.
Come, death, and welcome! Juliet wills it so.
25 How is't, my soul? Let's talk; it is not day.

**Juliet.** It is, it is! Hie hence, be gone, away!
It is the lark that sings so out of tune,

*she's trying to keep him there*

*happy*

*reverse psychology: I'm gonna die, but let's talk*

**Lines 12-28:** Capulet is so sure that Juliet will follow his wishes that he arranges the marriage to Paris without discussing it with her. Speculate about why he is so hasty here when he was reluctant for her to marry in Act One.

**10. against:** for.

**11. Afore me:** By my word!

**Line 2:** The nightingale sings at night, while the lark sings during the day.

**1. lace:** stripe.

**2. severing:** scattering.

**3. night's candles:** the stars.

**4. reflex:** reflection.

**5. Cynthia:** goddess of the moon.

**6. care:** desire.

From the film *Romeo and Juliet,* 1967, starring Leonard Whiting and Olivia Hussey.
Photofest, New York.

Straining harsh discords and unpleasing sharps.
Some say the lark makes sweet division;[7]
30  This doth not so, for she divideth us.
Some say the lark and loathed toad changed eyes;[8]
O, now I would they had changed voices too,
Since arm from arm that voice doth us affray,[9]
Hunting thee hence with hunt's-up[10] to the day!
35  O, now be gone! More light and light it grows.

**Romeo.** More light and light—more dark and dark our
woes!

[Enter Nurse, *hastily*.]

**Nurse.** Madam!

**Juliet.** Nurse?

**Nurse.** Your lady mother is coming to your chamber.
40  The day is broke; be wary, look about.

[*Exit*.]

**Juliet.** Then, window, let day in, and let life out.

**Romeo.** Farewell, farewell! One kiss, and I'll descend.

[*He starts down the ladder*.]

**Juliet.** Art thou gone so, my lord, my love, my friend?
I must hear from thee every day in the hour,
45  For in a minute there are many days.
O, by this count I shall be much in years
Ere I again behold my Romeo!

**Romeo.** Farewell!
I will omit no opportunity
50  That may convey my greetings, love, to thee.

**Juliet.** O, thinkst thou we shall ever meet again?

**Romeo.** I doubt it not; and all these woes shall serve
For sweet discourses in our time to come.

**Juliet.** O God, I have an ill-divining[11] soul!
55  Methinks I see thee, now thou art below,
As one dead in the bottom of a tomb.
Either my eyesight fails, or thou lookst pale.

**Romeo.** And trust me, love, in my eye so do you.
Dry sorrow drinks our blood.[12] Adieu! adieu!

[*Exit*.]

---

◆ **Lines 26-30:** Notice that the song of the lark and the dawn, generally associated with joy and hope, are despised by Juliet because they signal separation from Romeo.

**7. division:** melody

**8. some . . . eyes:** this phrase refers to a fable explaining why the toad has bright eyes but a harsh croak, and the lark has dull eyes but a lovely voice.

**9. affray:** frighten.

**10. hunt's-up:** hunters' morning song.

**11. ill-divining:** foreseeing evil.

◆ **Lines 54-56:** This is one of the most direct and compelling examples of foreshadowing in the play, as Juliet imagines Romeo dead.

**12. dry . . . blood:** sorrow was believed to dry up the blood.

60 **Juliet.** O Fortune, Fortune! all men call thee fickle.
If thou art fickle, what dost thou with him
That is renowmed[13] for faith? Be fickle, Fortune,
For then I hope thou wilt not keep him long
But send him back.

**Lady Capulet.** [*Within.*] Ho, daughter! are you up?

65 **Juliet.** Who is't that calls? It is my lady mother.
Is she not down so late, or up so early?
What unaccustomed cause procures[14] her hither?

[*Enter* Lady Capulet.]

**Lady Capulet.** Why, how now, Juliet?

**Juliet.**                          Madam, I am not well.

**Lady Capulet.** Evermore weeping for your cousin's
death?
70 What, wilt thou wash him from his grave with tears?
An if thou couldst, thou couldst not make him live.
Therefore have done. Some grief shows much of love;
But much of grief shows still some want of wit.

**Juliet.** Yet let me weep for such a feeling[15] loss.

75 **Lady Capulet.** So shall you feel the loss, but not the
friend
Which you weep for.

**Juliet.**                     Feeling so the loss,
I cannot choose but ever weep the friend.

**Lady Capulet.** Well, girl, thou weepst not so much for
his death
As that the villain lives which slaughtered him.

80 **Juliet.** What villain, madam?

**Lady Capulet.**                    That same villain Romeo.

**Juliet.** [*Aside.*] Villain and he be many miles asunder.—
God pardon him! I do, with all my heart;
And yet no man like he doth grieve my heart.

**Lady Capulet.** That is because the traitor murderer
lives.

85 **Juliet.** Ay, madam, from the reach of these my hands.
Would none but I might venge my cousin's death!

13. **renowmed:** renowned.

14. **procures:** leads.

◆ **Lines 72-73:** According to Lady Capulet, a moderate grief shows love, but too much grief evidences lack of intelligence.

15. **feeling:** deeply felt.

**Lady Capulet.** We will have vengeance for it, fear thou
    not.
    Then weep no more. I'll send to one in Mantua,
    Where that same banished runagate[16] doth live,
90    Shall give him such an unaccustomed dram
    That he shall soon keep Tybalt company;
    And then I hope thou wilt be satisfied.

**Juliet.** Indeed I never shall be satisfied
    With Romeo till I behold him—dead—
95    Is my poor heart so for a kinsman vexed.
    Madam, if you could find out but a man
    To bear a poison, I would temper[17] it;
    That Romeo should, upon receipt thereof,
    Soon sleep in quiet. O, how my heart abhors
100    To hear him named and cannot come to him,
    To wreak the love I bore my cousin Tybalt
    Upon his body that hath slaughtered him!

**Lady Capulet.** Find thou the means, and I'll find such a
    man.
    But now I'll tell thee joyful tidings, girl.

105  **Juliet.** And joy comes well in such a needy time.
    What are they, I beseech your ladyship?

**Lady Capulet.** Well, well, thou hast a careful[18] father,
    child;
    One who, to put thee from thy heaviness,
    Hath sorted out[19] a sudden day of joy
110    That thou expects not nor I looked not for.

**Juliet.** Madam, in happy time![20] What day is that?

**Lady Capulet.** Marry, my child, early next Thursday
    morn
    The gallant, young, and noble gentleman,
    The County Paris, at Saint Peter's Church,
115    Shall happily make thee there a joyful bride.

**Juliet.** Now by Saint Peter's Church, and Peter too,
    He shall not make me there a joyful bride!
    I wonder at this haste, that I must wed
    Ere he that should be husband comes to woo.
120    I pray you tell my lord and father, madam,
    I will not marry yet; and when I do, I swear

---

16. **runagate:** runaway.

◆ **Lines 87–92:** Lady Capulet tells Juliet of her plan to have Romeo poisoned, thinking that such vengeance will comfort Juliet in her grief for Tybalt.

17. **temper:** mix.

◆ **Lines 93–102:** Juliet is choosing her words carefully so that Lady Capulet will mistakenly think that Juliet wishes to see Romeo dead.

18. **careful:** considerate.

19. **sorted out:** chosen.

20. **in happy time:** indeed.

It shall be Romeo, whom you know I hate,
Rather than Paris. These are news indeed!

**Lady Capulet.** Here comes your father. Tell him so
   yourself,
125 And see how he will take it at your hands.

*[Enter Capulet and Nurse.]*

**Capulet.** When the sun sets the air doth drizzle dew,
   But for the sunset of my brother's son
   It rains downright.
   How now? a conduit,[21] girl? What, still in tears?
130 Evermore show'ring? In one little body
   Thou counterfeitst a bark, a sea, a wind:
   For still thy eyes, which I may call the sea,
   Do ebb and flow with tears; the bark thy body is,
   Sailing in this salt flood; the winds, thy sighs,
135 Who, raging with thy tears and they with them,
   Without a sudden calm will overset
   Thy tempest-tossed body. How now, wife?
   Have you delivered to her our decree?

**Lady Capulet.** Ay, sir; but she will none, she gives you
   thanks.
140 I would the fool were married to her grave!

**Capulet.** Soft! take me with you,[22] take me with you,
   wife.
   How? Will she none? Doth she not give us thanks?
   Is she not proud? Doth she not count her blest,
   Unworthy as she is, that we have wrought[23]
145 So worthy a gentleman to be her bridegroom?

**Juliet.** Not proud you have, but thankful that you have.
   Proud can I never be of what I hate,
   But thankful even for hate that is meant love.

**Capulet.** How, how, how, how, choplogic?[24] What is
   this?
150 "Proud"—and "I thank you"—and "I thank you not"—
   And yet "not proud"? Mistress minion[25] you,
   Thank me no thankings, nor proud me no prouds,
   But fettle[26] your fine joints 'gainst Thursday next
   To go with Paris to Saint Peter's Church,
155 Or I will drag thee on a hurdle[27] thither.
   Out, you green-sickness carrion![28] out, you baggage!
   You tallow-face!

---

♦ **Lines 116–123:** Juliet points out the haste of her father's decision and cleverly says she would rather marry Romeo, whom her mother thinks she hates. Compare her refusal to marry Paris with her obedient willingness to consider his proposal in Act One, Scene 3.

**21. conduit:** fountain.

♦ **Lines 130–137:** Capulet compares Juliet to a boat ("bark"), the sea, and the wind in the abundance of her tears and sighs of grief.

**22. take me with you:** explain what you mean.

**23. wrought:** arranged for.

**24. choplogic:** hair-splitting.

**25. mistress minion:** saucy miss.

**26. fettle:** make ready.

**27. hurdle:** a wooden frame used to convey criminals to execution.

**28. green-sickness carrion:** anemic lump of flesh.

**Lady Capulet.**                    Fie, fie; what, are you mad?

**Juliet.** Good father, I beseech you on my knees,

*[She kneels down.]*

Hear me with patience but to²⁹ speak a word.

160 **Capulet.** Hang thee, young baggage! disobedient wretch!
I tell thee what—get thee to church a Thursday
Or never after look me in the face.
Speak not, reply not, do not answer me!
My fingers itch.³⁰ Wife, we scarce thought us blest
165 That God had lent us but this only child;
But now I see this one is one too much,
And that we have a curse in having her.
Out on her, hilding!³¹

**Nurse.**                    God in heaven bless her!
You are to blame, my lord, to rate³² her so.

170 **Capulet.** And why, my Lady Wisdom? Hold your tongue,
Good Prudence. Smatter³³ with your gossips, go!

**Nurse.** I speak no treason.

**Capulet.**                    O, God-i-god-en!

**Nurse.** May not one speak?

**Capulet.**                    Peace, you mumbling fool!
Utter your gravity³⁴ o'er a gossip's bowl,³⁵
175 For here we need it not.

**Lady Capulet.**          You are too hot.

**Capulet.** God's bread!³⁶ it makes me mad. Day, night,
late, early,
At home, abroad, alone, in company,
Waking or sleeping, still my care hath been
To have her matched; and having now provided
180 A gentleman of princely parentage,
Of fair demesnes,³⁷ youthful, and nobly trained,
Stuffed, as they say, with honorable parts,³⁸
Proportioned as one's thought would wish a man—
And then to have a wretched puling³⁹ fool,
185 A whining mammet,⁴⁰ in her fortunes tender,⁴¹
To answer "I'll not wed, I cannot love;
I am too young, I pray you pardon me"!
But, an you will not wed, I'll pardon you.⁴²

---

**29. but to:** just long enough to.

**30. itch:** that is, to strike Juliet.

◆ **Lines 149-168:** Capulet is furious at Juliet for not wanting to marry Paris. He rages at her and calls her names. Evaluate his behavior here and compare your opinion now to your earlier concept of him as a father.

**31. hilding:** good-for-nothing.

**32. rate:** scold.

**33. smatter:** chatter.

◆ **Lines 168-173:** Notice that the nurse dares to speak up to her master in defense of Juliet.

**34. gravity:** wise words.

**35. gossip's bowl:** a hot punch.

**36. God's bread:** an oath on the sacred communion bread.

**37. demesnes:** wealth.

**38. parts:** qualities.

**39. puling:** whining.

**40. mammet:** doll.

**41. in her fortunes tender:** when good fortune is offered her.

◆ **Lines 185-187:** Notice how Capulet mocks what he supposes to be Juliet's reasons for not wanting to marry Paris. Remember that in Act One he himself said she was too young to marry.

**42. pardon you:** be glad to see you gone.

190 Graze where you will, you shall not house with me.
Look to't, think on't; I do not use to[43] jest.
Thursday is near; lay hand on heart, advise:[44]
An you be mine, I'll give you to my friend;
An you be not, hang, beg, starve, die in the streets,
195 For, by my soul, I'll ne'er acknowledge thee,
Nor what is mine shall never do thee good.
Trust to't.[45] Bethink you. I'll not be forsworn.[46]

[Exit.]

**Juliet.** Is there no pity sitting in the clouds
That sees into the bottom of my grief?
O sweet my mother, cast me not away!
200 Delay this marriage for a month, a week;
Or if you do not, make the bridal bed
In that dim monument where Tybalt lies.

**Lady Capulet.** Talk not to me, for I'll not speak a word.
Do as thou wilt, for I have done with thee.

[Exit.]

205 **Juliet.** O God!—O nurse, how shall this be prevented?
My husband is on earth, my faith in heaven.
How shall that faith return again to earth
Unless that husband send it me from heaven
By leaving earth? Comfort me, counsel me.
210 Alack, alack, that heaven should practice stratagems[47]
Upon so soft a subject as myself!
What sayst thou? Hast thou not a word of joy?
Some comfort, nurse.

**Nurse.**                    Faith, here it is.
Romeo is banisht; and all the world to nothing[48]
215 That he dares ne'er come back to challenge[49] you;
Or if he do, it needs must be by stealth.
Then, since the case so stands as now it doth,
I think it best you married with the County.
O, he's a lovely gentleman!
220 Romeo's a dishclout to him. An eagle, madam,
Hath not so green, so quick, so fair an eye
As Paris hath. Beshrew my very heart,
I think you are happy in this second match,
For it excels your first; or if it did not,
225 Your first is dead—or 'twere as good he were
As living here[50] and you no use of him.

**43. I do not use to:** I do not usually.

**44. advise:** be advised.

◆ **Lines 189-196:** Capulet asserts his right as a father to do as he pleases with his child. He threatens to disown Juliet—literally to throw her out in the streets—if she does not marry Paris.

**45. Trust to't:** Be assured of it.

**46. be forsworn:** break my vow.

◆ **Lines 206-209:** Juliet worries that she will violate her faith if forced to marry Paris while she is already married to Romeo.

**47. practice stratagems:** contrive violent deeds.

**48. all the world to nothing:** that is, the odds are all to nothing.

**49. challenge:** claim.

◆ **Lines 214-226:** The nurse advises Juliet to marry Paris even though she knows that Juliet is already married. Think about how this advice must make Juliet feel.

**50. here:** on earth.

**Juliet.** Speakst thou this from thy heart?

**Nurse.** And from my soul too; else beshrew them both.

**Juliet.** Amen!

230 **Nurse.** What?

**Juliet.** Well, thou hast comforted me marvelous much.
　　Go in; and tell my lady I am gone,
　　Having displeased my father, to Laurence' cell,
　　To make confession and to be absolved.

235 **Nurse.** Marry, I will; and this is wisely done.

*[Exit.]*

**Juliet.** Ancient damnation![51] O most wicked fiend!
　　Is it more sin to wish me thus forsworn,[52]
　　Or to dispraise my lord with that same tongue
　　Which she hath praised him with above compare
240　So many thousand times? Go, counselor!
　　Thou and my bosom[53] henceforth shall be twain.
　　I'll to the friar to know his remedy.
　　If all else fail, myself have power to die.

*[Exit.]*

**51. ancient damnation:** wicked old devil.

**52. forsworn:** guilty of breaking her marriage vow to Romeo.

**53. bosom:** inner thoughts.

◆ **Lines 236-243:** Juliet feels betrayed that the nurse would advise her to commit the sin of bigamy by being married to two men. Because she is now alone, with no one in the household to turn to, she decides to ask Friar Laurence for help. Note that like Romeo earlier, she considers suicide as a possible solution to her problem.

# Thinking About Act Three

## A PERSONAL RESPONSE

*sharing impressions*

**1.** What do you think about Juliet's refusal to marry Paris? Record your thoughts in your journal.

*constructing interpretations*

**2.** How is your opinion of the nurse's character affected by her actions in Act Three?

### Think about
- your opinion of her after you read Acts One and Two
- how she defends Juliet to Lord Capulet
- why she advises Juliet to marry Paris
- whether she acts out of love for Juliet

**3.** Which of Juliet's loyalties are most severely tested in this act?

### Think about
- her mixed feelings of hate and love when she learns of Tybalt's death
- changes in her relationship with her parents
- why her marrying Paris would be considered a sin

**4.** How well do you think Romeo handles difficult circumstances?

### Think about
- his behavior to Tybalt before and after Mercutio's death
- his behavior in Friar Laurence's cell
- his state of mind when he parts from Juliet

**5.** Which event in this act do you think causes the most problems for Romeo and Juliet, and why?

**6.** What advice do you think Friar Laurence will offer Juliet in Act Four?

## A CREATIVE RESPONSE

**7.** If Mercutio had killed Tybalt in the fight, instead of the other way around, what do you think might have happened?

**8.** How do the efforts of Capulet and Lady Capulet to comfort Juliet, ironically, add to the complications of the plot? Give specific examples of the comfort each parent tries to give Juliet.

**9.** The critic Northrop Frye writes that in Shakespeare's time male friendship was often considered more important than romantic love. Therefore, when Mercutio is killed, "Juliet drops out of Romeo's mind, for the first time since he saw her, and all he can think of now is vengeance on Tybalt for his friend's death. Once again, male friendship overrides love of women." Explain whether you agree with Frye's assessment, using details from the play to support your answer.

#  nalyzing the Writer's Craft

## IMAGERY

Find the passage at the end of Act One in which Romeo sees Juliet for the first time. Notice how Romeo associates Juliet with light and brightness in his description of her beauty.

**Building a Literary Vocabulary.** Imagery refers to words and phrases that re-create sensory experiences for a reader. Images can appeal to any of the five senses: sight, hearing, smell, taste, and touch. The majority of images are visual, stimulating pictures in the reader's mind. Visual images of light and dark predominate in *Romeo and Juliet* to emphasize the contrast between love and hate and to heighten drama.

For example, in Act One before Romeo meets Juliet, he is associated with darkness because of his brooding over Rosaline: he "shuts up his windows, locks fair daylight out,/And makes himself an artificial night." When he sees Juliet for the first time, however, Romeo exclaims, "O, she doth teach the torches to burn bright!/It seems she hangs upon the cheek of night/Like a rich jewel in an Ethiop's ear." Juliet figuratively lights up Romeo's life. In a larger sense the love between Romeo and Juliet is the only light in a dark world dominated by the hatred of the feud.

**Application: Interpreting Imagery.** As a class, divide into six groups, with each group assigned to examine one of the following passages, that contain images of light and darkness.

Act Two, Scene 2, lines 2-10

Act Two, Scene 2, lines 15-32

Act Three, Scene 2, lines 1-10

Act Three, Scene 2, lines 17-25

Act Three, Scene 5, lines 1-16

Act Three, Scene 5, lines 17-36

Each group should paraphrase the passage and explain the imagery in relation to what has happened in the play up to that point. Consider especially what light and dark represent and what contrast is emphasized. Then each group should present its paraphrase and analysis of imagery to the rest of the class. After the presentations decide as a class whether the meaning of the imagery stays consistent throughout Acts Two and Three or changes as the action unfolds.

## Connecting Reading and Writing

**1.** Write an **article** for a teen magazine stating whether you believe that Romeo and Juliet are an example of the perfect couple. In your article examine why they fell in love, the actions they take because of their love, and any similarities and differences in their personalities.

Option: Imagine that you run a fourteenth-century match making service. Write two **reports**, one describing Romeo to Juliet and the other describing her to him.

**2.** Choose one **scene** from the play so far and rewrite it with a contemporary setting—for example, you might change Capulet's feast to a high school prom. Ask a friend to read your scene and comment on how well the contemporary setting works.

Option: Write a **parody** of a scene by imitating Shakespeare's style while incorporating contemporary words and phrases. Share your parody with your friends.

# ACT FOUR

**SCENE 1** *[Friar Laurence's cell.]*

*[Enter Friar Laurence and Paris.]*

**Friar Laurence.** On Thursday, sir? The time is very short.
**Paris.** My father[1] Capulet will have it so,
    And I am nothing slow to slack his haste.[2]

*has already married Romeo to Juliet*

**Friar Laurence.** You say you do not know the lady's
    mind.
5    Uneven[3] is the course; I like it not.

**Paris.** Immoderately she weeps for Tybalt's death,
    And therefore have I little talked of love;
    For Venus smiles not in a house of tears.
    Now, sir, her father counts it dangerous
10    That she do give her sorrow so much sway,
    And in his wisdom hastes our marriage
    To stop the inundation of her tears,
    Which, too much minded by herself alone,
    May be put from her by society.
15    Now do you know the reason of this haste.

**Friar Laurence.** *[Aside.]* I would I knew not why it
    should be slowed.—
    Look, sir, here comes the lady toward my cell.

*[Enter Juliet.]*

**Paris.** Happily met, my lady and my wife!

**Juliet.** That may be, sir, when I may be a wife.

20  **Paris.** That may be must be, love, on Thursday next.

**Juliet.** What must be shall be.

**Friar Laurence.**           That's a certain text.

**Paris.** Come you to make confession to this father?

**Juliet.** To answer that, I should confess to you.

**Paris.** Do not deny to him that you love me.

25  **Juliet.** I will confess to you that I love him.

**Paris.** So will ye, I am sure, that you love me.

**Juliet.** If I do so, it will be of more price,

*Romeo*

## Guide for Interpretation

**1. father:** prospective father-in-law.

**2. nothing . . . haste:** not interested in moderating Capulet's eagerness for the marriage.

**3. uneven:** difficult.

◆ **Lines 6-15:** Note the irony that Paris has come to Friar Laurence to make arrangements to marry Juliet, whom the friar has already married to Romeo. Paris says that Capulet is hastening the marriage because he thinks it will lessen Juliet's sadness.

◆ **Lines 18-36:** In this passage Juliet cleverly counters Paris' probing comments without revealing her true feelings about him.

◆ **Line 24:** Note how confident Paris is in his approach to Juliet.

606 Romeo and Juliet

Being spoke behind your back, than to your face.

**Paris.** Poor soul, thy face is much abused with tears.

30 **Juliet.** The tears have got small victory by that,
For it was bad enough before their spite.[4]

**Paris.** Thou wrongst it more than tears with that report.

**Juliet.** That is no slander, sir, which is a truth;
And what I spake, I spake it to my face.

35 **Paris.** Thy face is mine, and thou hast slandered it.

**Juliet.** It may be so, for it is not mine own.
Are you at leisure, holy father, now,
Or shall I come to you at evening mass?

**Friar Laurence.** My leisure serves me, pensive daughter, now.
40 My lord, we must entreat[5] the time alone.

**Paris.** God shield[6] I should disturb devotion!
Juliet, on Thursday early will I rouse ye.
Till then, adieu, and keep this holy kiss.

*[Exit.]*

**Juliet.** O, shut the door! and when thou hast done so,
45 Come weep with me—past hope, past cure, past help!

**Friar Laurence.** Ah, Juliet, I already know thy grief;
It strains me past the compass of my wits.[7]
I hear thou must, and nothing may prorogue[8] it,
On Thursday next be married to this County.

50 **Juliet.** Tell me not, friar, that thou hearst of this,
Unless thou tell me how I may prevent it.
If in thy wisdom thou canst give no help,
Do thou but call my resolution wise
And with this knife I'll help it presently.[9]
55 God joined my heart and Romeo's, thou our hands;
And ere this hand, by thee to Romeo's sealed,
Shall be the label to another deed,
Or my true heart with treacherous revolt
Turn to another, this shall slay them both.
60 Therefore, out of thy long-experienced time,
Give me some present counsel; or, behold,
'Twixt my extremes[10] and me this bloody knife
Shall play the umpire, arbitrating that

4. **spite:** injury.

♦ **Lines 35-36:** In responding to Paris, Juliet implies that her face is not her own—or Paris'—because she belongs to another.

5. **entreat:** request.

6. **shield:** forbid.

7. **strains . . . wits:** exceeds the limits of my wisdom.

8. **prorogue:** postpone.

9. **presently:** at once.

♦ **Lines 50-59:** Rather than sign another wedding agreement ("deed"), Juliet threatens to kill herself.

10. **extremes:** misfortunes.

Which the commission[11] of thy years and art
65  Could to no issue of true honor bring.
Be not so long to speak. I long to die
If what thou speakst speak not of remedy.

**Friar Laurence.** Hold, daughter. I do spy a kind of hope,
Which craves as desperate an execution
70  As that is desperate which we would prevent.
If, rather than to marry County Paris,
Thou hast the strength of will to slay thyself,
Then is it likely thou wilt undertake
A thing like death to chide away this shame,
75  That copest[12] with death himself to scape from it;
And, if thou darest, I'll give thee remedy.

**Juliet.** O, bid me leap, rather than marry Paris,
From off the battlements of yonder tower,
Or walk in thievish ways,[13] or bid me lurk
80  Where serpents are; chain me with roaring bears,
Or shut me nightly in a charnel house,[14]
O'ercovered quite with dead men's rattling bones,
With reeky[15] shanks and yellow chapless[16] skulls;
Or bid me go into a new-made grave
85  And hide me with a dead man in his shroud—
Things that, to hear them told, have made me
      tremble—
And I will do it without fear or doubt,
To live an unstained wife to my sweet love.

**Friar Laurence.** Hold, then. Go home, be merry, give
      consent
90  To marry Paris. Wednesday is tomorrow.
Tomorrow night look that thou lie alone;
Let not the nurse lie with thee in thy chamber.
Take thou this vial, being then in bed,
And this distilled liquor drink thou off;
95  When presently through all thy veins shall run
A cold and drowsy humor;[17] for no pulse
Shall keep his native[18] progress, but surcease;
No warmth, no breath, shall testify thou livest;
The roses in thy lips and cheeks shall fade
100  To paly ashes, thy eyes' windows fall
Like death when he shuts up the day of life;
Each part, deprived of supple government,[19]
Shall, stiff and stark and cold, appear like death;
And in this borrowed likeness of shrunk death

11. **commission:** authority.

12. **copest:** bargains.

13. **thievish ways:** in roads where thieves hide out.
14. **charnel house:** shed where bones from old graves are stored.
15. **reeky:** stinking.
16. **chapless:** jawless.

◆ **Lines 77-88:** Juliet lists all the horrible things she would endure to avoid marrying Paris. Consider what this reveals about her state of mind.

◆ **Lines 89-120.** In this passage Friar Laurence outlines his plan to rescue Juliet from having to marry Paris. Note the details of his scheme and consider whether you think it is a good one.

17. **humor:** moisture.
18. **native:** natural.

19. **supple government:** ability to move.

105     Thou shalt continue two-and-forty hours,
        And then awake as from a pleasant sleep.
        Now, when the bridegroom in the morning comes
        To rouse thee from thy bed, there art thou dead.
        Then, as the manner of our country is,
110     In thy best robes uncovered[20] on the bier
        Thou shalt be borne to that same ancient vault
        Where all the kindred of the Capulets lie.
        In the mean time, against[21] thou shalt awake,
        Shall Romeo by my letters know our drift;[22]
115     And hither shall he come; and he and I
        Will watch thy waking, and that very night
        Shall Romeo bear thee hence to Mantua.
        And this shall free thee from this present shame,
        If no inconstant toy[23] nor womanish fear
120     Abate thy valor in the acting it.

**Juliet.** Give me, give me! O, tell not me of fear!

**Friar Laurence.** Hold! Get you gone, be strong and
       prosperous
       In this resolve. I'll send a friar with speed
       To Mantua, with my letters to thy lord.

125 **Juliet.** Love give me strength! and strength shall help
       afford.
       Farewell, dear father.

                                 *[Exeunt.]*

**SCENE 2** *[Capulet's house.]*

*[Enter Capulet, Lady Capulet, Nurse, and Servingmen.]*

**Capulet.** So many guests invite as here are writ.

                   *[Exit a Servingman.]*

      Sirrah, go hire me twenty cunning cooks.

**Servingman.** You shall have none ill, sir; for I'll try if
      they can lick their fingers.

5 **Capulet.** How canst thou try them so?

**Servingman.** Marry, sir, 'tis an ill cook that cannot
      lick his own fingers. Therefore he that cannot lick
      his fingers goes not with me.

**Capulet.** Go, begone.

                  *[Exit Servingman.]*

◆ **Lines 109-112:** As is the custom, after Juliet is discovered apparently dead, she will be taken to the tomb where her ancestors lie, laid on a stone slab or table within the open chamber, and covered with a shroud.

**20. uncovered:** with uncovered face.

**21. against:** before.

**22. drift:** intention.

**23. inconstant toy:** foolish whim.

10     We shall be much unfurnished[1] for this time.
     What, is my daughter gone to Friar Laurence?

**Nurse.** Ay, forsooth.

**Capulet.** Well, he may chance to do some good on her.
     A peevish[2] self-willed harlotry[3] it is.

*[Enter Juliet.]*

15     **Nurse.** See where she comes from shrift with merry look.

**Capulet.** How now, my headstrong? Where have you
      been gadding?
**Juliet.** Where I have learnt me to repent the sin
     Of disobedient opposition
     To you and your behests,[4] and am enjoined
20     By holy Laurence to fall prostrate here
     To beg your pardon. Pardon, I beseech you!
     Henceforward I am ever ruled by you.

**Capulet.** Send for the County. Go tell him of this.
     I'll have this knot knit up tomorrow morning.

25     **Juliet.** I met the youthful lord at Laurence' cell
     And gave him what becomed[5] love I might,
     Not stepping o'er the bounds of modesty.

**Capulet.** Why, I am glad on't. This is well. Stand up.
     This is as't should be. Let me see the County.
30     Ay, marry, go, I say, and fetch him hither.
     Now, afore God, this reverend holy friar,
     All our whole city is much bound[6] to him.

**Juliet.** Nurse, will you go with me into my closet[7]
     To help me sort such needful ornaments
35     As you think fit to furnish me tomorrow?

**Lady Capulet.** No, not till Thursday. There is time
      enough.
**Capulet.** Go, nurse, go with her. We'll to church
      tomorrow.
                *[Exeunt Juliet and Nurse.]*

**Lady Capulet.** We shall be short in our provision.
     'Tis now near night.

**Capulet.**           Tush, I will stir about,
40     And all things shall be well, I warrant thee, wife.
     Go thou to Juliet, help to deck up her.

**1. unfurnished:** unprepared.

**2. peevish:** stubborn.
**3. harlotry:** good-for-nothing girl.

**4. behests:** commands.
◆ **Lines 17-22:** Notice how Juliet begins to implement Friar Laurence's plan by promising to obey her father.

◆ **Line 24:** Speculate about why Capulet moves the wedding up a day.
**5. becomed:** suitable.

**6. bound:** indebted.

**7. closet:** private room.

I'll not to bed tonight; let me alone.
I'll play the housewife for this once. What, ho!<sup>8</sup>
They are all forth; well, I will walk myself
45    To County Paris, to prepare him up
Against tomorrow. My heart is wondrous light,
Since this same wayward girl is so reclaimed.

[Exeunt.]

**8. What, ho!:** Capulet calls for a servant.

## SCENE 3 *[Juliet's chamber.]*

*[Enter* Juliet *and* Nurse.*]*

**Juliet.** Ay, those attires are best; but, gentle nurse,
    I pray thee leave me to myself tonight;
    For I have need of many orisons<sup>1</sup>
    To move the heavens to smile upon my state,
5    Which, well thou knowest, is cross<sup>2</sup> and full of sin.

**1. orisons:** prayers.

**2. cross:** contrary.

*[Enter Lady Capulet.]*

**Lady Capulet.** What, are you busy, ho? Need you my
    help?
**Juliet.** No madam; we have culled<sup>3</sup> such necessaries
    As are behooveful<sup>4</sup> for our state tomorrow.
    So please you, let me now be left alone,
10    And let the nurse this night sit up with you;
    For I am sure you have your hands full all
    In this so sudden business.

**3. culled:** selected.

**4. behooveful:** fit.

**Lady Capulet.**        Good night.
    Get thee to bed and rest, for thou hast need.

[Exeunt Lady Capulet and Nurse.]

**Juliet.** Farewell! God knows when we shall meet again.
15    I have a faint cold fear thrills through my veins
    That almost freezes up the heat of life.
    I'll call them back again to comfort me.
    Nurse!—What should she do here?
    My dismal scene I needs must act alone.
20    Come, vial.
    What if this mixture do not work at all?
    Shall I be married then tomorrow morning?
    No, no! This shall forbid it. Lie thou there.

[Lays down a dagger.]

◆ **Lines 14–58:** In this long soliloquy Juliet expresses her fears and doubts about drinking Friar Laurence's potion, and tries to work up her courage to do so.

◆ **Lines 21–23:** Juliet places a dagger close by so that she can kill herself if the potion fails.

What if it be a poison which the friar
Subtly hath ministered<sup>5</sup> to have me dead,

**5. ministered:** provided.

Lest in this marriage he should be dishonored
Because he married me before to Romeo?
I fear it is; and yet methinks it should not,
30 For he hath still been tried[6] a holy man.
How if, when I am laid into the tomb,
I wake before the time that Romeo
Come to redeem me? There's a fearful point!
Shall I not then be stifled in the vault,
35 To whose foul mouth no healthsome air breathes in,
And there die strangled ere my Romeo comes?
Or, if I live, is it not very like
The horrible conceit[7] of death and night,
Together with the terror of the place—
40 As in a vault, an ancient receptacle
Where for this many hundred years the bones
Of all my buried ancestors are packed;
Where bloody Tybalt, yet but green in earth,[8]
Lies fest'ring in his shroud; where, as they say,
45 At some hours in the night spirits resort—
Alack, alack, is it not like that I,
So early waking—what with loathsome smells,
And shrieks like mandrakes[9] torn out of the earth,
That living mortals, hearing them, run mad—
50 O, if I wake, shall I not be distraught,
Environed with all these hideous fears,
And madly play with my forefathers' joints,
And pluck the mangled Tybalt from his shroud,
And, in this rage, with some great kinsman's bone
55 As with a club dash out my desp'rate brains?
O, look! methinks I see my cousin's ghost
Seeking out Romeo, that did spit his body
Upon a rapier's point. Stay,[10] Tybalt, stay!
Romeo, I come! this do I drink to thee.

*[She drinks and falls upon her bed within the curtains.]*


SCENE 4 *[Capulet's house.]*

*[Enter Lady Capulet and Nurse.]*

**Lady Capulet.** Hold, take these keys and fetch more
    spices, nurse.
**Nurse.** They call for dates and quinces in the pastry.[1]

◆ **Lines 24-29:** Note why Juliet fears the friar might have given her real poison and why she ultimately dismisses that fear.

**6. tried:** proved.

**7. conceit:** idea.

**8. green in earth:** recently buried.

◆ **Lines 30-54:** Juliet imagines awakening before Romeo's arrival in the tomb. She fears she will go mad from terror amid the corpses in the foul-smelling vault and dash her brains out in a fit of fear and madness.

**9. mandrakes:** plants that resemble the human form. The mandrake was thought to shriek and cause madness when dug up.

**10. stay:** stop.

◆ **Line 58:** Think about how a girl of thirteen would feel, having to face this moment alone. Note what sustains her in her decision to drink the potion.

**1. pastry:** pantry.

*[Enter Capulet.]*

**Capulet.** Come, stir, stir, stir! The second cock hath
    crowed,
    The curfew bell hath rung, 'tis three o'clock.
5    Look to the baked meats, good Angelica;
    Spare not for cost.

◆ **Line 5:** Angelica is the nurse's name.

**Nurse.**            Go, you cot-quean,[2] go,
    Get you to bed! Faith, you'll be sick tomorrow
    For this night's watching.

**2. cot-quean:** man who meddles with women's affairs.

**Capulet.** No, not a whit. What, I have watched ere now
10    All night for lesser cause, and ne'er been sick.

**Lady Capulet.** Ay, you have been a mouse-hunt[3] in your
    time;
    But I will watch you from such watching now.

**3. mouse-hunt:** woman chaser.

                *[Exeunt Lady Capulet and Nurse.]*

**Capulet.** A jealous hood, a jealous hood!

*[Enter three or four Servants, with spits and logs and
baskets.]*

                      Now, fellow,
    What is there?

15  **First Servant.** Things for the cook, sir; but I know not
    what.
    **Capulet.** Make haste, make haste. *[Exit Servant.]* Sirrah,
    fetch drier logs.
    Call Peter; he will show thee where they are.

**Second Servant.** I have a head, sir, that will find out logs
    And never trouble Peter for the matter.

20  **Capulet.** Mass,[4] and well said; a merry whoreson, ha!
    Thou shalt be loggerhead.[5] *[Exit Servant.]* Good faith,
    'tis day.
    The County will he here with music straight,
    For so he said he would. *[Music within.]* I hear him near.
    Nurse! Wife! What, ho! What, nurse, I say!

**4. Mass:** by the Mass.
**5. loggerhead:** blockhead.

*[Re-enter Nurse.]*

25  Go waken Juliet; go and trim her up.
    I'll go and chat with Paris. Hie, make haste,
    Make haste! The bridegroom he is come already:

Make haste, I say.

[*Exeunt.*]

**SCENE 5** [*Juliet's chamber. Curtains drawn around her bed.*]

[*Enter Nurse.*]

**Nurse.** Mistress! what, mistress! Juliet! Fast,[1] I warrant
  her, she.
  Why, lamb! why, lady! Fie, you slugabed!
  Why, love, I say! madam! sweetheart! Why, bride!
  What, not a word? You take your pennyworths now!
5  Sleep for a week; for the next night, I warrant,
  The County Paris hath set up his rest[2]
  That you shall rest but little. God forgive me!
  Marry, and amen. How sound is she asleep!
  I needs must wake her. Madam, madam, madam!
10  Ay, let the County take you in your bed!
  He'll fright you up, i' faith. Will it not be?

[*Opens the curtains.*]

  What, dressed and in your clothes and down again?
  I must needs wake you. Lady! lady! lady!
  Alas, alas! Help, help! my lady's dead!
15  O well-a-day that ever I was born!
  Some aqua vitae, ho! My lord! my lady!

[*Enter Lady Capulet.*]

**Lady Capulet.** What noise is here?

**Nurse.**                              O lamentable day!

**Lady Capulet.** What is the matter?

**Nurse.**                              Look, look! O heavy day!

**Lady Capulet.** O me, O me! My child, my only life!
20  Revive, look up, or I will die with thee!
  Help, help! Call help.

[*Enter Capulet.*]

**Capulet.** For shame, bring Juliet forth; her lord is come.

**Nurse.** She's dead, deceased; she's dead! Alack the day!

**Lady Capulet.** Alack the day, she's dead, she's dead, she's
  dead!

1. **fast:** fast asleep.

2. **set . . . rest:** is firmly resolved.

**Capulet.** Ha! let me see her. Out alas! she's cold,
25
Her blood is settled, and her joints are stiff;
Life and these lips have long been separated.
Death lies on her like an untimely frost
Upon the sweetest flower of all the field.

**Nurse.** O lamentable day!
30

**Lady Capulet.**          O woeful time!

**Capulet.** Death, that hath ta'en her hence to make me
wail,
Ties up my tongue and will not let me speak.

*[Enter Friar Laurence and Paris, with Musicians.]*

**Friar Laurence.** Come, is the bride ready to go to
church?
**Capulet.** Ready to go, but never to return.
35
O son, the night before thy wedding day
Hath death lain with thy wife. See, there she lies,
Flower as she was, deflowered by him.
Death is my son-in-law, Death is my heir;
My daughter he hath wedded. I will die
40
And leave him all. Life, living, all is Death's.

**Paris.** Have I thought long to see this morning's face,
And doth it give me such a sight as this?

**Lady Capulet.** Accursed, unhappy, wretched, hateful day!
Most miserable hour that e'er time saw
45
In lasting labor of his pilgrimage!
But one, poor one, one poor and loving child,
But one thing to rejoice and solace in,
And cruel Death hath catched it from my sight!

**Nurse.** O woe! O woeful, woeful, woeful day!
50
Most lamentable day, most woeful day
That ever ever I did yet behold!
O day! O day! O day! O hateful day!
Never was seen so black a day as this.
O woeful day! O woeful day!

**Paris.** Beguiled, divorced, wronged, spited, slain!
55
Most detestable Death, by thee beguiled,
By cruel cruel thee quite overthrown!
O love! O life! not life, but love in death!

**Capulet.** Despised, distressed, hated, martyred, killed!

◆ **Lines 28-29:** Consider this simile comparing Juliet's apparent death to what happens to a flower stricken by frost.

◆ **Lines 35-39:** Capulet describes death as a suitor who secretly married Juliet.

60    Uncomfortable³ time, why camest thou now
      To murder, murder our solemnity?⁴
      O child! O child! my soul, and not my child!
      Dead art thou, dead! alack, my child is dead,
      And with my child my joys are buried!

65    **Friar Laurence.** Peace, ho, for shame! Confusion's⁵ cure
              lives not
      In these confusions. Heaven and yourself
      Had part in this fair maid! now heaven hath all,
      And all the better is it for the maid.
      Your part in her you could not keep from death,
70    But heaven keeps his part in eternal life.
      The most you sought was her promotion,
      For 'twas your heaven she should be advanced;
      And weep ye now, seeing she is advanced
      Above the clouds, as high as heaven itself?
75    O, in this love, you love your child so ill
      That you run mad, seeing that she is well.⁶
      She's not well married that lives married long,
      But she's best married that dies married young.
      Dry up your tears and stick your rosemary⁷
80    On this fair corse, and, as the custom is,
      In all her best array bear her to church;
      For though fond nature bids us all lament,
      Yet nature's tears are reason's merriment.⁸

      **Capulet.** All things that we ordained festival
85    Turn from their office to black funeral—
      Our instruments to melancholy bells,
      Our wedding cheer to a sad burial feast;
      Our solemn hymns to sullen <u>dirges</u>⁹ change;
      Our bridal flowers serve for a buried corse;
90    And all things change them to the contrary.

      **Friar Laurence.** Sir, go you in; and, madam, go with him;
      And go, Sir Paris. Every one prepare
      To follow this fair corse unto her grave.
      The heavens do lower¹⁰ upon you for some ill;
95    Move them no more by crossing their high will.

              [*Exeunt* Capulet, Lady Capulet, Paris, *and* Friar.]

      **First Musician.** Faith, we may put up our pipes and be
              gone.

      **Nurse.** Honest good fellows, ah, put up, put up!

**3. uncomfortable:** distressing.
**4. solemnity:** festivity.

**5. confusion:** disaster.

**6. well:** in heaven.

**7. rosemary:** a symbol of immortality and enduring love, used at funerals and weddings.
**8. For though . . . merriment:** While mourning is natural, rejoicing is also reasonable because Juliet is in heaven.

**9. dirges** (dʉrj′ əz): slow, sad songs expressing grief for the dead.

♦ **Lines 84-90:** Consider whether you feel sympathy for the Capulets.

**10. lower:** frown.
♦ **Lines 94-95:** Notice that Friar Laurence tells the family not to cross heaven, which is punishing them for some reason. Think about what reasons he might have for encouraging them to accept Juliet's death without question.

For well you know this is a pitiful case.

[Exit.]

**Second Musician.** Ay, by my troth, the case may be
    amended.
[Enter Peter.]

100 **Peter.** Musicians, O, musicians, "Heart's Ease," "Heart's
    Ease"![11] O, an you will have me live, play "Heart's Ease."

**11. "Heart's Ease":** a
popular tune of the time.

**First Musician.** Why "Heart's Ease"?

**Peter.** Oh, musicians, because my heart itself plays "My
    heart is full of woe." O, play me some merry dump[12] to
105     comfort me.

**12. dump:** mournful tune.

♦ **Lines 100-142:** Peter, a
Capulet servant, has an
amusing argument with the
musicians who were to play
at Juliet's wedding. This long,
witty dialogue provides a
moment of comic relief for
the audience in contrast to
the shock and grief over
Juliet's apparent death.

**First Musician.** Not a dump we! 'Tis no time to play now.

**Peter.** You will not then?

**First Musician.** No.

**Peter.** I will then give it you soundly.

110 **First Musician.** What will you give us?

**Peter.** No money, on my faith, but the gleek.[13] I will give
    you the minstrel.[14]

**13. gleek:** mock or gibe.
**14. give . . . minstrel:** call
you rogues.

**First Musician.** Then will I give you the serving-creature.

**Peter.** Then will I lay the serving-creature's dagger on
115     your pate. I will carry no crotchets.[15] I'll re you, I'll fa[16]
    you. Do you note[17] me?

**15. carry no crotchets:** sing
no quarter notes; that is, put
up with none of your whims.
**16. re, fa:** notes of the scale.
**17. note:** heed.
**18. note us:** put us to
music.

**First Musician.** An you re us and fa us, you note us.[18]

**Second Musician.** Pray you put up your dagger, and put
    out your wit.

120 **Peter.** Then have at you with my wit! I will dry-beat you
    with an iron wit, and put up my iron dagger.[19] Answer
    me like men
        "When griping grief the heart doth wound,
        And doleful dumps the mind oppress,
125        Then music with her silver sound—"
    Why "silver sound"? Why "music with her silver sound"?
    What say you, Simon Catling?[20]

**19. I will . . . dagger:** I will
display my merciless wit.

**20. catling:** a catgut lute
string.

**First Musician.** Marry, sir, because silver hath a sweet
    sound.

130 **Peter.** Pretty! What say you, Hugh Rebeck?[21]

**Second Musician.** I say "silver sound" because musicians sound for silver.

**Peter.** Pretty too! What say you, James Soundpost?[22]

**Third Musician.** Faith, I know not what to say.

135 **Peter.** O, I cry you mercy! You are the singer.[23] I will say for you. It is "music with her silver sound" because musicians have no gold for sounding.[24]
    "Then music with her silver sound
    With speedy help doth lend redress."[25]

                              *[Exit.]*

140 **First Musician.** What a pestilent knave is this same!

**Second Musician.** Hang him, Jack! Come, we'll in here, tarry for the mourners, and stay[26] dinner.

                              *[Exeunt.]*

**21. rebeck:** a three-stringed violin.

**22. soundpost:** part of a violin.

**23. I cry . . . singer:** I beg your pardon; you are only a dumb singer.

**24. musicians . . . sounding:** musicians have no money.

**25. redress** (ri dres′): something done to make up for a wrong or injury.

**26. stay:** wait for.

# Thinking About Act Four

## A PERSONAL RESPONSE

*sharing impressions*

**1.** How do you feel about the way circumstances have worked out so far for Juliet? Describe your feelings in your journal.

*constructing interpretations*

**2.** What aspects of Juliet's character do you think are most apparent in this act?

### Think about
- how Juliet responds to Paris in Friar Laurence's cell
- how she behaves toward her family after she agrees to Friar Laurence's plan
- the different thoughts and feelings she expresses in her soliloquy before taking the potion

**3.** Explain whether you think Juliet was right to follow Friar Laurence's plan.

### Think about
- her hatred of the idea of marrying Paris and her love for Romeo
- her fears about the plan
- whom else she might have turned to for help

**4.** Do you feel sympathy for the Capulets, the nurse, or Paris when they express grief over Juliet's death? Why or why not?

## A CREATIVE RESPONSE

**5.** If Juliet had been too afraid to drink Friar Laurence's potion, what other plan could the friar have devised?

## A CRITICAL RESPONSE

**6.** Shakespeare's tragedies often include comic relief, humorous scenes in the course of a serious drama that relieve the emotional intensity. Explain whether you think this technique is used successfully in the play so far. Use specific examples from the play to support your answer.

**7.** The scholar G. B. Harrison writes, "Juliet begins as a demure girl who is prepared to listen respectfully to the advice of her mother. When she has fallen in love, she becomes suddenly a woman of great courage and resource, who will face even death and fantastic horror to regain her husband." Explain whether you agree with this assessment of Juliet.

**8.** Compare Juliet's options with the options of a teenager today who is feeling desperate over a conflict with her parents.

# ACT FIVE

## SCENE 1 [A street in Mantua.]

[Enter Romeo.]

**Romeo.** If I may trust the flattering truth of sleep,[1]
  My dreams presage[2] some joyful news at hand.
  My bosom's lord[3] sits lightly in his throne,
  And all this day an unaccustomed spirit
5  Lifts me above the ground with cheerful thoughts.
  I dreamt my lady came and found me dead
  (Strange dream that gives a dead man leave to think!)
  And breathed such life with kisses in my lips
  That I revived and was an emperor.
10  Ah me! how sweet is love itself possessed,
  When but love's shadows are so rich in joy!

[Enter Romeo's *servant*, Balthasar, *booted*.]

  News from Verona! How now, Balthasar?
  Dost thou not bring me letters from the friar?
  How doth my lady? Is my father well?
15  How fares my Juliet? That I ask again,
  For nothing can be ill if she be well.

**Balthasar.** Then she is well, and nothing can be ill.
  Her body sleeps in Capels' monument,[4]
  And her immortal part with angels lives.
20  I saw her laid low in her kindred's vault
  And presently took post[5] to tell it you.
  O, pardon me for bringing these ill news,
  Since you did leave it for my office,[6] sir.

**Romeo.** Is it e'en so? Then I defy you, stars!
25  Thou knowst my lodging. Get me ink and paper
  And hire posthorses. I will hence tonight.

**Balthasar.** I do beseech you, sir, have patience.
  Your looks are pale and wild and do import
  Some misadventure.

**Romeo.**           Tush, thou art deceived.
30  Leave me and do the thing I bid thee do.
  Hast thou no letters to me from the friar?

**Balthasar.** No, my good lord.

---

**1. flattering . . . sleep:**
pleasant dreams that seemed
true.

**2. presage:** foretell.

**3. bosom's lord:** heart.

♦ **Lines 6-9:** Note the details of
Romeo's dream, which he
interprets as a happy one.

**4. Capels' monument:** the
Capulet family tomb.

**5. took post:** rode hard.

**6. office:** duty.

♦ **Lines 24-26:** Romeo chooses
to defy his fate ("you, stars")
and return to Verona in spite
of the death sentence
awaiting him there. Note
Romeo's reaction here: he
does not weep and moan at
the news of Juliet's death, as
he did when he first learned
of his banishment in Act
Three. He acts quickly and
decisively.

he's angry
everything
possible has gone wrong

**Romeo.**                    No matter. Get thee gone
And hire those horses. I'll be with thee straight.

[*Exit* Balthasar.]

Well, Juliet, I will lie with thee tonight.
35  Let's see for means. O mischief, thou art swift
To enter in the thoughts of desperate men!
I do remember an apothecary,[7]
And hereabouts he dwells, which late I noted
In tattered weeds,[8] with overwhelming brows,
40  Culling of simples.[9] Meager were his looks,
Sharp misery had worn him to the bones;
And in his needy shop a tortoise hung,
An alligator stuffed, and other skins
Of ill-shaped fishes; and about his shelves
45  A beggarly account of empty boxes,
Green earthen pots, bladders, and musty seeds,
Remnants of packthread,[10] and old cakes of roses[11]
Were thinly scattered, to make up a show.
Noting this penury, to myself I said,
50  "An if a man did need a poison now
Whose sale is present[12] death in Mantua,
Here lives a caitiff[13] wretch would sell it him."
O, this same thought did but forerun my need,
And this same needy man must sell it me.
55  As I remember, this should be the house.
Being holiday, the beggar's shop is shut.
What, ho! apothecary!

[*Enter* Apothecary.]

**Apothecary.**                Who calls so loud?

**Romeo.** Come hither, man. I see that thou art poor.
Hold, there is forty ducats.[14] Let me have
60  A dram of poison, such soon-speeding gear[15]
As will disperse itself through all the veins
That the life-weary taker may fall dead,
And that the trunk[16] may be discharged of breath
As violently as hasty powder fired
65  Doth hurry from the fatal cannon's womb.

**Apothecary.** Such mortal[17] drugs I have; but Mantua's law
Is death to any he that utters[18] them.

**Romeo.** Art thou so bare and full of wretchedness

---

7. **apothecary:** one who sells herb mixtures and medicines.

8. **weeds:** clothes.

9. **culling of simples:** sorting herbs.

10. **packthread:** twine.

11. **cakes of roses:** small blocks of pressed rose petals, used in perfume.

12. **present:** immediate.

13. **caitiff:** miserable.

♦ **Lines 34-54:** Notice how quickly Romeo thinks of a plan to kill himself. Poison had been in his thoughts ever since he first saw the poor apothecary's shop.

14. **ducats:** gold coins.

15. **gear:** stuff.

16. **trunk:** body.

17. **mortal:** deadly.

18. **utters:** sells.

And fearest to die? Famine is in thy cheeks,
Need and oppression starveth in thine eyes,
Contempt and beggary hangs upon thy back:
The world is not thy friend, nor the world's law;
The world affords no law to make thee rich;
Then be not poor, but break it and take this.

75 **Apothecary.** My poverty but not my will consents.

**Romeo.** I pay thy poverty and not thy will.

**Apothecary.** Put this in any liquid thing you will
And drink it off, and if you had the strength
Of twenty men, it would dispatch you straight.

80 **Romeo.** There is thy gold—worse poison to men's souls,
Doing more murder in this loathsome world,
Than these poor compounds that thou mayst not sell.
I sell thee poison; thou hast sold me none.
Farewell. Buy food and get thyself in flesh.
85 Come, cordial[19] and not poison, go with me
To Juliet's grave; for there must I use thee.

[*Exeunt.*]

◆ **Lines 68-84:** Romeo plays on
the apothecary's poverty to
convince him to sell illegal
poison. Consider Romeo's
comparison of money to
poison in its effect on people.

**19. cordial:** a hearty
stimulant.

---

**SCENE 2** [*Verona. Friar Laurence's cell.*]

[*Enter Friar John.*]

**Friar John.** Holy Franciscan friar, brother, ho!

[*Enter Friar Laurence.*]

**Friar Laurence.** This same should be the voice of Friar
John.
Welcome from Mantua. What says Romeo?
Or, if his mind be writ, give me his letter.

5 **Friar John.** Going to find a barefoot brother out,
One of our order to associate[1] me,
Here in this city visiting the sick,
And finding him, the searchers[2] of the town,
Suspecting that we both were in a house
10 Where the infectious pestilence did reign,
Sealed up the doors, and would not let us forth,
So that my speed to Mantua there was stayed.

**Friar Laurence.** Who bare my letter, then, to Romeo?

**1. associate:** accompany.

**2. searchers:** health officers.

**Friar John.** I could not send it—here it is again—

15     Nor get a messenger to bring it thee,

    So fearful were they of infection.

**Friar Laurence.** Unhappy fortune! By my brotherhood,

    The letter was not nice,[3] but full of charge,[4]

    Of dear import; and the neglecting it

20     May do much danger. Friar John, go hence,

    Get me an iron crow[5] and bring it straight

    Unto my cell.

**Friar John.**           Brother, I'll go and bring it thee.

*[Exit.]*

**Friar Laurence.** Now must I to the monument alone.

    Within this three hours will fair Juliet wake.

25     She will beshrew[6] me much that Romeo

    Hath had no notice of these accidents;[7]

    But I will write again to Mantua,

    And keep her at my cell till Romeo come—

    Poor living corse, closed in a dead man's tomb!

*[Exeunt.]*

**SCENE 3** *[A churchyard with the* Capulets' *tomb.]*

*[Enter* Paris *and his* Page *with flowers and a torch.]*

**Paris.** Give me thy torch, boy. Hence, and stand aloof.

    Yet put it out, for I would not be seen.

    Under yond yew tree lay thee all along,[1]

5     Holding thine ear close to the hollow ground.

    So shall no foot upon the churchyard tread

    (Being loose, unfirm, with digging up of graves)

    But thou shalt hear it. Whistle then to me,

    As signal that thou hearst something approach.

    Give me those flowers. Do as I bid thee, go.

10 **Page.** *[Aside]* I am almost afraid to stand alone

    Here in the churchyard; yet I will adventure.

*[Withdraws.]*

**Paris.** Sweet flower, with flowers thy bridal bed I strew

*[He strews the tomb with flowers.]*

(O woe! thy canopy is dust and stones)

---

♦ **Lines 5-16:** Note how an accident of fate prevents Friar John from delivering Friar Laurence's letter informing Romeo of Juliet's faked death. Health officials refused to let Friar John travel because they believed he had been exposed to a contagious disease.

**3. nice:** trivial.

**4. full of charge:** very important.

**5. iron crow:** crowbar.

**6. beshrew:** blame.

**7. accidents:** happenings.

♦ **Line 29:** Think about how Friar Laurence's words "poor living corse [corpse]" apply to Juliet, who sleeps within the Capulet tomb.

**1. all along:** at full length.

15

Which with sweet water[2] nightly I will dew;    *Paris really loved her*
Or, wanting[3] that, with tears distilled by moans.
The obsequies[4] that I for thee will keep
Nightly shall be to strew thy grave and weep.

[*The* Page *whistles.*]

The boy gives warning something doth approach.
What cursed foot wanders this way tonight

20

To cross[5] my obsequies and true love's rite?
What, with a torch? Muffle me, night, awhile.

[*Withdraws.*]

[*Enter* Romeo *and* Balthasar *with a torch, a mattock (pickax), and a crowbar.*]

**Romeo.** Give me that mattock and the wrenching iron.
Hold, take this letter. Early in the morning
See thou deliver it to my lord and father.

25

Give me the light. Upon thy life I charge thee,
Whate'er thou hearest or seest, stand all aloof
And do not interrupt me in my course.
Why I descend into this bed of death
Is partly to behold my lady's face,

30

But chiefly to take thence from her dead finger
A precious ring—a ring that I must use
In dear employment.[6] Therefore hence, be gone.
But if thou, jealous,[7] dost return to pry
In what I farther shall intend to do,

35

By heaven, I will tear thee joint by joint
And strew this hungry churchyard with thy limbs.
The time and my intents are savage-wild,
More fierce and more inexorable[8] far
Than empty[9] tigers or the roaring sea.

40

**Balthasar.** I will be gone, sir, and not trouble you.

**Romeo.** So shalt thou show me friendship. Take thou
   that.
Live, and be prosperous; and farewell, good fellow.

**Balthasar.** [*Aside*] For all this same, I'll hide me
   hereabout.
His looks I fear, and his intents I doubt.

[*Withdraws.*]

45

**Romeo.** Thou detestable maw,[10] thou womb of death,

---

**2. sweet water:** perfume.
**3. wanting:** lacking.
**4. obsequies:** funeral rites.
◆ **Lines 12-17:** Notice Paris' genuine grief at Juliet's death.

**5. cross:** interfere with.

*says he's going to get a ring*

◆ **Lines 28-32:** Romeo lies to Balthasar about his reasons for entering the tomb.

**6. dear employment:** for an important purpose.
**7. jealous:** curious.

**Lines 32-39:** Romeo threatens to kill Balthasar if he interferes with Romeo's actions at the tomb. Note how the violence of the images echoes the violence of Romeo's mood.

**8. inexorable** (in eks' ə rə bəl): unyielding, relentless.
**9. empty:** hungry.

**10. maw:** stomach.

Gorged with the dearest morsel of the earth,
Thus I enforce thy rotten jaws to open,
And in despite[11] I'll cram thee with more food.

*[Romeo opens the tomb.]*

**Paris.** This is that banisht haughty Montague
50  That murdered my love's cousin—with which grief
It is supposed the fair creature died—
And here is come to do some villainous shame
To the dead bodies. I will apprehend[12] him.
Stop thy unhallowed toil, vile Montague!
55  Can vengeance be pursued further than death?
Condemned villain, I do apprehend thee.
Obey, and go with me; for thou must die.

**Romeo.** I must indeed; and therefore came I hither.
Good gentle youth, tempt not a desp'rate man.
60  Fly hence and leave me. Think upon these gone;
Let them affright thee. I beseech thee, youth,
Put not another sin upon my head
By urging me to fury. O, be gone!
By heaven, I love thee better than myself,
65  For I come hither armed against myself.
Stay not, be gone. Live, and hereafter say
A madman's mercy bid thee run away.

**Paris.** I do defy thy conjuration[13]
And apprehend thee for a felon here.

70  **Romeo.** Wilt thou provoke me? Then have at thee, boy!

*[They fight.]*

**Page.** O Lord, they fight! I will go call the watch.

*[Exit.]*

**Paris.** O, I am slain! *[Falls.]* If thou be merciful,
Open the tomb, lay me with Juliet.

*[Dies.]*

**Romeo.** In faith, I will. Let me peruse this face.
75  Mercutio's kinsman, noble County Paris!
What said my man when my betossed[14] soul
Did not attend[15] him as we rode? I think
He told me Paris should have married Juliet.
Said he not so? or did I dream it so?
Or am I mad, hearing him talk of Juliet,

**11. despite:** scorn.

◆ **Lines 45-48:** In this extended metaphor Romeo compares the tomb to a stomach that holds the "dearest morsel," Juliet. Think about what he means by saying he will "cram" the stomach with more food.

**12. apprehend:** arrest.

◆ **Lines 49-55:** Note the assumption Paris makes about Romeo's reason for coming to the Capulet tomb.

◆ **Lines 58-67:** Note Romeo's sincerity and gentleness toward Paris. He confides that he came to the tomb to die and earnestly tries to avoid a fight—"tempt not a desp'rate man." Romeo wants to spare Paris' life so that he will not die with another sin on his head.

**13. conjuration:** appeal.

**14. betossed:** upset.
**15. attend:** listen to.

To think it was so? O, give me thy hand,
One writ with me in sour misfortune's book!
I'll bury thee in a triumphant[16] grave.
A grave? O, no, a lantern,[17] slaughtered youth,
85  For here lies Juliet, and her beauty makes
This vault a feasting presence[18] full of light.
Death,[19] lie thou there, by a dead man interred.

[Lays Paris *in the tomb.*]

How oft when men are at the point of death
Have they been merry! which their keepers call
90  A lightning[20] before death. O, how may I
Call this a lightning? O my love! my wife!
Death, that hath sucked the honey of thy breath,
Hath had no power yet upon thy beauty.
Thou art not conquered. Beauty's ensign yet
95  Is crimson in thy lips and in thy cheeks,
And death's pale flag is not advanced there.
Tybalt, liest thou there in thy bloody sheet?
O, what more favor can I do to thee
Than with that hand that cut thy youth in twain
100  To sunder his that was thine enemy?
Forgive me, cousin! Ah, dear Juliet,
Why art thou yet so fair? Shall I believe
That unsubstantial Death is amorous,
And that the lean abhorred monster keeps
105  Thee here in dark to be his paramour?[21]
For fear of that I still will stay with thee
And never from this palace of dim night
Depart again. Here, here will I remain
With worms that are thy chambermaids. O, here
110  Will I set up my everlasting rest
And shake the yoke of inauspicious stars
From this world-wearied flesh. Eyes, look your last!
Arms, take your last embrace! and, lips, O you
The doors of breath, seal with a righteous kiss
115  A dateless[22] bargain to engrossing death!
Come, bitter conduct; come, unsavory guide!
Thou desperate pilot, now at once run on
The dashing rocks thy seasick weary bark!
Here's to my love! [*Drinks.*] O true apothecary!
120  Thy drugs are quick. Thus with a kiss I die.

[*Falls.*]

**16. triumphant:** glorious.

**17. lantern:** a dome with windows that give more light to the hall beneath.

**18. feasting presence:** a beautiful chamber where the queen held public court.

**19. Death:** Paris' corpse.

◆ **Lines 76-87:** Romeo feels kindly toward Paris even though he knows that Paris was supposed to marry Juliet. Romeo fulfills Paris' dying wish to be laid near Juliet, because two young men are both victims of the same cruel fate.

**20. lightning:** a revival of spirits.

◆ **Lines 97-101:** Romeo tells Tybalt's corpse that he will make amends for Tybalt's death by killing himself. He then asks forgiveness of Tybalt, his "cousin."

**21. paramour:** lover

◆ **Lines 109-120:** Romeo believes that death is the only escape from his unlucky fate. In the line "Come, bitter conduct; come, unsavory guide!" he speaks to the bottle of poison. As he drinks the poison, he makes a toast to his love.

**22. dateless:** eternal.

[*Enter Friar Laurence, with lantern, crowbar, and spade.*]

**Friar Laurence.** Saint Francis be my speed!²³ how oft
    tonight
Have my old feet stumbled at graves! Who's there?

        **23. speed:** help.

**Balthasar.** Here's one, a friend, and one that knows you well.

**Friar Laurence.** Bliss be upon you! Tell me, good my
    friend,
125  What torch is yond that vainly lends his light
To grubs and eyeless skulls? As I discern,
It burneth in the Capels' monument.

**Balthasar.** It doth so, holy sir; and there's my master,
One that you love.

**Friar Laurence.**     Who is it?

**Balthasar.**                 Romeo.

130  **Friar Laurence.** How long hath he been there?

**Balthasar.**                    Full half an hour.

**Friar Laurence.** Go with me to the vault.

**Balthasar.**               I dare not, sir.
My master knows not but I am gone hence,
And fearfully did menace me with death
If I did stay to look on his intents.

135  **Friar Laurence.** Stay then; I'll go alone. Fear comes
    upon me.
O, much I fear some ill unthrifty²⁴ thing.

        **24. unthrifty:** unlucky.

**Balthasar.** As I did sleep under this yew tree here,
I dreamt my master and another fought,
And that my master slew him.

**Friar Laurence.**         Romeo!

[*Stoops and looks on the blood and weapons.*]

140  Alack, alack, what blood is this which stains
The stony entrance of this sepulcher?
What mean these masterless and gory swords
To lie discolored by this place of peace?

[*Enters the tomb.*]

Romeo! O, pale! Who else? What, Paris too?
145  And steeped in blood? Ah, what an unkind hour

Is guilty of this lamentable chance!
The lady stirs.

[Juliet *rises*.]

  **Juliet.** O comfortable²⁵ friar! where is my lord?
I do remember well where I should be,
150    And there I am. Where is my Romeo?

  **Friar Laurence.** I hear some noise. Lady, come from
     that nest
Of death, contagion, and unnatural sleep.
A greater power than we can contradict
Hath thwarted our intents. Come, come away.
155    Thy husband in thy bosom there lies dead;
And Paris too. Come, I'll dispose of thee
Among a sisterhood of holy nuns.
Stay not to question, for the watch is coming.
Come, go, good Juliet. I dare no longer stay.

160  **Juliet.** Go, get thee hence, for I will not away.

[*Exit* Friar Laurence.]

What's here? A cup, closed in my true love's hand?
Poison, I see, hath been his timeless²⁶ end.
O churl! drunk all, and left no friendly drop
To help me after? I will kiss thy lips.
165    Haply²⁷ some poison yet doth hang on them
To make me die with a restorative.²⁸

[*Kisses him.*]

Thy lips are warm!

  **Chief Watchman.** [*Within*] Lead, boy. Which way?

  **Juliet.** Yea, noise? Then I'll be brief. O happy²⁹ dagger!

[*Snatches* Romeo's *dagger.*]

170    This is thy sheath; there rest, and let me die.

[*She stabs herself and falls.*]

[*Enter* Watchmen *with the* Page *of* Paris.]

  **Page.** This is the place. There, where the torch doth
    burn.

  **Chief Watchman.** The ground is bloody. Search about
    the churchyard.

**25. comfortable:** comforting.

◆ **Lines 151-159:** Startled by a noise, Friar Laurence tries to make Juliet leave the tomb. Notice how abruptly he tells her of Romeo's death and offers to put her in a convent. Remember that he planned the fake death because Juliet threatened to kill herself. Think about why he would abandon her in such desperate circumstances now.

**26. timeless:** untimely.

◆ **Lines 160-166:** Like Romeo earlier, Juliet does not weep over her lover's death but decisively searches for a way to join him.

**27. haply:** perhaps.

**28. restorative:** medicine.

**29. happy:** timely.

Go, some of you; whoe'er you find attach.[30]

*[Exeunt some of the* Watch.*]*

Pitiful sight! here lies the County slain;
175 And Juliet bleeding, warm, and newly dead,
Who here hath lain this two days buried.
Go, tell the Prince; run to the Capulets;
Raise up the Montagues; some others search.

*[Exeunt others of the* Watch.*]*

We see the ground whereon these woes[31] do lie,
180 But the true ground[32] of all these piteous woes
We cannot without circumstance descry.[33]

*[Re-enter some of the* Watch, *with* Balthasar.*]*

**Second Watchman.** Here's Romeo's man. We found
him in the churchyard.

**Chief Watchman.** Hold him in safety till the Prince
come hither.

*[Re-enter* Friar Laurence *and another* Watchman.*]*

**Third Watchman.** Here is a friar that trembles, sighs,
and weeps.
185 We took this mattock and this spade from him
As he was coming from this churchyard side.

**Chief Watchman.** A great suspicion![34] Stay the friar
too.

*[Enter the* Prince *and* Attendants.*]*

**Prince.** What misadventure is so early up,
That calls our person from our morning rest?

*[Enter* Capulet, Lady Capulet, *and others.]*

190 **Capulet.** What should it be, that they so shriek abroad?

**Lady Capulet.** The people in the street cry "Romeo,"
Some "Juliet," and some "Paris"; and all run,
With open outcry, toward our monument.

**Prince.** What fear is this which startles[35] in our ears?

195 **Chief Watchman.** Sovereign, here lies the County
Paris slain;
And Romeo dead; and Juliet, dead before,
Warm and new killed.

---

**30. attach:** arrest.

**31. woes:** the three bodies.

**32. ground:** reason.

**33. descry:** understand.

◆ **Line 184:** Note the distraught condition of the friar.

**34. A great suspicion:** A most suspicious thing.

◆ **Lines 191-193:** Just as the brawl in Act One disturbed the peace of the entire city, the deaths of Paris, Romeo, and Juliet cause widespread disruption in Verona.

**35. startles:** shouts.

**Prince.** Search, seek, and know how this foul murder
    comes.

**Chief Watchman.** Here is a friar, and slaughtered
    Romeo's man,
200   With instruments upon them fit to open
    These dead men's tombs.

**Capulet.** O heavens! O wife, look how our daughter
    bleeds!
    This dagger hath mista'en,[36] for, lo, his house[37]
    Is empty on the back of Montague,
205   And it missheathed in my daughter's bosom!

**Lady Capulet.** O me! this sight of death is as a bell
    That warns my old age to a sepulcher.

*[Enter* Montague *and others.]*

**Prince.** Come, Montague; for thou art early up
    To see thy son and heir now early down.

210 **Montague.** Alas, my liege, my wife is dead tonight!
    Grief of my son's exile hath stopped her breath.
    What further woe conspires against mine age?

**Prince.** Look, and thou shalt see.

**Montague.** O thou untaught! what manners is in this,
215   To press before thy father to a grave?

**Prince.** Seal up the mouth of outrage[38] for a while,
    Till we can clear these ambiguities
    And know their spring,[39] their head, their true descent;
    And then will I be general of your woes
220   And lead you even to death. Meantime forbear,
    And let mischance be slave to patience.[40]
    Bring forth the parties of suspicion.

**Friar Laurence.** I am the greatest, able to do least,
    Yet most suspected, as the time and place
225   Doth make against me, of this direful[41] murder;
    And here I stand, both to impeach and purge[42]
    Myself condemned and myself excused.

**Prince.** Then say at once what thou dost know in this.

**Friar Laurence.** I will be brief, for my short date of
    breath[43]
230   Is not so long as is a tedious tale.

**36. mista'en:** mistaken; that is, missed its right target.

**37. his house:** the dagger's sheath.

♦ **Lines 202-205:** Note Capulet's shock as he discovers his daughter—whom he believed to be dead and buried—newly stabbed.

**38. seal . . . outrage:** refrain from emotional outbursts.

**39. spring:** source.

**40. let . . . patience:** let patience control your hasty reactions.

**41. direful:** dreadful, terrible.

**42. impeach and purge:** accuse and clear (of guilt).

**43. short . . . breath:** the little life left me.

Romeo, there dead, was husband to that Juliet;
And she, there dead, that Romeo's faithful wife.
I married them; and their stol'n marriage day
Was Tybalt's doomsday, whose untimely death
235    Banisht the new-made bridegroom from this city;
For whom, and not for Tybalt, Juliet pined.[44]
You, to remove that siege of grief from her,
Betrothed and would have married her perforce
To County Paris. Then comes she to me
240    And with wild looks bid me devise some mean
To rid her from this second marriage,
Or in my cell there would she kill herself.
Then gave I her (so tutored by my art)
A sleeping potion; which so took effect
245    As I intended, for it wrought on her
The form of death. Meantime I writ to Romeo
That he should hither come as this dire night
To help to take her from her borrowed[45] grave,
Being the time the potion's force should cease.
250    But he which bore my letter, Friar John,
Was stayed by accident, and yesternight
Returned my letter back. Then all alone
At the prefixed hour[46] of her waking
Came I to take her from her kindred's vault;
255    Meaning to keep her closely at my cell
Till I conveniently could send to Romeo.
But when I came, some minute ere the time
Of her awaking, here untimely lay
The noble Paris and true Romeo dead.
260    She wakes; and I entreated her come forth
And bear this work of heaven with patience;
But then a noise did scare me from the tomb,
And she, too desperate, would not go with me,
But, as it seems, did violence on herself.
265    All this I know, and to the marriage
Her nurse is privy;[47] and if aught in this
Miscarried by my fault, let my old life
Be sacrificed, some hour before his time,
Unto the rigor of severest law.
270  **Prince.** We still have known thee for a holy man.
Where's Romeo's man? What can he say in this?

**Balthasar.** I brought my master news of Juliet's death;
And then in post[48] he came from Mantua
To this same place, to this same monument.

---

♦ **Lines 231-269:** As you read Friar Laurence's summary of what happened, think about the possible effect of his words on Montague and the Capulets, who knew nothing of their children's relationship.

**44. pined:** wasted away with grief and longing.

**45. borrowed:** temporary.

**46. prefixed hour:** time fixed in advance.

**47. is privy:** shared the secret.

**48. in post:** with full speed.

275 This letter he early bid me give his father,
And threatened me with death, going in the vault,
If I departed not and left him there.

**Prince.** Give me the letter. I will look on it.
Where is the County's page that raised[49] the watch?
280 Sirrah, what made[50] your master in this place?

**Page.** He came with flowers to strew his lady's grave;
And bid me stand aloof, and so I did.
Anon comes one with light to ope the tomb;
And by-and-by my master drew on him;
285 And then I ran away to call the watch.

**Prince.** This letter doth make good the friar's words,
Their course of love, the tidings of her death;
And here he writes that he did buy a poison
Of a poor pothecary, and therewithal
290 Came to this vault to die and lie with Juliet.
Where be these enemies? Capulet, Montague,
See what a scourge[51] is laid upon your hate,
That heaven finds means to kill your joys[52] with love!
And I, for winking[53] at your discords too,
295 Have lost a brace of kinsmen. All are punished.

**Capulet.** O brother Montague, give me thy hand.
This is my daughter's jointure,[54] for no more
Can I demand.

**Montague.** But I can give thee more;
For I will raise her statue in pure gold,
300 That whiles Verona by that name is known,
There shall no figure at such rate be set[55]
As that of true and faithful Juliet.

**Capulet.** As rich shall Romeo's by his lady's lie—
Poor sacrifices of our enmity!

305 **Prince.** A glooming peace this morning with it brings.
The sun for sorrow will not show his head.
Go hence, to have more talk of these sad things;
Some shall be pardoned, and some punished;
For never was a story of more woe
310 Than this of Juliet and her Romeo.

*[Exeunt.]*

**49. raised:** gave alarm to.
**50. made:** did.

**51. scourge** (skɵrj): punishment.

**52. your joys:** your children.

◆ **Lines 292-295:** Note that the Prince believes that events were directed by a higher power, "heaven." Think about whether you agree with him. Also consider what he means by "All are punished."

**53. winking:** shutting my eyes.

**54: jointure:** dowry, or property that a bride brings to her husband.

**55. at such . . . set:** be valued so highly.

# Thinking About Act Five

## A PERSONAL RESPONSE

*sharing impressions*

**1.** How do you feel about the suicides of the two young lovers? Write about your feelings in your journal.

*constructing interpretations*

**2.** Why do you think that Romeo and Juliet each choose suicide after learning about the other's death?

### Think about
- how quickly events have developed since their first meeting
- whether there are any adults they can turn to for help
- their belief in fate, mentioned throughout the play
- whether they have demonstrated good judgment in their earlier decisions

**3.** Do you think that fate or individual characters are more responsible for the deaths of Romeo and Juliet? Why?

### Think about
- how likely it is that their love could have overcome their families' hate
- whether other characters might have acted differently if they had known about Romeo and Juliet's marriage
- the extent to which accidents and coincidences contribute to the outcome
- what other choices Romeo and Juliet might have made

**4.** How do you think Romeo has changed by Act Five?

**5.** How would you judge Friar Laurence's behavior in this act?

## A CREATIVE RESPONSE

**6.** If Friar Laurence had stayed with Juliet until her parents came, do you think she still would have killed herself?

## A CRITICAL RESPONSE

**7.** Do you think that Shakespeare glorifies suicide in this play or condemns it? Use specific details from the play to support your answer.

**8.** What point do you think Shakespeare wanted to make by having Paris and Lady Montague also die in this act?

**9.** Do you think it is true to human nature that, with the deaths of their children, Capulet and Montague end the feud? Why or why not?

# *Analyzing the Writer's Craft*

## TRAGEDY AND PLOT

How would you describe the way that Romeo and Juliet face death?

**Building a Literary Vocabulary.** In drama, a tragedy is a particular kind of play in which events turn out disastrously for the main character or characters. Usually, the tragic hero or heroine dies at the end of the play, after facing death with courage and nobility of spirit. In contrast to Romeo's and Juliet's earlier fits of helpless weeping, their decisions to die are made without fear or complaint. Although Romeo and Juliet do display courage, some critics think that the lovers are pathetic, rather than tragic, figures because they give in to despair by committing suicide.

Because an intricate chain of events is needed to bring about the tragic end, plot is an important element in tragedy. The plot of a classic tragedy contains five stages: exposition, rising action, climax, falling action, and catastrophe. These stages can be charted on a plot diagram like the following:

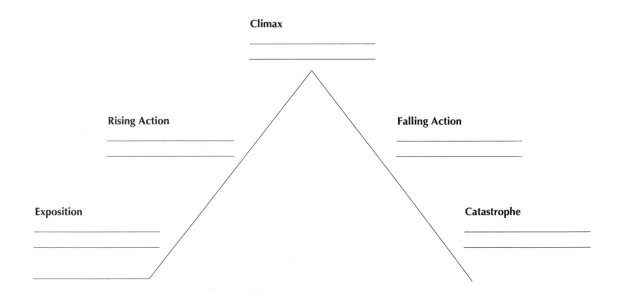

**Application: Diagramming the Plot of a Tragedy.** In groups of three or four, create a plot diagram for *Romeo and Juliet*, filling in the important details for each of the five stages. For example, under "Exposition" you would list the important introductory information presented in the prologue.

# Connecting Reading and Writing

**1.** From 1660 to nearly 1850, *Romeo and Juliet* was often performed with a happy ending in which the lovers live. Imagine that you have been asked to write a happy ending for your school to perform. Write a **proposal** in which you explain either how you would change the play to create such an outcome or why you would prefer to use Shakespeare's ending.

Option: Explain in an **essay** for your teacher what would be missed in a happy version of the play.

**2.** Compose **obituaries** for any two of the characters who die in the play, giving the facts of each person's life and death and commenting on his or her character.

Option: Write **epitaphs** to go on the tombs of each of the following characters: Mercutio, Tybalt, Paris, Romeo, Juliet, and Lady Montague.

**3.** Write an **editorial** on feuding that might appear in the Verona newspaper the day after Romeo and Juliet die. Use specific examples from the play to support your opinions.

Option: Write the **outline** for a speech to be presented to your class comparing the feud in *Romeo and Juliet* to a contemporary situation.

**4.** Prince Escalus has decided to put the parents on trial for negligence leading to their children's deaths. You have been called as a witness of the tragic events. Prepare a **written transcript** of your testimony explaining whether you think the adults or the teenagers are most responsible for the violent deaths in Verona.

Option: Create a chart illustrating several cause and effect relationships in the play and indicating your conclusions about who is ultimately responsible. Then write a **summary** of the information and conclusions shown on your chart.

**5.** Analyze three or four situations in the play in which characters who act on incomplete information trigger tragic events. Create a **chart** showing the characters, the information they lack, their actions, and the tragic repercussions of those actions. Share your chart with your study group.

Option: Write **notes** for an oral report on how human ignorance contributed to the tragedy of *Romeo and Juliet*.

# Biographies of Authors

***Maya Angelou*** (born 1928), although best known for her autobiographical books, has written poems, stage plays, screenplays, television specials, short stories, and magazine articles. She has also worked for newspapers in Egypt and Ghana. Angelou studied dance with Martha Graham, toured twenty-two countries in a production of the opera *Porgy and Bess,* directed and acted in off-Broadway shows, and served as a television narrator and interviewer. She has written and recorded songs and has composed musical scores for her screenplays. When time has permitted, Angelou has toured the country as a lecturer and visiting professor at various colleges and universities. During the 1960's, she worked with Dr. Martin Luther King, Jr., as a coordinator for the Southern Christian Leadership Conference.

***Isaac Asimov*** (born 1920) is almost a one-man encyclopedia. His more than three hundred books concern everything from science fact and fiction to history, Shakespeare, and the Bible. Asimov was born in the Soviet Union and moved with his parents to the United States when he was three years old. A brilliant student, he entered Columbia University at age fifteen and had his first science fiction story published by the time he was eighteen. Asimov permanently altered the genre of science fiction by the sheer volume and imaginative power of his works. In addition, he is the author of a number of science textbooks and a well-respected contributor to the field of robotics.

***Toni Cade Bambara*** (born 1939) had a remarkably varied education, ranging from a school for mimes in Paris and the University of Florence in Italy to the Katherine Dunham Dance Studio and the Harlem Film Institute in New York City. In the 1970's, Bambara became actively involved in social and political activities in the African-American community, where she is still deeply committed. Reviewers of her fiction remark on her distinctive style, which combines poetic rhythms and imagery with a street-talking slang. Bambara's first novel, *The Salt Eaters,* received the American Book Award in 1981, and her documentary film "The Bombing of Osage" has also won a number of awards.

***Matsuo Bashō*** (1644-1694) is known as the greatest poet of Japan. Early in his life, he went to work for a noble family and became the companion of the son. When the son died, Bashō was greatly upset. He left the family's service and became a wandering poet, teaching haiku to make a living. One day, according to legend, Bashō was out with some students. One of them suddenly announced that he had thought of a poem: "Pluck off the wings of a bright red dragonfly and there a pepper pod will be." Bashō informed the student that he would never be a poet. A poet, according to Bashō, would have created this image: "Add but the wings to a bright red pepper pod and there a dragonfly will be." Whether the story is true or not, it reflects the deep compassion for all living things that, along with his superb technical skills as a poet, made Bashō a major figure in world literature.

***William Blake*** (1757-1827) was born in London. At the age of fourteen he began his artistic career, not as a poet, but as a painter and engraver, working in the shop of a well-known master. It soon became clear, however, that Blake's creativity was not limited to copper plates and at twenty-six he published his first book of poetry. It was written in the bold, simple style that would mark all of his later work. The other hallmark of his art and life was his exceptional spirituality. Once, a visitor came upon Blake in his studio, looking intently at a point not far from him and then back to the pad where he was drawing. He looked and drew, alternately, until the visitor commented on it. Blake explained that Lot — the only survivor of the Biblical destruction of Sodom and Gomorrah — was sitting for his portrait.

***Gwendolyn Brooks*** (born 1917) has spent most of her life in Chicago. Although her background is middle-class, she identifies deeply with poor people and often makes them the subject of her poems and short stories. From the beginning, Brooks's poetry won praise for its simplicity and depth of feeling. *Annie Allen,* her second book, won the 1950 Pulitzer Prize. In 1969 she was named poet laureate of Illinois, and in 1985 she was appointed Poetry Consultant to the Library of Congress. When not writing poetry, Brooks has worked to support African-American community organizations, publishing ventures, and writing workshops.

***Yosa Buson*** (1716-1784) was a well-known Japanese painter as well as a great haiku poet. Born into a wealthy family in Kema, Japan, Buson left home at an early age to study with the masters of haiku. He traveled around Japan, staying with one teacher and then another, learning the many skills of this exquisite poetic form. Then, at the age of thirty-five, Buson settled in Kyoto to make his living as a painter and to continue working on his poetic technique. By the time he was in his sixties, he had gained a reputation as a highly respected poet. He wrote in the tradition of the great Bashō, but most critics agree he did not have Bashō's profound understanding of and compassion for all living beings. Buson's greatest contribution to the haiku tradition is probably his richly visual language that reflects the painter's love of detail and ornamentation.

***Truman Capote*** (1924-1984) spent his early years in the care of various southern relatives, including an elderly cousin, Miss Sook Faulk, who was the inspiration for "A Christmas Memory." Capote was sent to New York City for high school; he was a poor student, listless and uninterested in anything except writing. After graduation, he worked for *The New Yorker* magazine as a glorified errand boy, occasionally publishing a short story. Winning the O. Henry Short Story Award in 1943 and again in 1946 allowed him to concentrate on writing. His books were immediate successes; his novel *Breakfast at Tiffany's* was made into a popular movie in the 1960's. Capote spent six years on his most sensational book, *In Cold Blood,* which relates the true story of a mass murder in Kansas. His idea was to create a new literary form that combines fiction and journalism. He called his book a "nonfiction novel." Capote himself was as unique and eccentric as the characters he created. When not writing, he often socialized with an exclusive international crowd.

***Anton Chekhov*** (1860-1904) born in Taganrog, Russia, was by training a doctor, but the world has recognized him as one of the greatest playwrights in history. The young doctor's first plays were short comedies inspired by vaudeville and French farce. Later, he began to write longer and more serious works which were miserable failures at first. Then the director of the Moscow Art Theatre realized that Chekhov was writing a new, more realistic kind of play that demanded a new kind of acting. Out of that theater's productions of many of Chekhov's plays came a new appreciation of his unique vision. By the time of his death, Chekhov was a celebrated playwright and short story writer in Russia. He did not become internationally known until translations of his work began appearing after World War II.

***Eugenia Collier*** (born 1928) started teaching college English in 1955 but did not begin writing until fourteen years later. One of her first efforts, "Marigolds," won the Gwendolyn Brooks Short Story Award. Collier explains her new-found ability in this way: "After a conventional Western-type education, I discovered the richness, the diversity, the beauty of my black heritage. The fact of my blackness is the core and center of my creativity." Collier is making up for lost time with an outpouring of poems, stories, articles, and critical essays.

***Richard Connell*** (1893-1949) began his professional writing career at age ten by covering local baseball games for the newspaper his father edited. He attended Harvard University, where he was editor of both the college newspaper and *Lampoon,* the school's humor magazine. After graduation, Connell worked for newspapers and advertising agencies before becoming a fiction writer in 1919. He wrote film scripts and published several short story collections and novels.

***e.e. cummings*** (Edward Estlin Cummings) (1894-1962) was an innovative modern poet whose work influenced many later writers. As a young man, cummings volunteered for duty in France during World War I. When the fighting ended, he stayed in Paris to study art. He was a talented painter, and his search for new methods of expression is evident in his art, as it is in his poetry. In his poems he ignored rules of punctuation, capitalization, and spacing, running words together and stretching syllables out over several lines to create various rhythms and images. His intent was to coax meaning and dimension from the limitations of the printed word. At first, many critics condemned his work. Now, cummings is accepted as a major American poet.

***Guy de Maupassant*** (1850-1893) was born in France, the son of a stockbroker. From an early age, de Maupassant was interested in writing. However, he spent many years as a soldier and then as a government employee before he met with literary success. De Maupassant is known as one of the creators and early masters of the short story. "The Umbrella," "The Piece of String," and "The Necklace" are among his most famous works.

**Agnes de Mille** (born 1909) is a dancer, choreographer, and director whose autobiographical writings reflect her artistic experiences. Against the wishes of her family, de Mille studied dance and made her professional debut in 1929 with the *Ballet Rambert* international tour. Upon her return to the States in 1940, de Mille devoted herself to the opening of the American Ballet Theater (A.B.T.). She then began to choreograph, adding to her productions elements of American folk dance which became her trademark. De Mille has been awarded two Tony Awards (in 1947 and 1962) and the Capezio Dance Award. She most recently worked on an eighteen-month dance tour in celebration of A.B.T.'s fiftieth anniversary.

**Babette Deutsch** (1895-1982) published her first book of poetry in 1919. During the next sixty years, she became famous for her poetry, while at the same time writing novels, books for children, and literary criticism. From 1944 until her death, Deutsch was a lecturer in poetry at Columbia University in New York City.

**Emily Dickinson** (1830-1886) lived her entire life in Amherst, Massachusetts. During her early years, she led the typical life of an upper-class young girl in small-town New England. At age twenty-six, however, she suddenly withdrew from the world and rarely appeared in public again. It is thought that an unhappy love affair caused the great change in her personality. Throughout the next thirty years, Dickinson spent long hours in her room, secretly writing poetry on envelopes, paper bags, and other scraps of paper. She wrote more than seventeen hundred poems, of which only seven were published during her life. Although Dickinson used simple words and short stanzas, she displayed the originality of true genius. Today she is considered one of the most popular and influential of American poets.

**Daphne du Maurier** (1907-1989) was born in London into a family of writers and artists: her grandfather wrote novels, her uncle was a playwright, and her father won acclaim as a successful actor. Du Maurier first started writing to satisfy her own need for quiet and solitude. She soon gained a wide audience with her novels of romance tinged with mystery and suspense. Two of her works, the popular novel *Rebecca* and the short story "The Birds," attracted the attention of the great movie director Alfred Hitchcock, who made them into successful films.

**Loren Eiseley** (1907-1977) was an anthropologist by training but a poet by instinct and vision. His reputation rests on his ability to communicate the wonders and mysteries of natural science to ordinary people. Originally from Nebraska, Eiseley became a professor of anthropology at the University of Pennsylvania and curator of the Early Man collection at the University Museum. Eiseley wrote over twelve science books, narrated a television program called "Animal Secrets," and served as a consultant to numerous museums and foundations. He was the recipient of more than thirty-six honorary degrees and prizes.

***Robert Frost*** (1874-1963) was born to a family whose New England ancestors dated back eight generations. As a young man, Frost married and worked at odd jobs — as a mill hand, a shoe salesman, a farmer. When he was thirty-eight, his farm in New Hampshire failed, and he moved his family to England, where he concentrated on writing poetry. Frost had been writing poems since the age of fifteen with no success whatsoever; but as he neared the age of forty, his work began to receive recognition. His first two collections were praised in both Britain and the United States, and he returned home to New England. With each succeeding volume his stature in the literary world grew, and for the last forty years of his life he was considered one of the world's most important living poets. Frost was issued a special Congressional medal in 1960 and is the only American poet to win four Pulitzer Prizes. In 1961 he was asked to read his work at the inauguration of President John F. Kennedy.

***William Gibson*** (born 1914) is a novelist, poet, and dramatist, although his greatest recognition has come as a playwright. *Two for the Seesaw* had a long Broadway run and brought fame to Gibson and to his leading lady, Anne Bancroft. She also starred in his best-known play, *The Miracle Worker,* which Gibson originally wrote as a television script. He adapted it for the stage in 1959 and for film in 1962.

***Ellen Goodman*** (born 1941) grew up in Massachusetts. When she began writing a regular column for the Boston Globe she was quickly recognized for her wit and sharp insight into contemporary issues. Today her column is syndicated and appears in nearly four hundred newspapers across the country. Whether she is poking fun at athletes who appear in underwear advertisements or commenting on the problems of divorce, Goodman rewards her readers with both a high quotient of laughs and something to think about. In 1980, Goodman was awarded a Pulitzer Prize for her columns. She appears frequently on televison and radio as a commentator on current events, and her writing has been collected in a number of books.

***Eddy L. Harris*** is a young African-American journalist from St. Louis. In *Mississippi Solo,* his first book, he reveals much about himself and his observations of race relations in the United States.

***O. Henry*** (1862-1910) was the pen name of William Sidney Porter. As a young man, O. Henry went to Texas to work as a ranch hand. His fellow cowboys must have thought him odd, as he carried a small dictionary in one pocket and a book of poetry in the other. Eventually, he found work as a journalist and started his own humor weekly titled *The Rolling Stone.* When the publication failed, however, he found a job as a bank teller. Bookkeeping practices at the bank were careless and haphazard, and when a shortage was discovered, O. Henry was accused of embezzlement. He was almost certainly innocent and probably would have been acquitted, but he made the mistake of running away to Central and South America. When he returned two years later to visit his dying wife, he was quickly arrested and sentenced to three years in prison. While serving his term, he wrote stories under his pen name and continued writing upon his release. O. Henry turned out stories at an amazing rate, often one a week. Several collections were not even published until after his death.

**Langston Hughes** (1902-1967) was the first African American to earn his living solely from writing. Before becoming established as a writer, he worked as a farmer, cook, waiter, sailor, and doorman — a series of jobs that took him to more than eight countries. Hughes's first real recognition as a poet came to him when he was a hotel busboy. He left some of his poems at the table where poet Vachel Lindsay was dining. Lindsay was so impressed that he presented Hughes's work along with his own at poetry readings. In addition to the poetry for which he is best known, Hughes wrote novels, short stories, plays, song lyrics, and radio scripts. In his writing, he described the common people of Harlem, using their dialect and the jazz rhythms of their music. Hughes was active in helping young writers who came to him for advice.

**James Hurst** (born 1922) left the North Carolina farm where he was raised to study chemical engineering. After a short time he gave in to his love of music and began voice lessons at the Julliard School of Music. Hoping for an operatic career, Hurst went to Rome for additional study, but he soon realized that he had little chance for success. He returned to the United States where he worked as a bank clerk and wrote in his spare time. His first real recognition came in 1960 with the publication of "The Scarlet Ibis" in *The Atlantic Monthly.*

**Shirley Jackson** (1919-1965) is known primarily for her stories of psychological horror and evil, but she also wrote humorous stories, plays, and children's books. Born and raised in California, Jackson attended Syracuse University and settled in Vermont after marrying. Her husband and four children became the subjects of her humorous fictionalized autobiographies *Life Among Savages* and *Raising Demons*. She established her reputation as a writer of horror fiction with her short story "The Lottery" and her novel *The Haunting of Hill House.*

**Helen Keller** (1880-1968), born in Tuscumbia, Alabama, was a happy and normal baby until an illness left her blind and deaf at age two. By her own account, she lived the next five years like a wild animal. Then her father took her to Dr. Alexander Graham Bell, the inventor of the telephone, who recommended a teacher, Anne Sullivan. Sullivan communicated with Keller through touch and helped her to master reading and writing in Braille. The play *The Miracle Worker,* by William Gibson, is about Keller's discovery of the gift of language. As a teenager, Keller learned how to use her vocal cords. She attended Radcliffe College, graduating with honors. Dedicated to helping the blind, she raised funds, went on speaking tours, and visited more than twenty-five countries. The books she wrote have been translated into more than fifty languages.

**Jack Kerouac** (1922-1969) dropped out of college after a year, briefly worked as a merchant marine, and then traveled around the country doing physical labor. With the publication of his first work in 1950, Kerouac became the leader of the "beat" movement, an assortment of young people who rebelled against the commercialism and conventionalism of American life after World War II. The characters in Kerouac's novels opt out of the struggle to get ahead and set out to find happiness. Their goal — as well as methods that included sex, drugs, and Zen Buddhism — foreshadowed the countercultural movement of the 1960's.

***Martin Luther King, Jr.,*** (1929-1968) entered college at the age of fifteen and was ordained a minister at nineteen. He was only twenty-six years old when he organized the bus boycott in Montgomery, Alabama, to protest segregation, an act that brought him to national prominence. For the next thirteen years, King's courage, intelligence, and remarkable speaking ability were the moving forces behind the American civil rights movement. Under his leadership, the movement virtually eliminated segregation in public facilities. In 1964, King was awarded the Nobel Peace Prize. Four years later, he was assassinated. When his birthday was declared a national holiday, he became only the second American, after George Washington, to be given that honor.

***Doris Lessing*** (born 1919) began life in Persia, present-day Iran, where her father was stationed as a captain in the British army. She spent most of her youth on a farm in Rhodesia, now called Zimbabwe. These colonial experiences in the Middle East and Africa contributed to her awareness of racial and economic exploitation. Lessing is also known for her interest in feminist themes, and her novels and short stories have often focused on the changing situation for women.

***Denise Levertov*** (born 1923) grew up in England in an unusual atmosphere. Her father, a converted Russian Jew, became an Anglican minister who filled the house with thousands of books and dozens of temporary refugees, artists, and literary exiles. Her mother, a descendant of a mystical Welsh preacher, read classics to the family and provided all of Levertov's education. When Levertov was twelve years old, she sent some of her poems to poet T.S. Eliot, who thought them worthy enough to merit a long letter of advice. Her first collection of poetry was published when she was twenty-three. Her second did not appear until ten years later, after she had married an American soldier, moved to New York, and immersed herself in American culture. Since then Levertov has published many volumes of poetry. Much of her work, like "The Sharks," reveals an element of mystery in ordinary occurences.

***Beryl Markham*** (1902-1985) grew up on her father's farm in British East Africa, now called Kenya, playing with local Murani children and later hunting with Murani warriors. Her father taught her to breed and train race horses, but the young Markham's interest turned to the relatively new profession of aviation. In 1936 Markham's solo flight across the Atlantic Ocean, from east to west, earned her a ticker-tape parade in New York City and a place in the record books. After traveling for a while in the United States and spending a brief time in Hollywood in the 1940's, Markham returned to Africa. Aviation had changed after World War II and so had Africa, but Markham supported herself in the land that she loved by raising race horses once again.

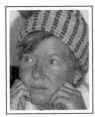

***Jean McCord*** (born 1924) has found time for writing even as she has pursued a variety of occupations, including time served in the Women's Army Corps. Her short stories have been published in *Seventeen* magazine and in *Best American Short Stories*.

**Patrick McManus** (born in 1933) currently lives in Washington state. His humorous pieces about the great outdoors have appeared frequently in such magazines as *Field & Stream, Reader's Digest,* and *Sports Illustrated.*

**Edna St. Vincent Millay** (1892-1950) was the first woman to win the Pulitzer Prize (1923). During the 1920's and 1930's, she was one of the best-known poets in the United States. Millay graduated from Vassar in 1917 and moved to Greenwich Village, where she supported herself doing translations, acting, and writing love stories under a pen name. Proclaiming that her "candle burns at both its ends," Millay was often considered the voice of a rebellious generation. Her poetry, however, was usually written in traditional poetic forms.

**David Nava Monreal** is a prize-winning poet who lives in California. His work has been anthologized in Chicano literature collections and in textbooks. "Moco Limping" was written about his own dog.

**Farley Mowat** (born 1921) spent much of his youth exploring the Canadian Arctic wilderness and continues to prefer the life of a naturalist. "I am a simple fellow," says Mowat, "and I like simple things. Cities give me the pip. Civilizations scare me." Not surprisingly, Mowat writes about the land, people, and animals he loves. He is often highly critical of those forces that endanger the environment, its creatures, and native peoples. After living with the Ihalmuit Eskimos for two years, he wrote *People of the Deer* to protest the Canadian government's treatment of the vanishing tribe. His book about wolves in the Artic, *Never Cry Wolf,* was made into a movie.

**Pablo Neruda** (1904-1973) won the Nobel prize for literature in 1971 and is considered by many to be the greatest Latin American poet of his time. He published his first poems when he was only seventeen. In his early work, Neruda movingly explores his own feelings; his later poetry is filled with dreamlike, often violent, images and symbols with very personal meanings. In addition to writing poetry, Neruda was active in politics. He was a member of the Chilean foreign service, served in the Chilean Senate from 1945 to 1948, and was ambassador to France in the early 1970's.

**Andre Norton** (born 1912) is the pen name of Alice Mary Norton. Norton began her career as a children's librarian but soon took a different direction. Trained in research and having a love for history, she began writing historical novels. Then in the 1950's, she started writing science fiction, shifting from a focus on the past to an interest in the future. This new form of fiction was rich territory for a writer with the talent for adventure stories that Norton had developed in her historical novels. Native Americans appear as major characters in several of her science fiction novels, such as *The Sioux Spaceman,* adding a special interest to these works. Some of her science fiction was written under the pen name of Andrew North.

***Gloria Oden*** (born 1923) was a senior editor of math, science, and language text-books before switching to a career of college teaching and poetry writing. Her work has appeared in numerous anthologies, and she has received two awards for creative writing.

***Liam O'Flaherty*** (1896-1984) was raised on the desolate Aran Islands off the west coast of Ireland. He signed up with the Irish Guards in 1915 but was discharged two years later after suffering severe shell shock in World War I. Returning to Dublin, O'Flaherty joined for a time in the Irish struggle for independence from Britain, then set out on a series of wan-derings. He worked in a London brewery, signed on as a seaman bound for Brazil, and lived in New York's Bowery district. Upon his return to Ireland in 1921, he began to write. The set-tings for O'Flaherty's stories are usually his native Aran Islands or Dublin.

***Dorothy Parker*** (1893-1967) is remembered best for her witty poems and short sto-ries. Readers delight in her ability to find humor in any situation. Parker's work appeared in many magazines, but she was most closely associated with *The New Yorker,* to which she contributed regularly for over thirty years. She also spent several years in Hollywood as a screen writer. Parker was a great champion of liberal causes and left the bulk of her estate to Dr. Martin Luther King, Jr., and the NAACP.

***Sylvia Plath*** (1932-1963) started writing at a very young age. Her short story "Initiation" was published in *Seventeen* magazine when she was only twenty years old. Although she occasionally wrote fiction, Plath primarily chose poetry to explore and express her troubled emotions. On the surface, her life was always successful. She gradu-ated with honors from Smith College, went to Cambridge University in England on a Fulbright Scholarship, met and married English poet Ted Hughes, and had two children. Her first book of poetry, *The Colossus,* was published in 1960, when she was twenty-seven. Three years later, however, Plath killed herself. In the last years of her life, she sometimes wrote two or three poems a day, trying to work out on paper the anger, terror, and anguish that had been with her since her father's death when she was eight. After Plath's death, Hughes edited several volumes of her poetry, letters, and fiction. In 1982, her work was awarded the Pulitzer Prize for poetry.

***Edgar Allan Poe*** (1809-1849) was born in Boston, the son of traveling actors. His father's desertion of the family followed by the death of his mother when he was only two years old marked the beginning of a tragic and unhappy life. The orphaned Poe was taken in by Mr. and Mrs. John Allan of Virginia, who gave him his middle name. Constant dis-agreements with his stepfather, though, made the arrangement difficult. After brief studies at the University of Virginia and a self-engineered dismissal from West Point, Poe sought work as a journalist. Although he received recognition for his biting, sarcastic literary reviews, money was scarce and Poe was often without funds for even food and heat. Poverty intensified his despair over the lingering illness and eventual death of his beloved wife, Virginia. Deeply depressed, Poe often sought escape in alcohol. Despite, or perhaps because of, his tragic life, he produced a body of work that continues to be both unique and popular. He was an innovator in the composition of the modern short story, and many critics also credit him with the invention of the detective story. His classic horror tales, such as "The Black Cat" and "The Tell-Tale Heart," established his reputation as a master of psychological terror and the macabre. Poe also wrote haunting poetry, such as "The Raven" and "Annabel Lee."

***Marjorie Kinnan Rawlings*** (1896-1953) wrote short stories at night while working for a newspaper during the day. Finally, in 1928 she purchased an orange grove in Florida where she farmed and wrote in solitude for almost twenty years. *The Yearling,* her most popular book, tells of a fourteen-year-old boy's passage from childhood to manhood. It was awarded the 1939 Pulitzer Prize and was eventually made into a movie. Rawlings produced many other novels and short stories, most set in Florida's scrub-pine back country. *Cross Creek,* a collection of nonfiction sketches about Rawlings's farm life and neighbors, was the basis for a movie.

***Theodore Roethke*** (1908-1963) grew up in Michigan, where his father and uncle owned a greenhouse. As a young poet, he sold his poems for a dollar each. Eventually, though, he earned almost every honor a writer dreams of achieving — two Guggenheim Fellowships, a Pulitzer Prize, and two National Book Awards. Along with writing, Roethke taught at many universities and sometimes coached varsity tennis as well. Roethke is an original, imaginative poet. His work ranges from childlike nonsense rhymes to complicated metaphors. Many of his subjects are drawn from the world of nature.

***Carl Sandburg*** (1878-1967) had a long and distinguished career as a poet, folklorist, and biographer. As a child, Sandburg attended school intermittently between various jobs as a harvester, milk truck driver, and barbershop helper. After serving in the Spanish-American War, he moved to Chicago and worked as a news reporter. Sandburg's first poetry collections, *Chicago Poems* and *Cornhuskers,* were published in 1914 and celebrated the energy and vitality of American life. These early poems established his fame as a poet of the people. He went on to publish several other poetry collections, four children's books, two collections of folksongs, and several biographies — including one of Lincoln, for which he won the Pulitzer Prize for history in 1940. Sandburg received the Pulitzer Prize for poetry in 1951.

***Richard Selzer*** (born 1928) did not set out to be a writer. Like playwright Anton Chekhov, Selzer was trained as a physician. Unlike Chekhov, however, Selzer decided to become a surgeon. He currently practices in New Haven, Connecticut, where he is also on the faculty of the Yale School of Medicine. Although Alexandre Dumas said that "a good surgeon operates with his hand, not with his heart," Selzer's literary work indicates clearly that both hand and heart are hard at work in his case. His experiences and attitudes are evident in his collection of short stories, *Rituals of Surgery,* which was published in 1974, as well as in his essays on medicine, which won him the National Magazine Award in 1975.

***Wallace Stevens*** (1879-1955) knew he did not have the stamina to endure the life of a struggling poet and so obtained a law degree after graduating from college. He practiced law for a while, then joined a Connecticut insurance firm, where he worked for the rest of his life. Throughout this time, Stevens wrote some of the most remarkable poems in American literature. He ultimately became a great influence on poets of his own and future generations.

**Frank R. Stockton** (1834-1902) was born in Philadelphia, Pennsylvania. He first became known as a writer of fairy tales, which were published in both magazines and books. Stockton helped edit *St. Nicholas,* a children's publication. He also wrote stories for adults. "The Lady, or the Tiger?" is by far the most widely read of Stockton's stories.

**Adrien Stoutenburg** (born 1916) worked as a librarian, reporter, and editor before turning to writing as a full-time career. Since 1951 she has published more than thirty books, including poetry, short stories, biographies, and novels. One of her most popular books, *American Tall Tales,* is a collection of folklore. Stoutenburg is also an accomplished artist, sculptor, and musician.

**Amy Tan** (born 1952) was not always the proud Chinese American that she is now. She recalls dreaming when she was young of making her features look more Western by having plastic surgery. It was not until she made her first trip to China in 1987 that Tan could truly accept both the Chinese and American cultures as her own. Though Tan won a writing contest at the age of eight, her identity as a writer was slow in coming, too. However, after successfully publishing some of her stories in magazines — "Two Kinds" was one of them — Tan combined those stories with others into a novel and called it *The Joy Luck Club,* which became a bestseller.

**Hernando Téllez** (1908-1966) is a Colombian diplomat and politician as well as a writer. Although known chiefly for his essays on social and political matters in South America, Téllez also published a collection of short stories, *Ashes for the Wind and Other Tales,* in 1950. One of the stories, "Lather and Nothing Else," has been widely translated and anthologized.

**James Thurber** (1894-1961) made a career out of poking fun at modern human beings and their complicated society. His humorous writings and cartoon drawings are peopled with small, frightened adults bowing under the weight of life's pressures. Sad-looking dogs and unmannerly children also live in the Thurber world. Much of his work first appeared in *The New Yorker,* with which he was associated for more than twenty-five years. Thurber's cartoons, essays, and short stories helped to create the magazine's sophisticated style. "The Secret Life of Walter Mitty" is one of the most popular of Thurber's short stories.

**Mark Twain** (1835-1910) was the pen name of Samuel Clemens, one of America's best and most loved humorists. Twain grew up in Hannibal, Missouri, on the Mississippi River. He loved the water and lived a wild and joyous boyhood. These experiences were the basis for his most popular books, *The Adventures of Tom Sawyer* and *The Adventures of Huckleberry Finn.* As a young man, Twain worked as a printer and then as a riverboat pilot. The Civil War, however, closed the river to travel, and Twain headed west where he was a prospector, adventurer, and eventually a journalist. At this time he first used his pen name, a riverboat term that means "the water marks the measuring twine at two fathoms."

***Kurt Vonnegut, Jr.*** (born 1922) once described a writer as "a person who makes his living with his mental disease." Whether the definition fits or not, Vonnegut writes wildly comic fiction about some of the blackest aspects of society. His concerns are the horrors of war, human brutality, and the crush of modern technology. Raised in the Midwest and armed with his father's advice to learn "something useful," Vonnegut went to college and studied biochemistry and anthropology. During World War II, he was captured by the German army. As a prisoner of war, he witnessed the Allied firebombing of Dresden. The total destruction of the city and 135,000 of its citizens is a memory that haunts Vonnegut and that appears repeatedly in his work, especially in his novel *Slaughterhouse-Five.* His first attempts at writing were incorrectly labeled science fiction and were virtually ignored by critics. With the 1963 publication of *Cat's Cradle,* however, he experienced instant popularity with critics and the reading public.

***David Wagoner*** (born 1926) successfully combines the career of a college professor at the University of Washington with that of a poet. He has published more than twenty collections of poetry and received many prizes, including Guggenheim and Ford Fellowships. Wagoner was raised in Indiana, which may explain his interest in fellow Hoosier John Dillinger. Most of Wagoner's poetry celebrates the coastal areas of the Pacific Northwest, where he currently lives.

***Alice Walker*** (born 1944) has come a long way from the small Georgia farm where she was raised. She has campaigned for welfare rights, helped in voter registration, and traveled to Kenya, Uganda, and the Soviet Union. She also has taught at Wellesley and Jackson State colleges and the University of Massachusetts. Her best-known novel is *The Color Purple,* which won the Pulitzer Prize and was made into a popular movie.

***Margaret Walker*** (born 1915) won the Yale Younger Poets Award in 1942 for her first book of poetry, *For My People.* In 1966 she published *Jubliee,* a carefully researched novel of slavery and the Civil War. Besides being a writer, Walker has been a social worker, magazine editor, college English instructor, and mother to four children. In 1968 she was named director of the Institute for the Study of the History, Life, and Culture of Black Peoples.

***Elinor Wylie*** (1885-1928) was born into a prominent social and political family. She spent her youth in Washington, D.C., where she studied painting and secretly wrote poetry, wavering between the two pursuits as possible careers. After a socially correct but unhappy marriage, Wylie set out for Europe alone and began to write seriously. She returned to America in 1916, and her poems began to appear in magazines. Eight years later, she was a famous person, the author of two successful poetry collections and a novel.

# Index of Essential Vocabulary

## A

abhorrence, 254, 258
admonition, 287, 290
adulation, 126, 129
adversary, 406, 416, 530, 537
adversities, 421, 425
affable, 4, 9
anecdote, 282, 283
anomalous, 110, 114
appalled, 313, 315
ascetic, 20, 21
aura, 222, 226
avenge, 406, 410
avenger, 27, 30
aversion, 446, 504

## B

beleaguered, 20, 21
benign, 222, 223

## C

calamity, 242, 243
carnivore, 294, 298
cavernous, 265, 269
commandeered, 421, 423
commercial, 362, 363

communion, 110, 113
compassion, 446, 498
comradeship, 64, 69
condone, 4, 11
conspiracy, 230, 233
contempt, 421, 431
contrition, 74, 75, 101, 107
courtiers, 185, 186

## D

dastardly, 45, 48
dauntless, 185, 186
deceitful, 342, 343
defiant, 74, 77
degenerate, 307, 309
degradation, 101, 107
delirium, 313, 317
depredation, 45, 51
derelict, 178, 180
derision, 313, 315
descrimination, 307, 308
desolation, 265, 269
devastated, 145, 151, 185, 186
dilapidated, 230, 231
dirges, 530, 616
disconsolate, 126, 127
discordant, 145, 149

discords, 307, 310
disdained, 406, 418
disjointed, 282, 283
dominant, 362, 364

# E

elect, 64, 65
empathy, 313, 316
enigmatic, 254, 255
enmity, 530, 559
ensanguined, 313, 316
exhilarates, 230, 231
exorbitant, 126, 131
exotic, 90, 96
expanse, 178, 181
expansively, 134, 140

# F

fanatic, 20, 21
feign, 530, 572
fiasco, 145, 151
foray, 27, 28
fortitude, 242, 243
frailty, 294, 296
futile, 4, 14, 101, 102

# G

gossamer, 178, 181
grotesque, 185, 188

# H

hemorrhage, 294, 296
heresy, 90, 98
hue, 392, 394

# I

imminent, 90, 94
impelled, 110, 113
imperative, 4, 14
impingement, 168, 173
importuned, 265, 271
impoverished, 101, 102
impudence, 446, 451
impudent, 45, 52
inaudible, 362, 363
inaugurating, 230, 231
incalculable, 168, 172
incessantly, 126, 127
inclusively, 222, 223
inconceivable, 134, 138
incredulity, 134, 140
incredulous, 74, 78, 287, 288
indelible, 27, 30
indulgent, 446, 448
inexorable, 254, 255, 531, 624
infallibility, 90, 95
infuse, 222, 225
ingenious, 313, 316
initiation, 64, 65
inscrutable, 265, 271
integrity, 110, 112
intoxicate, 287, 290
invalid, 90, 91
irreplaceable, 230, 239

# L

languishing, 307, 308

# M

malicious, 64, 67
manacles, 307, 308
manipulates, 168, 173

microcosm, 294, 295
militancy, 307, 309

# N

nape, 27, 28

# O

ominous, 242, 243

# P

palpable, 4, 5
pathetic, 282, 283
pauper, 126, 128
pedestrian, 254, 257
peremptory, 45, 49
perilous, 242, 244
pernicious, 530, 536
perverse, 101, 104
pestilence, 185, 186
phobia, 242, 243
plausible, 254, 255
plundered, 421, 424
poignantly, 101, 103
portentous, 530, 538
potent, 230, 234
potentialities, 265, 269
preludes, 145, 149
presentiment, 294, 297
prestige, 64, 71
presumes, 446, 475
pretense, 282, 283
privations, 126, 130
prodigious, 406, 408
prodigy, 145, 146
programming, 168, 169

# Q

quarry, 4, 7
quietude, 294, 295

# R

recalcitrant, 168, 174
redress, 530, 618
rejuvenated, 27, 29
remorse, 20, 23
renegade, 45, 51
reserve, 134, 136
resolute, 254, 255
resolve, 294, 295
restitution, 421, 433
ritual, 294, 295
rogues, 406, 410
ruse, 20, 23

# S

sacrilegious, 222, 224
sagacious, 185, 186
sage, 406, 414
scourge, 531, 632
scruples, 4, 11
segregation, 307, 308
severing, 230, 239
shun, 349, 351
sibilant, 313, 315
sinister, 368, 371
skeptically, 168, 174
slighted, 349, 350
spendthrift, 45, 52
stanched, 27, 30
stoicism, 101, 104
subsides, 392, 394
suffice, 392, 393
supplication, 74, 76
surreptitiously, 45, 50

# T

tactics, 406, 414
tangible, 4, 5, 185, 190
titanic, 406, 418
tribulations, 307, 309

# U

undeleterious, 45, 46
untenanted, 185, 190

# V

vermilion, 90, 98
vexation, 126, 127
voluptuous, 185, 186

# W

wanton, 313, 315
wary, 446, 487
wiles, 342, 343
wrath, 342, 343
wretchedly, 134, 139

# Index of Literary Terms

Allegory, 167, 191
Alliteration, 327, 335, 347
Autobiography, 221, 227, 228

Ballad, 341, 352, 357
Biography, 221, 227

Catastrophe, 525, 634
Character, 39, 44, 445
Characterization, 39, 44, 419
Climax, 3, 25-26, 31, 43, 525
Comic relief, 525, 557, 617, 619

Conflict, 3, 18, 32, 116, 154, 263, 445, 492

Description, 63, 72
Dialogue, 445
Drama, 445

Epic, 403
Epic hero, 403, 420
Epic simile, 403, 419, 429, 437
Epithet, 403, 417, 427, 430
Essay, 281, 285-86
Exposition, 525, 533, 634

Extended metaphor, 281, 299, 361, 367, 546, 625

Falling action, 525, 634
Figurative language, 125, 281, 361, 370, 380
    extended metaphor, 299, 361, 367, 546, 625
    hyperbole, 361
    metaphor, 292-93, 299, 361, 536
    simile, 154-55, 361, 538, 558, 562
Foil, 525, 579
Flashback, 89, 108, 445, 492
Foreshadowing, 89, 99, 424, 596

Hero, epic hero, 403, 420
Humor, 53, 246, 285
Hyperbole, 361

Imagery, 221, 227, 240-41, 292, 377, 388, 525, 604
Irony, 39, 53-54, 133, 143, 176, 191, 221, 246, 525, 593, 606

Metaphor, 281, 292-93, 299, 361, 536
    extended, 281, 299, 361, 367, 546, 625
Meter, 341, 348
Mood, 167, 191, 305, 319

Narrator, 89, 100, 183

Paradox, 525, 540, 554, 561, 586
Persuasion, 305, 311-12
Plot, 3, 19, 525, 634
Point of view, 89, 117
Psychological realism, 63, 73, 81

Repetition, 335
Rhyme, 341, 348
Rhythm, 341, 380
Rising action, 525, 634

Science fiction, 167, 177
Setting, 63, 82

Simile, 125, 154-55, 361, 364, 538, 558, 562, 615
epic simile, 403, 419
Soliloquy, 525, 563, 572, 577, 611
Speaker, 327, 330, 366, 395
Stage directions, 445, 469
Style, 253, 263
Suspense, 3, 19, 25
Symbol, 63, 72, 82, 99, 109, 132-33, 361, 435, 445, 509

Titles, 183
Theme, 125, 144, 177, 253, 272, 327, 332
Tone, 167, 184, 221, 240, 247, 327, 332
Tragedy, 525, 634

# Index of Writing Modes and Formats

Analysis. *See* Informative (expository) writing: Analysis

Classification. *See* Informative (expository) writing: Classification

Description. *See* Observation and description

Expository writing. *See* Informative (expository) writing

Expressive and personal writing
diary entry, 19, 32, 117, 229, 241, 510
essay, college application, 73
family tree, 333
journal, xv-xvii, 4, 27, 45, 64, 74, 90, 100, 101, 110, 126, 134, 145, 168, 178, 185, 222, 230, 242, 254, 265, 282, 294, 307, 313, 328, 333, 342, 349, 362, 368, 378, 383, 393, 407, 421, 446, 531
letter, 100, 117, 144, 264, 312, 382
monologue, 247
note, 117
oral history, 337
poem, 241, 382

Informative (expository) writing: Analysis
analysis of trial, 100
charts, 287, 358, 362, 368, 372, 382, 398, 635

cluster diagram, xviii, 109
exposition, 32
expository essay, 144
flowchart, 247, 300
informal outline, 300
instruction manual, 293
instructions, 312, 398
map, 273
notes, 635
outline, 117
poster, 32, 192
proverbs, 395
recommendation for a job, 117
story sequence map, xix, xx
summary, 635
teacher's note, 109
written transcript, 635

Informative (expository) writing: Classification
agenda, 510
calendar of events, 293
captions, 117, 312
chart, 184
comparison/contrast, 19, 54, 510
comparison/contrast essay, 217, 372, 395
comparison/contrast chart, xix, xx, 54
crossword puzzle, 184, 320
director's notes, 510
essay, 217, 395
expository essay, 54, 117, 184, 398

extended metaphor, 300, 372

footnotes, 184

game cards, 293

guidelines, 286

instruction manual, 293

letter, 177

notes, 82

outline, 144, 273, 635

pamphlet, 82

poster, 320

time line, xix, xx

Venn diagram, xx

want ad, 300

wanted poster, 177


Informative (expository) writing: Synthesis

cue cards, 312

exposition, 133

expository essay, 398

guidelines, 155

help wanted notice, 184

interview report, 273, 293

letter of advice, 155

note of warning, 144

notes for a speech, 133, 323

notes for monologue, 286

opinion survey report, 82, 264

oral presentation, 382

problem-solution essay, 510

proposal, 320

report, 82

sermon, 241

speech, 312

summary, 26, 155, 358, 438, 635

survey report, 264


Narrative and imaginative writing

anecdote, 54

article, 358

comic strip, 32, 247

dialogue, 109, 133, 155, 241, 382

diary entry, 54, 133

dramatic dialogue, 26

dramatic skit, 32, 155

first-person narrative, 372

humorous anecdote, 286

interview, 438

letter, 73, 133, 337, 438

lines or stanzas of poetry, 358

list for babysitter, 54

monologue, 286

narrative essay, 229

narrative poem, 133

outline for story, 133

poem, 73, 100, 337

proposal, 438

rap song, 19

reminiscence, 229

report, 32

scene, 32, 133, 184, 273, 605

script, 82, 109, 117, 192, 247, 264, 273

slogans, 395

song, 192

story, 155, 438

storyboard, 337

story-sequence map, xix, xx

testimony, 100


Observation and description

advertisement, 177

article, 293, 605

autobiographical sketch, 337

character sketch, 100, 144, 337, 398

description, 247, 300, 382

descriptive essay, 241

detective's report, 382

epitaphs, 635

essay, 273

eulogy, 26, 100

field guide, 293

field notes, 273

gossip column, 358

help-wanted ad, 398
interview, 19, 32, 54, 73, 247
metaphor, 300
newspaper article, 19, 144
notes for a speech, 177
obituaries, 635
outline, 177
poem, 26
press release, 300
reports, 605
setting description, 177
stage bill, 510
word search puzzle, 109

Persuasion
    advertisement, 184, 320
    book jacket, 382
    brochure, 521
    closing argument, 100
    debate notes, 438
    diary entry, 82, 177
    editorial, 73, 109, 264, 312, 510, 635
    essay, 264, 358, 635
    invitation, 398
    letter, 26, 395
    letter to a publisher, 54
    letter to the editor, 19, 372
    literary evaluation, 372
    persuasive essay, 273
    persuasive speech, 320
    petition, 312, 510
    phamphlet, 320
    poster, 264
    proposal, 109, 177, 438, 635
    radio advertisement, 293
    recommendation, 358
    review column, 54
    sermon, 109

song, 26
speech, 19, 73, 438

Reports (research)
    description, 247
    essay, 273, 358
    expository essay, 54
    guidelines, 155
    interview report, 273, 293
    literary evaluation, 510
    news report, 312
    opinion survey report, 82, 264
    review, 192, 286

Synthesis. See Informative (expository) writing: Synthesis

Writing about literature
    book review, 229, 438
    essay, 399
    evaluating art, 286
    evaluation, xxiii
    expository essay, 229, 241
    interpretating art, 144
    interpretation, 26
    interpretive poster, 229
    lecture notes, 229
    literary evaluation, 372, 510
    literary review, 192
    memo, 337
    parody, 192, 358, 605
    recommendation, 337
    responding as a character, xvii, xxii, 26, 73, 82, 100, 117, 133, 144, 177, 192, 229, 241, 247, 273, 319, 337, 358, 382, 398, 438
    review, 241, 286, 312
    review column, 54

# Index of Authors and Titles

*All Cats Are Gray*, 178
*An Ancient Gesture*, 439
Angelou, Maya, 222, 636
*Ape*, 338
Asimov, Isaac, 168, 636
Austin, Deborah, 373

Bambara, Toni Cade, 83
*Barbara Allen's Cruelty*, 349
Bashō, Matsuo, 359, 636
*The Bean Eaters*, 328
*Birches*, 392
*A Bird Came Down the Walk*, 383
*The Birds*, 193
Blake, William, 342, 637
Brooks, Gwendolyn, 328, 637
Buson, Yosa, 359, 637

Capote, Truman, 230, 637
*The Cave*, 156
Chekhov, Anton, 511, 638
*A Christmas Memory*, 230
Collier, Eugenia, 101, 638
Connell, Richard, 4, 638
cummings, e.e., 383, 638

*Dance to the Piper*, 248

*Dandelions*, 373
de Maupassant, Guy, 126, 638
de Mille, Agnes, 248, 639
Deutsch, Babette, 338, 639
Dickinson, Emily, 383, 639
*A Dog for All Seasons*, 301
du Maurier, Daphne, 193, 639

Eiseley, Loren, 265, 639
*Everybody Knows Tobie*, 118

*The Feeling of Power*, 168
*Fire and Ice*, 392
Frost, Robert, 392, 640

Garza, Daniel, 118
Gibson, William, 446, 640
Goodman, Ellen, 321, 640

*Haiku*, 359
Harris, Eddy, 274, 640
Henry, O., 45, 640
Herrera, Demetrio, 373
Hiroshi, Yoshino, 328
Homer, 406
*How to Tell a Story*, 282

Hughes, Langston, 40, 362, 641
Hurst, James, 90, 641

*I Have a Dream*, 306
*Initiation*, 64

Jackson, Shirley, 55, 641
*Jazz Fantasia*, 378
*John Dillinger*, 349

Keller, Helen, 287, 641
Kerouac, Jack, 359, 641
King, Martin Luther, Jr., 306, 642
*The Knife*, 294

*The Lady, or the Tiger?*, 33
*Lather and Nothing Else*, 27
Lessing, Doris, 74, 642
Levertov, Denise, 368, 642
*The Lie*, 134
*Lineage*, 333

McCord, Jean, 156, 642
McManus, Patrick, 301, 643
*Marigolds*, 101
Markham, Beryl, 254, 642
*A Marriage Proposal*, 511
*The Masque of the Red Death*, 185
Millay, Edna St. Vincent, 439, 643
*The Miracle Worker*, 446
*Mississippi Solo*, 274
*Moco Limping*, 338
Monreal, David Nava, 338, 643
*The Most Dangerous Game*, 4

*A Mother in Mannville*, 110
*Mother to Son*, 362
Mowat, Farley, 313, 643
*Mrs. Flowers*, 222
*My Delicate Heart Condition*, 83
*My Papa's Waltz*, 378

*The Necklace*, 126
Neruda, Pablo, 389, 643
*The Night the Bed Fell*, 242
Norton, Andre, 178, 643
*Nothing Gold Can Stay*, 392

*Obituary of a Bone Hunter*, 265
Oden, Gloria, 362, 644
*Ode to the Watermelon*, 389
*The Odyssey*, 406
O'Flaherty, Liam, 20, 644

Parker, Dorothy, 439, 644
*Penelope*, 439
Plath, Sylvia, 64, 644
Poe, Edgar Allan, 185, 644
*A Poison Tree*, 342
*The Possibility of Evil*, 55
*Primal Screen*, 321

*The Ransom of Red Chief*, 45
Rawlings, Marjorie Kinnan, 110, 645
*Rhinoceros*, 368
Roethke, Theodore, 378, 645
*Romeo and Juliet*, 530

Sandburg, Carl, 378, 645
*The Scarlet Ibis*, 90
*The Seeing See Little*, 287
Selzer, Richard, 294, 645
Shakespeare, William, 530
*The Sharks*, 368
*The Shooting of John Dillinger Outside the
    Biograph Theater, July 22, 1934*, 349
*The Sniper*, 20
*Spring is like a perhaps hand*, 383
Stevens, Wallace, 359, 645
Stockton, Frank R., 33, 646
Stoutenburg, Adrien, 368, 646
*Sunset Colors*, 328


Tan, Amy, 145, 646
Téllez, Hernando, 27, 646
*Thank You, M'am*, 40
*Through the Tunnel*, 74

Thurber, James, 242, 646
*The Tragedy of Romeo and Juliet*, 530
*Training*, 373
Twain, Mark, 282, 646
*Two Kinds*, 145


*Velvet Shoes*, 342
Vonnegut, Kurt, Jr., 134, 647


Wagoner, David, 349, 647
Walker, Alice, 333, 647
Walker, Margaret, 333, 647
*The Way It Is*, 362
*West with the Night*, 254
*A Whale for the Killing*, 313
*Women*, 333
Wylie, Elinor, 342, 647

## *Art Credits*

### Cover

*Philadelphia Triptych* (detail), 1982, Sally Bachman. Twining Weavers, Arroyo Seco, New Mexico.

### Author Photographs